Lecture Notes in Computer Science

Commenced Publication in 1973
Founding and Former Series Editors:
Gerhard Goos, Juris Hartmanis, and Jan van Leeuwen

Editorial Board

David Hutchison
Lancaster University, UK
Takeo Kanade
Carnegie Mellon University, Pittsburgh, PA, USA
Josef Kittler
University of Surrey, Guildford, UK
Jon M. Kleinberg
Cornell University, Ithaca, NY, USA
Alfred Kobsa
University of California, Irvine, CA, USA
Friedemann Mattern
ETH Zurich, Switzerland
John C. Mitchell
Stanford University, CA, USA
Moni Naor
Weizmann Institute of Science, Rehovot, Israel
Oscar Nierstrasz
University of Bern, Switzerland
C. Pandu Rangan
Indian Institute of Technology, Madras, India
Bernhard Steffen
University of Dortmund, Germany
Madhu Sudan
Massachusetts Institute of Technology, MA, USA
Demetri Terzopoulos
University of California, Los Angeles, CA, USA
Doug Tygar
University of California, Berkeley, CA, USA
Gerhard Weikum
Max-Planck Institute of Computer Science, Saarbruecken, Germany

Martin Gaedke   Michael Grossniklaus
Oscar Díaz (Eds.)

Web Engineering

9th International Conference, ICWE 2009
San Sebastian, Spain, June 24-26, 2009
Proceedings

 Springer

Volume Editors

Martin Gaedke
Chemnitz University of Technology
Faculty of Computer Science
Straße der Nationen 62, 09111 Chemnitz, Germany
E-mail: martin.gaedke@cs.tu-chemnitz.de

Michael Grossniklaus
Politecnico di Milano
Dipartimento di Elettronica e Informazione
Piazza Leonardo da Vinci 32, 20133 Milano, Italy
E-mail: grossniklaus@elet.polimi.it

Oscar Díaz
University of the Basque Country
Department of Computer Languages and Systems
Paseo de Manuel Lardizabal 1, 20018 San Sebastián, Spain
E-mail: oscar.diaz@ehu.es

Library of Congress Control Number: Applied for

CR Subject Classification (1998): H.5, H.4, K.6, D.2, C.2, H.3.5, H.5.3

LNCS Sublibrary: SL 3 – Information Systems and Application, incl. Internet/Web and HCI

ISSN	0302-9743
ISBN-10	3-642-02817-9 Springer Berlin Heidelberg New York
ISBN-13	978-3-642-02817-5 Springer Berlin Heidelberg New York

This work is subject to copyright. All rights are reserved, whether the whole or part of the material is concerned, specifically the rights of translation, reprinting, re-use of illustrations, recitation, broadcasting, reproduction on microfilms or in any other way, and storage in data banks. Duplication of this publication or parts thereof is permitted only under the provisions of the German Copyright Law of September 9, 1965, in its current version, and permission for use must always be obtained from Springer. Violations are liable to prosecution under the German Copyright Law.

springer.com

© Springer-Verlag Berlin Heidelberg 2009
Printed in Germany

Typesetting: Camera-ready by author, data conversion by Scientific Publishing Services, Chennai, India
Printed on acid-free paper   SPIN: 12711277   06/3180   5 4 3 2 1 0

Preface

As of 2009, the discipline of Web engineering is a well-established and mature field of research within the software engineering, database, information technology, and other related communities. By its very nature, Web engineering is, therefore, a multidisciplinary field that is beginning to establish ties even outside the domain of computer science. As a discipline, Web engineering systematically applies the knowledge of Web science to the development and evolution of Web-based applications and systems. This volume contains the proceedings of the 9th International Conference on Web Engineering (ICWE 2009), which was held in San Sebastián, Spain in June 2009. The ICWE conferences are among the most essential events of the Web engineering community. This fact is manifested both by the number of accomplished researchers that support the conference series with their work and contributions as well as by the continuing patronage of several international organizations dedicated to promoting research and scientific progress in the field of Web engineering.

ICWE 2009 followed conferences in Yorktown Heights, NY, USA; Como, Italy; Palo Alto, CA, USA; Sydney, Australia; Munich, Germany; Oviedo, Spain; Santa Fe, Argentina; and Cáceres, Spain. With San Sebastián as this year's venue, the conference series visits the country where it was originally launched in 2001 for the third time.

This year's call for papers attracted a total of 90 submissions from 33 countries spanning all continents of the world with a good coverage of all the different aspects of Web engineering. Topics addressed by the contributions include areas ranging from more traditional topics such as component-based Web engineering, model-driven Web engineering, navigation, search, Semantic Web, quality, and testing to novel domains such as the Web 2.0, rich internet applications, and mashups. All submitted papers were reviewed in detail by at least three members of the Program Committee which was composed of experts in the field of Web engineering from 23 countries. Based on their reviews, 22 submissions were accepted as full papers (24%) and 15 as short papers (22%). The program was completed by 8 posters and 10 demonstrations that were presented in dedicated sessions at the conference. Finally, the conference was also host to keynotes by James A. Hendler (Rensselaer Polytechnic Institute, USA), Jaideep Srivastava (University of Minnesota, USA), and Juan Jose Hierro (Telefonica, Spain) as well as an outstanding collection of four tutorials and four workshops.

We would like to express our gratitude to all the sponsors that supported ICWE 2009 financially, namely, the Regional Council of Gipuzkoa, the Association of Industries for Electronic and Information Technologies in the Basque Country (GAIA), LKS Co., and the University of the Basque Country (Summer Course Board). The conference would not have been possible without the endorsement of the International World Wide Web Conference Committee (IW^{3}C^2)

and the International Society for Web Engineering (ISWE). In this context, we would especially like to thank Bebo White and Geert-Jan Houben for their work as our liaisons to these two organizations. We are also indebted to the various Chairs (Josu Aramberri, Francisco Curbera, Florian Daniel, Peter Dolog, Jon Iturrioz, Oscar Pastor, Mario Piattini, Gustavo Rossi, Takehiro Tokuda, and Antonio Vallecillo) and to the local organizers who helped with their enthusiastic work to make ICWE 2009 a reality. Finally, a special thanks to all the researchers who contributed their work and participated in the conference. After all, as with any other conference, exchanging ideas and forging connections is what it is all about.

May 2009   Martin Gaedke
                                                          Michael Grossniklaus
                                                                  Oscar Díaz

Organization

General Chair

Oscar Díaz — University of the Basque Country, Spain

Program Chairs

Martin Gaedke — Chemnitz University of Technology, Germany
Michael Grossniklaus — Politecnico di Milano, Italy

Program Committee

Silvia Abrahão — Polytechnic University of Valencia, Spain
Virgilio Almedia — Federal University of Minas Gerais, Brazil
Boualem Benatallah — University of New South Wales, Australia
Maria Bielikova — Slovak University of Technology in Bratislava, Slovakia
Judith Bishop — University of Pretoria, South Africa
Marco Brambilla — Politecnico di Milano, Italy
Chris Brooks — University of San Francisco, USA
Jordi Cabot — University of Toronto, Canada
Fabio Casati — University of Trento, Italy
Sven Casteleyn — Vrije Universiteit Brussel, Belgium
Dan Chiorean — University Babes-Bolyai, Romania
Maria da Graça Pimentel — University of São Paulo, Brazil
Paul Dantzig — IBM T.J. Watson Research Center, USA
Peter Dolog — Aalborg University, Denmark
Schahram Dustdar — Vienna University of Techonology, Austria
Flavius Frasincar — Erasmus University of Rotterdam, The Netherlands
Dragan Gasevic — Simon Fraser University, Canada
Athula Ginige — University of Western Sydney, Australia
Angela Eck Soong Goh — Nanyang Technological University, Singapore
Jaime Gomez — University of Alicante, Spain
Mei Hong — Peking University, China
Geert-Jan Houben — Delft University of Technology, The Netherlands
Arun Iyengar — IBM, USA
Stanislaw Jarzabek — National University of Singapore, Singapore
Gerti Kappel — Vienna University of Technology, Austria

Nora Koch   Ludwig-Maximilians-Universität München,
                                   Germany
David Lowe   University of Technology Sydney, Australia
Ioana Manolescu   Inria Futurs, France
Maristella Matera   Politecnico di Milano, Italy
Emilia Mendes   University of Auckland, New Zealand
San Murugesan   University of Southern Cross, Australia
Moira C. Norrie   ETH Zurich, Switzerland
Luis Olsina   National University of la Pampa, Argentina
Satoshi Oyama   Kyoto Univerisity, Japan
Oscar Pastor   Polytechnic University of Valencia, Spain
Vicente Pelechano   Polytechnic University of Valencia, Spain
Claudia Pons   National University of la Plata, Argentina
Birgit Pröll   University of Linz, Austria
I.V. Ramakrishnan   Stony Brook University, USA
Simos Retalis   University of Crete, Greece
Gustavo Rossi   National University of la Plata, Argentina
Klaus-Dieter Schewe   Massey University, New Zealand
Daniel Schwabe   Pontifical Catholic University of Rio de
                                   Janeiro, Brazil
Weisong Shi   Wayne University, USA
Katsumi Tanaka   Kyoto University, Japan
Bernhard Thalheim   Christian Albrechts University Kiel, Germany
Giovanni Toffetti
   Carughi   Università della Svizzera Italiana, Switzerland
Takehiro Tokuda   Tokyo Institute of Technology, Japan
Riccardo Torlone   Univesità di Roma, Italy
Jean Vanderdonckt   Université Catholique de Louvain, Belgium
Petri Vuorimaa   Helsinki University of Technology, Finland
Vincent Wade   Trinity College Dublin, Ireland
Bebo White   Stanford Linear Accelerator Center, USA
Marco Winckler   Université Paul Sabatier, France
Bin Xu   Tsinghua University, China

Posters Chair

Florian Daniel   University of Trento, Italy

Posters Committee

Maria Bielikova   Slovak University of Technology in Bratislava,
                                   Slovakia
Alexander Birukou   University of Trento, Italy
Alessandro Bozzon   Politecnico di Milano, Italy
Sara Comai   Politecnico di Milano, Italy
Vincenzo D'Andrea   University of Trento, Italy

Federico Michele Facca	STI Innsbruck, Austria
Michael Grossniklaus	Politecnico di Milano, Italy
Nora Koch	Ludwig-Maximilians-Universität München, Germany
David Lowe	University of Technology Sydney, Australia
Maristella Matera	Politecnico di Milano, Italy
Moira C. Norrie	ETH Zurich, Switzerland
Giovanni Toffetti Carughi	Universitá della Svizzera Italiana, Switzerland
Jin Yu	Tiburon, USA

Demonstrations Chair

| Antonio Vallecillo | University of Malaga, Spain |

Demonstrations Committee

Silvia Abrahão	Polytechnic University of Valencia, Spain
Michel Chaudron	Eindhoven University of Technology, The Netherlands
Piero Fraternali	Politecnico di Milano, Italy
Nora Koch	Ludwig-Maximilians-Universität München, Germany
David Lowe	University of Technology Sydney, Australia
Alfonso Pierantonio	Università de L'Aquila, Italy
Vicente Pelechano	Polytechnic University of Valencia, Spain
Gustavo Rossi	National University of la Plata, Argentina
Fernando Sánchez-Figueroa	University of Extremadura, Spain
Manuel Wimmer	Vienna University of Techonology, Austria

Doctoral Consortium Chair

| Gustavo Rossi | National University of la Plata, Argentina |

Doctoral Consortium Committee

Sven Casteleyn	Vrije Universiteit Brussel, Belgium
Florian Daniel	University of Trento, Italy
Damiano Distante	Università Telematica Telma, Italy
Marí Escalona	University of Seville, Spain
Fernando Sánchez-Figueroa	University of Extremadura, Spain
Joan Fons	Polytechnic University of Valencia, Spain
Daniela Godoy	ISISTAN Research Institute, Argentina

Nora Koch   Ludwig-Maximilians-Universität München,
                            Germany
Luis Olsina   National University of la Pampa, Argentina
Gustavo Rossi   National University of la Plata, Argentina
Wieland Schwinger   Johannes Kepler University of Linz, Austria

Workshop Chairs

Peter Dolog   Aalborg University, Denmark
Takehiro Tokuda   Tokyo Institute of Technology, Japan

Tutorial Chair

Oscar Pastor   Polytechnic University of Valencia, Spain

Publicity Chair

Mario Piattini   University of Castilla-La Mancha, Spain

Industrial Chair

Francisco Curbera   IBM Research, USA

ISWE Conference Steering Committee Liaison

Geert-Jan Houben   Delft University of Technology,
                            The Netherlands

IW3C2 Liaison

Bebo White   Stanford Linear Accelerator Center, USA

Local Organization Chairs

Jon Iturrioz   University of the Basque Country, Spain
Josu Aramberri   University of the Basque Country, Spain

Additional Referees

Ahmed, Faisal   Bartalos, Peter   Cachero, Cristina
Al-Naymat, Ghazi   Beheshti, Seyed M. R.   Castillo, Claris
Baez, Marcos   Borodin, Yevgen   Covella, Guillermo
Barla, Michal   Brosch, Petra   Ferreira, Renato

Garg, Supriya
Garrigós, Irene
Gu, Zhifeng
Guabtni, Adnene
Gómez, Cristina
Hidders, Jan
Huang, Gang
Insfran, Emilio
Islam, Asiful
Jatowt, Adam
Jiao, Wenpin
Kawai, Hideki
Kotsis, Gabriele
Kroiss, Christian
Le, Duy Ngan
Leonardi, Erwin
Leone, Stefania
Li, Fei
Li, Ge

Luo, Sen
Mahmud, Jalal
Meinecke, Johannes
Melia, Santiago
Molina, Hernan
Moro, Mirella
Noack, Rene
Oyama, Satoshi
Paraschiv, Sergiu
Parra, Cristhian
Pereira, Adriano
Prates, Raquel
Puzis, Yury
Ravi, Jayashree
Retschitzegger, Werner
Sakr, Sherif
Schall, Daniel
Seidl, Martina
Silva-Lepe, Ignacio

Simko, Marian
van der Sluijs, Kees
de Spindler, Alexandre
Subramanian, Revathi
Syukur, Evi
Tan, Puay Siew
Torres, Victoria
Valverde, Francisco
Van Woensel, William
Veloso, Adriano
Vu, Hung
Wang, Yasha
Wimmer, Manuel
Wu, Qinyi
Yan, Yixin
Zapletal, Marco
Zhang, Lu
Zhang, Yan
Zhao, Junfeng

Table of Contents

Navigation

Process, Planning and Phases

Quality

Rich Internet Applications

Search

Testing

Web Services, SOA and REST

Web 2.0

Posters

Demonstrations

Fine-Grained Analysis of Web Tasks through Data Visualization

Gennaro Costagliola and Vittorio Fuccella

Department of Mathematics and Informatics,
University of Salerno
{gencos,vfuccella}@unisa.it

Abstract. This paper presents an approach for monitoring several important aspects related to user behaviour during the execution of Web tasks[1]. The approach includes the tracking of user interactions with the Web site and exploits visual data mining to highlight important information regarding Web application usage. In particular, our approach intends to be a *natural heir* of the approaches based on *clickstream* visualization, by integrating them with the visualization of page-level data and by improving them with the definition of ad-hoc *zoom* and *filter* operations. Furthermore, we present a theoretical framework to formally define our proposal. Lastly, in order to test the approach, a simple case-study for a particular practical usability evaluation has been carried out. To this aim, we built a prototypal system composed of a tracking tool, responsible for tracking user interactions and a visualization tool for task analysis.

1 Introduction

The analysis of user behaviour during Web navigation is a potentially fruitful source of important information. In particular, it has been extensively used for improving usability, but also to provide a better support to task users, i.e. by improving Web browsers and navigation tools [1], and to discover behavioural patterns in a given category of users [2].

The recent AJAX [3] technologies, provide us with detailed information regarding user behaviour, by allowing us to capture user interface events triggered on the client-side of Web applications. For example, with AJAX we can easily capture and record users' behaviour on complex interaction systems, such as Web forms, which are the primary medium for user input on the web [4].

Unfortunately, since interface events are not included in traditional server-side logs, they have scarcely been considered in the analysis of on line tasks for a long time, despite the richness of information regarding user behaviour they convey. From server logs, we can only elicit the *clickstream*, which is the

---

[1] This research has been partially supported by the grant "cofinanziamento per attrezzature scientifiche e di supporto, grandi e medie (2005)" from the University of Salerno.

M. Gaedke, M. Grossniklaus, and O. Díaz (Eds.): ICWE 2009, LNCS 5648, pp. 1–15, 2009.
© Springer-Verlag Berlin Heidelberg 2009

recording of what a computer user clicks on while Web browsing. Past systems, such as *WebQuilt* [5], in fact, relied on *clickstream* visualization, to graphically show Web users behaviour on Web tasks.

The availability of information on the user interactions with the Web interfaces should be effectively used for the previously mentioned purposes, in particular for usability evaluation. In literature, some attempts to integrate web server logs with client-side data for analysis purposes are present [6] [7], but, to our knowledge, no complete and effective visualization methods for Web task analysis, based on client-side data, have been proposed. In particular, usability analysis still largely employs the *think out loud* protocol, which has several disadvantages: to some extent, a user has to interrupt operations, when commenting; evaluators are expected to have special knowledge; subjects do not necessarily comment [8].

In this paper we present an approach for monitoring several important aspects related to user behaviour during the execution of Web tasks. The approach includes the tracking of user interactions with the Web site and exploits data visualization to highlight important information regarding Web application usage. In particular, our approach intends to be a *natural heir* of the approaches based on *clickstream* visualization: while for the existing approaches *clickstream* visualization is the final result, in our system its graph chart is only the starting point of a more comprehensive visual data mining process. To elaborate, it is our approach's *first level* of analysis. By applying a *zoom in* operation, we can deepen the analysis to a *second level* chart, showing the page-level interactions of the users. A *filter* operation is also defined. It allows the analyzer to visualize only a selection of the currently visualized user sessions involved in the task.

In order to define in an unambigous way the charts and the operations of filtering and zooming, the paper presents a theoretical framework. These operations, largely employed in visual data mining [9] are defined in the context of our approach. Lastly, we give a first glance at the way our approach can be used for detecting usability problems in Web pages. To this aim, we built a prototypal system and used it in a real life example. The example shows how our approach, by performing simple visual interactions, aids the analyst in detecting usability problems in Web tasks.

The rest of the paper is organized as follows: Section 2 contains a brief survey on works related to ours. The whole approach is presented in Section 3. The theoretical framework is presented in Section 4, whereas, in Section 5, we discuss the results of a case-study application. Several final remarks and a brief discussion on future work conclude the paper.

2   Related Work

Several approaches can be found in the literature that describe how to capture and visualize user behaviour in Web tasks. Most of them only rely on server log analysis. In recent years, there have been several attempts of integrating web server logs with client-side data, but only a few of them have resulted in an effective visual data mining method for user behaviour analysis.

Among the earliest methods there are those exploiting *clickstream* visualization. *WebQuilt* (2001), [5] employs *clickstream* visualization for highlighting the most used paths by the users to accomplish a given web task. A variant of the above method, called *DiskTree*, transforms the *clickstream* graph in a 2D tree, generally by simply running the Breadth First Search algorithm on it, and visualizes it in a disk, such that the root is located in the centre and the last level nodes on the circumference of the disk. Chi [10] used this approach for discovering usability defects in Web sites. Chen et al. [11] have improved this method by introducing operations and by describing a web graph algebra to manipulate and combine web graphs.

Specific approaches for the analysis of e-commerce systems capturing and visualizing user interface interactions are presented in [12,13,14]. In [12] it is presented a case study based on *ClickViz*. This system integrates *clickstream* data with user demographic information. The other two ones refine *clickstream* data by selecting specific web merchandising events from the web server log, such as: product impression, clickthrough, basket placement and purchase. In [14] the analysis is oriented to the product evaluation, which is shown through a starfield display [15], where it is possible to verify that user interest for the product is in tune with its visibility in the site. In [13], instead, an interactive parallel coordinate system is used to interpret and explore *clickstream* data, checking, i.e., how many sessions lead to a purchase and how many abandoned the site before.

Other approaches [16] [6] [8], focus on the use of mouse and gaze movements as implicit interest indicators. In particular, the paths of the mouse and of the user gaze are visualized in a video [8] or in a page screenshot [6] as lines overimposed to the image visualized on the screen at that moment.In [8] the approach is used in a usability study with 5 tasks where it is proved that the use of a video improves the think out loud protocol that would miss 11.6% of the entire user comments.

From a visualization point of view, our approach proposes a system similar to those visualizing the *clickstream*, significantly improving previous approaches with the appropriate integration of elements that visualize the additional client-side tracking information. This study originates from our previous experience on studying learners' strategies to complete tests by tracking their interactions with Web-based learning systems [17]. The current work is then a generalization of the previous one from a specific domain (e-learning) to the general case of web task analysis.

3   The Approach

In this section, we describe the approach for the analysis of user behaviour during online tasks. In particular, we have devised a new symbolic data visualization strategy, which is used within a KDD process to graphically highlight behavioral patterns related to the users activity in online tasks. The main two steps of our approach are *data collection* and *data visualization*.

3.1   Data Collection

The proposed approach aims to gather data concerning the users' activities during Web tasks. Gathering occurs by simply recording the interactions of the users with the Web site interface during navigation.

The data collection can be realized in a laboratory, with selected users, or during Web site usage, with real users. The case-study application results shown in section 5, refer to the first method only. The collected data carries information about the user session, the sequence of the pages loaded in the browser (*clickstream*) and the interactions of the users with the interactive elements contained in the pages, such as links and form fields. In particular, the information about a specific web task accomplished by several users is recorded in a log. During a session, the operations realized by a user in a specific task produce the following data:

1. information about the browser session: sessionID, IP address, username, information about the user agent, sequence of visited pages;
2. information about the visit of single pages: url of the page and timestamp of the loading and of the unloading events; the mouse movements and clicks, scrolling; presence and duration of inactivity time intervals (no interactions) during the page visit. Furthermore, the whole HTML code of the visited pages and the referenced resources are recorded;
3. events generated by the user interaction with the widgets of a page: duration of the interaction and sequence of events occurring in that interaction;

Given the hierarchical nature of the gathered data (session, page, page elements), we store data in XML format instead of storing it in plain text as in the usual log files. In this way the input for the next step (data visualization) is already partially elaborated.

3.2   Data Visualization

Data visualization is an important tool for Web task analysis. It has been widely employed for *clickstream* analysis, so far. Nevertheless, *clickstream* only includes high level information: it does not allow a deep analysis of user behaviour. In our approach, the data gathered in step 1 are visualized through a suite of charts showing the user actions during the web tasks at various levels of detail. The charts are analyzed both top-down and bottom-up following the different levels. The analysis from the higher level starts visualizing cumulative and most significant data of the whole task, and proceeds to more detailed views through *zoom* and *filter* operations applied by the analyzer through simple interactions with the charts. The *filter* operation can also be applied to the detailed views to expose particular user behaviours and, if needed, the analyzer can return to higher level views to consider the context in which these behaviours occur.

Our approach includes the visualization of charts, showing cumulative information of the sessions of the users participating to a given task, at two levels of deepening.

The **first level chart** represents *Clickstream* through a direct graph. The node set of the graph includes all the pages visited by at least one user while each edge is a transition between two pages. In our approach, as shown in Figure 6(i), to better associate the graph nodes to the visited pages, each node is represented through a thumbnail of the associated page. The color of the nodes background is forced to be in a gray scale (in order to represent the average time spent on the page) even in the event of a different color indicated by the Web page style settings. A direct edge is present between two nodes if at least one user has visited the pages represented by the two nodes in succession.

In our approach, pages requested from the same URL can be associated to different graph nodes. This happens since dinamically produced Web pages are often different, even when obtained by requesting the same URL. Two pages are regarded as different versions of the same page if their internal link structure is different. Graph nodes are visually arranged in a matrix. Nodes corresponding to different versions of the same page are shown in the same column, ordered descendingly by the number of sessions passing through the node. Further optimizations are performed in order to improve chart readability.

The **second level chart** is a deepening of the previous. It shows information regarding a visit of a single page. The used visual metaphor is a graph, as before. Nevertheless, this time the nodes represent the widgets (generally links and form fields) at least one user has interacted with. The chart is shown in transparency on the screenshot of the page, in order to highlight the widgets. A direct edge is present between two nodes if at least one user has interacted with the widgets represented by the two nodes in succession, that is, the user focus has directly passed from the first to the second widget, with no inner focuses on a third widget. At this level, previous and next pages are reported in the chart in two different columns, on the left and on the right of the currently zoomed page.

The association between visual cues and usage metrics is the following:

- **Node border thickness** represents the number of sessions passing through the node. A thicker border is for a node with a greater number of user accesses.
- **Node border color** represents the average number of passages through the node for each session (calculated only on the sessions which have at least one passage through the node). The color is reported in red scale: a darker red is for more passages.
- **Node internal background color** represents the average time spent on the node (in case of multiple passages in the same sessions, their durations are summed). The color is reported in gray scale: a darker gray is for a longer time.
- **Edge thickness** represents the number of sessions performing the transition.
- **Edge color** represents the average number of passages through the edge for each session (calculated only on the sessions which have at least one passage through the edge). The color is reported in gray scale: a darker gray (tending to black) is for more passages.

Since, compared to previous approaches, we increased the number of visual cues, we also made an effort to use them "consistently", thus guaranteeing a lower cognitive load while interpreting the charts [18]. Firstly, the above association is valid in both levels. Furthermore, other solutions have been adopted: cues on nodes and edges are always associated to measures related to pages and transitions, respectively; line thickness, line color and internal color are always associated to number of sessions, average number of passages in a session and time of a visit measures, respectively.

It is possible to go back and forth through the levels by applying *zoom* (*in* and *out*) operations. Furthermore, *filter* operations can be applied in order to construct the graph only by using a selection of the currently visualized user sessions involved in the task. In particular, the subset of the sessions which satisfy a selection condition: nodes and edges can be marked with *inclusive* or *exclusive* ticks, indicating that the sessions underlying the selected nodes and edges are included or excluded, respectively. *Inclusive* and *exclusive* ticks can be interactively added on the graph. The *inclusive filter* is used to select only the sessions passing through the marked elements, whilst the *exclusive filter* is used to select all the sessions except those passing through the marked elements. An *inclusive filter* can be applyed, i.e. to an outgoing edge on a node representing an error page in first level chart, in order to understand how a set of users recovered from the error. Conversely, an *exclusive filter* can be applied to a node representing the submit button of a form in the second level chart, in order to visualize only the form filling patterns of the users who abandoned the form (users who never submit the form). A sample of application of such a *filter* is shown in Figure 1.

Fig. 1. Sample of application of a *filter*. The submit button of the form has been marked with an *exclusive* tick.

4   Theoretical Framework

In this section we provide a framework to formally define the operations of *filter* and *zoom in*. In order to do so we need to explicitly define the notions of session and page-session and, then, model the first and second level charts as labelled graphs.

4.1   The First Level Chart

Given a set of pages A, a *session* S on A is defined by a sequence of pages $(p_0, p_1, \ldots, p_n)$ in A, where p_0 and p_n are the entry and exit pages, respectively, and the set of all the transitions (p_i, p_{i+1}) of successive pages in the sequence.

A *first level chart* for a set of sessions Σ is defined as a labelled direct graph $G_\Sigma(V, E)$ where V is the union set of all the pages occurring in the sessions, i.e., $V = \cup p$, for each $p \in S$ and for each $S \in \Sigma$, and E is the union set of all the transitions occurring in the sessions, i.e., $E = \cup(p_i, p_{i+1})$, for each $(p_i, p_{i+1}) \in S$ and for each $S \in \Sigma$.

Each transition and page in the graph is labelled by a tuple. These tuples generally represent the metrics to keep track of, such as the ones introduced in subsection 3.2. In this section, for sake of simplicity we will only refer to the label w of a transition t representing the number of sessions containing at least one occurrence of the transition, i.e., $w_t = |\{S \in \Sigma | t = (p_i, p_{i+1}) \in S\}|$.

For example, let us consider the set of pages $A = \{p, q, r, s, u\}$ and the following set of sessions on A:

$$\{S_1 = (p, q, s), S_2 = (p, r, p, q, s), S_3 = (p, r, p, q, s), S_4 = (p, u, p, q, s)\}$$

The resulting labelled graph is shown in Figure 2.

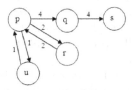

Fig. 2. A labeled direct graph modeling a first level chart

In the following we will use the term 'element' when referring to either a page (node) or a transition (edge) in a labeled direct graph.

The session filter operations. To define *filters* on a set of sessions we start by giving the notion of a *filter* based on a single element of the graph. We will then use this primitive *filter* to provide a general definition of complex *filters*.

Given a set of sessions Σ and an element e in G_Σ, we denote with Σ_e the set of all the sessions in Σ including e.

If we consider the previous example, Σ_r is $\{S_2 = (p, r, p, q, s), S_3 = (p, r, p, q, s)\}$ and $\Sigma_{(u,p)}$ is $\{S_4 = (p, u, p, q, s)\}$, leading, respectively, to Figures 3(i) and 3(ii).

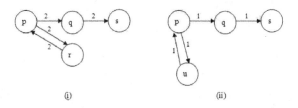

Fig. 3. Labeled direct graphs modeling Σ_r, (i), and $\Sigma_{(u,p)}$, (ii)

We can then define the *filter* operations: given a set of sessions Σ, a *filter on* Σ is defined by a set-theoretic expression on the set $\{\Sigma_e \in 2^\Sigma |\ e$ is an element in $G_\Sigma\}$ using the operations of union, intersection and complementation.

In particular, given a set M of (marked) elements in G_Σ, we can define, among the others, the following four *filters*:

- *union-inclusive filter*: for the selection of all the sessions of Σ with at least an element in M, (defined as $uif(\Sigma, M) = \cup_{e \in M} \Sigma_e$);
- *union-exclusive filter*: for the selection of all the sessions of Σ except for those with at least a marked element in M, (defined as $uef(\Sigma, M) = \Sigma - \cup_{e \in M} \Sigma_e$);
- *intersection-inclusive filter*: for the selection of all the sessions of Σ containing all the marked elements in M, (defined as $iif(\Sigma, M) = \cap_{e \in M} \Sigma_e$);
- *intersection-exclusive filter*: for the selection of all the sessions of Σ except for those containing all the marked elements in M, (defined as $ief(\Sigma, M) = \Sigma - \cap_{e \in M} \Sigma_e$).

Following the previous example, if we take $M = \{r, (u, p)\}$, as shown in Figure 4(i)), the application of the *union-inclusive filter* will filter out session S_1 producing the graph in Figure 4(ii), while the *union-exclusive filter* will filter out sessions S_2, S_3 and S_4 producing the graph in Figure 4(iii). The *intersection-inclusive filter* will filter out all the sessions while the *intersection-exclusive filter* will produce no filtering at all.

Note that the the *inclusive* and *exclusive filters* introduced in subsection 3.2 are formally defined by the intersection-inclusive and intersection-exclusive definitions above but the approach can be extended to support any other *filter*.

The session zoom-in operation. In order to define the *zoom-in* operation we first need to define the notion of page-session, i.e., the interactions of a user with a particular page extracted from the *clickstream*. This is very similar to the notion of session with the difference that we now deal with sequences of page-widgets.

Given a page p_i of a session S, a *page-session* P_{p_i} is a sequence ($w_0 = p_{i-1}, w_1, w_2, \ldots, w_{n-1}, w_n = p_{i+1}$), where each element w_i is a widget internal to page p_i. Pages p_{i-1} and p_{i+1} are the entry and the exit points of the

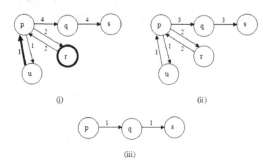

Fig. 4. Filter applications with $M = \{r, (u, p)\}$ (i): union-inclusion (ii) and union-exclusion (iii)

page-sessions, respectively. In the cases where p_{i-1} and p_{i+1} do not exist they are substituted by a dummy entry point and a dummy exit point, respectively. As with the definition of session, a page-session also includes all the transtions (w_i, w_{i+1}).

We can now give the definition of *zoom-in* operation: given a set of sessions Σ, and a page p of G_Σ, the *zoom-in operation* $zi(\Sigma, p)$ returns the the set of page-sessions $\Pi = \{P_p | p \in S \text{ and } S \in \Sigma\}$.

In other words a *zoom-in* operation extracts a page from the *clickstream* and makes explicit the user interactions with the page internal elements.

The following definitions are given for sake of completeness but they can be easily derived from the corresponding ones above.

4.2   The Second Level Chart

A *second level chart* for a set Π of page-sessions in p is formally described by a labeled direct graph $G_\Pi(V, E)$ where V is the union set of all the elements occurring in the page-sessions, i.e., $V = \cup_{w \in P} w$ for each $P \in \Pi$. E is the union set of all the transitions occurring in the page-sessions, i.e., $E = \cup(w_i, w_{i+1})$, for each w_i, $w_{i+1} \in S$ and for each $P \in \Pi$.

Each transition t in the graph G is labelled by a weigth w representing the number of page-sessions of Π containing at least one occurrence of the transition, i.e., $w_t = |\{P \in \Pi | t = (w_i, w_{i+1}) \text{ and } (w_i, w_{i+1}) \in P\}|$.

The page-session filter operations. Given a set of page-sessions Π and an element e of G_Π, we denote with Π_e the set of all the page-sessions in Π including e. The *filter* operations on Π can be analougously defined as done above on Σ.

5   The Case-study Application

In order to demonstrate the effectiveness of the approach, we have evaluated the usability of a simple Web task with respect to six students of the third year of the Laurea degree in Computer Science at the University of Salerno. The goal of this case-study is to gather preliminary data for a simple task and use our protoype to visually analyze them in order to discover eventual usability faults with respect to our sample. We chose a simple web task where few paths of few pages could be followed. Furthermore, the good variety of paths to be followed allowed us to reason on the cases of success, wrong input, and incomplete input.

Our users have been asked to perform an information seeking task on the Web site of the Italian ministry of universities and research (MIUR). In Italy, academic staff is hired by *concorsi* (national competitions). A national, discipline-related committee is responsible for choosing the winner candidate. The names of the committee's members are published through the Web site of the ministry. The starting URL for the procedure to search them is

http://reclutamento.miur.it/seleziona/commissioni.html.

A typical search can be performed by providing information such as the year of publication, the position and the discipline of the *concorso* and information

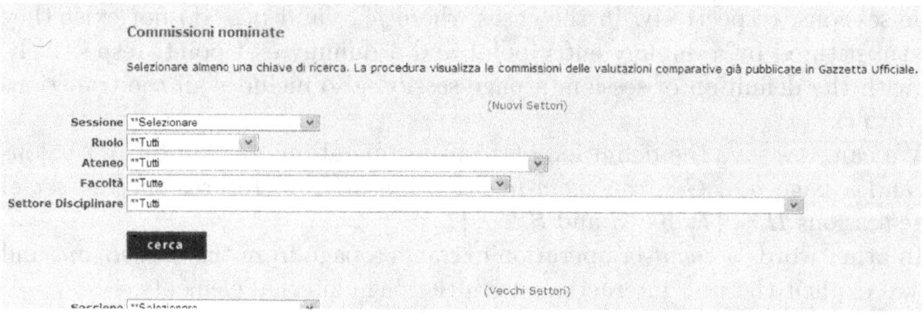

Fig. 5. The first form of the concorso committee search interface

about the organizing institution (university and/or faculty). All of the concorsi published in an year are grouped by sessions; in a year, from two to four sessions can be included. The search interface, shown in Figure 5, allows the seeker to specify one or more of the above data through two forms including five HTML select fields: *sessione*, *ruolo* (position) *ateneo* (university), *facoltà* and *settore disciplinare* (discipline). The two forms have identical structure but refer to the *concorsi* after and before the reform of the disciplines, respectively.

The statement of the task was the following: "search on the MIUR Web site the members of the committee of the *concorso* for the position of Researcher, discipline MAT/09 - Ricerca Operativa (Operative Research), published in 2007 at the University of Salerno, Faculty of Science".

The System. In order to carry out the case-study, we built a prototypal system. The system is composed of two main components: a *tracking tool*, responsible for tracking user interactions and saving the recording in a log file, and a visualization tool, responsible for aiding the analyzer to graphically inspect the log.

The tracking tool relies on the AJAX [3] technology in order to capture all of the users interactions with the user interface (running in the Web browser). It can be used as a framework to be instantiated in Web applications in order to track system users. Alternatively, it can be used as an external tool for tracking user behaviour on any Web site. The only requisite in the latter case, is to opportunely configure the Web browser to overcome security limitations, which do not allow the scripts to establish connections with external domains (cross-domain scripting security). The visualization tool is an *Integrated Analysis Environment*, in which a suite of interactive charts is combined with textual information presented under the form of tables, to perform a cross-data analysis.

Tracking. The test has been carried out in a laboratory equipped with PCs running a version of Firefox 3.x Web browser, opportunely configured to allow the interaction tracking. With an "authorization" by the webmaster of the analyzed site to insert our scripts in the pages, this step would have not been necessary. Relying on our approach, it was not necessary that the operator controlled the users during the execution of the task. Thus, the users were completely autonomous and performed the task at the same time. The operator was available for answering possible users' questions. The task only lasted a few minutes (except the time necessary to configure the browser), and produced a log file sized less than 100Mb.

Analysis. The produced log has been analyzed with the *visualization tool*. The analysis begins with the visualization of the first level chart (see Figure 6(i)), which summarizes in a single view all of the sessions of the six users who performed the task. The users visited pages from the following three URLs (the prefix http://reclutamento.miur.it/seleziona/ has been cut for brevity):

- A: *commissioni.html*: static Web page containing the search form.
- B: *find_commiss.pl*: dynamic Web page containing the search results. Three different versions of this page have been visited by the users.
   - B1: page containing the expected search result, with a link to the committee's page;
   - B2: page with no results;
   - B3: page containing an error message (mandatory data not specified) and a back link to A.
- C: *commiss_names.pl*: dynamic Web page containing task's final results, that is, the names of the committee's members.

By observing the image, we immediately note that the internal color of node A is darker than other nodes. This suggests that the average time spent on the page with the form is significantly greater than the time spent in checking the search results. Furthermore, nodes B2 and B3 have a lighter color (less time spent) and a thinner border (less visits). The image summarizes the sessions of our six users. In the following, we report in bold face their usernames (as chosen by them) and the sequence of visited pages.

alessia	A → B1 → C
gatto	A → B2 → A → B1 → C
lella	A → B1 → C
lulu	A → B2 → A → B1 → C
mirco	A → B3 → A → B1 → C
zanzibar	A → B3 → A → B1 → C

The three nodes on top of the chart shown in Figure 6(i) are those belonging to the *main flow*, that is, the users must visit the A → B1 → C path in order to successfully accomplish the task. In the case of our test, all of the users did. This can be argued by both inspecting the above sequences and observing the chart. In particular, we note that the nodes corresponding to the pages A, B1 and C have the same border thickness. So do the edges connecting A with B1 and B1 with C. The presence in the chart of pages B1 and B2 is sign of an expected behaviour from the users. The presence of page B3, which contains an error message stating that the required *sessione* field has not been set, is, instead, sign of a usability problem: the *sessione* field is not adequately marked as required in page A. The only cue that differentiates it from the other fields is a "(please) select!" message in the field. Not enough, we can argue, considering that two users out of six left the field blank. Furthermore, the instructions for

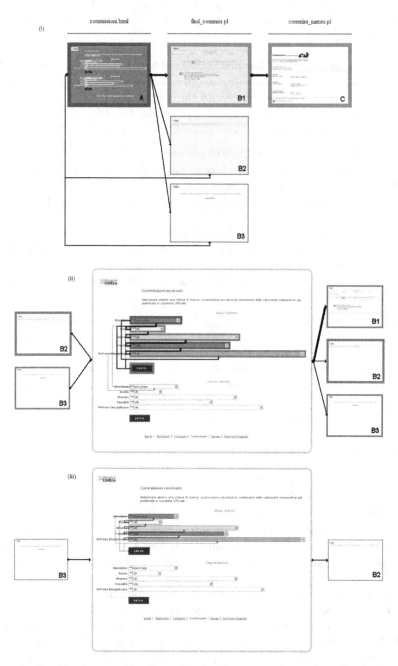

Fig. 6. A selection of screenshots from the visualization tool interface. (i) The first level chart; (ii) the second level chart obtained by zooming-in on page A; (iii) the same chart after the application of an *inclusive filter* on the edge going from B3 to the zoomed page.

filling the form in the upper part of the page state that it is required to "select at least one field", without specifying which one of them is required.

To have a more detailed insight into the situation, hopefully discovering other usability issues with respect to our sample, we start performing a *zoom* operation on page A, obtaining the chart shown in Figure 6(ii). The chart visualizes the 10 page-sessions reported in the following. Here, each field's identifier is composed of a form identifier (0 or 1) and the field name, separated with a dot. The *START* element denotes the dummy entry point (see Section 4.1).

alessia	START → 0.sessione → 0.ruolo → 0.settore → 0.sessione → 0.facolta → 0.ateneo → 0.cerca → B1
gatto	START → 0.ruolo → 0.ateneo → 0.facolta → 0.settore → 0.sessione → 0.cerca → B2
gatto	B2 → 0.sessione → 0.cerca → B1
lella	START → 0.sessione → 0.ruolo → 0.ateneo → 0.facolta → 0.facolta → 0.settore → 0.cerca → B1
lulu	START → 0.sessione → 0.ruolo → 0.ateneo → 0.facolta → 0.settore → 0.cerca → B2
lulu	B2 → 0.sessione → 0.cerca → B1
mirco	B3 → 0.sessione → 0.ruolo → 0.ateneo → 0.facolta → 0.settore → 0.sessione → 0.cerca → B1
mirco	START → 0.sessione → 1.sessione → 0.settore → 0.sessione → 0.ruolo → 0.ateneo → 0.facolta → 0.cerca → B3
zanzibar	START → 0.sessione → 0.ruolo → 0.facolta → 0.ateneo → 0.facolta → 0.settore → 0.cerca → B3
zanzibar	B3 → 0.sessione → 0.ruolo → 0.ateneo → 0.facolta → 0.settore → 0.cerca → B1

The page-sessions visualized in the image are all those passing through page A. Some sessions have more page-sessions satisfying this requirement, in particular all the sessions passing through B2 and B3, since the users had to fill the form again. To keep on analyzing the task, let's apply some *filters*. In particular, let's see what happens by applying an inclusive *filter* on the edge (B3, 0.sessione). By performing this action, we are only selecting the page-sessions that, coming from the error page (B3), have brought again to the starting page (A, the one with the form): A. The page-sessions are the following:

mirco	B3 → 0.sessione → 0.ruolo → 0.ateneo → 0.facolta → 0.settore → 0.sessione → 0.cerca → B1
zanzibar	B3 → 0.sessione → 0.ruolo → 0.ateneo → 0.facolta → 0.settore → 0.cerca → B1

In the resulting chart shown in Figure 6(iii), all of the form fields are highlited (in red). This means that, coming from the error page, the form has been completely reset, forcing the user to re-enter all the input fields. In a well designed interface, the values of the fields should have been kept. This is the second usability problem detected with respect to our sample. By analyzing the code of page B3, we realize that the link back to page A has been coded by the following HTML element:

<a href=http://reclutamento.murst.it/seleziona/commissioni.html> Torna indietro </a>

In order to keep the form values, the back link should have been implemented through a Javascript history.back() statement.

6   Conclusions

We have presented an approach for the analysis of Web tasks by means of Information Visualization. The approach significantly improves previous ones based on *clickstream* visualization. It enables several kinds of analysis in order to trigger the analyzer's attention on behavioral patterns of the users. In this way, the analyzer is provided with a powerful tool that lets him/her review the whole task. A theoretical framework has been defined in order to clearly define the basic elements of the approach and the semantics of the classical visual data mining operators such as *filters* and *zoom* with respect to our case. We have also presented a case-study to show how our approach aids the analyst in detecting usability problems in Web tasks.

We believe that much more patterns can be discovered than those highlited in this paper and that the approach can be used with more general objectives other than evaluating Web usability. Thus, we are planning to perform further experiments, aimed at discovering and classifying new Web usage patterns and at testing our approach in different case-studies. In particular, we are planning to test our approach with a larger number of users, trying also to address problems related to the visualization of large and dense graphs.

Furthermore, we would like to enrich the model with new visual representations to express further metrics not represented yet by the visual cues used in the current charts. Finally, we are adding new features to the prototype and testing it in order to obtain a stable and robust system.

References

1. Kellar, M.: An examination of user behaviour during web information tasks. PhD thesis, Dalhousie University, Dalhousie Univ., Halifax, Canada (2007)
2. Sellen, A.J., Murphy, R., Shaw, K.L.: How knowledge workers use the web. In: CHI 2002: Proceedings of the SIGCHI conference on Human factors in computing systems, pp. 227–234. ACM, New York (2002)
3. Murray, G.: Asynchronous javascript technology and xml (ajax) with the java platform (October 2006),
   http://java.sun.com/developer/technicalArticles/J2EE/AJAX/
4. Thompson, S., Torabi, T.: A process improvement approach to improve web form design and usability. In: DEXA 2007: Proceedings of the 18th International Conference on Database and Expert Systems Applications, Washington, DC, USA, pp. 570–574. IEEE Computer Society, Los Alamitos (2007)
5. Hong, J.I., Heer, J., Waterson, S., Landay, J.A.: Webquilt: A proxy-based approach to remote web usability testing. ACM Transactions on Information Systems 19, 263–285 (2001)

6. Atterer, R., Wnuk, M., Schmidt, A.: Knowing the user's every move: user activity tracking for website usability evaluation and implicit interaction. In: WWW 2006: Proceedings of the 15th international conference on World Wide Web, pp. 203–212. ACM, New York (2006)
7. Paganelli, L., Paternò, F.: Intelligent analysis of user interactions with web applications. In: IUI 2002: Proceedings of the 7th international conference on Intelligent user interfaces, pp. 111–118. ACM, New York (2002)
8. Nakamichi, N., Sakai, M., Shima, K., Hu, J., ichi Matsumoto, K.: Webtracer: A new web usability evaluation environment using gazing point information. Electron. Commer. Rec. Appl. 6(1), 63–73 (2007)
9. Keim, D.A.: Information visualization and visual data mining. IEEE Transactions on Visualization and Computer Graphics 8(1), 1–8 (2002)
10. Chi, E.H.: Improving web usability through visualization. IEEE Internet Computing 6(2), 64–71 (2002)
11. Chen, J., Sun, L., Zaïane, O.R., Goebel, R.: Visualizing and discovering web navigational patterns. In: WebDB 2004: Proceedings of the 7th International Workshop on the Web and Databases, pp. 13–18. ACM, New York (2004)
12. Brainard, J., Becker, B.: Case study: E-commerce clickstream visualization. In: IEEE Proceedings of Information Visualization 2001 (INFOVIS 2001), pp. 153–156. IEEE Computer Society, Los Alamitos (2001)
13. Cofino, T., Gomory, S., Lee, J., Podlaseck, M.: Method for graphically representing clickstream data of a shopping session on a network with a parallel coordinate system. U.S. Patent Office (2007), Patent number 7266510
14. Lee, J., Podlaseck, M.: Using a starfield visualization for analyzing product performance of online stores. In: EC 2000: Proceedings of the 2nd ACM conference on Electronic commerce, pp. 168–175. ACM, New York (2000)
15. Ahlberg, C., Shneiderman, B.: Visual information seeking: Tight coupling of dynamic query filters with starfield displays. In: ACM CHI Conference on Human Factors in Computing Systems, pp. 313–317. ACM Press, New York (1994)
16. Mueller, F., Lockerd, A.: Cheese: tracking mouse movement activity on websites, a tool for user modeling. In: CHI 2001: CHI 2001 extended abstracts on Human factors in computing systems, pp. 279–280. ACM, New York (2001)
17. Costagliola, G., Fuccella, V., Giordano, M., Polese, G.: Monitoring online tests through data visualization. IEEE Transactions on Knowledge and Data Engineering (2009 - to be printed)
18. Green, T.R.G., Petre, M.: Usability analysis of visual programming environments: A cognitive dimensions framework. Journal of Visual Languages and Computing 7, 131–174 (1996)

Exploring Automatic CSS Accessibility Evaluation

Amaia Aizpurua, Myriam Arrue, Markel Vigo, and Julio Abascal

Laboratory of Human-Computer Interaction for Special Needs, Informatika Fakultatea,
University of the Basque Country, Manuel Lardizabal 1, 20018 Donostia, Spain
amaia.aizpurua@ehu.es, myriam@si.ehu.es,
markel@si.ehu.es, julio@si.ehu.es

Abstract. Automatic evaluation tools are crucial for helping designers to develop accessible web content. However, most of the existing automatic tools are focused on evaluating the accessibility of (X)HTML code and do not consider style sheets. CSS provides mechanisms for separating content from display which is a requirement for accessible web documents. Although the use of CSS has become essential, sometimes its powerful mechanisms and functionalities may lead to a misuse. This paper presents an accessibility evaluation framework for verifying the correct application of CSS techniques. For this purpose, a flexible accessibility evaluation framework was selected and adapted to incorporate CSS test cases defined in WCAG 2.0. As a result of a detailed analysis, 6 different types of test cases were identified and a total number of 92 test cases were accommodated into the framework. This process has lead to obtain a flexible framework which performs more comprehensive automatic evaluations.

1 Introduction

One of the most important issues for improving accessibility of web content is to ensure that its structure is separated from the presentation. According to Paciello [1] *"by separating presentation from structure, specialized technologies used by people with disabilities can easily interpret the structure and render it properly to users"*. Therefore, web designers should use appropriate mechanisms for this purpose. In this sense, the World Wide Web Consortium (W3C)[1] recommends using Cascading Style Sheets (CSS)[2].

In recent years, the use of CSS has significantly increased. Designers are supposed to consider structure and presentation as two different aspects of web development by properly structuring web documents using only (X)HTML mark-up and defining its presentation in a separated CSS file. This process facilitates the development of web documents which are more accessible, easier to maintain, possible to navigate with screen readers, better indexed by search engine [2], etc. In addition, the use of CSS has other advantages regarding accessibility [3]:

---

[1] http://www.w3.org/
[2] http://www.w3.org/Style/CSS/

M. Gaedke, M. Grossniklaus, and O. Díaz (Eds.): ICWE 2009, LNCS 5648, pp. 16–29, 2009.
© Springer-Verlag Berlin Heidelberg 2009

- Allows designers to control the spacing, alignment, positioning, etc. of components without using (X)HTML structural elements for stylistic effects.
- Reduces required download time by preventing the use of images for positioning content such as invisible images.
- Provides control over font size, color and style avoiding the use of images to represent text.
- Allows users to override designers' styles.
- Provides techniques for including orientation mechanisms such as numbers or contextual clues, etc.

However, the use of CSS does not guarantee accessibility of web documents. For instance, when the designer defines rigid styles may disturb with the ones defined in users' personal style sheets. Therefore, mechanisms for evaluating the use of CSS are needed in order to ensure accessibility of web documents.

Web Content Accessibility Guidelines 1.0 (WCAG 1.0) [4] specify several CSS techniques [5] which are necessary for developing accessible web documents. In addition, the new version of this set of guidelines, WCAG 2.0 [6], defines evaluation procedures for ensuring CSS techniques [7] are correctly used. Automatic tools able to evaluate the correct use of these CSS techniques would be very useful as they are an essential help for web developers. Ivory and Hearst [8] highlight some advantages of using automatic tools:

- Evaluation process becomes less time demanding and consequently there is a reduction in costs.
- The detected errors are more consistent.
- Possibility for predicting the effort needed in the process in terms of time and economical costs.
- Spreads evaluation scope as it is possible to analyse diverse aspects of the interface in less time.
- Facilitates the process to evaluators with little experience in usability and accessibility evaluation.
- Facilitates comparing the adequacy of different user interface design alternatives.
- Facilitates incorporation of evaluation tasks during the development process.

Many automatic web accessibility evaluation tools exist though most of them focus on (X)HTML mark-up evaluation. The existing automatic evaluation tools for CSS are based on simple syntax verifications such as checking that relative units of measurement are used. The main objective of this work is to extend the evaluation of style aspects by adapting a flexible accessibility evaluation framework to incorporate WCAG 2.0 CSS techniques. For this purpose, a thorough analysis of CSS techniques has been done. It has been useful in order to detect similarities of these techniques with respect of (X)HTML ones. The paper is structured as follows: section 2 is devoted to the analysis of the CSS techniques evaluation coverage of existing accessibility evaluation tools; section 3 describes the analysis process of CSS techniques proposed in WCAG 2.0, in this process test cases are identified and classified; section 4 presents the evaluation process of CSS performed by the adapted evaluation framework; section 5 points out the limitations of current CSS evaluation procedures and conclusions are drawn in section 6.

2 Related Work

There are numerous accessibility evaluation tools. Diverse ways for classifying them can be found in the literature [8, 9, 10, 11]. For instance, they can be classified in two groups, remote or local, based on the location they are executed, on the local computer or on a server respectively. Other [12] studied the coverage of several evaluation tools in all the stages of the development process: specification, design, implementation and post-implementation.

However, the most relevant aspect of tools considered for this research work is their coverage of CSS techniques when evaluating web accessibility. W3C-Web Accessibility Initiative (WAI)[3] maintains a complete list of available evaluation tools[4] and it is possible to search for tools with specific characteristics, for instance their coverage of CSS techniques. According to this list there are 18 tools which meet the specified search criteria: they are free software and evaluate the accessibility of CSS based on WCAG 1.0. Some of them are specific tools which are focused on CSS evaluation while others are accessibility general tools which check some CSS techniques in addition to (X)HTML techniques. Nevertheless, most of them only incorporate a few aspects of CSS; for instance the W3C CSS Validation Service[5] is a specific tool which checks style sheets against the grammar, properties and values defined in the corresponding CSS specification. The CSS Analyser[6] tool by Juicy Studio checks the validity of the given CSS as well as the color contrast and the use of relative units. Hera[7] is an online general accessibility tool based on techniques defined in WCAG 1.0 and also checks some CSS related techniques from checkpoints such as "*3.2: Create documents that validate to published formal grammars*", "*3.3: Use style sheets to control layout and presentation*" or "*3.4: Use relative rather than absolute units in markup language attribute values and style sheet property value*". The evaluated aspects regarding CSS are basically related to checking the use of style sheets in the evaluated web page, validating its syntax against the corresponding formal grammar and verifying the use of relative units.

The aim of this research work is to extend the CSS techniques verified by automatic tools incorporating them into general accessibility evaluation tools in order to perform more comprehensive evaluations. There are several accessibility evaluation tools which are interesting to incorporate new techniques as they do not have to be recoded. They are based on flexible guidelines definition language which provides mechanisms for specifying testing cases. AccessEnable [13] and Kwaresmi [14, 15] are two examples. AccessEnable is a commercial tool which is not longer supported, whereas the GDL guidelines definition language used by Kwaresmi has been recently revised [16]. The locally executable version of TAW[8] offers several functionalities for defining personalized tests but they are limited to some regular expressions not sufficiently complete for accommodating CSS techniques testing

---

[3] http://www.w3.org/WAI/
[4] http://www.w3.org/WAI/ER/tools/Overview
[5] http://jigsaw.w3.org/css-validator/
[6] http://juicystudio.com/services/csstest.php#csscheck
[7] http://www.sidar.org/hera/
[8] http://www.tawdis.net

cases. More recently, Leporini et al. [17] have developed a new evaluation tool MAGENTA which is based on Guidelines Abstraction Language, GAL. Abascal et al. [18] proposed in 2004 the evaluation tool EvalAccess. Recently, the language for guidelines definition used by the tool, UGL (Unified Guidelines Language), was extended and revised in order to accommodate different types of sets of guidelines [19]. This framework has been selected for this research work since its proved flexibility. As far as the evaluation logic of evaluation tools is concerned, there is a growing trend towards using XML technology. XML query languages are very powerful due to their expressiveness and flexibility. Takata et al. [20] proposed a pseudo-XQuery language for accessibility evaluation purposes and XPath/XQuery sentences are defined to check WCAG guidelines in [21]. The use of this technology makes the implementation of the evaluation logic easier and, as a result, many lines of source code are saved.

3   Incorporating CSS into Accessibility Evaluation Process

The process described by Vanderdonckt in [22] has been taken as the basis of this work. The principal steps of the process are the following:

- Gather, combine and compile accessibility guidelines from different sources in order to develop a complete set of guidelines.
- Classify and order the obtained set of guidelines in one organizational framework.
- Develop a computational representation of the set of guidelines so guidelines can be specified and manipulated by software components.

As it can be observed, this process is focused on a complete analysis of sets of guidelines in order to obtain a computational representation flexible enough to accommodate different types of guidelines. In this case, different sets of guidelines have been analysed in order to detect the CSS techniques defined. This process is not simple as guidelines may have different formats, may contain different information and may be described with different level of detail [23, 24]. However, it has been simplified as the recently released WCAG 2.0 determines the exact evaluation procedure for each CSS technique. Depending of their evaluation procedure CSS techniques can be classified in three groups:

- Automatic tests: these problems should not require human judgment to check their validity. Therefore, their evaluation can be completely automatic.
- Manual or semi-automatic tests: human judgment is necessary to check potential problems associated to particular fragments of code implementing the page.
- Generic problems: human judgment is necessary to check potential problems that cannot be associated to any code fragments.

EvalAccess framework can manage these three types of tests. However, the most important types of tests are those that its evaluation can be totally or partially automated.

As a result of the analysis, 22 CSS techniques have been detected. 13 of those can be automatically or semi-automatically evaluated whereas 8 specify generic problems independent of any CSS code fragment and require human judgment. In addition, there is one CSS technique[9] which has no available tests. For the automatic and semi-automatic techniques a number of 92 test cases have been identified. Those test cases can be classified in 6 different types shown in Table 1.

Table 1. The detected different types of test cases for CSS techniques in WCAG 2.0

Id.	Test case name	Description	Example
1	Selector warning	Using a selector may cause accessibility problems and have to be tested manually	*WCAG 2.0 – C15 technique* `A :focus`
2	Property warning	Using a property may cause accessibility problems and have to be tested manually	*WCAG 2.0 – C25 technique* `*{color, background-color}`
3	Determined value	The value of a property has to be one of some specifically defined	*WCAG 2.0 – C13 technique* `*{font-size: xx-small, x-small, small, medium, large, x-large, xx-large, larger, smaller}`
4	Determined Part of Value	The value of a property must contain a determined value	*WCAG 2.0 – C12 technique* `*{font-size: *%}`
5	Value between two values	The value of a property must be between to values	*WCAG 2.0 – C21 technique* `P{line-height: 150% - 200%}`
6	Avoid determined part of value	Avoid a determined value for a property	*WCAG 2.0 – C20 technique* `DIV {width: cm, mm, in, pt, pc, px }`

The detected test cases can be easily represented by UGL, the guidelines specification language used by EvalAccess. This ensures a straightforward process for accommodating the new test cases into the evaluation framework simply by defining each one and incorporating this definition in UGL to the repository of EvalAccess. However, each test case type requires the specification of one XQuery template. The evaluation engine of EvalAccess will match the UGL document of each test case with the corresponding XQuery template. These templates will be completed with the necessary information contained in the UGL document. These completed XQuery templates will be those directly applicable evaluation queries which will be used by the evaluation engine.

---

[9] http://www.w3.org/TR/WCAG20-TECHS/css.html#C18

Figure 1 shows the XQuery template corresponding to test case no. 6 completed with the necessary information for the evaluation of the test case included as an example.

```
let $r:=//rule return(
if($r/selector='div') then
(let $p:= $r/declaration_block/declaration/property return(
if($p='width') then(
for $v in $s/descendant::value return(
if( (contains($v/text(), 'cm') or contains($v/text(), 'mm') or
contains($v/text(), 'in') or contains($v/text(), 'pt') or
contains($v/text(), 'pc') or contains($v/text(), 'px'))) then
('warn')
else ())) else ())) else ())
```

Fig. 1. XQuery template for CSS test-case no. 6 *"Avoid determined part of value"*

Note that some details of the XQuery sentence related to the results are omitted in order to enhance readability.

4   Evaluation Process of CSS Techniques

Figure 2 depicts the evaluation process of CSS techniques included in EvalAccess framework. Each component block in Figure 2 is described below:

1. The CSS Code Retriever obtains the content of a style sheet from the WWW. The obtained CSS code is then converted into XML. This pre-processing of CSS code is necessary since EvalAccess framework is prepared to evaluate (X)HTML code parsed into XML. For this purpose, a XML Schema for parsing CSS code has been developed.

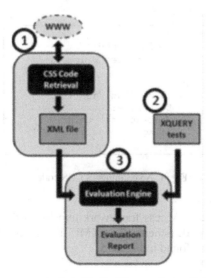

Fig. 2. Evaluation process included in EvalAccess for verifying CSS techniques

2.   The necessary XQuery templates are matched and completed with the information contained in UGL. This process leads to obtain all the XQuery sentences to be applied in the evaluation process.

3.   The code of the style sheet in XML format is evaluated against the XQuery sentences. As a result, detailed evaluation report, which contains information regarding errors, warnings, etc., is obtained. Since reports are formatted according to a specific XML Schema, they can be also exploited by external applications.

Figure 3 shows the defined XML Schema for representing the content of style sheets. As it can be appreciated, style sheets consist of a set of style rules which contains a selector and a declaration block. The last one will gather the attributes and the corresponding values that are defined for the selector element.

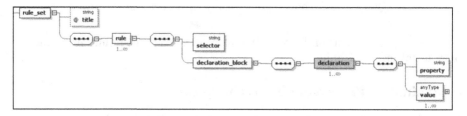

Fig. 3. XML Schema developed for parsing CSS code into XML

4.1   Example of the Evaluation Process

This section presents a detailed description of each necessary step in the evaluation process. For this purpose, a CSS code fragment has been selected as an example for illustrating the developed evaluation process. Figure 4 shows the CSS code fragment.

```
div{
        width: 350px;
        margin: 1em 0 1em 0;
}
#tag p{
        text-align: justify;
        font-size:10px;
        font-weight: bold;
        background-color: #FFFFFF;
}
```

Fig. 4. An example of CSS code

As mentioned above, EvalAccess framework transforms the CSS code into XML based on the developed XML Schema. The XML file corresponding to the example CSS code (Figure 4) can be found in Figure 5.

```
<?xml version="1.0"?>
<css xmlns:xsi="http://www.w3.org/2001/XMLSchema-instance"
xsi:noNamespaceSchemaLocation="file:///c:/schemaCSS.xsd">
    <rule_set title="C:\style">
        <rule>
                <selector>div</selector>
                <declaration_block>
                        <declaration>
                                <property>width</property>
                                <value>350px</value>
                        </declaration>
                        <declaration>
                                <property>margin</property>
                                <value>1em</value>
                                <value>0</value>
                                <value>1em</value>
                                <value>0</value>
                        </declaration>
                </declaration_block>
        </rule>
        <rule>
                <selector>#tag p</selector>
                <declaration_block>
                        <declaration>
                                <property>text-align</property>
                                <value>justify</value>
                        </declaration>
                        <declaration>
                                <property>font-size</property>
                                <value>10px</value>
                        </declaration>
                        <declaration>
                                <property>font-weight</property>
                                <value>bold</value>
                        </declaration>
                        <declaration>
                                <property>background-color</property>
                                <value>#FFFFFF</value>
                        </declaration>
                </declaration_block>
        </rule>
    </rule_set>
</css>
```

Fig. 5. XML representation of the CSS code in Figure 4

As it can be observed, the CSS code is analysed in order to detect the selectors and all the rules in terms of attributes and values applied to them. This information is inserted in a XML file. This XML transformation facilitates the application of the CSS test cases defined in the evaluation framework.

The 92 CSS test cases identified in WCAG 2.0 document are stored in UGL format in a repository. In this way, incorporation of new test cases or new versions of existing ones is quite straightforward.

Next figures, Figure 6, 7 and 8, show the UGL definition of different CSS test cases applied in the evaluation process and the generated XQuery sentences based on

```
<techniques id="C12">
  <type>CSS</type>
  <title>Using percent for font sizes</title>
  <description>The value of the property must contain a
  determined part of value
  </description>
  <test_case>
   <type>4</type>
   <evaluation_type>auto</evaluation_type>
   <evaluation_result>[error]</evaluation_result>
   <element>
       <label>#tag p</label>
       <attribute>
           <atb>[font-size]</atb>
           <test_a>value</test_a>
           <content analysis="=">[*%]</content>
       </attribute>
   </element>
  </test_case>
</techniques>
```

```
for $d in //rule/declaration_block/declaration return
if($d/property = "font-size") then
return
    if(not(contains(($d/value),  "%")))
    then ("error")
    else ()
```

Fig. 6. One test case for verifying WCAG 2.0 C12 CSS technique specified in UGL and the corresponding XQuery sentence

appropriate XQuery templates directly applied to the XML file containing the CSS code fragment.

Figure 6 contains the UGL specification of one test case for CSS technique C12 defined in WCAG 2.0. All the necessary information for completing the corresponding XQuery template is included in this specification. UGL provides mechanisms for determining the correspondence of one CSS test case with its XQuery template (*type* attribute of the *test_case* element). In this case, the corresponding XQuery template is the one defined for CSS test case type no.4 *"Determined Part of Value"* (see Table 1).

Figure 7 shows the UGL file and the generated XQuery sentence for the evaluation of one test case of WCAG 2.0 C19 CSS technique. The XQuery sentence is generated by including the necessary data in the XQuery template corresponding to CSS test case type no.3 *"Determined value"* (see Table 1).

Figure 8 shows UGL specification and XQuery sentence for verifying one of the test cases of WCAG 2.0 C25 CSS technique. XQuery sentence is generated by including the necessary data in the XQuery template corresponding to CSS test case type no.2 *"Property warning"* (see Table 1). In this case, a warning will be created if the XQuery sentence is proved to be true as the test case is of semi-automatic type. This is defined in UGL by *evaluation_result* attribute of *test_case* element.

```
<techniques id="C19">
  <type>CSS</type>
  <title>Specifying alignment either to the left OR right in
  CSS</title>
  <description>The value of the property has to be one of some
  specifically defined</description>
  <test_case>
    <type>3</type>
    <evaluation_type>auto</evaluation_type>
    <evaluation_result>[error]</evaluation_result>
    <element>
      <label>#tag p</label>
      <attribute>
      <atb>[text-align]</atb>
      <test_a>value</test_a>
      <content analysis="=">[left]</content>
      <content analysis="=">[right]</content>
      </attribute>
    </element>
  </test_case>
</techniques>
```

```
for $d in //rule/declaration_block/declaration return
if($d/property = "text-align") then
return
    if($d/value!="left" and $d/value!="right")
  then ("error")
```

Fig. 7. One test case for verifying WCAG 2.0 C19 CSS technique specified in UGL and the corresponding XQuery sentence. CSS test-case no. 3 *"Determined value"*

```
<techniques id="C25">
  <type>CSS</type>
  <title>Specifying borders and layout in CSS to delineate areas
  of a Web page while not specifying text and text-background
  colors</title>
  <description>It is recommended to avoid using the
  property</description>
  <test_case>
    <type>2</type>
    <evaluation_type>semi</evaluation_type>
    <evaluation_result>[warn]</evaluation_result>
    <element>
      <label>#tag p</label>
      <attribute>
      <atb> [background-color] </atb>
      <test_a>warning</test_a>
      </attribute>
    </element>
  </test_case>
</techniques>
```

```
for $d in //rule/declaration_block/declaration return
if($d/property = "background-color")
    then ("warn")
```

Fig. 8. One test case for verifying WCAG 2.0 C25 CSS technique specified in UGL and the corresponding XQuery sentence

Table 2. Evaluation results of the example CSS code fragment based on the described three test cases

Type	Selector	Attribute	Description	Technique Id	CSS code
Error	#tag p	font-size	The value of the property must contain a determined part of value	C12	`font-size:10px`
Error	#tag p	text-align	The value of the property has to be one of some specifically defined	C19	`text-align: justify`
Warning	#tag p	background-color	It is recommended to avoid using the property	C25	`background-color: #FFFFFF`

UGL specification of CSS test cases also provides useful information for creating the evaluation results report as the description and title of the test case is also available. The results obtained evaluating the example CSS code fragment according to the described three test cases are described in Table 2.

5   Limitations of CSS Evaluation

The main advantage of using style sheets is that they allow the separation of content from design, as recommended by the W3C. Separating markup and presentation is a crucial part of universal design paradigm. This architectural principle is the key for the evolution of the web in a wide range of aspects, such as accessibility, device independence, ubiquity and so on. Currently, it would be very difficult to fulfill the WCAG accessibility guidelines without using CSS.

However, CSS provides powerful mechanisms and functionalities which can lead to a misuse. In this sense, some practices may lead to confuse specialized technologies used by people with disabilities. For instance, the use of misusing (X)HTML structural elements for its expected visual effects, such as the TABLE element which is often used for stylistic purposes like positioning or alignment. On the contrary, style sheets may be used to imitate proper (X)HTML Markup. Elements such as headings, paragraphs and inline elements (STRONG, EM, etc) are sometimes replaced with inappropriate tags which are styled to simply look like markup elements. In order to avoid confusing specialized technologies, it is crucial to verify that CSS techniques are applied appropriately.

Even though this paper describes a useful evaluation framework for CSS techniques, there are several issues which have to be necessarily considered in order to perform comprehensive evaluations. For example, the presented framework evaluates the accessibility of a style sheet itself but it is more interesting to evaluate the result of applying the styles on a specific web page. In addition there are some aspects of CSS which make more difficult to foresee the final display of a web page, but they should be considered for ensuring accessibility of web documents:

- **Inheritance**[10]. CSS allows some properties applied to determined elements, to be inherited from those specified for the parent elements. Although all CSS properties cannot be inherited, the latter CSS specification introduced the *inherit* property value. This value allows the property to be inherited from a parent element in the document tree.

- **Cascading**[11]. Style sheets may belong to different agents: author, user and user-agent. The cascade is the property which allows having multiple styles from different sources merged together into one definitive style. It consists of a set of rules to determine the interaction among conflicting styles from different origins. Conflicts among styles happen when for the same element in a document a determined property is assigned contradictory values by different style sheets. Priority levels have been determined in order to solve these conflicts. They are based on three main factors: weight and origin, specificity of selectors and order of appearance. However, there are some mechanisms which can override the established priorities such as *!important* style rules, *@import* statement. Therefore, it is a complex task to foresee which style rules will be finally applied to the document.

- **Media selection**[12]. Media Types allow specifying how documents will be presented on different media, such as speech synthesizers, braille devices, printers, etc. The design of a web page to be displayed on a normal desktop screen may not be suitable for a printer, or a handheld device. There are several media types but by default, style sheets apply to all media types. Different ways can be used to make styles apply only to specific media types. The most commonly used methods are the use of the media attribute of the link or style tag, and the *@media* rule. Most of the styles are available to all media types, but some CSS properties are only designed for certain media. For example, the *font-size* style property does not make any sense in speech media. This means that the rules of the style sheets must be applied depending on the selected media.

- **Browser implementation differences**[13]. Although most browsers support style sheets, not all of them provide the same level of implementation[14]. Moreover, there are implementation differences among versions of the same browser. There are several mechanisms[15] to solve the CSS related browser bugs. Nevertheless, if those solutions are not applied and a design for a given web page is made for a determined browser, the content of the page can be inaccessible for persons using other browsers.

All these aspects should be considered in order to perform a more adaptive evaluation but it requires gathering more information about final users' environment, such as the

---

[10] http://www.w3.org/TR/CSS21/cascade.html#inheritance

[11] http://www.w3.org/TR/CSS21/cascade.html#cascade

[12] http://www.w3.org/TR/CSS21/media.html

[13] http://www.webreference.com/authoring/style/sheets/browser_support/

[14] http://www.quirksmode.org/css/contents.html

[15] http://websitetips.com/css/solutions/

browser model and version, access device used, existence of user defined style sheets, etc. Otherwise, evaluating accessibility of CSS for all possible interaction schemas becomes an excessively complex task.

6 Conclusions

In this paper we have presented a framework to evaluate accessibility of style sheets according to the CSS techniques specified in WCAG 2.0. For this purpose, a detailed analysis of CSS techniques has been performed. The framework itself has not been developed from scratch since one flexible accessibility evaluation framework was selected to accommodate the new CSS techniques. This allows extending the efficiency of the framework so that more comprehensive accessibility evaluation can be performed.

Unified Guidelines Language (UGL) is the basis of the framework. The use of this language guarantees that new CSS techniques will be easily incorporated into the framework. A total number of 92 CSS test cases have been defined in UGL and incorporated to the framework for their automatic verification.

This work involves an important step towards considering the web design in the accessibility evaluation process. However, the proposed framework only deals with the evaluation of CSS files and it does not consider some significant aspects inherent to the use of style sheets such as inheritance, cascading, differences in browser implementation, etc.

Comprehensive accessibility evaluations involve considering more aspects than only the CSS or the (X)HTML code. In this sense, it is necessary to predict the resulting display of combining an (X)HTML file with the applicable style sheets in a determined context of use (specific browser and version, access device, users' preferences, etc.). Nevertheless, this is a complex task and future work will be focused on trying to find better solutions in order to improve the accessibility evaluation process.

References

1. Paciello, M.G.: Web Accessibility for People with Disabilities. CMP books (2000)
2. Pemberton, S.: Accessibility is for Everyone. ACM Interactions 10(6), 4–5 (2003)
3. Jacobs, I., Brewer, J. (eds.): Accessibility Features of CSS. W3C Note, (August 4, 1999), http://www.w3.org/TR/CSS-access
4. Chrisholm, W., Vanderheiden, G., Jacobs, I. (eds.): Web Content Accessibility Guidelines 1.0, W3C Recommendation (May 5, 1999), http://www.w3.org/TR/WCAG10/
5. Chisholm, W., Vanderheiden, G., Jacobs, I. (eds.): CSS Techniques for Web Content Accessibility Guidelines 1.0, W3C Note (November 6, 2000), http://www.w3.org/TR/WCAG10-CSS-TECHS/
6. Caldwell, B., Cooper, M., Reid, L.G., Vanderheiden, G. (eds.): Web Content Accessibility Guidelines (WCAG) 2.0, W3C Recommendation (December 11, 2008), http://www.w3.org/TR/WCAG20/
7. Caldwell, B., Cooper, M., Reid, L.G., Vanderheiden, G. (eds.): Techniques for WCAG 2.0. CSS Techniques for WCAG 2.0, W3C Working Group Note (December 11, 2008), http://www.w3.org/TR/WCAG20-TECHS/css.html

8. Ivory, M.Y., Hearst, M.A.: The state of art in automating usability evaluations of user interfaces. ACM Computing Surveys 33(4), 470–516 (2001)
9. Ivory, M.Y., Mankoff, J., Le, A.: Using Automated Tools to Improve Web Site Usage by Users with Diverse Abilities. Information Technology and Society 1(3), 195–236 (2003)
10. Brajnik, G.: Comparing accessibility evaluation tools: a method for tool effectiveness. Universal Access in the Information Society 3(3-4), 252–263 (2004)
11. Abou-Zahra, S. (ed.): Selecting Web Accessibility Evaluation Tools (2006), http://www.w3.org/WAI/eval/selectingtools
12. Xiong, J., Farenc, C., Winckler, M.: Analyzing Tool Support for Inspecting Accessibility Guidelines During the Development Process of Web Sites. In: Weske, M., Hacid, M.-S., Godart, C. (eds.) WISE Workshops 2007. LNCS, vol. 4832, pp. 470–480. Springer, Heidelberg (2007)
13. Brinck, T., Hermann, D., Minnebo, B., Hakim, A.: AccessEnable: A Tool for Evaluating Compliance with Accessibility Standards. In: Automatically Evaluating the Usability of Web Sites, CHI Workshop (2002)
14. Beirekdar, A., Vanderdonckt, J., Noirhomme-Fraiture, M.: Kwaresmi - Knowledge-based Web Automated Evaluation with REconfigurable guidelineS optimization. In: Forbrig, P., Limbourg, Q., Urban, B., Vanderdonckt, J. (eds.) DSV-IS 2002. LNCS, vol. 2545, pp. 362–376. Springer, Heidelberg (2002)
15. Beirekdar, A., Vanderdonckt, J., Noirhomme-Fraiture, M.: A Framework and a Language for Usability Automatic Evaluation of Web Sites by Static Analysis of HTML Source Code. In: Proceedings of 4th Int. Conf. on Computer-Aided Design of User Interfaces CADUI 2002, ch. 29, pp. 337–348. Kluwer, Dordrecht (2002)
16. Vanderdonckt, J., Bereikdar, A.: Automated Web Evaluation by Guideline Review. Journal of Web Engineering. Rinton Press 4(2), 102–117 (2005)
17. Leporini, B., Paternò, F., Scorcia, A.: Flexible tool support for accessibility evaluation. Interacting with Computers 18(5), 869–890 (2006)
18. Abascal, J., Arrue, M., Fajardo, I., Garay, N., Tomás, J.: Use of Guidelines to automatically verify web accessibility. Universal Access in the Information Society 3(1), 71–79 (2004)
19. Arrue, M., Vigo, M., Abascal, J.: Including Heterogeneous Web Accessibililty Guidelines in the Development Process. In: Gulliksen, J., et al. (eds.) EIS 2007, vol. 4940, pp. 620–637. Springer, Heidelberg (2008)
20. Takata, Y., Nakamura, T., Seki, H.: Accessibility Verification of WWW Documents by an Automatic Guideline Verification Tool. In: Proceedings of the 37th Hawaii International Conference on System Sciences (2004)
21. Luque, V., Delgado, C., Gaedke, M., Nussbaumer, M.: WCAG Formalization with W3C Techniques. In: Lowe, D.G., Gaedke, M. (eds.) ICWE 2005. LNCS, vol. 3579, pp. 615–617. Springer, Heidelberg (2005)
22. Vanderdonckt, J.: Development milestones towards a tool for working with guidelines. Interacting with Computers 12, 81–118 (1999)
23. Abascal, J., Nicolle, C.: Why Inclusive Design Guidelines? In: Abascal, J., Nicolle, C. (eds.) Inclusive Design Guidelines for HCI, ch.1, pp. 3–13. Taylor & Francis, Abington (2001)
24. Mariage, C., Vanderdonckt, J., Pribeanu, C.: State of the Art of Web Usability Guidelines. In: Proctor, R., Vu, K. (eds.) The Handbook of Human Factors in Web Design, ch. 8, pp. 688–700. Lawrence Erlbaum, Mahwah (2005)

A Component-Based Approach for Engineering Enterprise Mashups

Javier López[1], Fernando Bellas[1], Alberto Pan[1], and Paula Montoto[2]

[1] Information and Communications Technology Department, University of A Coruña
Facultad de Informática, Campus de Elviña, s/n, 15071, A Coruña, Spain
{jmato,fbellas,apan}@udc.es
[2] Denodo Technologies, Inc.
Real 22, 3°, 15003, A Coruña, Spain
pmontoto@denodo.com

Abstract. Mashup applications combine pieces of functionality from several existing, heterogeneous sources to provide new integrated functionality. This paper presents the design of an enterprise-oriented mashup tool that fully supports the construction of mashup applications. Our tool provides generic, reusable components to engineer mashup applications. It includes components for accessing heterogeneous sources, a component to combine data from different sources and components for building the graphical interface. The user builds graphically the mashup application by selecting, customizing, and interconnecting components. Unlike other proposals we: (1) use the Data Federation/Mediation pattern (instead of Pipes and Filters pattern) to express the data combination logic, (2) follow the RESTful architectural style to improve component reusability, and (3) reuse Java standard portal technology to implement the graphical interface of the mashup application.

Keywords: Enterprise Mashups, Integration Patterns, Web Engineering.

1 Introduction

Mashup applications combine pieces of functionality from several existing, heterogeneous sources to provide new integrated functionality. Many research works and industrial tools have appeared during the last two years to ease the creation of mashups. In particular, mashup tools enable 'power users', which do not have programming skills, to build easily mashup applications to quickly respond to a personal or business need.

There are two key aspects in building a mashup application: (1) accessing data sources to obtain unified data and (2) building the graphical interface. Some tools are strong in the first aspect (e.g. [23][13][19]), and only include minimum graphical support to format the returned data. Other tools (e.g. [9][10][4]) support both aspects. Tools also differ in the type of mashup application they are oriented to. Some of them are hosted tools (e.g. [23][13]) that allow Internet users to build mashup applications ('consumer' mashups). Other tools (e.g. [9][10]) are enterprise-oriented and allow the

M. Gaedke, M. Grossniklaus, and O. Díaz (Eds.): ICWE 2009, LNCS 5648, pp. 30–44, 2009.
© Springer-Verlag Berlin Heidelberg 2009

construction of 'enterprise' mashups. Consumer-oriented tools include support to integrate a limited set of sources (typically, RSS/Atom feeds, and REST services) and provide basic graphical capabilities. Enterprise-oriented tools need to take into account many other types of sources, such as databases, SOAP services, and semi-structured HTML web sources, or even to extract parts of web pages (web clipping). Furthermore, the data combination logic and the requirements of the graphical interface are often much more complex.

In this paper we present the design of an enterprise-oriented mashup tool that fully supports the construction of mashup applications. Our tool provides generic, reusable components to engineer mashup applications. It includes components for accessing a great variety of sources ('source adaptors'), a component to combine data from different sources ('data mashup' component), and components for building the graphical interface ('widgets'). The user builds graphically the mashup application by selecting, customizing, and interconnecting components. For example, a data mashup component is connected to the source adaptors of the sources to be combined.

To the best of our knowledge, all existing tools use the Pipes and Filters pattern [8] to express the data combination logic of the data sources making up the mashup application. This pattern follows a 'procedural' approach that forces the user to implement the combination logic in terms of a pipe. Depending on how the end-user needs to query the data, more than one pipe may need to be implemented to optimally execute the query. Unlike current tools, our data mashup component uses a 'declarative' approach based on the Data Federation pattern [22]. Combination logic is graphically expressed as relational operations (such as joins, unions, projections, selections, and aggregations) over the data sources to be combined. When the end-user launches a query, the data mashup component can automatically compute all the possible execution plans to solve it and let the optimizer choose one. Conceptually, each execution plan can be seen as a pipe in the Pipes and Filters pattern.

Our architecture also makes emphasis in component reusability. Source adaptors and data mashup components implement the same RESTful [5] interface. Apart from the advantages intrinsic to the RESTful architectural style, this allows, for example, reusing a data mashup component as a source component. It also makes possible the construction of 'template' widgets that can analyze the meta-information (a WADL specification [21]) of a component and provide specific functionality at run-time.

Finally, unlike other proposals, we reuse standard Java portal technology to implement the graphical interface. In particular, widgets are implemented as portlets [12][15]. At the graphical interface level, a mashup application is implemented as a portal page composed of a number of widgets. Some of these widgets will be connected to data mashup components. Reusing standard Java portal technology allows aggregating heterogeneous widgets in a mashup application and using the portal's event bus to coordinate them.

The rest of the paper is structured as follows. Section 2 presents a running example to illustrate our approach to building enterprise mashup applications. Section 3 provides an overview of the mashup tool architecture. Sections 4 and 5 discuss the design of the architecture. Section 6 discusses related work. Finally, Section 7 presents conclusions and outlines future work.

2 A Running Example

This section presents a running example[1] to exemplify our approach to building enterprise mashup applications. In the example, Martin, a Sales Manager from Acme, Inc. needs to perform a typical task: discovering new potential customers. Acme, like many other companies, uses an on-demand CRM to store data about its customers. In particular, Acme uses salesforce.com (http://www.salesforce.com). Customer's data includes, apart from general company information, the satisfaction level with Acme products and the name of a business contact in such a company.

Martin, like many other professionals, uses LinkedIn (http://www.linkedin.com) to maintain information about their business contacts. LinkedIn is a business-oriented social network that does not only allow maintaining information about personal contacts but also to access contacts from other users. LinkedIn users may specify public information, such as, personal information (name and title) and general information about her/his company (name, industry, and address), and private information (e.g. phone and email). Another LinkedIn user can see public information of the contacts of any of her/his direct contacts.

To discover new 'leads' (i.e. potential customers), Martin intends to use the following strategy:

- Search current customers in salesforce.com. He may be interested in retrieving these customers by different criteria, such as satisfaction level, industry, geographic location, or even by the name of a business contact. For this example, we will assume that Martin wishes to find customers by satisfaction level and/or business contact name. For each customer he needs its satisfaction level and the name of the business contact. These business contacts are among the Martin's direct contacts in LinkedIn. We will call 'reference contacts' to these business contacts.
- For each reference contact, search in LinkedIn her/his business contacts (the 'leads'). Many of them will work in other companies and Martin intends to contact them by using the reference contact. Martin may want to analyze all the leads or only those fulfilling a set of criteria. For this example, we will assume that he may want to restrict the returned leads to those working in a company of a given industry.
- To perform a global analysis, Martin wants to classify all lead companies by industry, using a pie chart summary.
- Finally, for each lead company, Martin wants to locate it in a map to plan a visit (e.g. by using Google Maps) and obtain information about it (e.g. by using Yahoo! Finance).

Since the number of customers in salesforce.com (and LinkedIn network) is large and variable, Martin quickly realizes this task is large and tedious. Clearly, he needs an application that fully automates the task. Martin is not a programmer. In consequence, it is not feasible for him to build such an application. Even for a programmer, building this application is not easy since it involves the access to five

---

[1] We have implemented a running prototype of the architecture proposed in this paper and we have used it to create the mashup illustrated in this section. The mashup can be accessed at http://www.tic.udc.es/mashup-demo.

applications with heterogeneous, complex interfaces. Martin could solve his need using our mashup tool. This tool provides a set of generic, reusable components that can be customized and assembled to engineer mashup applications.

The first aspect he needs to resolve consists in obtaining the data. For each lead, Martin wishes to obtain:

- Data about the lead (name and title) and her/his company (name, industry, and address). This information is provided by LinkedIn.
- Data about the reference customer: satisfaction level and reference contact. This information is provided by salesforce.com.

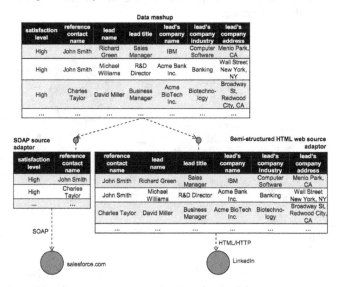

Fig. 1. Assembly of components to get the data of potential new customer companies

Fig. 1 shows how Martin solves the first aspect. The mashup tool provides 'source adaptor' components to access many kinds of sources. Source adaptors are non-visual components that allow accessing a source by providing a uniform interface to other components. Among others, the tool provides adaptors for data sources such as SOAP and semi-structured HTML web sources. All these data source adaptors allow seeing a data source as a web service that can be consulted through the uniform interface. The first one inspects a WSDL specification and invokes the appropriate operations. The second one uses web wrapper generation techniques to automate queries on a semi-structured HTML web source.

Martin selects the SOAP salesforce.com adaptor and configures it to obtain the data he needs. Then, he configures the semi-structured HTML web adaptor to automatically login with Martin's credentials in LinkedIn, fill in the search form with a reference contact name, navigate to the pages containing the public information of the leads and extract the target data.

To combine the data provided by salesforce.com and LinkedIn, Martin selects a 'data mashup' component and connects it to the previous two components. This component combines the data provided by both components, conceptually performing a JOIN operation by reference contact name. The data mashup component is also a non-visual component that allows seeing the resulting data as a web service that can be consulted through the same interface as the data source components.

The second aspect Martin has to deal with consists in building the graphical interface of the application. The interface consists in: (1) a form to query leads according to Martin's criteria, (2) a pie chart for classifying leads by industry, (3) a map to locate lead companies, and (4) a web clipping of Yahoo! Finance to obtain the information about them. The mashup tool provides generic visual components that fulfill Martin's requirements. He only needs to customize and to assembly them. We name 'widgets' to these visual components. Fig. 2 shows the assembly of widgets making up the graphical interface.

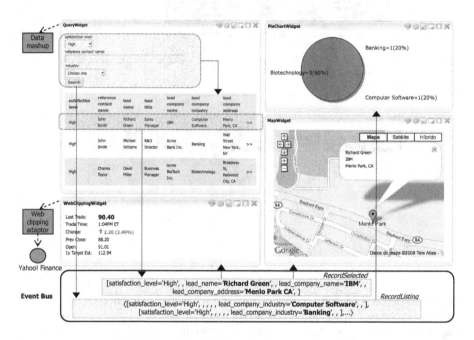

Fig. 2. Assembly of widgets in the example mashup

To provide the form for querying leads, Martin selects the 'query widget' and connects it to the data mashup component. This widget can analyze the meta-information provided by the data mashup component to find out its query capabilities (e.g. query parameters) and the schema of the returned data. From this information, it automatically generates an HTML form to allow querying the data mashup component, showing the results in an HTML table. In the example, the form has the following fields: satisfaction level, reference contact name, and industry.

To include the pie chart, Martin chooses the 'pie chart widget'. This widget generates a pie chart from a list of records using the values of one of the fields to classify them. In this case, Martin specifies this widget to receive the list of records displayed by the query widget and classify them by the industry field. How the pie chart widget receives the list of records? One approach would consist in Martin to explicitly create a link between the query widget and the pie chart widget. However, in the general case this could result in the user would have to create manually a network of links between all widgets sending a given type of object and all the widgets wishing to receive it. To overcome this problem, widgets communicate each other by using an event-based model. An event has a logical name (e.g. *RecordListing*) and data (e.g. the list of records). A widget subscribes to an event by specifying its name. Each time a widget publishes an event, the mashup tool delivers it to all subscribing widgets. In this case, the query widget generates the *RecordListing* event when it obtains the results and the pie chart widget is prepared to receive events containing a list of records. Martin personalizes the pie chart widget to subscribe it to the *RecordListing* event. The query widget also allows selecting one of the records in the result listing. Selecting a record causes the query widget to send the *RecordSelected* event containing the selected record.

To locate lead companies on a map, Martin selects the 'map widget'. This widget receives an event containing a record that must include an address field. This widget uses Google Maps to show the information contained in the record into a map. Martin personalizes the widget to subscribe it to the *RecordSelected* event and to specify the name of the field containing the address. This way, whenever the user selects a record in the query widget, its information is automatically placed in the map.

Finally, to get the clipping of a given company from Yahoo! Finance, Martin chooses the 'web clipping widget'. This widget allows accessing a web page to extract a block of markup. Since accessing a web page involves automatic navigation (maybe traversing several forms and links), this widget must be connected to a 'web clipping source adaptor'. Like a 'semi-structured HTML web adaptor', this adaptor performs automatic navigation. However, unlike that adaptor, a web clipping adaptor does not extract data but a block of markup (without interpreting its meaning). In consequence, Martin selects a web clipping adaptor and configures it to access Yahoo! Finance. He also customizes the web clipping widget to use the web clipping adaptor. Like the map widget, the web clipping widget is also prepared to receive an event containing a record that must include a field for the company name. Martin subscribes the web clipping widget to the *RecordSelected* event and specifies the name of the field containing the company name.

3 Overview of the Mashup Tool Architecture

Fig. 3 shows the architecture of our mashup tool. The design of the architecture breaks down the functionality in 'layers' and 'common services'. Layers represent main functional blocks and have the traditional meaning in software design. Common services represent services that are useful for several layers.

The goal of the 'Source Access Layer' is to let the higher level layers access heterogeneous sources by using a common interface. As justified in section 4, we use a RESTful interface. Internally, this layer provides a 'source adaptor' component for each possible type of source. Each adaptor maps the meta-model and access modes used by the underlying source to the RESTful interface. Our current implementation provides adaptors for accessing typical data sources, such as SOAP/REST web services, relational databases, and semi-structured HTML web pages. It also includes a special adaptor, 'web clipping source adaptor', to extract a block of markup of a HTML web source.

The 'Data Mashup Layer' allows defining 'views' combining one or several sources, which are accessed through the Source Access Layer interface. A 'view' has the same meaning as in databases. It is possible to define views as joins, unions, projections, selections, and aggregations of sources. As justified in section 4, we have chosen the Data Federation pattern to declaratively define the views. To this end, this layer provides the 'data mashup' component. The user connects this component to the source adaptors she/he needs. This layer (and in consequence the data mashup component) exposes the same RESTful interface to the higher level layer as the Source Access Layer. This allows reusing a data mashup component as a source adaptor, enabling to connect it to other data mashup components.

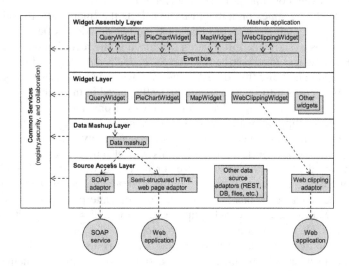

Fig. 3. Mashup tool's architecture

To support the construction of the graphical interface of the mashup application, the 'Widget Layer' provides visual components, which we call 'widgets' (query widget, pie chart widget, etc.). Some widgets are connected to data mashup components (e.g. the query widget). As explained in section 5, we have decided to use standard Java portal technology to implement this layer and the layer above it. In particular, widgets are implemented as portlets [12][15].

The 'Widget Assembly Layer' allows assembling several widgets to create the final, unified graphical interface of the mashup. Assembly capability implies 'aggregation' and 'coordination' of widgets. Aggregation refers to the capability of adding heterogeneous widgets into a mashup application. Coordination refers to enabling communication between widgets inside the mashup application.

Finally, our architecture distinguishes three services, namely 'registry', 'collaboration', and 'security' to facilitate the implementation of all layers. Our current implementation includes support for registry and security services. Basic registry capabilities include registering and searching components (individual sources, data mashups, widgets, and mashup applications). Additional registry capabilities include component lifecycle management (e.g. versioning) and community feedback (e.g. tagging, rating, etc.). The security service follows a role-based policy to specify and control the actions that can be taken on components. Finally, collaboration refers to the possibility of reusing knowledge automatically obtained by the tool in function of previous user interactions. This knowledge may be used to automatically or semi-automatically compose data mashups and widgets. We are currently working on adding this service to our tool.

4 Design of the Source Access and Data Mashups Layers

4.1 Access to Web Sources

In the Source Access Layer, semi-structured web sources require special attention. By semi-structured web sources, we refer to websites which do not provide any programmatic interface to access their contents and/or services.

In this case, this layer needs to use either web wrapper generation techniques [2][14] or web clipping techniques [1] to emulate a programmatic interface on top of the existing website. Web wrappers extract data from the target website in structured form. For instance, in our example, a web wrapper is used to automate the search for the contacts of a given reference customer in LinkedIn, extracting the structured data embedded in the HTML response pages. Our current implementation supports graphical generation of wrappers using the techniques proposed in [14].

In turn, web clipping automates the process of extracting target markup fragments from one or several pages in a website, providing reuse at the UI-interface level. In our example, the web clipping widget introduced in section 2 uses the web clipping adaptor provided by the Source Access Layer to obtain the desired Yahoo! Finance information. The web clipping adaptor automates the process of querying Yahoo! Finance (using the same automatic navigation techniques used for wrapper generation) and return the HTML markup corresponding to the fragment of the page containing the target information.

4.2 Interface Provided for the Source Access and Data Mashup Layers

Our approach reuses the RESTful architectural style [5] for the interface provided by the Source Access Layer and Data Mashups Layer. A RESTful web service allows accessing resources by using the standard HTTP methods GET, POST, PUT, and DELETE. Each resource is uniquely identified by a global URI. A RESTful interface presents several relevant advantages in the mashup environment:

- It supports both sources returning visual markup (such as HTML web sources used for web clipping) and sources returning structured data.
- Each individual data item obtained from a source/data mashup can be modeled as a resource accessible by a unique global URI. For instance, let us assume for the sake of simplicity that the fields *reference_contact_name* and *lead_name* uniquely identify an item returned by the data mashup of Fig. 1; then we could use a

URI such as *http://www.tic.udc.es/mashup_demo/leads?reference_contact_name=John+Smith&lead_contact_name=Richard+Green* to reference the lead contact named *Richard Green* obtained through the reference contact named *John Smith*.

- These resources can be read, updated, inserted, or removed by respectively issuing GET, POST, PUT, and DELETE HTTP requests on the URI of the resource. Of course, some resources may not admit some operations or may require authorization before executing them. Special URIs (e.g. *http://www.tic.udc.es/mashup_demo/leads?reference_contact_name=John+Smith*) can be constructed for executing queries by using the GET method.

- It promotes reuse at the resource granularity. Since each resource is identified by a global URI, any data mashup can link to a resource from another one just by including its URI. For example, let us suppose that, after creating the mashup application of section 2, Martin creates another mashup application to support tracking of the sales opportunities opened by using the first one. This second application could be based on a new data mashup gathering information from several sources and including in each opportunity a link to the original information that provoked it. For instance, if an opportunity came from the lead *Richard Green* of the reference contact *John Smith*, the new data mashup could include a link to *http://www.tic.udc.es/mashup_demo/leads?reference_contact_name=John+Smith&lead_contact_name=Richard+Green* in the returned information about the opportunity. Notice also how using links lets the higher layer or the application decide in an item-by item basis whether to pay the cost of obtaining the detail information or not.

- Using the unified interface provided by HTTP methods, lets third-party providers (proxies) transparently provide additional services (e.g. security, caching, etc.) to the clients invoking the sources and/or the data mashups.

To allow clients and higher layers to know the capabilities of a source/data mashup, we use the WADL language [21]. WADL[2] allows describing the resources offered by a RESTful web service, how they are connected, the data schema of the information associated to them, the HTTP methods supported by each resource and the parameters that can be used to invoke them.

4.3 Model Used for Expressing Data Combination Logic

The model used in the majority of mashups platforms to express data combination logic is based on the Pipes and Filters pattern [8]. A 'pipe' is composed of a series of interconnected components. Each component performs a specific operation such as accessing to sources, filtering input records, and/or merging input feeds. A connection from the component 'A' to the component 'B' denotes that the output from 'A' is the input to 'B'. Connections in such a model may be of several types and the most common are serial, joins, and forks. Components begin their execution when they have all their inputs available. This way, processing is propagated through the flow. The most commonly mentioned advantage of using this approach is simplicity in

---

[2] See http://www.tic.udc.es/mashup-demo/leads.wadl for the WADL specification of the data mashup shown in Fig. 1.

modeling these flows. It is assumed that pipes can be created by 'power users' which do not necessarily have programming skills.

However, we advocate for the Data Federation pattern to express data combination logic. This pattern has been extensively researched during the last decade to combine heterogeneous data. In this approach, the data combination logic is expressed as a 'view'. The view definition is written as a query (in SQL, for instance) over the data source schemas. Combination is expressed as relational operations like joins, unions, projections, selections, and aggregations. A graphical interface can allow users to create the view by interconnecting components that represent basic combination operations. This way, power users without programming skills can define views.

An important advantage of Data Federation pattern is its declarative nature. At run-time, when the user launches a query, the system automatically computes all the possible execution plans to solve it. The user can either manually choose the plan or let the system optimizer make the choice. The query capabilities supported by each source are also taken into account when generating the execution plans, so only the plans allowed by the source are generated. For instance, the LinkedIn source used in the example from section 2 requires a mandatory input parameter (the name of the person we want their contacts to be retrieved); therefore, only the execution plans satisfying that restriction will be generated for the data mashup in Fig. 1. To compute query plans having query capabilities into account and to choose the most optimal plan, we leverage on the techniques proposed in [17] and [7], respectively. Query capabilities of the sources are discovered at run-time using their WADL descriptions.

In turn, the Pipes and Filters pattern uses a 'procedural' approach: the system executes the pipe exactly as it was designed, following the flow path as defined. In fact, a pipe can be seen as the explicit definition of a particular query execution plan.

Let us go back to the running example introduced into the section 2 to highlight the differences between the Pipes and Filters pattern and the Data Federation pattern. Let us consider two different use case examples for Martin:

- **Example A:** Get all the leads that can be obtained from the *reference_contact_name John Smith*. In this case, the optimal way to solve it is by querying salesforce.com and LinkedIn in parallel using *John Smith* as the input parameter and merging the obtained records.

- **Example B:** Get all the leads that can be obtained from customers with high satisfaction level. In this other case, the system would query salesforce.com for contacts with a high satisfaction level. Then, for each customer retrieved, the system should search LinkedIn by using the *reference_contact_name* as the input parameter to obtain the data of the lead. The two sources need to be accessed sequentially because the query does not provide us with a value to fill in the mandatory input parameter of the LinkedIn data source.

Using the pipes and filter model, two different pipes would have to be created, each of which would solve one of the cases. The resulting pipes are shown in Fig. 4.

In turn, using the Data Federation pattern and given the source adaptors for salesforce.com and LinkedIn, the required data mashup can be modeled as a 'view' defined by a join operation between both data sources by the *reference_contact_name* attribute.

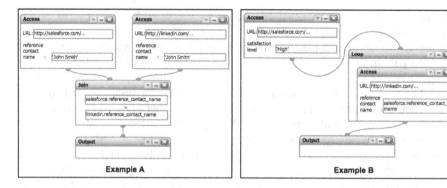

Fig. 4. Pipes and Filters approach

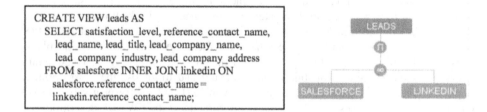

Fig. 5. Data Federation approach

Fig. 5 shows both the graphical representation of the data view created and its internal definition written in the SQL-like language used in our implementation to define views. Notice that in our implementation the user does not need to use SQL; the views are created using graphical wizards. The SQL expression defines an inner join between the views *linkedin* and *salesforce* (both exported by the Source Access Layer). Both example use cases shown above can be resolved by querying the 'Leads' view with queries such as:

```
select * from leads where reference_contact_name = 'John Smith'
select * from leads where satisfaction_level = 'High'
```

Notice that the user does not need to write these concrete queries at data mashup generation time. The data mashup component generates the WHERE clause automatically at run-time when it is accessed by the GET method, adding a condition for each parameter received in the request. Next, the data mashup component computes all possible execution plans and chooses the best one [7].

5   Design of the Widget and Widget Assembly Layers

Instead of creating yet another widget technology, we have reused standard Java portal technology [12][15] to implement individual widgets as portlets and mashup applications as portal pages. Portlets are interactive, web mini-applications which can be aggregated into portal pages. Any standards-compliant portlet (widget), local or remote to the portal, can be aggregated into a page. Portlets communicate each other in a decoupled way through the portal's event bus.

The meta-information provided by the WADL specifications of the data mashup instances enables the construction of 'template' widgets. Unlike 'specific' widgets, such as the pie chart or map widgets introduced in section 2, template widgets do not implement specific business functionality. Instead, they acquire business value at run-time. One such widget is the query widget mentioned in section 2. This widget analyzes the WADL specification of the mashup component it is connected to. In view mode, it discovers the query capabilities of a data mashup instance and generates a form containing a field for each query parameter. The WADL specification also specifies the schema (e.g. an XML Schema, RelaxNG, etc.) of the returned data. The schema is used to display the results (a list of records) in an HTML table. To connect an instance of the query widget to a particular data mashup, the user selects the edit mode and specifies the URL of its WADL specification.

Fig. 6. MapWidget's edit mode

Another important design aspect to make possible the construction of reusable widgets consists in treating events in a generic way, so that can be consumed by any interested widget. On the one hand, data contained in events must be modeled in a generic way. Taking up the example of Section 2, the query widget generates a *RecordListing* event when obtains the results. This event contains an array of *Record*. Each *Record* is an array of *RecordField*, being a *RecordField* a data structure containing the name and the value of an individual field in a record. The *RecordListing* event can be consumed by any widget expecting to receive an event containing an array of records, such as the pie chart widget. In the same way, when the user selects a particular record in the query widget, an event containing the record is generated, which can be consumed by any widget expecting to receive a record, such as the map and web clipping widgets.

On the other hand, it is necessary to provide a mechanism to subscribe a widget to an event and specify how to process it. To subscribe a widget to an event, it is necessary to specify the name of the event by using the portal capabilities. The widget can provide a wizard in the edit mode to specify how to process the event. For example, the map widget in the edit mode (see Fig. 6) lets the user specify the name of the field (in the record contained in the event) containing the address (needed to obtain the map coordinates) and the names of the fields to display in the 'balloon'. This way, the consumer widget (the map widget, in this case) does not assume particular names for the fields of the events it receives, improving its reusability.

6 Related Work

In the commercial arena, tools like Yahoo! Pipes [23] and Microsoft PopFly [13] are oriented to the construction of consumer mashups. They offer hosted tools that provide a set of user-configurable modules to create pipes to process RSS/Atom feeds and other types of REST web services. They also provide some support to show the output of the pipe using pre-created template widgets such as maps or photo albums. Therefore, the functionality they provide fits into the Data Mashup Layer and Widget Layer of our architecture; they do not provide support neither for assembling several widgets in a more complex mashup nor to access other kinds of data sources (such as databases or semi-structured web sources). Other key differences with our proposal include that they use the Pipes and Filters pattern to specify the data combination logic and they do not provide a standard interface between layers. Besides, since these tools are oriented to consumer mashups, the processing and displaying components they offer are not designed for enterprise environments.

There also exist a number of commercial tools that are exclusively oriented to enterprise data mashups. For instance, RSSBus [19] provides simple ESB (Enterprise Service Bus) functionality based on the Pipes and Filters pattern to generate mashups from a variety of enterprise sources such as REST web services, databases, content servers or CRM tools. All those source formats are imported as RSS feeds, which is the format that the platform natively uses. With respect to our proposal, on one hand, they do not deal with user interface issues; on the other hand, they rely on the Pipes and Filters pattern instead of the Data Federation pattern.

Like our proposal, JackBe [10] and IBM Mashup Center [9] provide functionality for creating both 'data mashups' and 'graphical user interfaces'. The architecture of both tools is similar: they use the Pipes and Filters pattern for data combination, support creating widgets from data combination components (similarly to our 'template' widgets), and allow assembling several widgets to build the graphical interface of the mashup application. All the languages and interfaces used by these tools are proprietary. Unlike these tools, we (1) opt for the Data Federation pattern instead of Pipes and Filters pattern, (2) rely on RESTful interfaces between layers, and (3) reuse standard portal technology.

Like our proposal, the Yahoo! Query Language (YQL) platform [24] allows querying web sources by using an SQL-like language. However, this platform only allows getting data from one individual web source. It is possible to query additional web sources, but only in nested queries to filter the values of the main web source by using the IN operator (like in SQL). In consequence, this platform could not be used to implement the data mashup component of our architecture. Furthermore, its approach is not truly declarative, since each YQL query has only one possible execution plan.

In academia, [25][3] present a framework to assembly several independently created widgets. The underlying model used is also event-based: widgets emit events in response to user actions; the events have attached meta-information that can be used to fill in the input parameters of the operations exposed by other widgets subscribed to the event. [6] and [11] also present proposals for event-based widget inter-communication. The first one is based on the OpenAJAX initiative [16], while the second one uses proprietary mechanisms. Neither of these proposals addresses the problem of data combination (the Data Mashup Layer of our architecture). Their proposals for widget inter-communication are conceptually similar to ours.

[20] proposes an approach for building mashups by example. Firstly, the user provides examples for the system to be able to create wrappers and perform transformations on the extracted data. Secondly, the system suggests the user to join different wrappers by detecting overlaps in the values extracted by them. The simplicity of use comes at the cost of powerfulness: the range of possible transformations is limited and the only way available to combine the data is using simple equijoin operations. In addition, the system only allows showing the results in an HTML table, and does not provide any way to combine several widgets.

MARIO [18] combines 'tagging' and automatic composition techniques to allow creating automatically pipes from a set of keywords ('tags') specified by the user. Although using automatic composition techniques is a promising idea, MARIO is limited to use RSS feeds as data sources and uses the Pipes and Filters pattern for data combination. Furthermore, it does not address the graphical interface.

Mash Maker [5] is another system that allows creating mashups without needing to have any technical knowledge. The system assumes that the user will create extractors for web sources and widgets to manipulate and visualize data. As normal users browse the web, Mash Maker suggests widgets that can be applied on the current page based on the experience from previous users. With respect to our proposal, Mash Maker uses a client-side approach heavily based on collaboration that fits better with consumer mashups than with enterprise mashups. In addition, the available components to extract, transform, and manipulate data are quite limited.

7 Conclusions and Future Work

In this paper we have presented the design of an enterprise-oriented, component-based mashup tool that fully supports the construction of mashup applications. The user builds graphically the mashup application by selecting, customizing, and interconnecting components. With respect to other tools, our approach presents the following advantages: (1) we use a declarative approach to express data combination logic based on the Data Federation pattern; (2) we use a RESTful approach to define the interface of source adaptors and data mashup components, which improves system flexibility; and (3) we reuse standard portal technology to improve reusability and interoperability at the graphical interface level.

We are now exploring automatic composition of data sources and the application of collaborative filtering techniques to suggest additional data sources and widgets during the mashup creation process.

References

1. Bellas, F., Paz, I., Pan, A., Diaz, O.: New Approaches to Portletization of Web Applications. In: Handbook of Research on Web Information Systems Quality, 270–285 (2008) ISBN: 978-1-59904-847-5
2. Chang, C.-H., Kayed, M., Girgis, M.R., Shaalan, K.F.: A Survey of Web Information Extraction Systems. IEEE Transactions on Knowledge and Data Engineering 18(10), 1411–1428 (2006)

3. Daniel, F., Matera, M.: Mashing Up Context-Aware Web Applications: A Component-Based Development Approach. In: Proceedings of the 9th International Conference of Web Information Systems Engineering, pp. 250–263 (2008)
4. Ennals, R.J., Brewer, E.A., Garofalakis, M.N., Shadle, M., Gandhi, P.: Intel Mash Maker: Join the Web. SIGMOD Record 36(4), 27–33 (2007)
5. Fielding, R.T., Taylor, R.N.: Principled Design of the Modern Web Architecture. ACM Transactions on Internet Technology 2(2), 115–150 (2002)
6. Gurram, R., Mo, B., Gueldemeister, R.: A Web Based Mashup Platform for Enterprise 2.0. In: Proceedings of the 1st International Workshop on Mashups, Enterprise Mashups and LightWeight Composition on the Web (MEM & LCW), pp. 144–151 (2008)
7. Hidalgo, J., Pan, A., Alvarez, M., Guerrero, J.: Efficiently Updating Cost Repository Values for Query Optimization on Web Data Sources in a Mediator/Wrapper Environment. In: Etzion, O., Kuflik, T., Motro, A. (eds.) NGITS 2006. LNCS, vol. 4032, pp. 1–12. Springer, Heidelberg (2006)
8. Hohpe, G., Woolf, B.: Enterprise Integration Patterns: Designing, Building, and Deploying Messaging Solutions. Addison-Wesley, Reading (2003) ISBN: 032120068
9. IBM Mashup Center, http://www.ibm.com/software/info/mashup-center
10. JackBe, http://www.jackbe.com
11. Janiesch, C., Fleischmann, K., Dreiling, A.: Extending Services Delivery with LightWeight Composition. In: Proceedings of the 1st International Workshop on Mashups, Enterprise Mashups and LightWeight Composition on the Web (MEM & LCW), pp. 162–171 (2008)
12. Java Community Process: Java Portlet Specification - Version 2.0, http://jcp.org/en/jsr/detail?id=286
13. Microsoft Popfly, http://www.popfly.com
14. Montoto, P., Pan, A., Raposo, J., Losada, J., Bellas, F., Carneiro, V.: A Workflow Language for Web Automation. Journal of Universal Computer Science 14(11), 1838–1856 (2008)
15. OASIS: Web Services for Remote Portlets Specification – Version 2.0, http://docs.oasis-open.org/wsrp/v2/wsrp-2.0-spec-os-01.html
16. OpenAjax, http://www.openajax.org
17. Pan, A., Alvarez, M., Raposo, J., Montoto, P., Molano, A., Viña, A.: A Model for Advanced Query Capability Description in Mediator Systems. In: Proceedings of 4th International Conference on Enterprise Information Systems, ICEIS, vol. I, pp. 140–147 (2002)
18. Riabov, A.V., Bouillet, E., Feblowitz, M., Liu, Z., Ranganathan, A.: Wishful Search: Interactive Composition of Data Mashups. In: Proceedings of the 17th International Conference on World Wide Web, pp. 775–784 (2008)
19. RSS Bus, http://www.rssbus.com
20. Tuchinda, R., Szekely, P., Knoblock, C.: Building Mashups by Example. In: Proceedings of the 13th international conference on Intelligent User Interfaces, pp. 139–148 (2008)
21. Web Application Description Language, https://wadl.dev.java.net
22. Wiederhold, G.: Mediators in the Architecture of Future Information Systems. IEEE Computer 25(3), 38–49 (1992)
23. Yahoo! Pipes, http://pipes.yahoo.com/pipes
24. Yahoo! Query Language, http://developer.yahoo.com/yql
25. Yu, J., Benatallah, B., SaintPaul, R., Casati, F., Daniel, F., Matera, M.: A Framework for Rapid Integration of Presentation Components. In: Proceedings of the 16th World Wide Web Conference, pp. 923–932 (2007)

Turning Web Applications into Mashup Components: Issues, Models, and Solutions

Florian Daniel[1] and Maristella Matera[2]

[1] University of Trento
Via Sommarive 14, 38100 Povo (TN), Italy
daniel@disi.unitn.it
[2] Politecnico di Milano - DEI
Via Ponzio 34/5, 20133 Milano, Italy
matera@elet.polimi.it

Abstract. Sometimes it looks like development for Web 2.0 is completely detached from the "traditional" world of web engineering. It is true that Web 2.0 introduced new and powerful instruments such as tags, micro formats, RESTful services, and light-weight programming models, which ease web development. However, it is also true that they didn't really substitute conventional practices such as component-based development and conceptual modeling.

Traditional web engineering is still needed, especially when it comes to developing components for mashups, i.e., components such as web services or UI components that are meant to be combined, possibly by web users who are not skilled programmers. We argue that mashup components do not substantially differ from common web applications and that, hence, they might benefit from traditional web engineering methods and instruments. As a bridge toward Web 2.0, in this paper we show how, thanks to the adoption of suitable models and abstractions, generic web applications can comfortably be turned into mashup components.

1 Introduction

Skilled web users who develop own applications online, so-called mashup applications, are a reality of today's Web. *Mashups* are simple web applications (most of the times even consisting of only one page) that result from the integration of content, presentation, and application functionality stemming from disparate web sources [1], i.e., mashups result from the integration of components available on the Web. Typically, a mashup application creates new value out of the components it integrates, in that it combines them in a novel manner thereby providing functionality that was not there before. For example, the housingmaps.com application allows one to view the location of housing offers from the Craigslist in Google Maps, a truly value-adding feature for people searching an accommodation in a place they are not yet familiar with.

While the value-adding combination of components is important for the *success* of a mashup application, it is also true that a mashup application can only

M. Gaedke, M. Grossniklaus, and O. Díaz (Eds.): ICWE 2009, LNCS 5648, pp. 45–60, 2009.
© Springer-Verlag Berlin Heidelberg 2009

be as good as its constituent parts, the *components*. That is, without high-quality components (e.g., UI components or web services) even the best idea won't succeed: users easily get annoyed by low-quality contents, weak usability, or, simply, useless applications.

In order to ease the task of developing mashups, a variety of *mashup tools* such as Yahoo Pipes [2], Google Mashup Editor [3], Intel Mash Maker [4,5], Microsoft Popfly [6] or IBM QEDWiki (now part of IBM Mashup Center [7]) have emerged, and they indeed facilitate the mashing up of components via simple, graphical or textual user interfaces, sets of predefined components, abstractions of technicalities, and similar. Some of these tools (e.g., Popfly) also provide the user with support for the creation of *own components* to be added into the spectrum of predefined components. Newly created components are then immediately available in the development environment, and users can mash them up just like any other component of the platform.

If we however have a look at programmableweb.com, one of the most renowned web sites of the mashup community, we can easily see (in the APIs section) that the *most popular components* (APIs) are for instance Google Maps, Flickr, YouTube, and the like. All names that guarantee best web engineering solutions and high-quality content. User-made components do not even show up in the main statistics, very likely due to the fact that most of them are rather toy components or, however, components of low quality or utility.

We argue that successful components are among the most important ingredients in the development of mashups (besides a well-designed composition logic, an aspect that we do not discuss in this paper). The development of components should therefore follow sound principles and techniques, like the ones already in use in web application engineering. In this paper, we show how generic web applications, developed with any traditional practice and technology, can be wrapped, componentized, and made available for the composition of mashups (in form of so-called *UI components* [8]). The conceived solution especially targets mashup tools or platforms that provide mashup composers with mashup-specific abstractions and development and runtime environments. We developed the ideas of this paper in the context of mashArt, a platform for the hosted development, execution, and analysis of lightweight compositions on the Web (our evolution of [8]), but the ideas proposed are simple and generic enough to be used straightforwardly in other mashup environments too.

1.1   Reference Development Scenario

Besides concerns such as IT security and privacy preservation, IT support for compliance with generic laws, regulations, best practices or the like is more and more attracting industry investments. In particular, business monitoring applications and violation root-cause analyses are gaining momentum. In this context, a company's compliance expert wants to mash up a business compliance management (BCM) application that allows him to correlate company-internal policies (representing rules and regulations the company is subject to) with business process execution and compliance analysis data and, in case of violations, to easily

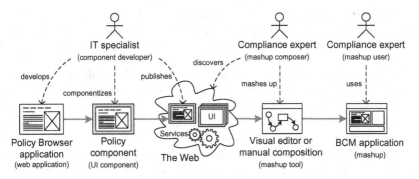

Fig. 1. Mashup scenario: developing, componentizing, and mashing up a component

identify the root cause of the problem (e.g., a business process). In order to populate the enterprise mashup system with the necessary components, the IT specialist wants to develop the necessary components for the mashup platform.

The overall scenario is depicted in Figure 1, where we focus on the development of the Policy component that will allow the compliance expert to browse the company-internal policies. The IT specialist (*component developer*) develops the Policy Browser application (*web application*) with his preferred development tool and following his choice of methodology. Then he componentizes the application (*UI component*) and publishes it on the Web (or only internally to the company). The compliance expert (in the role of *mashup composer*) then discovers the components he is interested in, mashes them up (with a *mashup tool*), and runs the BCM application (in the role of *mashup user*).[1]

1.2 Research Challenges and Contributions

In this paper, we focus on the *component developer* in the above scenario and specifically aim at assisting him in the development of the web application, its componentization for mashups, and its publication. In this context, this paper provides the following contributions, which are also the main research challenges in developing reusable components for the Web:

- We define a *UI component model* and a *description language* that abstract from implementation details and capture those features that characterize mashup components that come with an own UI (unlike web services or RSS/Atom feeds).
- We provide a simple *micro format* [9] for annotating generic, HTML-based web applications with instructions on how to componentize the application according to our UI component model.
- We provide for the *componentization* of applications by means of a generally applicable wrapping logic, based on the interpretation of descriptors and annotations.

---

[1] We here assume that the compliance expert acts as both mashup composer and mashup user, though in general these are conceptually distinct roles.

– We show how componentized applications can be used as constituent elements in generic compositions together with components, such as SOAP and RESTful services, RSS/Atom feeds, and other UI components.

We next introduce the design principles that we think should drive the development of mashup components (Section 2), and propose our component model for mashup components (Section 3). In Section 4, we discuss how to componentize web applications and introduce our component description language and our micro format for component annotation. In the same section, we show how annotated applications can be wrapped in practice and also provide some component design guidelines. Finally, in Section 5 we discuss related works, and in Section 6 we conclude the paper.

2   Mashup Components: Development Principles

From the development of our own mashup platform [8], we learned some principles that good mashups and mashup components should follow in order to succeed. Here we summarize the most important ones:

– *Developers, not users*: Developing good components is as tricky as developing good applications. Therefore, we stress the importance that component developers be skilled web programmers, while users may assume the roles of both mashup composer and mashup user (see Figure 1).
– *Complexity inside components*: Components may provide complex features, but they should not expose that complexity to the composer or the user. The interfaces the composers (APIs) and the users (UIs) need to deal with should be as appropriate and simple as possible. The internal complexity of components is up to the component developer.
– *Design for integration*: A component typically runs in an integrated fashion in choreography with other components. Components that come with their own UI (in this paper we concentrate on this kind of components) should therefore be able to run inside a DIV, SPAN, or IFRAME HTML element without impacting other components or the mashup application (e.g., due to code collision problems).
– *Stand-alone usability*: A component's executability and benefit should not depend on whether the component is integrated into a mashup application or not. Components should be executable even without any mashup platform available. This increases the return on investment of the component and also facilitates development (e.g., a component can be partly tested even without being mashed up).
– *Standard technologies*: In order to guarantee maximum compatibility and interoperability, a component should not rely on proprietary technologies. Especially for the development of components, we advocate the use of standard technologies (mashup tools, on the other hand, may also use proprietary technologies, as they typically do not aim at re-usability).

– *Abstract interface descriptions*: Similarly to WSDL for web services, component interfaces and their features should be described abstractly and hide their internal details from the composer and the user. Internally, components may then be implemented via multiple technologies and protocols.

We regard these principles as particularly important for the development of mashup components. The solutions proposed in the next sections aim at putting them into practice.

3 A Model for Mashup Components

Mashups are typically characterized by the integration of a variety of different components available on the Web. Among the most prominent component technologies we find, for example, SOAP/WSDL and RESTful web services, RSS/Atom feeds, and XML data sources. Most of these components rely on standard languages, technologies, or communication protocols. Yet, when it comes to more complex *UI components*, i.e., mashup components that are standalone applications with their own data, application, and presentation layer, no commonly accepted standard has emerged so far. We believe that a common high-level model for UI components might boost the spreading of mashup applications. Next we therefore present a component model that adequately captures the necessary features.

In Figure 2(a) we show the UML class diagram of our mashArt model for UI components. The main elements of the model are the user interface, events, and operations. The three elements allow us to explain our idea of UI component:

– *User interface/state*: The user interface (UI) of the component is the component's graphical front-end that is rendered to the user. In this paper, we focus on components with standard HTML interfaces rendered in a browser, though technologies like Flash or Java Swing could be used as well. The

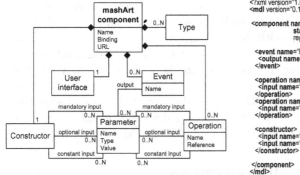

(a) UML class diagram of the UI component model.   **(b)** MDL descriptor of the Policy component.

Fig. 2. The mashArt UI component model with an example of component descriptor

UI enables the user's interaction with the component. In response to the user's actions, the component may change its *state* (e.g., by navigating to another page of the application). For instance, our Policy component could provide the user with the details of a given policy upon selection of the policy from a list. The UI shown to the user can be interpreted as the state of the interaction (e.g., before selection vs. after selection).

– *Events*: By interacting with the component, the user provides inputs that are interpreted by the component. User actions are commonly based on low-level events, such as mouse clicks, mouse moves, key strokes, and similar, that depend on the input device used to interact with the UI (e.g., the mouse or the keyboard). For the purpose of integration, however, UI components should abstract from such low-level events and publish only "meaningful" events to other components, i.e., events that provide information about the semantics of the interaction (we call them *component events*). Each time a user action, based on one or more low-level events, significantly changes the state of a component, a respective component event should be generated. In the case of the Policy component, the selection of a policy from the list should, for example, launch a component event (e.g., PolicySelected) informing other components about which policy has been selected.

– *Operations*: Not only the user should be able to change the internal state of a component. If a mashup comprises multiple components, these must typically be synchronized upon a user interaction with one of them, e.g., to align displayed content. Synchronization of components is one of the main features that characterize mashup applications (differently from traditional portals, which aggregate multiple portlets without however providing for their synchronization). Via operations, a UI component allows external actors (e.g., other components) to trigger state changes. That is, operations allow the mashup application to propagate a user interaction from one component to other components by mapping events to operations, thus providing for the synchronization of component states. One particular operation, the *constructor*, is in charge of setting up the component at startup.

The synchronization of components is *event-based*. Events generate outputs (parameters), operations consume them. We propose to use *parameters* that are simple name-value pairs, in line with the structure of the query string in standard URLs. At the UI layer, synchronization does not require the transportation of large amounts of data from one component to another (this is typically handled by web services at the application or data layer). Component events with simple synchronization information (e.g., the name or the identifier of a policy) suffice to align the state of components that are able to understand the meaning of the event and its parameters. Custom data types might also be specified.

4 Componentizing Web Applications

The above component model proposes the idea of "web application in the small", and abstracts the features of common web applications into the concepts of

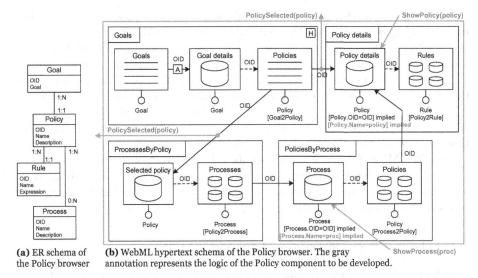

(a) ER schema of the Policy browser

(b) WebML hypertext schema of the Policy browser. The gray annotation represents the logic of the Policy component to be developed.

Fig. 3. WebML model of the Policy application to be componentized

state, events, and operations. In this section, we show how this abstraction can be leveraged to componentize a web application in a way that reconciles the application's standalone operation and it's use as mashup component. In particular, we propose three ingredients: (i) an *abstract component descriptor* in the mashArt Description Language (MDL), (ii) a *micro format* (the mashArt Event Annotation - MEA) for the annotation of the application with event information, and (iii) a *generic wrapper structure* able to support the runtime componentization of the application according to (i) and (ii).

We show the different concepts at work in the componentization of the Policy Browser application, which consists of a set of HTML pages. To easily describe the structure and logic of the application and to effectively highlight the concepts and constructs necessary for its componentization, in this paper we show the model of the application expressed according to the WebML notation [10] .

Figure 3(a) illustrates the WebML data schema that specifies the organization of the contents published by the Policy Browser application. Each *policy* consists of one or more *rules* and can be related to one or more business *processes*. Policies are classified according to the compliance *goals* regarding given legislations, laws, best practices, and similar.

Figure 3(b) shows the structure of the hypertext interface that allows one to browse the policies; the gray annotations represent the componentization logic, which we explain later. The schema specifies the pages that compose the application (the containers), the content units that publish content extracted from the application data source (the boxes inside the containers), and the links that enable both the user navigation (the arrows) and the transport of parameters (the labels) needed for the computation of units and pages.

The navigation starts from the home page Goals (identified by the H label), where the user sees a list of goals (Goals unit) and, for each selected goal (Goal details), a list of related policies (Policies unit). For each policy in the list, the user can navigate to the page Policy details, which shows the data of the selected policy (Policy details unit) and all the policy rules associated with it (Rules unit). The user can also follow a link leading to the page ProcessesByPolicy, which shows a short description of the selected policy (Selected policy) plus a summary of all the processes (Processes) related with that policy. The selection of a process leads the user to the page PoliciesByProcess, which shows the process details (Process unit) and the description of all the policies (Policies unit) related with that process. By selecting a policy, the user then reaches the Policy details page.

Such WebML hypertext schema describes the structure of the web application as it is perceived by the human users of the application. Componentizing this application instead means providing a programming interface (API), which can be used by a mashup application to programmatically interact with it.

4.1   The Mashart Description Language (MDL)

In order to instantiate the component model described in Section 3, we use MDL, an abstract and technology-agnostic description language for UI components, which is similar to WSDL for web services. Given an application that we want to componentize, MDL allows us to define a new component, to describe which are the events and operations that characterize the component, and to define data types and the constructor. There is no explicit language construct for the state of the component, which therefore is handled internally by the component in terms of the UI it manages. However, MDL allows us to describe state changes in the form of events and operations. MDL is an extension of UISDL [8].

The gray annotations of the schema in Figure 3(b) highlight the events and operations of the Policy component we would like to derive form the Policy Browser application. We suppose that the selection of a policy from the Policies unit in the Goals page corresponds to the event PolicySelected that carries the parameter policy (i.e., the name of a policy). This event will be used to synchronize the state of other components in the final BCM mashup (e.g., the process browser), so that all components show related data. The two links departing from the Policies index unit are both sources for this event: their navigation by a user implies the selection of a policy and, hence, launches the event.

Our Policy component also exposes two operations. The operation ShowProcess sets the name of the process to be shown to the value of the parameter proc. The effect of this operation is the computation and rendering of the page PoliciesByProcess with data about the selected process and its related policies. As represented in Figure 3(b), this corresponds to a navigation to the page PoliciesByProcess, with the name of the process defined by the value of the proc parameter. When the operation ShowProcess is enacted, the "implied" (optional) selector[2] "Process.Name=proc" replaces the other implied selector "Process.OID=OID", which

---

[2] In WebML, each unit inside a page is characterized by an *entity* of the data schema plus a *selector*. The selector is a parameterized condition identifying the entity instances to be displayed. Each unit also has a default selector that works with OIDs.

is instead based on the process OID transported by the user-navigated link entering the page. The operation ShowPolicy sets the name of the policy to be shown. Similarly to the previous operation, it enacts the computation and rendering of the page Policy details with the data about the policy identified by the policy parameter.

Figure 2(b) shows the MDL descriptor capturing this component logic. The XML snipped defines a UI component (binding attribute) named Policy, which is stateful and can be accessed via the URL in the url attribute. We do not need any custom data types. The descriptor specifies the event PolicySelected with its parameter policy and the two operations ShowProcess and ShowPolicy. Finally, the constructor specifies two parameters that allow the mashup composer to set up the number of policies visible at the same time and the start policy.

The descriptor in Figure 2(b) fully specifies the external behavior of our component. Of particular importance to the integration of a component is the ref attribute of operations: it tells us how to invoke operations. From the specification in Figure 2(b), we know that the operation ShowProcess is invoked via the following URL: `http://mashart.org/registry/234/PolicyBrowser/ShowProcess?proc=name`. With the descriptor only, we are however not yet able to derive how to intercept low-level events and how to translate them into component events. As described in the next section, for this purpose we have introduced a novel technique, the mashArt Event Annotation, for annotating the HTML of the application pages.

4.2   The Mashart Event Annotation (MEA)

Operations are triggered from the outside when needed, events must be instead raised in response to internal state changes. The generation of component events is tightly coupled with user interactions, that is, with the actions performed by the user during the component execution. A runtime mapping of low-level UI events onto component events is needed, in order to filter out those low-level events that raise component events, while discarding other low-level events.

We specify this mapping in the mashArt Event Annotation (MEA) *micro format*, which allows us to associate component events with low-level events by means of three simple annotations that can be added to HTML elements in form of *attributes*. Candidate HTML elements are all those elements that are able to generate low-level JavaScript (JS) events, such as click, mouse down, etc.). Table 1 summarizes the purpose of the three attributes, and gives examples about how they can be used to specify the PolicySelected event introduced above.

The event_name attribute, if specified and nonempty, gives a *name* to the component event that can be raised by the HTML element carrying the attribute. There might be multiple HTML elements raising the same event, i.e., an event with the same name (e.g., the policy might be selected by navigating a catalog of policies or by selecting it from a list of "Recently violated policies"). It is the responsibility of the developer to assure that a same event is used with the same meaning throughout the whole application.

Table 1. Annotation elements of the mashArt Event Annotation (MEA) micro format

Attribute	Purpose and description
event_name	Defines a component event and binds it to an HTML element. For instance, the markup <A href="..." **event_name="PolicySelected"**> Privacy Policy </A> specifies an HTML link that, if navigated, may raise the PolicySelected event.
event_binding	Binds a component event to a JavaScript event. For example, we can explicitly bind the PolicySelected event to a click as follows: <A href="..." event_name="PolicySelected" **event_binding="onClick"**> Privacy Policy </A>. Events are identified through the name of their JavaScript event handlers (e.g., onClick for a click). Multiple bindings can be specified by separating the respective JS event handlers with commas.
event_par	Specifies event parameters. A single event parameter is specified as follows: <A href="..." event_name="PolicySelected" event_binding ="onClick" **event_par="policy=PrivacyPolicy"**> Privacy Policy </A>. Multiple parameter can be specified by separating them with & symbols.

The event_binding attribute allows the developer annotating the application to specify which JS event actually triggers the component event. That is, the event_binding attribute specifies a binding of component events to native JS events. If no binding is specified for a given component event, the JS click event is used as *default binding*. This decision stems from the fact that in most cases we can associate events (and operations) with teh selection of hypertext links by means of mouse clicks.

Events may carry *parameters* that publish details about the specific event instance that is being raised. For example, our PolicySelected event will typically carry the name (or any other useful parameter) of the selected policy. If *multiple* parameters are required, this can be easily specified inside the event_par attribute using the standard URL parameter convention: paramter1=value1&parameter2= value2.... If an event can be raised by multiple HTML elements, it is the responsibility of the developer to guarantee that each event consistently carries the same parameters.

The generation of component events that do not derive from user interactions, and instead are based on some *component-internal* logic (e.g., a timer or asynchronous AJAX events), can be set up via hidden HTML elements. It is enough to annotate the element as described above, and, when the component event needs to be fired, to simulate the necessary low-level JS event on the hidden element.

It is important to note that the values for event parameters can be generated *dynamically* by the application to be componentized the same way it generates on-the-fly hyperlinks. It suffices to fill the value of the event_par attribute. The values of event_name and event_binding typically do not change during runtime, though this might be done as well.

4.3   The Runtime Componentization Logic

Once we have the MDL descriptor of the application and the application is annotated accordingly, we are ready to componentize, i.e., wrap, the application. The result of this process is typically a JavaScript object/function (other technologies, such as Flash or JavaFX, could be used as well) that provides programmatic access to the application, i.e., an API. The API renders the component's UI, generates events, enacts operations, and allows for the "instantiation" of the component inside an HTML DIV, SPAN, or IFRAME element (in the following we focus on DIVs only). Given the MDL descriptor and suitable event annotations, the wrapping logic is simple and generic, as illustrated in Figure 4.

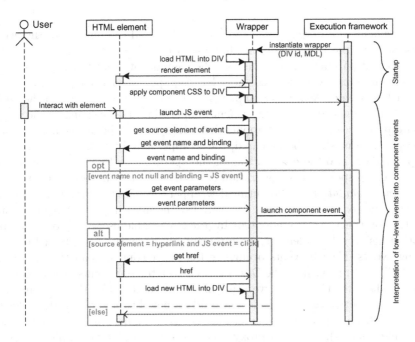

Fig. 4. Sequence diagram illustrating the wrapping logic for annotated applications

We distinguish between a startup phase and an event interpretation phase. During *startup*, the execution framework (either the mashup application or any mashup platform) instantiates the wrapper by passing the identifier of the HTML DIV element that will host the UI of the component along with the MDL descriptor of the component. The wrapper loads the application into the DIV and applies the component's CSS rules.

The *interpretation* of events is triggered by the user or by the internal logic of the component by generating a low-level JS event. Upon interception of such an event, the wrapper identifies the source element of the event and tries to access the event_name and event_binding attributes possibly annotated for the

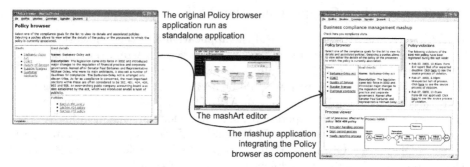

Fig. 5. The componentized Policy Browser application running in the BCM mashup

source element. If an event name can be retrieved and the binding of the event corresponds to the low-level event that has been raised, the wrapper gets the possible event parameters and launches the component event to the framework; otherwise, no action is performed. In order to support navigations, if a hyperlink element has been clicked, the wrapper loads the destination page into the DIV.

As discussed above, for the enactment of operations (state changes) the wrapper interprets the operations as application URLs that can be invoked. Therefore, if an operation needs to be executed, the wrapper simply packs the possible input parameters into the query string of the operation and performs the HTTP request. The response of the operation is rendered inside the DIV element.

The *implementation* of the outlined wrapper logic in JavaScript implies answering some technical questions. We here list the most important issues, along with the solutions we have adopted: In order to enable users to browse an application inside a DIV element, we intercept all JS events and check for page loading events. If such events occur, we take over control, load the new page via AJAX, and render it in the DIV. In order to intercept events, we set generic event handlers for the events we are looking for in the DIV. From a captured event we can derive the source element and its possible annotation. In order to load a page from a remote web server (JavaScript's sandbox mechanism does not allow direct access), we run a proxy servlet on our own server, which accesses the remote page on behalf of the wrapper, a common practice in AJAX applications. In order to handle CSS files when instantiating a component, we load the component's CSS file and associate its formatting instructions to the DIV that hosts the component. In order to avoid the collision of JavaScript code among components, the wrapper, and the mashup application, we pack each component into an own object and instantiate it inside an isolated scope.

Figure 5 shows at the left hand side the Policy Browser application running in a browser. After componentization of the application for our mashArt platform, at the right hand side the figure shows the final result: the BCM mashup, which uses the Policy component to synchronize other two components displaying compliance violations and affected process models.

4.4   Component Development Guidelines

The above approach shows how to componentize a web application starting from its HTML markup. In order for an application to support an easy and effective componentization, it is good that application developers follow a few rules of thumb when developing applications: The *layout* of the application should support graceful transformations, e.g., by discarding fixed-size tables or by providing for the dynamic arrangement of layout elements (floating). The use of *frames* is prohibited, if the developer aims at wide use of the final component. *CSS style rules* should focus on the main characteristics of the application's appearance and foresee the cascaded integration of the component's rules with the ones of the mashup application. For instance, absolute positioning of elements is deprecated, and background colors, border colors, and similar should be inherited from the component's container. Finally, *JavaScript code* (e.g., for dynamic HTML features) should be designed with integration in mind. For example, if HTML elements are to be accessed, it is good to access them via their identifiers and not via their element type, as, once integrated into a mashup application, other elements of the same type will be used by other components as well.

Actually, these guidelines apply the same way to the development of generic web applications. However, in the case of applications that are componentized, their violation might even stronger degrade the usability of the final component.

5   Related Works

The current scenario in the development of mashup environments is mainly characterized by two main challenges [11]: (i) the definition of mechanisms to solve composition issues, such as the interoperability of heterogeneous components or their dynamic configuration and composition, and (ii) the provision of easy-to-use composition environments. All the most emergent mashup environments [2,3,7,6,5] have proposed solutions in this direction. However, very often they assume the existence of ready-to-use components, thus neglecting the ensemble of issues related to the development of quality components.

Some works concentrate on the provision of domain-specific, ready-to-use mashup components (see for example [12]) allowing developers to extend their applications with otherwise complicated or costly services. Some other works go in the direction of enabling the configuration of *visualization widgets* inside very specific programming environments (see for example [13]). The resulting contributions address the needs of very specific domains. In general, as can be observed in the most widely used mashup tools, there is a lack of support for the (easy) creation of components; more specifically, the componentization of web applications, as proposed in this paper, is largely uncovered.

Very few environments provide facilities for the creation of mashup components. For example, Microsoft Popfly [6] includes the so-called *Popfly block creator*, an environment for the definition of components (*blocks* in the Popfly terminology). Besides describing the block logic (properties and exposed operations) in an XML-based format, the creation of a new block requires writing ad hoc JavaScript code implementing the component logic. This could prevent developers (especially those not acquainted with JavaScript) to build own blocks.

Based on a different paradigm, Intel MashMaker [4,5] also offers support for component creation. Users are enabled to personalize arbitrary web sites, by adding on the fly *widgets* that provide visualizations of data extracted from other web sites. The approach is based on the concept of *extractors*, which, based on XPath expressions formulated by developers, enable the extraction of structured data from a web page, from RDF data, or from the HTML code. Once extractors have been defined or selected from a shared repository (extractors can be shared among multiple users), MashMaker is able to suggest several ways in which data can be integrated in the currently visited page, for example in the form of *linked data* (a preview of the source page is shown if a link to that page is included in the current page), or by using *visualization widgets* (simple text, images, dynamic maps, etc.). Visualization widgets can be selected from a shared server-side repository; alternatively users can create their own widgets, by defining web pages in (X)HTML and JavaScript. Each widget is then described through an XML-based configuration file that specifies information about the widget, including links to the HTML files providing for the widget's visualization.

With respect to the Popfly solution, MashMaker proposes a more intuitive paradigm (from the users' perspective) for the creation of components. However, both environments ask the developer to become familiar with their proprietary environments and languages. Also, the adopted description languages are based on models that work well only within their mashup platform. The solution proposed in this paper tries to overcome these shortcomings.

6   Conclusion

In this paper, we have shown that the development of mashup components does not mandatorily require mashup- or platform-specific implementations or complex, low-level concepts web developers are not familiar with. In some cases, it suffices to equip an HTML web application with an abstract component descriptor (MDL) and a set of event annotations (MEA), in order to allow everyone to wrap the application and use it as a component. The combined use of MDL and MEA allows one to derive a proper API toward a full-fledged application, unlike other approaches that rather focus on the extraction of data (e.g., MashMaker).

The wrapper logic described in this paper is very general and can be easily implemented for a variety of mashup tools and platforms. In order to wrap an unlimited number of applications, it is enough to implement the wrapper once. Annotated applications can then be reused by multiple mashups, a feature that adds value to the original applications. The benefit for component developers is that they can use their preferred IDEs, web development tools, or programming languages and only need to abstractly describe and annotate their applications.

The described technique intrinsically helps them to respect our principles for good mashup components.

A point to be highlighted is that conceptual modeling methods can easily be extended to allow component developers to annotate the conceptual models instead of the HTML code of an application. MEA annotations and MDL descriptors can then be generated from the models, along with the actual code of the application. This elevates the componentization concerns to a higher level of abstraction – the one provided by the adopted conceptual model – and further speeds up component development. For instance, our first experiments show that generating MDL and MEA from WebML schemas is feasible.

It is important to note that the proposed approach also works if no annotation or description is provided at all. We can still wrap the application and integrate it into a composite application, without however supporting events and operations. Ad hoc events and operations can be managed by the mashup developer by extending the generic wrapper with additional code adding the necessary logic to the wrapped application from the outside.

As a next step, on the one hand we plan to develop an environment for the creation of mashup components as described in this paper, so as to guide the developer (or the skilled web user) in the description and annotation of existing web applications. On the other hand, we need to investigate further how to enable data passing of complex data structures (e.g., an XML file) and how to solve interoperability problems that might arise when integrating UI components with web services. We are however confident that the ideas introduced in this paper will accommodate the necessary extensions.

References

1. Yu, J., Benatallah, B., Casati, F., Daniel, F.: Understanding UI Integration: A survey of problems, technologies. Internet Computing 12, 44–52 (2008)
2. Yahoo!: Pipes (2009), http://pipes.yahoo.com/pipes/
3. Google: Google Mashup Editor (2009), http://code.google.com/intl/it/gme/
4. Ennals, R., Garofalakis, M.N.: MashMaker: Mashups for the Masses. In: Chan, C.Y., Ooi, B.C., Zhou, A. (eds.) SIGMOD Conference, pp. 1116–1118. ACM, New York (2007)
5. Intel: MahMaker (2009), http://mashmaker.intel.com/web/
6. Microsoft: Popfly (2009), http://www.popfly.com/
7. IBM: Mashup Center (2009), http://www-01.ibm.com/software/info/mashup-center/
8. Yu, J., Benatallah, B., Saint-Paul, R., Casati, F., Daniel, F., Matera, M.: A Framework for Rapid Integration of Presentation Components. In: Proc. of WWW 2007, pp. 923–932. ACM Press, New York (2007)
9. Microformats.org: Microformats (2009), http://microformats.org/about/
10. Ceri, S., Fraternali, P., Bongio, A., Brambilla, M., Comai, S., Matera, M.: Designing Data-Intensive Web Applications. Morgan Kaufmann Publishers Inc, San Francisco (2002)

11. Makela, E., Viljanen, K., Alm, O., Tuominen, J., Valkeapaa, O., Kauppinen, T., Kurki, J., Sinkkila, R., Kansala, T., Lindroos, R., Suominen, O., Ruotsalo, T., Hyvonen, E.: Enabling the Semantic Web with Ready-to-Use Mash-Up Components. In: First Industrial Results of Semantic Technologies (2007)
12. Benslimane, D., Dustdar, S., Sheth, A.: Services Mashups: The New Generation of Web Applications. IEEE Internet Computing 12, 13–15 (2008)
13. Tummarello, G., Morbidoni, C., Nucci, M., Panzarino, O.: Brainlets: "instant" Semantic Web applications. In: Proc. of the 2nd Workshop on Scripting for the Semantic Web (2006)

Tagging-Aware Portlets

Oscar Díaz, Sandy Pérez, and Cristóbal Arellano

ONEKIN Research Group, University of the Basque Country,
San Sebastián, Spain
{oscar.diaz,sandy.perez,cristobal-arellano}@ehu.es
http://www.onekin.org

Abstract. A corporate portal supports a community of users on cohesively managing a shared set of resources. Such management should also include social tagging, i.e. the practice of collaboratively creating and managing tags to annotate and categorize content. This task involves to know both *what* to tag (hence, the rendering of the resource content) and *how* to tag (i.e. the tagging functionality itself). Traditionally both efforts are accomplished by the same application (*Flickr* is a case in point). However, portals decouple these endeavours. Tagging functionality is up to the portal, but content rendering can be outsourced to third-party applications: the portlets. Portlets are Web applications that *transparently* render their markup through a portal. The portal is a mere conduit for the portlet markup, being unaware of what this markup conveys. This work addresses how to make portlets tagging-aware, i.e. portlets that can be seamlessly plugged into the portal tagging infrastructure. The main challenge rests on consistency at both the back-end (i.e. use of a common structure for tagging data, e.g. a common set of tags), and the front-end (i.e. tagging interactions to be achieved seamlessly across the portal using similar rendering guidelines). Portlet events and *RDFa* annotations are used to meet this requirement. A running example in *WebSynergy* illustrates the feasibility of the approach.

Keywords: tagging, portlets, Web portals, RDFa, WSRP, Liferay.

1 Introduction

Corporate portals play a three-fold role. As a means by which to manage and access content, portals play the role of content managers. As the mechanism to integrate third party applications using portlets or gadgets, portals can be regarded as front-end integrators. Finally, portals also offer a conduit for on-line communities. It is in this third role where the importance of incorporating social networking facilities in current portal engines emerges. Portals, to a bigger extent than other Web applications, have the notion of community deeply rooted inside its nature. Specifically, corporate portals are borne to support the employees within an organization. Therefore, it is just natural to integrate social networking into these portals (hereafter referred to as just "portals"). Among social networking activities, this paper focuses on social tagging.

Social tagging brings sociality into tagging. Attaching labels to resources is no longer a secluded activity, but seeking or tagging resources is achieved based on previous inputs from the community, and this activity, in turn, serves to build the community itself by clustering users based on tag preferences.

M. Gaedke, M. Grossniklaus, and O. Díaz (Eds.): ICWE 2009, LNCS 5648, pp. 61–75, 2009.
© Springer-Verlag Berlin Heidelberg 2009

Traditional tagging sites such as *Delicious, Youtube* or *Flickr* can be characterized as being *self-sufficient* and *self-centered*. The former implies that all it is need for tagging (i.e. the description of the resource, the tag and the user) is kept within the tagging site. *Delicious* keeps the bookmark URL, the tags and the user community as assets of the site. On the other hand, self-centeredness indicates that all *Delicious* care about is its own resources, tags and users. No links exists with other tagging sites, even if they tag the same resources (e.g. *CiteULike*).

This situation changes when moving to a portal setting. A hallmark of portals is integration. Rather than providing its own services, a portal is also a conduit for external applications. So offered applications are technically known as *portlets* [3]. Portlets can be locally deployed or be provided remotely through third-party providers. For instance, a portal can offer the possibility of blogging, purchasing a book, or arranging a trip, all without leaving the portal. Some of these portlets can be built in house whereas others can be externally provided by third parties (e.g. *Amazon* or *Expedia*). The portal mission is to offer a common gateway that hides such distinct origins from the user. This has important implications on the way tagging can be incorporated into portals, namely:

- portals are not self-sufficient. Taggers (i.e. the portal community) and tags are portal assets. However, and unlike self-sufficient tagging sites, portals could not hold the description of all tag-able resources. For instance, the description of the books or hotels offered through the portal could be remotely kept by e.g. *Amazon* and *Expedia*, respectively. This outsource of content description does not imply that the external resources are not worth tagging. This leads to distinguish between two actors: *the resource provider*, which keeps the content of the tag-able resources (e.g. book description in the case of *Amazon*), and *the resource consumer* (i.e. the portal), which holds the tagger community and the tags,
- portals are not self-centered. Traditional tagging sites are "tagging islands": each site keeps its own tagging data. Providing an integrated view of these heterogeneous tagging silos is at the user expenses. By contrast, portals strive to glue together heterogeneous applications. This effort implies offering a consistent set of tags no matter the resource nor the portlet through which the tagging is achieved. That is, our expectation is that employees would use a similar set of tags no matter the portlet that holds the tagged resource.

Based on these observations, consistency is identified as a main requirement, i.e. tagging should be seamlessly achieved across the portal, regardless of the type (messages, books, hotels, etc), or origin (i.e. *Amazon, Expedia*, etc) of the resource. This consistency is two-fold. *"Back-end consistency"* implies the use of a common structure for tagging data, e.g. a common set of tags. On the other hand, *"front-end consistency"* entails tagging interactions to be achieved seamlessly and cohesively across the portal using similar rendering recourses and aesthetic guidelines.

To this end, we present a novel architecture to support tagging capabilities as a portal commodity. This implies that portlets should be engineered to be plugged into this commodity rather than building their own tagging functionality. In the same way, that portlets adapt their rendering to the aesthetic guidelines of the hosting portal, tagging through portlets should also cater for the peculiarities of the consumer portal. The paper presents how these ideas have been borne out for the *WebSynergy* portal engine, using *RDFa* annotations and a publish/subscribe mechanism. The running example is available for consultation at `http://tagging.onekin.org/`.

The rest of the paper is organized as follows. Section 2 reviews tagging in current portal engines. Section 3 provides a brief on portlets. The different actors that interact during tagging are introduced in Section 4. Back-end consistency and front-end consistency are the topics of Sections 5 and 6, respectively. A revision and some conclusions end the paper.

2   Tagging in Current Portal Engines

Motivation for bringing tagging at the working place admits a two-fold perspective. From the company's viewpoint, tagging is an affordable approach to account for knowledge sharing and retention in the context of an organization, preventing leaking critical data outside the company [4]. From an employee's perspective, distinct studies [10,2,7] conclude that individual motivations for tagging at the working place, such as creating a personal repository or re-finding one's own resources, remained important. Additionally, tagging is also a means for professional promotion, community construction and information dissemination. Indeed, tags can serve distinct purposes: identifying what the resource is about (e.g. descriptive tags such as *"ajax"*), identifying what it is (e.g. *"book"*); identifying who owns it (e.g. *"peter"*); refining categories (e.g. *"beginning"*); identifying qualities (e.g. *"interesting"*), self reference (e.g. *"myfavorite"*) or task organizing (*"toRead"*, *"forDevelProject"*) [5]. Some of these purposes really turn fully useful in a working context. Tagging a resource as *"forDevelProject"* makes *social* sense if there are other users that share the same project. Insights suggest that "people need concepts and words in common in order to engage in collective actions. Tagging services in general appear to offer a means for achieving such common ground. Tagging services within a work-oriented enterprise would seem to be a particularly promising setting for people to engage in the co-construction of their common understandings" [8]. Tagging emerges as a main opportunity not only for resource self-organization but also for community construction.

Portal engine vendors are well-aware of this fact, and include tagging among their offerings. Tagging can come in different flavours: (1) tagging as part of an external application (i.e. a portlet) offered by the portal, (2) tagging as a portal functionality offered as a separated service, and (3), tagging as a portal commodity which it is not intended to work on its own but for other services to plug into. All three approaches can co-exist in the same portal. The difference stems from who is the owner of the tagging data, and what is the scope of tagging (see Table 1).

Tagging as part of an integrated application. This is the trivial case where the application being integrated (e.g. an external portlet) offers tagging capabilities on its own. Both tagged resources and tagging data are kept by the portlet. The only difference with traditional tagging sites such as *Flickr*, is that now tagging is achieved *through* the portal but not *by* the portal.

Tagging as a portal functionality. This is the approach currently supported by most vendors. The portal is regarded as a content manager. The portal owns the resources,

Table 1. Tagging through portals

Tagging as ...	Tagging Data Owner	Tagging Scope
...part of an external application	application	resources of the application
... portal functionality	portal	resources *kept by* the portal
... portal commodity	portal	resources *offered through* the portal

and provides functionality for tagging. Tagging is restricted to those resources within the realm of the portal. *Liferay* illustrates this approach. *Liferay* allows users to tag web content, documents, message board threads, wiki article, blog posts, etc. Users can then capitalize on their tagging efforts through two *Liferay* applications (delivered as portlets): the *TagsAdmin* portlet and the *AssetPublisher* portlet. The former permits tag addition and organization into categories. The second portlet creates tag-based views out of tag-based queries. Notice however, that all tag-able content should be within the realm of the *Liferay* portal.

Tagging as a portal commodity. Rather than as content managers, portals are now envisaged as integration platforms. As such, portals offer commodities for easing the integration of heterogeneous applications (e.g. the *Single Sign-On* commodity is a popular example[1]). Likewise, we advocate for tagging services to be offered as a commodity. Portlets then plug into this commodity. This is, tagging services are up to the portal but offered through the companion portlets. This insight, its grounds and feasibility, make up the contribution of this work.

3 A Brief on Portlets

Traditional data-oriented Web Services facilitate the sharing of the business logic, but suggest that Web service consumers should write a presentation layer on top of this business logic. By contrast, presentation-oriented Web Services (a.k.a. *portlets*) do deliver markup (a.k.a. *fragments*) rather than a data-based XML document. A fragment is then a piece of XHTML or other markup language, compliant with certain rules that permit a fragment to be aggregated with other portlets' fragments to build up a complete portal page. The aim is for full-fledged applications (not just functions) to provide both business logic and presentation logic as a Web component, easily pluggable into distinct Web applications (e.g. portals).

Portlets can be either local or remote to the hosting portal. This brings component-based development to the portal realm where different teams can be in charge of supporting a given functionality (supported as a portlet) that is later deployed locally at the portal. However, where the notion of portlet gets its full potential is when portlets are deployed remotely, provided by third parties. This scenario requires portlet interoperability, and here is when the *Web Services for Remote Portlets* (WSRP) specification [9] come into play. WSRP specifies a protocol and a set of interfaces that allows portals to consume and publish portlets as Web Services.

---

[1] This commodity enables a user to log in once at the portal, and gain access to the available applications being offered through the portal without being prompted to log in again.

Additionally, the Java Portlet Specification [6] follows a model of separating concerns in different lifecycle methods, like *processAction, processEvent, render*. This provides a clean separation of the action semantics from the rendering of the content. During the process action, the portlet can change its state. Next, during the rendering phase, the portlet generates the fragment. Since a portal page can contain several portlets, a *render()* petition is forwarded to each of the participating portlets, each of them returning a fragment. The portal builds a "quilt page" out of these fragments, and renders it back to the user.

4 The Actors

Being content managers, portals can keep their own resources. Additionally, portals are also integration platforms, making external resources available through *portlets*. Figure 1 provides a snapshot of a portal page offering two portlets: *LibraryPortlet* and *AllWebJournalPortlet* that render content on books and publications, respectively. Both books and publications are kept outside the portal realm. The running example is available at http://tagging.onekin.org/.

Notice that both portlets, regardless of their different providers, offer the same set of tags. That is, tagging adapts to the hosting portal. This also implies that if the very same portlet is offered through a different portal then, the rendered tag set will be distinct since tags reflect the projects, roles and ways of working of the organization at hand.

This provides grounds for tagging to be supported as a portal commodity, and introduces three actors in portal tagging, namely: **portlets**, which provide the tag-able resources; **the portal**, which embodies the portal users as potential taggers; and **the tagging commodity**, i.e. a portal component that provides tagging utilities. This paper looks at two such tagging functionalities: tag assignment and tag-based querying.

However, the existence of three different actors should not jeopardize one of the portal hallmarks: interaction consistency across the portal. Tagging should be homogenously achieved throughout the portal, no matter where the resource resides (i.e. which portlet renders it). Additionally, and on top of the portal mandate, the desire

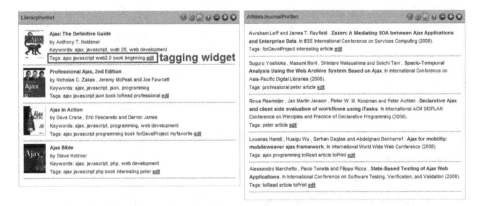

Fig. 1. A portal page offering two portlets (i.e. *LibraryPortlet* and *AllWebJournalPortlet*)

for tag consistency emerged as a major request among portal users, (e.g. "how will others find my content if I don't use the same tags over and over?") as drawn from a recent study [10].

This consistency is two-fold. "Back-end consistency" implies the use of a common structure for tagging data, e.g. a common set of tags. On the other hand, "front-end consistency" entails tagging interactions to be achieved seamlessly and cohesively across the portal using similar rendering guidelines. Next sections delve into the details.

5 Back-End Consistency

Back-end consistency implies tagging data to be a portal asset rather than being disseminated across different silos. Tagging data basically refers to tags, taggers and tag-able resources. Both, taggers and tags, are naturally held by the portal. However, tag-able resources can be outside the portal realm. Although tagging could become a portal duty, some tag-able resources would still be provided by third-party portlets. Therefore, a mechanism is needed for portlets to make the portal aware of their tag-able resources.

The main means for portlet-to-portal communication is the markup fragment that the portlet delivers to the portal. Here, the portal is a mere conduit for portlet markups. Portals limit themselves to provide a common skin and appropriate decorators to portlet

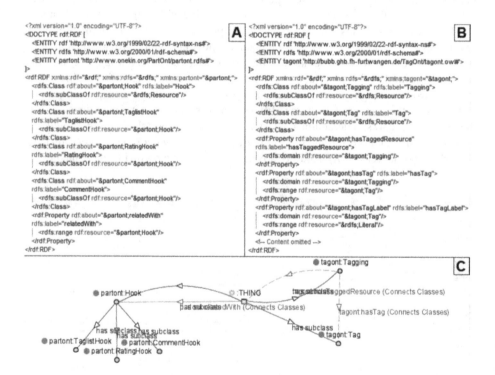

Fig. 2. The *PartOnt* (a) and the *TagOnt* (b) ontologies together with their *Protégé* rendering counterparts (c).

fragments, being unaware of what this markup conveys. We propose to annotate this markup with tagging concerns using *RDFa* [1].

RDFa is a W3C standard that provides syntax for communicating structured data through annotating the XHTML content. In our case, *RDFa* offers a means for the portlet provider to communicate the portlet consumer the existence of tag-able resources. The idea is to capitalize on the fragment layout to annotate tag-able resources.

Firstly, an ontology is defined which is later used to annotate the fragment. This ontology should serve to indicate both *what* to tag and *where* to tag (see later). This is the aim of *PartOnt* (*Part*icipatory *Ont*ology), an ontology that aims at capturing manners in which users engage in the participatory web. One of these ways is of course, tagging. Rather than defining its own concepts, *PartOnt* capitalizes on existing ontologies that already formalize some of these notions. Specifically, *PartOnt* benefits from *TagOnt*, an ontology that captures tagging by describing resources, tags, taggers, tagging time, etc [11]. Figure 2 shows these ontologies, both the RDF code and the *Protégé* rendering counterpart.

These ontologies are then used to annotate the portlet markup. An example is shown in Figure 3. The JSP script outputs a *LibraryPortlet* fragment. Book data (i.e. title, authors, etc) are rendered as table rows (*TR*), where book keywords are iteratively enclosed within SPAN elements. All of the table cells are wrapped within a table (*<table>*) which in turns is wrapped in another table together with the book-cover image.

This markup is then annotated along the previous ontologies. Specifically, the following structural HTML elements are annotated [2]:

```
<jsp:useBean id="library" scope="request" class="java.util.ArrayList" />
<div  xmlns:books="http://www.onekin.org/library/"
      xmlns:partont="http://www.onekin.org/PartOnt/partont.rdfs#"
      xmlns:tagont="http://bubb.ghb.fh-furtwangen.de/TagOnt/tagont.owl#">

    <c:forEach var="book" items="${library}">
        <table about="[books:${book.id}]"><tr>
            <td><!-- BOOK'S PAPERBACK IMAGE --> </td>
            <td>
                <table>
                    <tr><td><!-- BOOK'S TITLE --></td></tr>
                    <tr><td><!-- BOOK'S AUTHORS --></td></tr>
                    <tr><td typeof="tagont:Tagging">
                        <div rel="tagont:hasTaggedResource" resource="[books:${book.id}]"/>
                        Keywords:
                        <span rel="tagont:hasTag">
                            <c:forEach var="keyword" items="${book.keywords}">
                                <span typeof="tagont:Tag" property="tagont:hasTagLabel">
                                    <c:out value="${keyword}"/>
                                </span>
                            </c:forEach>
                        </span>
                    </td></tr>
                    <tr><td>
                        <div style="display:none;" rel="partont:relatedWith"
                                                    typeof="partont:TaglistHook" />
                    </td></tr>
                </table>
            </td>
        </tr></table>
    </c:forEach>
</div>
```

Fig. 3. JSP that delivers a fragment markup with annotations along the *TagOnt* and *PartOnt* ontologies

- HTML element that embodies a tag-able resource. In our example, this corresponds to the outer *<table>* element. This element now includes an *"about"* attribute which denotes the existence of a tag-able resource. The identifiers of tag-able resources are supported as *Uniform Resource Identifiers* (URIs). Following Semantic Web practices, these URIs are created by concatenating a namespace with a resource's key,
- HTML element that conveys potential tags. In this case, we identify keywords as playing such role. This implies to annotate the *<span>* element with the *"tagont:Tag"* annotation. These tags are provided for the portal's convenience, and they are expected to describe the resource content. It is up to the portal to incorporate these tags as suggestions during tagging. These portlet-provided tags should not be mistaken with those provided by the portal users.

These annotations permit the portlet consumer (i.e. the portal) to become aware of resources and tags coming from external sources. This external data is incorporated into the portal not when it is rendered but when it is tagged. When the first tag is added, the portal check if the resource ID is already in the tagging repository (see later Figure 4).

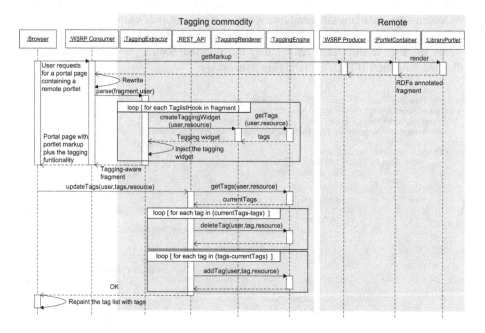

Fig. 4. Interaction diagram: *base requests* vs. *tagging requests*

However, resource IDs and tags are not introduced in the tagging repository right away. Rather, the tagging commodity should include a *"cleaning module"*

---

[2] As far as this work is concerned, we ignore the resource content (i.e. we do not annotate e.g. titles or authors of book resources). All the portal needs to know is that a tag-able resource is being rendered. The details about the rendering itself are left to the portlet.

to ascertain whether two tags/resources really stand for the same notion. For instance, the same resource can be offered as a book in *LibraryPortlet* and as a publication in *AllWebJournalPortlet*. Likewise, this resource can be tagged as *"ServiceOrientedArchitecture"* in one place and *"SOA"* in the other. This cleaning module will provide some heuristics to ascertain the equality of resources and tags being offered in different forms by different resource providers. This effort is akin to the view of the portal as an *integration* platform, and an argument in favour of tagging being conducted through the portal rather than as a disperse activity performed at each resource provider.

6 Front-End Consistency

Portals are a front-end technology. Much of their added value (and investment) rests on how content is rendered and navigated. In this context, presentation consistency is a must to hide the diverse sources that feed the portal. Tagging wise, consistency mandates tagging interactions to be seamlessly and coherently achieved across the portal. This would not be much of a problem if tagging were only up to the portal. But, this paper highlights that portal tagging is a joint endeavour among the portal and the companion portlets. Rendering wise, this coupling can be achieved at the portlet place (through markup portions referred to as *widgets*) or at the portal place (using a publish/subscribe approach with local portlets). Next subsections address each of these approaches.

6.1 Front-End Consistency through Widgets

Seamlessness calls for tagging to be conducted at the place tag-able resources are rendered (side-by-side rendering). This place is the portlet fragment. But portlets should not deliver their own tagging functionality since a premise of this work is that such functionality should be provided by the portal. But, portals are traditionally mere proxies for the portlet markup. Tagging however, requires portals to take a more active role. Besides skins and decorators, portals now become the purveyors of tagging widgets to be injected into the portlet markup.

The question is how can the portal know where to inject these widgets? Annotations are again used for this purpose. Specifically, the *PartOnt* ontology includes a *Hook* class, with a subclass *TaglistHook* that denotes an extension point for adding markup to update the tag list. This class annotates the HTML element that plays the "hook" role. Figure 3 shows our sample fragment where this role is played by a *<div>* element. At execution time, the portal locates the "hooks" and injects the tagging widget (see later).

Markup coming from the portlet should be seamlessly mixed together with markup coming from the portal so that the user is unaware of the different origins. After all, this is the rationale behind letting the portlet specify the tagging hooks: injecting the extra markup in those places already foreseen by the portlet designer so that the final rendering looks harmonious. However, the distinct markup origins become apparent to the portal which needs to propagate the user interactions to the appropriate target. Specifically, *base requests* (i.e. those with the portlet markup) are propagated to the portlet provider, while *tagging requests* (i.e. those with the tagging widget) are processed by the tagging commodity.

Figure 4 provides an overview of the whole process where these two types of interactions are distinguished:

1. *base request.* According with the WSRP standard, user interactions with portlet markup are propagated till reaching the appropriate portlet. In return, the portlet delivers a markup, now annotated with tagging metadata,
2. content annotation processing. At the portal place, the tagging commodity (specifically an *RDFa* parser) extracts both tag-able resources and tags conveyed by the actual markup. This data is kept at the tagging repository.
3. *hook* annotation processing. If the markup also holds *"TaglistHook"* annotations, the tagging commodity (specifically, a markup renderer) outputs the appropriate widget to be injected at the hook place. The markup renderer can need to access the tagging repository, e.g. to recover the tags currently associated with a given resource.
4. markup rendering. The original markup has now become a tagging-aware fragment, i.e. a fragment through which tagging can be conducted,
5. *tagging request.* Now, the user interacts with the tagging markup (e.g. requesting the update of the tag set). This petition is directed to the tagging commodity which checks the additions and removals being made to the tag set kept in the repository. In return, the tagging commodity repaints the tagging markup.

As the previous example illustrates, the co-existence of markups from different origins within the same portlet decorator brings an Ajax-like style to markup production. In Figure 4, lines with solid triangular arrowheads denote synchronous communication whereas open arrowheads stand for asynchronous communication. Specifically, the tagging request is asynchronously processed.

6.2   Front-End Consistency through Local Portlets

Previous subsection illustrates the case of a tagging functionality (e.g. tag update) to be achieved at the portlet place. However, other services can be directly provided by the portal but in cooperation with the companion portlets. Tag-based querying is a case in point.

Comprehensive querying implies the query to expand across resources, no matter their origin. A query for resources being tagged as *"forDevelProject"* should deliver books (hence, provided by the *LibraryPortlet* portlet), publications (hence, supplied by the *AllWebJournalPortlet* portlet), post blogs (locally provided), etc being tagged as used in this project. Such a query can be directly answered through the tagging repository that will return the set of resource identifiers meeting the query condition.

However, portals are a front-end technology. Providing a list of identifiers is not a sensible option when an end user is the addressee. Rather, it is the content of resource what the user wants to see. We need then to *de-reference* these identifiers. Unfortunately, the tagging repository can not "de-reference" those identifiers. The portal owns the tagging data. But it is outside the portal realm to know the resource content as well as

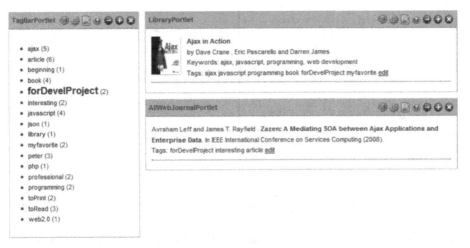

Fig. 5. Split query processing. Query specification goes through *TagBarPortlet*: the tag selected by the user is highlighted. Query outcome is delegated to the portlets holding the resource content, i.e. *LibraryPortlet* and *AllWebJournalPortlet*.

how this content is to be rendered. This is the duty of the resource providers, i.e. the portlets. Therefore, the portal can not accomplish the whole query processing on its own since this also involves content rendering.

Figure 5 illustrates this situation. First, a mean is needed for the user to express the query. For the sake of this paper, a simple portlet has been built: *TagBarPortlet*. This portlet consults the tagging repository, renders the tags available, and permits the users to select one of theses tags. The selection has two consequences. First, the selected tag is highlighted. Second, and more important, the companion portlets synchronize their views with this selection, rendering those resources that were tagged with the selected tag *at this portal*. This last point is important. The very same portlet can be offered through different portals. Hence, the same resource (e.g. a book) can be tagged at different places (i.e. through distinct portals). When synchronized with the *TagBarPortlet* of portal P1, the portlet just delivers those resources being tagged through portal P1.

This scenario again requires a means for portal-to-portlet communication. Previous section relies on the rendering markup as the means of communication. This was possible because the data flew from the portlet to the portal. However, now identifiers/tags go the other way around: from the portal to the portlets. To this end, we follow a publish/subscribe approach where data flows from the publisher (i.e. the portal, better said, the portal representative, i.e. *TagBarPortlet*) to the subscriber (e.g. *LibraryPortlet* and *AllWebJournalPortlet*). The availability of an event mechanism in the Java Portlet Specification [6] comes to our advantage.

Portlet events are intended to allow portlets to react to actions or state changes not directly related to an interaction of the user with the portlet. Portlets can be both event producers and event consumers. Back to our sample case, the query-specification portlet, i.e. *TagBarPortlet*, fires the appropriate event that is broadcasted by the portal to the resource-provider portlets to make then aware of the tag

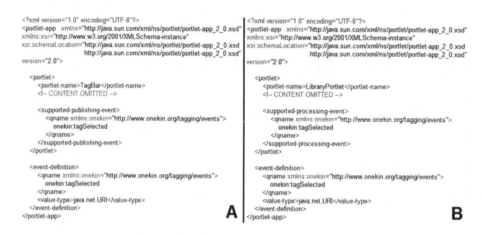

Fig. 6. *portlet.xml* configuration files for *TagBarPortlet* and *LibraryPortlet*. Both portlets know about the *tagSelected* event

being selected. Publications and subscriptions are parts of the portlet definition and hence, expressed in the configuration file *portlet.xml*. Figure 6 shows those files for *TagBarPortlet* and *LibraryPortlet*. The former defines a published event, *tagSelected*, whereas *LibraryPortlet* acknowledges the capacity to process *tagSelected* events.

Processing *tagSelected* occurrences imply rendering the content of the so-tagged resources at the portlet place. For instance, *LibraryPortlet* should produce markup for those books being tagged with the tag provided in the event payload. However, *LibraryPortlet* holds the resource content but ignores how they have been tagged. This tagging data is kept at the portal. Therefore, the portlet needs to get such data from the tagging commodity. As a result, the tagging-commodity URL is included as part of the event payload, so that the portlet can construct a REST petition asking which of *its* resources are so-tagged at *this* portal. Therefore, the very same portlet can process *tagSelected* occurrences coming from different portals and hence, whose payloads refer to different URLs[3]. In this way, portlet interoperability is preserved.

Figure 7 provides the global view. First, the user selects *"forDevelProject"* as the tag to be used as the filtering criteria. This request is handled by *TagBarPortlet* that signals a *tagSelected* occurrence. The portal forwards this occurrence to their subscribers: *LibraryPortlet* and *AllWebJournalPortlet*. Processing *tagSelected* involves first, to query the *TaggingEngine* about the so-tagged resources. To this end, the *REST_API* provides the *getResourceByTag* method. This method outputs a list of resource identifiers for which the *LibraryPortlet* should locally retrieve the content and produce the markup. This process is accomplished for all the resource-provider portlets. This ends the state changing logic phase of the portlet lifecycle.

---

[3] An alternative design would have been for *TagBarPortlet* to recover itself all resorce identifiers that exhibit the selected tag, and include the whole set of identifiers as part of the event payload. On reception, the portlet filters out its own resources. However, this solution does not scale up for large resource sets. Additionally, the option of restricting the payload to just those resources of the addressee portlet forces to have a dedicated event for each portlet.

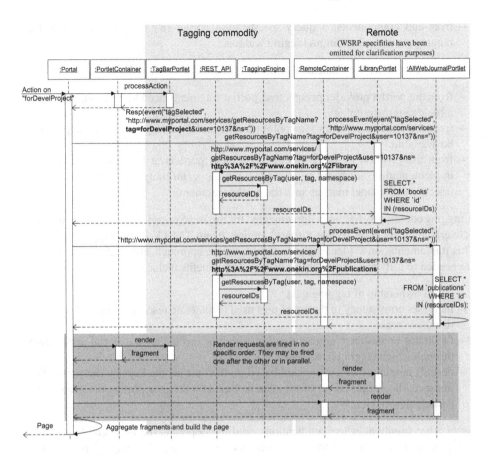

Fig. 7. Handling a *tagSelected* occurrence

The rendering phase builds up the portal page out of the portlet fragments. This implies sending the *render()* request to each of the portlets of the page, assembling the distinct markups obtained in return, and render the result back to the user. For our sample case, the outcome is depicted in Figure 5.

7 Revision and Conclusions

This work argues for portal tagging to be a joint endeavour between resource providers (i.e. portlets) and resource consumers (i.e. portals). Additionally, portlets are reckoned to be interoperable, i.e. deliverable through different portals. These observations advocate for tagging to be orthogonally supported as a crosscut on top of portlets, i.e. a portal commodity. Driven by two main functionalities, tag update and tag-based querying, this paper identifies main components of such a commodity:

- back-end components: a tagging engine, a tagging extractor (in our case, a *RDFa* parser) and a cleaning module,

- front-end components: a query-specification portlet (e.g. *TagBarPortlet*) and a tagging renderer that output tagging widgets.

This work explores the technical requirements of such solution, namely:

- from the portlet provider perspective, portlet fragments need to be annotated along a basic tagging ontology,
- from the portlet consumer viewpoint (i.e. the portal), a tagging commodity should be available,
- from the position of the container of remote portlets at the portal, the WSRP implementation needs to be extended for the *getMarkup* method to cater for injections of widget markup into the portlet fragment.

A tagging commodity has been implemented for the *WebSynergy*[4] portal engine, a Sun's deliverable of the open-source *Liferay*[5] engine, using TASTY as the tagging engine[6]. This implementation evidences the feasibility of the approach, although real test cases are needed to fully test scalability problems. The benefits include:

- portal ownership of tagging data,
- increases consistency in the set of tags used to annotate resources, regardless of the resource owner,
- facilitates consistency among tagging activities, no matter the portal application through which tagging is achieved,
- permits tagging to be customized based on the user profile kept by the portal. For instance, the suggested set of tags can be based on the user profile, the projects he participates in, etc.

As in other situations where applications need to cooperate, the main challenge rests on agreeing in common terms and protocols. In our case, this mainly implies the standardization of the tagging ontology, and the REST API.

Acknowledgements.   This work is co-supported by the Spanish Ministry of Education, and the European Social Fund under contract TIN2008-06507-C02-01/TIN (MODELINE), and the Avanza I+D initiative of the Ministry of Industry, Tourism and Commerce under contract TSI-020100-2008-415. Pérez enjoys a doctoral grant from the Basque Government under the "Researchers Training Program", and Arellano has a doctoral grant from the Spanish Ministry of Science & Education.

References

1. Adida, B., Birbeck, M.: RDFa Primer. Technical report, W3C Working Group (2008), http://www.w3.org/TR/xhtml-rdfa-primer/
2. Ames, M., Naaman, M.: Why we tag: motivations for annotation in mobile and online media. In: CHI 2007: Proceedings of the SIGCHI Conference on Human Factors in Computing Systems, pp. 971–980 (2007)

---

[4] https://portal.dev.java.net/

[5] http://www.liferay.com/

[6] http://microapps.sourceforge.net/tasty/

3. Díaz, O., Rodríguez, J.J.: Portlets as Web Components: an Introduction. Journal of Universal Computer Science, 454–472 (2004)
4. DiMicco, J., Millen, D.R., Geyer, W., Dugan, C., Brownholtz, B., Muller, M.: Motivations for social networking at work. In: CSCW 2008: Proceedings of the ACM 2008 Conference on Computer Supported Cooperative Work, pp. 711–720 (2008)
5. Golder, S.A., Hubermann, B.A.: The Structure of Collaborative Tagging System. In: CoRR (2005)
6. Java Community Process (JCP). JSR 286: Portlet Specification Version 2.0 (2008), http://www.jcp.org/en/jsr/detail?id=286
7. Millen, D.R., Yang, M., Whittaker, S., Feinberg, J.: Social bookmarking and exploratory search. In: ECSCW 2007: Proceedings of the Tenth European Conference on Computer Supported Cooperative Work, pp. 21–40 (2007)
8. Muller, M.J.: Comparing tagging vocabularies among four enterprise tag-based services. In: GROUP 2007: Proceedings of the 2007 International ACM Conference on Supporting Group Work, pp. 341–350 (2007)
9. OASIS. Web Services for Remote Portlets (WSRP) Version 2.0 (2008), http://www.oasis-open.org/committees/wsrp/
10. Thom-Santelli, J., Muller, M.J., Millen, D.R.: Social tagging roles: publishers, evangelists, leaders. In: CHI 2008: Proceeding of the twenty-sixth annual SIGCHI Conference on Human Factors in Computing Systems, pp. 1041–1044 (2008)
11. Knerr, T.: Tagging Ontology - Towards a Common Ontology for Folksonomies, http://tagont.googlecode.com/files/TagOntPaper.pdf

Trust and Reputation Mining in Professional Virtual Communities*

Florian Skopik, Hong-Linh Truong, and Schahram Dustdar

Distributed Systems Group, Vienna University of Technology
Argentinierstr. 8/184-1, A-1040 Vienna, Austria
{skopik,truong,dustdar}@infosys.tuwien.ac.at

Abstract. Communication technologies, such as e-mail, instant messaging, discussion forums, blogs, and newsgroups connect people together, forming virtual communities. This concept is not only used for private purposes, but is also attracting attention in professional environments, allowing to consult a large group of experts. Due to the overwhelming size of such communities, various reputation mechanisms have been proposed supporting members with information about people's trustworthiness with respect to their contributions. However, most of today's approaches rely on manual and subjective feedback, suffering from unfair ratings, discrimination, and feedback quality variations over time.

To this end, we propose a system which determines trust relationships between community members automatically and objectively by mining communication data. In contrast to other approaches which use these data directly, e.g., by applying natural language processing on log files, we follow a new approach to make contributions visible. We perform structural analysis of discussions, examine interaction patterns between members, and infer social roles expressing motivation, openness to discussions, and willingness to share data, and therefore *trust*.

1 Introduction

The concept of virtual (or online) communities is quite common today and frequently used not only for private concerns, but also in professional working environments. Online platforms such as discussion forums, blogs, and newsgroups are regularly utilized to get introduced into new things, to find solutions for particular problems, or just to stay informed on what's up in a certain domain. Virtual communities are rapidly growing and emerging, and thus, lots of spam and dispensable comments are posted in their forums or sent via e-mail, polluting fruitful discussions. Several mechanisms have been proposed to handle this problem, such as collaborative filtering of comments and global reputation of users based on feedback mechanisms. However, because these concepts rely on manual and subjective human feedback, they suffer from several drawbacks [1], including

---

* This work is mainly supported by the European Union through the FP7-216256 project COIN.

M. Gaedke, M. Grossniklaus, and O. Díaz (Eds.): ICWE 2009, LNCS 5648, pp. 76–90, 2009.
© Springer-Verlag Berlin Heidelberg 2009

unfair ratings, low incentives for providing feedback, and quality variations of ratings over time.

Collaborative Environments. Especially, where mentioned communication technologies are regularly embedded to connect e-professionals together, such as in professional virtual communities (PVCs), and where successful collaboration is critical for business, we identified the need for more sophisticated reputation methods. Moreover, in modern working environments, where virtual teams consisting of members from different departments or even companies work together, personally unknown to each other, various complex social factors affect the overall collaboration success. These factors can be expressed by one composite and abstract concept: *trust*. Trusted relationships between colleagues are vital to the whole collaboration and a prerequisite for successful work. A recent report about the roles of trust in today's business world [2] discovers that besides professional skills expressed as experience, expertise and competence, soft skills, such as the willingness to exchange information, motivation and communication skills, are at least equally important. Such social skills can be discovered and evaluated in typical computer-supported discussions, common in online communities, including threaded forum discussions, instant messaging chats, and e-mail conversation.

The Autonomic Cycle. Our overall motivation for trust determination is to apply an autonomic management cycle [3] consisting of four phases (monitoring, analyzing, planning, executing), which enable the adaptation of collaboration environments and personalization of applications with respect to trust between participants. In this cycle, the collaboration behavior, such as the communication culture, the execution of tasks and the coordination of e-workers is monitored by the system and their relationships are determined by analyzing logging data and structural profiles. Depending on particular situations, different available metrics are aggregated and interpreted as trust, which enables the maintenance of a trust network. This trust network is utilized to plan further collaboration, e.g., influences work partner selection or the assignment of tasks. After that, when people perform the actual work, their collaboration is monitored by the system, which closes the loop. In this paper we focus particularly the *monitoring phase* and the *analyzing phase*.

Contributions. We show an approach for automatic inference of trust between online discussion participants. To this end, we propose a system which collects and merges data from various sources, define the notion of discussion trust, and cover related concepts, including the definition of user roles and an interaction network. The main contribution is the design of a mining algorithm, which we evaluate with a real data set.

Paper Structure. The rest of the paper is organized as follows. In Sect. 2 we consider related work. Sect. 3 is about harnessing trustworthy sources of data in PVCs. We describe trust and roles in discussions in Sect. 4, a mining algorithm using these concepts to calculate relationships based on observed communication in Sect. 5, and network-based trust inference in Sect. 6. We prove our approach with extensive experiments on real data in Sect. 7 and conclude in Sect. 8.

2   Related Work

Welser et al. [4] provides interesting studies about social roles in online discussion groups and participants' behaviors. Furthermore, Nonnecke et al. [5] and Meyer et al. [6] research the meaning of online communication and differences between traditional face-to face and threaded discussions. McLure-Wasko and Faraj [7] investigate the motivation for knowledge sharing in online platforms, and Rheingold [8] comprehensively examines the concept of virtual communities. The article [2] in The Economist draws the importance of trust in business communication, and shows that various factors which directly influence trust between individuals are based on communication.

Until now various computational trust models have been developed, as summarized by Massa in [9]. Though they are useful to deal with trust propagation, aggregation and evaluation over time, it is mostly assumed that initial trust relationships are manually determined by people. For example, the well-known TrustRank model [10] for ranking web sites with respect to their trustworthiness, needs a set of trusted web sites to be initially defined and is then able to inherit trust to further linked pages automatically.

We interpret previous communications between people as interactions and rank them according to their trustworthiness in the originating network. There are several graph based ranking algorithms, including PageRank [11], HITS [12], and Eigentrust [13]. However, in contrast to these algorithms, which operate on top of an existing network, our approach tackles the challenges beneath, i.e. creating the network based on discussion data. To this end, we develop a mining algorithm to gather individual trust relationships based on observed communications, considering detailed analysis of online discussion platforms such as Gomez et al. [14] for Slashdot.

3   Trustworthy Sources of Data

Most common online communication platforms, such as vBulletin[1], integrate reputation systems which either rank users based on simple metrics, including their posting count, or enable users to reward ('thank') others directly. In contrast to this approach, we reward the vitality of *relationships* between users and then derive the user gradings by aggregating relationship gradings. This enables us to utilize global metrics calculated from all available data, such as the overall discussion effort of a particular user with respect to the whole community, but also local metrics considering data restricted to particular users only, such as the discussion effort between two specific users. Utilizing local metrics is particularly of interest when the amount of controversial users is high [15]. With our system a user does not get one globally valid trust rank, but may be graded from each individual's view.

We developed a pluggable architecture (Fig. 1) - part of VieTE [16] - which utilizes various communication data sources through standard protocols, such as

---

[1] http://www.vbulletin.com

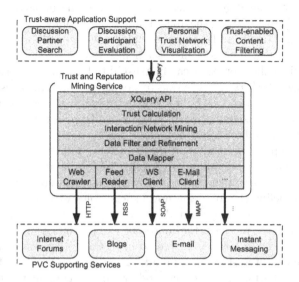

Fig. 1. Architectural overview of the trust and reputation mining service

RSS feeds, SOAP, and e-mail. The obtained data is mapped to a generic communication schema, pre-processed and refined, and finally an interaction network, modeling the relationships between users emerging from communication, is built. Based on this network, trust between individuals and reputation from the community's view can be inferred and queried through a dedicated interface. We understand the inferred *discussion trust* to represent one dimension of general trust in PVCs, applicable in a wide range of differently organized communities. Other dimensions of trust may base on the fulfillment of service level agreements or the reliability of task execution, which are out of scope of this paper.

4   Trust and Roles in Virtual Community Discussions

In discussions we can intuitively distinguish between information providers and information consumers. Especially in online discussions we can easily track who provides information, e.g., by posting a comment in a forum or writing an e-mail to a group of people. In contrast to that, determining information consumers is tricky. We can never be sure, that people read received e-mails or new comments in a forum, even when they open forum entries in their browsers. However, if somebody replies to a particular comment, then we can certainly assume, s/he has read the message and found it worth for discussion. Thus the replier can be identified as an information consumer, but as an information provider as well.

In our approach we track exactly this discussion behavior and define, that whenever one replies to a comment of another one, an interaction between them takes place. We process these interactions and build a notion of trust on top.

We apply Mui's definition of trust [17], which states that trust is *"a subjective expectation an agent has about another's future behavior based on the history of their encounters"*. We extend this definition by the notion of context, which means trust is established by considering past interactions in particular situations as widely agreed [18,19,20]. In the area of online discussions, contextual information is for instance the overall discussion topic or the type of forum being used.

Particularly, in discussions it may seem intuitive, that the more comments somebody provides the more s/he can be trusted to be a good discussion partner. On the other side *lurkers* [5], referring to people just watching discussions but not actually participating, can be less trusted regarding their 'openness'. They lack the willingness to exchange information, motivation or communication skills, thus they are bad collaborators.

However, a simple comment count does not truly reflect if somebody's statements are real contributions and worth reading and discussing. Thus, we consider threaded structures as well and analyze how comments are recognized by others. To this end, we define the following novel social roles within discussion scenarios: (i) **Activator:** The role of an *Activator* reflects, that the more replies a discussion participant receives, the more one's comments seem to to be worth for discussion, thus one can be trusted to have the competencies and skills to provide comments, interesting for a broad base of participants. (ii) **Driver:** The role of a *Driver* reflects, the more somebody replies to comments, the more s/he can be trusted to actively participate in a discussion, thus s/he represents a 'driver' evident for a fruitful discussion. (iii) **Affirmed Driver:** An *Affirmed Driver* is defined as a Driver whose contribution is affirmed. This is the case if there is at least one reply to a driver's comment.

According to these roles, *discussion trust* is a measure for the contribution to discussions expressing the willingness to provide information and support, but does not reflect that a particular participant offers a valid information or posts the truth. For this purpose, at least natural language processing and analyzing semantic meanings are required [21,22], which is out of scope of this paper.

5   Discussion Mining Approach

We developed a mining algorithm to determine the contribution of people in discussions. However, in contrast to common approaches, we neither reward the participants directly (e.g., their number of provided comments), nor we utilize subjective feedback, but we mine interactions to reward particularly the relationships between each pair of discussion participants.

We make the following assumptions: (i) The notion of time can be neglected, which means our algorithms do not determine how trust relations change over time. We determine trust relations for one particular point in time, based on short history data. Temporal evaluations, e.g. by applying moving averages, temporal weighting functions or sliding windows, have to be set up on top of our approach and is out of scope of this paper. (ii) We do not apply natural language processing. Thus, we accept introducing noise and small errors by rewarding users who post useless comments (i.e., spam). In the evaluation part we show that this is no disadvantage if we rely on larger amounts of data. We further assume that in PVCs spam occurs less frequently than in open internet forums.

5.1   Interaction Network Definition

We utilize a widely adopted graph model to reflect discussion relationships between users. However, we further incorporate context awareness in this model to allow trust determination with respect to different situations on top of the created interaction network.

This network is modeled as a directed multigraph $G = \langle V, E \rangle$ where each vertex $v, w \in V$ represents a user and the edges reflect relationships based on previous interactions between them. A relationship $e_{vw}^{Ctx} \in E$, as defined in (1), is described by various *metrics* such as the number of recent interactions, their weights and communication scores, with respect to particular situations described by context elements Ctx.

$$e_{vw}^{Ctx} = \langle v, w, Ctx, metrics[name, value] \rangle \ . \tag{1}$$

5.2   Discussion Mining Algorithm

We develop an algorithm which weighs the communication relations based on discussions between each pair of participants. For environments supporting threaded discussion structures as common in online forums or newsgroups, we argue that somebody who provides a comment in a discussion thread, is not only influenced by the comment s/he directly replies, but to a certain extent also by other preceding ones in the same chain of discussion. Thus, we interpret a thread to be similar to a group discussion and establish relationships between participants posting in one chain. Figure 2(a) shows a structured discussion thread where every box represents a comment provided by the annotated participant. For the highlighted comment provided by x, arrows show exemplary which interactions between participants take place. The comment provider x honors the attracting comments of w and u, and rewards the driving contribution of u, v, and y. If only affirmed drivers shall be rewarded, then the relation to y (dashed lines) is skipped, because nobody has been attracted by its comment. The weights of interactions is calculated by the interaction reward function $f_i(dt, c1, c2)$, where dt is the discussion tree, and the interaction from the author of comment $c1$ to the author of $c2$ is rewarded. We initially set $f_i(dt, c1, c2) = \frac{1}{dist(c1, c2)}$, where $dist()$ determines the distance between two comments (direct replies have $dist = 1$). However, considering further comment attributes, including time intervals between a comment and its replies or the number of replies a single comment attracts, may improve the expressiveness according to trust. All interactions between two particular participants are aggregated and directed weighted relations are created in the graph model shown in Fig 2(b).

Algorithms 1. and 2. describe formally the mode of operation. According to (1) each edge in the interaction model can have various metrics. Currently we apply *count*, which is the amount of interactions between two participants based to their

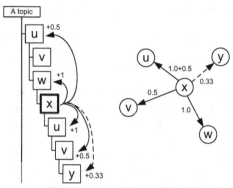

(a) Discussion thread (b) Mapping for user x

Fig. 2. Mapping from a discussion thread to the interaction network model

discussion behavior, and *strength* which is the sum of the weights of all interactions between them. We utilize the function incMetric(name, edge, value) to increment the metric specified by name of the given edge by a certain value.

In Algorithm 1. relations from a comment's provider to the providers of preceding comments are established due to their activator role. Algorithm 2. establishes relations to the providers of child comments due to driving behavior. The function providerOf() returns the identity of a comment provider, parentCommentOnLevel() determines the parent comment on the specified level ($level = dist(c1, c2)$), and childCommentsOnLevel() provides child comments.

Algorithms 1. and 2. are applied for every comment and reward the provider's contribution to the overall discussion. This process can be further improved by additionally rewarding common communication patterns as well. This means, if v provides a comment replied by w, and v replies to w's comment, then a real bidirectional communication can be observed.

Algorithm 1. Function for rewarding the relations to the activators of a comment

Require: discussionThread, graphModel, comment, Ctx
  commentProvider ← providerOf(comment)
  for level = 1 to configMaxLevelUp **do**
    parentComment ← parentCommentOnLevel(comment, level)
    if $\nexists$ parentComment **or** providerOf(parentComment) = commentProvider **then**
      break
    end if
    parentCommentProvider ← providerOf(parentComment)
    if $\nexists$ edge(commentProvider, parentCommentProvider, Ctx) **then**
      createEdge(commentProvider, parentCommentProvider, Ctx)
    end if
    incMetric(strength, edge(commentProvider, parentCommentProvider, Ctx), 1/level)
    incMetric(count, edge(comentProvider, parentCommentProvider, Ctx), 1)
    level ← level + 1
  end for
  return graphModel

Algorithm 2. Function for rewarding the relations to the drivers of a comment

---

Require: discussionThread, graphModel, comment, Ctx
    commentProvider ← providerOf(comment)
    for level = 1 to configMaxLevelDown **do**
        childComments ← childCommentsOnLevel(comment, level))
        if ∄ childComments **then**
            break
        end if
        for all childComment ∈ childComments **do**
            childCommentProvider ← providerOf(childComment)
            if childCommentProvider = commentProvider **then**
                break
            end if
            if ∄ edge(commentProvider, childCommentProvider, Ctx) **then**
                createEdge(commentProvider, childCommentProvider, Ctx)
            end if
            incMetric(strength, edge(commentProvider, childCommentProvider, Ctx), 1/level)
            incMetric(count, edge(commentProvider, childCommentProvider, Ctx), 1)
        end for
        level ← level + 1
    end for
    return graphModel

---

6   Trust Network Model

6.1   Trust Inference

Similar to previous approaches [23,24] trust is determined on top of the created interaction network, depending on the notions of confidence and reliability. We define that the confidence of user v in user w with respect to context Ctx can be derived from the previously described graph model by using a confidence function $c_{vw}^{Ctx} = f_c(G, v, w, Ctx)$.

Reliability, expressing the certainty of v's confidence in w with respect to context Ctx, is determined by a reliability function $r_{c_{vw}^{Ctx}} = f_r(G, v, w, Ctx)$. The value of $r_{c_{vw}^{Ctx}} \in [0,1]$ is basically influenced by the number and type of interactions which were used to calculate confidence, and expresses the reliability of the confidence value between totally uncertain and fully affirmed.

With the confidence of v in w and its reliability we calculate trust τ_{vw}^{Ctx} of v in w according to (2).

$$\tau_{vw}^{Ctx} = c_{vw}^{Ctx} \cdot r_{c_{vw}^{Ctx}} . \tag{2}$$

6.2   Trust Aggregation and Reputation

Aggregation of trust, often referred to as reputation, refers to (i) the combination of trust values of a group of users in one user to build a view of trust from a community's perspective, or (ii) the combination of trust values calculated for different contexts between two users to get a notion of trust for a broader context or (iii) the combination of (i) and (ii) to get a kind of general community trust in one user.

Equation (3) is applied to determine aggregated trust T_a of a group $M = \{v_i\}$ of users in one particular user w with respect to a set of context elements $Ctxs$. The weighting factor calculated by f_a can be configured statically or obtained dynamically depending on individual properties of M's elements, e.g., trust of long-term users have a higher impact on reputation than those of newbies.

$$T_{a_{Mw}}^{Ctxs} = \frac{\sum_{v_i \in M} \sum_{Ctx_j \in Ctxs} \tau_{v_i w}^{Ctx_j} \cdot f_a(v_i, w, Ctx_j)}{\sum_{v_i \in M} \sum_{Ctx_j \in Ctxs} f_a(v_i, w, Ctx_j)} \quad . \tag{3}$$

6.3   Contextual Description

We distinguish two different subtypes of contextual elements: (i) *Provenance Context* describing the situation of interactions for which an edge is created, e.g., the domain of the discussion topic, or the used forum, and (ii) *Calculation Context* depicting the situation for which trust is calculated, e.g. for suggesting a discussion partner in a particular domain. Furthermore, calculation context may dynamically determine $f_i()$, $f_c()$, $f_r()$, and $f_a()$. The detailed design of the context models depend on the available information determined by the environment and area of application. We show an exemplary configuration of the trust network model in the evaluation part of this paper.

7   Evaluation

7.1   Preparing Evaluation Data

For the evaluation of our approach, we compare the output of the proposed algorithm with real users' opinions. Because our developed system is new and currently not utilized by a wide range of users, we need a dataset which offers structured discussions in various contexts and information about the real contribution of users. We fetched an appropriate dataset with the required characteristics from the famous Slashdot[2] community.

Slashdot is a platform which offers the ability to discuss a wide variety of topics classified in different subdomains. One nice feature is the moderation system allowing experienced users to rate the postings of other users on a scale between -1 and 5. We interpret this score as human feedback which provides information about the quality of comments and thus, when considering all posts, the average discussion quality of a person.

We developed a Web crawler to capture threaded discussions in the subdomains *Your Rights Online (yro)* and *Technology (tech)* from January 2007 to June 2008. We selected these two subdomains due to their diversity, expressing different expertises of people discussing there. The subdomain in which a discussion takes place is reflected by the context of a discussion: ctx=$\{yro \mid tech\}$. Users may have established discussion relationships with respect to either *yro*, or *tech*, or both.

---

[2] http://slashdot.org

We have to ensure to compensate all impacts which degrade the quality of the data set and suitability for the tests. First, we remove all comments posted by anonymous users, because there is no meaningful way to map this data to particular nodes of the interaction graph model. Second, if not changed from the default settings, the Slashdot UI hides low scored comments automatically. Therefore, there is no way to distinguish if a particular comment is not replied because it is simply poor and not worth a discussion, or if it is not replied because it is hidden and thus never read. Hence, we remove low scored comments from the data set. Third, we remove all posts which potentially haven't been rated by others.

Initially the captured data set consists of 49.239 users and 669.221 comments in the given time period. After applying all steps of reduction we map the discussions to the graph model, consisting of 24.824 nodes and 343.669 edges. In the experiments we rank each user relatively to the others based on how much their discussion skills can be trusted by the rest of the community. Because our presented trust calculation method fully relies on the connectivity of a node within the graph, we have to ensure that the filtering procedures do not distort this property. Figure 3 shows the degree of connection for each node for the full data set and for the reduced one. The distribution follows a common power law function, and when applying the reduction steps, the characteristics of the user distribution and their connectivity basically do not change.

7.2   Trust Network Model Configuration

By applying the presented mapping approach we are able to grade discussion relationships between any two users v and w in the graph G with respect to the subdomain, reflected by context ctx=$\{yro \mid tech\}$.

Trust is determined by confidence and reliability as described in Sect. 6. To this end we define $f_c(G, v, w, Ctx) = strength$ to be a function which simply returns the discussion strength from v to w in a specific subdomain. We define a notion of confidence from v in w to be fully reliable if there are at least max_{ia} interactions with respect to the same subdomain. If $f_r(G, v, w, Ctx) = \frac{count}{max_{ia}}$

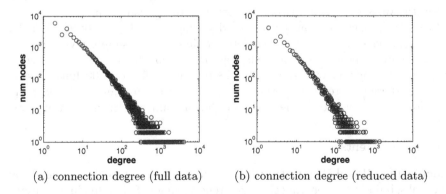

(a) connection degree (full data)   (b) connection degree (reduced data)

Fig. 3. Degree distribution

is greater than 1 we set $f_r(G, v, w, Ctx) = 1$. We configure $max_{ia} = 10$ per year, which is the same amount of posts as identified in [14] to be required to calculate representative results. For trust aggregation we apply all single input trust values having the same weight $f_a(v, w, Ctx) = 1$.

For the sake of clarity we apply only the simple functions defined above, however, more complex functions can be set up, which consider similarities between subdomains, the amount of interactions compared to well-known community members or symmetry of trust relationships, just to name a few.

Furthermore, we set $configMaxLevelUp = 3$, $configMaxLevelDown = 3$ and reward bidirectional communication, i.e., post-reply-post patterns, with $bidiR = 1$ extra point. By further increasing the number of levels for rewarding, the values indicating discussion strength between the users will increase as well. However, this does not highly influence the relative rankings of users.

7.3 Evaluation Approach

We evaluate our trust mining algorithm approach by comparing its results with trust values derived from the feedback of real users. We introduce the following terminology:

Link rank: The link rank of a user is calculated by our mining algorithm considering the strength of connections to others based on their nested comments within discussions. We interpret this measure as trust and argue, that it directly reflects a user's willingness to share information and support others (driver role), and attitude to highly recognized contributions (activator role).

Score rank: The score rank of a user is calculated by averaging his/her posting scores, thus we utilize direct human feedback. We interpret the score rank as trust and argue, that users may trust posters with high average posting score more to deliver valuable contributions, than others.

Obviously both ranking methods rely on the same social properties, which reflect the value of contribution a user provides to the community.

First of all, we clarify that our proposed scoring method does not only depend on the number of posts and is completely different from simply giving reward points for every posted comment such as in common Internet forums. Figure 4 depicts the number of posts within 18 month of the top1000 linked users. However, there is a trend that frequently posting users are ranked higher, there is obviously no strong correlation between the link rank and the number of posts.

7.4 Experiments

Calculating Global Reputation. In our first experiment we determine global link ranks, built by aggregating the link strength values of all individual relations within the network for each user over all contexts. Besides this, we determine the

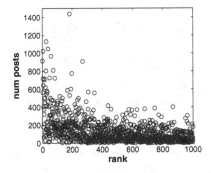

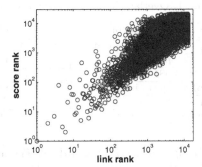

Fig. 4. Link rank compared to number of posts for top1000 linked users

Fig. 5. Link rank compared to score rank for each user

global score rank as well. This means we rank each user two times: once with our algorithm based on discussion structures, and once based on humans' feedback score. For determining score ranks we degrade users' average scores by the factor $\frac{postcount}{numMinposts \cdot numMonth}$, if they posted less than $numMinposts$ posts a month to make sure that rarely posting users are not scored too high. During experiments we found out that $numMinposts = 10$ per month seems to be the value to reach the highest value for the Pearson correlation coefficient (0.77) between the results of both ranking methods for the given data set, as shown in Fig. 5.

We further calculate the Dice similarity coefficient depicted in (4), which is defined as the amount of elements included in both of two sets, in our case the sets of top scored users (TopXS) and top linked users (TopXL), where X={10,25,50,100,1000} determining the size of the sets.

$$s = \frac{2 \cdot |\text{TopXS} \cap \text{TopXL}|}{|\text{TopXS}| + |\text{TopXL}|} . \tag{4}$$

Table 1 shows how many percent of the top linked users and top scored users overlap after different time intervals. Obviously, the more data is used for trust calculation the more the resulting top linked users get similar to the top scored ones, which means we receive preciser results. After 18 month we finish with an overlap between 45 and 60 percent, for the top10 to top50 and approximately 65 to 70 percent for larger groups. Furthermore, we compare the amount of the top10 scored (Top10S) users who are also in the top25, top50, top100, and top1000 (TopXL) of the top linked users. The top10 scored users are the users scored best by others, and thus are most trusted to provide meaningful information. Table 1 shows that after 4 month 90 to 100 percent of the top10 scored users are included in the top50 linked users.

We conclude, that for the given data set we are able to find a similar set of users, who are trusted to post high quality comments, when ranked either by the average of posting scores (scoreRank) or by the discussion structure and reply behavior (linkRank).

Table 1. Overlap similarities (OSim) of top linked and top scored users in percent

OSim after month:	01	02	03	04	06	10	14	18
Top10|TopS10 in TopL10	10|10	30|30	30|30	30|30	40|40	50|50	60|60	50|50
Top25|TopS10 in TopL25	32|50	36|40	48|70	60|80	52|80	48|70	44|70	44|90
Top50|TopS10 in TopL50	28|50	34|60	40|80	50|90	54|100	58|90	62|100	60|100
Top100|TopS10 in TopL100	36|90	42|90	46|90	48|100	58|100	66|100	70|100	64|100
Top1000|TopS10 in TopL1000	61|100	61|100	66|100	64|100	64|100	66|100	68|100	70|100
number of users x1000	2.5	4.9	6.4	7.9	11	15	18	20

Enabling Context Dependent Trust Ranking. In a second experiment we consider the discussion context. Discussions in the utilized dataset take place either in subdomain `yro` or `tech`. We show that it is reasonable to calculate trust for particular situations reflected by context. We use six month of data from January 2008 to July 2008 because in this interval the amount of discussions and user distribution in both subdomains are nearly the same, thus results cannot be influenced by the number of posts. Then we rank each user two times with our algorithm, once for discussions in `yro` and once for `tech`. We rank only users with more than 10 posts, which we defined earlier as the absolute minimum for being trustworthy. There are in sum 14793 different users, where 5939 are only active in `yro` and 6288 in `tech`. Other users participate in discussions in both subdomains and thus, are ranked two times.

In Fig. 6 we compare how users are ranked with respect to both subdomains. There is an amount of approximately 40 users who are both, in the top100 wrt. `yro` and in the top100 wrt. `tech`, hence these people are highly trusted independent from the subdomain. However, there are around 60 users in the top100 of one subdomain but badly ranked in the other one, or not participating in discussions in the other subdomain at all. They are located in Fig. 6 in the top-left quadrant for `yro` and in the bottom-right for `tech` respectively.

We conclude that between the sets of top100 trusted users wrt. each subdomain there is less overlapping than diversity. These results show the usefulness of considering contextual data.

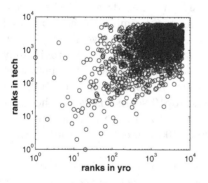

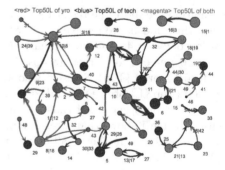

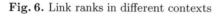

Fig. 6. Link ranks in different contexts   **Fig. 7.** Trust network (color online)

Determining Individual Trust. In contrast to reputation, which is mostly defined to be determined by the aggregated opinion of others, trust relies on personal experiences. As described in [14] in typical online communities there exist several clusters of users, which are tightly interconnected, but sparsely connected to other clusters.

Compared to most common reputation systems, which maintain only one global rank for each user from a global point of view, we are able to consider trust relations from an individual view as well. Hence, for a particular user there remain three possibilities to determine which users can be trusted: (i) trust users with highest reputation from a global view (with or without respect to context), (ii) trust the users who are directly connected strongest by utilizing local metrics (however, these users may have only an average global reputation) or (iii) combine both possibilities.

In Figure 7 we removed all connections with strength ≤ 5, and all users who are either not in the top50L users of *yro* (red), *tech* (blue), or both (magenta), or not connected to anyone else. Therefore, the most trusted users and their strongest connections remain. The size of the circles representing users depends on their rank they received in either *yro* (red), *tech* (blue) or both (magenta), and the thickness of the lines reflect the connection strength. Obviously the trust graph splits into several only sparsely interconnected components. This justifies applying local metrics and selecting partners to trust with respect to strong personal relationships, instead of using global ranks only.

8 Conclusion and Future Work

In this paper we proposed a system for collecting communication data and performing trust determination within virtual communities. We demonstrated how our mining algorithm is able to determine trust relationships between users, after they contributed a while within the community. In the evaluation part we showed, that taking these trust relationships into account, the algorithm is able to find sets of trusted users, which are similar to sets of users top rated by humans. We further proved the usefulness of the concept of context awareness and considering local trust relationships.

In the next steps we plan to extend our framework to utilize more data sources. Especially in service-oriented collaborative working environments not only communication data, but task execution, resource utilization, and Web service invocation logs are further possible sources for better expressing the diversity of trust. We prepare our approach to be used in a project in the sector of networked enterprises to test it under real conditions and to enable research about influences of diverse interaction metrics on trust.

Furthermore, we plan to implement mechanisms to detect malicious attacks, such as artificially pushing a user's reputation rank. The evolvement of trust over time, currently neglected by our algorithm, may provide a valuable source of information about the long-term reputation of discussion participants.

References

1. Jøsang, A., Ismail, R., Boyd, C.: A survey of trust and reputation systems for online service provision. Decision Support Systems 43(2), 618–644 (2007)
2. The Economist: The role of trust in business collaboration. An Economist Intelligence Unit briefing paper sponsored by Cisco Systems (2008)
3. IBM: An architectural blueprint for autonomic computing. Whitepaper (2005)
4. Welser, H.T., Gleave, E., Fisher, D., Smith, M.: Visualizing the signatures of social roles in online discussion groups. Journal of Social Structure 8 (2007)
5. Nonnecke, B., Preece, J., Andrews, D.: What lurkers and posters think of each other. In: HICSS (2004)
6. Meyer, K.A.: Face-to-face versus threaded discussions: The role of time and higher-order thinking. Journal for Asynchronous Learning Networks 7(3), 55–65 (2003)
7. McLure-Wasko, M., Faraj, S.: Why should i share? examining social capital and knowledge contribution in electronic networks. MIS Quarterly 29(1), 35–57 (2005)
8. Rheingold, H.: The Virtual Community: Homesteading on the electronic frontier, revised edition. The MIT Press, Cambridge (2000)
9. Massa, P.: A survey of trust use and modeling in real online systems (2007)
10. Gyngyi, Z., Garcia-Molina, H., Pedersen, J.: Combating web spam with trustrank. In: VLDB, pp. 576–587 (2004)
11. Page, L., Brin, S., Motwani, R., Winograd, T.: The pagerank citation ranking: Bringing order to the web. Technical report, Stanford University (1998)
12. Kleinberg, J.M.: Authoritative sources in a hyperlinked environment. Journal of the ACM 46(5), 604–632 (1999)
13. Kamvar, S.D., Schlosser, M.T., Garcia-Molina, H.: The eigentrust algorithm for reputation management in p2p networks. In: WWW, pp. 640–651 (2003)
14. Gomez, V., Kaltenbrunner, A., Lopez, V.: Statistical analysis of the social network and discussion threads in slashdot. In: WWW, pp. 645–654. ACM, New York (2008)
15. Massa, P., Avesani, P.: Controversial users demand local trust metrics: An experimental study on epinions.com community. In: AAAI, pp. 121–126 (2005)
16. Skopik, F., Truong, H.L., Dustdar, S.: VieTE - enabling trust emergence in service-oriented collaborative environments. In: WEBIST, pp. 471–478 (2009)
17. Mui, L.: Computational models of trust and reputation: Agents, evolutionary games, and social networks. Ph.D thesis, Massachusetts Institute of Technology (December 2002)
18. Grandison, T., Sloman, M.: A survey of trust in internet applications. IEEE Communications Surveys and Tutorials 3(4) (2000)
19. Marsh, S.P.: Formalising trust as a computational concept. Ph.D thesis, University of Stirling (April 1994)
20. McKnight, D.H., Chervany, N.L.: The meanings of trust. Technical report, University of Minnesota (1996)
21. Wanas, N.M., El-Saban, M., Ashour, H., Ammar, W.: Automatic scoring of online discussion posts. In: WICOW, pp. 19–26. ACM, New York (2008)
22. Feng, D., Shaw, E., Kim, J., Hovy, E.H.: Learning to detect conversation focus of threaded discussions. In: HLT-NAACL. The Association for Computational Linguistics (2006)
23. Billhardt, H., Hermoso, R., Ossowski, S., Centeno, R.: Trust-based service provider selection in open environments. In: SAC, pp. 1375–1380. ACM, New York (2007)
24. Huynh, T.D., Jennings, N.R., Shadbolt, N.R.: An integrated trust and reputation model for open multi-agent systems. Autonomous Agents and Multi-Agent Systems 13(2), 119–154 (2006)

A Structured Approach to Data Reverse Engineering of Web Applications

Roberto De Virgilio and Riccardo Torlone

Università Roma Tre, Italy
{devirgilio,torlone}@dia.uniroma3.it

Abstract. The majority of documents on the Web are written in HTML, constituting a huge amount of legacy data: all documents are formatted for visual purposes only and with different styles due to diverse authorships and goals and this makes the process of retrieval and integration of Web contents difficult to automate. We provide a contribution to the solution of this problem by proposing a structured approach to data reverse engineering of data-intensive Web sites. We focus on data content and on the way in which such content is structured on the Web. We profitably use a Web data model to describe abstract structural features of HTML pages and propose a method for the segmentation of HTML documents in special blocks grouping semantically related Web objects. We have developed a tool based on this method that supports the identification of structure, function, and meaning of data organized in Web object blocks. We demonstrate with this tool the feasibility and effectiveness of our approach over a set of real Web sites.

1 Introduction

With the growth of the Internet, Web applications have become the most important means of electronic communication, especially for commercial enterprisers of all kinds. Unfortunately, many Web applications are poorly documented (or not documented at all) and poorly structured: this makes difficult the maintenance and the evolution of such systems. This aspect, together with the growing demand to reimplement and evolve legacy software systems by means of modern Web technologies, has underscored the need for Reverse Engineering (RE) tools and techniques for the Web. Chikofsky describes RE as *"the process of analyzing a subject system to identify the system's components and their interrelationships and create representations of the system in another form or at a higher level of abstraction"* [6]. The Data Reverse Engineering (DRE) emerged from the more general problem of reverse engineering: while RE operates on each of the three main aspects of an information system (data, process, and control), DRE concentrates on data and on its organization. It can be defined as a collection of methods and tools supporting the identification of structure, function, and meaning of data in an software application. In particular, DRE aims at recovering the semantics of the data, by retrieving data structures and constraints, and relies on *structured* techniques to model, analyze, and understand existing

M. Gaedke, M. Grossniklaus, and O. Díaz (Eds.): ICWE 2009, LNCS 5648, pp. 91–105, 2009.
© Springer-Verlag Berlin Heidelberg 2009

applications of all kinds. It is widely recognized that these techniques can greatly assist for system maintenance, reengineering, extension, migration and integration and motivate the add-on of a framework supporting the complete process of data reverse engineering of Web applications. In this scenario, several approaches have been proposed to convert HTML Web pages into more or less structured formats (e.g. XML or relational tables). Usually, these approaches leverage the structural similarities of pages from large Web sites to automatically derive data *wrappers* (see [12] for a survey). Most of them rely on hierarchy-based algorithms that consider any two elements as belonging to the same item when their corresponding HTML tags are located under a common parent tag in the DOM tree [8,16]. However, when the HTML structure of a Web page became more complicated, an item with several elements can be extracted incorrectly: related elements may be visually positioned closely but textually located under different parent tags in the tree hierarchy. Moreover, the result of the reverse engineering process is a repository of data (e.g., a collection of relational tables) that is poorly processable without user supervision mainly because they take into account the semantics of data only to a limited extent.

In this framework, we propose a structure discovery technique that: (i) identifies blocks grouping semantically related objects occurring in Web pages, and (ii) generates a logical schema of a Web site. The approach is based on a page segmentation process that is inspired by a method to group elements of a Web page in blocks according to a cognitive visual analysis [5]. Visual blocks detection is followed by a pattern discovery technique that generates structural blocks that are represented in a conceptual model, called Web Site Model (WSM) [9]. This model generalizes various (data and object oriented) Web models and allows the representation of the abstract features of HTML pages at content, navigation and presentation levels. Content and presentation are linked to these blocks to produce the final logical schema of the Web site.

An important aspect of our approach is that we face with a highly heterogeneous collection of HTML documents. Specifically, we start from the observation that even if HTML documents are heterogeneous in terms of how topic specific information is represented using HTML markups, usually the documents exhibit certain domain-independent properties. In particular, an HTML document basically presents two types of elements: *block elements* and *text elements*. The former involve the document structure (i.e. headings, ordered/unordered lists, text containers, tables and so on), the latter refer to text inside block elements (e.g., based on font markups). Together, these elements specify information at different levels of abstraction. We distinguish several types of blocks due to their functionality in the page: (i) visual or cognitive, (ii) structural and (iii) Web object. Starting from the visual rendering of a Web page, it is straightforward to divide the page in well-defined and well-identifiable sections according to the cognitive perception of the user. In these *visual blocks* we identify a set of *patterns* that represent structures aggregating information. Each pattern is a collection of tags. For instance the pattern HTML-BODY-UL-LI identifies a *structural block* that organizes related information as a list. By grouping patterns, we identify several *Web object blocks* representing aggregations of information in the page that give hints on the grouping of semantically related objects. Each Web object block represents a particular hypertextual element that organizes and presents a content with a specific layout. We have developed a tool, called RE-VERSEWEB, implementing the above mentioned methods to semi-automatically identify structure, function, and meaning of Web data organized in Web object blocks. REVERSEWEB has been used to perform experiments on publically available Web sites.

The paper is structured as follows. In Section 2 we present some related works. In Section 3 we introduce the page segmentation technique to individuate visual and structural blocks. In Section 4 we illustrate how we can identify blocks and produce a logical description of the Web site. In Section 5 we show an architecture of the tool and a number of experimental results and finally, in Section 6, we sketch concluding remarks and future works.

2   Related Work

The literature proposes many methods and tools to analyze Web page structures and layout, with different goals.

UML based approaches. The majority of Web Application reverse engineering methodologies and tools rely on the Unified Modeling Language (UML). UML-based techniques provide a stable, familiar environment to model components as well as the behavior of applications. Among them, Di Lucca et al. have developed the Web Application Reverse Engineering (WARE) tool [10], a very well documented example to RE. The approach is based on the Goals, Models and Tools (GMT) paradigm of Benedussi and makes use of the Conallen UML extensions to represent information as package diagrams (use-case diagrams for functional information, class-diagrams for the structure, and sequence-diagrams for the dynamic interaction with the Web Application). Chung and Lee [7] also adopt the Conallen extensions. They represent the Web content in terms of a component diagram and the Web application in terms of a package diagram. In general, all of these approaches focus on the behavior and interaction with a Web Application, rather than on its organization.

Ontology based approaches. The basic idea of these approaches is to model a Web application by means of an schema. Among them, Benslimane et. al [3] and Bouchiha et. al. [4] have proposed OntoWare, whose main objective is the generation of an ontological, conceptual representation of the application. The authors criticize other approaches to reverse engineering because they do not provide adequate support to knowledge representation (a position also supported by Du Bois [11]). The ontological approach provides a high level analysis of a Web Application but usually depends on the specific domain of interest. In most cases, data extraction can only be done after a user intervention aimed at building the domain ontology by locating and naming Web information [2].

Usually, the ontology based approaches rely on a specific formalism to represent the structures extracted from Web pages. Lixto [2] is a tool for the generation of wrappers for HTML and XML documents. Patterns discovered Lixto are here expressed in terms of a logic-based declarative language called Elog.

Source code based approaches. Ricca and Tonella have proposed ReWeb [13], a tool for source code analysis of Web Applications. They use a graph model to represent a Web application and focus on reachability, flow and traversal analysis. The outcome of the analysis is a set of popup windows illustrating the evolution of the Web Application. Vanderdonckt et al. [15] have developed VAQUISTA, a framework to reverse engineering the interface of Web applications. The aim of this work is to facilitate the migration of Web Application between different platforms. VAQUISTA performs a static analysis of HTML pages and translates them into a model describing the elements of the HTML page at different levels of abstraction. Antoniol et. al. [1] use an RMM based methodology. The authors apply an RE process to identify logical links which are then used to build a Relationship Management Data Model (RMDM). From the RMDM an Entity-Relationship model is then abstracted. This is the end point of the reverse engineering process. In general, all of these solutions produce a logical description of a specific aspect of a Web application (mainly related to the presentation).

3   Extraction of Page Structure

3.1   Overview

Our approach is related to recent techniques for extracting information from the Web [12]. As for most of these proposals, we start from the observation that data published in the pages of large sites usually (i) come from a back-end database and (ii) are embedded within shared HTML templates. Therefore the extraction process can rely on the inference of a description of the shared templates. Though this approach is applicable on Web documents, it does not exploit the hypertext structure of Web documents. Our work focuses on discovering this structure as well. Some research efforts show that users always expect that certain functional part of a Web page (e.g., navigational links, advertisement bar and so on) appears at certain position of a page[1]. Additionally, there exist blocks of information that involve frequent HTML elements and have a higher coherence. That it to say, in Web pages there are many unique information features, which can be used to help the extraction of blocks involving homogeneous information.

To this aim we define a Data Reverse Engineering (DRE) process composed by the following steps:

– *Page Segmentation*: each Web page in a Web site is segmented in several blocks according to the visual perception of a user. Each resulting visual block of a Web page is isolated and through an analysis of the DOM associated with blocks, a set of structural patterns are derived. Differently from

---

[1] For more details see http://www.surl.org/

other approaches, this step combines a computer vision approach (to understand the perception of users) with a DOM structure extraction technique
(which conveys the intention of Web authors).

– *Schema Discovery*: the derived patterns of each Web page, grouped in visual
  blocks, suggest the clustering of pages in the Web site. Each cluster represents aggregations of semantically related data and is represented by a set
  of structural patterns. Usually, a wrapper is generated to automate the extraction of patterns and to structure the Web content associated with them
  according to a logical model (e.g, the relational model). Differently from
  these solutions, in this step we make use of a conceptual model to represent
  Web data at content, navigation and presentation levels. The patterns of
  each cluster are mapped into constructs of this model. Finally, based on this
  conceptual representation, a logical schema of the Web site is extracted.

In the rest of this section, we will describe in detail the page segmentation phase,
providing algorithms to compute the structural patterns. In the next section we
will illustrate the schema discovery technique.

3.2   Page Segmentation

We start by exploiting the semi-structured nature of Web documents described
in terms of their document object model (DOM) representation. Note that DOM
poorly reflects the actual semantic structure of a page. However the visual page
layout structuring is more suitable to suggest a semantic partitioning of a page.
Therefore, we make use of the VIPS approach (Vision-based Page Segmentation)
[5], taking advantage from DOM trees and visual cues. The main idea is that:
(i) semantically related contents are often grouped together, and (ii) the page
usually divides the content by using visual separators (such as images, lines, and
font sizes). VIPS exploits the DOM structure and the visual cues and extracts
information blocks according to the visual perception. The output of VIPS associates with each is Web page a partitioning tree structure over *visual blocks*
(VBs). The resulting VBs present a high *degree of coherence*, meaning that they
convey homogeneous information within the page. Then we assign an XML description to the tree: each VB is identified by the path from the root of the page
in its DOM representation (considering also the available styling information
of class or id referring to the associated Cascading Style Sheet or CSS) and
is characterized by the position in the page. For instance, Figure 1 shows the
resulting partitioning tree and XML description of the home page of Ebay[2].

Let us consider the visual block VB2_1 of Figure 1: it organizes information
using an unordered list of items. Figure 2 shows an extract of DOM and CSS
properties for VB2_1. The next phase analyzes each identified VB and discovers
repeated patterns representing aggregations of information with a shared structure. More in detail, in each VB we label any path from the root of VB to a node
using an hash code. A preorder traversal generates a sequence V representing a
vector of hash codes, as shown in Figure 2.

---

[2] http:\www.ebay.com

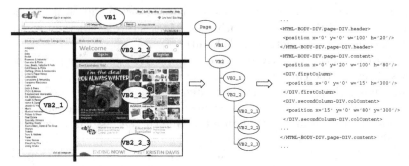

Fig. 1. Visual Partitioning of a Web page

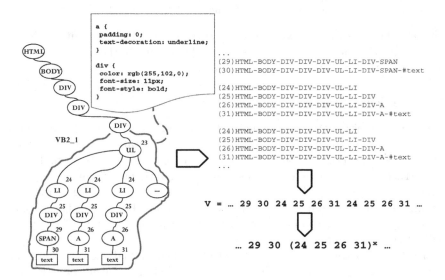

Fig. 2. Pattern searching

Finally we group repeated paths that represent patterns to identify. To this aim we use an algorithm, called *path-mark* that gets inspiration from the dictionary-based compression algorithm LZW [14]. Algorithm 1. illustrates the pseudo-code of path-mark.

The algorithm manages a queue Q and a sequence V, and returns a map M where each group of hash codes has assigned the number of its occurrences in V. We generate V, initialize Q and M (lines $4-5$) and make use of a window (win) to scan the subsequences to analyze (line 7). win varies from one to half of the length of V. So we extract a candidate subsequence ($actual$) of win length and insert it in Q (lines $9-11$). We compare $actual$ with the top subsequence ($previous$) in Q, previously analyzed, and if they are equal we count the number of consecutive occurrences ($counter$) of $actual$ in the rest of V moving with a win scale. At the end we assign $counter$ to $actual$ in M (lines $12-22$). Otherwise we extract another subsequence and iterate the algorithm from the line 8. Referring

---

Algorithm 1. Path-Mark

1: **Input:** A visual block VB
2: **Output:** A Map of occurring patterns in VB, each one related to its occurrences
3: **begin**
4:    $V \leftarrow HASHPREORDER(VB)$ // V is a sequence
5:    $EMPTY(M), EMPTY(Q)$ // M is a map and Q a queue
6:    $seq\_length \leftarrow LENGTH(V)$
7:    **for** win from 1 to $\frac{seq\_length}{2}$ **do**
8:       **for** $index$ from 0 to $seq\_length - win$ **do**
9:          $previous \leftarrow DEQUEUE(Q)$
10:          $actual \leftarrow SUBSEQUENCE(V, index, index + win)$
11:          $ENQUEUE(Q, actual)$
12:          **if** $actual = previous$ **then**
13:             $counter \leftarrow counter + 1$
14:             $internal \leftarrow index + win$
15:             **while** $internal < seq\_length$ **do**
16:                $next \leftarrow SUBSEQUENCE(V, internal, internal + win)$
17:                **if** $actual = next$ **then** $counter \leftarrow counter + 1$
18:                **else**$INSERT(M, actual, counter)$
19:                **end if**
20:                $internal \leftarrow internal + win$
21:             **end while**
22:          **end if**
23:       **end for**
24:    **end for**
25:    **return** M
26: **end**

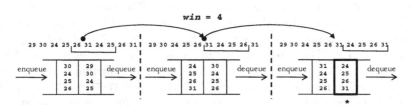

Fig. 3. An execution of Path-Mark

---

to the example of Figure 2, we show an execution of the algorithm in Figure 3 with $win = 4$.

Our algorithm returns a grouping such as: $(\ldots, 29, 30, (24, 25, 26, 31)^x, \ldots)$. This means that $(24, 25, 26, 31)$ is a repeated path HTML-BODY-DIV-DIV-DIV-UL-LI-DIV-A that presents a pattern UL-LI-DIV-A, where HTML-BODY-DIV-DIV-DIV is the root of the container VB2_1.

4   Schema Discovery

In the previous section we have presented a technique to segment a Web page into structural blocks representing aggregations of semantically related data. The following step consists of generating a logical schema matching the discovered patterns making use of the Web Site Model described in [9].

To this purpose, we get inspiration from the idea of Crescenzi et al. [8]: a Web page p can be considered as a couple $\{ID, VB\}$, where ID is an identifier and VB is the set of visual blocks, resulting by the VIPS segmentation. Each VB_i is

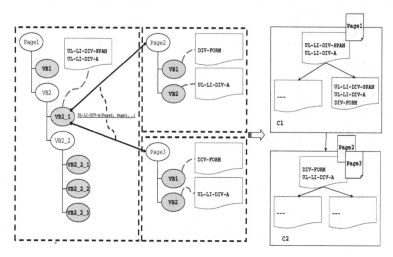

Fig. 4. From pages to clusters

a collection of patterns $pt_1, pt_2, \ldots$, identified by the path-mark algorithm shown
in the previous section. So we define the *page schema* of a Web page p as the
union of all patterns occurring in each visual block. Then we call *link collection*
in a Web page p all node-to-link patterns together with all the URLs that share
that pattern. For instance consider the Web pages *Page1*, *Page2* and *Page3* in
left side of Figure 4. They are described in terms of a tree of visual blocks. Each
block is associated with a set of patterns, identified by Algorithm 1. Both *Page2*
and *Page3* have a page schema described by the set {DIV-FORM, UL-LI-DIV-A}
and the link collection {UL-LI-DIV-A$\{url_1, url_2, \ldots\}$}. *Page1* is associated with
the link collection {UL-LI-DIV-A$\{Page2, Page3, \ldots\}$}.

We can establish a partial ordering between page schemas by introducing
the notions of *subsumption* and *distance*. Given two page schemas ps_1 and ps_2,
we say that ps_1 is subsumed by ps_2, $ps_1 \lhd ps_2$, if each pattern pt in ps_1 also
occurs in ps_2. The distance between two page schemas is defined as the normal-
ized cardinality of the symmetric set difference between the two schemas. Let
us consider again ps_1 and ps_2, then $dist(ps_1, ps_2) = \frac{|(ps_1 - ps_2) \cup (ps_2 - ps_1)|}{|ps_1 \cup ps_2|}$. Note
that if $ps_1 = ps_2$ (that is, the schemas coincide), then $dist(ps_1, ps_2) = 0$. If
$ps_1 \cap ps_2 = \emptyset$ (the schemas are disjoint), then $dist(ps_1, ps_2) = 1$. Based on the
notions of page schema, subsumption and distance we then define a notion of
cluster as a collection of page schemas: a cluster is a tree $\{N_C, E_C, r_C\}$ where (i)
N_C is a set of nodes representing page schemas, (ii) E_C is a set of edges (n_i, n_j)
such that $n_i \lhd n_j$, and (iii) r_C is the root. In a cluster, a page schemas ps_i is
parent of a page schema ps_j if $ps_i \lhd ps_j$, therefore the root of a cluster represents
the most general page schema in the cluster. Each page schema is associated with
a set of Web pages that match with it. To maintain clusters we use a threshold dt. Given a cluster C and a page schema ps and the set of associated pages, ps

can be inserted in C if $dist(ps, r_C)$ is lower than the given threshold dt[3]. For instance, in right side of Figure 4 there are the clustering of *Page1*, *Page2* and *Page3*. Now we can define also a notion of *cluster link*: given a cluster C_1 and one of its pattern node-to-link pt, consider the link collections of the Web pages in C associated with pt. We say that there exists a cluster link L between C_1 and the cluster C_2 if there are links in the link collections associated to pt that point to pages in C_2.

A relevant step in schema discovery is the computation of a useful partition of Web pages in clusters, such that pages in the same cluster are structurally homogeneous. Whereupon a crawler navigates a Web site starting from the home page and an agglomerative clustering algorithm groups pages into classes. We have designed an algorithm that builds a set of clusters incrementally. Algorithm 2. shows the pseudo code.

Algorithm 2. Compute Clusters

Require: n: max size of selected links subset
Require: dt: distance threshold for candidate selection
```
 1: Input: Starting Web page p0
 2: Output: the set of Clusters CL
 3: begin
 4:   EMPTY(CL), EMPTY(Q) // CL is a set and Q a queue
 5:   INSERT(p0, CL, dt)
 6:   Q ← LINKCOLLECTION(p0)
 7:   while Q is not empty do
 8:       lc ← DEQUEUE(Q)
 9:       W ← PAGES(lc, n)
10:       H ← ∅
11:       while W is not empty do
12:           W − {p}
13:           INSERT(p, CL, dt)
14:           H ∪ LINKCOLLECTION(p)
15:       end while
16:       while H is not empty do
17:           H − {lc′}
18:           ENQUEUE(Q, lc′)
19:       end while
20:   end while
21:   return CL
22: end
```

The input of the algorithm is the home page p_0 of the Web site, which is the first member of the first cluster in the set CL (line 5). The output is the set of computed clusters CL. From p_0 we extract its link collections, and push them into a priority queue Q (line 6). Then, the algorithm iterates until the queue is empty. At each iteration a link collection lc is extracted from Q (line 8), and a subset W of the pages (n) pointed by its links is fetched (line 9)[4]. Then the pages in W are grouped according to their schemas (lines 11-15). The function $INSERT(p, CL, dt)$ inserts a page p into a cluster of CL all the pages whose page schema has a distance from the root r_C lower than the threshold dt. Basically, we extract the page schema ps of p, by using the path-mark algorithm, and select

---

[3] On the basis of our experiments, we have set $dt = 0.4$.

[4] We assume that is sufficient to follow a subset of the potentially large set of links to determine the properties of the entire collection.

the cluster C in CL whose root has the minimum distance from ps (lower than dt). If there is no cluster satisfying these properties, we add to CL a new cluster having ps as root.

Starting from the root of C, we insert ps (and p) into C as follows: (i) if there is no child n of the root r_C of C such that $n \lhd ps$, then (a) ps becomes the child of r_C, and (b) each child n of r_C such that $p \lhd n$ becomes child of ps; (ii) otherwise, we insert ps in the sub-tree of C having as root the child n of r_C such that (a) $n \lhd ps$, and (b) the distance between ps and n is minimum. Once ps has be inserted in C, we move each n'' such that (i) $ps \lhd n''$ and (ii) n'' is at the same level of ps, as a child of ps.

Then, we extract the link collections of p and update the queue Q (lines 16-19). In this process we assume that the links that belong to the same link collection lead to pages that are similar in structure or with minor differences in their schemas. Then we assign a priority to link collections by visiting the fewest possible pages: an higher priority is given to link collections that have many instances of outgoing links from the cluster. This means that long lists in a page are likely to point pages with similar content (this is particularly true when they are generated by a program), and therefore the next set of pages will provide an high support to discover another cluster.

The final step of the schema discovery process consists of representing each cluster according to our Web Site Model (WSM) [9]. The idea is to identify a set of *container tags* representing candidates to be mapped. In particular we refer to HTML tags that bring to information content in a Web page such as `UL,TABLE,DIV,BODY,....` Each pattern rooted in a tag container will be translated into a metacontainer using a particular navigational structure (Index, Guided Tour or Entry). We fix a set of heuristics for each construct of our model. Referring to the example of Figure 2 we map the pattern `UL-LI-DIV-A` into an Inde because we have a heuristic that maps a pattern `UL-LI-#-A` with an Index. Each metacontainer is identified by the path from the root to the container tag in the DOM and presents several properties representing the occurring patterns into the block. Then, we organize the data content according to the information content associated to each pattern, and the presentation according to the style properties associated in the Cascading Style Sheet, organized then in WOTs. The root of each cluster is the representative page schema to describe in WSM. As a example, Figure 5 shows the Web object blocks associated with the root of cluster C_1 shown in Figure 4 and the corresponding implementation in a relational DBMS.

5   Experimental Results

On the basis of the methodologies and techniques above described, we have designed a tool for data reverse engineering of data intensive Web applications called REVERSEWEB. Figure 6 shows the architecture of the tool.

The main modules of the tool are¿ (i) a *PreProcessor (PP)* and (ii) a *Semantic Engine (SE)*. The PP module is responsible to communicate with the

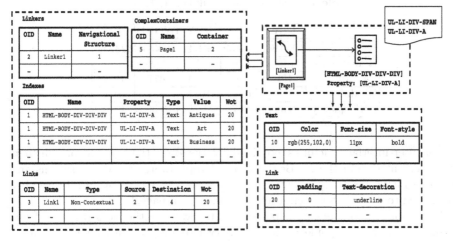

Fig. 5. An example of Web object blocks

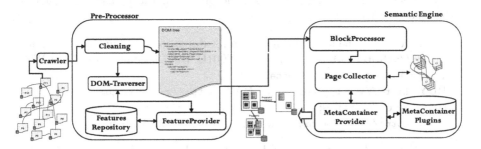

Fig. 6. The Architecture of REVERSEWEB

crawler, to process a Web page by using a cleaner (Tidy available at http://tidy.sourceforge.net/) and a *DOM traverser*, and to produce a structural segmentation of the page. This segmentation is supported by a *Feature Provider* that selects in a repository the segmentation feature to apply (i.e. VIPS and Path-Mark). This choice makes the segmentation step modular and extensible. The resulting XML description (as shown in Section 3.2) is taken as input by the SE module that is responsible to map discovered patterns to metaconstructs of our Web Site Model. The *Block Processor* supports the *Page Collector* to produce and manage the clusters of pages. The resulting set of clusters are taken as input by the *MetaContainer Provider* component that processes the representative page schemas, maps single pattern to a construct by using a repository of *Plugins*, containing the different heuristics, and returns the final logical schema.

REVERSEWEB has a Java implementation. The crawling is multi-threading makes use of an internal browser. The GUI has been realized with the SWT toolkit[5]), which has been designed to provide an efficient and portable access

---

[5] http://www.eclipse.org/swt/

Table 1. Experimental Results on 1000 pages

	DIA	EBAY	BUY	WORD	NBA
R .total (sec)	1050,80	2209,39	4589,95	1045,51	1232,68
R .avg (sec)	1,05	2,30	7,57	1,06	1,25
Page dim	471	1108	2054	477	1827
BF dim	179	631	1047	171	804
DRE quality	0,38	0,57	0,51	0,36	0,44

to the user-interface facilities provided by the operating system on which it is implemented, and the NetBeans Visual Graph Library[6]. All algorithms and heuristics have been implemented in Java. The CSS steady state Library[7] has been used to parse the presentation properties of a page.[8]

Plenty of experiments have been done to evaluate the performance of our framework using an Apple computer xServer, equipped with an Intel Core 2 Duo 1.86 Ghz processor, a 4 GB RAM, and a 500 GB HDD Serial ATA. These experiments rely on crawling 1000 pages and producing the logical page schemas of the following Web sites:

1. DIA, the Department of Informatics and Automation of Roma Tre University (http://web.dia.uniroma3.it/), and WORD, the Dictionary translator Web Site (http://www.wordreference.com);
2. BUY (http://www.buy.com) and EBAY (http://www.ebay.com), two famous e-commerce Web sites;
3. NBA (http://www.nba.com), a well known basketball Web site.

We measured the *average elapsed time* to produce a logical schema and the *accuracy* of the result. In the table 1, for each Web site we show (i) the real time in seconds (R. total) to produce a logical schema, (ii) the average time in seconds (R. avg) to reverse a Web page, (iii) the average page dimension (Page dim) in terms of number of nodes in the DOM, (iv) the average amount of nodes in the DOM of the Web page, involved in the Web object blocks (correctly computed) of the final page schema (BF dim) and (v) the *DRE quality*. The DRE quality measures the accuracy to determine a correct set of Web object blocks as follows. We have adopted the following performance measure: $P_r = \frac{Page_{dim} - BF_{dim}}{Page_{dim}}$ where $Page_{dim}$ is the retrieved portion of a Web site and BF_{dim} is the relevant portion. Basically, P_r is the fraction of the Web site portion retrieved that is not relevant to the schema information need. In other words P_r is the fraction of the Web site portion containing Web content that user will not query.

Then, we define the DRE quality results as: $DRE_{quality} = 1 - P_r$. This coefficient measures the effectiveness of the resulting logical schema. It compares the average amount of nodes involved in the final schema with the average number

---

[6] http://graph.netbeans.org/

[7] http://cssparser.sourceforge.net/

[8] More details on REVERSEWEB can be found at http://mais.dia.uniroma3.it/ ReverseWeb, where an alpha version of the tool is publically available.

of nodes for page. More specifically, the percentage of DOM nodes in a page involved in the final schema. This coefficient is in a range [0,1]. If DRE quality is too close to zero, this means that the system was not able to identify significant blocks. Conversely, if the DRE quality is too close to one, the system had difficulties to prune unmeaningly blocks. We have experimentally determined that the best values of DRE quality are in the range [0.2,0.6].

The table provides interesting information about the structure of the analyzed Web sites. DIA, WORD and NBA present the lowest values of R. total. This is a consequence of the regular structure and homogeneity of information blocks in the pages. Moreover they present an optimal DRE quality. EBAY and BUY have higher elapsed times, due to their irregular structure of pages, relevant heterogeneity of published information and great amount of non informative nodes (e.g. banner, spots, and so on), typical in e-commerce Web sites. These results are supported also by diagrams: Figure 7 illustrates the number of Web object blocks and the average elapsed time with respect to the increasing number of DOM nodes in a Web page for the Web sites BUY and NBA. They underline the effectiveness and the add-on of our framework. In Figure 7 is shown the trend of the number of Web object blocks with respect to the increasing number of page nodes. NBA presents an average of 5 blocks for page. This implies that the Web site presents a regular (and complex) structure. The regularity of the site is due to common structure of the published information (regarding basketball teams) and this is close to the reality. This regularity is also supported by the stable average of the elapsed time, shown in Figure 7. Conversely, BUY presents a variable structure of pages with an increasing trend of Web object blocks and

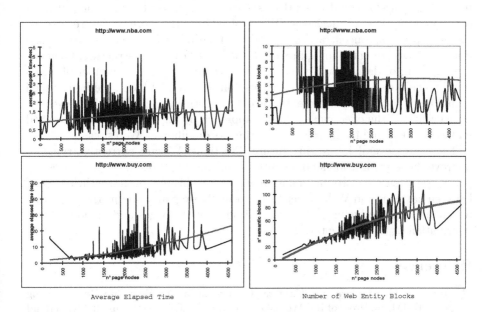

Fig. 7. Average elapsed time and Number of Web object blocks

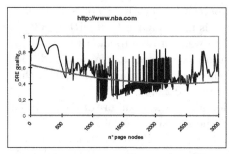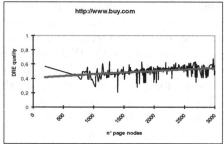

Fig. 8. DRE quality

elapsed times. This is due to the different structure of published information with (i.e., very different products such as art, Hi-Tech and so on). The DRE quality is very good in all Web sites. It presents the best values for DIA, WORD and NBA, over which REVERSEWEB worked linearly. In Figure 8 we present the trend of DRE quality with respect to the increasing number of visited nodes. NBA starts with high values, due to the initial computation of clusters. However, as the number of visited nodes increases, the performance improves and converges to an average of 0,44. BUY has an average of 0,51. In summary, plenty of experiments have confirmed the effectiveness of our framework to detect the organization of a Web site.

6   Conclusions and Future Work

In this paper we have addressed the issue to Data Reverse Engineering (DRE) of data-intensive Web Applications. DRE evolved from the more generic reverse engineering process, concentrating on the data of the application and on its organization. We have presented an approach to the identification of structure, function, and meaning of data in a Web site. The approach relies on a number of structured techniques (such as page segmentation) and model-based methods aimed at building a conceptual representation of the existing applications. Moreover, we have evaluated the effectiveness of our approach by implementing a tool, called REVERSEWEB, and facing several experiments on different Web sites.

There are several interesting future directions. We are currently trying to improve the segmentation step, by introducing new features in the preprocessing phase. We intend to introduce a notion of polymorphism to optimize the mapping between patterns and Web object blocks. Finally we plan to refine the clustering technique by introducing a distance notion between pages and exploiting this information in the segmentation phase.

References

1. Antoniol, G., Canfora, G., Casazza, G., De Lucia, A.: Web Site Reengineering using RMM. In: Proc. of Int. Workshop on Web Site Evolution, Zurich, Switzerland (2000)

2. Baumgartner, R., Flesca, S., Gottlob, G.: Visual Web Information Extraction with Lixto. In: Proc. of the 27th Int. Conf. on Very Large Data Bases (VLDB 2007), Roma, Italy (2001)
3. Benslimane, S.M., Benslimane, D., Malki, M., Amghar, Y., Hassane, H.S.: Acquiring owl ontologies from data-intensive web sites. In: Proc. of Int. Conf. on Web Engineering (ICWE 2006), Palo Alto, California, USA (2006)
4. Bouchiha, D., Malki, M., Benslimane, S.M.: Ontology based Web Application Reverse Engineering Approach. INFOCOMP Journal of Computer Science 6(1), 37–46 (2007)
5. Cai, D., Yu, S., Wen, J.R., Ma, W.Y.: Extracting Content Structure for Web Pages based on Visual Representation. In: Zhou, X., Zhang, Y., Orlowska, M.E. (eds.) APWeb 2003. LNCS, vol. 2642, pp. 406–417. Springer, Heidelberg (2003)
6. Chikofsky, E.J., Cross, J.H.: Reverse Engineering and Design Recovery: A Taxonomy. IEEE Software 7(1), 13–17 (1990)
7. Chung, S., Lee, Y.S.: Reverse Software Engineering with UML for Web Site Maintenance. In: Proc. of the 1th Int. Conf. on Web Information Systems Engineering (WISE 2000), Hong Kong, China (2000)
8. Crescenzi, V., Merialdo, P., Missier, P.: Clustering Web pages based on their structure. Data Knowl. Eng. 54(3), 279–299 (2005)
9. De Virgilio, R., Torlone, R.: A Meta-model Approach to the Management of Hypertexts in Web Information Systems. In: ER Workshops (WISM 2008) (2008)
10. Di Lucca, G.A., Fasolino, A.R., Tramontana, P.: Reverse engineering Web applications: the WARE approach. Journal of Software Maintenance 16(1-2), 71–101 (2004)
11. Du Bois, B.: Towards a Reverse Engineering Ontology. In: Proc. of the 2th Int. Workshop on Empirical Studies in Reverse Engineering (WESRE 2006), Benevento, Italy (2006)
12. Laender, A., Ribeiro-Neto, B., Da Silva, A., Teixeira, J.S.: A brief survey of web data extraction tools. ACM SIGMOD Record 31(2), 84–93 (2002)
13. Ricca, F., Tonella, P.: Understanding and Restructuring Web Sites with ReWeb. IEEE Multimedia 8(2), 40–51 (2001)
14. Tao, T., Mukherjee, A.: LZW Based Compressed Pattern Matching. In: Proc. of the 14th Data Compression Conf (DCC 2004), Snowbird, UT, USA (2004)
15. Vanderdonckt, J., Bouillon, L., Souchon, N.: Flexible reverse engineering of Web Pages with VAQUISTA. In: Proc. of the 8th Working Conf. on Reverse Engineering (WCRE 2001), Stuttgart, Germany (2001)
16. Wong, T.-L., Lam, W.: Adapting web information extraction knowledge via mining site-invariant and site-dependent features. ACM Transactions on Internet Technology 7(1), 6 (2007)

Harnessing the Power of Semantics-Based, Aspect-Oriented Adaptation for AMACONT

Matthias Niederhausen[1], Kees van der Sluijs[2], Jan Hidders[3],
Erwin Leonardi[3], Geert-Jan Houben[2,3], and Klaus Meißner[1]

[1] Technische Universität Dresden, Chair of Multimedia Technology,
01062 Dresden, Germany
{matthias.niederhausen,kmeiss}@tu-dresden.de
[2] Eindhoven University of Technology
P.O. Box 513, NL-5600 MB Eindhoven, The Netherlands
k.a.m.sluijs@tue.nl
[3] Delft University of Technology
P.O. Box 5031, NL-2600 GA Delft, The Netherlands
{a.j.h.hidders,e.leonardi,g.j.p.m.houben}@tudelft.nl

Abstract. Adaptivity in web applications raises several concerns. One demands it to be decoupled from the actual application and at the same time wants to use very domain-specific terms for dividing the audience into groups. Two current trends, aspect-oriented programming and semantic web technologies, fit these requirements like a glove. In this paper, we present the AMACONT web modeling framework and use it as an example of how to extend such a framework to make use of these powerful technologies. The underlying concepts, however, can be applied to the modeling of adaptivity in general.

Keywords: adaptation, aspect-oriented programming, semantic data.

1 Introduction

The concerns that must be considered when developing a web application are numerous and often change over time, by current trends on the Web or the availability of new technologies. Two such concerns that have emerged in the last years are the demand for adaptivity to the context (e.g., serving content that has been prepared for a special audience), and the need to actually model this context exploiting rich, semantics-based models. While an application designer typically addresses the audience in a high-level and often domain-specific way (e.g., "premium customers"), the existing frameworks do rarely offer facilities for easily improving and extending this context model. Further, in most cases the web application as such does already exist and its application and adaptation logic should be extended with these additional concerns. This raises the question of how an existing web framework can be extended to provide accordant support.

In this paper, we present AMACONT, a web modeling framework that has its roots in a component-based document format. We show how we extended the existing

M. Gaedke, M. Grossniklaus, and O. Díaz (Eds.): ICWE 2009, LNCS 5648, pp. 106–120, 2009.
© Springer-Verlag Berlin Heidelberg 2009

AMACONT framework with two independent mechanisms – aspect-oriented adaptation modeling and semantics-based adaptation – for addressing the concerns of adaptivity and context modeling. We believe that aspect orientation is a useful technique to model aspects of an application that stem from separate concerns and appear throughout the whole application, such as privacy and security. We further argue that semantics-based adaptation can help to bridge granularity differences, e.g., between some available, detailed individual customer information and the "premium customer" classification – the rules for this classification can be more flexibly encoded in an ontology. Also it allows for easier and more flexible inclusion of additional knowledge from external ontologies such as customer preferences or product information, a type of flexibility still lacking in most existing web engineering methods. The approach that we take for extending the previous component-based document transformer gives a general recipe for extending web application development tools with aspect-orientation and semantic context modeling.

2 A Document Format for Adaptive Web Applications

AMACONT aims at enabling web engineers to design web applications tailored to users' varying needs, device capabilities and context data such as the users' location. As such, it is comparable to other web application design methods like SHDM, WebML, WSDM, UWE, OO-H, OOWS and Hera-S (for a survey on these web modeling approaches, cf. [11]). These methods typically separate concerns in the design process by distinguishing several distinct, but related models. A typical distinction is made into the following phases: (1) the underlying data model of the data that is to be presented, (2) the application model that describes the web application logic and (3) the presentation model that describes the exact lay-out and presentation of the web pages. Moreover, they all either allow the (semi-)automatic generation of code from their models or can interpret and execute them directly.

AMACONT provides a document format and a runtime environment, allowing for both static and dynamic adaptations of content, layout and structure. Furthermore, mechanisms for modeling dynamically changing context information like users' device capabilities, preferences and locations are provided in order to guarantee that adaptation is based on up-to-date context models.

2.1 Document Format

Targeting reuse of content, AMACONT employs a component-based document format to model adaptive web applications [5]. As Figure 1 shows, components in AMACONT can be classified into three different layers, with an orthogonal fourth Hyperlink layer.

The most basic components stem from the bottom layer of *Media Components*. Examples of such elements are text fragments, images, CSS stylesheets and videos.

Often there are fragments that are closely related and typically used in conjunction, like an image with a textual caption. By defining such semantic groups on the *Content Unit* layer of AMACONT, authors can structure their applications.

Finally, there is the *Document Component* layer. It allows to structure a web application further by grouping Content Units into larger components and further into

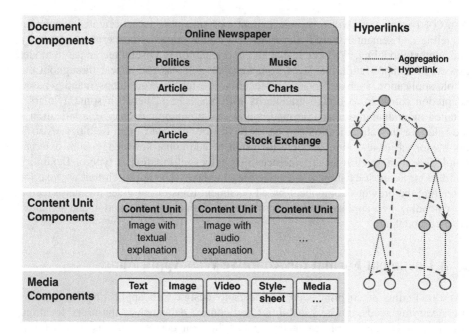

Fig. 1. The AMACONT Component Model

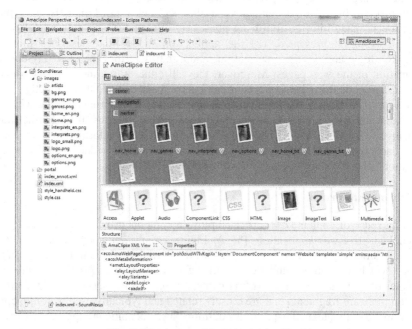

Fig. 2. The AmaArchitect Authoring Tool

web pages. AMACONT allows arbitrarily complex subcomponents, so that authors have the freedom to organize their page structure in any way they want. Note that web pages in AMACONT can be either modeled by structuring one document accordingly or by splitting the definition up into a number of documents, similar to HTML files.

Orthogonal to these three layers, the *Hyperlink* layer is spanned. Hyperlinks in AMACONT can reference components from all three levels. Thereby, it is easy to create a link starting from a composed page element. Links can target either an AMACONT file or an arbitrary component – or any custom URL.

In order to allow authors to easily create AMACONT applications, an Eclipse-based authoring tool, the AmaArchitect[1] has been designed and is constantly being improved. Figure 2 shows a screenshot of the tool, where in the middle, depending on the currently edited component, a specialized editor is shown. In the picture, this is an editor visualizing the document structure of the project's index page. At the bottom, we also have a quick XML overview of the currently selected component.

The next section explains how adaptivity can be defined on top of such a base document model in AMACONT.

2.2 Basic Adaptivity

As many other prominent web engineering approaches, AMACONT allows authors to specify adaptation by the means of alternative document fragments, called *variants*.

Variants can be defined for any components (or fragments thereof) on the four component layers. To this end, an adaptation construct must be created, consisting of two general parts: a *variants container* and a *selection condition header*. As its name suggests, the variants container contains alternatives for a given fragment, whereas the number of alternatives is not limited. Such a variant can also be empty, leading to the fragment's removal. The selection condition header specifies the contextual circumstances for showing each variant. At runtime, these conditions are evaluated to determine the variant to select. The details of this process are discussed in Section 2.3.

By using variants, authors can specify static adaptation, i.e., chose from variants that are known at design time. However, it is often desirable to include data that is only available at runtime or that changes over time, e.g., database contents. In this case, the actual content must be queried anew every time someone sends a request. To this end, AMACONT has been extended with a dynamic content engine that builds on component templates. Component templates are structured just like regular AMACONT components, allowing for a seamless integration of dynamic content. The difference, however, is that in their body they can refer to previously defined data fields. These data fields are typically defined in the component's head, by the means of an SQL query. It is possible to access the data fields of queries of all parent elements, which allows for an arbitrary nesting of queries. Further, component templates can be iterated: multiple copies of such a component are instantiated, each filled with different concrete values. By combining these features, it is possible to create dynamic linked lists (e.g., a list of all book authors together with all their books).

The next section explains the pipelined process of adapting and serving an AMACONT document in response to an HTTP request.

---

[1] The tool can be downloaded at http://www.hyperadapt.net/AmaArchitect/

2.3 Publication Process

For each user request, the respective AMACONT document which contains variants for all defined adaptation is fetched from the component repository and transformed in various steps, according to the current context. To the overall process there are three central elements: *document generation, context modeling* and *context acquisition*. Figure 3 shows an overview of the whole process, while the following subsections deal with the details of each component.

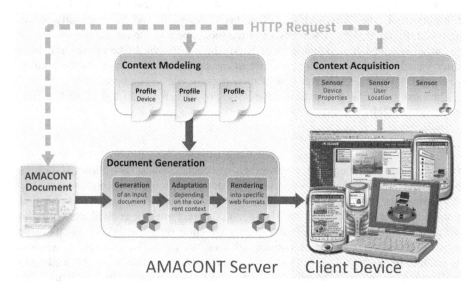

Fig. 3. The AMACONT Publication Process

2.4 Context Acquisition

Whenever a request is sent to an AMACONT web application, this request per se contains some context data on the client, e.g., preferred content language and used browser. As this little context information can hardly serve for rich adaptation, AMACONT deploys additional *sensor components* on the client, embedded as Java or JavaScript fragments into delivered pages. Sensor components can determine simple data like the available screen resolution or track more complex information like the user's interactions with the page, or his location.

2.5 Context Modeling

On the server, the gathered sensor information is processed by the *context modeling components*. An important component within the context modeling is the *user modeling* [6]. It provides user modeling strategies that require explicit feedback (e.g., filling out questionnaires) as well as an automatic modeling mechanism that allows an implicit analysis of user interactions. Context modeling also comprises *device modeling* components that process sensed device capabilities. In addition, AMACONT also provides *location modeling* mechanisms that can be used to develop and deploy location-based services [7].

In order to be accessible by a broad range of web applications, AMACONT offers an extensible *context model*. It stores data in different context profiles. Each profile relies on CC/PP[2], an RDF grammar for describing device capabilities and user preferences in a standardized way. Context modeling and sensor components for user, device and location profiles have already been implemented and are in detail presented in [7]. In order to support the addition of further context modeling techniques, the framework provides generic extension mechanisms for adding new sensor components and context modelers.

2.6 Document Generation

Each requested document passes the publication pipeline where it is adapted according to the context model. To this end, elements are removed from the document containing all variants to eventually leave only the desired, adapted information. The last step of the pipeline carries out the transformation to a specific output format, such as XHTML or WML. The resulting document can then be delivered to the specific target device where it is rendered accordingly. For a detailed description of the adaptation pipeline, see [6].

3 Leveraging Aspect-Orientation for Modeling Adaptation

The variant-based adaptation concept in AMACONT presented in the previous section allows for a maximum flexibility, but reduces the overall reusability in the web application. As variants contain altered duplicates of the original component to cater for the special needs of users or devices, there is lots of duplicate content in the web application, which the author has to change consistently when making changes. Additionally, in an adaptive web application variants are spread all over the documents, missing some sort of connection that groups them by their goal (e.g., grouping all variants that cater for adaptation to the user's device). In order to maximize reusability and embrace the evolution of web applications, we extended AMACONT with a second concept for modeling adaptation: aspect-orientation. We argue that this allows us to separate the adaptation model from the rest of the application while offering an intuitive grouping mechanism for adaptation fragments.

3.1 Fundamentals of Aspect-Oriented Adaptation

Aspect-oriented programming (AOP) has been designed for "classic" desktop applications. The paradigm that AOP proposes is separation of concerns. Code that is spread throughout an application (i.e., logging or access restriction) is outsourced into isolated modules called *aspects*. These aspects are automatically merged with the *base application* (i.e., the application without the orthogonal concerns) at a later time, in a process called *weaving*.

---

[2] Composite Capability/Preference Profiles, http://www.w3.org/Mobile/CCPP/

3.2 Aspect-Orientation in Other Web Application Models

The idea of aspect orientation can already be found in UWE, where specific types of adaptation such as link hiding, link annotation and link generation were separated into different aspects ([1]). Also the UML-based WebML was redesigned with aspect-oriented features for the purpose of modeling ubiquitous web applications ([10]). AMACONT mainly differs from these approaches in that we transfer the AOP concept to the level of XML documents, allowing arbitrary transformations.

3.3 Aspect-Orientation in AMACONT

AMACONT employs traditional AOP concepts: the base is a regular web application, that is, typically without adaptivity. On top of such existing web applications, authors can instantiate *adaptation concerns* (Figure 4) that group adaptation on a requirement-level. Typical examples of adaptation concerns are *device independence*, *location awareness*, *internationalization* or *role-based access*.

Because concerns offer only a high level view, adaptation is further subdivided into *adaptation aspects*. These are medium-sized adaptation fragments that allow authors to impose an order on the weaving process, which is needed for a predictable result, as the weaving order generally plays a decisive role in AOP (e.g., see [9]).

Finally, the smallest possible piece of adaptation is an *advice*. Advices describe how to transform a given component within an AMACONT document. To this end, they may instantiate *adaptation patterns*, i.e., reusable transformations that resemble typical adaptation techniques like the ones identified by the hypermedia community ([3, 4]). The adaptation patterns available to the author differ, depending on the adaptation concern he is working on. We already have implemented a number of patterns, e.g., *first sentence elision*, *image rescaling* or *layout change* for instant use. Still, authors are free to define their very own patterns to achieve any adaptation effect they want. Advices also contain an adaptation precondition, similar to classic variants, that specifies the circumstances under which to perform the transformation. Finally, advices are connected to the web application via their *pointcut*. The pointcut, expressed in XPath, is a reference to one or many AMACONT components. Therefore, it is possible to easily apply one advice to an arbitrary number of components.

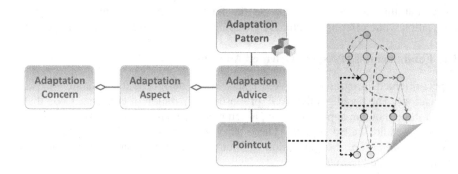

Fig. 4. Aspect Model of AMACONT Adaptation

An adaptation model based on aspects can be stored either for every AMACONT document or for the whole web application. The aspect weaver then has the task to merge this model with the base application.

3.4 Aspect Weaving in AMACONT

For weaving aspects, AMACONT offers two general choices: weaving at design time and weaving at run time.

Design time weaving offers one obvious advantage: Because it is a one-time process of generating alternative variants, it creates only a neglectable overhead. Then, at run time the server only needs to decide which (pre-made) variant to choose for a user. However, the greatest disadvantage of design time weaving is the inability to cover dynamic adaptation. For example, it is not possible to insert a user's name into the document, because that data is not known at design time.

In contrast, run time weaving shows opposite characteristics: Working with dynamic data is no longer a problem, while the downside is that it requires weaving at every request, thus reducing performance. But weaving at run time offers some more advantages: depending on the server load, it becomes possible to "deactivate" costly aspects temporarily. Moreover, it is possible to create alternative aspect configurations that are chosen dynamically based on the context. For example, authors could model three different levels of location awareness and base the selection on whether the user is a paying customer.

With aspect-oriented adaptation, web engineers are able to nicely separate adaptation from the rest of the web application. However, adaptation preconditions still show a semantic gap. While the AMACONT context model can only supply generic information on the user, his device and context, adaptation authors typically think in terms of higher granularity, e.g., "all returning customers from around Dresden". In the next two sections, we present a new approach for bridging this gap.

4 Semantics-Based Adaptation

One of the important issues in improving and making adaptation more sophisticated is to incorporate semantic web technology in AMACONT, allowing us to specify the meaning of the data by using meta-data and ontologies, and define their relationship. This enables applications to tie, exchange, and reuse data from different external data sources, including the data resources on the Web. Consequently, this is useful to reduce the knowledge load for adaptation conditions, as well as to simplify queries, or even use knowledge that is not available at design time. The semantic web technology also makes reasoning about the data by applications possible, allowing the semantic gap between data to be bridged. Therefore, by exploiting the semantic web technology, AMACONT is able to provide adaptation in a richer and more flexible way. And even though some work has been done on utilizing external knowledge for adaptation purposes (e.g., [8]), we do not know of another approach that applied external knowledge to simplify adaptation.

In order to make the semantic information of data accessible to the applications, they have to be represented in a machine-accessible format. W3C has released the

Resource Description Framework (RDF, cf. http://www.w3.org/RDF), a standard data model for representing meta-data and describing the semantics of information in a machine-accessible way. RDF defines statements about information resources in the form of subject-predicate-object expressions called *triples*. As the subject of one statement can be the object of another, a collection of statements forms a directed, labeled graph. There are several syntaxes to represent RDF, like an XML serialization, but obviously the interesting concept is the graph-based model that lies behind it. RDF statements can be stored in RDF repositories like Jena (cf. http://jena.sourceforge.net) or Sesame (cf. http://www.openrdf.org). For accessing information stored in RDF repositories, there are several RDF query languages (e.g., SeRQL [2] and SPARQL (cf. http://www.w3.org/TR/rdf-sparql-query)).

In this project, we use SPARQL as the RDF query language that is a W3C standard. As an example of a simple SPARQL query, consider the following:

```
PREFIX geo: <http://www.geography.org/schema.rdf>
SELECT ?capital ?country
WHERE { ?x    geo:cityname ?capital ;
              geo:isCapitalOf       ?y .
        ?y    geo:countryname       ?country ;
              geo:isInContinent     geo:Africa . }
```

The PREFIX clause is used to define namespace prefixes. The namespace geo is bound to the a URL that specifies geographical domain concepts. The SELECT clause lists the variables for which bindings will be returned. Note that variable names are always preceded with "?". The WHERE clause provides the graph patterns to be matched against the data graph. The ";" notation is used to list triples that start with the same subject. So, the above query looks for a city object ?x with the name ?capital. Furthermore, ?x is the capital of country ?y, and ?y must have the name ?country and be in the continent of Africa. Finally, it returns all combinations of ?capital and ?country for which these triples exist.

We now look at how we use a semantics-based adaptation extension in AMACONT to overcome granularity issues. Let us first look at the problem at hand, by looking at an example. Suppose we want to select the language in which we present pages in our application, based on where a user lives. In this way we could choose to give someone who lives in Germany a German version of the page, and other users the English version of the page. However, suppose we have a user model that contains the following location information about a user (in abbreviated TURTLE[3] syntax):

```
:userJohn    :livesin    :cityX
             a           :city;
             :cityname   "Dresden" .
```

In other words, we only know in this case that user "John" lives in a city called "Dresden". The question is now where we get the knowledge from to understand that Dresden lies in Germany so that we should give user "John" the German version of the page. One possible solution would be of course to extend the user model so that it

---

[3] Cf. http://www.w3.org/TeamSubmission/turtle/

also contains the information that user "John" also lives in the country of Germany, and ask the user for this information. However, this would bother the user with additional questions while we could already deduce the country from the city. Even though it might still be possible to ask the user in this concrete example, one can easily think of cases where this is not viable or even possible (e.g., if the information is not known at design time). Another possibility would be to extend the adaptation query with an enumeration of all German cities, which obviously is also not really viable as it would be extremely laborious to write such queries and their performance would suffer dramatically. We take another approach by exploiting the knowledge of RDF and OWL ontologies (cf. http://www.w3.org/2001/sw) to solve our granularity problem. Many of such ontologies are freely available on the Web and can be reused for our purposes.

We consider an example in which we add multilinguality via aspect orientation. Given that we have an application in default English with a set of text objects in English, we added translations of those objects in German with a derived name pattern de/%name%. We can now add the following aspect-oriented adaptation:

```
<aspect id="ML1" concern="Internationalization">
    <advice>
        <pointcut>
            <condition>
                <aada:Sparql>
                  SELECT ?country
                  WHERE {   $CurrentUser :livesin ?country
                            a :country ;
                            :name "Germany" . }
                </aada:Sparql>
            </condition>
            <target>
                <xpath>//AmaTextComponent</xpath>
            </target>
        </pointcut>
        <pattern id="ReplaceComponentByName">
            <parameter id="replacePattern">de/%name%</parameter>
        </pattern>
    </advice>
</aspect>
```

This aspect oriented adaptation condition expresses that if the user is from Germany (denoted by the SPARQL query to the user model), we want to replace all (English) text elements by their German translation (with path de/%text%). If the user is not from Germany we just present the default English text (and thus do not adapt anything). Please note here that $CurrentUser is an AMACONT variable (denoted by the $-sign) that is substituted at run time with the actual identifier for the current user.

We now have to deal with the fact that the {:livesin ?country} pattern is not in our user model. Therefore, we first select an appropriate ontology that allows making the semantic connection we need, in our case between a city and the country it resides in. A good candidate for this case is the GeoNames Ontology[4]. This ontology simply provides us with additional knowledge:

---

[4] Cf. http://www.geonames.org/ontology/

```
geo:6551127 geo:Name        "Dresden, Stadt" ;
            geo:inCountry   geo:DE .
```

In plain English this means that we have an object with id "6551127", which apparently represents the city of Dresden and has a direct property which connects it to Germany ("DE") via the geo:inCountry property. This is a very fortunate simple example, as every location within a country has this inCountry element. However, it could also be necessary to follow more complex paths. If we need more information about the country of Germany (e.g., its population), we would have to follow the complete chain

Germany » Saxony » Regierungsbezirk Dresden » Kreisfreie Stadt Dresden » Dresden, Stadt

to find the Germany URL, namely geo:2921044.

As we can via this ontology make the connection between Dresden and Germany, we can conclude that the user lives in Dresden and *therefore* in Germany. In order to achieve that, we of course need to do some configuration in AMACONT.

We first need to align the location name in our local ontology (e.g., "Dresden") with the location name in the geo ontology (e.g., "Dresden, Stadt"). If these concepts are identical (for instance, by design), then no further configuration is needed in AMACONT. Otherwise, we can make a manual alignment for every user, or a (semi-) automatic alignment. The last can be configured by specifying two SPARQL queries.

We then first specify the following construct in our AMACONT configuration to indicate an alignment step:

```
:align [ sourceConceptQuery "query1 details" ;
         targetConceptQuery "query2 details" ; ]
```

Now we fill in the query details. For the source concept we specify which concept in the UM we want to connect with a target concept of our specialized ontology. In simple cases we allow for simple declarations like for "query1" in this case:

```
?city a um:City
```

Here we specify that we want to select all concepts of type city of the UM vocabulary, i.e., the only variable. For "query2", the target concepts, we specify a (somewhat simplified) SPARQL query of how to find the aligned city in the geo ontology. In this query we can align the result by using it for query1, referring to it by the variable $city. The "query2" could then look like this:

```
SELECT ?feature
WHERE {
        ?feature    a               geo:Feature ;
                    geo:featureCode geo:P.PPL ;
                    geo:name        ?name ;
                    geo:population  ?population .

        FILTER (regex(?name, $city))
    }
ORDER BY DESC(?population)
```

In this query we are looking for a "feature" (in GeoNames terminology) that has the featureCode geo:P.PPL (code for city) and the name should contain the original city name indicated by the AMACONT variable $city in the FILTER clause. Note that we assume that the target location here contains the city name of the source as a substring (i.e., this might be a limitation for more complex searches that cannot be expressed like this). We also include "?population" in our search to solve ambiguity issues. Suppose that there are more cities in the world that are called Dresden (actually six such cities/towns exist in the USA), so we have to find a heuristic to determine the most probable target concept. For our example, we use the heuristic that the most populated city is the most probable one. We order the results by population and, in the case of more than one result, we use the first result as the target concept.

We have now aligned concepts in our user model to concepts in our helping ontology. After alignment we want to specify a reasoning rule that defines how knowledge in the helping ontology extends the knowledge in our user model. In our case, we define an entailment rule that specifies that if a user lives in a city, he also lives in the country in which that city is located. This rule is basically of the form:

$$
\left.\begin{array}{l}
<\,?X\ :\text{livesin}\ ?Y> \\
<\,?Y\ \text{rdf:type}\ :\text{city}> \\
<\,?Y\ \text{geo:inCountry}\ ?Z>
\end{array}\right\} \Rightarrow \left\{\begin{array}{l}
<\,?X\ :\text{livesin}\ ?Z> \\
<\,?Z\ \text{rdf:type}\ :\text{country}>
\end{array}\right.
$$

This (syntactically simplified) inference rule specifies that if X lives in Y of type city, then X also lives in the country in which Y is located. By applying this entailment rule, we can deduce that John who lives in Dresden, also lives in Germany and thus should get the German welcome page. With this configuration, AMACONT can now effectively use the external ontology to solve granularity issues in our user model.

5 Implementation

Both the proposed aspect-oriented modeling approach and the semantics-based adaptation have been implemented in AMACONT's publication pipeline, enabling authors to make use of the new features.

For aspect orientation, we extended the document generation pipeline by adding another transformation component before the adaptation transformer (Figure 5, green parts have been added/extended). This way, we can weave adaptation aspects at runtime, but still allow authors to use the more generic static variants, which are then processed by the existing adaptation transformer.

The aspect weaver takes as input an AMACONT document together with an adaptation description. It then tries to match the advice's pointcuts as specified in the adaptation description with the components in the input document. The following code snippet shows an extract from the aspect-oriented adaptation definition, resizing all images in the navigation bar if the user accesses the application with his PDA.

```
<aspect id="RI1" concern="ResolutionIndependence">
    <advice>
        <pointcut>
            <condition>
                <adaptationclass>Device_PDA</adaptationclass>
            </condition>
            <target>
                <xpath>//*[@id="nav"]/aco:AmaImageComponent</xpath>
            </target>
        </pointcut>
        <pattern id="ReduceImageSizeByTranscoding">
            <parameter id="ratio">0.5</parameter>
        </pattern>
    </advice>
</aspect>
```

If a match is found, the advice's transformation is executed, modifying the affected components. Advices are executed one after another, depending on the order specified by the author.

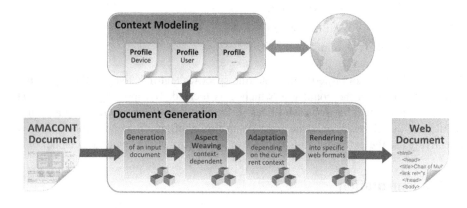

Fig. 5. The Extended AMACONT Document Generation Pipeline

In order to add the new semantic web capabilities, we have chosen to base our implementation on the open-source RDF framework Sesame[5]. Sesame offers a good level of abstraction on connecting to and querying of RDF storages, similar to JDBC.

We have extended both the existing adaptation transformer and the new dynamic weaver to not only support terms that rely on the local context model, but also to process SPARQL statements. These statements are evaluated at runtime, replacing AMACONT variables and finally querying the corresponding SPARQL endpoint.

Queries can be added to conditions of both variants and adaptation advices by encapsulating them via the new Sparql element in an If term:

---

[5] http://www.openrdf.org/

```
<aada:Sparql>
  SELECT ?conceptVisits
  WHERE { $CurrentUser    :livesin?country
                          a         :country ;
                          :name     "Germany" . }
</aada:Sparql>
```

The SPARQL syntax itself is not touched, just extended with the notion of AMACONT variables (denoted with a preceding $), which are replaced before running the query.

6 Conclusion and Future Work

In this paper we have presented methods for extending an existing web application framework with orthogonal facilities for adding adaptivity and for extending the user context modeling with semantics. To this end, we have applied aspect-oriented techniques to the modeling of adaptivity on the one hand and concepts and technologies from the semantic web for building and accessing a rich context on the other hand. We have illustrated this in terms of AMACONT, but these techniques are suitable for enhancing web application frameworks in general.

As a continuation of our work, we plan to further combine both worlds by allowing authors to use semantic web techniques for specifying the content of a web application. An example use case for this is displaying Wikipedia pages of local sights. By using an ontology, sights within a greater area around the user's location (not only within the same city) can be recommended in a tourist guide. Aspect-orientation can then be used to add adaptation on top of such content, providing support for orthogonal adaptivity on all three application layers: content, structure and presentation. Another point is evaluation of the system's performance, especially measuring scalability. In our implementation we found no performance issues given that we use a relatively straightforward application and mid-sized ontology. However, as Semantic Web reasoning applications typically run into scalability issues, we want to explore the scalability limits of our approach. Finally, we plan to extend our authoring tool, AmaArchitect, to provide authors with means for dealing with the new semantic context. Authors could thus browse datasources and select from the concepts and relations available there.

Acknowledgements. Part of this work is funded by the German Research Foundation (DFG) within the project "HyperAdapt".

References

[1] Baumeister, H., Knapp, A., Koch, N., Zhang, G.: Modelling adaptivity with aspects. In: Lowe, D.G., Gaedke, M. (eds.) ICWE 2005. LNCS, vol. 3579, pp. 406–416. Springer, Heidelberg (2005)

[2] Broekstra, J., Kampman, A.: An RDF Query and Transformation Language. Springer, Heidelberg (2006)

[3] Brusilovsky, P.: Adaptive navigation support. In: Brusilovsky, P., Kobsa, A., Nejdl, W. (eds.) Adaptive Web 2007. LNCS, vol. 4321, pp. 263–290. Springer, Heidelberg (2007)

[4] Bunt, A., Carenini, G., Conati, C.: Adaptive content presentation for the web. In: Brusilovsky, P., Kobsa, A., Nejdl, W. (eds.) Adaptive Web 2007. LNCS, vol. 4321, pp. 263–290. Springer, Heidelberg (2007)

[5] Fiala, Z., Hinz, M., Meißner, K., Wehner, F.: A component-based approach for adaptive dynamic web documents. Journal of Web Engineering 2(1&2), 058–073 (2003)

[6] Hinz, M., Fiala, Z.: Amacont: A system architecture for adaptive multimedia web applications. In: Workshop XML Technologien für das Semantic Web (XSW 2004), Berliner XML Tage (October 2004)

[7] Hinz, M., Pietschmann, S., Fiala, Z.: A framework for context modeling in adaptive web applications. IADIS International Journal of WWW/Internet 5(1) (June 2007)

[8] Krištofič, A., Bieliková, M.: Improving adaptation in web-based educational hypermedia by means of knowledge discovery. In: HYPERTEXT 2005: Proceedings of the sixteenth ACM conference on Hypertext and hypermedia, pp. 184–192. ACM, New York (2005)

[9] Nagy, I., Bergmans, L., Aksit, M.: Composing aspects at shared join points. In: NODe/GSEM, pp. 19–38 (2005)

[10] Schauerhuber, A., Wimmer, M., Schwinger, W., Kapsammer, E., Retschitzegger, W.: Aspect-oriented modeling of ubiquitous web applications: The aspectwebml approach. In: Engineering of Computer-Based Systems, 2007. ECBS 2007, Tucson, Arizona. 14th Annual IEEE Proceedings of the 14th Annual IEEE International Conference and Workshops on the Engineering of Computer-Based Systems, pp. 569–576. IEEE Computer Society, Los Alamitos (2007)

[11] Schwinger, W., Retschitzegger, W., Schauerhuber, A., Kappel, G., Wimmer, M., Pröll, B., Cachero Castro, C., Casteleyn, S., De Troyer, O., Fraternali, P., Garrigos, I., Garzotto, F., Ginige, A., Houben, G.J., Koch, N., Moreno, N., Pastor, O., Paolini, P., Pelechano Ferragud, V., Rossi, G., Schwabe, D., Tisi, M., Vallecillo, A., van der Sluijs, K., Zhang, G.: A survey on web modeling approaches for ubiquitous web applications. International Journal of Web Information Systems 4(3), 234–305 (2008)

Model-Driven Web Engineering for the Automated Configuration of Web Content Management Systems

Jurriaan Souer[1], Thijs Kupers[1], Remko Helms[2], and Sjaak Brinkkemper[2]

[1] GX, Wijchenseweg 111, Nijmegen, The Netherlands
{jurriaan.souer,thijs.kupers}@gxwebmanager.com
http://www.gxwebmanager.com
[2] Department of Information and Computing Sciences,
Utrecht University, Utrecht, The Netherlands
{r.w.helms,s.brinkkemper}@cs.uu.nl
http://www.cs.uu.nl

Abstract. With the growing use of Web Content Management Systems for the support of complex online business processes, traditional implementation solutions proofed to be inefficient. Specifically the gap between business requirements and the realized Web application should be closed. This paper presents the development of a modeling tool for the automated configuration of Web Content Management Systems (WCM) which aims to reduce the complexity and increase the transparency of implementations. It allows business users to configure the business processes without technical support. We combine fragments of existing Web Engineering methods and specify an abstract and concrete syntax based on a domain model and end user analysis. The resulting WebForm Diagram has been implemented in a prototype and validated by subject matter experts. This research is part of a project to develop the Web Engineering Method (WEM) which provides an overall method towards a full coverage of the specification, design, realization, implementation and maintenance of WCM-based Web applications.

1 Introduction

The World Wide Web has evolved towards a platform for sophisticated enterprise applications and complex business processes. In result, the effort of time specifying and developing these Web applications reflects the complexity of these applications and business processes. An industry solution to improve development time and stability is a Web Content Management (WCM) system which is product software with out-of-the-box functionalities and allow for specific customizations [26].

Customizing WCM systems to implement business processes is a difficult task. In this context we developed the Web Engineering Method (WEM) as a method to manage and control web applications and web sites based on WCM systems [28]. WEM describes a complete development and implementation process of Web Engineering based on WCM systems as defined by Kappel et al [8]: requirements analyses, design, implementation, testing, operation, and maintenance of high-quality Web applications [25].

The central problem we are addressing in this paper is that there is a gap between the requirements analysis in WCM implementations (usually defined by business users or

M. Gaedke, M. Grossniklaus, and O. Díaz (Eds.): ICWE 2009, LNCS 5648, pp. 121–135, 2009.
© Springer-Verlag Berlin Heidelberg 2009

online marketers) and the realization of those requirements (usually done by technical developers or software engineers). Therefore our leading research question is: 'how to automatically configure a WCM System based on requirements'. Note that we do not try to create a WCM system, but configure an exsisting WCM for the development of Web Applications. We focus on the configuration of business processes and defined the following goals:(1) Develop an unambiguous form definition to model a business process; (2) Automatically configure a WCM system based on the business process model; and (3) Generate a business process model based on a configured WCM system. This paper presents a new approach for an automated configuration of WCM systems using a modeling tool. The contribution of this research consists of a Model Driven Engineering (MDE) approach for the configuration of WCM software and a unique concrete and abstract syntax to model WCM systems. Secondly, we implement the MDE specification as a prototype and used it to model an actual project situation.

The rest of this paper is organized as follows: In Section 2 we introduce the Web-Form Diagram which is the result of this research. Section 3 elaborates on the problem area analysis which resulted in the WebForm Diagram including a domain model, a user analysis and a comparison of existing web engineering methods. In section 4 we formally specify the WebForm Diagram and describe the development of a prototype which is evaluated in section 5. Finally conclusion and future work are discussed in Section 6.

2   The WebForm Diagram

The WebForm Diagram is a visual language for the specification of online business processes. It is developed to cover all online form variables within a web-based application.

As an example of the realized WebForm Diagram we refer to Figure 1 that models a user registration scenario from a real life case: it illustrates how a new user can enter his account information, some personal information and after validation by e-mail and text messaging he is allowed to enter the registered area. However, there are some conditions which the system and user should meet and during the process some system processes and database access are initialized. The purpose of this research is to allow functional users to model such a form and automatically configure a WCMS to support this process. We detail this form in the following sections.

2.1   Steps, Routers, Validation, and Handlers

In the WebForm Diagram, the screens of the form dialogue which are actually presented on a Website are called **steps** and are visualized with rounded rectangles. A single step can have multiple *formfields* such as text input, list item, checkbox, etc. A typical first step of a user registration process has two formfields: desired username and password. The form displayed in Figure 1, has 5 steps starting with 'Account Info'. Individual formfields are not displayed in this top level view of the WebForm Diagram. However, the diagram allows users to detail steps.

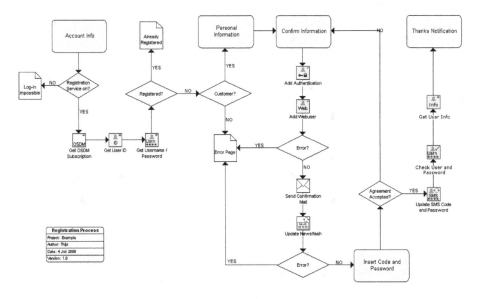

Fig. 1. Example of a business process modeled with the WebForm Diagram

Steps are connected with **routers** which are visualized by arrows between steps. After each step, a form is routed to another step. In the form in Figure 1, after the user enters his username and password in the 'Account info' step the system will try to route him to the step 'Personal Information'.

The flow of the routers depends on certain conditions which are known as **validations**. These validations are visualized with a diamond. For example, the user can only register when the registration service is set to 'on' which is the first validation after step 'Account Info' in Figure 1. Otherwise he will be routed to the web page 'Log-in Impossible'.

Between steps, the WebForm Diagram can perform actions which we call **handlers** and are visualized with a small square containing an icon inside representing the functional behavior of the handler. A handler can for example access a database to check the user id, send a confirmation e-mail or check the user credentials with an authorization server by SOAP.

Hence a complete online business process is a logical flow of steps which are routed in the correct way, with validated input fields and correct handling of the data.

2.2 Formalizing the WebForm Diagram

To develop our WebForm Diagram, we formally specified the syntax to define the logic. The WebForm Diagram relies on the Model Driven Engineering paradigm [10]. MDE is in accordance with the objectives of this research: configuration of a software system based on a model [20]. MDE uses models as a primary artifact in the development process and consists of a Domain Specific Modeling Language (DSML) and a transformation mechanism [29] reflecting the structure, behavior or requirements of a given domain and transforms the model into different implementations respectively.

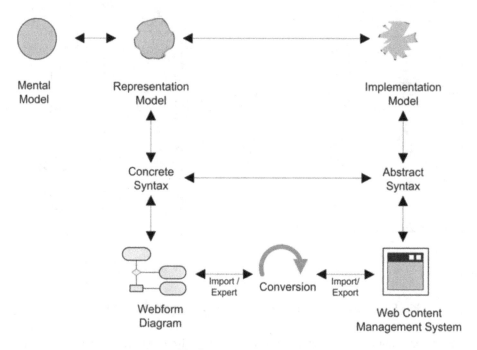

Fig. 2. Research Approach

A DSML is a graphical and executable specification language that is specialized to model concepts within a given domain by means of notations and abstractions. To develop our WebForm Diagram we therefore analyze the problem area with the following three activities: (1) what needs to be modeled, using domain modeling [7];(2) what is the expected outcome, with user analysis as defined by [4] resulting in a mental model, a representation model and an implementation model; and (3) Comparing concepts of existing models to identify key concepts which we could use in our model. Similar to Situational Method-Engineering [2], [17], we selected method fragments from existing modeling languages and assembled our new modeling language out of these fragments.

The DSML in this research consists of a comprehensive abstract syntax and an understandable concrete syntax with a graphical notation [6]. The concrete syntax resembles the representation model of the end user and the abstract syntax represents the objects which need to be configured in the WCM System. We developed the model as a prototype based on the graphical notation of the concrete syntax which we resulted in the WebForm Diagram. The prototype is developed in MetaEdit+ since it allows us to build our own specific development environment. The definition can be exported into an XML format and is converted into the WCMs compliant XML which by itself can be imported into the WCM system. An overview of the approach is illustrated in Figure 2.

The evaluation consists of both a functional assessment in which we used the prototype tool to define a real project situation, and an expert validation in which we interviewed end users.

3 Problem Area Analysis

This research has been carried out within GX, a software vendor of Web Content Management system. GX develops GX WebManager, a Web Content Management System based on open standards such as OSGi as implemented in Apache Felix, Spring MVC and the Java Content Repository by Apache JackRabbit.

3.1 Domain Model

We use a domain model to analyze the elements and their relationships. Domain Modeling helps identify the key concepts which need to be modeled as well as generalizations which relates the entities on a higher abstraction level and is a meta-model of the objects of the modeling language. A relevant functional component within the WCMS – in the context of this research – is the 'Advanced Form Module': a functional component which allows editors to develop business processes based on advanced forms.

Using a domain model, we identified all the elements that need to be modeled by the WebForm Diagram and is the foundation of the abstract syntax.

3.2 User Analysis

In the next step we identified the expected model by interviewing end-users using a threefold model as proposed by Cooper [4]: **Mental model** providing the system, its components and the way they interact from an End-user (or functional) perspective; **Implementation model** reflecting the actual system implementation composing of all

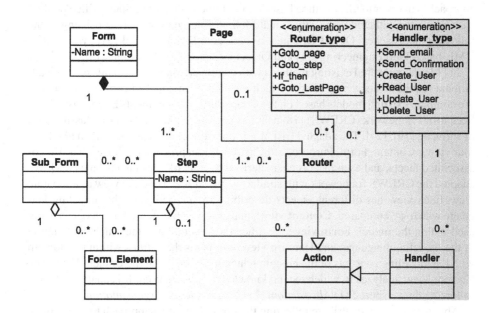

Fig. 3. Excerpt of Domain Model

components, their relationships and the way they interact; and **Representation Model** representing the implementation to the end-users. One should try to create a representation model as close to the mental model as possible [5]. Within a modeling language, the representation model consists of the graphical notation.

We interviewed six users (3 senior technical architects and 3 senior functional consultants). All six users defined a form as a set of *Steps* on the one hand, and a *Flow* defining the order of the steps on the other hand. They visualized it as a set of square blocks (the steps) with arrows in between (representing the order of the steps, or 'flow'). After they defined the steps and the flow on a high level they started to specify the steps in detail. In other words: the users expected at least 2 levels of abstraction: (1) high level defining the steps and the flow between the steps, and (2) a more detailed level specifying the contents of the step. Each step has multiple input fields from a certain type (e.g. text field, password field, radio button, etc), buttons and information. Two architects suggested adopting Business Process Modeling Language (BPMN) as a solution for the modeling language especially since WCM systems are often integrated into other systems and BPMN is a well known standard for defining processes [23] and used within Web Engineering [1]. When a router was conditional, a diamond was suggested with multiple outbound lines. The users did not have any clear ideas how to cope with database connections and handlers except for the idea of using an object to define that there should be a handler on that specific place. With the user analysis we identified the mental model of the end users.

3.3   Comparing Existing Models

In this section we describe a comparison and selection of web application modeling approaches in order to fill a method base. We continue with our previously filled method base which we gathered using Situational Method-Engineering [17] , consisting of the following approaches: Object Oriented Hypermedia Design Model [21], WebML[3], UML-based Web Engineering [11] and Object Oriented Web Solutions [15].

In [14] we compared existing methods with a comparison matrix. In this research additional requirements were gathered which resulted in an adjusted comparison matrix. We compare existing models based on the Cooperative Requirements Engineering With Scenarios Framework (CREWS) [18] as it has been successfully used for classification of software [19], [24]. The adapted CREWS framework classifies modeling methods by four views: Content, Form, Purpose, and Customization process. Each view has a set of associated facets, and each facet is characterized by a set of relevant attributes [24]. We adapted the CREWS framework with similar views, adding a domain view as a separate view. Each view has different aspects describing the properties of the modeling language which we compared. **Content view**: analyzes which existing knowledge is being used within the model; **Form view**: identifies the structure and the graphical notation of the modeling language; and **Domain view**: compares the entities within the domain with the modeling concepts of the modeling language. We detail the Content View. The Content View analyzes to which extend knowledge is being used. It is analyzed on the following three aspects: (1) *Abstraction*, (2) *Context* and (3) *Argumentation*.

Abstraction has one attribute reflecting the possibility of an approach to incorporate different abstraction levels. There are three possible values for this attribute: Flexible (multiple levels possible), Fixed (multiple levels possible, but when a level is chosen it cannot be changed) or Unique (only one level). In our case, the preferred value is 'Flexible' since the user analysis asked for a multiple detailed abstraction.

Context consists of three operators: Internal (model the internal system), Interaction (model the interaction between the system and its environment) and Contextual (model the environment and its context). In our case, the preferred values are 'Internal' and 'Interaction' since the scope of this research is modeling the user interaction (business processes) and the configuration of an internal system.

Argumentation consists of an 'Argument' which defines if the model allows for providing arguments. The preferred value in our case is 'Argument' set to TRUE since it would allow end users to provide arguments for their decisions.

An example of the Content View table is displayed in Figure 1. Based on the Content View we conclude that the Business Process Model (OOWS) and the Activity Diagram (UWE) are the most suitable.

Table 1. Content View Table

Aspect	Attribute	OOHDM		WebML	UWE	OOWS	Preferred
		User Interaction Diagram	Coceptual Class Schema	Business Process Diagram	Activity Diagram	Business Process Model	
Abstraction	Abstraction	Unique	Unique	Flexible	Flexible	Flexible	Flexible
Context	Intern	–	TRUE	TRUE	TRUE	TRUE	TRUE
	Interaction	TRUE	–	–	TRUE	TRUE	TRUE
	Contextual	–	–	–	TRUE	–	
Argumentation	Argument	–	TRUE	–	TRUE	TRUE	TRUE

Similar to the CREWS framework we made a Form view and a Domain view. We concluded based on the Form View that – again – both the Activity Diagram (UWE) and the Business Process Model (OOWS) are interesting because of their functional perspective. In the Domain View, we compared the entities from the earlier defined Domain Model with the concepts of the different approaches. Our modeling language will be a construct of multiple modeling languages. Formally defined:

$$MM \subseteq \left(\bigcup_{i=1}^{n} MM_i \right) \cup MM_{new}$$

where $MM_1, MM_2, \ldots, MM_n$ are the meta models of the analyzed modeling languages and MM is the meta model of our new modeling language. MM_{new} reflects the elements which are not covered by the selected meta models but which are necessary within our new modeling language. The relationship between the entities of the Domain Model and the meta model is defined by function *map*.

$$map : MM \to D$$

Each entity within the Domain Model should be defined in the meta model. We therefore define the following:

$$\forall d \in D(\exists m \in MM[map(m) = d])$$

Based on the Domain View, the Conceptual Class Schema (OOHDM) seems useful, although it lacks the diversity of entities which makes it hard for business users to use it. The Activity Diagram (UWE) and the Business Process Model (OOWS) provide good possibilities to define the flow of a form. However, they do not provide a way to define the different elements within a form. The Business Process Diagram (WebML) is somewhere in between: it provides the possibilities to define the different elements within the form, but is not that sophisticated for defining the form flow.

Taken all three views in account, we conclude that the Activity Diagram (UWE) and the Business Process Model (OOWS) are the closest to our target modeling language: they provide a way to define the interaction between user and the system, have multiple abstraction levels, a functional perspective and have a strong focus on defining the flow of the form. However, they lack the possibility to define the different elements within the form. The User Interaction Diagram (OOHDM) is more suitable in this particular area because it represents the form elements in a compact and well-organized way. Also the UML Class Diagram (being used by most of the Web Engineering methods) can define different form elements. The Business Process Diagram from WebML has other possibilities to model these forms, but has a less compact notation to define the user interaction with the system.

We therefore selected the Business Process Model, the User Interaction Model and the UML Class Diagram as the base models for our modeling language.

4   Specifying the WebForm Diagram

To allow end users to define models which precisely express their expectations of the business process, and automatically translate models into the configuration of a WCM system as defined by its architecture, we need to formally specify our model. Similar to any other modeling language the WebForm Diagram consists of syntax and semantics. The syntax defines the rules, constructs and its decomposition where the semantics defines the meaning and interpretation of the constructs. The syntax and notation should be separated when developing a graphical language [6]. We therefore use a concrete and abstract syntax similar to the author in [4]. We elaborate on the concrete and abstract syntax in the following sections.

4.1   Concrete Syntax

The graphical notation of the concrete syntax is the representation model of the Web-Form Diagram. It should therefore match the mental model of the user which defined a web form in concepts of steps, routers, formfields and dependencies. More formalized we define form f in the following nonuple:

$$f = \{N, S, FE, V, H, C, P, B, E\}$$

Where form f consists of: N is the set of nodes, S the set of steps, FE the set of form elements, V the set of validators, H the set of handlers, C the set of conditions, P the set of web pages, B the set of blocks, and E the set of edges. We elaborate on one element to illustrate how the elements are defined – it goes beyond the scope of this paper to elaborate on each of these elements.

Form Element: A Form element is similar to a Data Entry (User Interaction Diagram) or an Attribute (UML). It is a superclass of elements which are presented to a visitor in a single step of the business process. The set of form elements *FE* can be defined as a union of different formfields where *INPUT* is the set of input types, *BUTTON* the set of buttons and *INFO* the set of information elements. Each step has zero or more form fields in a specific order. The function *fields* provides a set of form elements for a given step:

$$fields : S \rightarrow \acute{S}(FE)$$

where *Ś(FE)* is the set of all possible tuples of form elements. The function *fields* has the following characteristics: each form element is linked to one single step. This can be formalized in the following axiom:

$$\forall f \in FE \, \forall s_1, s_2 \in S \, \forall i, j \in \mathbb{N}$$
$$[occ(f, fields(s_1), i) \wedge occ(f, fields(s_2), j) \Rightarrow s_1 = s_2]$$

The function *occ()* determines if an element f exists on position i within the given sequence and since form element can only exist *once* within a single step we add the following characteristic:

$$\forall f \in FE \, \forall s \in S \, \forall i, j \in \mathbb{N}$$
$$[occ(f, fields(s), i) \wedge occ(f, fields(s), j) \Rightarrow i = j]$$

Similar to the definition of the formelement, we defined all the other elements of the Form.

4.2 Abstract Syntax

Where the concrete syntax corresponds to the representation model, the abstract syntax is a representation of the implementation model and is a formalization of the Domain Model. There are similarities between the Abstract and the Concrete Syntax, such as *Steps*, *Validation rules*, *Handlers*, *parameters* and *pages*. However, when validation rules and handlers which are connected to a single step are configured within the WCM, they are executed in a consecutive order. Edges are therefore transformed into one of two different concepts: a sequential number or a *router*. The sequential number defines the order of execution from the formvalidations, handlers and routers. An edge which leads to a different *step* or *page* will be transformed into a *router* since it will route to a new step or a page. The actual configuration of the router depends on the conditions of the object. An examples is that a user will only be routed under certain preconditions. Formalized, the WebForm Diagram f' is a septupel:

$$f' = \{N', S', FE', V', H', R', P'\}$$

Where form f' consists of: N' is the set of nodes, S' the set of steps, FE' the set of form elements, V' the set of validators, H' the set of handlers, R' the set of router, and P' the set of edges. Note that Conditions, Blocks and Edges as defined in the concrete syntax are defined within this definition. An Edge for instance is translated into a Router in the abstract syntax. Also in the Abstract Syntax, there are axioms defining the constraints. Example: each router can only be attached to one single step.

$$\forall r \in R' \forall s_1 \, s_2 \in S'$$

$$[r \in routersS'(s_1) \land r \in routersS'(s_2) \implies s_1 = s_2]$$

4.3 WebForm Diagram Modeling Tool

We have defined the concrete and abstract syntax. We then developed a modeling tool to implement the WebForm Diagram as a prototype. To build our prototype of the WebForm Diagram we used MetaEdit+ [9]. This application is both proven in building a CASE tool as well as providing computer aided support for method engineering [27].

The integration of MetaEdit+ and the WCMS is facilitated by XML: the WebForm is exported from MetaEdit+ as an XML file. This XML file however is MetaEdit+ specific which we transform into an XML resembling the Concrete Syntax (GXML). We then translate the Concrete Syntax (GXML) into the WCMS compliant XML (GXML') using a conversion tool. Since it is a prototype, we have written the conversion in general-purpose languages Java and XSLT. The GXML' can be imported into the WCM system. The transformation process works both ways: WCM form definitions can be exported to XML and can be transformed and imported into back into MetaEdit+.

5   Evaluation

We evaluated the WebForm diagram from a functional assessment to see if business users were able to develop a business process in a modeling tool to automatically configure a WCMS, thereby closing the requirements gap and making the implementation more transparent. The reduction in complexity is determined by interviewing experts on the matter.

5.1   Case Validation

To test the application in a real life situation, we took a real case situation and implemented a business process from an existing website using the WebForm Diagram. The complete implementation has been tested both ways: i.c. Designing a WebForm Diagram in MetaEdit+, XML transformation and importing it into the WCMS; and the same process in the opposite order to visualize a defined WebForm in MetaEdit+. The organization of the case is a large Dutch telecommunications provider which provides telephone, internet and television services to individuals and organizations within the Netherlands.

A WebForm Diagram is modeled by a business user, exported into the MetaEdit+ specific XML, transformed the exported XML and then imported into the WCMS. The import went without any problems and the resulting form in the WCMS is displayed in

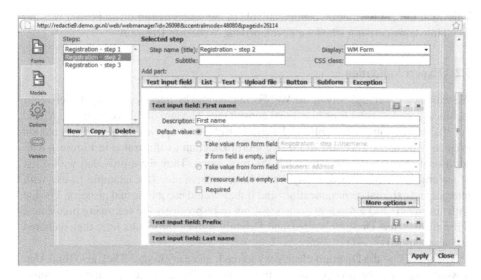

Fig. 4. WebForm Diagram converted into a WCMS Form Module

Figure 4. The form had the correct configuration of handlers and routers which could also be tested by registering a new user using the newly configured form.

To gain transparency of a WCMS implementation, we also validated the process in the opposite direction: creating a WebForm Diagram based on an existing form configuration in the WCMS. This process is slightly more difficult since not all aspects of the existing form can be extracted into an XML. The form we use for this validation is a user sign in form allowing users to access a secure page. This form consists of two steps: Step 1 allows the user to enter his credentials (username/password) and submit them to the web application. Although the form is not that complex, it is an often used business process in online transactions. If the credentials are correct the user will be routed to step 2, the secure page. If the credentials are not correct he will be routed back to the sign in page and will get an error message. We exported this form and transformed it back to the MetaEdit+ specific XML and imported it to present the WebForm Diagram without any problems.

Based on the functional validation, some limitations concerning this implementation where identified preventing it from putting it directly into practice. Within the WCM system, there is an extensive library of existing handlers and routers. Still, in projects new handlers and routers are sometimes developed for project specific purposes (e.g. connect to a specific customer legacy system). These routers and handlers are not available by default in the WebForm Diagram. This resulted in a change in the WebForm Diagram: a new placeholder handler during the modeling phase which needs to be configured or developed within the WCM System afterwards. A second limitation we found when we visualized a web form based on a predefined form definition: some routers were conditional based on volatile information (e.g. user specific session information).

This conditional information is not available in the router definition and can it was not taken into consideration when we developed the WebForm Diagram.

5.2 Expert Validation

We validated the complexity of the WebForm Diagram by interviewing eight users: four technical architects and four functional consultants. The aim of this validation is to find out if the users find the WebForm Diagram useful and applicable in implementation projects. The users were shown the WebForm Diagram as illustrated in Figure 1 with additional abstraction layers to detail the form steps. They were provided with a list of statements addressing usability, suitability, transparency (for example to use with internal and external communication) and if they would use it in actual projects. The list with statements had a 4-points scale resulting in respectively the following predicates: Strongly disagree, Disagree, Agree, and Strongly Agree. The results were then gathered and summarized.

The users find the Diagram clear, easy to read, and easy to use. They also think that it would improve the transparency within projects. The architect and the consultants are convinced that it would improve the requirements analysis and design with the end customer. Using this model will improve the validity of the requirements since the customer will probably understand such a diagram easier then the written descriptions. The architect can also use the model to check whether all relevant information is available for the implementation of a business process. However, they are not yet convinced that the handlers and validators will help the design phase much. The general opinion is that it depends much on how it is visualized in the modeling tool. They agree however that this visualization should keep a balance of usable icons but not an overload of details. Other icons in the diagram are quite abstract yet useful. They all agree that a WebForm Diagram will improve the visibility of a form and that end users will gain insight. They also state that they want to use the modeling tool if they have the proper tools supporting it. However, a remark is made concerning the fact that the current application as developed in MetaEdit+ is not web based in contrast with the WCM system. It would therefore require a rebuild in a web based environment to get it into production.

6 Related Work

In the field of Web Engineering, there are several research groups working on the development of MDE products. We briefly elaborate on four relevant research groups.

One research which started early with MDE is the Object-Oriented Hypermedia Design Method (OOHDM) as proposed by Schwabe and Rossi [21], [22]. OOHDM comprises of four steps: conceptual modeling, navigational design, abstract interface design and implementation. These activities are performed in a mix of incremental, iterative and prototype-like way. In OOHDM a clear separation is made between on the one hand navigation and the other hand presentation. OOHDM has introduced powerful navigational concepts for contexts, personalization and user interaction.

Koch et al. describe the UML-based Web Engineering (UWE) approach in [12]. UWE is an object-oriented, iterative and incremental approach for the development of web applications. The development process of UWE consists of five phases: inception, elaboration, construction, transition and maintenance. The approach focuses mainly on customized and adaptive systems and also do not take content management and integration of external sources into account.

Pastor et al. describe different methods with the Object-Oriented Web-Solutions Modeling approach. OOWS provides mechanisms to deal with the development of hypermedia information systems and e-commerce applications in web environments [16]. OOWS strongly focuses on the generation of the required Web Application and less about managing the content and the application afterwards. OOWS extends OO-method by means of a navigation model, a presentation model and a user categorization. OOWS comprises of two main activities: system specification and solution development. Similar to our framework: the OOWS approach is supported by a commercial tool called OlivaNova.

Ceri et al. describe in [3] their Web Modeling Language (WebML), a notation for specifying complex web sites at a conceptual level. In line with the definition of Web Engineer, the WebML approach consists of seven phases: requirements specification, data design, hypertext design, architecture design, implementation, testing and evaluation and maintenance and evolution. The WebML method is supported by a commercial Model Driven development environment called WebRatio that allows modeling and automatic generation of Web interface applications.

These models are used within our research. We compared these models based on the Cooperative Requirements Engineering With Scenarios Framework (CREWS) [18].

7   Conclusion

The purpose of this research is to reduce complexity and increase the transparency of the development of online business processes supported by Web Content Management Systems. To achieve these goals, we defined modeling tool to automate the configuration of Web Content Management Systems with a strong focus on defining the business processes. Based on user analysis and domain modeling, we presented the WebForm Diagram which utilizes fragments of established Web Engineering methods. The WebForm Diagram consists of an abstract and concrete syntax resembling the implementation model and the mental model respectively. We developed a prototype of the model in MetaEdit+ and were able to automatically configure the WCMs. Several abstraction layers in the WebForm Diagram supports the different process steps in the implementation project. We validated the WebForm Diagram by means of a prototype validation and an expert evaluation. The results from both the prototype and user evaluation were positive and promising. However, the validation presented some technical limitations which need to be addressed. The most important limitation was the fact that the modeling tool was not yet Web enabled. Another aspect to consider is the fact that we use general-purpose languages such as Java and XLST in the prototype to transform the different models while upcoming model-to-model transformations seem promising [13]. We believe that we have made an improvement in an approach for WCMS-based Web Engineering and that concepts of this research can be applied beyond the scope of WCMS. Future research includes further development of the WEM Framework and refinement of the modeling tool to support the automated configuration of WCMS.

References

1. Brambilla, M., Preciado, J.C., Linaje, M., Sanchez-Figueroa, F.: Business process-based conceptual design of rich internet applications. In: ICWE 2008: Proceedings of the 2008 Eighth International Conference on Web Engineering, Washington, DC, USA, 2008, pp. 155–161. IEEE Computer Society, Los Alamitos (2008)
2. Brinkkemper, S.: Method engineering: Engineering of information systems development methods and tools. Journal of Information and Software Technology 38(4), 275–280 (1996)
3. Ceri, S., Fraternali, P., Bongio, A., Brambilla, M., Matera, M.: Designing Data Intensive Web Applications. Morgan Kaufmann, San Francisco (2003)
4. Cooper, A.: About Face 3: The Essentials of Interaction Design. Wiley, New York (2007)
5. Fein, R.M., Olson, G.M., Olson, J.S.: A mental model can help with learning to operate a complex device. In: CHI 1993: INTERACT 1993 and CHI 1993 conference companion on Human factors in computing systems, pp. 157–158. ACM, New York (1993)
6. O. M. Group. Unified modeling language: Infrastructure, version 2.0.(2005), http://www.omg.org/docs/formal/05-07-05.pdf
7. Kang, K.C., Cohen, S.G., Hess, J.A., Novak, W.E., Peterson, A.S.: Feature-oriented domain analysis (foda) feasibility study. Technical report, Carnegie-Mellon University Software Engineering Institute (November 1990)
8. Kappel, G., Prll, B., Reich, S., Retschitzegger, W.: Web Engineering: The Discipline of Systematic Development of Web Applications. Wiley, New York (2006)
9. Kelly, S., Lyytinen, K., Rossi, M.: Metaedit+: A fully configurable multi-user and multi-tool case and came environment. In: CAiSE 1996: Proceedings of the 8th International Conference on Advances Information System Engineering, London, UK, pp. 1–21. Springer, Heidelberg (1996)
10. Kent, S.: Model driven engineering. In: Butler, M., Petre, L., Sere, K. (eds.) IFM 2002. LNCS, vol. 2335, pp. 286–298. Springer, Heidelberg (2002)
11. Koch, N.: A comparative study of methods for hypermedia development. Technical Report 9905, Institut für Informatik der LMU (1999)
12. Koch, N., Kraus, A.: The expressive power of uml-based web engineering. In: Proceedings of IWWOST 2002, pp. 105–119 (2002)
13. Koch, N., Meliá, S., Moreno, N., Pelechano, V., Sanchez, F., Vara, J.M.: Model-driven web engineering. Upgrade-Novática Journal (English and Spanish), Council of European Professional Informatics Societies (CEPIS) IX(2), 40–45 (2008)
14. Luinenburg, L., Jansen, S., Souer, J., van de Weerd, I., Brinkkemper, S.: Designing web content management systems using the method association approach. In: Proceedings of the 4th International Workshop on Model-Driven Web Engineering (MDWE 2008), pp. 106–120 (2008)
15. Pastor, O., Fons, J., Pelechano, V., Abrahao, S.: Conceptual modelling of web applications: The oows approach. In: Mendes, E., Mosley, N. (eds.) Web Engineering: Theory and Practice of Metrics and Measurement for Web Development (2006)
16. Pastor, Ó., Abrahão, S., Fons, J.: An object-oriented approach to automate web applications development. In: Bauknecht, K., Madria, S.K., Pernul, G. (eds.) EC-Web 2001. LNCS, vol. 2115, pp. 16–28. Springer, Heidelberg (2001)
17. Ralyté, J., Brinkkemper, S., Henderson-Sellers, B.: Situational method engineering: Fundamentals and experiences. In: Proceedings of the IFIP WG 8.1 Working Conference, vol. 38(4), pp. XII + 368 (2007)
18. Rolland, C., Achour, C.B., Cauvet, C., Ralyté, J., Sutcliffe, A., Maiden, N., Jarke, M., Haumer, P., Pohl, K., Dubois, E., Heymans, P.: A proposal for a scenario classification framework. Requir. Eng. 3(1), 23–47 (1998)

19. Rolland, C., Prakash, N.: Bridging the gap between organisational needs and erp functionality. Requir. Eng. 5(3), 180–193 (2000)
20. Schmidt, D.C.: Guest editor's introduction: Model-driven engineering. Computer 39(2), 25–31 (2006)
21. Schwabe, D., Rossi, G.: The object-oriented hypermedia design model. Commun. ACM 38(8), 45–46 (1995)
22. Schwabe, D., Rossi, G., Barbosa, S.D.J.: Systematic hypermedia application design with oohdm. In: HYPERTEXT 1996: Proceedings of the the seventh ACM conference on Hypertext, pp. 116–128. ACM, New York (1996)
23. Smith, H.: Business process management–the third wave: business process modelling language (bpml) and its pi-calculus foundations. Information & Software Technology 45(15), 1065–1069 (2003)
24. Soffer, P., Golany, B., Dori, D.: Erp modeling: a comprehensive approach. Inf. Syst. 28(6), 673–690 (2003)
25. Souer, J., Honders, P., Versendaal, J., Brinkkemper, S.: A framework for web content management system operation and maintenance. Journal of Digital Information Management (JDIM), 324–331 (2008)
26. Souer, J., van de Weerd, I., Versendaal, J., Brinkkemper, S.: Situational requirements engineering for the development of content management system-based web applications. Int. J. Web Eng. Technol (IJWET) 3(4), 420–440 (2007)
27. Tolvanen, J.-P., Rossi, M.: Metaedit+: defining and using domain-specific modeling languages and code generators. In: OOPSLA 2003: Companion of the 18th annual ACM SIGPLAN conference on Object-oriented programming, systems, languages, and applications, pp. 92–93. ACM Press, New York (2003)
28. van de Weerd, I., Brinkkemper, S., Souer, J., Versendaal, J.: A situational implementation method for web-based content management system-applications: method engineering and validation in practice. Software Process: Improvement and Practice 11(5), 521–538 (2006)
29. van Deursen, A., Klint, P., Visser, J.: Domain-specific languages: an annotated bibliography. SIGPLAN Not. 35(6), 26–36 (2000)

Bridging Test and Model-Driven Approaches
in Web Engineering

Esteban Robles Luna[1,2], Julián Grigera[1], and Gustavo Rossi[1,2]

[1] LIFIA, Facultad de Informática, UNLP, La Plata, Argentina
{esteban.robles,julian.grigera,gustavo}@lifia.info.unlp.edu.ar
[2] Also at CONICET

Abstract. In the last years there has been a growing interest in agile methods and their integration into the so called "unified" approaches. In the field of Web Engineering, agile approaches such as test-driven development are appealing because of the very nature of Web applications, while model-driven approaches provide a less error-prone code derivation; however the integration of both approaches is not easy. In this paper, we present a method-independent approach to combine the agile, iterative and incremental style of test-driven development with the more formal, transformation-based model-driven Web engineering approaches. We focus not only in the development process but also in the evolution of the application, and show how tests can be transformed together with model refactoring. As a proof of concept we show an illustrative example using WebRatio, the WebML design tool.

1 Introduction

Agile methods [7, 16] are particularly appealing for Web applications, given their short development and life-cycle times, the need of small multidisciplinary development teams, fast evolution, etc. In these methods applications are built incrementally, usually with intense feedback of different stakeholders to validate running prototypes.

Unfortunately most solid Model-Driven Web Engineering (MDWE) approaches, even claiming to favor incremental and iterative development, use a more formal[1] and waterfall style of development. Web engineering methods like UWE [14], WebML [6], OOWS [18], OO-H [9] or OOHDM [22] define a set of abstract models such as content (called also data or application), navigation and presentation model, which allow the generation of running applications by automatic (error free) model transformations. This approach is attractive because it raises the abstraction level of the construction process, allowing developers to focus on conceptual models instead of code. The growing availability of techniques and tools in the universe of model-driven development (e.g. transformation tools) adds synergy to the approach.

---

[1] While Agile approaches might be also "formal" (see [7]), more popular ones tend to encourage a handcrafted style.

M. Gaedke, M. Grossniklaus, and O. Díaz (Eds.): ICWE 2009, LNCS 5648, pp. 136–150, 2009.
© Springer-Verlag Berlin Heidelberg 2009

Many agile methods seem to follow a different direction. For example Test-Driven Development (TDD) uses small cycles to add behavior to the application [3]. The cycle starts with a set of requirements expressed with use cases [11] or user stories [13] that describe the application's expected behavior informally. The developer abstracts concepts and behavior, and writes a set of meaningful test cases which will fail on their first run, prior to the implementation. Then, he writes the necessary code to make the tests pass and run them again, until the whole test suite passes. The process is iterative and continues by adding new requirements, creating new tests and running them to check that they fail, then writing code to make them pass, and so on. In these cycles the developer might have to refactor [8] the code when necessary.

This strategy gives a good starting point for the development process, because developers specify the programs expected behavior first, making assertions about the return values right before the development itself begins. The process follows the idea of "Test first, by intention" [13], which is based on two key principles:

- Specify program's behavior (test first), and write code only when you have a test that doesn't work.
- Write your code without thinking about *how* to do a thing, instead think about *what* you have to do (intention).

Moreover, when using a static typed language like Java, the tests code may not even compile, as the involved classes and methods still don't exist. Thus, writing the tests first, guides us to create the classes and methods of the domain model. TDD allows better communication among different stakeholders, as short cycles favor the permanent evaluation of requirements and their realization in incremental prototypes. TDD is also claimed to reduce the number of problems found on the implementation stage [21] and therefore its use is growing fast in industrial settings [15].

In the Web Engineering area, efforts to integrate agile and model-driven development styles are just beginning [2], and most methods lack clear heuristics of how to improve the development life-cycle with the incorporation of these new ideas.

In this paper we present a novel, method-independent approach, to bridge the gap between TDD and MDWE approaches. The overall process has the same structure as TDD, but instead of writing code, we generate it from the well-known content, navigational and presentation models using a MDWE tool. We also create automated tests (that can be run without manual interaction) and deal with Web refactoring interventions [17]. These navigational and presentation tests allow us to manage evolution in a TDD fashion. Also, like in traditional TDD, we specify the application's behavior prior to its development in terms of tests, and use them to specify the application models, as they express (and validate) the expected functionality. We also relax some of the assumptions in TDD (based on its inherent bottom-up approach), as they are not appropriated for highly interactive applications. We illustrate our approach showing how to use these ideas in the context of the WebML methodology, using the WebRatio [24] tool.

The main contributions of the paper are the following:

- We present a novel TDD-like process to improve Model-Driven Web Engineering.
- We propose the use of black box interaction tests as essential elements for validating the application's navigational and interface behavior.

- We present an approach for dealing with navigation and interface test evolution during the refactoring process.

It should be noticed that our focus is in the development process and not in the tests themselves. Rather, we see tests as tools for driving the web application's construction and evolution.

The structure of the paper is the follows: In Section 2 we review some related work; In Section 3 we present our approach, and using a case study we explain how we map requirements into test models, and how the cycle proceeds after generating the application. We end the technical description of our approach by discussing, in Section 4 and 5, refactoring issues, both in the application and in the test models. Finally, we conclude and present some further work we are pursuing.

2   Related Work and Discussion

The advantages of using agile approaches in Web application development processes have been early pointed out in [16]. The authors not only argue in favor of agile approaches, but also propose a specific one (AWE) that, being independent of the underlying Web engineering method, could in theory be used with any of them. However, AWE is "just" a process; it does not indicate how software artifacts are obtained or how the process is supposed to be integrated in a model-driven development style.

Most Web Engineering methods such as WebML, UWE, OOHDM, OOWS or OO-H, have already claimed to use incremental and iterative styles, though support for specific agile approaches has not been reported yet in the literature.

In the broader field of software engineering, agile approaches have flourished, though most of them are presented as being centered in coding, much more than in the modeling and design activities. An interesting and controversial point of view in this debate can be found in [19], in which the author proposes to use an extreme "non-programming" approach, by only using models as development artifacts. In this arena, Test-Driven Development has been presented as one of the realizations of Extreme Programming [13], where tests are developed previously to code. In a recent paper [12] however, the authors clearly indicate that TDD is also appropriated as a design technique, and show examples in which TDD is used beyond "extreme" approaches.

The interest of using TDD in interactive applications is relatively new, given that the artifacts elicited from tests are usually "far" from the interface realm, and also because unit testing [4], which focuses on individual classes, is unsuitable for complex GUIs. In [1], the authors present a technique for organizing both the code and the development activities to produce fully tested GUI applications from customer stories. Similarly, [20] proposes to use TDD as an approach to develop Web applications, focusing on the development of the different parts of the MVC triad, again emphasizing coding more than modeling.

Also, in relation to our approach, as TDD makes a heavy use of requirements models, it is important to say that most Web engineering approaches have either automatic ways or explicit heuristics to derive content and navigation models from requirements documents; particularly, in OOWS [18], the conceptual model can be generated from requirements using model-to-model transformations; earlier in [5], the authors have presented an attractive way to map use cases into navigation models in the context of OO-H and UWE, giving much more relevance to the requirement documents. The concept of Navigation Semantic Unit in [5] has inspired our idea of Navigation Unit Testing (see Section 3).

In a different direction, though still related with our ideas, [10] show how to systematically generate test cases from requirements, particularly from use cases. These proposals however deal with tests as usual in non-agile processes, therefore running them against a "final" application, instead of profiting from them during the whole development process.

3   An Overview of Our Approach

In the TDD approach, new functionality is specified in terms of automated tests derived from individual requirements, and then the code to make them pass is written. A further step involves refactoring this code by removing duplication, for example. Obviously TDD does not deny the need to perform a thorough testing process of the final application; the tests in TDD are a perfect start to assess how the application fulfills the client's requirements beyond its correctness.

Our approach follows the same structure, but given the nature of Web applications instead of focusing on unit testing, we emphasize the use of navigation and interaction level tests, which we first run against user interface (UI) mockups using a black box approach. We then replace the coding by a modeling step, generating the code using a MDWE tool. We also add an intermediate step to adapt the tests, in order to trim the differences between the mockups and the generated application prototype.

Even though we face application generation using MDWE tools, this stage of our process differs slightly from the conventional model-driven approach, as we work at a very fine granularity level: in the extreme case, we build models for one requirement at a time, generating tested and running prototypes incrementally, leading each requirement through a lightweight version of a full MDWE step. In this way, we come closer to the TDD short-cycle style, while still profiting from the advantages of working with models.

Briefly explained, our approach mixes TDD and MDWE techniques to make Web development more agile. We first gather user requirements with use cases [11], User Interaction Diagrams (UIDs) [22] and presentation mockups [25]. Then, we choose a use case and derive an interaction test against the related presentation mockup, with which we specify the navigation and UI interaction prior to the development. We next get a running prototype of the application by creating models and generating code in a short MDWE cycle, and check its correctness using the test. Should these tests fail, we would go back to tweak the models, regenerate the application and run them back again, repeating the process until they pass. As in TDD, the complete method is repeated with all use cases, until a full-featured prototype is reached. Fig. 1 shows a simplified view of our approach, confronting it with the "traditional" TDD.

While the application evolves, tests will also help to check that functionality is preserved after applying navigation and presentation refactorings (i.e. usability improvements that don't alter the application behavior [17]).

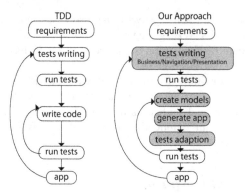

Fig. 1. TDD life cycle comparison

In the following subsections we illustrate the approach with the development of TDDStore, a simplified online bookstore, similar to Barnes&Noble. As we use WebML and WebRatio, which support data-intensive applications, we focus mainly on navigation and UI tests, also contemplating some business operations.

3.1 Capturing Requirements with Mockups and UIDs

Similarly to a MDWE approach, we begin gathering and modeling the set of requirements. Particularly, we propose employing use cases, UIDs and mockups. With these artifacts, the analyst can easily specify UI, navigation and business requirements that the application must satisfy. For each use case, we specify the corresponding UID that serves as a partial, high-level navigation model, and provides abstract information about interface features. As an example of an interaction diagram, we show in Fig. 2 the UID corresponding to the case when the user is presented with a list of books, indicated with "…" in state 1, containing some information about each book ("title, author…") , and selects a book from the list (transition marked with 1) to see the full book details (state 2).

Fig. 2. UID for simple navigation

Using UI mockups, we agree with the client on broad aspects of the application look and feel, prior to the development. This is a very convenient way for interacting with stakeholders and gathering quick feedback from them. There are two additional reasons to use UI mockups: we will perform UI and navigational tests against them, and they will become the application's final look and feel.

In Fig. 3.a we show an initial and simplified mockup of our application's main page, where all books are listed. Fig. 3.b shows a mockup for the book details page. In the

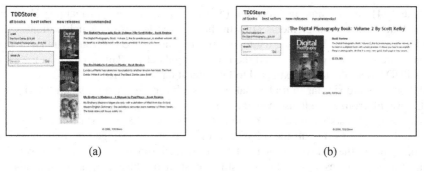

Fig. 3. a) Books list mockup; b) Book details mockup

next sub-section we show how to specify a test against this mockup to verify the UID in Fig. 2. To make the example realistic, we also included some other features in the mockup, though they will be tested in further iterations, when being involved in a use case and UID.

3.2 Writing Tests

Mockups and UIDs help to understand the expected behavior of the application. UIDs refine use cases to show how the user interacts with the application, and mockups complement UIDs to give a sample of the application look and feel. However, these useful tools fall short to provide by themselves an artifact capable of being run to validate the application's expected behavior. By incorporating interaction tests, we provide a better way to validate the application.

Following the process we create a test for the mentioned use case, using as a basis the UID in Fig. 2 and the mockup in Fig. 3. For the sake of clarity and concreteness instead of an abstract test specification, we tie our description to a standard test tool like Selenium [23], to specify the interactions between the user and the application (other similar tools can be used for this task). These tests rely on the DOM structure of the tested document, so they are agnostic of the process by which the application has been generated, as well as the applied styles. The following test validates that the UI shows the book list and the navigation between the book list and the book's detail:

```
public class BookListTestCase extends SeleneseTestCase {
    public void testBookListToProdDetailNav() throws Exception {
(1)   sel.open("file:///dev/bookstore/Mockups/books-list.html");
(2)   assertEquals("all books", sel.getText("//div[@id='tb']/p[1]"));
(3)   sel.click("link=The Digital Photography Book");
(4)   sel.waitForPageToLoad("30000");
(5)   sel.assertLocation("/bookDetail*");
(6)   assertEquals("The Di...", sel.getText("//div[@id='prod']/h2"));
(7)   assertEquals("The ...", sel.getText("//div[@id='p-d']/p[1]"));
(8)   assertEquals("+ Add to...", sel.getText("//div[@id='p-d']/a"));
    }
}
```

The test begins by opening the page (the mockup file) (1) and asserting that a specific element has some content (2); in this way we can assert that we are in the book list page. Then we specify to click on a specific link (3) and wait until the page is loaded (4) and validate our location (5) thus validating our navigation. Then, we assert that several html elements contain the specific text (6-8) which validates that the UI has changed. When we try to run the test using the Selenium runner it fails because we have not yet developed the running application. This scenario is the same as in TDD where the test is expected to fail after it has been written.

These tests are similar to traditional unit tests but performed on small "navigation units" arising from a single use case, so we call them navigation unit tests.

This kind of tests simulate user interactions (click on a link, fill a text box, etc.) and add assertions about the elements of the page. Navigation unit tests are independent of the MDWE tool used because they run using a web browser. We found this type of tests suitable for testing most of the business, navigation and UI logic as perceived by the user. However, in complex Web applications there are many scenarios in which unit and integration tests [4] (the usual TDD type of tests) should be used. One example is the integration between Web applications using Web services. Another one are application's behaviors performed "in the shadows" (e.g. support for the shipping process in an e-store). In both cases, interaction tests are not useful because the user might not be interacting with the application. We don't include these examples as illustrations as they are not novel in TDD. For these tests our approach remains unchanged: specify a test (e.g. a unit test), check that it fails, specify the corresponding models (e.g. using WebML units, UWE classes, etc.), generate the application, etc.

At this point, we can start using our design artifacts (mockups and UIDs) to derive the application, navigation and presentation models.

3.3 Deriving Design Models

Once requirements have been (at least partially) gathered, and the tests specified for a particular use case, the next step is to generate a running application. As mentioned before, here is where we differ from a pure TDD approach, as we chose to use a MDWE tool, instead of writing code. Throughout the development of our proofs of concept we have used the WebML's MDD tool, WebRatio [24]. We will concentrate on the navigational (hypertext) model for several reasons; first, it is the distinctive model in Web applications; besides we want to emphasize the differences between typical TDD and TDD in Web applications and show how navigation unit tests work. Additionally, as said before, WebRatio's (and WebML) content model is a data and not an object-oriented model, thus some of the typical issues in TDD (originally devised to work with classes and methods) do not apply exactly as they were conceived, as we discuss below.

A first data model is derived using the UIDs as a starting point, identifying the entities needed to satisfy the specified interactions, e.g. by using the heuristics described in [22]. As Web Ratio supports the specification of ER models at this stage of the development, the application behavior will be specified later, in the so-called logic model. Following with our example, we need to build an application capable of listing books, and exhibiting links to their corresponding details pages, so the book and author entities come out immediately from the UID in Fig. 2. Then, we map the navigation sequence in the UID to a WebML hypertext diagram, as shown in Fig. 4.

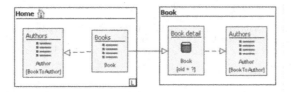

Fig. 4. WebML diagram for the UID

WebRatio is now ready to generate the application. Once we have a running prototype, we can adapt the tests (this process is detailed in section 3.4) and run them to check if the models (and therefore the application) conform with the requirements.

Finally, we need to adjust the application's presentation. WebML does not define a presentation model; instead presentation is considered like a document transformation from a WebML specification of a page into a specific language page like JSP or ASP.NET. In another methodology, the mockups and UIDs would be used to also specify the presentation model. Since we already had developed mockups for our current UID, this part of the process is straightforward: we only need to slice up the mockup, and input it as an XHTML template into WebRatio. We can run the tests again to ensure no interaction is corrupted while the template is being modified.

3.4 Test Adaptation

After building the models, we need to make sure the implementation generated from them is valid according to the requirements specification. In particular, we want to confirm that business, navigation and UI behavior are correct with respect to the tests defined in section 3.2. However, if we try to run the tests as they are written, they will fail because they still reference mockups files, and although the layout may be the same, the location in terms of an XPath expression [26] may have changed.

On one hand, the generation may have renamed the URLs of each page. For instance, if we chose to transform templates into JSP pages, URLs change their names to end with ".jsp". We can prevent this scenario by defining the name of the mockups upfront, according to the technology. Another problem may arise if we use components that generate HTML code in a different way than what we had expected. We face this problem, for example, when we display a collection of objects using WebRatio`s Table component. This could be also prevented by using a customized template, in which we manually iterate over the collection of objects.

Although both scenarios could be prevented, we should consider the case in which they are not. In that situation we must adapt the test to the current implementation. Fortunately, the adaptation of tests is easy to perform manually, and its mechanics can be automated in a straightforward way. As an example, we show how to adapt the test of section 3.2 to be compliant to the current implementation.

```
public class BookListTestCase extends SeleneseTestCase {
    public void testBookListToProdDetailNav() throws Exception {
(1)    sel.open("http://127.0.0.1:8180/TDDStore/page1.do");
(2)    assertEquals("all…", sel.getText("//div[@id='page1FB']/p[1]"));
(3)    sel.click("link=The Digital Photography Book");
```

```
(4)   sel.waitForPageToLoad("30000");
(5)   sel.assertLocation("/page2*");
(6)   assertEquals("The ...", sel.getText("//div[@id='p2FB']/h2"));
(7)   assertEquals("The D...", sel.getText("//div[@id='p2FB']/p[1]"));
(8)   assertEquals("+ Add to...", sel.getText("//div[@id='p2FB']/a"));
    }
}
```

In the above test we first changed the URL to start the test by just finding the right URL and changing it (1, 5). Then, as the layout of the list of products has changed due to the derivation process of WebRatio, the XPath expressions we had used are no longer valid as WebRatio has included a different DOM structure. This can be changed for example by accessing the url with a tool such as the XPather plugin [27]. Just right click over the item, shown in XPather and then copy the XPath expression to the test (2, 6-8). Next we can re-run the test, and verify it succeeds.

3.5   Towards a New Iteration

Having our iteration complete (i.e. all tests run correctly), we are ready to add new functionality to the application. We will incorporate the possibility of adding a book to a shopping cart, so we go through the same steps of the first example:

1. Model the new requirements, with use cases and UIDs.
2. Create a new mockup if necessary, or extend a previous one.
3. Write a new navigation unit test for the added functionality and run it against the corresponding mockup.
4. Upgrade the model and generate the application, implementing the new functionality to make the tests pass.
5. Adapt the new test, as previously shown in section 3.4
6. Run the new test and check that the new functionality has been correctly added. If the test fails, then go back to step 3 until it passes.

In order to introduce the new add-to-cart functionality we need to illustrate the interaction with a new UID (1) that slightly extends the one in Fig. 2 with a new navigational transition with the product being added to the cart. We need to expand the book details mockup by adding an "add to cart" link (2). Then we write the test in the same way as we did previously on section 3.2.

```
public class BookListTestCase extends SeleneseTestCase {
    public void testAddBookToShoppingCart() throws Exception {
(1)   sel.open("file:///dev/bookstore/Mockups/books-list.html");
(2)   assertEquals("The D...", sel.getText("//div[@id='p-i']/h4/a"));
(3)   sel.click("//div[@id='product-info']/a");
(4)   sel.waitForPageToLoad("30000");
(5)   assertEquals("The Dig...", sel.getText("/ul[@id='s-p']/li[1]"));
(6)   sel.assertLocation("/cart*");
    }
}
```

The test above opens the book list (1) and asserts the name of the product. Then clicks on the "add to cart" link of the product (3) and waits for the page to load (4). It asserts that the selected book has been added to the cart by asserting that the book's title is present in the shopping cart page (5) and that navigation has succeeded (6).

As we show in Fig. 5, an extended WebML hypertext diagram including the AddToCart operation is derived from the new UID.

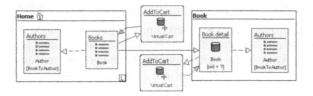

Fig. 5. Upgraded WebML diagram

We regenerate the application and run the whole test suite against the derived application. Notice that the test suite will be composed of the previously adapted test, and the new one after the corresponding adaptation.

4   Dealing with Application Evolution

Web applications tend to evolve constantly and in short periods of time; the evolution is driven mainly by two reasons:

- New requirements: Generally, new requirements arise because of clients or users' requests to enhance the application's functionality. For example, the book store's owner may want to categorize books, which would require defining new model elements (entities, page types, links, etc).
- Web refactorings: We might want to improve the application's usability, by either modifying the interface or the navigation facilities. This kind of model changes, usually driven by non-functional requirements (usability, accessibility, etc), have been called elsewhere Web model refactorings [17]. Web refactorings may eventually occur in a TDD cycle, for example if the developer notices an opportunity to improve the user experience.

Next, we analyze both cases and show how we deal with them during the test-driven development process.

4.1 New Requirements

After the application has been deployed (or even during its development), the client may want to add new functionality, such as organizing books in categories. New requirements have to be described using the artifacts we have previously mentioned (UIDs, mockups) and following the process we have summarized in Section 3.5:

1. Add the label that shows the category name of the book, to the mockup of books list and books' details.
2. Add the assertions to the adapted tests of the books list and books' details pages, with the XPath expression obtained from the mockups.
3. Run the tests and ensure they fail.

4. Enhance the domain, navigation and the UI models (entities, units and templates in WebRatio) to show the category.
5. Generate the application.
6. Run the tests (adapt them if necessary). If they fail go back to step 4.

After finishing this cycle, we will have a new requirement added to the application and a new test that validates the UI of the book list and book detail pages. Obviously, we might want to navigate through categories but the process remains similar just by adding some new use cases and UIDs before 2 and building the corresponding tests.

4.2 Web Refactorings

Web refactorings seek to improve application's usability with small model changes. A catalog of such refactorings has been presented in [17]. In order to illustrate the process we selected a fairly simple one, *Turn Information into Link*, which consists in converting a text string into a link leading to a page with information about the object represented by the text. In our case, we will enhance the authors' names on the book details page and transform them into links, leading to a list of their books . Once again, we will follow the steps of our approach as follows:

1. Refactor the book details mockup to show a link where each author name appears, as shown in Fig. 6.

Fig. 6. Refactored book details mockup

2. Transform the UI test of the book detail page (3) by changing the XPath expression. Previously it was an h2 element, but now it is a link, so we have to change it to an a element. Also, add a test to validate the navigation from the book detail to the author page (8-13).

```
public class BookDetailTestCase extends SeleneseTestCase {
    public void testBookDetailUI() throws Exception {
(1)    sel.open("http://127.0.0.1:8180/TDDStore/page2.do?oid=2");
(2)    assertEquals("The ...", sel.getText("//div[@id='p2FB']/h2[1]"));
(3)    assertEquals("Sc...", sel.getText("//div[@id='prod-d']/a"));
(4)    assertEquals("Book R...", sel.getText("//div[@id='p2FB2']/h3"));
(5)    assertEquals("The ...", sel.getText("//div[@id='p2FB2']/p[1]"));
(6)    assertEquals("$19.99", sel.getText("//div[@id='p2FB2']/p[2]"));
(7)    assertEquals("+ Add t...", sel.getText("//div[@id='p2FB2']/a"));
    }
    public void testBookDetailNavigationToAuthor() throws Exception {
(8)    sel.open("file:///dev/bookstore/Mockups/books-detail.html ");
(9)    assertEquals("Scott Kelby", sel.getText("//div[@id='p-d']/a"));
(10) sel.click("//div[@id='p-d']/a");
```

```
(11)  sel.waitForPageToLoad("30000");
(12)  assertEquals("Books f...",  sel.getText("//div[@id='p-1']/h2"));
(13)  sel.assertLocation("/byAuthor*");
    }
}
```

3. Run the tests and ensure they fail.
4. Modify the corresponding WebML hypertext model and the corresponding presentation
5. Derive the application.
6. Run the tests (adapt them if necessary). If they fail go to step 4.

At the end of this cycle we have a complete refactoring applied over the application and tests transformed and added to the test suite. We next show how we can automate this kind of tests transformations.

5 Towards Automated Test Evolution

During the development cycle, "old" tests should always succeed (except that some already processed requirement has changed dramatically). However, Web refactorings pose a new challenge for the developer: even not being originated by new requirements, they can make navigation tests fail, as they might (slightly) change the navigational and/or interface structure of the application. In other words, and as shown in 4.2, tests must be adapted to be useful after a refactoring, i.e. to correctly assess if it was safely performed. Fortunately, refactorings can be catalogued, because, as well as design patterns, they record and convey good design practices. Therefore, it is feasible to automate the process of test transformation. This refactoring-driven transformation of tests must be performed after the mockup and UIDs have been modified to show the new expected behavior. To transform a test we need to follow these steps:

1. Select the test transformation associated with the refactoring of the catalogue to be applied.
2. Configure the test transformation with UID's, mockups, location of tests and specific parameters of the transformation (e.g. a specific element's location).
3. Apply the test transformation.

There are many strategies to transform tests; we next explain one of them, as it comprises defining a model for tests, which can be useful for other further tasks, such as linking tests' components to design model elements, for example to improve traceability. To achieve automatic tests transformation, we first need to abstract the concepts involved in a Web test. A Web test is a sequence of interactions and assertions that aim to validate the application's behavior. An interaction allows the user to interact with the application. For example: click a link, click a button, type a text on an input field, check a checkbox, etc. Assertions allow ensuring that a predicate is valid in the current context. There are many possible assertions over a Web page such as assertTitle, assertTextPresent, etc. A Web test could be then abstracted using the simplified model shown in Fig. 7.

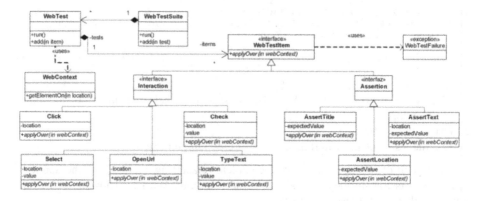

Fig. 7. Web Test Model

Individual tests can be abstracted, from their source code to an instance of the model, in a straightforward way by using a parser. When tests are mapped onto a set of objects, they can be easily manipulated. For instance, adding a title assertion to a test is as simple as creating a new instance of the AssertTitle class and adding it to the WebTest instance. Web test transformations are then designed and coded with objects, and thus the algorithm that performs the transformation can be coded and encapsulated in a class. Once the test transformation has been applied, we translate objects back into the test text using a pretty printing algorithm. We omit here the explanation of the parsing and pretty printing phases, as they are outside the scope of the paper. As an example we show the algorithm of the Turn Information Into link [17] test transformation that can be summarized in the following steps:

1. Request the location of the test.
2. Request the location of the text.
3. Change the location of the AssertText instance of the text. If no assertion is pointed by the user, create a new instance of the AssertText class.
4. Create a new WebTest instance. Create an OpenUrl instance (pointing to the mockup) and clone the AssertText instance of 3. Add both instances to the WebTest.
5. Create a Click and Wait instances pointing to the location of the new link and add it to the WebTest instance.
6. Request the expected location and a text that identifies the new location.
7. Create an AssertText and AssertLocation instances with the corresponding requested values.

The result of applying the algorithm looks similar to the result shown in section 4.2, but instead of testBookDetailNavigationToAuthor, the new test is called testNavigationTextToLink1. Using this approach we can automate the process of Web test transformation based on the catalogue of refactorings we want to apply.

6 Concluding Remarks and Further Work

We have presented a novel approach to integrate test-driven development into model-driven web engineering methods. Our approach can be used with any of the existing methods, though to illustrate its feasibility we have used WebML and WebRatio as a proof of concept. We have briefly explained the main steps of our approach and showed some advanced aspects, such as tests transformations during the Web refactoring stage. We have also shown that most activities related to tests evolution can (and indeed should) be automated. To our knowledge, our proposal is the first to bridge the gap between model-driven approaches and test-driven development, and particularly in the Web engineering field. We retain the agile style of TDD that focuses on short cycles, each one aimed at implementing a single requirement, to validate the generated prototype. However, we work at a higher level of abstraction (i.e. with models) leaving code generation to the support tool.

While TDD is usually, due to its strong relationship with coding, a handcrafted and therefore error-prone activity, integration with model-driven approaches opens an interesting space for improvement. We are now working on several directions: first we are making field experiences to measure the impact of the integration on development costs and quality aspects. While both TDD and model-driven development improve software construction, we believe that our approach tends to synergize the benefits more than just summing them up. From a more technical point of view we are working in the integration of tools for TDD in different MDWE tools. These tools include: Selenium and XPather for developing test cases, and Selenium RC to make a one click away the generation and running of the whole test suite (currently done manually). We are also planning to use an object-oriented approach (like UWE), together with its associated tool to research deeper in the relationships between typical unit testing in TDD (focused on object behaviors) and our navigation unit testing, which focuses more on navigation and user interactions. Automatic generation of tests from UIDs by using transformations or strategies like the one described in [10], and improving traceability between tests and models are also important items in our research agenda.

References

1. Alles, M., Crosby, D., Erickson, C., Harleton, B., Marsiglia, M., Pattison, G., Stienstra, C.: Presenter First: Organizing Complex GUI Applications for Test-Driven Development. In: AGILE 2006, pp. 276–288 (2006)
2. Ambler, S.W.: The object primer: agile modeling-driven development with UML 2.0. Cambridge University Press, Cambridge (2004)
3. Beck, K.: Test Driven Development: By Example. Addison-Wesley Signature Series (2002)
4. Binder, R.V.: Testing Object-Oriented Systems: Models, Patterns, and Tools. Addison-Wesley Longman Publishing Co., Inc., Amsterdam (1999)
5. Cachero, C., Koch, N.: Navigation Analysis and Navigation Design in OO-H and UWE. Technical Report. Universidad de Alicante, Spain (April 2002),
   http://www.dlsi.ua.es/~ccachero/papers/ooh-uwe.pdf
6. Ceri, S., Fraternali, P., Bongio, A.: Web Modeling Language (WebML): A Modeling Language for Designing Web Sites. Computer Networks and ISDN Systems 33(1-6), 137–157 (2000)

7. Eleftherakis, G., Cowling, A.: An Agile Formal Development Methodology. In: SEEFM 2003 Proceedings 36 (1 de 12) (2003)
8. Fowler, M., Beck, K., Brant, J., Opdyke, W., Roberts, D.: Refactoring: Improving the Design of Existing Code. Addison-Wesley Professional, Reading (1999)
9. Gómez, J., Cachero, C.: OO-H Method: extending UML to model web interfaces. In: van Bommel, P. (ed.) Information Modeling For internet Applications, pp. 144–173. IGI Publishing, Hershey (2003)
10. Gutiérrez, J.J., Escalona, M.J., Mejías, M., Torres, J.: An approach to generate test cases from use cases. In: Proceedings of the 6th international Conference on Web Engineering. ICWE 2006, Palo Alto, California, USA, July 11 - 14, vol. 263, pp. 113–114. ACM, New York (2006)
11. Jacobson, I.: Object-Oriented Software Engineering: A Use Case Driven Approach. ACM Press/Addison-Wesley (1992)
12. Janzen, D., Saiedian, H.: Does Test-Driven Development Really Improve Software Design Quality? IEEE Software 25(2), 77–84 (2008)
13. Jeffries, R.E., Anderson, A., Hendrickson, C.: Extreme Programming Installed. Addison-Wesley Longman Publishing Co., Inc., Amsterdam (2000)
14. Koch, N., Knapp, A., Zhang, G., Baumeister, H.: UML-Based Web Engineering, An Approach Based On Standards. In: Web Engineering, Modelling and Implementing Web Applications, pp. 157–191. Springer, Heidelberg (2008)
15. Maximilien, E.M., Williams, L.: Assessing test-driven development at IBM. In: Proceedings of the 25th international Conference on Software Engineering, Portland, Oregon, May 03 - 10, pp. 564–569. IEEE Computer Society, Los Alamitos (2003)
16. McDonald, A., Welland, R.: Agile Web Engineering (AWE) Process: Multidisciplinary Stakeholders and Team Communication. In: Web Engineering, pp. 253–312. Springer, US (2002)
17. Olsina, L., Garrido, A., Rossi, G., Distante, D., Canfora, G.: Web Application evaluation and refactoring: A Quality-Oriented improvement approach. Journal of Web Engineering 7(4), 258–280 (2008)
18. Pastor, O., Abrahão, S., Fons, J.: An Object-Oriented Approach to Automate Web Applications Development. In: Bauknecht, K., Madria, S.K., Pernul, G. (eds.) EC-Web 2001. LNCS, vol. 2115, pp. 16–28. Springer, Heidelberg (2001)
19. Pastor, O.: From Extreme Programming to Extreme Non-programming: Is It the Right Time for Model Transformation Technologies? In: Bressan, S., Küng, J., Wagner, R. (eds.) DEXA 2006. LNCS, vol. 4080, pp. 64–72. Springer, Heidelberg (2006)
20. Pipka, J.U.: Test-Driven Web Application Development in Java. In: Objects, Components, Architectures, Services, and Applications for a Networked World, vol. 1, pp. 378–393. Springer, US (2003)
21. Rasmussen, J.: Introducing XP into Greenfield Projects: lessons learned. IEEE Softw. 20(3), 21–28 (2003)
22. Rossi, G., Schwabe, D.: Modeling and Implementing Web Applications using OOHDM. In: Web Engineering, Modelling and Implementing Web Applications, pp. 109–155. Springer, Heidelberg (2008)
23. Selenium web application testing system, http://seleniumhq.org/
24. The WebRatio Tool Suite, http://www.Webratio.com
25. VanderVoord, M., Williams, G.: Feature-Driven Design Using TDD and Mocks. In: Embedded Systems Conference Boston (October 2008)
26. XML Path Language (XPath), http://www.w3.org/TR/xpath
27. XPather - XPath Generator and Editor, https://addons.mozilla.org/en-US/firefox/addon/1192

A Requirement Analysis Approach for Using i* in Web Engineering

Irene Garrigós, Jose-Norberto Mazón, and Juan Trujillo

Lucentia Research Group
Department of Software and Computing Systems – DLSI
University of Alicante, Spain
{igarrigos,jnmazon,jtrujillo}@dlsi.ua.es

Abstract. Web designers usually ignore how to model real user expectations and goals, mainly due to the large and heterogeneous audience of the Web. This fact leads to websites which are difficult to comprehend by visitors and complex to maintain by designers. In order to ameliorate this scenario, an approach for using the i* modeling framework in Web engineering has been developed in this paper. Furthermore, we also present a traceability approach for obtaining different kind of design artifacts tailored to a specific Web modeling method. Finally, we include a sample of our approach in order to show its applicability and we describe a prototype tool as a proof of concept of our research.

1 Introduction

In the last decade, the number and complexity of websites and the amount of information they offer is rapidly growing. In this context, introduction of Web design methods and methodologies [1,2,3,4,5] have provided mechanisms to develop complex Web applications in a systematic way. To better accommodate the individual user, personalization of websites has been also introduced and studied [6,7,8,9]. However, due to the idiosyncrasy of the audience, traditionally methodologies for Web engineering have not taken into serious consideration the requirement analysis phase. Actually, one of the main characteristics of Web applications is that they typically serve large and heterogeneous audience, since respectively i) everybody can access to the website and ii) each user has different needs, goals and preferences. Interestingly, this is the opposite situation from the traditional software development where the users are well known.

Therefore, current effort for requirement analysis in Web engineering is rather focused on the system and the needs of the users are figured out by the designer. This scenario leads us to websites that do not assure *real* user requirements and goals, thus producing user disorientation and comprehension problems. There may appear development and maintenance problems for designers, since costly, time-consuming and rather non-realistic mechanisms (e.g. surveys among visitors) should be developed to improve the already implemented website, thus increasing the initial project budget.

M. Gaedke, M. Grossniklaus, and O. Díaz (Eds.): ICWE 2009, LNCS 5648, pp. 151–165, 2009.
© Springer-Verlag Berlin Heidelberg 2009

To solve these drawbacks, in this paper, a complementary viewpoint should be adopted: modeling which are the expectations, intentions and goals of the users when they are browsing the site and determining how they can affect the definition of a suitable Web design. The main benefit of our point of view is that the designer will be able to make decisions from the very beginning of the development phase. These decisions could affect the structure of the envisioned website in order to satisfy needs, goals, interests and preferences of each user or user type. To this aim, we propose to use the i* modeling framework [10,11], one of the most valuable approaches for analyzing stakeholders' goals and how the intended system would meet them. This framework is also very useful for reasoning about how stakeholders' goals contribute to the selection of different design alternatives. However, although i* provides mechanisms to model stakeholders and relationships between them, it should be adapted for Web engineering, since the Web domain has special requirements that are not taken into account in traditional requirement analysis approaches. These requirements are related to the three main features of Web applications [12]: navigational structure, user interface and personalization capability.

Bearing these considerations in mind, in this paper, we present an approach for specifying requirements in the context of a Web engineering method [8] improving the development of Web applications by using i* models. Also we provide the designer with a set of guidelines to define these models. Moreover, the main conceptual models are derived from this requirements specification using QVT (Query/View/Transformation) rules [13]. In this way, designers will not have to create these models from scratch but obtaining a first tentative model that ensures user requirements and then they only have to refine these models, saving time and development effort.

The remainder of this paper is structured as follows: our approach for requirement analysis in Web engineering and how to trace these requirements to the Web design is presented in Sect. 2. Section 3 describes an example of applying our approach. Section 4 describes related work. Finally, in Sect. 5, we present our conclusions and sketch some future work.

2   Modeling Requirements in Web Engineering

In this section, we present a proposal which provides a way of specifying requirements using i* in the context of A-OOH *(Adaptive Object Oriented Hypermedia method)* [8]. A-OOH is the extension of the OO-H modeling method [2], which includes the definition of adaptation strategies. This approach has also been extended with UML-profiles so all the conceptual models are UML-compliant (see Sect. 2.1). We use A-OOH for demonstration purposes but the proposal could be applied to any Web modeling method. Traceability from the specified requirements to the different conceptual models is also studied (see Sect. 2.2). Designers will have to focus on specifying the requirements and will just have to refine the generated conceptual models in order to adjust them.

2.1   Specification of Requirements

The development of Web applications involves different kind of stakeholders with different needs and goals. Interestingly, these stakeholders depend on each other to achieve their goals, perform several tasks or obtain some resource, e.g. *the Web administrator relies on new clients for obtaining data in order to create new accounts.* In the requirements engineering community, goal-oriented techniques, such as the i* framework [10,11], are used in order to explicitly analyze and model these relationships among multiple stakeholders (actors in the i* notation). The i* modeling framework has been proven useful for representing (i) intentions of the stakeholders, i.e. their motivations and goals, (ii) dependencies between stakeholders to achieve their goals, and (ii) the (positive or negative) effects of these goals on each other in order to be able to select alternative designs for the system, thus maximizing goals' fulfilment.

Next, we briefly describe an excerpt of the i* framework which is relevant for the present work. For a further explanation, we refer the reader to [10,11]. The i* framework consists of two models: the strategic dependency (SD) model to describe the dependency relationships (represented as ⁃D⁃) among various actors in an organizational context, and the strategic rationale (SR) model, used to describe actor interests and concerns and how they might be addressed. The SR model (represented as $\vcenter{\hbox{⌒}}$) provides a detailed way of modeling internal intentional elements and relationships of each actor (○). Intentional elements are goals (○), tasks (◇), resources (▢) and softgoals (◯). Intentional relationships are means-end links (⇾) representing alternative ways for fulfilling goals; task-decomposition links (—+) representing the necessary elements for a task to be performed; or contribution links (⟶) in order to model how an intentional element contributes to the satisfaction or fulfillment of a softgoal. A sample application of the i* modeling framework is shown in Fig. 1, which represents the SR model of our case study (see Sect. 3) for the client stakeholder. The main goal of the client is to *"buy books"*. In order to do this, the client should *"choose a book to buy"* and *"provide his/her own data"*. The task *"choose a book to buy"* should be decomposed in several subtasks: *"consult books"*, *"search for a specific book"*, *"consult recommended books"*. These tasks can have positive or negative effects on some important softgoals. For example, while *"consult books"* helps to satisfy the softgoal *"obtain more complete information"*, it hurts the softgoal *"reduce selection time"*. Moreover, *"consult books"* can be further decomposed according to the way in which the book data is consulted.

Although i* provides good mechanisms to model actors and relationships between them, it needs to be adapted to the Web engineering domain to reflect special Web requirements that are not taken into account in traditional requirement analysis approaches, thus being able to assure the traceability to Web design. Web functional requirements are related to three main features of Web applications [12] (besides of the non-functional requirements): navigational structure, user interface and personalization capability. Furthermore, the required data structures of the website should be specified as well as the required (internal)

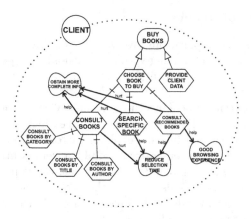

Fig. 1. Modeling the client in an SR model

functionality provided by the system. Therefore, in this paper, we use the taxonomy of Web requirements presented in [12]:

Content Requirements. With this type of requirements the content that the website presents to its users is defined. Some examples might be: "book information" or "product categories". Other kind of requirements may need to be related with one or more *content requirements*.

Service Requirements. This type of requirement refers to the internal functionality the system should provide to its users. For instance: "register a new client", "add product", etc.

Navigational Requirements. A Web system must also define the navigational paths available for the existing users. Some examples are: "consult products by category", "consult shopping cart", etc.

Layout Requirements. Requirements can also define the visual interface for the users. For instance: "present a different style for teenagers", etc.

Personalization Requirements. We also consider personalization requirements in this approach. The designer can specify the desired personalization actions to be performed in the final website (e.g. "show recommendations based on interest", "adapt font for visual impaired users", etc.)

Non-Functional Requirements. In our approach the designer can also model non-functional requirements. These kind of requirements are related to quality criteria that the intended Web system should achieve and that can be affected by other requirements. Some examples can be "good user experience", "attract more users", "efficiency", etc.

Once this classification has been adopted, the i* framework needs to be adapted. As the considered Web engineering approach (A-OOH) is UML-compliant, we have used the extension mechanisms of UML to (i) define a profile for using i* within UML; and (ii) extend this profile in order to adapt *i** to specific Web domain terminology. Therefore, new stereotypes have been added

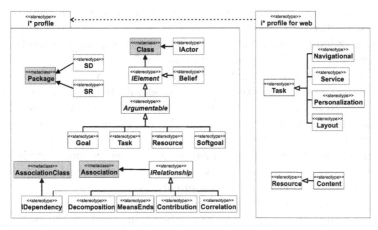

Fig. 2. Overview of the UML profiles for $i*$ modeling in the Web domain

according to the different kind of Web requirements (see Fig. 2): *Navigational, Service, Personalization* and *Layout* stereotypes extend the *Task* stereotype and *Content* stereotype extends the *Resource* stereotype. It is worth noting that non-functional requirements can be modeled by directly using the softgoal stereotype.

Finally, several guidelines should be provided in order to support the designer in defining i* models for Web domain.

1. Determine the kind of users for the intended Web and model them as actors. The website is also considered as an actor. Dependencies among these actors must be modeled in an SD model.
2. Define actors' intentions by using i* techniques in an SR model [14]: modeling goals, softgoals, tasks and resources, and the relationships between them.
3. Annotate tasks as navigational, service, personalization or layout require-ments. Also, annotate resources as content requirements. It is worth noting that goals and softgoals should not be annotated.

2.2   Traceability to Web Design

Once the requirements have been defined they can be used to derive the con-ceptual models for the website. Typically, Web design methods have three main models to define a Web application: a *Domain model*, in which the structure of the domain data is defined, a *Navigation model*, in which the structure and behavior of the navigation view over the domain data is defined, and finally a *Presentation model*, in which the layout of the generated hypermedia presenta-tion is defined. To be able to model personalization at design time two additional models are needed: a *Personalization model*, in which personalization strategies are specified, and a *User model*, in which the structure of information needed for personalization is described.

As aforementioned, the conceptual models of the A-OOH method are derived from requirements. Once these models are derived the designer has only to refine them, avoiding the task of having to create them from scratch. Due to space constraints, in this work, the focus is on the Domain and Navigation models. However, an skeleton of the Presentation, User and Personalization models could also be generated from the requirements specification.

Since the i* framework does not well support traceability to other design artifacts by its own, domain-oriented mechanisms should be considered to perform this task [15]. In our approach, the new stereotypes presented in the previous subsection allow us to prepare models for this traceability phase. We have detected several i* patterns [16] in order to define a set of QVT transformation rules to map elements from the SR metamodel to their counterparts in the A-OOH metamodel. They are applied with a certain order as shown in Fig. 3, where the transformation workflow is summarized.

After analyzing and modeling the requirements of the website according to the guidelines presented in the previous subsection, the Domain model (DM) and Navigational model (NM) are generated from the specified requirements. Before explaining each of the derivations, we briefly introduce the A-OOH DM and NM so the reader can easily follow the derivation of them.

Deriving the Domain model. The A-OOH DM is expressed as a UML-compliant class diagram. It encapsules the structure and functionality required of the relevant concepts of the application and reflects the static part of the system. The main modeling elements of a class diagram are the classes (with their attributes and operations) and their relationships.

Table 1 summarizes how DM elements are mapped from the SR model. To derive a preliminary version of the DM we take into account two types of requirements defined in Sect. 2 content and service requirements. We have detected several patterns in the i* models and we have used these patterns to define several

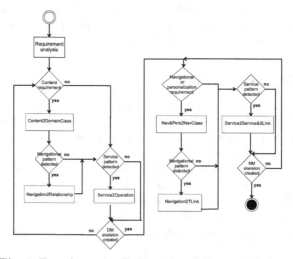

Fig. 3. Transformation Rules: Traceability to Web design

Table 1. Derivation of the Domain model

i* element	A-OOH element
Content Requirement	Class
Service Pattern	Operation
Navigational Pattern	Association between classes

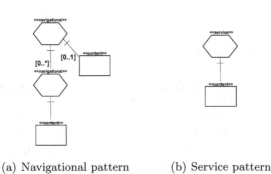

(a) Navigational pattern   (b) Service pattern

Fig. 4. Patterns

transformation rules in QVT. Specifically, three transformation rules are defined in order to derive the DM from the SR model:

- *Content2DomainClass* By using this transformation rule, each content requirement is detected and derived into one class of the DM.
- *Navigation2Relationship* Preliminar relations into classes are derived from the relations among goals/tasks with attached resources by applying this rule. To generate the associations in the DM we have to detect a *navigational pattern* in the SR model of the *website* stakeholder. In Fig. 4(a) we can see that the *navigational pattern* consists of a navigational root requirement (i.e. task) which can contain one or more navigational requirements attached. Each of the navigational requirement can have attached a resource (i.e. content requirement). The classes mapped from the resources we find in such pattern will have an association relation between them.
- *Service2Operation* This transformation rule detects a *service pattern*, i.e. a service requirement with an attached content requirement in the SR model (see Fig. 4(b)). In this case each service requirement is transformed into one operation of the corresponding class (represented by the content requirement). In this QVT rule (shown in Fig. 5), a service pattern is detected and transformed into the corresponding elements in the target model.

Once the DM skeleton has been obtained it is left to the designer to refine it, who will also have to specify the most relevant attributes of the classes, identify the cardinalities and define (if existing) the hierarchical relationships.

After the preliminar DM is created, a skeleton of the NM is also derived from the specified requirements. This diagram enriches the DM with navigation and interaction features. It is introduced next.

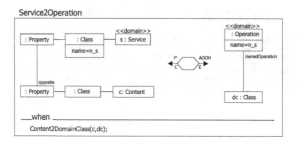

Fig. 5. QVT transformation rule for the service pattern

Deriving the Navigational model. The A-OOH Navigational model is composed of Navigational Nodes, and their relationships indicating the navigation paths the user can follow in the final website (Navigational Links).

There are three types of Nodes: (a) Navigational Classes (which are view of the domain classes), (b) Navigational Targets (which group the model elements which collaborate in the fulfilment of every navigation requirement of the user) and (c) Collections (which are (possible) hierarchical structures defined in Navigational Classes or Navigational Targets. The most common collection type is the C-collection (Classifier collection) that acts as an abstraction mechanism for the concept of menu grouping Navigational Links). Navigational Links (NL) define the navigational paths that the user can follow through the system. A-OOH defines two main types of links: Transversal links (which are defined between two navigational nodes) and Service Links(in this case navigation is performed to activate an operation which modifies the business logic and moreover implies the navigation to a node showing information when the execution of the service is finished).

To derive the NM we take into account the content requirements, service requirements and the navigation and personalization requirements. We also take into consideration the patterns detected (see Fig. 4) in order to develop several QVT transformation rules. In Tab. 2 we can see a summary showing how the different requirements are derived into elements of the NM. In the right part of Fig. 3 we can see the different transformation rules that are to be performed in order to derive a preliminar Navigation model. In this case we also define three transformation rules:

– *Nav&Pers2NavClass:* By using this rule, a "home" navigational class is added to the model, which is a C-collection representing a Menu grouping navigational links. From each navigational and personalization requirement with an associated content requirement a navigational class (NC) is derived. From the "home" NC a transversal link is added to each of the generated NCs.
– *Navigation2TLink:* This rule checks the *navigational pattern*, if it is detected, then a transversal link is added from the NC that represents the root navigational requirement to each of the NCs representing the associated navigational requirements.

Table 2. Derivation of the Navigation model

i* element	A-OOH element
Navigation and Personalization Requirements	Navigational Class
Navigation Pattern	Transversal Links
Service pattern	Operation + Service Link with a target Navigational Class

– *Service2Service&SLink:* Finally, the *service pattern* is checked by applying this transformation rule. If a service pattern is found, then an operation to the class representing the resource is added and service link is created from each of the operations, with a target navigational class which shows the termination of the service execution.

Finally, the derived NM could be refined by the designer in order to specify complementary elements for the desired navigation paths.

3   Sample Application of Our Approach

In this section, we provide an example of our approach based on a company that sells books on-line. In this case study, a company would like to manage book sales via an online bookstore, thus attracting as many clients as possible. Also there is an administrator of the Web to manage clients.

3.1   Requirements Specification

Three actors are detected that depend on each other, namely *"Client"*, *"Administrator"*, and *"Online Bookstore"*. A client depends on the online bookstore in order to *"choose a book to buy"*. The administrator needs to use the online bookstore to *"manage clients"*, while the *"client data"* is provided by the client. These dependencies are modeled by an SD model (see Fig. 6). Once the actors have been modeled in an SD model, their intentions are specified in SR models.

The SR model for the client actor was previously explained in Sect. 2.1. The SR model of the online bookstore is shown in Fig. 6. The main goal of this actor is to *"manage book sales"*. To fulfill this goal the SR model specifies that two tasks should be performed: *"books should be sold online"* and *"clients should be managed"*. We can see in the SR model that the first of the tasks affects positively the softgoal *"attract more users"*. Moreover, to complete this task four subtasks should be obtained: *"provide book info"* (which is a navigational requirement), *"provide recommended books"* (which is a personalization requirement), *"search engine for books"*, and *"provide a shopping cart"*. We can observe that some of these tasks affect positively or negatively to the non-functional requirement *"easy to maintain"*: *"Provide book information"* is easy to maintain, unlike *"provide recommended books"* and *"use a search engine for books"*. The navigational requirement *"provide book information"* can be decomposed into several navigational requirements according to the criteria used to sort the data. These data

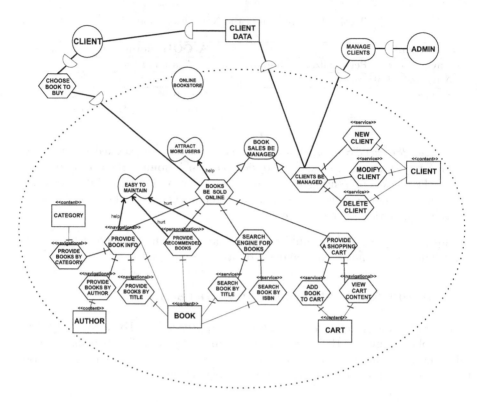

Fig. 6. Modeling the online bookstore in an SR model and the SD model

is specified by means of content requirements: *"book"*, *"author"* and *"category"*. The personalization requirement *"provide recommended books"* is related to the content requirement *"book"* because it needs the book information to be fulfilled. The task *"search engine for books"* is decomposed into a couple of service requirements: *"search book by title"* and *"search book by ISBN"*, which are also related to the content requirement *"book"*. In the same way, the task *"provide a shopping cart"* is decomposed into two service requirements: *"add book to cart"* and *"view cart content"*. These service requirements are related to the content requirement *"cart"*. Finally, the task *"clients be managed"* is decomposed into three service requirements: *"new client"*, *"modify client"* and *"delete client"*, which are related to the content requirement *"client"*.

3.2 Traceability to Domain and Navigational Models

In Fig. 7 we can see the derived Domain model from the specified requirements. As explained in Sect. 2.2 to derive the Domain model we take into account the content and service requirements as well as the existence of service or navigational patterns. In this case we can see that five domain classes are created by applying the *Content2DomainClass* transformation rule: one class is generated for each content requirement specified in the SR model. Moreover, we detect three service patterns (see Fig. 4(b)), so operations are added to the classes *client, cart* and *book* by executing the *Service2Operation* rule. Finally we detect that the *Provide Book Info* requirement follows the navigational pattern as we can see in Fig. 4(a). In this case the rule *Navigation2Relationship* adds associations among all the resources found in this pattern. The generated Domain model is shown in Fig. 7.

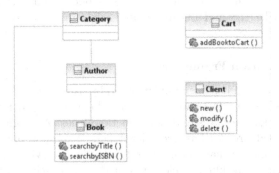

Fig. 7. Traceability to Domain model

In the case of the Navigational model, the rule *Nav&Pers2NavClass* is performed adding a home page with a collection of links (i.e. menu). Afterwards, one NC is created for each navigational and personalization requirement with an attached resource, in this case we have five NC created from navigational and

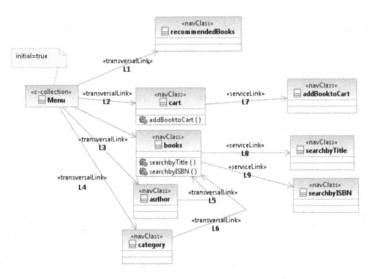

Fig. 8. Traceability to Navigation model

personalization requirements. From the menu, a transversal link to each of the created NCs is added (L1 to L4).

The next step is checking the navigational and service patterns. In this example, we find a navigational pattern (see Fig.4(a)) applying the *Navigation2TLink* it implies creating a transversal link from the NCs created by the associated navigational requirements, to the NC that is represented by the root navigational requirement. In this case two links are added: L5 and L6.

Finally, as we are referring to the website stakeholder, we find three service patterns from which the operations of the NCs books and cart are added and the service links L7, L8 and L9 are created with an associated target NC by applying the *Service2Service&SLink*.

3.3   Implementation Framework

The presented approach has been implemented by using the *Eclipse development platform* [17]. *Eclipse* is a framework which can be extended by means of plugins in order to add more features and new functionalities. A plugin that supports both of the defined profiles has been developed. This new plugin implements several graphical and textual editors (Fig. 9 shows an overview of the tool). The palette for drawing the different elements of i* can be seen on the right-hand side of this figure. A sample SR model is shown in the center of the figure. Traceability rules are also being defined and tested in our prototype.

4   Related Work

Few approaches have focused on defining an explicit requirement analysis stage to model the user. We can stress the following:

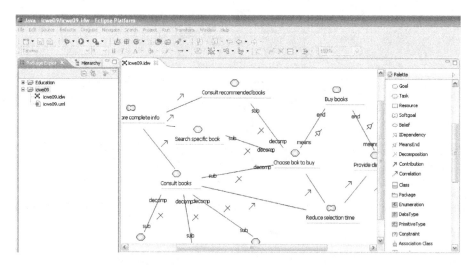

Fig. 9. Screenshot of our prototype

NDT[12] considers a complete taxonomy for the specification of Web requirements. It allows to specify requirements by means of use cases diagrams and templates. It uses a different template for each requirement type they consider, so requirements and objectives are described in a structured way. UWE [7] also describes a taxonomy for requirements related to the Web. It proposes extended use cases, scenarios and glosaries for specifying requirements. WebML [5] also proposes the use of use case diagrams combined with activity diagrams and semi-structured textual description. WSDM [3] is an audience driven approach in which they do a classification of the requirements and the audience. These classes are represented with a diagram in which they are related. Then they are modeled into detail in a Task model using concurrent task trees. OOHDM [18] capture the requirements in use case diagrams. They propose the use of UIDs (user interaction diagrams) for defining the requirements deriving them from the Use cases. OOWS [19] focuses on the specification of tasks. They extend the activity diagrams with the concept of interaction point to describe the interaction of the user with the system.

Furthermore traceability from the requirements to conceptual models is an important issue to bridge the gap between requirements and Web design. There are two approaches to the author's knowledge that support this in some way: OOWS provides automatic generation of (only) navigation models from the tasks description by means of graph transformation rules. NDT [20] defines a requirement metamodel and allows to transform the requirements model into a content and a navigational model by means of QVT rules. Our approach of traceability resembles NDT since we have also adopted QVT in order to obtain design artifacts from Web requirements, but we have kept the benefits of the i* framework by means of the defined profiles and patterns.

However, some of these approaches present the following drawbacks: (i) they do not take into consideration a complete taxonomy of requirements which is suitable in Web applications, or (ii) they consider non-functional requirements in an isolated manner, or (iii) they mainly focus on design aspects of the intended Web system without paying enough attention to Web requirements. Furthermore, none of them perform the analysis of the users' needs. Requirements are figured out by the designer, it may be needed to re-design the website after doing usability and satisfaction tests to the users. Modeling users allow us ensuring that the Web application satisfies real user needs and goals and the user is not overwhelmed with functionalities that he does not need or expect and he does not miss functionalities that were not implemented.

To the best of our knowledge, the only approaches that use goal oriented techniques have been presented in [21,22]. They propose a complete taxonomy of requirements for the Web and use the i* notation to represent them. Unfortunately, they do not benefit from every i* feature, since they only use a metamodel that has some of its concepts, e.g. means-end, decomposition or contribution links from i* are not specified in the approach presented in [21].

5   Conclusions and Future Work

Websites require special techniques for requirement analysis in order to reflect, from early stages of the development, specific needs, goals, interests and preferences of each user or user type. However, Web engineering field does not pay the attention needed to this issue. We have presented a goal oriented approach on the basis of the i* framework to specify Web requirements. It allows the designer to make decisions from the very beginning of the development phase that would affect the structure of the envision website in order to satisfy users.

Moreover, the following guidelines are provided to the designer to properly define i* models for the Web domain: (i) discovering the intentional actors (i.e. Web users and the Web application) and their dependencies in an SD model, (ii) discovering their intentional elements, thus defining SR models for each one, and (iii) annotating intentional elements with Web concepts. We can use this model to check the current website or to make the appropriate decision to build a new one. Moreover, we have defined a set of transformation rules in order to assure the traceability from requirements to the conceptual models. Although this approach is presented in the context of the A-OOH modeling method it can be applied to any Web modeling approach.

Our short-term future work consists of completing the transformation rules in order to obtain the rest of the A-OOH models (i.e. presentation and personalization models).

Acknowledgements. This work has been partially supported by the ESPIA project (TIN2007-67078) from the Spanish Ministry of Education and Science, and by the QUASIMODO project (PAC08-0157-0668) from the Castilla-La Mancha Ministry of Education and Science (Spain). Jose-Norberto Mazón is funded by the Spanish Ministry of Education and Science under a FPU grant (AP2005-1360).

References

1. Casteleyn, S., Woensel, W.V., Houben, G.J.: A semantics-based aspect-oriented approach to adaptation in web engineering. In: Hypertext, pp. 189–198 (2007)
2. Cachero, C., Gómez, J.: Advanced conceptual modeling of web applications: Embedding operation interfaces in navigation design. In: JISBD, pp. 235–248 (2002)
3. Casteleyn, S., Garrigós, I., Troyer, O.D.: Automatic runtime validation and correction of the navigational design of web sites. In: Zhang, Y., Tanaka, K., Yu, J.X., Wang, S., Li, M. (eds.) APWeb 2005. LNCS, vol. 3399, pp. 453–463. Springer, Heidelberg (2005)
4. Koch, N.: Software engineering for adaptive hypermedia systems: Reference model, modeling techniques and development process. Softwaretechnik- Trends 21(1) (2001)
5. Ceri, S., Manolescu, I.: Constructing and integrating data-centric web applications: Methods, tools, and techniques. In: VLDB, p. 1151 (2003)
6. Rossi, G., Schwabe, D., Guimarães, R.: Designing personalized web applications. In: WWW, pp. 275–284 (2001)

7. Koch, N.: Reference model, modeling techniques and development process software engineering for adaptive hypermedia systems. KI 16(3), 40–41 (2002)

8. Garrigós, I.: A-OOH: Extending Web Application Design with Dynamic Personalization. Ph.D thesis, University of Alicante, Spain (2008)

9. Daniel, F., Matera, M., Morandi, A., Mortari, M., Pozzi, G.: Active rules for runtime adaptivity management. In: AEWSE (2007)

10. Yu, E.: Modelling Strategic Relationships for Process Reenginering. Ph.D thesis, University of Toronto, Canada (1995)

11. Yu, E.: Towards modeling and reasoning support for early-phase requirements engineering. In: RE, pp. 226–235 (1997)

12. Cuaresma, M.J.E., Koch, N.: Requirements engineering for web applications - a comparative study. J. Web Eng. 2(3), 193–212 (2004)

13. QVT Language: http://www.omg.org/cgi-bin/doc?ptc/2005-11-01

14. i* wiki: http://istar.rwth-aachen.de

15. Estrada, H., Rebollar, A.M., Pastor, O., Mylopoulos, J.: An empirical evaluation of the * framework in a model-based software generation environment. In: Dubois, E., Pohl, K. (eds.) CAiSE 2006. LNCS, vol. 4001, pp. 513–527. Springer, Heidelberg (2006)

16. Strohmaier, M., Horkoff, J., Yu, E.S.K., Aranda, J., Easterbrook, S.M.: Can patterns improve i* modeling? two exploratory studies. In: Paech, B., Rolland, C. (eds.) REFSQ 2008. LNCS, vol. 5025, pp. 153–167. Springer, Heidelberg (2008)

17. Eclipse: http://www.eclipse.org/

18. Schwabe, D., Rossi, G.: An object oriented approach to web-based applications design. TAPOS 4(4), 207–225 (1998)

19. Valderas, P., Pelechano, V., Pastor, O.: A transformational approach to produce web application prototypes from a web requirements model. Int. J. Web Eng. Technol. 3(1), 4–42 (2007)

20. Koch, N., Zhang, G., Cuaresma, M.J.E.: Model transformations from requirements to web system design. In: ICWE, pp. 281–288 (2006)

21. Bolchini, D., Paolini, P.: Goal-driven requirements analysis for hypermedia-intensive web applications. Requir. Eng. 9(2), 85–103 (2004)

22. Molina, F.M., Pardillo, J., Álvarez, J.A.T.: Modelling web-based systems requirements using wrm. In: WISE Workshops, pp. 122–131 (2008)

Automating Navigation Sequences in AJAX Websites

Paula Montoto, Alberto Pan, Juan Raposo, Fernando Bellas, and Javier López

Department of Information and Communication Technologies, University of A Coruña
Facultad de Informática, Campus de Elviña s/n 15071 A Coruña, Spain
{pmontoto,apan,jrs,fbellas,jmato}@udc.es

Abstract. Web automation applications are widely used for different purposes such as B2B integration, automated testing of web applications or technology and business watch. One crucial part in web automation applications is to allow easily generating and reproducing navigation sequences. Previous proposals in the literature assumed a navigation model today turned obsolete by the new breed of AJAX-based websites. Although some open-source and commercial tools have also addressed the problem, they show significant limitations either in usability or their ability to deal with complex websites. In this paper, we propose a set of new techniques to deal with this problem. Our main contributions are a new method for recording navigation sequences supporting a wider range of events, and a novel method to detect when the effects caused by a user action have finished. We have evaluated our approach with more than 100 web applications, obtaining very good results.

Keywords: Web automation, web integration, web wrappers.

1 Introduction

Web automation applications are widely used for different purposes such as B2B integration, web mashups, automated testing of web applications or business watch. One crucial part in web automation applications is to allow easily generating and reproducing navigation sequences. We can distinguish two stages in this process:

- Generation phase. In this stage, the user specifies the navigation sequence to reproduce. The most common approach, cf. [1,9,11], is using the 'recorder' metaphor: the user performs one example of the navigation sequence using a modified web browser, and the tool generates a specification which can be run by the execution component. The generation environment also allows specifying the input parameters to the navigation sequence.
- Execution phase. In this stage, the sequence generated in the previous stage and the input parameters are provided as input to an automatic navigation component which is able to reproduce the sequence. The automatic navigation component can be developed by using the APIs of popular browsers (e.g. [9]). Other systems like [1] use simplified custom browsers specially built for the task.

Most existing previous proposals for automatic web navigation systems (e.g. [1,9,11]) assume a navigation model which is now obsolete to a big extent: on one

M. Gaedke, M. Grossniklaus, and O. Díaz (Eds.): ICWE 2009, LNCS 5648, pp. 166–180, 2009.
© Springer-Verlag Berlin Heidelberg 2009

hand, the user actions that could be recorded were very restrictive (mainly clicking on elements and filling in form fields) and, on the other hand, it was assumed that almost every user action caused a request to the server for a new page.

Nevertheless, this is not enough for dealing with modern AJAX-based websites, which try to replicate the behavior of desktop applications. These sites can respond to a much wider set of user actions (mouse over, keyboard strokes, drag and drop...) and they can respond to those actions executing scripting code that manipulates the page at will (for instance, by creating new graphical interface elements on the fly). In addition, AJAX technology allows requesting information from the server and repainting only certain parts of the page in response.

In this paper, we propose a set of new techniques to build an automatic web navigation system able to deal with all this complexity. In the generation phase, we also use the 'recorder' metaphor, but substantially modified to support recording a wider range of events; we also present new methods for identifying the elements participating in a navigation sequence in a change-resilient manner.

In the execution phase, we use the APIs of commercial web browsers to implement the automatic web navigation components (the techniques proposed for the recording phase have been implemented using Microsoft Internet Explorer (MSIE) and the execution phase has been implemented using both MSIE and Firefox); we take this option because the approach of creating a custom browser supporting technologies such as scripting code and AJAX requests is effort-intensive and very vulnerable to small implementation differences that can make a web page to behave differently when accessed with the custom browser. In the execution phase, we also introduce a method to detect when the effects caused by a user action have finished. This is needed because one navigation step may require the effects of the previous ones to be completed before being executed.

2 Models

In this section we describe the models we use to characterize the components used for automated browsing. The main model we rely on is DOM Level 3 Events Model [3]. This model describes how browsers respond to user-performed actions on an HTML page currently loaded in the browser. Although the degree of implementation of this standard by real browsers is variable, the key assumptions our techniques rely on are verified in the most popular browsers (MSIE and Firefox). Therefore, section 2.1 summarizes the main characteristics of this standard that are relevant to our objectives. Secondly, section 2.2 states additional assumptions about the execution model employed by the browser in what regards to scripting code, including the kind of asynchronous calls required by AJAX requests. These assumptions are also verified by current major browsers.

2.1 DOM Level 3 Events Model

In the DOM Level 3 Events Model, a page is modelled as a tree. Each node in the tree can receive events produced (directly or indirectly) by the user actions. Event types exist for actions such as clicking on an element (*click*), moving the mouse cursor over it (*mouseover*) or specifying the value of a form field (*change*), to name a few. Each node can register a set of event listeners for each event type. A listener executes arbitrary code (typically written in a script language such as Javascript). Listeners have the entire page tree accessible and can perform actions such as modifying existing nodes, removing them, creating new ones or even launching new events.

The event processing lifecycle can be summarized as follows: The event is dispatched following a path from the root of the tree to the target node. It can be handled locally at the target node or at any target's ancestors in the tree. The event dispatching (also called event propagation) occurs in three phases and in the following order: capture (the event is dispatched to the target's ancestors from the root of the tree to the direct parent of the target node), target (the event is dispatched to the target node) and bubbling (the event is dispatched to the target's ancestors from the direct parent of the target node to the root of the tree). The listeners in a node can register to either the capture or the bubbling phase. In the target phase, the events registered for the capture phase are executed before the events executed for the bubbling phase. This lifecycle is a compromise between the approaches historically used in major browsers (Microsoft IE using bubbling and Netscape using capture).

The order of execution between the listeners associated to an event type in the same node is registration order. The event model is re-entrant, meaning that the execution of a listener can generate new events. Those new events will be processed synchronously; that is, if l_i, l_{i+1} are two listeners registered to a certain event type in a given node in consecutive order, then all events caused by l_i execution will be processed (and, therefore, their associated listeners executed) before l_{i+1} is executed.

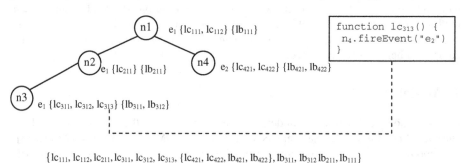

$\{lc_{111}, lc_{112}, lc_{211}, lc_{311}, lc_{312}, lc_{313}, \{lc_{421}, lc_{422}, lb_{421}, lb_{422}\}, lb_{311}, lb_{312}\, lb_{211}, lb_{111}\}$

Fig. 1. Listeners Execution Example

Example 1: Fig. 1 shows an excerpt of a DOM tree and the listeners registered to the event types e_1 and e_2. The listeners in each node for each event type are listed in registration order (the listeners registered for the capture phase appear as l_{cxyz} and the ones registered for the bubbling phase appear as l_{bxyz}). The figure also shows what listeners and in which order would be executed in the case of receiving the event-type e_1 over the node n_3, assuming that the listener on the capture phase l_{c313} causes the event-type e_2 to be executed over the node n_4.

DOM Level 3 Events Model provides an API for programmatically registering new listeners and generating new events. Nevertheless, it does not provide an introspection API to obtain the listeners registered for an event type in a certain node. As we will see in section 3.1, this will have implications in the recording process in our system.

2.2 Asynchronous Functions and Scripts Execution Model

In this section we describe the model we use to represent how the browser executes the scripting code of the listeners associated to an event. This model is verified by the major commercial browsers.

The script engine used by the browser executes scripts sequentially in single-thread mode. The scripts are added to an execution queue in invocation order; the script engine works by sequentially executing the scripts in the order specified by the queue.

When an event is triggered, the browser obtains the listeners that will be triggered by the event and invokes its associated scripts, causing them to be added to the execution queue. Once all the scripts have been added, execution begins and the listeners are executed sequentially.

The complexity of this model is slightly increased because the code of a listener can execute asynchronous functions. An asynchronous function executes an action in a non-blocking form. The action will run on the background and a callback function provided as parameter in the asynchronous function invocation will be called when the action finishes.

The most popular type of asynchronous call is the so-called AJAX requests. An AJAX request is implemented by a script function (i.e. in Javascript, a commonly used one is *XMLHTTPRequest*) that launches an HTTP request in the background. When the server response is received, the callback function is invoked to process it.

Other popular asynchronous calls establish timers and the callback function is invoked when the timer expires. In this group, we find the Javascript functions *setTimeout(ms)* (executes the callback function after ms milliseconds) and *setInterval(ms)* (executes the callback function every ms milliseconds). Both have associated cancellation functions: *clearTimeout(id)* and *clearInterval(id)*.

It is important to notice that, from the described execution model, it is inferred the following property:

Property 1: The callback functions of the asynchronous calls launched by the listeners of an event will never be executed until all other scripts associated to that event have finished.

The explanation for this property is direct from the above points: all the listeners associated to an event are added to the execution queue first, and those listeners are the ones invoking the asynchronous functions; therefore, the callback functions will always be positioned after them in the execution queue even if the background action executed by the asynchronous call is instantaneous.

3 Description of the Solution

In this section we describe the proposed techniques for automated web navigation. First, we deal with the generation phase: section 3.1 describes the process used to record a navigation sequence in our approach. Section 3.2 deals with the problem of identifying the target DOM node of a user action: this problem consists in generating a path to the node that can be used later at the execution phase to locate it in the page and section 3.3 deals with the execution phase.

3.1 Recording User Events

The generation phase has the goal of recording a sequence of actions performed by the user to allow reproducing them later during the execution phase.

A user action (e.g. a click on a button) causes a list of events to be issued to the target node, triggering the invocation of the listeners registered for them in the node and its ancestors, according to the execution model described in the previous section. Notice that each user action usually generates several events. For instance, the events generated when the user clicks on a button include, among others, the mouseover event besides of the click event, since in order to click on an element it is previously required to place the mouse over it. Recording a user action consists in detecting which events are issued, and in locating the target node of those events.

In previous proposals, cf. [1,6,9], the user can record a navigation sequence by performing it in the browser in the same way as any other navigation. The method used to detect the user actions in these systems is typically as follows: the recording tool registers its own listeners for the most common events involved in navigations (mainly clicks and the events involved in filling in form fields) in anchors and form-related tags. This way, when a user action produces one of the monitored event-types e on one of the monitored nodes n, the listener for e in n is invoked, implicitly identifying the information to be recorded.

Nevertheless, the modern AJAX-based websites can respond to a much wider set of user actions (e.g. placing the mouse over an element, producing keyboard strokes, drag and drop...); in addition, virtually any HTML element, and not only traditional navigation-related elements, can respond to user actions: tables, images, texts, etc.

Extending the mentioned recording process to support AJAX-based sites would involve registering listeners for every event in every node of the DOM tree (or, alternatively, registering listeners for every event in the root node of the page, since the events execution model ensures that all events reach to the root). Registering listeners for every event has the important drawback that it would "flood" the system by recording unnecessary events (e.g. simply moving the mouse over the page would generate hundreds of *mouseover* and *mouseout* events); recall that, as mentioned in section 2, it is not possible to introspect what events a node has registered a listener for; therefore, it is not possible to use the approach of registering a listener for an event-type e only in the nodes that already have other listeners for e.

Therefore, we need a new method for recording user actions. Our proposal is letting the user explicitly specify each action by placing the mouse over the target element, clicking on the right mouse button, and choosing the desired action in the contextual menu (see Fig. 2). If the desired action involves providing input data into an input element or a selection list, then a pop-up window opens allowing the user to specify the desired value (see Fig. 2). Although in this method the navigation recording process is different from normal browsing, it is still fast and intuitive: the user simply changes the left mouse button for the right mouse button and fills in the value of certain form fields in a pop-up window instead of in the field itself.

This way, we do not need to add any new listener: we know the target element by capturing the coordinates where the mouse pointer is placed when the action is specified, and using browser APIs to know what node the coordinates correspond to. The events recorded are implicitly identified by the selected action.

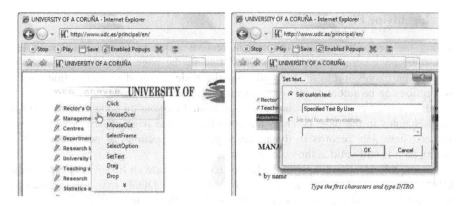

Fig. 2. Recording Method

Our prototype implementation includes actions such as *click*, *mouseover*, *mouseout*, *selectOption* (selecting values on a selection list), *setText* (providing input data into an element), *drag* and *drop*. Since each user action actually generates more than one event, each action has associated the list of events that it causes: for instance, the *click* action includes, among others, the events *mouseover*, *click* and *mouseout*; the *setText* action includes events such as *keydown* and *keyup* (issued every time a key is pressed) and *change* (issued when an element content changes).

This new method has a problem we need to deal with. By the mere process of explicitly specifying an action, the user may produce changes in the page before we want them to take place. For instance, suppose the user wishes to specify an action on a node that has a listener registered for the *mouseover* event; the listener opens a pop-up menu when the mouse is placed over the element. Since the process of specifying the action involves placing the mouse over the element; the page will change its state (i.e. the pop-up menu will open) before the user can specify the desired action. This is a problem because the process of generating a path to identify the target element at the execution phase (described in detail in section 3.2) cannot start until the action has been specified. But, since the DOM tree of the page has already changed, the process would be considering the DOM tree after the effects of the action have taken place (the element may even no longer exist because the listeners could remove it!).

We solve this problem by deactivating the reception of user events in the page during the recording process. This way, we can be sure that no event alters the state of the page before the action is specified. Once the user has specified an action, we use the browser APIs to generate on the target element the list of events associated to the action; this way, the effects of the specified action take place in the same way as if the user would have performed the action, and the recording process can continue.

Another important issue we need to deal with is ensuring that a user does not specify a new action until the effects caused by the previous one have completely finished. This is needed to ensure that the process for generating a path to identify at the execution phase the target element of the new action has into account all the changes in the DOM tree that the previous action provokes. Detecting the end of the effects of an action is far from a trivial problem; since it is one of the crucial issues at the execution phase, we will describe how to do it in section 3.3.

3.2 Identifying Elements

During the generation phase, the system records a list of user actions, each one performed on a certain node of the DOM tree of the page. Therefore, we need to generate an expression to uniquely identify the node involved in each action, so the user action can be automatically reproduced at the execution phase.

An important consideration is that the generated expression should be resilient to small changes in the page (such as the apparition in the page of new advertisement banners, new data records in dynamically generated sections or new options in a menu), so it is still valid at the execution stage.

To uniquely identify a node in the DOM tree we can use an XPath [15] expression. XPath expressions allow identifying a node in a DOM tree by considering information such as the text associated to the node, the value of its attributes and its ancestors. For our purposes, we need to ensure that the generated expression on one hand identifies a single node, and on the other hand it is not too specific to be affected by the formerly mentioned small changes. Therefore, our proposal tries to generate the less specific XPath expression possible that still uniquely identifies the target node. The algorithm we use for this purpose is presented in section 3.2.1.

In addition, the generated expressions should not be sensible to the use of session identifiers, to ensure that they will still work in any later session. Section 3.2.2 presents a mechanism to remove session identifiers from the generated expressions.

3.2.1 Algorithm for Identifying Target Elements

This section describes the algorithm for generating the expression to identify the target element of a user action.

As it has already been said, the algorithm tries to generate the less specific XPath expression possible that still uniquely identifies the target node. More precisely, the algorithm first tries to identify the element according to its associated text (if it is a leaf node) and the value of its attributes. If this is not enough to uniquely identify the node, its ancestors (and the value of their attributes) will be recursively used. The algorithm to generate the expression for a node n consists of the following steps:

1. Initialize $X_{(n)}$ (the variable that will contain the generated expression) to the empty string. Initialize the variable n_i to the target node n.

2. Let m be the number of attributes of n_i, T_{ni} be the tag associated to n_i and t_{ni} be its associated text. Try to find a minimum set of r attributes $\{a_{ni1},...,a_{nir}\}_{r<=m}$, of $_{ni}$ such that the following expression ('+' represents the concatenation of two strings):

    "//" + T_{ni} [@$a_{ni1}=v_{ni1}$ and... and @$a_{nir}=v_{nir}$ and @text()=t_{ni}] + $X_{(n)}$+"/"

    uniquely identify n. (NOTE:The fragment and $text()=t_{ni}$ of the expression would only be added if n_i is a leaf node, since only leaf nodes have associated text).

3. If the set is found then

    3.1) return the expression from step 1.

    else

    3.2) Let $\{a_{ni1},...,a_{nim}\}$ be the set of all attributes of n_i. Set $X_{(n)} = $ "/"+T_{ni} [@$a_{ni1}=v_{ni1}$ and... and @$a_{nim}=v_{nim}$ and @text()=t_{ni}] + $X_{(n)}$; that is, we add conditions by all the attributes of n_i to the expression.

4.   If n_i is not the root of the DOM tree then

    4.1)   Set $n_i=parent(n_i)$ and go to step 1

    else

    4.2)   Obtain the relative position j of n in the page with respect to all the nodes verifying the current expression $X_{(n)}$. Return "/" + $X_{(n)}$ + [j] + "/".

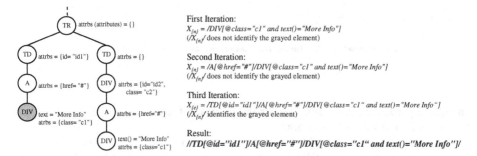

Fig. 3. Algorithm for Identifying Target Elements Example

Fig. 3 shows an example sub-tree and the $X_{(n)}$ value in each iteration of the algorithm to generate the XPath expression to identify the grayed *DIV* node.

Now, we provide further detail about some of the steps. The step 1 of the algorithm tries to identify the minimum set of attributes of the currently considered node n_i, that allow completing the identification of n. To do this, we add attributes one by one until either n is uniquely identified or all the attributes of n_i, have been added. To decide the order in which we add the attributes, we have defined an order for the attributes of each HTML tag based on its estimated selectivity (that is, how much they contribute to narrow the selection). For instance, we consider the *id* and *name* attributes highly selective for all HTML tags and the *href* attribute highly selective for the *A* tag, while we consider the class attribute as of low selectivity.

Step 3.2 considers the case when the algorithm reaches the root, and the generated expression still does not uniquely identify n. In that case, the algorithm adds to the XPath expression the relative position in the page of n with respect to the rest of elements identified by the expression.

3.2.2   Removing Session IDs
Many websites use session identifiers in URL attributes to track user sessions. In these sites, the values of attributes containing URLs may vary in each session. Since our method to identify target elements at the execution phase relies on attribute values, this causes a problem for our approach.

Our prototype implementation recognizes the main standard formats for including session identifiers in URLs. Unfortunately, many websites do not use any standard, but include the session identifier using arbitrary query parameters.

Therefore, we propose an algorithm to generalize the value of attributes containing URLs. The algorithm is based on two observations: 1) a query parameter acting as session identifier must take the same value in all the URLs of the page in which it appears; 2) if a query parameter takes the same value in all URLs with the same host

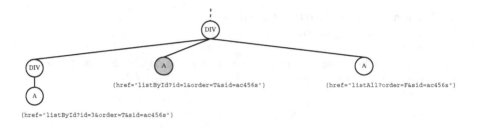

//A[matches(@href,"listById?id=1&order=[^&=]+&sid=[^&=]+")]/

Fig. 4. Removing Session IDs Example

and query parts, then it is irrelevant for the purpose of identifying an element in the DOM tree by the value of its attributes.

The basic idea of the algorithm derives directly from the above observations: find all the query parameters that take the same value in all the URLs in which they appear and ignore their values for identification purposes. Although some of the identified query parameters may not be session identifiers, according to observation 2 it is safe to ignore their values anyway.

Fig 4 shows a simple example of the algorithm where *n* is the grayed node in the figure. The query parameters named *order* and *sid* take the same value in all the URLs with the same path (in the example the page does not contain other URLs with the same path). Therefore, they are considered irrelevant for node identification purposes. (NOTE: *matches()* is XPath function for applying regular expressions).

3.3 Execution Phase

The generation phase generates a program capturing the navigation sequence recorded by the user. The execution phase runs the program in the automatic navigation component.

A first consideration is that we opt to use the APIs of commercial web browsers to implement the automatic web navigation components instead of building a simplified custom-browser. The main reason for taking this option is that web 2.0 sites make an intensive use of scripting languages and support a complex event model. Creating a custom browser supporting those technologies in the same way as commercial browsers is very effort-intensive and, in addition, is extremely vulnerable to small implementation differences that can make a web page to behave differently when accessed with the custom browser than when accessed with a "real" browser. Our techniques for the execution phase have been implemented in both MSIE and Firefox.

To reproduce an action in the navigation sequence, there are three steps involved:

1. Locating the target node in the DOM tree of the page.
2. Generating the recorded event (or list of events) on the identified node.
3. Wait for the effects of the events to finish. This is needed because the following action can need the effects of the previous ones to be completed (e.g. the action *n+1* can generate an event on a node created in the action *n*).

The implementation of 1) and 2) is quite straightforward using browser APIs and given the output of the recording process. Step 1) uses the XPath expression produced by the process described in section 3.2, and step 2) uses the events recorded in the process described in section 3.1.

In turn, step 3) is difficult because browser APIs do not provide any way of detecting when the effects on the page of issuing a particular event have finished. These effects can include dynamically creating or removing elements in the DOM tree, maybe also having into account the response to one or several AJAX requests to the server. Previous works have addressed this problem by establishing a timer after the execution of an event before continuing execution. This solution has the usual drawbacks associated to a fixed timeout in a network environment: if the specified timeout is short, then when the response to an asynchronous AJAX request is slower than usual (or even if the machine is very heavily loaded), the sequence may fail. If, in turn, we use a higher timeout valid even in those circumstances, then we are introducing an unnecessary delay when the server is responding normally.

The remaining of this section explains the method we propose to detect when the effects caused directly or indirectly by a certain event have finished. This way, the system waits the exact time required. The correctness of the method derives from the assumptions stated in section 2, which are verified by the major commercial browsers.

The method we use to detect when the effects of an event-type e generated on a node n have finished consists of the following steps:

1. We register a new listener l to capture the event e in n. The code of the listener l invokes an asynchronous function specifying the callback function cf. What asynchronous function is actually invoked in l is mainly irrelevant; for instance, in Javascript, we can simply invoke $setTimeout(cf,0)$. Notice that as consequence of property 1 in section 2, it is guaranteed that cf will be executed after all the listeners triggered by the execution of e have finished. Therefore, if the listeners had not made any other asynchronous call, then the control arriving to cf would indicate that the effects of e had finished and the navigation sequence execution could continue. Nevertheless, since the listeners can actually execute other asynchronous calls, this is not enough.
2. To be notified of every asynchronous call executed by the listeners triggered by e, we redefine those asynchronous functions providing our own implementation of them (for instance, in Javascript we need to redefine $setTimeout$, $setInterval$ and the functions used to execute AJAX requests such as $XMLHTTPRequest$). The template of our implementation of each function is shown in Fig 5. The function maintains a counter that is increased every time the function is invoked (the counter is maintained as a global variable initialized to zero for every emitted event). After increasing the counter, the function calls the former standard implementation of the asynchronous function provided by the browser but substituting the received callback function by a modified one (the new_cf function created in Figure 5). This new callback function invokes the original callback function and then decreases the counter. This way, the counter always takes the value of the number of currently active calls.
3. When the callback function cf from step 1 is executed, it polls the counters associated to the asynchronous functions. When they are all 0, we know the asynchronous calls have finished and execution can proceed.

4. There may be some cases where the effects of *e* actually never finish. This is for instance the case when the *setInterval* function is used. This function executes the callback function at specified time intervals and, therefore, its effects last indefinitely unless the function *clearInterval* is used. In the generation-phase, if the *setInterval* calls are not cleared after a certain timeout, the system notifies it to the user so she/he can specify the desired action, which can be to wait a fixed time or wait for a certain number of intervals to complete.

```
old_asyncFunction = standardAsyncFunction;
new_asyncFunction = new function(param1,param2,…,paramn,cf) {
    counter++;       //counter is a global variable
    new_cf = new function() {
      result = cf();
      counter--;
      if (counter==0) {
          notifyEndAsyncFunctions();
      }
      return result;
    };
    old_asyncFunction(param1,param2,…,paramn,new_cf);
};
standardAsyncFunction = new_asyncFunction;
```

Fig. 5. Asynchronous Function Redefinition

In addition of the possible effects of an event in the current page, the event can also make the browser (or a frame inside the page) navigate to a new page. When the new page/frame is loaded (this can be detected using browser APIs), the load event is generated; this event has as target the body element of the page. Before continuing the execution of the navigation sequence, we need to wait until the end of the effects of the load event have finished, using the same technique used for the rest of events.

4 Evaluation

To evaluate the validity of our approach, we tested the implementation of our techniques with a wide range of AJAX-based web applications. We performed two kinds of experiments:

1. We selected a set of 75 real websites making extensive use of scripting code and AJAX technology. We used the prototype to record and reproduce one navigation sequence on each site. The navigation sequences automated the main purpose of the site. For instance, in electronic shops we automated the process of searching products; in webmail sites we automated the process required to access e-mails.
2. Some of the main APIs for generating AJAX-based applications such as Yahoo! User Interface Library (YUI) [16] and Google Web Toolkit (GWT) [4] include a set of example websites. At the time of testing, GWT included 5 web applications and YUI included 300 examples. We recorded and executed 12 navigation sequences in the web applications from GWT ensuring that every interface element from the applications was used at least once. In the case of YUI, we recorded 40 sequences in selected examples (choosing the more complex examples). This second group of tests is useful because many real websites use those toolkits.

Table 1. Experimental Results

Website	Played	Website	Played	Website	Played
www.a9.com/java	✓	www.fidelityasap.com	✓	www.optize.es	✓
www.abebooks.com	✓	www.fnac.es	✓	www.paginasamarillas.es	✓
www.accorhotels.com	✓	www.gmail.com	✓	www.penguin.co.uk	✓
www.addall.com	✓	www.gongdiscos.com	✓	people.yahoo.com	✓
www.voyages-sncf.com	✓	www.hotelopia.es	✓	code.jalenack.com/periodic	✓
www.alitalia.com/ES_ES/	✓	www.hotelsearch.com	✓	www.pixmania.com	✓
www.allbooks4less.com	✓	www.iberia.com	✓	www.planethome.de	✓
www.amadeus.net	✓	www.iit.edu	✓	www.priceline.com	✓
www.amazon.com	✓	www.imdb.com/search	✓	www.renault.es	✓
store.apple.com	✓	www.infojobs.net	✓	www.renfe.es	✓
www.atrapalo.com	✓	www.jet4you.com	✓	www.reuters.com	✓
autos.aol.com	✓	www.laborman.es	✓	www.rumbo.es	✓
www.balumba.es	✓	www.landrover.com	✓	www.shop-com.co.uk	✓
www.barnesandnoble.com	✓	www.es.lastminute.com	✓	www.sparkassen-immo.de	✓
www.bookdepository.co.uk	✓	www.marsans.es	✓	www.sterling.dk	✓
www.booking.com	✓	www.meridiana.it	✓	www.ticketmaster.com	✓
www.carbroker.com.au	✓	www.msnbc.msn.com	✓	tudulist.com	✓
www.casadellibro.com	✓	www.muchoviaje.com	✓	www.tuifly.com/es	✓
www.cervantesvirtual.com	✓	www.musicstore.com	✓	es.venere.com	✓
www.cia.gov	✓	www.myair.com	✓	www.viajar.com	✓
controlp.com	✓	www.mymusic.com	✓	www.vuelosbaratos.es	✓
www.digitalcamerareview.com	✓	www.es.octopustravel.com	✓	www.webpagesthatsuck.com	✓
www.ebay.es	✓	www.ofertondelibros.com	✓	news.search.yahoo.com/news/advanced	✓
www.edreams.es	✓	www.okipi.com	✓	news.yahoo.com	✗
www.elcorteingles.es	✓	vols.opodo.fr	✓	mail.yahoo.com	✓

The techniques proposed for the recording phase have been implemented using MSIE and the execution phase has been implemented using both MSIE and Firefox. In each group of experiments, we recorded the navigation sequences on MSIE and executed them using both MSIE and Firefox. The execution on MSIE allows us to measure the effectiveness of our techniques in both the recording and execution phases. We execute the sequences in Firefox to check that the algorithm presented in section 3.3 is valid in both browsers. Since MSIE and Firefox usually build different DOM trees for the same pages, in some cases the XPath expression generated by the recording in MSIE were manually modified to fit the DOM tree in Firefox. Notice that this is not a limitation of our approach: it only highlights the issue that the browser used for the recording and execution phase should be the same.

The results of the evaluation were encouraging (see Table 1). In the first set of experiments (real websites), 74 of 75 sequences were recorded and executed fine.

In the case of *news.yahoo.com*, the XPath expression generated to identify an element used an URL with a query parameter which changed every time the page was reloaded. This parameter is not a session identifier since it changes its value during the same session. If the recorded XPath expression is modified manually to ignore the value of this parameter, then the sequence works correctly. To solve problems like this, we could include redundant localization information; this way, if an element cannot be identified using the "minimal" expression, then we can still use the other information to search the nearest match in the page ([1] uses a similar idea that could be extended to deal with these cases, although they do not use other necessary information, such as hierarchical information). Another option is allowing the user to provide several examples of the same sequence for detecting those parameters.

The second group of tests was completely successful in GWT applications, while in the YUI case only one sequence could not be recorded. The problem was that the *blur* event was not being generated with the *setText* action. Once this was corrected, the sequence could be recorded.

5 Related Work

WebVCR [1] and WebMacros [11] were pioneer systems for web navigation sequences automation using the "recorder metaphor". Both systems were only able to record a reduced set of events (clicks and filling in form fields) on a reduced set of elements (anchors and form-related elements). In the execution phase they relied on HTTP clients that lacked the ability to execute scripting code or to support AJAX requests. Furthermore, the techniques they used for identifying the target elements of user actions were based on the text associated to the elements and the value of some specific pre-configured attributes (e.g. *href* for *A* tags and *src* for *FORM* tags).

Wargo [9] introduced using a commercial browser as execution component, thus supporting websites using scripting languages and guaranteeing that the websites will behave in the execution phase in the same way as when a human user accesses it. Nevertheless, it still showed the remaining previously mentioned problems.

Instead of using the "recorder" metaphor, in SmartBookmarks [6] the macros are generated retroactively; when the user reaches a page and bookmarks it, the system tries to automatically find the starting point of the macro. In order to do this, SmartBookmarks permanently monitors the user actions. As it was explained in section 3.1, recording user actions in the browser as the user navigates forces to either restrict the set of monitored events or suffering from an "event-flooding" problem. SmartBookmarks only supports the events click, load and change. Another drawback is that it relies on timeouts to determine when to continue executing the sequence. HtmlUnit [5] is an open-source tool for web applications unit testing. HtmlUnit does not provide a recording tool; instead, the user needs to manually create the navigation sequences using Java coding. In addition HtmlUnit uses its own custom browser instead of relying on conventional browsers. Although their browser has support for many Javascript and AJAX functionalities, this is vulnerable to small implementation differences that can make a web page to behave differently when accessed with the custom browser.

Selenium [13] is a suite of tools to automate web applications testing. Selenium uses the recorder metaphor through a toolbar installed in Firefox. It is only able to record a reduced set of events. To identify elements, Selenium uses a system based on the text or generates an XPath expression that does not try to be resilient to small changes. Another drawback is that Selenium does not detect properly the end of the effects caused by a user action in the recording process.

Sahi [12] is another open-source tool for automated testing of web applications. Sahi includes a navigation recording system and it allows the sequences to be executed in commercial browsers. To use Sahi, the user configures its navigator to use a proxy. Every time the browser requests a new page, the proxy retrieves it, adds listeners for monitoring user actions, and returns the modified page. Using a proxy makes the recording system independent of the web browser used. Nevertheless, using a proxy does not allow using approaches where the user explicitly indicates the actions to record; therefore, as discussed previously, it forces to choose between either monitoring only a reduced set of events or suffering from "event flooding". Sahi only supports recording events such as click and change. Other events such as *mouseover* can be used at the execution phase if the user manually codes the navigation scripts. Another drawback is that they do not detect the end of the effects caused by a user action, using timeouts instead.

In the commercial software arena, QEngine [10] is a load and functional testing tool for web applications. QEngine also uses the recorder metaphor through a toolbar installed in MSIE (also used as execution component). In addition of the most typical events supported by the previously mentioned systems, QEngine also supports a form of explicitly specifying *mouseover* events on certain elements, consisting in placing the mouse over the target element for more than a certain timeout (avoiding this way the "flooding" problem). Nevertheless, they do not capture other events such as *mouseout* or *mousemove*. To identify elements, they use a simple system based on the text, attributes and relative position of the element. While this may be enough for application-testing purposes where changes are controlled, it is not enough to deal with autonomous web sources. In addition, as previous systems, QEngine does not detect the end of the effects of an action. iOpus [7] is another web automation tool that uses the recorder metaphor. Their drawbacks with respect to our proposal are almost identical to those mentioned for QEngine.

Kapow [8] is yet another web automation tool oriented to the creation of mashups and web integration applications. Kapow uses its own custom browser. Therefore, in our evaluation it showed to be vulnerable to the formerly mentioned drawback: small implementation differences can make a web page to behave differently. For instance, from the set of 12 sequences from Google Web Toolkit we used in our tests, the Kapow browser could only successfully reproduce 1 of them. To identify the target elements, Kapow generates an XPath expression that tries to be resilient to small changes, although the details of the algorithm they use have not been published.

With respect to the algorithm to identify target elements, [2,14] have also addressed the problem of generating change-resilient XPath expressions. In those approaches, the user provides several example pages identifying the target element; and the system generalizes the expression by examining the differences between them. In our case, that would force the user to record the navigation sequence several times. We believe that process would be much more cumbersome to the user.

6 Conclusions

We have presented a set of new techniques to record and execute web navigation sequences in AJAX-based websites. Previous proposals show important limitations in the range of user actions that they can record and execute, the methods they use for identifying the target elements of user actions and/or how they wait for the effects of a user action to finish. Our techniques have been successfully implemented using both MSIE and Firefox. Our main contributions are a new method for recording navigation sequences able to scale to a wider range of events and a novel method to detect when the effects caused by a user action (including the effects of scripting code and AJAX requests) have finished, without needing to use inefficient timeouts. We have also evaluated our approach with more than 100 web applications, obtaining a high degree of effectiveness.

References

1. Anupam, V., Freire, J., Kumar, B., Lieuwen, D.: Automating web navigation with the WebVCR. In: Proceedings of WWW 2000, pp. 503–517 (2000)
2. Davulcu, H., Yang, G., Kifer, M., Ramakrishnan, I.V.: Computational Aspects of Resilient Data Extraction from Semistructured Sources. In: Proc. of ACM Symposium on Principles of Database Systems (PODS), pp. 136–144 (2000)
3. Document Object Model (DOM) Level 3 Events Specification, http://www.w3.org/TR/DOM-Level-3-Events/
4. Google Web Toolkit, http://code.google.com/webtoolkit/
5. HtmlUnit, http://htmlunit.sourceforge.net/
6. Hupp, D., Miller, R.C.: Smart Bookmarks: automatic retroactive macro recording on the web. In: Proc. of ACM Symposium on User Interface Software and Technology (UIST 2007) (2007)
7. iOpus, http://www.iopus.com
8. Kapow, http://www.openkapow.com
9. Pan, A., Raposo, J., Álvarez, M., Hidalgo, J., Viña, A.: Semi automatic wrapper-generation for commercial web sources. In: Proc. of IFIP WG8.1 Working Conference on Engineering Information Systems in the Internet Context 2002, pp. 265–283 (2002)
10. QEngine, http://www.adventnet.com/products/qengine/index.html
11. Safonov, A., Konstan, J., Carlis, J.: Beyond Hard-to-Reach Pages: Interactive, Parametric Web Macros. In: Proc. of the 7th Conference on Human Factors & the Web (2001)
12. Sahi, http://sahi.co.in/w/
13. Selenium, http://seleniumhq.org/
14. Lingam, S., Elbaum S.: Supporting End-Users in the Creation of Dependable Web Clips. In: Proc. of WWW 2007, pp. 953–962 (2007)
15. XML Path Language (XPath), http://www.w3.org/TR/xpath
16. Yahoo! User Interface Library (YUI), http://developer.yahoo.com/yui

Modelling and Verification of Web Navigation [*]

Zuohua Ding[1], Mingyue Jiang[1], Geguang Pu[2], and Jeff W. Sanders[3]

[1] Center of Math Computing and Software Engineering, Zhejiang Sci-Tech University
Hangzhou, Zhejiang, 310018, P.R. China
zouhuading@hotmail.com, jiang_my@126.com
[2] Software Engineering Institute, East China Normal University
Shanghai, 200062, P.R. China
ggpu@sei.ecnu.edu.cn
[3] International Institute for Software Technology
Unite Nations University, P.O. Box 3058, Macao
jeff@iist.unu.edu

Abstract. Web navigation model provides a dynamic view for web modelling. It is useful for clarifying requirements and specifying implementation behaviors of systems from design intensions. In this paper, we propose a formal model to describe web navigation of user behaviors, where link activities play an important role. Several issues have been considered in our model, such as web browser effects, adaptive navigation, frame communication etc. After the link activity model is established, we use model checker SPIN to check whether there exist problems such as such as broken links, dead ends, missed reply pages, reachability of pages etc. This method can help us to analyze user behaviors, meanwhile it provides us a way to expose design faults in web systems.

Keywords: Web Modelling, Link Analysis, Requirement Engineering, Model Checking.

1 Introduction

Recently, various web modelling approaches are proposed to model web applications. There are two main different concerns for conceptual modelling of web applications: information modelling and navigation modelling. Information modelling describes the contents of web applications and it is considered as from static point of view such as [1]. Navigation modelling pictures the navigation capabilities, i.e., the paths on which users can traverse to explore the information required, and it is considered as from dynamic point of view. Examples can be found in [9]. We regard these two approaches are complement to each other. This paper is concerned with navigation modelling of web applications.

As the work [6] indicated, navigation models are useful for clarifying requirements and specifying implementation behaviors of systems. There are a few web navigation models proposed [1,9,11,2,5,3], such as the models based on extended

---

[*] Zuohua Ding is supported by NNSFC (No.90818013). Geguang Pu is partially supported by NNSFC (No.60603033) and Qimingxing Project (No. 07QA14020).

M. Gaedke, M. Grossniklaus, and O. Díaz (Eds.): ICWE 2009, LNCS 5648, pp. 181–188, 2009.
© Springer-Verlag Berlin Heidelberg 2009

UML notation [8], Statecharts [6], navigation map [4] [10], etc. While taking the advantages of these models, we still need to consider some issues which may not be considered by the existing navigation modelling or in the information modelling in the web design phase:

- Web browser effects. In addition to the navigation provided by hyperlinks, web browsers can provide additional navigation functions that is out of control of the web pages, such as scrolling, back button, forward buttons and a history list. Static design model cannot include these navigation information.
- Adaptive navigation. In this situation, the next page also depends on the user's mode, for example whether he is a customer or an administrator, or depends on what pages the user has visited previously.
- Frame communication. For example, synchronization between continuous and static documents (i.e., scenes and pages). Since in principle pages are not ordered, their ordering comes as a result of scene ordering and scene-page relationships.

Generally speaking, the navigation of a web application is the possible sequences of web pages a user can visit. To handle the above issues, we present a formal dynamic behavior model for specifying the behavior of the navigation by *link point* activities. Through our approach, the navigation model is defined rigorously. The developer of the web application can better understand the application requirements and the implementation behavior with this proposed model and thus can develop web applications in a rigorous way.

2   A Formal Navigation Model

In the navigation, users navigate from a web page to the other by clicking on a hyperlink. A hyperlink can be in the form of text strings, graphcs or video, activated explicitly by users, using a mouse click for example. Hyperlinks can also be included in client side program/scripts (such as Javascripts, VBScript, Java and ActiveX), to be invoked automatically by the browser on some predefined events. Examples of these events include timeout, mouse movements and window focus.

The place where the user clicks the hyperlink is called link point. Here we give a formal definition for link point.

Definition 1 (Link Point). *A link point lp is a tuple defined as follows:*

$$(currentLink, nextLink, linkState,$$
$$variable\_set, action\_name, duration\_time)$$

where

- *currentLink(cl) is a string indicating the URL that the current page is located.*
- *nextLink(nl) is a string indicating the URL that the next page is located.*
- *linkState(ls) indicates that the link is statically or dynamically defined, enabled or disabled.*

- *variable_set(vs)* *indicates that after clicking the hyperlink, these variables information will be brought to the next page, such as login user data.*
- *action_name(an)* *denotes the action name with this link, which is mostly specified by web designers.*
- *duration_time(dt)* *denotes the interaction time between web servers and users after the link is clicked, which is actually a performance property decided by the deployment environment.*

Based on the states of link point, we can classify the link points as Type I, Type II and Type III. Type I link point must have new user input data which will be passed to the next page. For example, when a user clicks login button, he needs to input login name and password. Login button is the link point and some user id will be generated (maybe login name) for the next page. Another example is the search button. Key words are the values for the search button. Key words will be passed to the next page. Type II link point does not need any user input, but it will bring user information to the next page implicitly. For example, after a user logins to an online shopping web site, user id will be passed from one page to another page when the current user surfs for products. Type III link point only breaks down the user session. For instance, if a user clicks a logout link, the session built up earlier is closed and the user data is removed. Type I link point is denoted by $lp\bullet$, Type II link point is denoted by $lp\circ$, and Type III link point is denoted as $lp\times$.

2.1 Syntax

To specify the behaviors of users, we attempt to design an activity calculus to describe the web navigation behaviors performed by users. Because link point clicking reflects the intended behaviors of users, we design this activity calculus based on link points. It is easy to see that the sequence of link points is the same as the navigation path. The syntax of the activity calculus is defined as follows.

$$
\begin{array}{lll}
NE ::= & p\,\bullet & \text{(Type I)} \\
       & \mid p\circ & \text{(Type II)} \\
       & \mid p\times & \text{(Type III)} \\
       & \mid \mathsf{skip} & \text{(Skip)} \\
       & \mid \mathcal{B}p & \text{(back action)} \\
       & \mid \mathcal{F}p & \text{(forward action)} \\
       & \mid \mathcal{R}p & \text{(refresh action)} \\
       & \mid NE\,;\,NE & \text{(Sequence)} \\
       & \mid NE\triangleleft\triangleright NE & \text{(nondeterminism)} \\
       & \mid NE\triangleleft b\triangleright NE & \text{(Conditional)} \\
       & \mid b*NE & \text{(Loop)} \\
       & \mid NE\parallel NE & \text{(Parallel)}
\end{array}
$$

Without confusion, we use the same notations $p\,\bullet$, $p\circ$ and $p\times$ for both link points and link activities here. Activity skip does nothing but terminates. $\mathcal{B}p$ is back operation which will clear all the user inputs on the page p. $\mathcal{F}p$ is forward operation which will not generate any user data, or bring any data to page p. $\mathcal{R}p$ is refresh operation which may change some link state from disable one to enabled one on the page p.

Action $NE \triangleleft \triangleright NE$ means that the user can randomly choose the link points. Action $NE \parallel NE$ denotes two link points may be performed in parallel. Note that $b * NE$ denotes loop activity, where b represents the boolean expressions, which depends on the variable values of link points or the history of variable values. Loop activity can specify the repeated actions performed by users.

2.2 Operational Semantics

The operational semantics of the link activities is presented in this subsection. We use the classical Labelled Transition System (LTS) to define an operational semantics, and the small-step operational semantics is adopted as well. The transition label a can be the link activity or the internal action τ.

The configuration of the transition system is designed as $\langle NE, \mathcal{E}, ST, LR, CL \rangle$, where NE is the link activity; $\mathcal{E}$ is the global activity trace in which each element is a link activity, and for instance, trace $< a, b, c >$ denotes that the user first performs link a and link b sequently, and then performs links c afterwards. The trace can help the user keep the visiting history list; ST represents the global state of link activities, which is a function of link variables; LR records the set of relations among link activities, which will be increased gradually based on the link activities performed by users; and CL stands for the current link activities.

Trace $\mathcal{E}$ has two types: one is for security and is bounded, denoted as $\mathcal{E}_s$; the other is for doing things, and is unbounded, denoted as $\mathcal{E}_t$. We use $\mathcal{E}^\frown a$ to represent the resulted trace after adding activity a to the end of $\mathcal{E}$, $\mathcal{E} \setminus a$ to represent the resulted trace after removing the top sequence composed by activity a in $\mathcal{E}$, and $a \in \mathcal{E}$ to represent that the activity a is contained in the trace $\mathcal{E}$.

The transitions of Type I and Type II activities are the following. The activating of Type II link will add the activity $\circ$ to the queue $\mathcal{E}$, while the activating of Type I link will add the activity $\bullet$ to the global queue $\mathcal{E}$.

$$\langle p\circ, \mathcal{E}, ST, LR, CL \rangle \xrightarrow{\circ} \langle skip, \ \mathcal{E}^\frown\circ, ST, LR \cup (CL, p\circ), p\circ \rangle$$

$$\langle p\bullet, \mathcal{E}, ST, LR, CL \rangle \xrightarrow{\bullet} \langle skip, \ \mathcal{E}^\frown\bullet, \mathsf{ud}(ST), LR \cup (CL, p\bullet), p\bullet \rangle$$

where predicate ud updates the global state based on link variables.

If Type III activity is performed, then the top sequence of activities $\bullet$ will be removed from the global trace. For example, in the queue, from the top we have $\bullet\bullet\circ\circ\ldots$, then $\bullet\bullet$ will be removed.

$$\langle p\times, \mathcal{E}, ST, LR, CL \rangle \xrightarrow{\tau} \langle skip, \ \mathcal{E} \setminus \bullet, \mathsf{ze}(ST), LR \cup (CL, p\times), p\times \rangle$$

where symbol $\mathcal{E} \setminus a$ represents the resulted trace after removing the top sequence of activity a in $\mathcal{E}$; and predicate ze sets the link variables to null.

The parallel expression has two cases. In the first case, if one part of the parallel structure moves to a new state, then the whole parallel structure will move to a corresponding state.

$$\frac{\langle NE_1, \mathcal{E}, ST, LR, CL \rangle \xrightarrow{a} \langle NE_1', \mathcal{E}', ST', LR', CL' \rangle}{\langle NE_1 \parallel NE_2, \mathcal{E}, ST, LR, CL \rangle \xrightarrow{a} \langle NE_1' \parallel NE_2, \mathcal{E}', ST', LR', CL' \rangle}$$

$$\frac{\langle NE_2, \mathcal{E}, ST, LR, CL \rangle \xrightarrow{a} \langle NE_2', \mathcal{E}', ST', LR', CL' \rangle}{\langle NE_1 \parallel NE_2, \mathcal{E}, ST, LR, CL \rangle \xrightarrow{a} \langle NE_1 \parallel NE_2', \mathcal{E}', ST', LR', CL' \rangle}$$

The second case is that if both parts in parallel structure terminate, then the whole parallel structure terminates as well.

$$\frac{}{\langle skip \parallel skip, \mathcal{E}, ST, LR, CL \rangle \xrightarrow{\tau} \langle skip, \mathcal{E}, ST, LR, CL \rangle}$$

The following rules are for operations $\mathcal{B}, \mathcal{F}$ and $\mathcal{R}$:

$$\frac{}{\langle \mathcal{B}p, \mathcal{E}, ST, LR, CL \rangle \xrightarrow{\mathcal{B}} \langle skip, \mathcal{E}^\frown \mathsf{bpair}, ST', LR, \mathsf{bpair} \rangle}$$

where element bpair is the most recent link point which, as the first element, forms a pair with CL in relation set LR. $ST' = ST \oplus (p.\{variable = null\})$.

$$\frac{}{\langle \mathcal{F}p, \mathcal{E}, ST, LR, CL \rangle \xrightarrow{\mathcal{F}} \langle skip, \mathcal{E}^\frown \mathsf{fpair}, ST', LR, \mathsf{fpair} \rangle}$$

where element fpair is the most recent point link which, as the second element, forms a pair with CL in relation set LR. $ST' = ST \oplus (p.\{variable = null\})$.

$$\frac{}{\langle \mathcal{R}p, \mathcal{E}, ST, LR, CL \rangle \xrightarrow{\mathcal{R}} \langle skip, \mathcal{E}^\frown CL, ST', LR, CL \rangle}$$

where $ST' = ST \oplus (p.linkState = enable)$.

The first expression means that if clicking back button, then (only) the user input on the last page will be removed. The second expression means that if clicking the forward button, then the user input (including null) will be forwarded to the next page. The third expression means to reset the link to the enable state, meanwhile automatically to set the duration time to the default.

3   SPIN Checking Navigation Model

In this section we discuss the use of the SPIN model checker [7] to check the navigation behaviors specified by our formal model. The input language of SPIN is called Promela, a modelling language for finite-state concurrent processes. SPIN model checker verifies (or falsifies, by generating counter- examples) LTL properties of Promela specifications using an exhaustive state space search.

We have defined some rules to translate our navigation model to Promela description. Due to the limited space, we only give some examples to illustrate our method.

- Conditional Choice $NE1 \triangleleft b \triangleright NE2$. Let $NE1$ and $NE2$ be two links, then

```
if
    :: b->atomic{NE1.nextlink='x';...};
    :: else->atomic{NE2.nextlink='y';...};
fi
```

- Nondeterministic Choice $NE1 \triangleleft \triangleright NE2$. Let $NE1$ and $NE2$ be two links, then

```
if
    //atomic1
    :: exp1->atomic{NE1.nextlink='x';...};
    //atomic2
    :: exp2->atomic{NE2.nextlink='y';...};
fi
```

Based on the transformation rules defined above, we have developed a prototype to support the automatic verification of web navigation. Some verification properties have been defined and can be automatically verified by SPIN. The properties that pass (are never violated) will return true, and for those that fail will give counterexample(s).

1) **Dead end.** For each page, we check the number of links:

```
assert(linkNumber!=0 || backState==true);
```

Once the linknumber is 0 and the backState is false, then we reach a dead end.

2) **Broken link.** We will define a global array to record all the pages being visited. After the navigation ends, if there still exist some pages not being visited, then we have broken links in this model.

3) **Navigation not complete.** We define the following sentence to check if $\mathcal{E}_s$ and $\mathcal{E}_{t1}$ still have some •:

```
assert(empty(Es) && empty(Et1));
```

4) **Reachability.** We define a global variable with initial value 0. Once a link is clicked, the variable value increases 1. Thus the link number of a page can be obtained from this global variable.

5) **Not removed data.** We define the following sentence to check the variable values on the page to see if the values are null:

```
assert(var!='0');
```

We have used SPIN to check two navigation models from Amazon and Elsevier Web systems. For the first example, we check if there exist not removed user data for the Back operation and not complete navigation for the one time navigation. For the first one, we add the following statements:

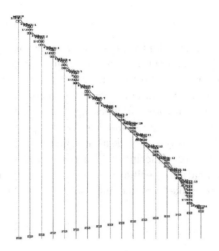

Fig. 1. SPIN checking Amazon

```
Back(var); Assert(var=='0');
```

For the second one, we check wether the following property is obeyed:

```
assert(empty(Es) && empty(Et1));
```

The simulation result is shown in Figure 1. The execution stops at the statement $assert(empty(Es)\,\&\&\,empty(Et1))$, which indicates that this assert statement is violated, and thus we have not complete navigation. We do not have not removed user data. The verification result is as the following:

```
pan: assertion violated ((q_len(Es)==0)
     &&(q_len(Et1)==0)) (at depth 161)
pan: wrote pan_in.trail
```

The result shows that at least one of the two channels Es and $Et1$ is not empty since either $q\_len(Es)! = 0$ or $q\_len(Et1)! = 0$ or both. Thus the navigation is not complete.

For the example of Elsevier submission system, we check the not complete navigation property by adding the following statements:

```
assert(empty(Es) && empty(Et1));
```

The execution will stop at the statement $assert(empty(Es)\&\&empty(Et1));$. This implies that we have not complete navigation. The verification result is as the following:

```
pan: assertion violated ((q_len(Es)==0)
     &&(q_len(Et1)==0)) (at depth 72)
pan: wrote pan_in.trail
```

The result shows that at least one of the two channels Es and $Et1$ is not empty. Thus the navigation is not complete.

4   Conclusion

We have proposed a formal model to specify web navigation precisely. The implementation semantics of the formal model is also presented. Based on the semantics of this model, we may simulate the user behaviors, and more importantly, we can find whether the user behaviors conform to the intentions of the system designers. To support the automatic checking of navigation model, we employ SPIN to check our navigation model and several properties can be checked. As the future work, we may study the click-action flow and use data mining skill to retrieve the natural language descriptions for these actions from log file, so that we can check the application-specific properties of the web navigation model. We will also continue to make our checking tool more scalable for web designers.

References

1. Alfaro, L.: Model Checking the World Wide Web. In: Berry, G., Comon, H., Finkel, A. (eds.) CAV 2001. LNCS, vol. 2102, pp. 337–349. Springer, Heidelberg (2001)
2. Baumeister, H., Knapp, A., Koch, N., Zang, G.: Modelling Adaptivity with Aspects. In: Lowe, D.G., Gaedke, M. (eds.) ICWE 2005. LNCS, vol. 3579, pp. 406–416. Springer, Heidelberg (2005)
3. Ceri, S., Daniel, F., Demaldé, V., Facca, F.M.: An Approach to User-Behavior-Aware Web Applications. In: Lowe, D.G., Gaedke, M. (eds.) ICWE 2005. LNCS, vol. 3579, pp. 417–428. Springer, Heidelberg (2005)
4. Conallen, J.: Building Web Applications with UML. Addison-Wesley, Reading (2002)
5. Deutsch, A., Sui, L., Vianu, V.: Specification and verification of data-driven Web applications. Journal of Computer and System Sciences 73, 442–474 (2007)
6. Han, M., Hofmeister, C.: Modeling and Verification of Adaptive Navigation in Web Applications. In: ICWE 2006, Palo Alto, California, USA, July 11-14, pp. 329–336 (2006)
7. Holzmann, G.J.: Basic Spin Manual (1980), http://cm.bell-labs.com/netlib/spin/whatispin.html
8. Koch, N., Baumeister, H., Hennicker, R., Mandel, L.: Extending UML to Model Navigation and Presentation in Web Applications. In: Workshop on Modelling Web Applications in UML, UML 2000, New York, UK (October 2000)
9. Ricca, F., Tonella, P.: Analysis and Testing of Web Applications. In: Proc. of 23rd Int. Conference on Software Engineering, Toronto, Ontario, Canada, May 2001, pp. 25–34 (2001)
10. Rational Software, Pearl Circle Online Auction Reference Application Software Architecture Document, Issue 0.2, Rational Software (2001)
11. Winckler, M., Palanque, P.: Statewebcharts: A Formal Description Technique Dedicated To Navigation Modelling of Web Applications. In: Jorge, J.A., Jardim Nunes, N., Falcão e Cunha, J. (eds.) DSV-IS 2003. LNCS, vol. 2844, pp. 61–76. Springer, Heidelberg (2003)

Context-Driven Hypertext Specification

Sara Comai, Davide Mazza, and Elisa Quintarelli

Dipartimento di Elettronica e Informazione
Politecnico di Milano, Italy
{comai,mazza,quintare}@elet.polimi.it

Abstract. The aim of the paper is the introduction of a compositional methodology for specifying context-driven hypertexts, that is the possibility to filter the available -usually too rich- knowledge and personalize the hypertext specification according to the notion of context. We use a methodology and a context model, recently proposed in the database literature, to tailor data on the basis of some predefined aspects on the user, the environment, and the possible scenarios, and we adapt them to specify also the hypertext schemata of the target application. The applicability of the work is shown on a running example and the advantages w.r.t. well known approaches for designing Web applications are highlighted.

1 Introduction

Current Web sites show a great amount of data to users. In order to show only the information that is really of interest and reduce the confusion produced by meaningless data, users have usually access to a filtered subset of the overall data. Filtering often depends on the particular context in which the user operates. For example, when using mobile devices the information to retrieve and to visualize is smaller in terms of the quantity of data sent at each request with respect to the data usually provided to the client during desktop navigation. The notion of context also depends upon the characteristics of the user, i.e., his profile, or on the basis of predefined access rights. More in general, we can state that the information about a target application domain can be seen by the user from *different points of view*.

In this paper we introduce the notion of *context* to define the *views* on the available data that can be delivered to the user in that particular context. Then, according to the characteristics of the user or to the situation in which he operates (i.e., considering the current context), the appropriate view of data is provided.

We propose a general approach, where the context becomes the element driving the specification of the Web application:

- context-driven views are defined over the data; in particular, different context perspectives can be considered separately, each associated with a particular subset of the entire dataset.
- The hypertext is configured with respect to a (set of) contextual aspect(s). Given a context configuration involving different contextual aspects, the actual view over the data is obtained as a combination of the views defined for the involved aspects.

M. Gaedke, M. Grossniklaus, and O. Díaz (Eds.): ICWE 2009, LNCS 5648, pp. 189–196, 2009.
© Springer-Verlag Berlin Heidelberg 2009

The paper is organized as follows: Section 2 presents a case study that will be used throughout the paper; Section 3 describes the context model and explains how the context-driven views can be specified; Section 4 exemplifies the use of contexts within an hypertext model. Section 5 compares the proposed approach with related work. Finally, in Section 6 conclusions are drawn.

2 Running Example

The scenario considered in this work is the internship service offered by a university: companies propose internships for students; professors supervise the internships and assign them to students. A Web site collects information about the internships proposed by the companies. A predefined professor (called *operator*) selects the appropriate internships for his faculty and approves them. Students can choose and book internships from the list of the available ones. In this scenario, the internships and the related information that can be seen by an operator depend on their status. For example, when the operator wants to analyze the proposed internships (s)he could be interested in their content and duration, while for assigned internships (s)he could be rather interested in the details, such as the name of the assigned student; for concluded internships also the evaluation becomes important.

The application Web site relies on a central relational database, whose schema is partially shown in Figure 1.

STUDENT(<u>stud_id</u>, lastname, firstname, birthdate, faculty)
PROFESSOR(<u>prof_id</u>, lastname, firstname, position, faculty)
COMPANY(<u>VATcode</u>, name, address, city, phone, fax, website)
INTERNSHIP(<u>id</u>, title, company, duration, location, visible, student, note, tutor, evaluation, faculty)
DOC(<u>internship,student,date,document</u>, document_type)
EXAM(<u>course,student</u>, date, mark)

Fig. 1. Relational schema of the running example

3 The CDT Context Model and the Contextual Views

In order to determine the contextual data associated with each context, in a scenario where different database users, situations, and other elements (called *dimensions*) determine the relevant portions of data, we use the methodology proposed in [2], which is based on three components: a *context model*, a set of *partial views* and an *operator* for combining the former ones to derive the final view(s) associated with each context.

The context model used to represent all the possible contexts for a given scenario is the Context Dimension Tree (CDT). A tree-based structure represents the dimensions used to tailor the available data (represented by black filled circles) and their values (represented by white filled circles).

The children of the root node represent the main dimensions used to filter the data; for each of these nodes a subtree is created, increasing the detail-level adopted to tailor data. The CDT of our application scenario, gathering contents about internships, students,

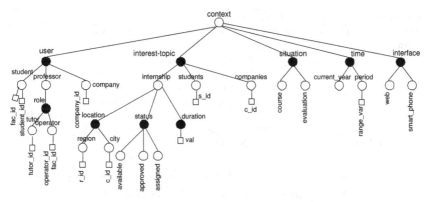

Fig. 2. The CDT for the internships in a university scenario

companies, and professors is reported in Figure 2. The dimensions used to filter the information are *user, interest-topic, situation, time,* and *interface.*

Possible values for the *user* dimension are student, professor, company; in each session, and hence for each possible context, the application may be accessed only by one of these roles. The user dimension is represented with a black circle; its possible values are represented as white siblings and are mutually exclusive. The same criterion applies to the other dimensions. For the *interest-topic* dimension the following mutually exclusive values can be introduced: internship, students, companies. Moreover, when considering the internship node, there are several aspects that can be identified for further refining the selection of interesting data: *status, duration, location;* these aspects, which are graphically represented as sibling black nodes, are not mutually exclusive, since they provide different characterizations of the same concept. Thus, a concept may be characterized by several aspects (i.e. sub-dimensions), and each aspect may be constituted by different concepts. In the CDT there are also attribute nodes, which are leaves, graphically represented as rectangles; attributes are used to select data according to a specific run-time generated value, e.g., to identify a specific student.

In order to identify a portion of data to be tailored from the entire data set, to be made available to the user on the basis of his current context, a tuple composed by one or more nodes for (a subset of) the dimensions is selected, choosing a single white sibling and any number of black siblings. The tuple is called *context.* An example of context defined on the CDT reported in Figure 2 is:

$$\langle\, \texttt{role} : \texttt{operator}(\$\texttt{operator\_id}, \$\texttt{fac\_id}), \texttt{status} : \texttt{assigned}\,\rangle \qquad (1)$$

The context is related to an *operator* professor who wants to analyze assigned internships proposed in his faculty, in order to visualize students and tutors.

Given the possible and meaningful contexts, the designer can then *associate them with the relevant portions of the information domain.* This step can be performed in a compositional way: (1) for each single concept of the CDT the designer specifies a partial view on the global schema, i.e., the portion of schema that is relevant for that concept; (2) given a context (composed of a set of concepts), its view is obtained by means of an algorithm that automatically combines the partial views of its elements.

Context Element	Partial View
role : operator(\$operator_id, \$fac_id)	$\{\sigma_{faculty=\$fac\_id}$STUDENT, PROFESSOR, COMPANY, $\sigma_{faculty=\$fac\_id}$INTERNSHIP$\}$
status : assigned	$\{$STUDENT $\bowtie_{stud\_id=student}$ INTERNSHIP, PROFESSOR $\bowtie_{prof\_id=tutor}$ INTERNSHIP, COMPANY $\bowtie_{VATcode=company}$ INTERNSHIP, $\sigma_{student!=NULL \wedge tutor!=NULL}$(INTERNSHIP), DOC $\bowtie_{internship=id}$ $(\sigma_{student!=NULL \wedge tutor!=NULL}$(INTERNSHIP)), EXAM $\bowtie$ $(\sigma_{student!=NULL \wedge tutor!=NULL}$(INTERNSHIP))$\}$
status : available	$\{$STUDENT, PROFESSOR, COMPANY $\bowtie_{VATcode=company}$ INTERNSHIP, $\sigma_{visible=FALSE}$(INTERNSHIP)$\}$

Fig. 3. Partial views associated with context elements

Figure 3 shows some partial views, expressed as sets of relational algebra expressions, and relation names, of some elements, including the one defined by (1). As an example, we can see that the partial view of the *role* operator contains the students of the faculty of the considered operator (identified at run-time by the value of two parameters related to his personal identifier and the faculty name), the information about the professors and the companies, and the internships proposed for his faculty.

The combination of the partial views into the final view of a specific context can be performed automatically by means of the so-called Double Intersection operator [2], defined as follows.

The **Double Intersection operator** $\cap\!\!\!\cap$, between two sets of relational algebra expressions $\mathcal{A}$ and $\mathcal{B}$ (i.e. two partial views), applies the classical intersection operator $\cap$ to pairs of expressions e_A and e_B, belonging to $\mathcal{A}$ and $\mathcal{B}$, respectively, each one of the form $\Pi_{Att_i}\sigma_{cond_i}(R)$, or $\Pi_{Att_i}\sigma_{cond_i}(R \bowtie S_i)$. In order to reduce them to a common schema, the intersection is performed on their projection over the intersection of their schemata.

Considering our running example, the view assigned to the context (1) is obtained by applying the Double Intersection operator to the two partial views in Figure 3 corresponding to the operator role and assigned status elements, and is:

$$\{ \ \sigma_{faculty=\$fac\_id}\text{STUDENT} \bowtie_{stud\_id=student} \text{INTERNSHIP},$$
$$\text{PROFESSOR} \bowtie_{prof\_id=tutor} \text{INTERNSHIP},$$
$$\text{COMPANY} \bowtie_{VATcode=company} \text{INTERNSHIP},$$
$$\sigma_{student!=NULL \wedge faculty=\$fac\_id \wedge tutor!=NULL}(\text{INTERNSHIP})\}$$

4   Context-Driven Hypertext

In a Web application, the hypertext can exploit the approach described in the previous section to show the data that are relevant in a specific context. In the following, we will exemplify the approach on the WebML [4] model.

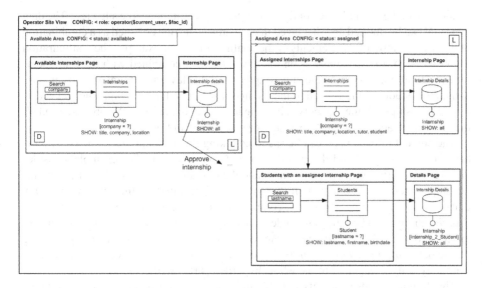

Fig. 4. The operator site view with context configurations

The specification of the hypertext can be extended with *context configurations*, to associate the whole hypertext -or a fragment thereof- with the context dimensions in which it operates. Considering the WebML concepts, the configuration may apply to any level of its hierarchical structure: to a site view, to an area, to a single page or nested sub-page. At each level, the context tuple is obtained as a combination of the context configurations specified at the current level and at all its super-levels; such a combination can be automatically computed by combining the partial views of the context dimensions specified in the combined configuration. In this way, the specification of the retrieval of data performed by the units/components of the page can be simplified and specified on top of the context view.

Figure 4 shows a fragment of the site view of the operator, associated with different configurations. Configurations are graphically indicated by the keyword *CONFIG*. In this example, a configuration is specified for the whole site view: the site view can see only the data associated with the operator dimension, and in particular, related to the specific current operator user, which is indicated by the session variable *$current_user*[1], and to his faculty (variable *$fac_id*): this means that all the data shown in the site view are constrained on the operator, according to the partial view of the operator *role* in Fig. 3. In particular, the site view can display data retrieved only from the Student, Professor, Company, and Internship relations; only the internships and the students belonging to the same faculty of the operator can be queried.

The operator site view contains different areas, each one configured with respect to other context dimensions, like, for example, the status of the internship, which can be available, or assigned. Each area inherits also the configurations of its higher-level

---

[1] For the specification and management of session variables in WebML the reader may refer to [4].

containers, in the example the configuration that applies at the whole site view. The data view that can be queried and displayed in each area is the one obtained as a combination of the partial views of the elements of the configuration. For example, the configuration *CONFIG:* $<$ *status : assigned* $>$ on the area *Assigned*, combined with the role operator configuration, constrains the area to query and display only the internships already assigned to students and related to the faculty of the operator, the companies related to those internships, all the students belonging to the same faculty of the operator, and all the professors, according to the partial views described in Fig. 3.

The content of each page can be specified taking into account that some constraints have already been defined through the context configurations. For example, consider the *Available Internships* page: in this page the operator can see the list of all the internships entered by companies in the system (represented by the *Internships* index unit), possibly filtering them by the company name (the filtering is represented by the *Search* entry unit). Then, from the index, the operator may select a particular internship to see its details (*Internship details* data unit) and decide for its approval, by clicking on the outgoing link *Approve internship* that will record the approval (for the sake of simplicity, only a fragment of the whole hypertext is reported).

The designer needs to specify only the information that is associated with the filtering and the selection operations, while the actual content of each single content unit will depend on the configuration. For example, the index unit *Internships* specifies only the selectors corresponding to the search facility; its query expressed in relational algebra is:

$$\Pi_{title,company,location,tutor} \sigma_{company=\$company} \text{INTERNSHIP}$$

This query is combined with the partial views related to the `role : operator` and `status : available`, by applying the Double Intersection explained in Section 3. The final view for the *Internships* index unit will be

$$\Pi_{title,company,location,tutor} \sigma_{company=\$company \land faculty=\$fac\_id \land visible=false} \text{INTERNSHIP}$$

The same hypertext fragment specified inside the *Assigned Internships* page, which is associated with the configuration `status : assigned`, will produce a different content: the query expressing the filtering in this case will be combined with the partial views related to the `role : operator` and `status : assigned`, producing the final view:

$$\Pi_{title,company,location,tutor}$$
$$\sigma_{company=\$company \land faculty=\$fac\_id \land studente!=NULL \land tutor!=NULL} \text{INTERNSHIP}$$

The same applies to the page *Students with an assigned internship*, which allows one to search and display the list of students "to whom an internship has been assigned". In this case, the base query of the *Students* index unit

$$\Pi_{lastname,firstname,birthdate} \sigma_{lastname=\$lastname} \text{STUDENT}$$

will be combined with the corresponding partial views `role : operator` and `status : assigned` producing the following final view:

$\Pi_{lastname,firstname,birthdate}$
$\sigma_{lastname=\$lastname}$STUDENT $\bowtie_{stud\_id=student}$ INTERNSHIP

Notice that the hypertext specification results simplified: all the predicates induced by the context are factorized in the configuration and the hypertext specifies only the desired structure to access the information (typically, using patterns) and the predicates that do not depend on the context (like, e.g., the predicates associated with the search functionalities).

5 Related Work

In this paper we have shown how data and hypertext views can be combined by means of configurations of specific context dimensions and operators that combine the different dimensions. In literature, several works define context models and the mechanisms to use them.

In the database field, the use of context over the data has been introduced in [1,2,7,9]: these systems focus on a *data-tailoring-oriented* perspective and aim at the reduction of the size of the retrieved data by means of contextual preferences. The tailoring process personalizes the retrieved data, thus enhancing the precision of the tailored information, according to the user information needs. In our paper the focus is instead on the reuse of the same hypertext view, tailored to different kinds of users and/or to different points of views. For a survey on the use of context in the database field see [1].

Also in the Web field, several context-aware systems have been proposed in literature. In most of the works the context is associated with the possibility of adapting the application, from different perspectives: adapting the content to be shown, the navigational paths the user has to follow, or the presentation features (see [8] for a complete survey). Looking at the first perspective, also adaptive and context-aware systems *tailor* the data to show in a particular context and therefore present some commonalities with our proposal.

Considering the most recent context-aware systems [3,5], they extend the personalization mechanism also to other contexts, such as, for example, the devices used to access the application (e.g., mobile devices), thus offering a more generalized mechanism like in the present approach. However, such systems focus on the acquisition of context data, on their update and on their monitoring, and define reactive behaviors that support adaptivity and can be seen as complementary to our approach.

The proposal presented in [6] also deals with the selection of the content to be presented to the user in a particular context. The approach is based on the definition of multi-variant objects, i.e., the same objects can have different versions (e.g., one version for each language in a multi-lingual Web application, one version of each target user group, a free and a non-free version of the data, and so on). The context information is then used to identify the right variant to be shown to the user. Although similar, our proposal determines the context characteristics, but instead of choosing a particular variant, we compose the final view starting from partial initial views. Moreover, we do not apply it at run-time, but our focus is on using the context at design-time to tailor data in the hypertext specification.

6 Conclusions

In this paper we have proposed a methodology for the specification of hypertexts, where the possible context dimensions and values play an important role in the definition of the portions of data that can be delivered to the user. In particular, we have introduced a context data model, as a mean to identify all the possible contexts and the corresponding partial data views. The hypertext specification can exploit such contexts to configure and constrain its content with respect to the corresponding data views.

As future work we plan to integrate the proposed methodology into a prototype, where the partial data views can be specified graphically, and the hypertext model visualizes the (combined) data view that results from the configuration.

References

1. Bolchini, C., Curino, C., Quintarelli, E., Schreiber, F.A., Tanca, L.: A data-oriented survey of context models. In: SIGMOD Record (2008) (to appear)
2. Bolchini, C., Quintarelli, E., Rossato, R.: Relational data tailoring through view composition. In: Parent, C., Schewe, K.-D., Storey, V.C., Thalheim, B. (eds.) ER 2007. LNCS, vol. 4801, pp. 149–164. Springer, Heidelberg (2007)
3. Ceri, S., Daniel, F., Matera, M., Facca, F.M.: Model-driven development of context-aware web applications. ACM Trans. Internet Techn. 7(1) (2007)
4. Ceri, S., Fraternali, P., Bongio, A., Brambilla, M., Comai, S., Matera, M.: Designing Data-Intensive Web Applications. Morgan Kaufmann Publishers Inc., San Francisco (2002)
5. De Virgilio, R.D., Torlone, R.: A framework for the management of context data in adaptive web information systems. In: ICWE 2008 Eighth International Conference on Web Engineering, pp. 261–272 (2008)
6. Grossniklaus, M., Norrie, M.C.: Using object variants to support context-aware interactions. In: AEWSE (2007)
7. Kaenampornpan, M., O'Neill, E.: An integrated context model: Bringing activity to context. In: Proc. Workshop on Advanced Context Modelling, Reasoning and Management (2004)
8. Schwinger, W., Retschitzegger, W., Schauerhuber, A., et al: International Journal of Web Information Systems 4(3), 234–305 (2008)
9. Yang, S.J.H., Huang, A., Chen, R., Tseng, S.-S., Shen, Y.-S.: Context model and context acquisition for ubiquitous content access in ulearning environments. In: IEEE Int. Conf. Sensor Networks, Ubiquitous, and Trustworthy Computing, vol. 2, pp. 78–83 (2006)

Feature-Based Engineering of Compensations in Web Service Environment

Michael Schäfer[1] and Peter Dolog[2]

[1] L3S Research Center, University of Hannover,
Appelstr. 9a, D-30167 Hannover, Germany
Michael.K.Schaefer@gmx.de
[2] IWIS — Intelligent Web and Information Systems,
Aalborg University, Department of Computer Science,
Selma Lagerloefs Vej 300, DK-9220 Aalborg East, Denmark
dolog@cs.aau.dk

Abstract. In this paper, we introduce a product line approach for developing Web services with extended compensation capabilities. We adopt a feature modelling approach in order to describe variable and common compensation properties of Web service variants, as well as service consumer application requirements and constraints regarding compensation. The feature models are being used in order to configure the compensation operations that are applied. In this way, we ensure that the compensation actions are limited to the prescribed ones, and the infrastructure which uses them can be adapted easily in case environment conditions change.

Keywords: Software Product Lines, Feature Model, Web Services, Compensations, Business Activities, Transactions.

1   Introduction

Web service environments are being used to connect clients and service providers and to establish and maintain conversations between them. Businesses adapt and change their business processes and operations, and they perform transactions with different clients at different times. Their services are accessed by third parties in a concurrent way. Concurrent access to services and changes regarding business processes imply that *service providers* should provide different variants of their services to satisfy the varying needs of different clients and to enable forward recovery for business transactions by replacement with another suitable variant if certain conditions are met. Also, *clients/service consumers* should be able to cover criteria in requirements and constraints assuming that the operations can change and can be replaced by other operations if a failure occurs or certain conditions are met.

We propose a feature based method for engineering compensations in Web service environments. We adopt a method and a modelling technique based on feature models described previously in UML [4]. The infrastructure which utilizes the models is based on our compensation environment described in [10].

M. Gaedke, M. Grossniklaus, and O. Díaz (Eds.): ICWE 2009, LNCS 5648, pp. 197–204, 2009.
© Springer-Verlag Berlin Heidelberg 2009

The infrastructure uses the XML schema used also within the eclipse plugin for feature oriented domain analysis [1] to provide the technical means for runtime decisions about compensations. The paper provides an evidence on how to a software product line method can be adapted for a novel application area which addresses real complex situations in business to business interactions. It also provides an evidence that the variability descriptions can be utilized by a middleware for the decisions about compensations, where the descriptions specify a client's requirements and constraints regarding compensation handling on the one hand, as well as the offered compensation capabilities of a service provider on the other hand.

The remainder or the paper is structured as follows. A feature modeling based method for web service compensation engineering is discussed in Section 2. Section 3 discusses service provider capabilities conceptual and feature modelling. Section 4 discusses client requirements conceptual and feature modelling, algorithm which ranks providers according to a matching score between capability and compensation model and requirements model, as well as resulting restriction model which serves as a contract between the client and the provider. Section 5 discusses it in the context of related work. Section 6 concludes the paper with a summary and proposal for further work.

2   Feature Based Development for Compensations

Software product line methodologies [8] employ a common process pattern. *Domain Engineering* is a process in which the commonality and variability of the product line are defined and realized. *Application Engineering* is a process subsequent to the domain engineering in which the applications of the product line are built by reusing domain artifacts and exploiting the product line's variability.

The domain engineering activities in Web service environments are realized by different independent service providers. The application engineering activities are realized by different parties as well, employing service selection mechanisms and matchmaking to fit particular business activities when utilizing Web services from different providers. Some of the variable features of the Web services can be considered at runtime. Therefore, the software product line engineering process can be tailored to the Web service environment with extended compensation capabilities as follows. Service provider tasks are (capabilities and compensations engineering):

- *Service Domain Analysis* — is a domain engineering process where variabilities and commonalities between service variants are designed to support compensations based on failures or based on different constraints and requirements;
- *Service Domain Design and Implementation* — different service features are mapped onto an implementation and an architecture for service provisioning where some of the features need not to be exposed to the public and some of the variabilities may be left to runtime adaptation.

Client/service consumer tasks are (Requirements and Restrictions):

- *Business Application Analysis and Design* — is an application engineering task which may be performed by a party external to the service provider and involves the definition of requirements for and constraints on the Web service compensations;
- *Retrieving the Abstract Web Services* — is an application engineering task in which a designer looks for and retrieves Web services which are required to perform business to business conversations;
- *Defining Client Side Compensations* — is an application engineering task in which a designer defines a variability for compensations which will be exploited at runtime if more Web services with similar capabilities have been found, or an alternative Web service has been defined by an application developer;
- *Implementing Client Side Compensations and Functionalities* — is an application engineering task in which the additional compensations are implemented at the client side, as well as additional operations for which there was no Web service found are realized by an application developer.

As a means for analysis and design we adopt a *feature modelling* approach and a methodology from [3]. *Feature models* are *configuration views* on concepts from conceptual models. The *conceptual model* describes the main concepts of a domain and linguistic relationships between them. *Web service capabilities or client requirements* main concepts are therefore placed into the *application domain conceptual model* and the *compensation concepts* are placed into the *environment conceptual model*. The *functionality feature model* as well as the *compensation feature model* describe the configuration views. Subsequently, the functionality and compensation models are merged to describe the offered capabilities by a service provider, or requested functionalities and restrictions regarding compensations by a service consumer. Different algorithms can then be employed by different middlewares and abstract service to match feature models of a client and service provider, and to trigger forward recovery by utilizing compensation actions agreed on by the consumer and the provider.

3   Capabilities and Compensations of Service Providers

Capability Conceptual and Feature Model. The capabilities conceptual model describes the concepts from a service application domain and relationships between them. In our case for example, the capabilities conceptual model contain concepts related to payroll processing such as salary, salary transfer, tax, tax rates, employee, and so on. The UML class diagram is used to model such conceptual model.

The capability feature model specifies the capabilities of an abstract service. This model can be provided in the public description of the service and can be used in the client's search process for services that fulfill his requirements. The functionality feature model describes the features of the abstract service that constitute the offered operations that can directly be used in the business process, e.g. the booking of a flight. It can be defined as a normal feature model.

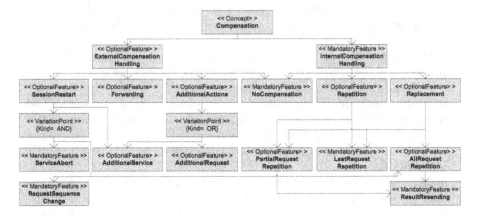

Fig. 1. The compensation feature model

Compensations Conceptual and Feature Model. In order to describe the available compensation types, a conceptual model is created, which constitutes the basis for the feature models in the extended transaction environment. The result is the *compensation concept model*, usually modeled by a class diagram. The basic concept used in such a model is the *Compensation*, which defines the required compensatory operations for a specific situation in a *CompensationPlan*. Each plan consists of one or more single *CompensationActions*.

The *compensation feature model* describes the configuration aspect of the mandatory and optional features of the compensation concept, and is depicted in Figure 1. It will be used in the next step to define service-specific feature models.

The two main features of this model are the *InternalCompensationHandling* and the *ExternalCompensationHandling* features. They structure the available compensation types as features according to their application: *Repetition* and *Replacement* are only available for internal compensation purposes, while *SessionRestart*, *Forwarding* and *AdditionalActions* are only available for external compensation operations. The exception to this separation is *NoCompensation*, which is the only common compensation feature. Only two of these features are mandatory, the *NoCompensation* and the *InternalCompensationHandling* feature. This is due to the fact that the default compensation action is inactivity: If no rule or compensation capabilities exist, then the service has to fail without any other operations. Accordingly, the ability to perform external compensations is only optional.

The *Repetition* feature contains the subfeatures *LastRequestRepetition* (mandatory) and *PartialRequestRepetition* (optional). *LastRequestRepetition* is mandatory, because even if partial request resending is applied, it will be necessary to resend the last request. Likewise, the *Replacement* feature requires that after the replacement of a concrete service has been performed at least the last request will be resent. Both, the resending of a part of the requests or all requests, requires that it is possible to resend new results to the client. Therefore, the *ResultResending* feature is mandatory.

The *SessionRestart* feature has as an optional subfeature the invocation of an additional service (*AdditionalService*), and requires via an AND variation point the *ServiceAbort*, *RequestSequenceChange*, and *AllRequestRepetition* subfeatures. The capability to abort the service, to change the request log, and to resend all requests is needed in order to perform the session restart, and therefore these three features have to be included. Within an externally triggered compensation, it is possible to invoke additional services and to create and send additional requests to the concrete service. That is why *AdditionalActions* includes the *AdditionalService* and *AdditionalRequest* subfeatures. They are connected via an OR variation point, as the *AdditionalActions* feature needs at least one of these two features.

Merging Capabilities and Compensations. The service provider provides at the end only one model to one client. The model is merged from capabilities and compensation feature model. The capability feature model can be extended with a special attribute: A *costs* attribute can be added to each feature. The provider can thus define how much the execution of a specific feature will cost.

4   Requirements and Restrictions of Client Application

Requirements Feature Model. The client creates a requirement description in order to be able to initiate a search for a suitable abstract service. The specification is being done in the same way as the definition of the capability feature model described in the previous section: A common model is being created that includes the required functionality and compensation features. This model is called the *requirement feature model*. However, although the basic process of creating the requirement feature model is the same, the interpretation of the mandatory/optional properties differs. A mandatory feature *has* to be provided by the service and is thus critical for the comparison process, while an optional feature *can* be provided by the service, and is seen as a bonus in the evaluation of the available services.

Model Comparison Algorithm. In the client's search process, each abstract service's capability feature model will be compared to the client's requirement feature model. We define a comparison algorithm which makes it possible to automatically assess the available services and to decide which ones meet the requirements. Our algorithm is a variant of graph matching algorithm on attributed graph [9]. The feature models are attributed graphs where each node is a feature with an attribute stating whether a feature is mandatory or optional. We make use of these attributes in comparing requested capability graph (feature model) with provided capability graph (feature model). The two models are the input for the algorithm, which iteratively compares them and calculates a numerical *compatibility score*. The basic algorithm of comparing the two models functions as follows:

- Using the requirement feature model as a basis, the features are compared stepwise. In this process, it is necessary that the same features are found in the same places, as the same feature structure is expected.
- Each mandatory feature from the requirement model has to be found in the capability feature model as well. A mandatory feature that is found in the capability feature model will not change the compatibility score. If the capability model is missing a mandatory feature, the comparison fails and a negative score is returned to indicate that the service does not fulfill the minimum requirements.
- Each optional feature of the requirement model can be part of the capability model, but does not have to. However, each optional feature that can be found in the capability model counts as a bonus added to the compatibility score. This accounts for the fact that an abstract service that provides more than the absolutely required features is better, as it can more easily be used in different applications and environments.
- Additional features in the abstract service's capability model like the specification of additional services used in the compensation process have to be defined in the correct place, i.e. as a subfeature of the *AdditionalService* feature. Any other additional features will lead to a failure of the comparison.

The compatibility score that is returned by the comparison algorithm describes the degree to which the abstract service fulfills the requirements specified by the client. The requirement model's mandatory features do not increase the compatibility score if they are found in the capability model, because they constitute the minimum requirements. Therefore, an abstract service that provides only the mandatory features has a compatibility score of *0*, although it meets the client's requirements. Each optional feature provided by the service increases the score by a predefined value. The default value for this is *1*, so an abstract service that offers all mandatory features and 5 optional ones has a score of *5*. The higher the compatibility score of an abstract service is, the better it meets the requirements of the client. Using this simple score, it is possible to compare different abstract services and their offered capabilities.

Restriction Feature Model. After the client has found and decided upon the necessary abstract services that offer the required functional and compensation features, a contract will be exchanged or negotiated with each service. A vital part of this contract is the specification which compensation features the abstract service is allowed to use for the purpose of processing internal and external compensations. While it is of course possible to apply this restriction by simply searching for abstract services that are able to perform only the allowed compensation actions, such an approach significantly reduces the available services. Moreover, it is quite possible that a client wants to use the same abstract service in multiple applications, each application having its own rules regarding the compensatory actions that are permitted. Therefore, it is beneficial to use a *restriction feature model* that can be part of the contract, and to which the abstract service dynamically adapts its compensation operations.

When the abstract service wants to invoke a specific compensation action, it will first consult the contract's restriction feature model. If the compensation action is part of the model, then the abstract service is allowed to use it. This way, the service can dynamically adapt to the requirements of each single client. It is possible to use an optional attribute in the restriction feature model in order to further restrict the execution of compensatory actions by the abstract service. The client can add a *maxCosts* attribute to the *InternalCompensationHandling* and *ExternalCompensationHandling* features, which specifies the maximum costs that may be spent by the abstract service for internal and external compensation handling, respectively. Using this approach, it is possible to define a "budget" for internal or external compensation handling.

Feature Model Specification for Middleware. The *FeaturePlugin* [1] for Eclipse has been applied to create the compensation feature model to be able to obtain an XML version of the feature models to be used by our transactional environment. This feature model is used as a basis for the specification of capability and requirement feature models, by changing the mandatory/optional features, or by deleting parts of the model. A restriction feature model can be created in a convenient way as a configuration of the predefined compensation feature model. While doing so, the plug-in monitors the constraints and thus guarantees that the resulting restriction feature model is valid with respect to the properties of the features as well as the feature group cardinalities.

5   Related Work

A product line approach for composite service-oriented systems has been envisioned in [2]. Our approach contributed to the issues of service selection, exception handling and quality factors identified in that paper in the context of service compensations. A pattern based variability has been employed for development of composite service-oriented systems in [7]. Our approach is based on feature models for variability description. The compensation mechanisms, engineering methodology and infrastructure can be used as a supplement to the method presented in [7]. [5] studies product lines in the context of adaptive composite service oriented systems. Our approach can be used as a supplement to provide compensations in such environment to support forward error recovery. [11] defines an atomicity-equivalent process algebra to define public views over business processes involved in B2B conversations. Views are used to check whether the processes are still in an atomicity sphere; i.e. the process is guaranteed to terminate with semantics all or nothing. Our approach allows for other semantics to satisfy clients at least partially though we need to study the properties of termination further. [6] deals with graph matching for feature composition from partial feature models as well. In our approach we do not compose feature models, we try to find out which service fits the client requested capability.

6 Conclusion and Future Work

We have described a software product line approach to be used for Web service transactions in order to control the use of compensatory actions. The compensation feature model has been introduced that structures the compensation types and activities. This model has subsequently been used in order to define the feature models for service capabilities, requirements, and restrictions.

It is necessary to run additional experiments with different scenarios, and to further analyze the usability of feature models. It is interesting to study the use of ontologies in the models. The extensions of the model comparison algorithm should also be studied.

References

1. Antkiewicz, M., Czarnecki, K.: Featureplugin: Feature modeling plug-in for eclipse. In: OOPSLA 2004 Eclipse Technology eXchange (ETX) Workshop (2004)
2. Capilla, R., Topaloglu, N.Y.: Product lines for supporting the composition and evolution of service oriented applications. In: Eighth Intl. Workshop on Principles of Software Evolution in conjunction with ESEC/FSE 2005 (2005)
3. Dolog, P., Nejdl, W.: Using UML-based feature models and UML collaboration diagrams to information modelling for web-based applications. In: Baar, T., Strohmeier, A., Moreira, A., Mellor, S.J. (eds.) UML 2004. LNCS, vol. 3273, pp. 425–439. Springer, Heidelberg (2004)
4. Dolog, P.: Engineering Adaptive Web Applications: A Domain Engineering Framework. VDM Verlag Dr. Müller (2008), http://www.vdm-publishing.com/
5. Hallstein, S., Stav, E., Solberg, A., Floch, J.: Using product line techniques to build adaptive systems. In: SPLC 2006. 10th Intl. Software Product Line Conf. (2006)
6. Jayaraman, P.K., Whittle, J., Elkhodary, A.M., Gomaa, H.: Model composition in product lines and feature interaction detection using critical pair analysis. In: Engels, G., Opdyke, B., Schmidt, D.C., Weil, F. (eds.) MODELS 2007. LNCS, vol. 4735, pp. 151–165. Springer, Heidelberg (2007)
7. Jiang, J., Ruokonen, A., Systä, T.: Pattern-based variability management in web service development. In: ECOWS 2005. Third European Conf. on Web Services (2005)
8. Pohl, K., Böckle, G., van der Linden, F.: Software Product Line Engineering. Springer, Heidelberg (2000)
9. Rozenberg, G.: A Handbook of Graph Grammars and Computing by Graph Transformation: Application Languages and Tools. World Scientific Publishing Company, Singapore (1997)
10. Schäfer, M., Dolog, P., Nejdl, W.: Environment for flexible advanced compensations of web service transactions. ACM Transactions on Web 2(2) (April 2008)
11. Ye, C., Cheung, S.C., Chan., W.K.: Publishing and composition of atomicity-equivalent services for b2b collaboration. In: ICSE 2006: Proceedings of the 28th Intl. Conf. on Software Engineering. ACM, New York (2006)

Product Line Development of Web Systems with Conventional Tools*

Miguel A. Laguna, Bruno González-Baixauli, and Carmen Hernández

Department of Computer Science, University of Valladolid,
Campus M. Delibes, 47011 Valladolid, Spain
{mlaguna,bbaixauli,chernan}@infor.uva.es

Abstract. Development of software product lines is a challenge for small organizations. Although the use of feature models is necessary to manage variability, we propose to use conventional tools for the rest of development activities. Traceability between the features and the UML architectural models is achieved by means of the package merge mechanism of UML 2. A similar strategy is applied at the implementation level, using packages of partial classes. The combination of these techniques and conventional IDE tools make the developments of product lines easier as it removes the need for specialized tools and personnel. This article reports a successful experience with these techniques in the domain of web applications.

Keywords: Software Product Lines, Feature Model, Variability, Traceability.

1 Introduction

Software product lines (SPL) are a proven reuse approach in industrial environments, based on the idea that each product of the SPL can be built from a common set of assets [3]. However, this approach is complex and requires a great effort by the companies that take it on [5]. The research we carry out aims to simplify the change from a conventional development process into one that benefits from the product line advantages in small and medium enterprises (SME).

As specific SPL development techniques, we must pay special attention to the variability and traceability aspects at each abstraction level. We need models that represent the product line and a mechanism to obtain the configuration of features that represent the best combination of variants for a specific application. There is wide agreement about using feature diagrams in some of their multiple versions like FODA [10] or FORM [9] to fulfill those requirements. A feature diagram is a tree, where the root node is the *concept*. The edges are used to decompose this concept into more detailed features by several types of decompositions.

Additionally, we must connect the optional features with the related variation points of the architectural models that implement the product line through traceability links. This explicit connection allows the automatic instantiation of the domain framework in each specific application, selecting or not the optional parts with respect to the particular functional and non-functional user requirements. However, this

* This work has been founded by the Junta de Castilla y León (VA-018A07 project).

M. Gaedke, M. Grossniklaus, and O. Díaz (Eds.): ICWE 2009, LNCS 5648, pp. 205–212, 2009.
© Springer-Verlag Berlin Heidelberg 2009

traceability is not easily managed for several reasons [13]. An optional feature can be related to several elements in a UML model and vice versa. On the other hand, the same basic modeling mechanisms of variability (the specialization in class diagrams or the <<extend>> relationship in use cases) are used to express two variability levels: the design of the product line architecture and the design of a specific application that also has variations (for example two valid and alternative payment forms within a sales system). The solution to this problem has been achieved by modifying or adapting the UML structural and behavioral models, moving from the standard. The works of Gomaa [8] and Clauß [4] are examples of this approach, using stereotypes. Another solution proposed by Czarnecki in [6], consists of annotating the UML models with *presence conditions*, so that each optional feature is reflected in one or several parts of a diagram. All these solutions involve UML modifications. One of our initial restrictions was to maintain unchanged the UML meta-model, in order to use conventional CASE tools to model the product line. Other obligations were to locate at one point on the model all the variations associated to each optional feature or to separate the SPL variability from the variability of the specific applications.

In a previous work [11], we proposed the UML 2 package merge mechanism to represent the SPL architectural variations. This mechanism permits a clear traceability between feature and UML models to be established, associating a package to each optional feature, so that all the necessary changes in the model remain located. Therefore, the architectural model (including structural –class diagrams-, behavioral - use cases-, and dynamic –interaction diagram- models) is built starting from a *Base* package that gathers the common SPL aspects. Then, each variability point detected in the feature model originates a package, connected through a <<merge>> relationship with its parent package. These packages will be combined or not, when each product is derived, according to the selected feature configuration.

To support the approach, we have developed a Feature Modeling Tool (FMT[1]) and integrated it into Visual Studio, using the Microsoft DSL tools. The aim was to introduce product line as one of the project types provided by the development platform. Figure 1 shows the feature explorer view and the configuration tool (Figure 4 in Section 3 depicts a general view). The interface and underlining meta-model of FMT is similar to the *fmp* plug-in [1] and compatible with it, allowing the direct import of *fmp* models. The advantages of FMT are direct integration into the Visual Studio IDE and the possibility of visual representation and manipulation of features and *mutex/require* constraints. As additional benefits, the package structure of the product line and the configuration files can be directly generated.

To test the proposal in realistic situations, this article reports the practical experience with these techniques in the development of an e-commerce product line, as a representative example of web systems. A distinctive characteristic is the use of conventional CASE and IDE tools. In particular, we have used .NET and MS Visual Studio as development platform, with the FMT tool incorporated into the platform. Personnel involved vary from granted postgraduate students to undergraduates working on their term projects, but they are not specialists in SPL development. Sections 2 and 3 of this article are devoted to the description of the case study analysis and design and Section 4 concludes the article and outlines future work.

---

[1] http://www.giro.infor.uva.es/FeatureTool.html

2   Case Study: e-Commerce

The starting point has been the feature model proposed by Lau in [12], where a complete domain analysis using feature models is accomplished. However, the SPL is not implemented, providing us with a starting point to contrast the technique, since the packages that we must implement are imposed by an external independent study. The aim was not to implement hundreds of packages, but to reach a result with enough variability to show that it is possible to develop a functional product line in the web systems domain using a conventional development platform. Figure 1 (left) shows the initially selected features. Some of them are mandatory, as *Catalog, Product Information* and *Categories*. Others can be incorporated or not to the final product as *Shipping* and *Billing Address* or *Multilevel Categories*.

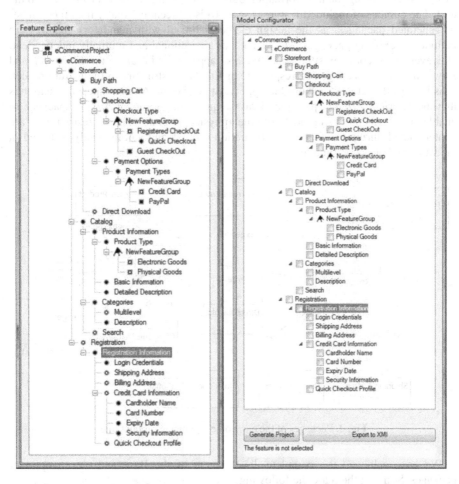

Fig. 1. FMT details of the e-Commerce product line: features tree-view and configuration tool

At this moment, the common part of the product line and a dozen packages have been developed. Therefore, we can already generate hundreds of e-commerce systems, from a minimal combination (that is, the simplest purchase process) to a typical portal with registered users, shopping cart, credit card secure payment, catalogs with multiple categories, search criteria, etc. The developed packages form a basic product family, but it continues growing with the successive packages in development.

3   Product Line Design and Implementation

The design has respected the basic ideas of the architecture proposed by Lau in [12], but organizing them in packages. The basic model of the product line is shown in Figure 2. This structure is automatically generated (in XMI format) from the Feature Modeling Tool using the transformation defined in [11] and now incorporated into the tool. The number of included features (near 40) is noticeably greater than the number of generated packages, as the design elements linked with mandatory features are included in existing packages. Most packages are optional and mutually independent. However, more complex situations have also appear: for instance, the *Electronic* and *Physical Product* packages correspond to an OR (1..2) structure in the feature model. This implies that at least one product type must be chosen. Another special situation is that the *Physical Product* package always requires the *Shipping Address* package to enable the effective shipment of the physical items. These restrictions are contemplated during the feature configuration process and automatically reflected in the valid packages combinations.

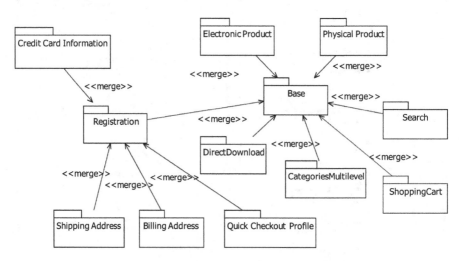

Fig. 2. Packages of the electronic commerce product line

We have achieved the complete development of the Base and eleven optional packages. Some of them are the following:

- *CategoryMultilevel* Package (supports multi-level categories in the catalog)
- *Search* Package (implements multiple criteria searches)

- *DirectDownload* Package (an electronic product can be directly downloaded)
- *ShoppingCart* Package (visualizes the detail of the products added to the cart at any time)
- *ElectronicProduct* and *PhysicalProduct* Packages (at least one must be included to enable the purchase process)

Other packages enable registration facilities, including a simplified payment process, when the user facilitates its payment preferences.

To trace the relationships between the different levels, this package organization is used throughout the development cycle of the product line: features, requirements (use cases and domain models), design (classes and interaction diagrams), and finally implementation. To extend traceability to the implementation, we use the concept of partial class of some languages. For example, C# permits to organize a project in packages with partial classes and, later, when two or more packages that contain classes with the same name are selected, the compilation process combines them in a unique class. The approach reproduces the same strategy used in requirements and design levels at the implementation level. Consequently, once the packages have been implemented, to derive a concrete application, we must uniquely indicate the selected packages corresponding to the feature configuration to the compiler. Thus, the goal of one-to-one traceability from features to code is achieved. The actual implementation of the e-commerce PL has been done using the .NET/ ASP as platform, C# as language, and Microsoft Visual Studio (including FMT) as IDE tool. In addition to domain classes, the implementation details must also solve two main problems: the user interface and data persistence. In the case of persistence, a pragmatic solution has been adopted, using a database that contains all the possible tables and columns. We continue working on the right solution: the *ad hoc* generation of the database schema as a part of the automated product configuration process. Consequently, the methods that handle access to the database use partial data structures, so that some columns of the database tables remain unused.

As for the user interface problem, we have used a combination of templates, cascade style definition files, and dynamic containers. In ASP.NET, it is possible to create master pages that (combined with .css files) serve as templates to the web system. Since we are not developping a closed application, each concrete product in the SPL will possibly have a different main page from the view point of final users. The variability mechanism of the template is achieved by using dynamic containers (*ContentPlaceHolder*) that will be filled in a dynamic way as specified in the code of each concrete application. As shown in Figure 3, each template is built from several pieces. The most interesting parts are on the left, where the different menus are, and the central part, corresponding to the specific content of the page. In both cases, a dynamic editable container has been used. To fill the containers, the methods of the associated C# classes (code behind in .NET terminology) add the needed dynamic controls, as well as their particular behavior. At the time of the configuration of each final product of the SPL, the compiler must recognize the necessary packages and the corresponding dynamic controls. To achieve this, a set of XML based configuration files are used to indicate paths, packages, etc. In addition to the default configuration files provided by the platform, other specific files have been added to each package. Thus, each page builds itself in a systematic way, using a name convention and the information about the necessary controls.

Fig. 3. Design view of a template with two dynamic containers

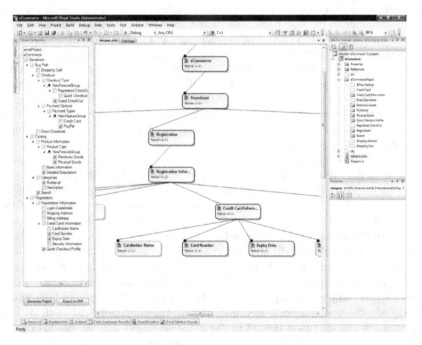

Fig. 4. Configuration process of the e-commerce product line with the detail of the selected (yellow) packages in the *solutions* explorer (right)

Figure 4 shows the way the packages are organized and configured. The available packages and their relationships are managed inside the IDE platform. In fact, the selection process is done using the FMT *configuration tool* (left part of Figure 4) and this selection is automatically reflected in the Visual Studio *solution explorer* (packages of the right part of Figure 4). Once selected and validated, the project configuration is set and the compiler generates the final specific product that can be deployed and installed in minutes in the production server.

The results include the generation of several hundreds of variants, simply configuring and recompiling the SPL project into a concrete product. All the products include the basic purchase process, but specific products can include: Registered users, electronic or physical products, search facilities, credit or *PayPal* secure payment methods, etc. The details of how to install and to configure a product can be consulted in [7]. In Figure 5, two examples of final products with different degrees of complexity can be appreciated. To summarize, a realistic e-commerce product line has been developed, using a seamless approach, based on UML package merging and partial classes. At the same time, the necessary implementation techniques to handle variability at code level have been established. In general, the experience with graduate students has been satisfactory as they have reached the objectives with a reasonable effort (three to four months, four students working part time).

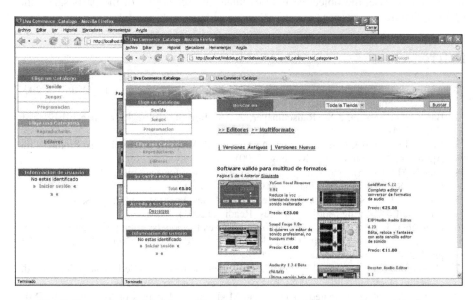

Fig. 5. Two variants of the electronic commerce product line as seen in a web browser

4   Conclusions

In this work the feasibility of a product line development approach in the web applications domain has been shown. The use of package merge and partial class mechanisms enables the automated generation of each product from the features configuration. Furthermore, the use of conventional CASE and IDE tools can simplify the adoption of this paradigm, avoiding the necessity of specific tools and techniques as in previous alternatives. The approach has been successfully applied to the design and implementation of an e-Commerce product line, based on a previous feature analysis published in the literature. As a part of this work, a Feature Modeling Tool have been developed and incorporated into the Visual Studio IDE. This direct integration allows generating automatically (through XMI standard files) the UML package model structure and configuring the final products from the Feature Modeling Tool. Therefore, the configuration process is more transparent and straightforward for the application engineers.

Some commercial tools, such as Big-Lever Gears (www.biglever.com) or pure::variants (www.pure-systems.com) offer similar functionalities. Batory et al. have developed AHEAD, a set of java based tools that implements the *Feature Oriented Programming* paradigm [2]. Though these solutions are valid, the learning of new modeling or implementation techniques and the need of specialized CASE and IDE tools represent barriers for the adoption of the product line approach in many organizations; we therefore believe that the solution presented here improves the abovementioned proposals.

Current work includes the development of other product lines (in particular in the domain of non-lucrative associations), and the enrichment of the e-commerce case study. In this case, the objective is to evaluate the scalability of the proposal as the optional features increase.

References

1. Antkiewicz, M., Czarnecki, K.: Feature modeling plugin for Eclipse. In: OOPSLA 2004 Eclipse technology exchange workshop (2004)
2. Batory, D., Sarvela, J.N., Rauschmayer, A.: Scaling Step-Wise Refinement. IEEE TSE (June 2004)
3. Bosch, J.: Design & Use of Software Architectures. Adopting and Evolving a Product-Line Approach. Addison-Wesley, Reading (2000)
4. Clauß, M.: Generic modeling using Uml extensions for variability. In: Workshop on Domain Specific Visual Languages at OOPSLA (2001)
5. Clements, P.C., Northrop, L.: Software Product Lines: Practices and Patterns. SEI Series in Software Engineering. Addison-Wesley, Reading (2001)
6. Czarnecki, K., Antkiewicz, M.: Mapping Features to models: a template approach based on superimposed variants. In: Glück, R., Lowry, M. (eds.) GPCE 2005. LNCS, vol. 3676, pp. 422–437. Springer, Heidelberg (2005)
7. García Gil, C., Izquierdo, Á., Juan, C.: Desarrollo de una Línea de Producto Software de comercio electrónico. PFC (2008), http://giro.infor.uva.es
8. Gomaa, H.: Object Oriented Analysis and Modeling for Families of Systems with UML. In: ICSR6, pp. 89–99 (2000)
9. Kang, K., Kim, S., Lee, J., Kim, K.: FORM: A Feature-Oriented Reuse Method with Domain-Specific Reference Architectures. Annals of Software Eng. 5, 143–168 (1998)
10. Kang, K.C., Cohen, S., Hess, J., Nowak, W., Peterson, S.: Feature-Oriented Domain Analysis (FODA) Feasibility Study. Technical Report, CMU/SEI-90-TR-21 (1990)
11. Laguna, M.A., González-Baixauli, B., Marqués, J.M.: Seamless Development of Software Product Lines: Feature Models to UML Traceability. In: GPCE 2007 (2007)
12. Lau, S.: Domain Analysis of E-Commerce Systems Using Feature-Based Model Templates., MSc Thesis, ECE Department, University of Waterloo, Canada (2006)
13. Sochos, P., Philippow, I., Riebish, M.: Feature-oriented development of software product lines: mapping feature models to the architecture. In: Weske, M., Liggesmeyer, P. (eds.) NODe 2004. LNCS, vol. 3263, pp. 138–152. Springer, Heidelberg (2004)

An Empirical Study on the Use of
Web-COBRA and Web Objects to
Estimate Web Application Development Effort

Sergio Di Martino[1], Filomena Ferrucci[2], and Carmine Gravino[2]

[1] University of Napoli "Federico II" Via Cinthia, I-80126 Napoli, Italy
dimartino@na.infn.it
[2] University of Salerno, Via Ponte Don Melillo, I-84084 Fisciano (SA), Italy
{fferrucci,gravino}@unisa.it

Abstract. We have performed a replication of a previous study in order to
further assess the effectiveness of Web-COBRA method, with the Web Objects
measure, in predicting Web application development effort. The results of the
empirical analysis confirm the interesting results of the previous study.

Keywords: Effort estimation method, Web-COBRA, Web applications.

1 Introduction

In the field of Web Engineering many techniques have been proposed to predict the
effort required for the development of an application, and among them Web-COBRA
is of particular interest, thanks to its ability to combine experts knowledge with a
formal estimation model [21]. Web-COBRA is an adaptation of COBRA [4] and the
key issue of these two methods is to exploit experts' knowledge, gathered in a
controlled way, for identifying the main factors that can influence the development
cost for a specific software company/domain, and this information is used to "adjust"
the estimations coming from a model that exploits a size measure as cost driver.

To date, the effectiveness of Web-COBRA has been assessed only in one previous
study, which exploited a dataset of 12 Web applications, sized using Web Objects, a
measure proposed by Reifer specifically for Web applications [20]. Web Objects add
four new Web-related components to the five function types of the Function Point
Analysis method [10], namely Multimedia Files, Web Building Blocks, Scripts, and
Links. The analysis performed in [21] provided interesting results and encouraged us
to further analyze the effectiveness of Web-COBRA in combination with Web
Objects. In particular, we have replicated that study in a different context, by
considering a dataset of 15 bigger Web applications developed by an Italian software
company.

The remainder of the paper is organized as follows. In Section 2 we report on the
empirical analysis we performed together with a discussion of the gathered results.
Section 3 contains a description of related work, while Section 4 concludes the paper
giving final remarks and suggestions on future work.

M. Gaedke, M. Grossniklaus, and O. Díaz (Eds.): ICWE 2009, LNCS 5648, pp. 213–220, 2009.
© Springer-Verlag Berlin Heidelberg 2009

2 Empirical Study

We start by describing the dataset employed in the empirical study and the differences with respect the dataset used in the previous analysis. Then, we report on the empirical analysis and discuss the results.

2.1 Dataset Description

The empirical study we present in this paper is based on a dataset coming from a medium-sized software company operating in Italy, whose core business is the development of enterprise information systems, mainly for local and central government. The company has about fifty employees and a turnover of about 5M €. It is certified ISO 9001:2000, and it is also a certified partner of Microsoft and Oracle.

Data used in the study are related to a set of 15 Web applications, including e-government, e-banking, Web portals, and Intranet applications. They have been developed by exploiting different Web-oriented technologies, such as J2EE, ASP.NET, etc... Oracle has been the most commonly adopted DBMS, but also SQL Server, Access and MySQL have been employed in some applications.

Table 1 provides some descriptive statistics about the considered dataset, taking into account the size (in terms of Web Objects), the actual effort (in terms of person-hours), and the peak staff (in terms of people involved in the project). Moreover, it also reports the statistics of the dataset considered by Ruhe *et al.* for the first assessment of Web-COBRA [21]. They used 12 Web applications, such as B2B, intranet or financial, developed between 1998 and 2002 by a small Australian software development company, with about twenty employees. The most of these projects were new developments, even if there were also enhancements, and re-development projects.

Table 1. Descriptive statistics of effort (in terms of person/hours), and size (in terms of Web Objects), and peak staff

	Min	Max	Median	Mean	Std. Dev.
Current study					
Web Objects	465	2,258	611	1,474.87	543.42
Effort	1176	3,712	1389	2,677.87	827.12
Peak Staff	6	7	6	6.2	0.4
Ruhe *et al.*'s study					
Web Objects	67	792	Un-Know	284	227
Effort	267	2,504	Un-Know	883	710
Peak Staff	2	6	Un-Know	3	1.5

The 15 Web applications considered in our replication are of the same kind, but they are more recent, being developed between 2003 and 2006. Other differences are related to the size of the applications and the size of the team. Indeed, in mean, the applications considered in this replication are 5.2 times bigger than the ones of Ruhe *et al.*, in terms of Web Objects. Moreover, the development teams considered in this replication are in mean 2 times bigger than the ones of Ruhe *et al.*

2.2 The Empirical Analysis

In order to apply the Web-COBRA method, we first identified and quantified the cost factors and then we collected data from Web application involved in our case study.

Regarding the identification and quantification of cost factors, a large number of cost drivers may affect the development cost of software applications. To select the set of the cost drivers that result significant for the considered domain [4], [21], we drafted an initial list, basing on a review of the literature on Web effort/cost estimation, including the cost factors identified in [21]. This preliminary list was submitted to five experts of the software company involved in our empirical study. Then a Delphi method [14] was adopted until they agreed on the final set of cost drivers. They were asked to comment, basing on their experience, on the clarity of the factors (to avoid that different project managers could interpret them in different ways), on their completeness (to avoid that some key factors might not be considered), and on relevance for the Web application development domain, working also to reduce as much as possible redundancies and overlaps. A final list of 10 cost drivers was devised. They are reported in Table 2. It is worth noting that this list includes four cost factors employed by Ruhe *et al.* in [21]: Novelty of Requirements, Importance of Software Reliability, Novelty of Technology, and Developer's Technical Capabilities. Then, the experts were asked to quantify the cost factors, specifying their minimal, most likely, and maximal inducted overhead (see Table 2). Again, a Delphi method was used to obtain a single representative triple for each cost factor.

Table 2. Identified cost factors and their influence

Cost factor	Minimal	Most likely	Maximal
Novelty of Requirements (CF1)	10%	35%	70%
Importance of Software Portability (CF2)	7%	25%	60%
Importance of Software Reliability (CF3)	5%	20%	60%
Importance of Software Usability (CF4)	7%	30%	65%
Importance of Software Efficiency and Performance (CF5)	7%	20%	50%
Novelty of Technologies (CF6)	5%	25%	65%
Integration/Interaction with legacy systems (CF7)	20%	35%	70%
Temporal Overlap with other projects (CF8)	10%	35%	60%
Productivity of the adopted technological platform (CF9)	15%	45%	65%
Developer's Technical Capabilities (CF10)	10%	35%	65%

In the second step, the relationship between the cost overhead and the development cost was modeled by using the Ordinary Least Squares Regression (OLSR) and employing past data of the company. The information on the cost overhead for each project p was obtained by the sum of all the triangular distributions of cost factors of p, given their minimal, most likely, and maximal values indicated by project managers. In particular, for each cost factor, the project manager specified its influence on the Web application by means of a value in the range 0..3, where 0 means that no influence was due to that factor, and 3 represents the highest impact. The descriptive statistics of the cost factors are shown in Table 3.

Table 3. Descriptive Statistics of cost factors

	Min.	Max.	Mean	Median	Std. Dev.
CF1	0	2	0.933	1	0.700
CF2	0	1	0.333	0	0.488
CF3	0	3	0.533	0	0.915
CF4	0	3	1.067	1	1.033
CF5	0	1	0.133	0	0.352
CF6	0	3	0.867	0	1.125
CF7	0	3	1.400	1	0.828
CF8	1	3	1.800	2	0.676
CF9	1	3	1.800	2	0.775
CF10	1	1	1.000	1	0

The information on Effort, Size (expressed in terms of Web Objects), and co_overhead was then exploited to build an estimation model and validate it. Observe that Web-COBRA assumes that the relationship between effort and size is linear [21]. We performed the required statistical tests to verify this linearity in our dataset. Moreover, the size of a Web application was modeled as an uncertain variable, which underlies a triangular distribution, and an uncertainty of 5% was considered in [21]. Then, we applied a leave-1-out cross validation, by performing 15 steps, where at each step the original dataset was partitioned into a training set of 14 Web applications and a validation set consisting of the remaining application. The training set was used to determine the estimation model and the validation set to assess the obtained estimates. Moreover, we ran a Monte Carlo simulation (considering 1000 iterations) that allowed us to use the relationship between cost overhead and effort together with the causal model in order to obtain a probability distribution of the effort for the new project [21]. Then, the mean value of the distribution was used as the estimated effort value.

To evaluate the accuracy of the obtained estimations, we employed some widely used summary measures, namely MMRE, MdMRE, and Pred(0.25) [6], together with boxplots of absolute residuals [13]. Table 4 contains the results we obtained, which highly fit the acceptable thresholds defined in [6] since MMRE (and MdMRE) values are less than 0.25 and Pred(0.25) value is greater than 0.75. This means that the mean error of the estimates we obtained is less than 25%, and that at least 75% of the estimated values fall within 25% of their actual values.

Table 4. Descriptive accuracy evaluation

	MMRE	MdMRE	Pred(0.25)
Web-COBRA with Web Objects	0.14	0.11	0.87
MeanEFH	0.34	0.27	0.47
MedianEFH	0.33	0.24	0.60

As suggested by Mendes and Kitchenham [18], we also compared MMRE, MdMRE, and Pred(0.25) with the mean of effort (i.e., MeanEFH) and the median of effort (i.e., MedianEFH) across all the dataset of past projects, as estimated value. The aim is to have a benchmark to assess whether the estimates obtained with Web-COBRA are significantly better than the trivial estimates based on the mean or median effort of all the previous projects. Indeed, if the estimates obtained with mean or median effort are similar to those obtained with the employed method then for the software company it could be more useful to simply use the mean or the median effort of the past developed applications rather than dealing with complex estimation techniques [18]. The results in Table 4 reveal that the values of MMRE and Pred(0.25) for MeanEFH and MedianEFH do not match the acceptance thresholds suggested in [6]. The boxplots of absolute residuals depicted in Figure 1 confirm that the estimations achieved by using Web-COBRA with Web Objects are better than those obtained using MeanEFH and MedianEFH. Indeed, the box length and the tails of the boxplot for Web-COBRA are smaller than those of boxplots for MeanEFH and MedianEFH. Furthermore, the median of boxplot for Web-COBRA is more close to zero than the other two boxplots.

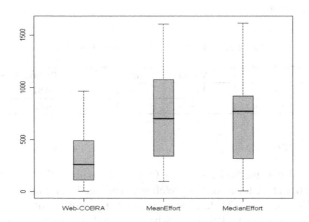

Fig. 1. The boxplots of absolute residuals

As suggested in [13], we also tested the statistical significance of the results obtained from the proposed models by using paired absolute residuals. To this end, we performed both the T-Test and the Wilcoxon test to verify the following null hypothesis: "the two considered population have identical distributions". The analysis revealed that the absolute residuals obtained using Web-COBRA and Web Objects were significantly better than those obtained using MeanEFH and MedianEFH.

To have an indication of the practical/managerial significance of these results we analyzed the effect size, which has many advantages over the use of tests of statistical significance alone since "whereas p-values reveal whether a finding is statistically significant, effect size indicates practical significance" [11]. Employing the Wilcoxon test and the T-test, the effect sizes was determined by using the formula: $r = Z\text{-score} / \sqrt{N}$, where N is the number of observations. The statistics on effect size revealed that all results statistically significant were also practical significant according to the widely used Cohen's benchmarks [5]. Indeed, medium effect sizes were highlighted (i.e., $50 < r < 0.80$).

2.3 Comparison with the Previous Case Study

As for comparison with the previous empirical study, in Table 5 we have reported the values of the summary statistics on the prediction accuracy obtained in the previous research on Web-COBRA [21]. We can observe that the MMRE and Pred(0.25) values we obtained are slightly better than those of [21]. Thus, the analysis reported in the present paper has confirmed the results of [21] showing the effectiveness of Web-COBRA in combination with Web Objects to estimate Web application development effort. Moreover, our results extend the ones in [21], showing the scalability of the method. Indeed, as discussed in Section 2.1 the Web applications used in our empirical study have larger sizes than the Web applications used in [21]. Thus, our results suggest that Web-COBRA and Web Objects turn out to be good for estimating larger Web applications, too.

Table 5. Comparison with the results of [21]

	MMRE	MdMRE	Pred(0.25)
Our result	0.14	0.11	0.87
Ruhe et al. result	0.17	0.15	0.75

3 Related Work

Besides Web-COBRA method and Web Objects measure, other approaches were proposed in the literature for estimating Web applications development effort.

The COSMIC method [7] has been applied to Web applications by some researchers in the last years [9], [15], who exploited as estimation technique the OLSR. In particular, Mendes *et al.* applied the COSMIC approach to Web sites, i.e., without server-side elaborations [15]. Using data about 37 Web systems developed by academic students, they constructed an effort estimation model by applying OLSR. However, this model did not provide good estimations and replications of the study were highly recommended by Mendes *et al.* to find possible biases in the application of the method. Subsequently, the observation that dynamic Web applications are characterized by data movements (from a Web server to the client browser) suggested to apply the principles of the COSMIC method to size this type of Web applications [9]. An empirical study based on the use of 44 Web applications developed by academic students, was performed to assess the COSMIC approach [9]. The effort estimation model obtained by employing the OLSR provided encouraging results.

Some authors investigated the usefulness of size measures specific for Web applications such as number of Web pages, media elements, internal links, etc. [1], [3], [8], [15], [16], [17]. Several studies were conducted to investigate and compare the effectiveness of these measures in combination with estimation techniques like Linear and Stepwise Regression, Case-Based Reasoning, Regression Tree, and Bayesian Networks [2], [3], [8], [16], [17], [19]. In particular, in [16] a dataset of 37

Web systems developed by academic students was exploited and the empirical results suggested that Stepwise Regression provided statistically significant superior predictions than the other techniques when using length size measures, such as number of Web pages, number of new media. By employing the same dataset, in [17] the Regression Tree gave worse results than Stepwise Regression and Case-Based Reasoning, and the authors highlighted that the models obtained with Linear and Stepwise Regression generally gave statistically significant better results than Case-Based Reasoning and Regression Tree. On the contrary, a study exploiting a dataset containing data on 15 Web software applications developed by a single Web company (the ones also employed in the empirical study presented in this paper) revealed that none of the employed techniques (i.e., Stepwise Regression, Regression Tree, and Case-Based Reasoning) was statistically significantly superior than others [8]. Recently, Mendes and Mosley investigated the use of Bayesian Networks for Web effort estimation using the Web applications of the Tukutuku database [19]. In particular, they employed two training sets, each with 130 Web applications, to construct the models while their accuracy was measured using two test sets, each containing data on 65 Web applications. The analysis revealed that Manual Stepwise Regression provided significantly better estimations than any of the models obtained by using Bayesian Networks and is the only approach that provided significantly better results than the median effort based model.

Baresi and Morasca proposed a different approach defining several measures on the basis of attributes obtained from design artifacts [3]. They reported on a case study, and two replications, conducted with students of an advanced university class, that highlighted the impact of some attributes, obtained from artifacts designed with W2000, on the total effort required for designing Web applications. It is worth noting that, in our empirical study, Web applications were not automatically obtained from design documents, thus our focus was on the effort to develop Web applications.

Abrahão and Pastor proposed the OOmFPWeb method [1] which maps the Function Points concepts into the primitives used in the conceptual modeling phase of OOWS, a method for producing software for the Web. In a recent work, an initial validation of the proposed size measure was described [2].

4 Conclusions

In this paper we have investigated the use of Web-COBRA proposed in [21] for estimating Web application development effort. In particular, we have replicated a previous case study [21], by applying Web-COBRA in combination with the Web Objects measure and exploiting data from 15 industrial Web applications developed by an Italian software company. The empirical analysis has not only confirmed the effectiveness of Web-COBRA and Web Objects in estimating development effort, but has also shown their ability to scale, dealing with bigger applications.

In the future, we intend to further assess Web-COBRA by considering a different contest. Moreover, we plan to apply Web-COBRA using COSMIC as size measure [7]. Indeed, Web-COBRA's authors suggested to employ COSMIC or Web Objects, however in [21] only Web Objects approach was used.

References

[1] Abrahão, S.M., Pastor, O.: Measuring the functional size of Web applications. International Journal of Web Engineering and Technology 1(1), 5–16 (2003)

[2] Abrahão, S.M., Pastor, O., Poels, G.: Evaluating a Functional Size Measurement Method for Web Applications: An Empirical Analysis. In: Proceedings of International Software Metrics Symposium (METRICS 2004), pp. 358–369 (2004)

[3] Baresi, L., Morasca, S.: Three Empirical Studies on Estimating the Design Effort of Web Applications. Transaction On Software Engineering and Methodology 16(4) (2007)

[4] Briand, L., El Emam, K., Bomarius, F.: COBRA: A Hybrid Method for Software Cost Estimation, Benchmarking, and Risk Assessment. In: Proceedings of the International Conference on Software Engineering (ICSE 1998), pp. 390–399 (1998)

[5] Cohen, J.: Statistical Power Analysis for the Behavioral Science. Lawrence Erlbaum Hillsdale, New Jersey (1988)

[6] Conte, D., Dunsmore, H.E., Shen, V.Y.: Software engineering metrics and models. The Benjamin/Cummings Publishing Company, Inc. (1986)

[7] COSMIC. Web site (2007), http://www.cosmicon.com

[8] Costagliola, G., Di Martino, S., Ferrucci, F., Gravino, C., Tortora, G., Vitiello, G.: Effort estimation modeling techniques: a case study for Web applications. In: Proceedings of International Conference on Web Engineering (ICWE 2006), pp. 9–16 (2006)

[9] Costagliola, G., Di Martino, S., Ferrucci, F., Gravino, C., Tortora, G., Vitiello, G.: A COSMIC-FFP: Approach to Predict Web Application Development Effort. Journal of Web Engineering 5(2), 93–120 (2006)

[10] IFPUG, Function point counting practices manual, release 4.2.1 (2004)

[11] Kampenes, V., Dybå, T., Hannay, J.E., Sjøberg, D.I.K.: A Systematic Review of Effect Size in Software Engineering Experiments. Information and Software Technology 4(11-12), 1073–1086 (2007)

[12] Kitchenham, B.A., Pfleeger, S.L., Pickard, L.M.: Case Studies for Method and Tool Evaluation. IEEE Software 12(4), 52–62 (1995)

[13] Kitchenham, B.A., Pickard, L.M., MacDonell, S.G., Shepperd, M.J.: What accuracy statistics really measure. IEE Proceedings – Software 148(3), 81–85 (2001)

[14] Linstone, H.A., Turoff, M.: The Delphi Method: Techniques and Applications. Addison-Wesley Publishing Co. Inc. (1975)

[15] Mendes, E., Counsell, S., Mosley, N.: Comparison of Web Size Measures for Predicting Web Design and Authoring Effort. IEE Proceedings-Software 149(3), 86–92 (2002)

[16] Mendes, E., Counsell, S., Mosley, N., Triggs, C., Watson, I.: A Comparative Study of Cost Estimation Models for Web Hypermedia Applications. Empirical Software Engineering 8(2), 163–196 (2003)

[17] Mendes, E., Counsell, S., Mosley, N., Triggs, C., Watson, I.: A Comparison of Development Effort Estimation Techniques for Web Hypermedia Applications. In: Proceedings of International Software Metrics Symposium (METRICS 2002), pp. 131–140 (2002)

[18] Mendes, E., Kitchenham, B.: Further Comparison of Cross-company and Within-company Effort Estimation Models for Web Applications. In: Proceedings of International Software Metrics Symposium (METRICS 2004), pp. 348–357 (2004)

[19] Mendes, E., Mosley, N.: Bayesian Network Models for Web Effort Prediction: A Comparative Study. IEEE Transactions on Software Engineering (August 1, 2008), http://doi.ieeecomputersociety.org/10.1109/TSE.2008.64

[20] Reifer, D.: Web-Development: Estimating Quick-Time-to-Market Software. IEEE Software 17(8), 57–64 (2000)

[21] Ruhe, M., Jeffery, R., Wieczorek, I.: Cost estimation for Web applications. In: Proceedings of the International Conference on Software Engineering (ICSE 2003), pp. 285–294 (2003)

An Extensible Monitoring Framework for Measuring and Evaluating Tool Performance in a Service-Oriented Architecture

Christoph Becker, Hannes Kulovits, Michael Kraxner, Riccardo Gottardi, and
Andreas Rauber

Vienna University of Technology, Vienna, Austria
http://www.ifs.tuwien.ac.at/dp

Abstract. The lack of QoS attributes and their values is still one of
the fundamental drawbacks of web service technology. Most approaches
for modelling and monitoring QoS and web service performance focus
either on client-side measurement and feedback of QoS attributes, or on
ranking and discovery, developing extensions of the standard web service
discovery models. However, in many cases, provider-side measurement
can be of great additional value to aid the evaluation and selection of
services and underlying implementations.

We present a generic architecture and reference implementation for
non-invasive provider-side instrumentation of data-processing tools exposed as QoS-aware web services, where real-time quality information is
obtained through an extensible monitoring framework. In this architecture, dynamically configurable execution engines measure QoS attributes
and instrument the corresponding web services on the provider side. We
demonstrate the application of this framework to the task of performance
monitoring of a variety of applications on different platforms, thus enriching the services with real-time QoS information, which is accumulated
in an experience base.

1 Introduction

Service-oriented computing as means of arranging autonomous application components into loosely coupled networked services has become one of the primary
computing paradigms of our decade. Web services as the leading technology in
this field are widely used in increasingly distributed systems. Their flexibility and
agility enable the integration of heteregoneous systems across platforms through
interoperable standards. However, the thus-created networks of dependencies
also exhibit challenging problems of interdependency management. Some of the
issues arising are service discovery and selection, the question of service quality
and trustworthiness of service providers, and the problem of measuring quality-
of-service (QoS) attributes and using them as means for guiding the selection of
the optimal service for consumption at a given time and situation.

Measuring quality attributes of web services is inherently difficult due to the
very virtues of service-oriented architectures: The late binding and flexible integration ideals ask for very loose coupling, which often implies that little is

M. Gaedke, M. Grossniklaus, and O. Díaz (Eds.): ICWE 2009, LNCS 5648, pp. 221–235, 2009.
© Springer-Verlag Berlin Heidelberg 2009

known about the actual quality of services and even less about the confidence that can be put into published service metadata, particularly QoS information. Ongoing monitoring of these quality attributes is a key enabler of service-level agreements and a prerequisite for building confidence and trust in services.

Different aspects of performance measurement and benchmarking of web services have been analysed. However, most approaches do not provide concrete ways of measuring performance of services in a specific architecture. Detailed performance measurement of web services is particularly important for obtaining quality attributes that can be used for service selection and composition, and for discovering bottlenecks to enable optimization of composite service processes.

The total, round-trip-time performance of a web service is composed by a number of factors such as network latency and web service protocol layers. Measuring only the round-trip performance gives rather coarse-grained measurements and does not provide hints on optimization options. On the other hand, network latencies are hard to quantify, and the run-time execution characteristics of the software that is exposed as a service are an important component of the overall performance.

Similar to web service quality criteria and service selection, these run-time execution characteristics of a software tool are also an important criterion for the general scenario of Commercial-off-the-Shelf (COTS) component selection. Our motivating application scenario are the component selection procedures in digital preservation planning. In this domain, a decision has to be taken as to which tools and services to include for accomplishing the task of keeping specific digital objects alive for future access, either by converting them to different representations or by rendering them in compatible environments, or by a combination of both. The often-involved institutional responsibility for the curation of digital content implies that a carefully designed selection procedure is necessary that enables transparent and trustworthy decision making.

We have been working on a COTS selection methodology relying on empirical evaluation in a controlled experimentation setting [2]. The corresponding distributed architecture, which supports and automates the selection process, relies on web services exposing the key components to be selected, which are discovered in corresponding registries [1].

This COTS selection scenario shows many similarities to the general web service selection problem, but the service instances that are measured are used mainly for experimentation; once a decision is taken to use a specific tool, based on the experimental evaluation through the web service, it might be even possible to transfer either the data to the code or vice versa, to achieve optimum performance for truly large-scale operations on millions of objects.

The implications are that

1. Monitoring the round-trip time of service consumption at the client does not yield sufficient details of the runtime characteristics;
2. Provider-side runtime characteristics such as the memory load produced by executing a specific function on the server are of high interest;

3. Client-side monitoring is less valuable as some of the main parameters determining it, such as the network connection to the service, are negotiable and up to configuration and production deployment.

While client-side measurement is certainly a valuable tool and necessary to take into account the complete aspects of web service execution, it is not able to get down to the details and potential bottlenecks that might be negotiable or changeable, and thus benefits greatly from additional server-side instrumentation. Moreover, for large-scale library systems containing millions of objects that require treatment, measuring the performance of tools in detail can be crucial.

In this paper, we present a generic and extensible architecture and framework for non-invasive provider-side service instrumentation that enables the automated monitoring of different categories of applications exposed as web services and provides integrated QoS information. We present a reference implementation for measuring the performance of data processing tools and instrumenting the corresponding web services on the provider side. We further demonstrate the performance monitoring of a variety of applications ranging from native C++ applications and Linux-based systems to Java applications and client-server tools, and discuss the results from our experiments.

The rest of this paper is structured as follows. The next section outlines related work in the areas of web service QoS modelling, performance measurement, and distributed digital preservation services. Section 3 describes the overall architectural design and the monitoring engines, while Section 4 analyses the results of practical applications of the implemented framework. Section 5 discusses implications and sets further directions.

2   Related Work

The initially rather slow takeup of web service technology has been repeatedly attributed to the difficulties in evaluating the quality of services and the corresponding lack of confidence in the fulfillment of nun-functional requirements. The lack of QoS attributes and their values is still one of the fundamental drawbacks of web service technology [21,20].

Web service selection and composition heavily relies on QoS computation [18,6]. A considerable amount of work has been dedicated towards modelling QoS attributes and web service performance, and to ranking and selection algorithms. A second group of work is covering infrastructures for achieving trustworthiness, usually by extending existing description models for web services and introducing certification roles to the web service discovery models. Tian describes a QoS schema for web services and a corresponding implementation of a description and selection infrastructure. In this framework, clients specify their QoS requirements to a broker, who tests them agains descriptions published by service providers and interacts with a UDDI registry [25]. Industry-wise, IBM's Web Service Level Agreement (WSLA) framework targets defining and monitoring SLAs [14].

Liu presents a ranking algorithm for QoS-attribute based service selection [16]. The authors describe the three general criteria of execution duration (round-trip time), execution price, and reputation, and allow for domain-specific QoS criteria. Service quality information is collected through accumulating feedback of the requesters who deposit their QoS experience. Ran proposes a service discovery model including QoS as constraints for service selection, relying on third-party QoS certification [21]. Maximilien proposes an ontology for modelling QoS and an architecture where agents stand between providers and consumers and aggregate QoS experience on behalf of the consumers [17]. Erradi presents a middleware solution for monitoring composite web service performance and other quality criteria at the message level [7].

Most of these approaches assume that QoS information is known and can be verified by the third-party certification instance. While this works well for static quality attributes, variable and dynamically changing attributes are hard to compute and subject to change. Platzer discusses four principal strategies for the continuous monitoring of web service quality [20]: provider-side instrumentation, SOAP intermediaries, probing, and sniffing. They further separate performance into eight components such as network latency, processing and wrapping time on the server, and round-trip time. While they state the need for measuring all of these components, they focus on round-trip time and present a provider-independent bootstrapping framework for measuring performance-related QoS on the client-side [22,20].

Wickramage et. al. analyse the factors that contribute to the total round trip time (RTT) of a web service request and arrive at 15 components that should ideally be measured separately to optimize bottlenecks. They focus on web service frameworks and propose a benchmark for this layer [26]. Her et. al. discuss metrics for modelling web service performance [11]. Head presents a benchmark for SOAP communication in grid web services [10]. Large-scale client-side performance measurement tests of a distributed learning environment are described in [23], while Song presents a dedicated tool for client-side performance testing of specific web services [24].

There is a large body of work on quality attributes in the COTS component selection domain [5,4]. Franch describes hierachical quality models for COTS selection based on the ISO/IEC 9126 quality model [13] in [9].

Different categories of criteria need to be measured to automate the COTS selection procedure in digital preservation [2].

- The quality of results of preservation action components is a highly complex domain-specific quality aspect. Quantifying the information loss introduced by transforming the representation of digital content constitutes one of the central areas of research in digital preservation [3].
- On a more generic level, the direct and indirect costs are considered.
- For large-scale digital repositories, process-related criteria such as operational aspects associated with a specific tool are important. To these criteria pertain also the performance and scalability of a tool, as they can have significant impact on the operational procedures and feasibility of implementing a specific solution in a repository system.

In the preservation planning environment described in [1], planning decisions are taken following a systematic workflow supported by a Web-based application which serves as the frontend to a distributed architecture of preservation services.

To support the processes involved in digital preservation, current initiatives are increasingly relying on distributed service oriented architectures to handle the core tasks in a preservation system [12,8,1].

This paper builds on the work described above and takes two specific steps further. We present a generic architecture and reference implementation for non-invasively measuring the performance of data processing tools and instrumenting the corresponding web services on the provider side. We demonstrate the performance monitoring of a variety of applications ranging from native C++ applications on Linux-based systems to Java applications and client-server tools, and discuss results from our experiments.

3   A Generic Architecture for Performance Monitoring

3.1   Measuring QoS in Web Services

As described in [20], there are four principle methods of QoS measurement from the technical perspective.

- *Provider-side instrumentation* has the advantage of access to a known implemementation. Dynamic attributes can be computed invasively within the code or non-invasively by a monitoring device.
- *SOAP Intermediaries* are intermediate parties through which the traffic is routed so that they can collect QoS-related criteria.
- *Probing* is a related technique where a service is invoked regularly by an independent party which computes QoS attributes. This roughly corresponds to the certification concept described in the previous section.
- *Sniffing* monitors the traffic on the client side and thus produces consumer-specific data.

Different levels of granularity can be defined for performance-related QoS; some authors distinguish up to 15 components [26].

In this work, we focus on measuring the *processing time* of the actual service execution on the provider-side and describe a non-invasive monitoring framework. In this framework, the invoked service code is transparently wrapped by a flexible combination of dynamically configured monitoring engines that are each able of measuring specific properties of the monitored piece of software. While these properties are not in any way restricted to be performance-related, the work described here primarily focuses on measuring runtime performance and content-specific quality criteria.

3.2   Monitoring Framework

Figure 1 shows a simplified abstraction of the core elements of the monitoring design. A `Registry` contains a number of `Engines`, which each specify which

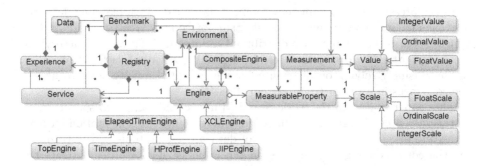

Fig. 1. Core elements of the monitoring framework

aspects of a service they are able to measure in their `MeasurableProperties`. These properties have associated `Scales` which specify value types and constraints and produce appropriate `Value` objects that are used to capture the `Measurements` associated with each property. The right most side of the digram shows the core scales and values which form the basis of their class hierarchies.

Each `Engine` is deployed on a specific `Environment` that exhibits a certain performance. This performance is captured in a benchmark score, where a `Benchmark` is a specific configuration of services and benchmark `Data` for a certain domain, aggregating specific measurements over these data to produce a representative *score* for an environment. The benchmark scores of the engines' environments are provided to the clients as part of the service execution metadata and can be used to normalise performance data of software across different service providers.

A registry further contains `Services`, which are, for monitoring purposes, not invoked directly, but run inside a monitoring engine. This monitoring execution produces a body of `Experience` for each service, which is accumulated through each successive call to a service and used to aggregate QoS information over time. It thus enables continuous monitoring of service quality. Bootstrapping these aggregate QoS data happens through the benchmark scoring, which can be configured specifically for each domain.

`CompositeEngines` are a flexible form of aggregating measurements obtained in different monitoring environments. This type of engine dispatches the service execution dynamically to several engines to collect information. This is especially useful in cases where measuring code in real-time actually changes the behaviour of that code. For example, measuring the memory load of Java code in a profiler usually results in a much slower performance, so that simultaneous measurement of memory load *and* execution speed leads to skewed results. Separating the measurements into different calls leads to correct results.

The bottom of the diagram illustrates some of the currently deployed performance monitoring engines.

1. The `ElapsedTimeEngine` is a simple default implementation measuring elapsed (wall-clock) time.

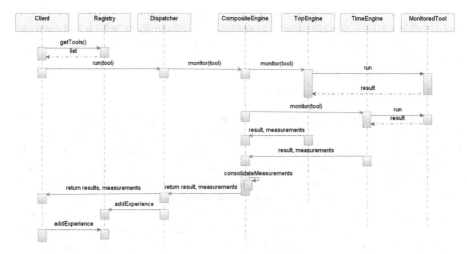

Fig. 2. Exemplary interaction between the core monitoring components

2. The TopEngine is based on the Unix tool *top*[1] and used for measuring the memory load of wrapped applications installed on the server.
3. The TimeEngine uses the Unix call *time*[2] to measure the CPU time used by a process.
4. Monitoring the performance of Java tools is accomplished by a combination of the HProfEngine and JIPEngine, which use the *HPROF*[3] and *JIP*[4] profiling libraries, for measuring memory usage and timing characteristics, respectively.
5. In contrast to these performance-oriented engines, the XCLEngine, which is currently under development, is measuring a very different QoS aspect. It quantifies the quality of file conversion by measuring the loss of information involved in file format conversion. To accomplish this, it relies on the eXtensible Characterisation Languages (XCL) which provide an abstract information model for digital content which is independent of the underlying file format [3], and compares different XCL documents for degrees of equality.

Additional engines and composite engine configurations can be added dynamically at any time. Notice that while the employed engines 1-4 in the current implementation focus on performance measurement, in principle any category of dynamic QoS criteria can be monitored and benchmarked.

Figure 2 illustrates an exemplary simplified flow of interactions between service requesters, the registry, the engines, and the monitored tools, in the case of a composite engine measuring the execution of a tool through the Unix tools *time* and *top*. The composite engine collects and consolidates the data; both

---

[1] http://unixhelp.ed.ac.uk/CGI/man-cgi?top
[2] http://unixhelp.ed.ac.uk/CGI/man-cgi?time
[3] http://java.sun.com/developer/technicalArticles/Programming/HPROF.html
[4] http://jiprof.sourceforge.net/

the engine and the client can contribute to the accumulated experience of the registry. This allows the client to add round-trip information, which can be used to deduct network latencies, or quality measurements computed on the result of the consumed service.

3.3 Performance Measurement

Measuring run-time characteristics of tools on different platforms has always been difficult due to the many peculiarities presented by each tool and environment. The most effective way of obtaining exact data on the behaviour of code is instrumenting it before[19] or after compilation [15]. However, as flexibility and non-intrusiveness are essential requirements in our application context, and access to the source code itself is often not even possible, we use non-invasive monitoring by standard tools for a range of platforms. This provides reliable and repeatable measurements that are exact enough for our purposes, while not necessitating access to the code itself. In particular, we currently use a combination of the following tools for performance monitoring.

- *Time.* The unix tool `time` is the most commonly used tool for measuring actual processing time of applications, i.e. CPU time consumed by a process and its system calls. However, while the timing is very precise, the major drawback is that memory information is not available on all platforms. Depending on the implementation of the `wait3()` command, installed memory information is reported zero on many environments[5].
- *Top.* This standard Unix program is primarily aimed at continuos monitoring of system resources. While the timing information obtained is not as exact as the `time` command, `top` measures both CPU and memory usage of processes. We gather detailed information on a particular process by starting `top` in batch mode and continually logging process information of all running processes to a file. After the process to be monitored has finished asynchronously (or timed out), we parse the output for performance information of the monitored process.

  In principle, the following process information provided by top can be useful in this context.
  - Maximum and average *virtual memory* used by a process;
  - Maximum and average *resident memory* used;
  - The used *percentage of available physical memory* used; and
  - The *cumulative CPU time* the process and its dead children have used.

  Furthermore, the *overall CPU state* of the system, i.e. the accumulated processing load of the machine, can be useful for detailed performance analysis and outlier detection.

As many processes actually start child processes, these have to be monitored as well to obtain correct and relevant information. For example, when using *convert* from ImageMagick, in some cases the costly work is not directly performed by the

---

[5] http://unixhelp.ed.ac.uk/CGI/man-cgi?time

convert-process but by one of its child processes, such as GhostScript. Therefore we gather all process information and aggregate it.

A large number of tools and libraries are available for profiling Java code.[6] The following two open-source profilers are currently deployed in our system.

- The *HProf* profiler is the standard Java heap and CPU profiling library. While it is able to obtain almost any level of detailed information wanted, its usage often incurs a heavy performance overhead. This overhead implies that measuring both memory usage and CPU information in one run can produce very misleading timing information.
- In contrast to HProf, the *Java Interactive Profiler (JIP)* incurs a low overhead and is thus used for measuring the timing of Java tools.

Depending on the platform of each tool, different measures need to be used; the monitoring framework allows for a flexible and adaptive configuration to accomodate these dynamic factors. Section 4.1 discusses the relation between the monitoring tools and which aspects of performance information we generally use from each of them. Where more than one technique needs to be used for obtaining all of the desired measurements, the composite engine described above transparently forks the actual execution of the tool to be monitored and aggregates the performance measurements.

4 Results and Discussion

We run a series of experiments in the context of a digital preservation scenario comparing a number of file conversion tools for different types of content, all wrapped as web services, on benchmark content. In this setting, candidate services are evaluated in a distributed SOA to select the best-performing tool. The experiments' purpose is to evaluate different aspects of both the tools and the engines themselves:

1. *Comparing performance measurement techniques.* To analyse the unavoidable variations in the measurements obtained with different monitoring tools, and to validate the consistency of measurents, we compare the results that different monitoring engines yield when applied to the same tools and data.
2. *Image conversion tools.* The ultimate purpose of the system in our application context is the comparative evaluation of candidate components. Thus we compare the performance of image file conversion tools on benchmark content.
3. *Accumulating average experience on tool behaviour.* An essential aspect of our framework is the accumulation of QoS data about each service. We analyse average throughput and memory usage of different tools and how the accumulated averages converge to a stable value.

---

[6] http://java-source.net/open-source/profilers

4. *Tradeoffs between different quality criteria.* Often, a trade-off decision has to be made between different quality criteria, such as compression speed versus compression rate. We run a series of tests with continually varying settings on a sound conversion software and describe the resulting trade-off curves.

Table 1 shows the experiment setups and their input file size distribution. Each server has a slightly different, but standard x86 architecture, hardware configuration and several conversion tools installed. Experiment results in this section are given for a Linux machine running Ubuntu Linux 8.04.2 on a 3 GHz Intel Core 2 Duo processor with 3GB memory. Each experiment was repeated on all other applicable servers to verify the consistency of the results obtained.

4.1   Measurement Techniques

The first set of experiments compares the exactness and appropriateness of measurements obtained using different techniques and compares these values to check for consistency of measurements. We monitor a Java conversion tool using all available engines on a Linux machine. Figure 3 shows measured values for a random subset of the total files to visually illustrate the variations between the engines. On the left side, the processing time measured by top, time, and the JIP profiler are generally very consistent across different runs, with an empirical correlation coefficient of 0.997 and 0.979, respectively. Running HProf on the same files consistently produces much longer execution times due to the processing overhead incurred by profiling the memory usage. The right side depicts

Table 1. Experiments

Experiment	Files	File sizes	Total input volume	Tool	Engines
1	110 JPEG images	Mean: 5,10 MB Median: 5,12 MB Std dev: 2,2 MB Min: 0,28 MB Max: 10,07MB	534 MB	ImageMagick conversion to PNG	Top, Time
2	110 JPEG images	Mean: 5,10 MB Median: 5,12 MB Std dev: 2,2 MB Min: 0,28 MB Max: 10,07MB	534 MB	Java ImageIO conversion to PNG	HProf, JIP
3	110 JPEG images	Mean: 5,10 MB Median: 5,12 MB Std dev: 2,2 MB Min: 0,28 MB Max: 10,07MB	534 MB	Java ImageIO conversion to PNG	Time, Top
4	312 JPEG images	Mean: 1,19 MB Median: 1,08 MB Std dev: 0,68 MB Min: 0,18 MB Max: 4,32MB	365MB	ImageMagick conversion to PNG	Time, Top
5	312 JPEG images	Mean: 1,19 MB Median: 1,08 MB Std dev: 0,68 MB Min: 0,18 MB Max: 4,32MB	365MB	Java ImageIO conversion to PNG	HProf, JIP
6	56 WAV files	Mean: 49,6 MB Median: 51,4 MB Std dev: 12,4 MB Min: 30,8 MB Max: 79,8 MB	2747MB	FLAC unverified conversion to FLAC, 9 different quality/speed settings	Top, time
7	56 WAV files	Mean: 49,6 MB Median: 51,4 MB Std dev: 12,4 MB Min: 30,8 MB Max: 79,8 MB	2747MB	FLAC verified conversion to FLAC, 9 different quality/speed settings	Top, time

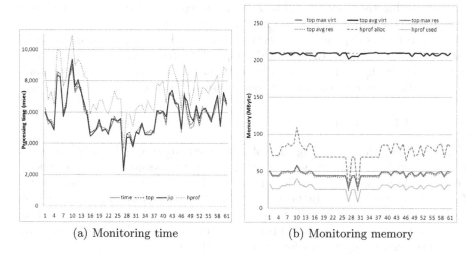

(a) Monitoring time   (b) Monitoring memory

Fig. 3. Comparison of the measurements obtained by different techniques

different memory measurements for the same experiment. The virtual memory assigned to a Java tool depends mostly on the settings used to execute the JVM and thus is not very meaningful. While the resident memory measured by Top includes the VM and denotes the amount of physical memory actually used during execution, HProf provides figures for memory used and allocated within the VM. Which of these measurements are of interest in a specific component selection scenario depends on the integration pattern. For Java systems, the actual

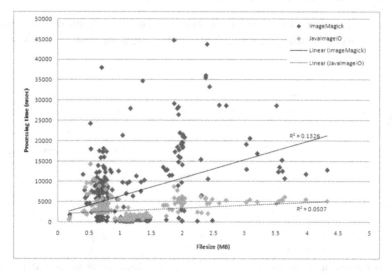

Fig. 4. Runtime behaviour of two conversion services

memory within the machine will be relevant, whereas in other cases, the virtual machine overhead has to be taken into account as well.

When a tool is deployed as a service, a standard benchmark score is calculated for the server with the included sample data; furthermore, the monitoring engines report the average system load during service execution. This enables normalisation and comparison of a tool across server instances.

4.2   Tool Performance

Figure 4 shows the processing time of two conversion tools offered by the same service provider on 312 image files. Simple linear regression shows the general trend of the performance relation, revealing that the Java tool is significantly faster. (However, it has to be noted that the *conversion quality* offered by ImageMagick is certainly higher, and the decision in our component selection scenario depends on a large number of factors. We use an approach based on multi-attribute utility theory for service selection.)

4.3   Accumulated Experience

An important aspect of any QoS management system is the accumulation and dissemination of experience on service quality. The described framework automatically tracks and accumulates all numeric measurements and provides aggregated averages with every service response. Figure 5 shows how processing time and memory usage per MB quickly converge to a stable value during the initial bootstrapping sequence of service calls on benchmark content.

4.4   Trade-off between QoS Criteria

In service and component selection situations, often a trade-off decision has to be made between conflicting quality attributes, such as cost versus speed or

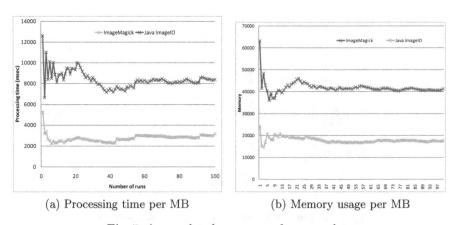

(a) Processing time per MB   (b) Memory usage per MB

Fig. 5. Accumulated average performance data

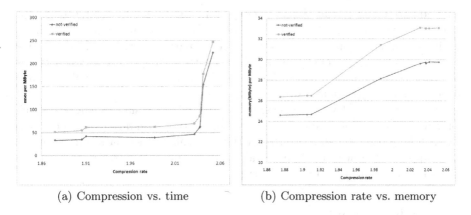

(a) Compression vs. time   (b) Compression rate vs. memory

Fig. 6. QoS trade-off between compression rate and performance

cost versus quality. When using the tool Free Lossless Audio Codec (FLAC)[7], several configurations are available for choosing between processing speed and achieved compression rate. In a scenario with massive amounts of audio data, compression rate can still imply a significant cost reduction and is thus a valuable tweak. However, this has to be balanced against the processing cost. Additionally, the option to verify the encoding process by on-the-fly decoding and comparing the output to the original input provides integrated quality assurance and thus increased confidence at the cost of increased memory usage and lower speed.

Figure 6 projects compression rate achieved with nine different settings against used time and used memory. Each data point represents the average achieved rate and resource usage over the sample set from Table 1. It is apparent that the highest settings achieve very little additional compression while using excessive amounts of time. In terms of memory, there is a consistent overhead incurred by the verification, but it does not appear problematic. Thus, in many cases, a medium compression/speed setting along with integrated verification will be a sensible choice.

5   Discussion and Conclusion

We have described an extensible monitoring framework for enriching web services with QoS information. Quality measurements are transparently obtained through a flexible architecture of non-invasive monitoring engines. We demonstrated the performance monitoring of different categories of applications wrapped as web services and discussed different techniques and the results they yield.

While the resulting provider-side instrumentation of services with quality information is not intended to replace existing QoS schemas, middleware solutions and requester-feedback mechanisms, it is a valuable complementary addition that enhances the level of QoS information available and allows verification of

---

[7] http://flac.sourceforge.net/

detailed performance-related quality criteria. In our application scenario of component selection in digital preservation, detailed performance and quality information on tools wrapped as web services are of particular value. Moreover, this provider-side measurement allows service requesters to optimize access patterns and enables service providers to introduce dynamic fine-granular policing such as performance-dependant costing.

Part of our current work is the extension to quality assurance engines which compare the output of file conversion tools for digital preservation purposes using the XCL languages [3], and the introduction of flexible benchmark configurations that support the selection of specifically tailored benchmarks, e.g. to calculate scores for data with certain characteristics.

Acknowledgements

Part of this work was supported by the European Union in the 6th Framework Program, IST, through the PLANETS project, contract 033789.

References

1. Becker, C., Ferreira, M., Kraxner, M., Rauber, A., Baptista, A.A., Ramalho, J.C.: Distributed preservation services: Integrating planning and actions. In: Christensen-Dalsgaard, B., Castelli, D., Ammitzbøll Jurik, B., Lippincott, J. (eds.) ECDL 2008. LNCS, vol. 5173, pp. 25–36. Springer, Heidelberg (2008)
2. Becker, C., Rauber, A.: Requirements modelling and evaluation for digital preservation: A COTS selection method based on controlled experimentation. In: Proc. 24th ACM Symposium on Applied Computing (SAC 2009), Honolulu, Hawaii, USA. ACM Press, New York (2009)
3. Becker, C., Rauber, A., Heydegger, V., Schnasse, J., Thaller, M.: A generic XML language for characterising objects to support digital preservation. In: Proc. 23rd ACM Symposium on Applied Computing (SAC 2008), Fortaleza, Brazil, vol. 1, pp. 402–406. ACM Press, New York (2008)
4. Carvallo, J.P., Franch, X., Quer, C.: Determining criteria for selecting software components: Lessons learned. IEEE Software 24(3), 84–94 (2007)
5. Cechich, A., Piattini, M., Vallecillo, A. (eds.): Component-Based Software Quality. Springer, Heidelberg (2003)
6. Dustdar, S., Schreiner, W.: A survey on web services composition. International Journal of Web and Grid Services 1, 1–30 (2005)
7. Erradi, A., Maheshwari, P., Tosic, V.: Ws-policy based monitoring of composite web services. In: ECOWS 2007: Proceedings of the Fifth European Conference on Web Services, Washington, DC, USA, pp. 99–108. IEEE Computer Society, Los Alamitos (2007)
8. Ferreira, M., Baptista, A.A., Ramalho, J.C.: An intelligent decision support system for digital preservation. International Journal on Digital Libraries 6(4), 295–304 (2007)
9. Franch, X., Carvallo, J.P.: Using quality models in software package selection. IEEE Software 20(1), 34–41 (2003)

10. Head, M.R., Govindaraju, M., Slominski, A., Liu, P., Abu-Ghazaleh, N., van Engelen, R., Chiu, K., Lewis, M.J.: A benchmark suite for soap-based communication in grid web services. In: Proceedings of the ACM/IEEE SC 2005 Conference Supercomputing, 2005, p. 19 (November 2005)
11. Her, J.S., Choi, S.W., Oh, S.H., Kim, S.D.: A framework for measuring performance in service-oriented architecture. In: International Conference on Next Generation Web Services Practices, pp. 55–60. IEEE Computer Society, Los Alamitos (2007)
12. Hunter, J., Choudhury, S.: PANIC - an integrated approach to the preservation of complex digital objects using semantic web services. International Journal on Digital Libraries: Special Issue on Complex Digital Objects 6(2), 174–183 (2006)
13. ISO: Software Engineering – Product Quality – Part 1: Quality Model (ISO/IEC 9126-1). International Standards Organization (2001)
14. Keller, A., Ludwig, H.: WSLA framework: Specifying and monitoring service level agreements for web services. Journal of Network and Systems Management 11(1), 57–81 (2003)
15. Larus, J.R., Ball, T.: Rewriting executable files to measure program behavior. Software: Practice and Experience 24(2), 197–218 (1994)
16. Liu, Y., Ngu, A.H., Zeng, L.Z.: Qos computation and policing in dynamic web service selection. In: WWW Alt. 2004: Proceedings of the 13th international World Wide Web conference on Alternate track papers & posters, pp. 66–73. ACM, New York (2004)
17. Maximilien, E.M., Singh, M.P.: Toward autonomic web services trust and selection. In: ICSOC 2004: Proceedings of the 2nd international conference on Service oriented computing, pp. 212–221. ACM, New York (2004)
18. Menascé, D.A.: Qos issues in web services. IEEE Internet Computing 6(6), 72–75 (2002)
19. Nethercote, N., Seward, J.: Valgrind: a framework for heavyweight dynamic binary instrumentation. SIGPLAN Not. 42(6), 89–100 (2007)
20. Platzer, C., Rosenberg, F., Dustdar, S.: Enhancing Web Service Discovery and Monitoring with Quality of Service Information. In: Securing Web Services: Practical Usage of Standards and Specifications, Idea Publishing Inc. (2007)
21. Ran, S.: A model for web services discovery with qos. SIGecom Exch. 4(1), 1–10 (2003)
22. Rosenberg, F., Platzer, C., Dustdar, S.: Bootstrapping performance and dependability attributes of web services. In: International Conference on Web Services (ICWS 2006), pp. 205–212 (2006)
23. Saddik, A.E.: Performance measurements of web services-based applications. IEEE Transactions on Instrumentation and Measurement 55(5), 1599–1605 (2006)
24. Song, H.G., Lee, K.: Performance Analysis and Estimation Tool of Web Services. In: Business Process Management, sPAC (Web Services Performance Analysis Center). LNCS, vol. 3649, pp. 109–119. Springer, Heidelberg (2005)
25. Tian, M., Gramm, A., Ritter, H., Schiller, J.: Efficient selection and monitoring of qos-aware web services with the ws-qos framework. In: Proceedings. IEEE/WIC/ACM International Conference on Web Intelligence, WI 2004, pp. 152–158 (September 2004)
26. Wickramage, N., Weerawarana, S.: A benchmark for web service frameworks. In: 2005 IEEE International Conference on Services Computing, July 2005, vol. 1, pp. 233–240 (2005)

A Quality Model for Mashup Components

Cinzia Cappiello[1], Florian Daniel[2], and Maristella Matera[1]

[1] DEI - Politecnico di Milano
Via Ponzio 34/5, 20133 Milano, Italy
{cappiell,matera}@elet.polimi.it
[2] University of Trento
Via Sommarive 14, 38100 Povo (TN), Italy
daniel@disi.unitn.it

Abstract. Through web mashups, web designers with even little programming skills have the opportunity to develop advanced applications by leveraging components accessible over the Web and offered by a multitude of service providers. So far, however, component selection has been merely based on functional requirements only, without considering the quality of the components and that of the final mashup. The quality in this context results from different factors, such as the software API, the contents, and the user interface.

In the literature, quality criteria for the different aspects have been proposed and analyzed, but the adaptability and dynamicity that characterize the mashup ecosystem require a separate and focused analysis. In this paper, we analyze the quality properties of mashup components (APIs), the building blocks of any mashup application, and define a quality model, which we claim represents a valuable instrument in the hands of both component developers and mashup composers.

1 Introduction

Modern Web 2.0 applications are characterized by a high user involvement: users are supported in the creation of contents and annotations, but also in the "composition" of applications starting from contents and functions that are provided by third parties. This last phenomenon is known as *Web mashups*, and is gaining popularity even under users with only little programming skills.

Mashups integrate heterogeneous *components* available on the Web, such as RSS/Atom feeds, Web services, content wrapped from third party web sites, or programmable APIs (e.g., Google Maps). Components may have a proper user interface that can be reused to build the interface of the composite application, they may provide computing support, or they may just act as plain data sources. Several mashup tools currently support the easy mashup of components, by offering visual environments where users can select pre-defined components and combine them by specifying models that abstract from technology and implementation details.

The success of a mashup is certainly influenced by the added value that the final combination of components is able to provide. However, it is self-evident

M. Gaedke, M. Grossniklaus, and O. Díaz (Eds.): ICWE 2009, LNCS 5648, pp. 236–250, 2009.
© Springer-Verlag Berlin Heidelberg 2009

that the quality of the final combination is strongly influenced by the quality of each single component, especially if we consider the current nature of mashups: single pages where, apart from the choreography logics, the overall functionality and application behavior directly derive from the single components.

If we look at components as standalone modules, then we can say that their quality is determined by the attributes that traditionally characterize software quality. A selection and/or specialization of such attributes is however needed to capture the peculiarities deriving from the components' intended use, i.e., their combination within mashups. This factor leads us to consider components as black boxes exposing their programmatic interfaces (APIs) to the audience of mashup developers.

We strongly believe that, as for any other software product, the component-internal quality is a relevant issue, and as such it must be taken into account during component development. Nevertheless, we argue that, as also confirmed by an experimental analysis conducted on the huge set of APIs published in the programmableweb.com repository (http://www.programmableweb.com), for the purpose of mashup composition some external features strongly affect the component success and diffusion.

In the light of the previous observations, in this paper we discuss the quality of mashups based on a *component-driven* approach. We recognize the validity of consolidated models and metrics for the component-internal quality. Our novel contribution is a further quality perspective, which is especially oriented toward the production of successful components. More specifically, we look at *mashup components* and their *APIs* in an isolated fashion and identify those individual features (e.g., the documentation, the ease of use of the API, the content provided through the API, and so on) that are likely to contribute to the success of a component. The challenge lies in the identification of those dimensions that really affect the adoption of an API.

The paper is organized as follows. In the next section, we provide the necessary context of the paper, i.e., we describe the typical mashup scenario. In Section 3 we introduce the ISO standard for software quality, one of the starting points of our work, and we also discuss some related works. In Section 4 we look at the mashup scenario from a quality perspective and provide our own quality model for mashup components. In Section 5 we report on our first experiments, and in Section 5 we conclude the paper with a final discussion and an outlook over our future work.

2   The Mashup Development Scenario

In order to clarify the roles and artifacts we will be referring to in this paper, in Figure 1 we illustrate the typical mashup scenario that spans from the production of single *mashup components* to the integration of components into a final *mashup application*. We explicitly highlight the involved *actors* and some of the development challenges.

The *Component Developer* who wants to create a new component has to cope with two complementary concerns, i.e., functional and non functional

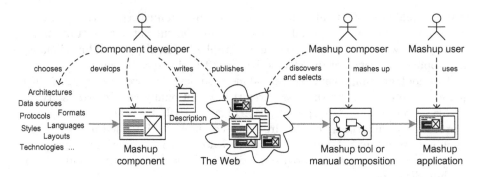

Fig. 1. The scenario for mashup API development

requirements. In this paper we concentrate on the non functional aspects and trust that the developer correctly implements all necessary functionalities.

From a non functional perspective, building a component implies taking decisions regarding the architectural style (e.g., SOAP service vs. RESTful service vs. UI component), the programming language (e.g., client side vs. server side technologies), the data formatting logic (e.g., XML vs. JSON), and so on. In addition to the functional features, all these aspects affect the "appeal" of the component from the point of view of the mashup composer that wants to include the component into a mashup application. The component developer should therefore aim at maximizing, among others, the components's interoperability, ease of use, attractiveness, and so on. Hence, based on the above considerations, the developer builds the component, provides a description or a documentation for its use (at least, ideally), and then publishes the components and its description on the Web (if any).

The *mashup composer* integrates the component into a mashup application. He typically browses the Web in search for components that suit his mashup idea, both in terms of functionality and quality provided. That is, the composer discovers components and selects the "good" ones. In doing this, he may take into account not only his own needs (e.g., a simple programming API and simple data formats for easy integration), but typically he also tries to guess the needs and the expectation of the final mashup user. Of course, a composer only selects components that will also be appealing to the users of the final mashup.

Developing good mashup components is therefore a challenging task, that requires the component developer to take into account the expectations of both the potential mashup composers and the potential mashup users. We say "potential", as it is typically not easy to fully predict who the real consumers of a component will be, once it is published on the Web. The challenge we focus on in this paper is therefore to understand how to assess the quality of a mashup component and, therefore, how to develop high-quality components.

In the rest of the paper, we assume that a *mashup component* is the logical entity that a component developer provides to the mashup composer. Physically, the component is accessed via proper *APIs*, i.e., programming interfaces that are characterized for instance by a programming language, a data format, and a communication protocol. A single component might come with multiple APIs. For instance, a component might be used via both a RESTful API or a SOAP/WSDL API.

3   Rationale and Background

A *quality model* consists of a selection of quality characteristics that are relevant for a given class of software applications and/or for a given assessment process. Quality models are drivers of quality assessment: assessment methods relying on well-defined quality models have the merit of establishing systematic frameworks in which the different quality dimensions are identified, precisely decomposed into quantifiable attributes, and then properly measured [1].

A relevant contribution to the definition of quality models comes from a family of ISO/IEC standards that focus on the quality of software systems and on its assessment. The standard ISO 8402-86 [2] defines quality as the "totality of features and characteristics of a software product that relate to its ability to satisfy stated or implied needs". As reported in Table 1, more concretely the standard ISO/IEC 9126-1 [3] defines quality as the combination of six characteristics that represent the attributes of a software product by which its quality can be described and evaluated. For each characteristic, the standard also specifies a set of finer-grained sub-characteristics with a granularity that fits well the principal need underlying the standard definition, i.e., quantifying the quality of software by means of metrics.

The standard ISO/IEC 9126-1 also distinguishes among different perspectives:

- *Internal Quality* is based on a *white box* model that considers the intrinsic properties of the software functionality, independently of the usage environment and the user interaction, and is measured directly on the source code and its control flow.
- *External Quality* is based on a *black box* model and is related to the behavior of the software product in a given running environment.
- *Quality in use* refers to the capability of a system to enable specified users to achieve specified goals with effectiveness, productivity, safety, and satisfaction in specified contexts of use.

Based on the above framework, several works have proposed quality models for traditional Web applications (see for example [4,5,6]). Few proposals also concentrate on modern Web 2.0 applications. For example, in [7], the authors extend the ISO 9126-1 standard, and discuss the internal quality, external quality, and quality in use of Web 2.0 applications. The authors also recognize the existence of some additional factors related to the quality of contents. This dimension is indeed central in Web 2.0, due to the increasing amount of user-authored information.

There is a lack of proposals for the quality of mashups. In a sense, this is because the quality of mashups can be mainly characterized by the external quality-in-use perspective, which is exhaustively covered by the huge research

Table 1. Definition of quality characteristics in the ISO/IEC 9126 standard [3]

Characteristics	Definition	Sub-characteristics
Functionality	A set of attributes that bear on the existence of a set of functions and their specified properties. The functions are those that satisfy stated or implied needs.	Suitability, Accuracy, Interoperability, Compliance, Security.
Reliability	A set of attributes that bear on the capability of software to maintain its level of performance under stated conditions for a stated period of time.	Maturity, Fault Tolerance, Recoverability.
Usability	A set of attributes that bear on the effort needed for use, and on the individual assessment of such use, by a stated or implied set of users.	Understandability, Learnability, Operability.
Efficiency	A set of attributes that bear on the relationship between the level of performance of the software and the amount of resources used, under stated conditions.	Time Behaviour, Resource Behaviour.
Maintainability	A set of attributes that bear on the effort needed to make specified modifications.	Analysability, Changeability, Stability, Testability.
Portability	A set of attributes that bear on the ability of software to be transferred from one environment to another.	Adaptability, Instalability, Conformance, Replaceability.

on Web application usability. We however believe that beyond quality in use, other issues that are strictly related to the quality of the individual components must be considered.

Similarly to the other works described above, our model is derived from the quality attributes defined by the ISO standard. We however add a specific perspective, which allows us to concentrate on the external quality of components, i.e., on the set of properties that affect the component's quality as perceived by the mashup composer (not necessarily the final mashup user). It is worth noting that other works focused on API quality in the more general SOA (Service-Oriented Architecture) domain, by specifically addressing the set of external factors that increase the ease of use of an API (the so-called *API usability*) [8,9,10], such as the quality of API documentation [10]. Our approach capitalizes on these contributions but tries to go beyond, since it considers a broader set of external quality factors – not only usability –, all having impact on the success of mashup components.

4   A Reference Quality Model

By definition, the publication of mashup components through APIs hides their internal complexity and, therefore, also their internal details. After a component

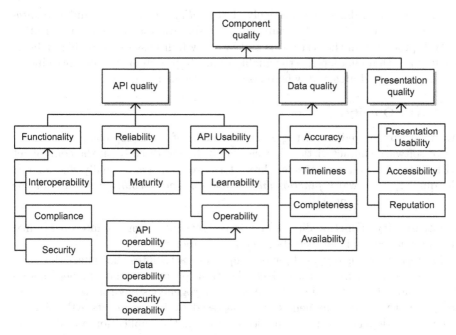

Fig. 2. The quality model for mashup components

has been deployed, external quality factors are the ones that drive the evaluation of the component's suitability for integration into a mashup application. This is also confirmed by a preliminary analysis that we have performed on the huge set of data available on **programmableweb.com**, a Web site that publishes data about APIs (e.g., links to the URLs for API download, descriptions, comments, user ratings, how-tos, etc.) and their use within mashups. We wrapped the data available on the site,[1] and analyzed them to identify possible correlations between observable API properties (e.g., the programming language, the number of supported protocols, the availability of documentation, etc.) and the component's usage in mashups. We discovered that the availability of *how-to* items (links to Web pages supplying information on how to install and use the component) has the strongest correlation with the diffusion of the component. This result, which is not surprising if we consider that Web 2.0 mashup composers typically prefer *easy-to-combine* components over complex components, led us to concentrate more specifically on the component-external quality.

Provided that the component-internal quality must be taken into account and must be assessed in accordance with the principles and methods traditionally adopted for software quality, in the rest of this section we concentrate on the external quality of components and illustrate our reference quality model. Figure 2 gives an overview of the addressed quality attributes, which we organize

---

[1] For more details on the wrapper and the analysis of the downloaded data the reader is referred to [11].

along three main dimensions, namely *API quality*, *Data quality* and *Presentation quality*, which recall the traditional "presentation-logic-data" organization of Web products. In the rest o this section we will discuss them, by highlighting the features that characterize the quality of mashup components and introducing fine-grained attributes and, where possible, assessment metrics.

4.1   API Quality

An important ingredient of the external quality of a mashup component is the set of software characteristics that can be evaluated directly on the component API. In this section, we consider three attributes that traditionally characterize the quality of software, *functionality*, *reliability*, and *usability*, revisited for the analysis of component APIs.

Functionality. Functionality can be refined by considering the interoperability, the compliance, and the security level of a component.

Interoperability is one of the most important attributes that affect the quality of a mashup component. In fact, the diffusion of a component depends on its capability to be used in different and heterogeneous environments. The interoperability of a component can be assessed by inspecting its API, since it particularly depends on the technologies used at the application and data layers. At the application layer, a mashup component can be provided through several APIs developed by using different technologies, such as different protocols or languages. The higher the number of the offered APIs for a given mashup component, the higher its interoperability. At the data layer, interoperability is affected by the number of data formats accepted for information exchange. Thus, the interoperability of a mashup component can be defined as:

$$Interoperability_{comp} = |P_{comp}| + |L_{comp}| + |DF_{comp}|$$

where $P_{comp} \subset \mathcal{P}$, $L_{comp} \subset \mathcal{L}$, and $DF_{comp} \subset \mathcal{DF}$ are the subsets of protocols, languages, and data formats used by the specific component. $\mathcal{P}$, $\mathcal{L}$, and $\mathcal{DF}$ are the sets of possible protocols, languages, and data formats that can be used for the development of mashup components. The analysis of the information contained in programmableweb.com allowed us to identify these sets. Table 2, for instance, summarizes the most prominent technologies found on programmableweb.com; the data are based on the descriptions provided by the component developers.

Table 2. Most used technologies in mashup component development

Protocols	REST, SOAP
Languages	Javascript, PHP
Data Formats	Atom, RSS, Gdata, JSON, XML, Parameter-Value

Some data formats are also standard (e.g., Atom, RSS, GData) and this increases the interoperability level and gives also the possibility to assess the *compliance* dimension as follows:

$$Compliance_{comp} = std(DF_{comp}) : DF_{comp} \rightarrow [0;1]$$

where $std(DF_{comp})$ produces 1 when at least one of the data formats supported by the component is a standard data format, and 0 if none of the supported data formats is standard.

The *security* of a component is related to the protection mechanism that is used to rule the access to the offered functionalities. We distinguish between two aspects: *SSL support* and *authentication mechanisms*. A component might provide access to its features with or without SSL support. That is, the component might allow for encrypted communications, which improves security, or not. As for the authentication mechanism, we distinguish between no authentication, API key, developer key, and user account. If the component requires mashup composers to use an API key, this means that the composer typically needs to use an access key that is specific to the mashup application the component will be running in. The key can usually be generated on the component provider's web site (for instance, Google Maps adopts this technique). A developer key, instead, requires the mashup composer to be registered personally as developer on the web site of the component provider (eBay for instance uses this techniques), while a user account requires the mashup composer to also be a registered user of the component provider (e.g., this is necessary to integrate PayPal features into mashups). In Figure 3 we show a graphical representation of the security metric, along with two examples.

Formally, it is possible to define the security metric as

$$SEC_{comp} = SSL_{comp} + AUT_{comp}$$

where SSL_{comp} is a boolean value that indicates the use of SSL inside the component, while AUT_{comp} is a number between 1 and 4 that indicates the type of authentication method according to some complexity values, as defined in Figure 3. The score of the security metric is calculated on the basis of the actual requirements the mashup composer poses to the component. For instance, if a composer at most wants to use a developer key with SSL support, a component that imposes the use of a user account does not add any value. Instead, a component that only provides an API key or no SSL support does not meet the requirements. According to this, we assign the value that corresponds to the composer's expectation if the component meets or exceeds the expectation, and lower values to components that do not meet the expectations (see highlighted values in Figure 3).

Reliability. The black-box approach does not allow one to evaluate the level of performance of a component under stated conditions for a stated period of time. Reliability can be evaluated in terms of *maturity*, by considering the available

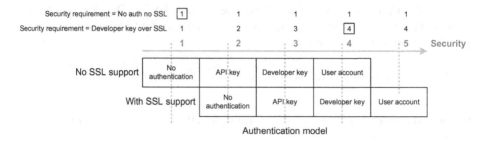

Fig. 3. Security mechanisms adopted by mashup components

statistics of usage of the component together with the frequency of its changes and updates:

$$Maturity_{comp} = max(1 - \frac{CurrentDate_{comp} - LastUseDate_{comp}}{\frac{CurrentDate_{comp} - CreationDate_{comp}}{|V_{comp}|}}; 0)$$

where V_{comp} is the set of versions available for a specific mashup component.

API Usability. Within the API quality dimensions, usability refers to the ease of use of the API.[2] API usability can be measured in terms of: *understandability*, *learnability*, and *operability*. Given our black box approach, *learnability* and *understandability* can be evaluated by considering the component documentation. Particularly relevant in the mashup scenario is the support offered to mashup composers by means of examples, API groups, blogs, or forums, and any other kind of documentation. The availability of each type of support contributes to increase these quality attributes.

Operability also affects the ease of use of a component. It depends on the complexity of the technologies used at the application and data layers, and of the adopted security mechanisms. The operability of technologies at the application level can be evaluated by considering the diffusion and the interaction overhead of both protocols and languages used in the API development. In fact, the diffusion of a protocol or a language enables the diffusion of a common knowledge that supports its use. In the same way, the operability of a component is higher when the interaction with the available API is easier. For example, the adoption of a protocol is more complex than the direct invocation of an object method, since dedicated standards and protocols might have to be used for the data exchange. In Figure 4(a) we show a method to estimate the operability of the most common technologies generally adopted at the application level.

Similarly, operability at the data layer can be evaluated by analyzing the data formats offered by the component along two aspects: the need for a parsing, meaning that further transformations are needed before the component can be integrated in the final mashup, and the use of a standard format. Figure 4(b) describes a method to assess the operability of the most common data formats.

---

[2] We will discuss presentation usability later in this section.

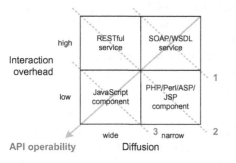

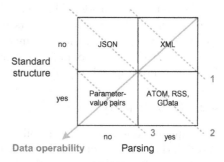

(a) A metric to measure operability of API types

(b) A metric to measure the operability of data formats

Fig. 4. Operability of the technologies used at the application and data level

The security operability and the actual level of security are instead inversely proportional. The higher the level of security, the lower the security operability. This is due to the consideration that operating a restrictive security solution is more demanding than less restrictive security solutions. Figure 5 represents the different degrees of security operability that can be identified by considering the security mechanisms typically adoptable in a mashup component.

In general, once the above technologies have been classified using the described criteria, it is possible to define clusters and characterize them with an operability level. As shown in Figure 4, technologies in the same cluster are associated with the same operability value. For example, in our analysis described in Figure 4, we use the following function family: $OP(T_{comp}) : T_{comp} \rightarrow OPV$, where $T_{comp} = \{P_{comp}, L_{comp}, DF_{comp}, SEC_{comp}\}$ includes the technologies used by a mashup component at the application and data layers and the adopted security mechanisms, and $OPV \subset \mathbb{N}$ is the set of operability values defined for each technology. Since a component can be offered by using different APIs and thus more application and data technologies have to be evaluated, the overall operability measure can be defined as:

$$OP_{comp} = max(OP(P_{comp} \cup L_{comp})) + max(OP(DF_{comp})) + max(OP(SEC_{comp}))$$

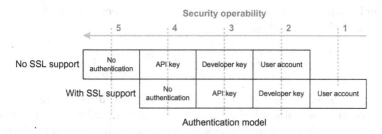

Fig. 5. Operability of the security mechanisms

The first term considers the technologies characterizing the application layer of the component; the second refers to the data layer; and the last term refers to the security mechanism implemented by the component. For each addend, we only consider the maximum operability value, as we think this characterizes best the overall operability of the component.

4.2 Data Quality

Data quality refers to the suitability of the data provided by the components through their APIs (both the information supplied to the final mashup users and the data exchanged between APIs for their choreography within the mashups). It mainly refers to data *accuracy*, *completeness*, and *timeliness*. Accuracy and completeness assess data along their correctness and numerical extension [12][13], while timeliness evaluates the validity of data along time [14]. In this context, it is also important to consider *data availability* because of data usage restrictions often applied by mashup component developers (e.g., some components limit the number of allowed requests per day).

Accuracy. It is defined as the degree with which data are consistent with the part of the real world that they have to represent. More formally, accuracy is defined as a correctness measure typically expressed in terms of proximity of a value v returned by the mashup component to a value v' considered as correct [12]. The evaluation of the accuracy dimension can be difficult if reference values are not available. In this case, digital sources can be compared, and accuracy problems are often revealed by inconsistencies among values stored in the different sources.

Completeness. It is defined as the degree with which a given data collection produced by the component includes all the expected data values. The assessment of the completeness can be performed by considering the ratio between the amount of data received and the amount of data expected:

$$Completeness = 1 - \left(\frac{Number\ of\ Missing\ values}{Total\ number\ of\ values} \right)$$

Timeliness. Represents the degree with which data are updated. It expresses how current (up-to-date) exchanged data are for the users that use them. Data can be indeed useless because they are *late* for a specific task. A measure of timeliness is defined in [14] as:

$$Timeliness = \max \left(0, 1 - \frac{currency}{volatility} \right)^{s}$$

where the exponent s controls the sensitivity of timeliness to the currency-volatility ratio. The value of the exponent is, indeed, related to the context (task-dependent), and it absorbs the subjectivity introduced with the judgment of who analyzes data.

With this definition, the value of timeliness ranges between 0 and 1, and expresses the temporal validity of data that users access. The validity is calculated by using the ratio between *currency* and *volatility*. Currency provides the "age" of data considering the creation time or the last update, while volatility is a static dimension that expresses the average period of validity of data in a specific context [14]. Temporal valid data are those data that are not "expired" when users read them.

Availability. In the SOA domain, a general assumption is to increase as much as possible the level of availability. A common practice in the definition of usage licenses for mashup components is to introduce some form of limitations. For example Google maps allows each IP up to 50,000 geocode requests per day. If, from the user perspective, this can be considered a restriction, it can be a necessary action to prevent service abuses leading to service availability pitfalls. A trade off solution must be carefully designed, so as to maximize possible quality advantages, without reducing the component's attractiveness.

4.3 Presentation Quality

Presentation quality refers to all those attributes that characterize the user experience and therefore relate to the user interface aspects that the mashup users go through when they access and use the final mashup application. It especially applies to UI components, i.e., those components that, differently form pure web services, are also provided with a presentation layer.

For this dimension, we focus on three quality attributes, i.e., *usability*, *accessibility*, and *reputation*.

Presentation usability. In some cases, mashup components are provided with a presentation layer, i.e., a user interface (UI) where some widgets provide a visualization for the component produced data and also allow some form of interaction. Despite the simplicity of such UIs, usability of the presentation mechanisms must be taken into account. All the usability attributes and metrics already defined for Web UIs can be taken into account [15,4,16]. Particular emphasis must be devoted to factors such as the *understandability* and *learnabilty*, i.e., the provision of easy-to-understand presentations for data and easy-to-learn interaction mechanisms, and the *compliance* with standard interaction mechanisms. The *attractiveness* of presentations also needs to be addressed. With this respect, RIA interfaces can provide suitable solutions.

Accessibility. All the features supporting the access by any class of users and technology must be addressed. The component UI should be therefore designed by taking into account well-know accessibility criteria, such as those defined by the W3C Web Accessibility Initiative (WAI) [17]. Just to mention few, different APIs enabling different presentation modalities should be provided for the same components, so that its contents and functions can be rendered on devices with different capabilities. Multimedia contents should be augmented with textual descriptions, so that they can be presented even through alternative browsing technologies, such as screen readers assisting impaired users. Finally, components and the resulting mashups should be accessible through different types of hardware devices, from voice-based devices to small-size or black and white screens.

Reputation. Reputation is the degree with which a component is perceived as reliable. In the Web, most of the user actions are driven by reputation: users simply access and trust the information provided by reliable institutions and/or authors. In the mashup scenario, this trend is observable as well. Our analysis of the programmableweb.com data revealed that the most diffused components are those distributed by well-known, and therefore credible, providers (e.g., Google). Therefore, in the quality evaluation of a mashup component the credibility of the organization/person that publishes and advertises it cannot be neglected.

Form the component developer perspective, it is also important to achieve a reasonable level of reputation. Certainly, reputation is positively affected by the component documentation, especially if it is available in different formats and distributed through different channels (including blogs, forums, wikies, etc.), by the compliance of presentation mechanisms with the most diffused standards, and in general by the attitude to maximize all the quality attributes previously discussed, to meet the user (both mashup composer and mashup user) expectations.

5 Discussion

The current mashup ecosystem is characterized by a strong growth, by a strong focus on technologies, by few really value-adding mashups, and by a generally low quality of both components and mashups. The ecosystem is still in its infancy, yet the trend toward so-called "enterprise mashups" (as, for example, those supported by companies like IBM or JackBe), which go beyond 1-page Web user mashups, is real. Understanding which factors determine or influence the quality of mashups and – of particular interest to this paper – of mashup components represents a first step toward valuable mashups.

As illustrated in the scenario at the beginning of this paper, developing good, i.e., high-quality, mashup components is not a trivial task. Besides the pure functional features of a component, there are many design decisions (e.g., regarding programming languages, communication protocols, data formats, and the like) that need to be taken and that influence the quality and the success of a component. Developing a mashup component requires the component developer to take into account at least two different stakeholders, i.e., the mashup composer, who might want to include the component into his mashup, and the mashup user, who will use the component in the mashup. This is peculiar, and differentiates mashup component development from traditional development: developers of conventional APIs (e.g., Web services or object libraries) typically only need to take into account the need of developers who will use their API, as the APIs do not expose an interface that is directly operated by users; developers of Web applications, instead, rather need to take into account the users of their application, as a Web application is typically not accessed also via an API. Mashup component development, instead, must take into account the expectations of both and, hence, design decisions are harder.

In this paper, we looked at component development from an external perspective, that is, from the perspective of the mashup composer or the mashup user, and we characterized the observable properties of components in terms of a component-specific quality model. The model is based on both our own experience with the development of components and mashups, and experimental evidence gathered by analyzing data from programmableweb.com. For the actual assessment of the quality properties, we provided – where possible – metrics.

We claim that the defined model and metrics contain valuable knowledge that (i) creates an awareness of the problem of today's general low-quality in mashups and mashup components, (ii) assists the mashup composer in selecting components that effectively suit his mashup needs (focusing not only on hard functional requirements), and (iii) provides the component developer with guidelines about how to take into account the needs of both the mashup composer and the mashup user. The described model can indeed be used by the component developer as a methodology for the selection of appropriate languages, protocols, data formats, etc., compatibly with the functional requirements of the component and updated (if necessary) according to the pace of the Web 2.0.

As a next step, the model will be validated by applying it to a significant number of mashup components. We would like to "rank" mashup components (e.g., by looking at the mashups and components in programmableweb.com), in order to assess correlations among their quality properties, possibly also taking into account their use within mashups. We are also planning some formal experiments to validate our metrics against inspection-based evaluations by a pool of expert developers. We will also extend the model to cover the quality of mashups, which we believe is tightly related with the quality of the components they integrate.

References

1. Fenton, N.E., Pfleeger, S.L.: Software metrics: a rigorous and practical approach. PWS Publishing, Boston (1997)
2. ISO: ISO 8402:1994. Quality Management and Quality Assurance - Vocabulary (1986)
3. ISO/IEC: ISO/IEC 9126-1 Software Engineering. Product Quality - Part 1: Quality model (2001)
4. Calero, C., Ruiz, J., Piattini, M.: A Web Metrics Survey Using WQM. In: Koch, N., Fraternali, P., Wirsing, M. (eds.) ICWE 2004. LNCS, vol. 3140, pp. 147–160. Springer, Heidelberg (2004)
5. Malak, G., Badri, L., Badri, M., Sahraoui, H.A.: Towards a Multidimensional Model for Web-Based Applications Quality Assessment. In: Bauknecht, K., Bichler, M., Pröll, B. (eds.) EC-Web 2004. LNCS, vol. 3182, pp. 316–327. Springer, Heidelberg (2004)
6. Olsina, L., Covella, G., Rossi, G.: Web Quality. In: Web Engineering, pp. 109–142. Springer, Heidelberg (2005)
7. Olsina, L., Sassano, R., Mich, L.: Specifying Quality Requirements for the Web 2.0 Applications. In: Proc. of IWWOST 2008, pp. 56–62 (2008)

8. Ko, A.J., Myers, B.A., Aung, H.H.: Six learning barriers in end-user programming systems. In: VL/HCC, pp. 199–206. IEEE Computer Society, Los Alamitos (2004)
9. Ellis, B., Stylos, J., Myers, B.A.: The Factory Pattern in API Design: A Usability Evaluation. In: ICSE, pp. 302–312. IEEE Computer Society, Los Alamitos (2007)
10. Jeong, S.Y., Xie, Y., Beaton, J., Myers, B., Stylos, J., Ehret, R., Karstens, J., Efeoglu, A., Busse, D.K.: Improving Documentation for eSOA APIs through User Studies. In: Proc. of the Second International Symposium on End User Development (IS-EUD 2009), Siegen, Germany, March 2–4 (2009)
11. Cappiello, C.: Analyzing the Success of Mashup Components. Technical report, Politecnico di Milano (2009)
12. Redman, T.: Data Quality for the Information Age. Artech House (1996)
13. Wang, R., Strong, D.: Beyond Accuracy: What Data Quality Means to Data Consumers. Journal of Management Information Systems 12 (1996)
14. Ballou, D., Wang, R., Pazer, H., Tayi, G.: Modeling Information Manufacturing Systems to Determine Information Product Quality. Management Science 44 (1998)
15. Nielsen, J.: Web Usability. New Riders, Indianapolis (2000)
16. Matera, M., Rizzo, F., Carughi, G.T.: Web Usability: Principles and Evaluation Methods. In: Web Engineering, pp. 109–142. Springer, Heidelberg (2005)
17. Consortium, W.: Wai guidelines and techniques. Technical report (2007), http://www.w3.org/WAI/guid-tech.html

Towards the Discovery of
Data Quality Attributes for Web Portals*

Carmen Moraga[1], Mª Ángeles Moraga[1], Coral Calero[1], and Ángélica Caro[2]

[1] Alarcos Research Group – Institite of Information Technologies & Systems,
Dept. Information Technologies & Systems – Escuela Superior de Informática,
University of Castilla-La Mancha, Spain
Carmen.Moraga@alu.uclm.es,
{MariaAngeles.Moraga,Coral.Calero}@uclm.es
[2] Department of Computer Science and Information Technologies,
University of Bio Bio, Chillán, Chile
mcaro@ubiobio.cl

Abstract. The Internet has become in a place for the exchange and publication of data. Nowadays, Web portals serve as an important means to access information. In this context, the concepts of quality in general and of data quality in particular are highly relevant. The objective of this paper is to carry out a systematic literature review (SLR) in order to discover the state-of-the art in data quality for Web portals, and to evaluate the evolution of data quality since 2006, when another SLR was carried out, and in which a PDQM (Portal Data Quality Model) was defined. As a result, 39 attributes have been considered relevant for the assessment of data quality in Web portals.

Keywords: Data/Information quality, Web portals, data quality attributes.

1 Introduction

One of the aims of many web portals is to select, organize and distribute content (information or other services and products) in order to satisfy their users/customers [1]. However, unnecessary, out of date or erroneous data are also included. Data quality is an actual factor in competitiveness.

Bearing in mind the importance of data quality, the main goal of this paper is to discover the state-of-the-art in Web portal data quality through a systematic literature review (SLR). This SLR is based on a previous SLR [2], which covered the years 1996 to 2005, and in which 33 attributes considered to be relevant for Web portal data quality were chosen. These attributes were then used to define a quality model for the assessment of Web portal data quality, namely PDQM (Portal Data Quality Model), in [3]. The SLR which is presented here covers 2006 to the end of 2008. The objective of this SLR is to establish the evolution of Web portal data quality

---

* This work is part of the projects: INCOME (PET2006-0682-01) from Ministerio de Educación and IVISCUS (PAC08-0024-5991) from the Consejería de Educación y Ciencia (JCCM) and DQNet (TIN2008-04951-E) supported by the Spanish Ministerio de Educación y Ciencia.

M. Gaedke, M. Grossniklaus, and O. Díaz (Eds.): ICWE 2009, LNCS 5648, pp. 251–259, 2009.
© Springer-Verlag Berlin Heidelberg 2009

attributes. As a result, it will be possible to evaluate whether the PDQM attributes are still valid and to identify new relevant attributes.

This paper is organized as follows. In Section 2, the SLR process, including the planning and conduction phases, is presented. The main results obtained from the SLR are reported in Section 3. Finally, our conclusions and future works are outlined in Section 4.

2   Review Process

This section details the activities performed in each of the two main phases of the procedure for performing an SLR, as proposed by [4]: "Planning the review" and "Conducting the review".

a) **Planning the review:** The most important pre-review activities are identified by the research questions(s) that the systematic review will address, and by producing a review protocol (i.e. plan) which defines the basic review procedures. In this phase, the following steps have been carried out:

1. Identification of the need for a review: The SLR has been planned in an attempt to identify the most important attributes related to Web data quality. Therefore, the main goal of our SLR is to discover the state-of-the-art in data quality for the Web since 2006.

2. Specifying the research questions. The following research questions (see Table 1) guided the design of the review process.

Table 1. Research Questions

Research Questions	Main Motivation
RQ1: "Which Web data quality attributes are addressed by researchers?"	To identify the Web data quality attributes which have been researched in the Web context
RQ2: "From which point of view is the Web data quality analyzed?"	To discover whether the Web data quality is from the manager's, programmer's or consumer's/user's perspective
RQ3: "In what context is the Web data quality evaluated?"	To identify whether the work is focused on the Web in general, a Web site or a Web portal
RQ4: "Is a quality model defined?"	To evaluate whether a set of attributes and the relationships between them have been defined
RQ5:"Do any measures for Web data quality exist?"	To discover whether measures are defined
RQ6: "Does a tool which supports the proposed approach exist?"	To determine whether a tool that assesses Web data quality exists.

3. Developing a review protocol. The development of the review protocol is the most relevant activity of the review process, since it establishes the basis of the search.

Source selection. The planned list of sources with which to carry out the SLR review was: 1.- Digital libraries; 2.- Grey literature comprises some papers considered to be relevant by experts which were not included in the aforementioned digital sources, and 3.- The manual revision of the Conference Proceeding of WISE (Web Information Systems Engineering) and ICWE (International Conference on Web Engineering) of 2006 and 2007.

Search string. The following strings were defined: 1) "data quality" AND web; 2) "information quality" AND web; 3) ("data quality" and web) and ("information quality");

4) web and ("information quality" or "data quality"); 5) ("data quality" and web) AND (aspect OR dimension OR characteristic OR factor OR criterion OR criteria OR attribute OR model); 6) ("information quality" and web) AND (aspect OR dimension OR characteristic OR factor OR criterion OR criteria OR attribute OR model). The results obtained by using search strings 3, 4, 5 and 6, are very similar in the majority of cases. This signifies that the terms "Data Quality" and "Information Quality" are used interchangeably in literature.

Inclusion and Exclusion criteria. The inclusion criteria defined for this review were papers that present approaches or proposals that: a)were written in English, b)were published after 2005, c)identified a set of data quality characteristics, attributes or measures. And the following were defined as exclusion criteria: a) the work is previous to 2006, b) the paper is not within the scope of data quality in the Web, c) the paper does not propose a data quality attribute, or is not relevant, d) it does not contain the terms 'data quality' or 'information quality' either in the title or in the abstract e) studies are only available in the form of abstracts or Powerpoint presentations, f) duplicate studies, g) quality is not a part of the contributions of the paper.

b) Conducting the review: Once the protocol has been agreed, the review can begin. In this phase, the following steps have been made:

1. Selection of primary studies. The search process was completed on 31/12/2008 in the digital libraries previously mentioned, and 4105 papers were found. Many of the papers were eliminated owing to the fact that the use of different search strings in the digital libraries had caused them to be duplicated. Once these papers had been discarded, 1332 papers remained. These papers were then analyzed. This was done by first analysing the title and the abstract, and a total of 173 papers were selected. The full texts were then read, and once the inclusion and exclusion criteria had been applied, 69 papers were obtained.

2. Data extraction and monitoring. Once the primary studies had been chosen, the extraction of the relevant information for this SLR was stored in a data extraction form which was structured as follows: a) Data of the paper, including the search engine, title, year, type of publication and authors; b) Data of the classification, considering the following dimensions: quality attributes, point of view, context, application domain, quality model, measure and tool.

3   Results

This section provides an in depth presentation of the "Reporting the review" phase.
For the purpose of our analysis, the papers were classified in order to answer the research questions listed in Table 1.

Our classification will hereafter be used in this section to present the answers to each research question.

RQ1: "Which Web data quality attributes are addressed by researchers?"
A total of 130 attributes were initially obtained. Bearing in mind that our objective is to select the set of most relevant attributes, the attributes which did not contain descriptions were first discarded. 20 attributes were thus eliminated. Next, we

analyzed the attributes specific to Web Site or Web that could be applicable for Web portals. 63 attributes were defined for data quality in the Web or in a Web site. However, after studying their applicability to the Web portal context only 22 attributes were selected. We then analyzed the definition of the attributes and detected that there were different names which were related to the same concept.

A total of 39 attributes related to data quality attributes were eventually selected (see Table 2).

Table 2. Attributes by origin

Attributes not obtained in our SLR (for authors other than those of [2])	Attributes obtained in our SLR also included in [2]			New attributes obtained in our SLR and not in [2]
Customer Support	Accessibility	Consistent Representation	Reliability	Effectiveness
Documentation	Accuracy	Currency	Reputation	Efficiency
Duplicates	Amount of data	Ease of operation	Security	Readability
Expiration	Applicability	Interactivity	Specialization	Usability
Flexibility	Attractiveness	Interpretability	Timeliness	Usefulness
Response Time	Availability	Novelty	Understandability	Verifiability
Traceability	Believability	Objectivity	Validity	
	Completeness	Organization	Value-added	
	Concise Representation	Relevancy		

As was previously stated, in [2] the best attributes for Web portals were selected, but this selection was made in 2005. Therefore, we wish to make a comparison between the PDQM attributes and the attributes detected in our SLR. The main findings of this comparison are shown in Table 2. Note that there is a set of attributes which was only selected in [2]. These attributes are presented in the first column. The second column shows the attributes which were chosen both in this paper and in PDQM. Finally, the last column presents 6 attributes which have been added in this paper as a result of the SLR.

Table 3 presents the data quality attributes. The table shows the selected papers. The attributes which appear in the papers under the same name have been marked with an "X", and those which have a different name but explain the same concept have been marked with a "□". References are detailed in Appendix Table I.

RQ2: "From what point of view is the Web data quality analyzed?"
In this paper, we consider that data quality can be analyzed from three points of view: manager, programmer and consumer. Fig 1 summarizes the number of papers for each point of view.

We can deduce that the majority of the papers are related to the consumer or user. This signifies that researchers are more concerned about the quality of the data with which the consumer is provided. We can therefore affirm that it is necessary to make an effort to study the data quality from the other perspectives, since all the perspectives are obviously related.

RQ3: "In which context the Web data quality is evaluated?"
As was previously stated, in order to attain a wide knowledge of data quality attributes the following contexts were included: Web portal, Web site and the Web in general. However, each attribute has been reviewed, and only those which are of interest in the context of Web portal data quality have been selected. Fig 2 illustrates the classification of papers according to their context. It must be stressed that Web sites are studied more frequently than Web portals.

Table 3. Quality attributes investigated in the context of SPL

Accessibility	Accuracy	Amount of data	Applicability	Attractiveness	Availability	Believability	Completeness	Concise Representation	Consistent Representation	Currency	Customer Support	Documentation	Duplicates	Ease of operation	Effectiveness	Efficiency	Expiration	Flexibility	Interactivity	Interpretability	Novelty	Objectivity	Organization	Readability	Relevancy	Reliability	Reputation	Response Time	Security	Specialization	Timeliness	Traceability	Understandability	Usability	Usefulness	Validity	Value-added	Verifiability	References
X	X						X		□																	□					X				X				R1
X						X	X											X																	X				R2
	X								□				X									X																	R3
			□																																			□	R4
	X			X			X		□	X				X	X					X					□	□							□	X		X		R5
X																																	□				X	R6
X						X																																	R7
								X																															R8
X									X																						X				□				R9
X						□																	X									X							R10
X	X	X	X	X	X	X	X	X	X	X	X	X	X	X		X	X	X	X	X	X		X	X	X	X	X	X	X	X	X			X	X			R11
X	X	X	X	X	X	X	X	X	X	X	X	X	X	X		X	X	X	X	X	X		X	X	X	X	X	X	X	X			X	X	X			R12
X							X	X	□	X													X				X				X				X	X			R13
X						X	X	X									X						□		X											X	R14
	X						□		□																														R15
							X		□																	□													R16
X																										X				X		X		X				R17
X			□		X																			X						X	□							R18
X							X			□																			□	X	□							R19
	X						□																	X							X	□						R20
	X							X																X						X	X							R21
	X							X																X														R22
□							□																															R23
	X			X												X								X			X							X	X			R24
					X									□	□																			X				R25
X	X	X	X	X	X	X	X	X	X	X	X	X	X	X		X	X	X	X	X	X		X	X	X	X	X	X	X	X			X	X			R26
																							X		X	X				X		X					X	R27
X					X	X	X	□	□														X		X					X		X					X	R28
X				X			□																							X								R29
X					X																																	R30
X	□				X	X	X	X										X		X			X		X		□		X		X				X	R31
	X					□									X															X	□		X				R32
	X		□		X																		X							X	X							R33
X	□		□		X	X	X	X				□					X		X			□	X	X				X	X	□		X			X	R34
X			X				□																														R35
															X							□		X	X									X			R36
																						□		X	X							X	X				R37
X						X																		X														R38
X						X																		X														R39
						X □																																R40
X							X																X															R41
					□			□															□						□			□						R42
X					X					X													□	X			X	X		X								R43
X			□		X																		X							X								R44
					□																		X	X						X			X		X		R45
							X																X							X								R46
X	X				□	X									X						□		X						X			X	□				R47
X			X		□	X									X			X																			R48
X																							X							X			X				R49
X	□	X			X	□			X			□					X					□	X	X					X								R50
X																						□							X		X						R51
X	X	X	X	X	X	X	X	X	X	X	X	X	X		X	X	X	X	X	X	X		X	X	X	X	X	X	X	X			X	X	X	X	R52
X	X					X		□												□		X	X						X	X	X						R53
X	X				□	X	□																X	□						X						X	X	R54
X	X	X	X	X	X	X	X	X	X	X	X	X		X	X	X	X	X	X	X	X		X	X	X	X	X	X	X	X			X	X		X	X	R55
X					X	X		X														X		X						□			X				R56
X	X	X	X	X	X	X	X	X	X	X	X	X		X	X	X	X	X	X	X	X		X	X	X	X	X	X	X	X			X	X	X	X	R57
X	X	X	X	X	X	X	X	X	X	X	X	X		X	X	X	X	X	X	X	X		X	X	X	X	X	X	X	X			X	X	X	X	R58
X						X																	X							X							R59
X	X	X			X	□	X	X		X			X		X	X			X		X	X			X		X	X		X		X	X	□		X	X	R60
X	X				□	X	□																X	X	□										X	X	R61
X					X	□																	□														R62
X					X	□																	□														R63
X					X			X												X	□		X	□								□	X				R64
X			□		□																		□							X				X			R65
					□																																R66
X					□																	X			X												R67
X	□		X		□		□												X			X						X					X			R68
X					X																		X							X							R69

RQ4: "Is a quality model defined?"

With regard to whether a quality model is proposed, as Fig 3 shows, 60% of the works defined a quality model. This means that there is a tendency towards covering all the aspects related to quality, and that the works are not limited to the simple definition of attributes.

RQ5: "Do measures for Web data quality exist?"
Only 22% of the papers do not include measures, as is shown in Fig 4. Therefore, unlike the situation of some years ago, researchers have now realized the importance of measurement and almost all the proposals define measures with which to assess the data quality level. We believe that this is a very positive aspect, since without measures it is obviously not possible to evaluate quality.

RQ6: "Does a tool with which to support the proposed approach exist?"
The proposal was considered to contain a tool when the authors affirmed that a new tool had been created or when one or several existing tools could support their proposal. Only 8 of the 69 selected papers provided a support tool, which represents 12% of the total.

In conclusion, we can state that although the majority of the proposals define measures (as was mentioned in the previous section), their assessment it not automated. This reveals the difficulty of automating the proposed measures. Hence, as a future work it will be necessary to work on the automation of measure assessment.

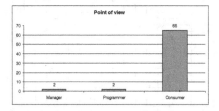

Fig. 1. Papers according to whose point of view they are directed towards

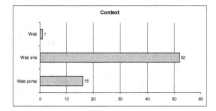

Fig. 2. Papers according to their context

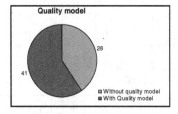

Fig. 3. Proposals with a quality model

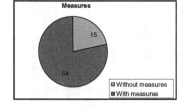

Fig. 4. Proposals which define measures

4   Conclusions and Future Works

In this paper, a systematic literature review has been carried out in order to obtain the portal data quality attributes that have been proposed in literature.

Moreover, the realization of this SLR has led us to certain conclusions. Firstly, the majority of the papers study Web data quality from the consumer's perspective, and more effort should therefore be made to study this from the other perspectives. Secondly, it should be noted that Web sites are studied more frequently than Web portals. Thirdly, more than half the proposals define a quality model. This means that there is a tendency towards covering all the aspects related to quality and that the works are not limited to the simple definition of attributes. Fourthly, it is also of interest to stress that researchers have realized the importance of measurement, and that almost all the proposals define measures with which to assess the data quality level.

Without measures it is obviously not possible to evaluate quality. However, these measures are not easy to calculate automatically since only 12% of the proposals have developed a tool for their assessment.

Finally, in comparison with the previous work [2], we conclude that a greater number of papers related to data quality attributes were selected, and a greater number of attributes were identified. We have therefore included all the attributes of [2] and have added other attributes detected in this SLR which we consider to be relevant to our study.

In the future we shall compare both the data quality attributes obtained and SQUARE [5]. Since some PDQM attributes are now obsolete and are included in this work, it is necessary to review and analyze the possibility of discarding them. In order to do this, we shall first study the data quality attributes of SQUARE [5], and shall then analyze both the attributes obtained in this SLR and the PDQM attributes, which will eventually be compared in order to select the most relevant attributes.

References

1. Domingues, M.A., Soares, C., Jorge, A.M.: A Web-Based System to Monitor the Quality of Meta-Data in Web Portals. In: IEEE/WIC/ACM International Conference on Web Intelligence and Intelligent Agent Technology (WI-IATW 2006), pp. 188–191 (2006)
2. Caro, A., Calero, C., Caballero, I., Piattini, M.: A proposal for a set of attributes relevant for Web portal data quality. Software Quality Journal 16, 513–542 (2008)
3. Caro, A., Calero, C., Caballero, I., Piattini, M.: Defining a data quality model for web portals. In: Aberer, K., Peng, Z., Rundensteiner, E.A., Zhang, Y., Li, X. (eds.) WISE 2006. LNCS, vol. 4255, pp. 363–374. Springer, Heidelberg (2006)
4. Kitchenham, B., Charters, S.: Guidelines for performing systematic literature reviews in software engineering. Technical Report EBSE-2007-01, School of Computer Science and Mathematics, Keely University (2007)
5. [ISO/IEC-FDIS-25012]: Software engineering - Software product Quality Requirements and Evaluation (SQuaRE) - Data quality model (2008)

Appendix

Table I. References of the SLR

ACM

R1: Nichols, D.M., Chan, C., Bainbridge, D., McKay, D., Twidale, M.B.: A lightweight metadata quality tool. In: JCDL '08:Proceedings of the 8th ACM/IEEE-CS joint conference on Digital libraries. (2008)

R2: Gelman, I., A.Barletta, A.L.: A "quick and dirty" website data quality indicator, (2008)

R3: Scaffidi, C., Myers, B., Shaw, M.: Topes: reusable abstractions for validating data. In: ICSE '08: Proceedings of the 30th international conference on Software engineering. (2008)

R4: Caro, A., Calero, C., Caballero, I., Piattini, M.: Defining a quality model for portal data. In: ICWE '06: Proceedings of the 6th international conference on Web engineering. (2006)

R5: Costa, C.J., Nhampossa, J.L., Aparicio, M.: Wiki content evaluation framework. In: SIGDOC '08: Proceedings of the 26th annual ACM international conference on Design of communication. (2008)

R6: Kitter, A.R.E. K.: Harnessing the wisdom of crowds in wikipedia: quality through coordination. In: CSCW '08: Proceedings of the ACM 2008 conference on Computer supported cooperative work. (2008)

R7: Wilkinson, D.M., Huberman, B.A.: Cooperation and quality in wikipedia. In: WikiSym '07: Proceedings of the 2007 international symposium on Wikis. (2007)

R8: McKnight, D.H.Kacmar, C.J.: Factors and effects of information credibility. In: ICEC '07: Proceedings of the ninth international conference on Electronic commerce. (2007)

R9: Rodgers, W., Negash, S.: The effects of web-based technologies on knowledge transfer. Communications of the ACM. 50, 117-122 (2007)

R10: Belanger, F., Fan, W., Schaupp, L.C., Krishen, A., Everhart, J., Poteet, D.Nakamoto, K.: Web site success metrics: addressing the duality of goals. Communications of the ACM. 49 (2006)

IEEE

R11: Caro, A., Calero, C., Enriquez de Salamanca, J., Piattini, M.: Refinement of a Tool to Assess the Data Quality in Web Portals. In: Seventh International Conference on Quality Software (QSIC 2007). (2007)

R12: Caro, A., Calero, C., Mendes, E., Piattini, M.: A Probabilistic Approach to Web Portal's Data Quality Evaluation. In: 6th International Conference on the Quality of Information and Communications Technology (QUATIC 2007). (2007)

R13: Vorochek, O., Biletskiy, Y.: Toward Assessing Data Quality of Ontology Matching on the Web. In: Fifth Annual Conference on Communication Networks and Services Research (CNSR '07). (2007)

R14: Domingues, M.A., Soares, C., Jorge, A.M.: A Web-Based System to Monitor the Quality of Meta-Data in Web Portals. In: 2006 IEEE/WIC/ACM International Conferences on Web Intelligence and Intelligent Agent Technology - Workshops. (2006)

R15: Yin, X., Han, J.Yu, P.S.: Truth Discovery with Multiple Conflicting Information Providers on the Web. IEEE Transactions on Knowledge and Data Engineering. 20, 796-808 (2008)

R16: Prat, N., Madnick, S.: Measuring Data Believability: A Provenance Approach. In: Proceedings of the 41st Annual Hawaii International Conference on System Sciences (HICSS 2008). (2008)

R17: Hadaya, P.,, Ehier, J.: Online Purchasing of Simple Retail Goods: The Impact of e-Service Quality as Provided by Electronic Commerce Functionalities. In: Proceedings of the 41st Annual Hawaii International Conference on System Sciences (HICSS 2008). (2008)

R18: Tate, M., Evermann, J., Hope, B., Barnes, S.: Perceived Service Quality in a University Web Portal: Revising the E-Qual Instrument. In: 40th Annual Hawaii International Conference on System Sciences (HICSS'07). (2007)

R19: Prestipino, M., Aschoff, F.-R., Schwabe, G.: How up-to-date are Online Tourism Communities? An Empirical Evaluation of Commercial and Non-commercial Information Quality. In: 40th Annual Hawaii International Conference on System Sciences (HICSS'07). (2007)

R20: Rabjohn, N., Cheung, C.M.K.Lee, M.K.O.: Examining the Perceived Credibility of Online Opinions: Information Adoption in the Online Environment. In: Proceedings of the 41st Annual Hawaii International Conference on System Sciences (HICSS 2008). (2008)

R21: Lin, H., Fan, W., Wallace, L., Zhang, Z.: An Empirical Study of Web-Based Knowledge Community Success. In: 40th Annual Hawaii International Conference on System Sciences (HICSS'07). (2007)

R22: Schaupp, L.C., Fan, W., Belanger, F.: Determining Success for Different Website Goals. In: Proceedings of the 39th Annual Hawaii International Conference on System Sciences (HICSS'06) Track 6. (2006)

R23: McKnight, H., Kacmar, C.: Factors of Information Credibility for an Internet Advice Site. In: Proceedings of the 39th Annual Hawaii International Conference on System Sciences (HICSS'06) Track 6. (2006)

R24: Franch, X., Quer, C., Canton, J.A., Salietti, R.: Experience Report on the Construction of Quality Models for Some Content Management Software Domains. In: Seventh International Conference on Composition-Based Software Systems (ICCBSS 2008). (2008)

OTHER

R25: Mich, L.: Subjectivity in Web site quality evaluation: the contribution of Soft Computing. In: Workshops of 7th International Conference on Web Engineering. (2007)

R26: Caro, A., Calero, C., Sahraoui, H.A., Piattini, M.: A Bayesian Network to represent a data quality model. International Journal Information Quality. 1, 272-294 (2007)

SCIENCE DIRECT

R27: Lee, J., Park, D.-H., Han, I.: The effect of negative online consumer reviews on product attitude: An information processing view. Electronic Commerce Research and Applications. 7, 341-352 (2008)

R28: Bizer, C., Cyganiak, R.: Quality-driven information filtering using the WIQA policy framework. Web Semantics: Science, Services and Agents on the World Wide Web. 7, 1-10 (2009)

R29: Prybutok, V.R., Zhang, X., Ryan, S.D.: Evaluating leadership, IT quality, and net benefits in an e-government environment. Information & Management. 45, 143-152 (2008)

R30: Gonçalves, M.A., Moreira, B.L., Fox, E.A., Watson, L.T.: "What is a good digital library?" – A quality model for digital libraries. Information Processing & Management. 43, 1416-1437 (2007)

R31: Herrera-Viedma, E., Peis, E., Morales-del-Castillo, J.M., Alonso, S., Anaya, K.: A fuzzy linguistic model to evaluate the quality of Web sites that store XML documents. International Journal of Approximate Reasoning. 46, 226-253 (2007)

R32: Chung, W., Bonillas, A., Lai, G., Xi, W., Chen, H.: Supporting non-English Web searching: An experiment on the Spanish business and the Arabic medical intelligence portals. Decision Support Systems. 42, 1697-1714 (2006)

R33: Barnes, S.J., Vidgen, R.T.: Data triangulation and web quality metrics: A case study in e-government. Information & Management. 43, 767-777 (2006)

R34: Chung, W.: Studying information seeking on the non-English Web: An experiment on a Spanish business Web portal. International Journal of Human-Computer Studies. 64, 811-829 (2006)

R35: Chen, C.-C., Wu, C.-S., Wu, R.C.-F.: e-Service enhancement priority matrix: The case of an IC foundry company. Information & Management. 43, 572-586 (2006)

R36: Grigoroudis, E., Litos, C., Moustakis, V.A., Politis, Y., Tsironis, L.: The assessment of user-perceived web quality: Application of a satisfaction benchmarking approach. European Journal of Operational Research. 187, 1346-1357 (2008)

R37: Tsakonas, G., Papatheodorou, C.: Exploring usefulness and usability in the evaluation of open access digital libraries. Information Processing & Management. 44, 1234-1250 (2008)

R38: Kim, D.J., Steinfield, C., Lai, Y.-J.: Revisiting the role of web assurance seals in business-to-consumer electronic commerce. Decision Support Systems. 44, 1000-1015 (2008)

R39: Kim, D.J., Ferrin, D.L., Rao, H.R.: A trust-based consumer decision-making model in electronic commerce: The role of trust, perceived risk, and their antecedents. Decision Support Systems. 44, 544-564 (2008)

R40: Robins, D., Holmes, J.: Aesthetics and credibility in web site design. Information Processing & Management. 44, 386-399 (2008)

R41: Wang, Y., Liu, Z.: Automatic detecting indicators for quality of health information on the Web. International Journal of Medical Informatics. 76, 575-582 (2007)

R42: Wang, Y.-S., Wang, H.-Y., Shee, D.Y.: Measuring e-learning systems success in an organizational context: Scale development and validation. Computers in Human Behavior. 23, 1792-1808 (2007)

R43: Yen, B., P.J-H., H., Wang, M.: Toward an analytical approach for effective Web site design: A framework for modeling, evaluation and enhancement. Electronic Commerce Research and Applications. 6, 159-170 (2007)

R44: Ahn, T., Ryu, S.I., H.: The impact of Web quality and playfulness on user acceptance of online retailing. Information & Management. 44, 263-275 (2007)

R45: Song, J., Jones, D., Gudigantala, N.: The effects of incorporating compensatory choice strategies in Web-based consumer decision support systems. Decision Support Systems. 43, 359-374 (2007)

R46: Lee, Y, .Kozar, K.A.: Investigating the effect of website quality on e-business success: An analytic hierarchy process (AHP) approach. Decision Support Systems. 42, 1383-1401 (2006)

R47: Kang, Y.-S., Kim, Y.J.: Do visitors' interest level and perceived quantity of web page content matter in shaping the attitude toward a web site? Decision Support Systems. 42, 1187-1202 (2006)

R48: Sillence, E., Briggs, P., Harris, P., Fishwick, L.: A framework for understanding trust factors in web-based health advice. International Journal of Human-Computer Studies. 64, 697-713 (2006)

Table I. (*continued*)

R49: Éthier, J., Hadaya, P., Talbot, J., Cadieux, J.: B2C web site quality and emotions during online shopping episodes: An empirical study. Information & Management. 43, 627-639 (2006)

R50: De Wulf, K., Schillewaert, N., Muylle, S., Rangarajan, D.: The role of pleasure in web site success. Information & Management. 43, 434-446 (2006)

R51: Zviran, M., Glezer, C., Avni, I.: User satisfaction from commercial web sites: The effect of design and use. Information & Management. 43, 157-178 (2006)

SCOPUS

R52: Calero, C., Caro, A., Piattini, M.: An applicable data quality model for web portal data consumers. World Wide Web. 11, 465-484 (2008)

R53: Cheung, C.M.K., Lee, M.K.O.: The structure of web-based information systems satisfaction: Testing of competing models. Journal of the American Society for Information Science and Technology. 59, 1617-1630 (2008)

R54: Stvilia, B., Twidale, M.B., Smith, L.C., Gasser, L.: Information quality work organization in Wikipedia. Journal of the American Society for Information Science and Technology. 59, 983-1001 (2008)

R55: Caro, A., Calero, C., Caballero, I., Piattini, M.: A proposal for a set of attributes relevant for Web portal data quality. Software Quality Journal. 16, 513-542 (2008)

R56: Kelton, K., Fleischmann, K.R., Wallace, W.A.: Trust in digital information. Journal of the American Society for Information Science and Technology. 59, 363-374 (2008)

R57: Caro, A., Calero, C., Piattini, M.: Development process of the operational version of PDQM. Lecture Notes in Computer Science. LNCS 4831, 436-448 (2007)

R58: Caro, A., Calero, C., Caballero, I., Piattini, M.: Defining a data quality model for web portals. 7th International Conference on Web Information System Engineering (WISE 2006) Lecture Notes in Computer Science. Vol. 4255, 363-374 (2006)

R59: Moraga, A., Calero, C., Piattini, M.: Comparing different quality models for portals. Online Information Review. 30, 555-568 (2006)

R60: Caro, A., Calero, C., Caballero, I., Piattini, M.: A first approach to a data quality model for web portals. Lecture Notes in Computer Science. LNCS 3982, 984-993 (2006)

R61: Ehmann, K., Large, A., Beheshti, J.: Collaboration in context: Comparing article evolution among subject disciplines in Wikipedia. First Monday. 13 (2008)

R62: Verbert, K., Ochoa, X., Duval, E.: The ALOCOM framework: Towards scalable content reuse. Journal of Digital Information. 9 (2008)

R63: Verbert, K., Duval, E.: Evaluating the ALOCOM approach for scalable content repurposing. Lecture Notes in Computer Science. LNCS 4443, 325-336 (2007)

R64: Metzger, M.J.: Making sense of credibility on the web: Models for evaluating online information and recommendations for future research. Journal of the American Society for Information Science and Technology. 58, 2078-2091 (2007)

R65: Dondio, P., Barrett, S.: Computational trust in web content quality: A comparative evaluation on the Wikipedia project. Informatica. 31, 151-160 (2007)

R66: Hong, T.: The influence of structural and message features on web site credibility. Journal of the American Society for Information Science and Technology. 57, 114-127 (2006)

WILEY

R67: Herrera-Viedma, E., Pasi, G., Lopez-Herrera, A.G., Porcel, C.: Evaluating the information quality of Web sites: A methodology based on fuzzy computing with words. Journal of the American Society for Information Science and Technology. 57, 538-549 (2006)

R68: Katerattanakul, P., Siau, K.: Factors affecting the information quality of personal Web portfolios. Journal of the American Society for Information Science and Technology. 59, 63-76 (2008)

R69: Chiu, C.-M., Chiu, C.-S., Chang, H.-C.: Examining the integrated influence of fairness and quality on learners' satisfaction and Web-based learning continuance intention. Information Systems Journal. 17, 271-287 (2007)

Script InSight: Using Models to Explore JavaScript Code from the Browser View

Peng Li and Eric Wohlstadter

University of British Columbia
{lipeng,wohlstad}@cs.ubc.ca

Abstract. As Web programming standards and browser infrastructures have matured, the implementation of UIs for many Web sites has seen a parallel increase in complexity. In order to deal with this problem, we are researching ways to bridge the gap between the browser view of a UI and its JavaScript implementation. To achieve this we propose a novel JavaScript reverse-engineering approach and a prototype tool called Script InSight. This approach helps to relate the semantically meaningful elements in the browser to the lower-level JavaScript syntax, by leveraging context available during the script execution. The approach uses run-time tracing to build a dynamic, context-sensitive, control-flow model that provides feedback to developers as a summary of tracing information. To demonstrate the applicability of the approach we present a study of an existing open-source Web 2.0 application called the Java Pet Store and metrics taken from several popular online sites.

Keywords: Reverse-Engineering, Software Maintenance, Rich Internet Applications, JavaScript.

1 Introduction

The user interface (UI) is a key aspect of most Web sites. As Web browser programming standards such as JavaScript and the W3C Document Object Model (DOM) have matured, the implementation of UIs for many sites has seen a parallel increase in complexity. These rich Web applications have the advantage of providing a seamless and interactive experience for end-users. However, these applications also require more development effort to build and maintain than older Web UI. As the Web has become more interactive and complex, we are researching a more interactive, model-based approach for Web application reverse-engineering and debugging.

Most existing work on modeling of UI-intensive Web applications focuses on development but not specifically maintenance and debugging. For example, [1] introduces a framework for the integration of presentation components in mashup applications. Trigueros et al. present a model driven approach, the RUX-Model, for the design of rich Internet applications [2]. Valderas et al. introduce an approach to support the coordinated work between Web UI designers and analysts during the development of a Web application [3]. In [15], Rossi et al. use a model-driven approach to transform conventional Web applications into rich Internet applications

M. Gaedke, M. Grossniklaus, and O. Díaz (Eds.): ICWE 2009, LNCS 5648, pp. 260–274, 2009.
© Springer-Verlag Berlin Heidelberg 2009

by applying refactoring at the model level. Meliá et al. propose a model-driven development methodology which extends a traditional Web modeling methodology for use with the Google Web Toolkit [16]. Some research in software maintenance and reverse-engineering has been used for testing of Ajax applications [14], but not specifically for interactive debugging, as we focus on in this paper.

As with any complex software development task, creating a user interface requires an iterative cycle of design and implementation. Starting with an initial design, an interface would first be prototyped and then refined over several cycles into a final product. At each stage, some design decisions may need to be reconsidered and the implementation adjusted accordingly. The UI might even evolve after the release of an application in order to fix bugs or add new features.

After each cycle, developers can determine the quality of the current application by executing the implementation and evaluating the UI appearance and functionality in a Web browser. If they notice anything wrong with the browser view of the UI, they would need to map the problem back to some part of the implementation, to enact the appropriate change.

Unfortunately, reversing engineering a rich interactive Web page and mapping the appearance or behavior of some element in the Web page to the corresponding implementation can be quite difficult. This is because today's Web UI are stateful and reactive. Their appearance and behavior vary over time based on mutations of state made from JavaScript. This problem is exacerbated by the fact that a developer working on the UI might not have written the original code for all parts of the Web site. In that case, they may need to dig through unfamiliar code to try and reverse-engineer the source. This process is especially difficult since code for some systems on the Web is poorly documented. As described by Hassan et al. [4], "Currently, [code] inquiries can only be answered by scanning the source code for answers using tools such as grep, consulting documentation, or asking senior developers."

In order to deal with this problem, we are researching an interactive approach to bridge the gap between the browser view of a UI and the JavaScript piece of the implementation. This is motivated by the fact that the browser view is usually easy to understand and semantically meaningful, unlike the implementation code. We want to help developers use the live UI as an entry-point into the lower-level implementation details.

To achieve this, we propose a novel JavaScript tracing approach. To a first approximation, when a change is made by a script statement to a visual DOM attribute (e.g. color, height, etc...), we record a link between the effected browser element and the code responsible. The intuition is that a developer can now easily navigate through the code by hyperlinking directly from browser elements. However, a basic implementation of this approach is vulnerable to two problems.

First, mapping semantically meaningful events, such as the mutation of a visual attribute directly to a location in the source code (e.g. a statement) may not be helpful, because that one statement might be reused for several different purposes in the execution of the script. For example, informing a developer that an attribute was changed in a "setter" method for that attribute provides little useful information. The "setter" method could be called many times in the execution of a script, in different contexts, for a variety of different purposes.

For this reason we are researching the use of context-sensitivity to help provide a mapping. A context-sensitive approach captures not only the execution of individual statements, but also the state of the call stack, which can help distinguish between multiple executions of the same statement.

Second, the visual behavior of a Web page (e.g. the way widgets are animated) is often achieved by a set of coordinated DOM attribute mutations. For example, a button's appearance may change to reflect the button is active when a panel is closed, and change again to reflect it is inactive when the panel is open. The changes to the button appearance and panel appearance have a causal relationship. If a developer wants to change the widget animation they may need to make coordinated changes to several DOM nodes. For this reason we are researching the use of a custom control-flow model, the *DOM mutation graph* (DMG), that developers can use to leverage their understanding of these causal relationships, seen in the browser view, in mapping from the browser view to script source code.

To demonstrate our approach of using this DMG to explore script code, we present a study of an existing open-source Web 2.0 application called the Java Pet Store [9] and metrics taken from several popular online sites. We show how this model is used to understand animation effects in the application which require coordinated changes to several page elements. The metrics taken from other pages provide evidence supporting the need for context-sensitivity in Web application reverse-engineering.

The rest of the paper is organized as following: Section 2 presents a motivating example and an overview of our approach, Section 3 presents technical details, Section 4 presents metrics from online sites, Section 5 presents a further detailed example, and in Section 6 we give related work and we conclude in Section 7.

2 Motivating Example and Approach Overview

In order to motivate our approach, we use a case-study of an existing open-source Web application called Java Petstore 2.0 (henceforth, JPS). This online pet store offers the end-user several interactive widgets to control the application, as shown in Figure 1. Here we see the "Catalog Browser" page from which the end-user can browse prospective pets. This one page alone makes use of 1232 lines of JavaScript code spread across 3 files.

Running down the left-side of the page is an *accordion bar*. This widget is a stylized tree-view for browsing categories of pets and their respective sub-categories (e.g. the specific kinds of cats). The table rows for the categories interactively expand/deflate to reveal/hide sub-categories when the mouse cursor is positioned/removed from a category name. This "accordion" animation requires JavaScript programming to mutate the DOM in an event loop. In Figure 1, the "Cats" row is expanded and the other categories remain deflated.

Consider the perspective of a front-end developer who would like to make changes to this Web page. They have to remember or understand how the 1232 lines of code is mapped to elements of the page and their behavior.

In the original JPS, each *accordion row* is expanded and deflated at a constant speed. Here we consider a change task where a front-end developer wants to change the animation to accelerate at a decreasing/increasing rate when a row is expanding/deflating. During the task the developer is confronted with three problems.

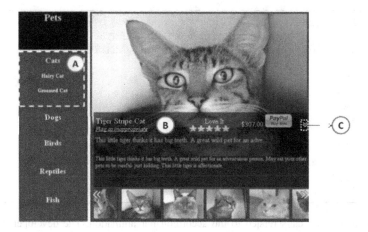

Fig. 1. A snapshot for the "Catalog Browser" from the Java Pet Store. Label (A) is an expanded accordion row, "Cats". The labels (B) and (C) will be described later, in Section 4.

First, they would need to determine which DOM nodes and which attributes of those nodes are responsible for the animation. This could be difficult because the implementation details could vary. For example, the animation might involve any combination of style attributes such as `height`, `top`, `clip`, etc...

Second, suppose a developer figures out that `height` is the key to change the animation. However, when they search through the code, there are two assignment statements to the height of some node in the JavaScript implementation. One of them is shown in Figure 2 and another one turns out not to be relevant. By looking at each statement individually, it is not always clear if the statement is relevant to the task at hand. They may also have to search the code to understand the *calling context* of each height setting statement. In other words, the function calls which lead to the statement's execution.

```
Row.prototype.setHeight = function(nH) {
    this.h = nH;
    this.div.style.height = nH + "px";
}
```

Fig. 2. The function `setHeight` on its own lacks the calling context which is needed to properly associate the function with the accordion bar animation

Third, suppose the developer determines the function as shown in Figure 2 contains the assignment statement they are interested in. In order to create the new acceleration/deceleration effect, they would want to change the argument value that was passed to a function call to `setHeight`, but not the definition of the `setHeight` code itself. But now, when a developer searches `setHeight` in the code, they find two places where the `setHeight` function is called, as shown in Figure 3. Each one is relevant for the change task, but for different reasons.

```
147. if(...) {
148.    nHeight = nHeight + INCREMENT;
149.    divs[nExpandIndex].setHeight(nHeight);
150.    if(...) {
151.       if(...)  {
152.          ...
153.       }
154.    else {
155.          oHeight = oHeight - INCREMENT;
156.       }
157.       divs[oExpandIndex].setHeight(oHeight);
158.    }
159. }
```

Fig. 3. Two function calls related to the accordion bar animation. The developer will need information to disambiguate the purpose of each function call. Some code is elided for illustration purposes.

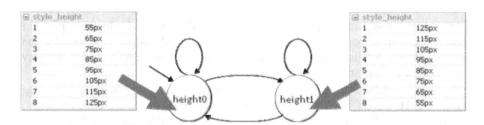

Fig. 4. The abstract behavior of an accordion row presented as a DMG. The two traces of the height values (overlayed on the model with block arrows, in the figure simply for illustration) show the information displayed to a developer when selecting one of the two nodes in the model.

After some investigation, they may find that the first one (line 149) is involved with expanding an accordion row and the second (line 157) is involved with the deflating.

Using our proposed approach, a developer could have chosen to see a model of the accordion row's execution. The model generated by our tool is shown in Fig. 4. In the model, each node represents a statement that mutated some visual DOM attribute and the calling context in which that statement execution. Notice that the model contains two nodes, although we are only concerned with one source code statement (the height setting statement in Fig. 2). From the model a developer could determine that the animation was created by alternating, repeated executions of the context represented by height0, followed by repeated executions of the context represented by height1.

By selecting each node in our tool, the developer can perform two functions. First, the developer can view a trace of the values which were set in each context. From the trace, it is clear which one is responsible for expanding and which one is responsible for deflating. Having the information in mind, the developer can hyperlink to the corresponding source for the one they are interested in. In the model, `height0` links to the executions of Fig.2, which were made from line 149 in Fig 3; `height1` links to the following repeated executions of Fig. 2, which were made from line 157 in Fig. 3.

Now, the developer can find the correct locations to change argument values for each call to implement the desired acceleration/deceleration change. In the remainder of the paper we describe more precisely the details regarding using a DMG for exploring JavaScript code using Script InSight.

3 Implementation Details

Our prototype is implemented as a JavaScript front-end, to execute within a standard Web browser, and a separate HTTP proxy executable. A developer using our tool will install and point their browser to the HTTP proxy which provides instrumentation of existing JavaScript code. First, we describe our prototype tool from a developer's perspective to provide an overview of the lower-level details involved in our run-time tracing infrastructure, which is described in Section 3.1. The DMG model presentation for UI execution history is presented in Section 3.2.

Using Script InSight, developers can switch the Web browser between normal execution mode and inspection mode. In script inspection mode, a developer can select an element in the browser view. For example, the developer might select a particular image or table row they are interested in. Next, a list of the event handlers that have affected that node during execution are displayed. When the developer selects one of the handlers, a DMG of its previously recorded behavior is displayed.

By selecting a node in the DMG, the developer is hyperlinked to the file for the associated JavaScript statement in a special text editor, as shown in Figure 5. In the editor, the cursor position is set for the line number of the statement for convenience. This text editor includes a drop-down menu for the developer to navigate the calling context for a given statement execution. This allows the developer to jump up and down the call stack that was captured precisely for that instance of statement execution in the trace history.

3.1 Tracing JavaScript Execution

Run-time tracing is implemented as a set of JavaScript functions which are called by tracing code injected into existing scripts. Scripts are intercepted and manipulated by a client-side HTTP proxy. We use the open-source Rhino [10] JavaScript compiler framework to convert scripts into an abstract syntax tree (AST) which is then transformed to add the tracing code. In the remainder of this section we describe the details of this tracing procedure.

During program execution, our tool monitors a subset of the JavaScript statements executed. We refer to these statements as DOM *mutators*. A *DOM mutator* is a JavaScript statement which mutates the state of the DOM. This can be either by directly setting an attribute of a node (e.g. `node.id = 'submit'`) or through any one of the functions in the W3C DOM standard (e.g. `node.appendChild(..)`).

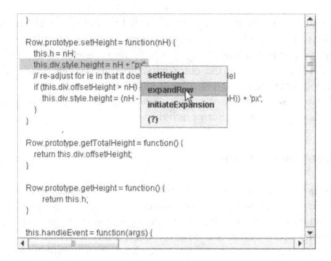

Fig. 5. Selecting a function call location from the calling context. The (?) entry references an anonymous JavaScript event handler function. A mutation of the `style.height` attribute for some DOM node was made in the function `setHeight` which is shown at the top of call stack. This mutation corresponds to the `height0` node from Fig. 4. The stack contents serve to distinguish this execution of `setHeight` from those corresponding to node `height1`.

For example, in JPS, the `height` attribute of some nodes is mutated dynamically. Our tool records this fact so that a developer concerned with an animation concerning the height can quickly locate the corresponding implementation.

In many cases, dynamic information is needed to distinguish the calling context in which some statement executed. For this reason, our tool captures the calling context of each DOM mutator execution instance. The *DOM Mutator Context* is an ordered list containing the location of all JavaScript function calls active at the moment of execution for some DOM mutator. This context captures the path of function calls from some event handler invoked by the browser, to the statement.

Consider an example from eBay where JavaScript library code is used to build "widgets". These widgets are an aggregation of DOM nodes which are encapsulated behind a high-level widget interface.

Suppose a developer is interested in a particular instance of an eBay drop-down menu. They might wish to modify the parameters that were used in the construction of the menu. Using our tool they could click on some part of the menu to be hyper-linked to the DOM mutator where that part of the menu was created. However, since these nodes were created as an internal part of the widget library, the developer would not want to actually change the library code but rather find where it was called from for this menu instance. This could be achieved using the captured context modeled in the DMG.

3.2 DOM Mutation Graph

Many Web 2.0 and Ajax style sites use JavaScript to control dynamic UI effects and animations. We want to help developers navigate directly to the code responsible for controlling this part of the UI. In this case, it could be hard for a user to determine precisely the moment when the UI transitioned between states which are responsible for creating the effect or animation.

To help developers review mutations in an animation which occur over the span of some time, we need to consider the history of DOM mutations related to each DOM node attribute. Our tracing infrastructure captures a complete trace of all DOM mutator contexts, including the value (e.g. 10, 'red', 'http://..') which is assigned by the mutator for each context. However, it is well known that dynamic traces can sometimes overwhelm a user with a large magnitude of data, making the information not valuable.

To abstract large execution traces for developers, we designed a mechanism to represent JavaScript execution as a variation of a traditional control-flow model, the DOM mutation graph. Each DMG is an abstract representation of the execution history for a specific instance of a JavaScript event handler (e.g. `onclick`, `onhover`). This execution history captures all mutations made during the activation of the handler (i.e. while the handler is on the call stack).

We use this partitioning of trace information because each particular event-handler is commonly responsible for creating one particular animation or dynamic effect on the page. Scoping the generation of models to align with event-handlers, allows a developer to focus on a particular animation or effect, and the way it may affect multiple attributes of multiple DOM nodes, in a coordinated fashion.

Our model is similar to traditional control-flow models, such as a control-flow graph or call-graph, in that each node represents some implementation level artifact. However, we consider only the set of statements which affect the visual appearance of the UI and distinguish those statements based on dynamic context information. These statements serve as a bridge between the browser view and the implementation. This is because a developer can plainly observe their effect from the live UI.

In the model, each node corresponds to a mutator context, abstracting over all the particular values which may have been assigned in that context. The trace of concrete mutations, including the attribute values assigned, can be retrieved by interrogating each node (as illustrated in Fig. 4). Edges in the model correspond to the sequencing of statement execution. A directed edge is created from node, u, to node, v, if there is a trace entry for u followed by a trace entry for v. This allows the model[1] to become a bridge between the flow of changes that a developer can see directly in the browser, and the implementation which is causing those changes.

Using the DMG as a bridge is effective because the implementation-level statements which can cause visual changes to the UI in standards-compliant Web applications are limited to a standard set of HTML/CSS attributes and DOM operations. Thus we are able to capture, and focus on, just these attributes and operations. If implementation code was non-standardized or able to directly draw to the browser window using pixel-level operations, such a mapping would be much more difficult or even impossible to create.

4 JavaScript Metrics

In order to better understand if our approach is truly motivated by the complexity of today's JavaScript implementations for several existing Web applications, we gathered

---

[1] To generate the visual appearance of the model, we use a GraphViz-based extension for Firefox.

Table 1. (**# of Files**) lists the number of JavaScript files downloaded for each page and (**Total Lines**) is the sum of their file line counts (in some cases the code is obfuscated so we cannot give an accurate estimate of non-commented lines of code). (**Context**) lists the average number of distinct contexts which a mutator statement was executed in (standard deviation in parentheses) / and the total number of DOM mutator statements executed for the page after the slash. (**Memory**) is the original memory used by Firefox for page execution / with the memory used for our instrumented page after the slash.

Web Page	# of Files	Total Lines	Context (see caption)	Memory (MB)
Petstore	3	1,232	2.2 (1.6) /118	36 / 38
eBay	4	19,682	1.5 (.84) /43	40 / 44
Facebook	7	37,310	1.7 (1.3) /485	68 / 72
Yahoo	1	10,218	2.3 (1.4) /164	42 / 43
Amazon	4	5,903	2.0 (.95) /91	45 / 46
Priceline	9	11,667	3.5 (1.8) /73	38 / 40

metrics from JPS and several popular Web sites. These measurements were taken using Mozilla Firefox 3.0.3 for Microsoft Windows.

Table 1 shows four columns of metrics for each page. The second column, number of files, counts the JavaScript files which were referenced by the page. The total lines, column three, is the sum of the files sizes (in terms of lines) for those files.

The column labeled Context describes information about the DOM mutator statements which were executed. The first number lists the average number of distinct calling contexts in which a statement executed. For example, considering the Petstore, each assignment statement to a DOM attribute was executed in 2.2 different contexts on average. The second number shows the standard deviation. The third number lists the total number of DOM mutator statements executed for the page.

The final column lists the memory usage of Firefox with a page loaded, after having its UI exercised; first without our tool in use and second with our tool being used. Memory consumption is discussed further in Section 4.2.

For JPS we use the Catalog Browser which has already been described in detail. The eBay page is a simple list of results for searching auctions related to "iPods". The FaceBook page is the default "Profile" page for a new Facebook user. For Yahoo, Amazon, and Priceline, we used the default homepages.

We took the metrics by triggering a measurement function injected into the code. Since these metrics measure properties of the JavaScript execution, we needed to exercise the UI of the page before taking measurements. We did this by simply manually manipulating any part of the UI which did not cause the page to be changed (hence losing the script state for the page).

4.1 Discussion

By looking at the results for the Context metrics, we see for which pages our calling context capture could be useful. Here we see that these pages either: frequently execute mutators in more than one context and/or execute some mutators in many different contexts.

In general, we see that it was common for a mutator of a DOM node to be used in more than one context. At first this could seem unintuitive because even most interactive Web pages tend to have a large amount of static content. However, this makes sense since we are only including mutations made in the JavaScript code and not any HTML attributes which are set in the static HTML or HTML generated by the server. If some attribute was going to be set only one time and never mutated, it would make sense that the developer chose to generate the value on the server. Thus for JavaScript execution, the reuse of code from different contexts appears to be prominent for these pages.

Developers working on a particular Web page without the help of a model, will need to create a mental map which connects an element of the Web page to a particular location in code. This would currently be done in an ad-hoc fashion. Two possible examples are as follows.

First, a developer could scan the code to identify relevant code. From the # of files and total LOC in Table 1, we believe that this approach is not scalable. There is simply too much code to consider across the files.

Second, a developer could associate an identifier such as a JavaScript function name or file with each element of the Web page. For example, they might use a particular file for all "information pane" functions. In this way, when they want to work on some code related to a particular element, they could use a text-based search to find the relevant code. However this one-to-one mapping does not appear scalable in light of the Context metrics from Table 1, because a distinct page element may be associated with code reused by several elements or for different purposes. Next, in Section 5 we turn to an example in our JPS case-study to demonstrate how our approach could be leveraged to deal with these problems.

4.2   Performance Considerations

Since our tool collects a history trace of DOM mutations, we wanted to determine how much memory overhead was used for the example Web pages in Table 1. These measurements are listed in last column. Here we see that the amount of memory used was never more than 4MB. Since we only exercised the parts of the UI that were obvious to us, it is possible we had missed some button, menu, or other widget that was not clearly marked. Still, since the amount of memory used was small relative to that in today's desktop machines, we did not consider this to be a large issue.

Certainly the memory used will depend on the code for the page itself. For example, looking back at Fig. 4, we see that the history for expanding and deflating one accordion bar, one time, required 16 trace entries. If JPS was programmed differently, this number could certainly increase but we believe that JPS and the example pages in Table 1 are a fair representation of UI programming practices for many of today's Web applications.

We have used our tool extensively in the exploration of JPS and also as part of collecting the measurements for Table 1. Using the tool we did not notice any perceptible slow down caused by the run-time tracing while interacting with the page.

5 Catalog Browser Example

In order for us to be able to describe some details of our study in depth, we choose to focus on the "Information Pane" (B) and "Collapse Button" (C) on the Catalog Browser page of JPS in Fig. 1.

In this section, we will first introduce the behavior of this information pane and collapse button at a high level. Then, we will give a more low level description from the developer's perspective. Finally, we describe the model that is generated by using our approach to bridge these two different perspectives. A developer can use this model as linked from the browser view, to quickly get into the script programming details.

The information pane (B) describes the detail information for a selected pet (e.g. name, description and rating). This widget is mapped to a `div` element in the DOM. In Fig 1., the information pane appears raised, partially obscuring a pet image. When the pane is lowered, it appears to slide behind the scrollbar (positioned beneath it). This animation is performed by mutating `clip`, `height`, and `top` attributes in coordination.

The collapse button (C) controls the raising and lowering of the information pane. It is an `img` element in the DOM. There are two places in JavaScript which set the `src` attribute. The collapse button's icon is changed to a down arrow when the information pane becomes fully raised and changed to an up arrow when the information pane becomes fully lowered.

Table 2 summarizes the three mutated attributes of the information pane and one attribute of the collapse button. Each attribute is mutated in two contexts, which correspond to each of the nodes in Fig. 6. The figure encapsulates changes made to multiple attributes of multiple DOM nodes, to show the flow of execution which was monitored.

Table 2. The various contexts in which attributes of the information pane and collapse button are mutated. The trace information of value changes associated which each context are shown in the second column (some are elided for illustration). Note that as is common, the coordinate for `top` is measured as the pixel distance from the top of the screen, hence it is decreasing. The clip value actually includes four coordinates but only one changes in this example so the others are elided.

DOM Mutator Context	Trace Values
height0	[75px...177px]
top0	[452px...350px]
clip0	[75px...177px]
src0	up-to-down.gif
height1	[177px...75px]
top1	[350px...452px]
clip1	[177px...75px]
src1	down-to-up.gif

From Fig. 6, we can see that the two sets of nodes related to the information pane (at the top and bottom of the figure) are separated by the nodes related to the button icon, which reflects the raising and lowering of the information pane. For each set of information pane attributes, the mutation of the three different attributes, height, top, clip have been executed continuously in an event-loop, shown by the recursive edges out of clip0 and clip1.

By examining the trace of values captured for different DMG nodes we can observe the changes which occur to create the raising and lowering effect. For example, by looking at the entry in Table 2 for height0. Here we see the height increases. Without examining the source code, we can already tell that this context is responsible for raising the information pane.

After discerning this information, then by an understanding of the information pane and collapse button behavior from the browser view, and examining the topology of the flow relationships between the DMG nodes, we can plainly determine that src0 is the context responsible for setting the image of the down arrow; top0 and clip0 must then be responsible for part of the information pane raising effect; so then, height1, top1, and clip1 must be responsible for the lowering effect; and finally we can surmise that src1 changes the down arrow to up arrow. Now, we can link to the code associated with any of the DMG nodes we are interested in for performing any changes during maintenance or debugging.

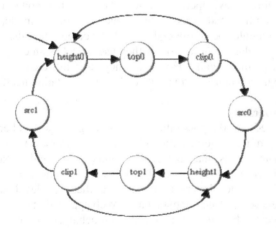

Fig. 6. The flow of the information pane and collapse button presented as a DMG; each node corresponds to the entries from Table 2

6 Related Work

JavaScript Programming Tools
Due to the popularity of Ajax based applications, there is an increasing demand for JavaScript programming tools. One representative tool for developing Ajax applications is the Firebug [13] extension for the Mozilla Firefox browser. Using

Firebug, a developer can simply click on a rendered element in the browser and be hyperlinked to an expanded tree-view of the corresponding DOM element. Now, a developer can inspect the low-level attributes of that specific DOM object and also understand its context relative to its ancestor and children objects.

Although this practice is useful, Firebug still does not provide any help for the developer to understand the connection between a DOM node and the JavaScript which acts on the DOM. Essentially, our research addresses this mapping between the DOM and JavaScript which is not addressed in existing practice.

GUI Maintenance

In [11], McMaster et al. present how to use calling context information collected during a GUI program's execution to solve the GUI test suite reduction problem (i.e. finding a minimal satisfactory test set). Their research considers two GUI test cases to be equivalent if they generate the same set of call stacks after execution. This new call-stack coverage criterion can be used to address the challenges for GUI-intensive applications, which are difficult to be handled by some other criteria such as statement or branch coverage. Similar with their research, we also use calling context to distinguish two artifacts. However, our research is used to resolve the ambiguity of the different UI changes instead of GUI test cases, for example, accordion row expanding and deflation.

In [17], Michail introduced a tool to provide GUI-guided browsing of source. Their objective was to allow developers to find where in the code a feature was implemented, based on how code was related to the GUI. For example, to find "spell checking" code, they could locate the code which executed when the spell checking menu was selected. Similar to our approach, they use a GUI as an entry-point into the lower-level implementation details. However, they user the GUI to understand its relation to other program features and not the GUI implementation itself.

Model-Based Approaches

Several projects looked into the possibility of recovering a high-level architecture for a Web application from its implementation [4, 12]. In [4], Hassan and Holt describe a set of semi-automated tools that parse the source code and binaries of Web applications and extract relations between the different components to create a model. Their model helps Web developers to understand the high level architecture of traditional HTML and server-side template based Web applications.

Using a finite state machine model to present GUI behavior has been studied in [7]. Their paper describes a Java toolkit called SwingStates which is used to assist in the development of GUIs for non-expert developers. The novel part of their research is that they use finite-state machines to describe the behavior of interactive UI systems. However, their research is concerned about how to create a user interface instead of reversing engineering from an existing UI.

In [8], Shehady and Siewiorek introduced how to use a Variable Finite State Machine (VFSM) interface model to present the behavior of the user interface. Each node in the VFSM is the state of the GUI, and an edge represents the possible events that can be triggered in that state. This model is useful for determining the flow of user-triggered events which change the state of the GUI. In contrast, our model is useful for mapping the live DOM nodes which make up the GUI to implementation-level statements.

Ali et al. introduces a tool called CrawlJax in [14]. Their research uses a dynamic approach to crawl Ajax based applications by triggering the event handlers in the code. After crawling, a state-flow graph is constructed. In this graph, each node represents the snapshot of the DOM tree for a Web UI after some event handler is triggered; each edge in the state-flow graph represents the clickable elements that transform one state to another state. This state-flow graph can be used to provide automated testing of Ajax applications. Similar to the research in the previous paragraph, their research is not concerned with providing a mapping for a programmer to the implementation level details of the UI.

7 Conclusion

In this paper we have studied the problem of JavaScript implementation complexity for interactive Web UI. These details of the UI are easy to understand from the perspective of the Web browser view but can be hard to map to the related code. We proposed an approach which leverages execution history and calling context so that developers can explore the code from the browser view. The DMG model was introduced to present the obtained history and context information to developers for a better understanding of the behavior of the UI. We presented some script complexity metrics for popular Web sites to further motivate the need for our interactive script development approach. We found that many of the sites that we measured included significant complexity based on the number of calling contexts for a given statement. To demonstrate how the DMG could help, we presented examples from the open-source Java Pet Store Ajax application.

References

1. Yu, J., Benatallah, B., Saint-Paul, R., Casati, F., Daniel, F., Matera, M.: A framework for rapid integration of presentation components. In: Proc. of the International Conference on the World-Wide Web (2007)
2. Trigueros, M.L., Preciado, J.C., Sánchez-Figueroa, F.: A Method for Model Based Design of Rich Internet Application Interactive User Interfaces. In: Proc. of the International Conference on Web Engineering, pp. 226–241 (2007)
3. Valderas, P., Pelechano, V., Pastor, O.: Introducing Graphic Designers in a Web Development Process. In: Krogstie, J., Opdahl, A.L., Sindre, G. (eds.) CAiSE 2007 and WES 2007. LNCS, vol. 4495, pp. 395–408. Springer, Heidelberg (2007)
4. Hassan, A., Holt, R.: Architecture recovery of web applications. In: Proc. of the International Conference on Software Engineering (2002)
5. Dojo JavaScript Toolkit, http://dojotoolkit.org/
6. jQuery JavaScript Library, http://jquery.com/
7. Appert, C., Beaudouin-Lafon, M.: SwingStates: adding state machines to Java and the Swing toolkit. Softw. Pract. Exper. 38(11), 1149–1182 (2008)
8. Shehady, R.K., Siewiorek, D.P.: A Methodology to Automate User Interface Testing Using Variable Finite State Machines. In: Proc. of the International Symposium on Fault-Tolerant Computing, pp. 80–88 (1997)

9. Java Pet Store, Sun Microsystems,
    `http://java.sun.com/developer/releases/petstore/`
10. Rhino JavaScript compiler framework. Mozilla,
    `http://www.mozilla.org/rhino/`
11. McMaster, S., Memon, A.M.: Call Stack Coverage for GUI Test-Suite Reduction. In: Proc of the International Symposium on Software Reliability Engineering, pp. 33–44 (2006)
12. Ricca, F., Tonella, P.: Analysis and Testing of Web Applications. In: Proc. of the International Conference on Software Engineering, pp. 25–34 (2001)
13. FireBug, `http://getfirebug.com/`
14. Mesbah, A., Bozdag, E., Deursen, A.V.: Crawling AJAX by Inferring User Interface State Changes. In: Proc. of the International Conference on Web Engineering, pp. 122–134 (2008)
15. Rossi, G., Urbieta, M., Ginzburg, J., Distante, D., Garrido, A.: Refactoring to Rich Internet Applications. A Model-Driven Approach. In: Proc. of the International Conference on Web Engineering, pp. 1–12 (2008)
16. Meliá, S., Gómez, J., Pérez, S., Díaz, O.: A Model-Driven Development for GWT-Based Rich Internet Applications with OOH4RIA. In: Proc. of the International Conference on Web Engineering, pp. 13–23 (2008)
17. Michail, A.: Browsing and searching source code of applications written using a GUI framework. In: Proc. of the International Conference on Software Engineering (2002)

A Conceptual Framework for User Input Evaluation in Rich Internet Applications

Matthias Book, Tobias Brückmann, Volker Gruhn, and Malte Hülder

Applied Telematics/e-Business Group, University of Leipzig
Klostergasse 3, 04109 Leipzig, Germany
{book,brueckmann,gruhn,huelder}@ebus.informatik.uni-leipzig.de

Abstract. The more complex an application's user interface is, the more important is the need to guide users filling out the forms—typically by highlighting invalid input, showing/hiding or enabling/disabling particular fields according to business rules. In Rich Internet Applications, these reactions are expected to occur virtually immediately. We discuss aspects to be considered for consistent reactions to user input, and describe how evaluation rules can be formulated for model-driven development.[1]

1 Introduction

The user interfaces (UIs) of web-based information systems tend to mirror the complexity of their underlying business processes: In areas as diverse as e.g. market research, insurance claims or reinsurance underwriting, users need to enter a lot of structured data that must obey a variety of domain-specific constraints.

To support users in working efficiently with complex forms, UIs typically react to input with local changes in individual UI widgets (text fields, list boxes etc.) such as making the user aware of invalid input by highlighting affected widgets, decreasing visual complexity by hiding unnecessary widgets, or guiding users by enabling or disabling input in particular widgets. Rich Internet Applications (RIAs) enable instantaneous input evaluation and interface updates, and can thus provide immediate feedback and guidance to users.

In this paper, we discuss the aspects that influence a UI's reaction to user input (Sect. 2), and present a behavior model that includes dependencies between UI reactions such as handling incomplete input, prioritizing validation issues, and considering visibility in validation (Sect. 3). For use in practice, we briefly describe our Cepheus framework that automatically generates evaluation logic following this model based on rules specified by domain experts, eliminating the need for manual implementation (Sect. 4). We conclude with an overview of related work (Sect. 5) and a summary of our contributions (Sect. 6).

---

[1] This work was supported by a technology support grant from the European Regional Development Fund (ERDF) and funds of the Free State of Saxony. The Applied Telematics/e-Business Group is endowed by Deutsche Telekom AG.

M. Gaedke, M. Grossniklaus, and O. Díaz (Eds.): ICWE 2009, LNCS 5648, pp. 275–282, 2009.
© Springer-Verlag Berlin Heidelberg 2009

2   Specification of Input Evaluation

2.1   Interface and Data Model

A web application's interface model is characterized foremost by the **UI widgets** displayed on its pages. Often, multiple widgets will jointly describe a particular semantic entity from the business domain (e.g. a group of radio buttons for 1-of-n selection, or a group of text fields for entering elements of a postal address). To model such relationships, we allow widgets to be contained in hierarchically nested **containers** that also govern the layout of the interface's **pages**.

To store the entered content, all widgets must be bound to **variables** in the application's data model. While widgets can only produce string input (as this is the serialized format universally used to exchange data between web application components), the data model's variables have certain **types** (e.g. Boolean, integer, floating-point, text, date etc.).

2.2   Evaluation Aspects and Rules

To formulate rules governing the evaluation of the information in the interface and data model, several orthogonal aspects have to be considered: Evaluation rules can serve different **purposes**—in this paper, we will focus on deciding *validity*, *visibility*, and *availability* of widgets, which are usually closely tied to UI **reactions** such as *highlighting* violating widgets, *hiding* invisible widgets, and *disabling* (e.g. "graying out") unavailable widgets, respectively.[2]

At the core of each evaluation rule must be an **expression** that describes the actual evaluation of certain values in order to arrive at a decision for one of the above purposes. While such an expression may consist of nested terms performing *comparisons*, *arithmetic*, *boolean* or *string operations* on literals or variables from the data model, it must ultimately resolve to a boolean value indicating the outcome of the decision.

Regardless of its purpose, any evaluation rule must relate to certain **subjects** on which the respective reaction shall be effected. For increased flexibility, we allow that subjects can not only be individual *widgets*, but also groups of widgets contained directly or transitively in a particular *container*. Note that the subject widgets do not necessarily need to correspond to the expression's input variables.

For the purpose of input validation, we must consider several additional characteristics. First, we can distinguish several **levels** of validation that depend on each other: The most basic level is checking for the *existence* of any input in a required field. Next, the *technical* check concerns whether a particular input string can be converted to the associated variable's type. Finally, performing any *domain-specific* validation of the input is only sensible if the previous two validation levels were satisfied.

---

[2] We can also conceive other purposes of user input evaluation, such as deciding on navigation options. However, we will focus on the above-mentioned purposes here since their reactions are more interrelated with each other, and they pose more interesting challenges in RIAs as they may impact a page's Document Object Model immediately, as opposed to navigation choices.

Our experience shows that in practice, it may be inconvenient or even impossible for the user to satisfy all validation rules immediately—rather, we identified four common **triggers** upon which different sets of validation rules can be sensibly checked and enforced: Validation may occur upon a widget's *"blurring"* (i.e. losing focus) when the cursor is moved to another widget; upon *leaving* a page in order to jump to the next or previous page in the dialog; upon *saving* the data entered so far as a draft version, in order to prevent data loss or continue working on the dialog at a later time; and finally upon *committing* all entered data in order to complete a task in a business process. By staging the validation through associating rules with appropriate triggers, developers can strike a balance between business requirements and usability considerations, ensuring data integrity while maintaining users' flexibility in working with the application.

In a similar vein, experience shows that typically not all rule violations are equally serious: Depending on the business semantics of a rule, developers may choose to associate a certain **severity** to it. We distinguish informative, warning and error rules in our evaluation specification, in order to tailor the interface's reactions to different severities, as we will see in the following section.

When formulating input evaluation rules, developers need to specify all of the above aspects (expression, subjects, level, trigger and severity) for the purpose of validation. In visibility and availability rules, only the expression and subjects must be specified, as their evaluation is always triggered immediately upon a widget's blurring, and we cannot distinguish different levels and severities.

3   Behavior of Input Evaluation

Having introduced the elements of input evaluation rules that developers need to specify at design-time, we will now discuss how these static specifications govern the dynamic behavior of an application at run-time, and how different rules affect each other. Anytime an evaluation is triggered, we need to (1) update the data model with the contents of those widgets that are technically valid; (2) validate the data model according to domain rules, and update the list of known issues; and (3) update the UI to reflect visibility, availability and issues of widgets.

In the following subsections, we will describe these steps in more detail. In this process, three data structures will be dynamically updated at run-time: The **contents** currently entered into the widgets of the interface model, the **values** currently stored in the variables of the data model, and the identified **issues**, i.e. the subset of all validation rules that are currently violated by any given input.

3.1   Data Model Update

Any time an evaluation is triggered (i.e. upon leaving a field or a page, or before saving or committing the dialog's data), we first need to update the data model according to the contents entered into the widgets affected by the trigger. The evaluation logic needs to implement the following algorithm for this purpose:

> IF a widget is visible AND contains input THEN
>   IF the input has the expected type THEN
>   store the input in the variable associated with the widget
>   ELSE leave the associated variable's current value unchanged
> ELSE render the associated variable undefined

This way, we ensure that input is only included in the data model if its type is actually suitable for storage there; that incorrect input cannot overwrite previously stored data; and that any absence of input is reflected in the data model.

3.2 Data Model Validation

In the previous step, we have ensured that only technically sound input (i.e. input of the proper type) is accepted into the application's data model. Now, we still need to check if that data complies with the existence and domain-specific rules, and potentially signal any validation issues.

Existence Validation. When checking existence validation rules, we must not just check for the presence of content in a widget, but also take into account whether that widget is actually visible: We define that an existence rule is satisfied iff the respective widget contains input or is invisible. By taking the visibility into account when checking required fields, we eliminate the need for the developer to explicitly specify this connection in every rule, as it would be nonsensical to require input in a field we have hidden.

Domain-Specific Validation. When checking domain-specific properties, we need to arrive at a validation result in a way that takes both business rules and usability factors into account: In complex forms, subjects to which the validation pertains may be invisible, or variables on which the validation depends may still be undefined as the user makes his way through the form. We therefore define that a domain-specific validation rule is satisfied iff its expression evaluates to *true* or all its subjects are invisible. In evaluating the rule's expression, we should strive to arrive at a meaningful result even if some of the input variables are still undefined. In our model, any non-Boolean term that encounters an undefined parameter will therefore return an "undefined" result. In a Boolean OR term, meanwhile, we consider undefined parameters as *false* values, and in a Boolean AND term, as *true* values, in order to let the result depend only on the other operand, thereby neutralizing the undefined part of the expression. This way, a term that returns an undefined result due to missing input parameters has no effect, so any empty widgets are not validated until they are filled—a behavior that we would intuitively expect from a dialog that is not yet filled completely. (Of course, an empty widget declared as required input would already be reported as invalid by the existence rules discussed before.)

Issue Tracking. To react to all validation issues consistently, regardless of when they occurred, we keep track of all rule violations in a central set. Anytime an evaluation is triggered, we perform the following two updates on this set:

1. add rules just found to be violated upon this triggering occasion
2. remove rules found to satisfied

By considering the triggering occasion when adding, but not when removing issues, we ensure that rule violations are not admonished until the time deemed appropriate by the developer, but that they are removed immediately when the violation is remedied. We found this behavior more intuitive for users than maintaining an old error message until the next trigger occasion, even when the user had already fixed the problem.

3.3   User Interface Reaction

Finally, our behavior model must define how the UI reacts to the various conditions that arise from validation results, visibility and availability of widgets:

Issue Notifications. We found it intuitive to signal validation issues in two ways: At the top of each page, the UI displays a concise list of human-readable explanations for all violations that were identified on the current and other pages. In case a particular set of subjects violates several rules, we display only the most severe issue to reduce clutter. To further aid the user in identifying invalid input, we highlight the respective widgets in a color corresponding to the severity (e.g. red for errors, orange for warnings, blue for information). Two relationships influence this coloring scheme: Firstly, if the subject of a rule is not an individual widget, but a container, the issue is assumed to apply to all directly and transitively contained widgets, which are all colored accordingly. Secondly, if a subject is affected by several issues (through several rules or inclusion in an affected container), it will be colored according to the most severe issue applying to it.

Visibility. In formulating the evaluation algorithms earlier, we have already relied on an indication of whether a particular subject is currently visible, but still need to define precisely how that decision is made: For any given subject (i.e. widget or container), we define that it is visible iff all visibility rules applying directly to it are satisfied, and if the container that it is contained in is visible. Note that this condition implies transitive dependency on the visibility of all containers in a subject's nesting hierarchy, allowing developers to conveniently hide or show whole groups of semantically related widgets if necessary.

Availability. Whether a widget is "grayed out" or editable is determined by availability rules that are specified and evaluated analogously to visibility rules. While visibility affects the data model, availability is a pure interface reaction that does not affect how data is validated or stored. The navigation buttons found on each page (typically, for navigating forward and backward in a dialog wizard, saving a draft of the current data, or committing it for further processing) are a special case insofar as they are implicitly associated with availability rules that do not need to be specified by developers: While a page contains validation errors triggered by leaving a field, the "previous page" and "next page" buttons are unavailable; while errors triggered by leaving a page are present, the "save draft" button is unavailable; and during the presence of errors triggered by trying to save a draft, the "commit" button is unavailable, to prevent entering, storing or committing invalid input.

4   Implementation

The input evaluation logic described in the previous section was implemented in our Cepheus framework that generates presentation, validation and persistence logic from models created by domain experts in a visual editor. As Fig. 1 shows, views (based on the ICEfaces framework [1]) and evaluation rules are derived from the specifications at deploy-time. At run-time, the views will trigger validation, visibility and availability checks based on the specified rules and the values entered into the data model, and update the presentation accordingly by highlighting, showing, hiding or graying out the GUI widgets.

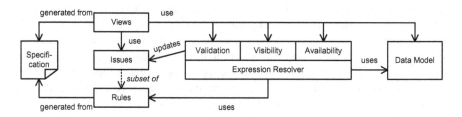

Fig. 1. Architectural overview of input evaluation in Cepheus

The screenshot in Fig. 2 illustrates an example system's behavior, where the visibility of the last three questions depends on the answer to the first question, and the allowed expenses have been limited to a certain amount that is exceeded here. Any changes in the input fields that affect the visibility or validation rules are immediately reflected in the user interface.

At this time, we have only anecdotal data about the time and effort savings that can be gained when using the Cepheus editor and framework instead of manual implementation. Initial experiences from employing a Cepheus prototype in an industry project from the market research sector (which is characterized by the need for frequent roll-outs of new web-based questionnaires) back our expectations that enabling domain experts to specify user interface layout and validation directly can reduce the time to market, since no transfer of domain knowledge to application programmers is required. Regarding performance implications, we do not expect a significant impact since all necessary rule-checking code is generated at deploy-time, so no expensive parsing occurs at run-time.

5   Related Work

Virtually all approaches for modeling and developing web applications provide means for realizing some form of input validation. To name just a few, in

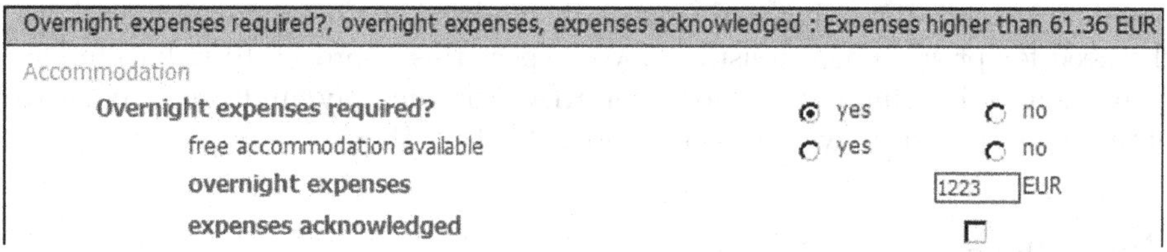

Overnight expenses required?, overnight expenses, expenses acknowledged : Expenses higher than 61.36 EUR

Accommodation

Overnight expenses required?	⊙ yes	○ no
free accommodation available	○ yes	○ no
overnight expenses		1223 EUR
expenses acknowledged		☐

Fig. 2. Screenshot excerpt from a Cepheus-based application

WebML [2], validity predicates are properties of entry units in the hypertext model, using an expression language that supports comparisons of input fields with constants or other field contents. UWE [3] enables designers to specify when and where fields should be validated in its process flow and process structure models, but leaves the actual implementation of these rules to the developer. OO-H [4] provides means for validating the type of input fields; its "visible" and "hidden" attributes however have slightly different semantics from our approach.

Recently, these approaches have also been extended to support the modeling of RIAs: Comai and Toffetti Carughi [5] discussed how to extend WebML to capture more fine-grained user interaction with page elements; Meliá et al. [6] introduced corresponding structural and behavioral models in OOH4RIA; and Preciado et al. [7] combined UWE with the RUX-Method, an approach that focuses especially on the spatial, temporal and interaction aspects of Rich Internet Applications [8]. However, the validation models do not seem to have changed in the extension of these approaches' scopes.

Looking at representatives of popular web application frameworks, Struts provides a number of built-in validators for simple type and range checking, and allows the formulation of more flexible expressions in the `validator.xml` file [9]. In Spring, developers can provide custom validation classes implementing the `Validator` interface [10]. The Seam framework [11] relies on constraints defined in the data model using the Hibernate Validator. Common AJAX frameworks such as ICEfaces [12] or RichFaces [13] typically provide means for adding validation rules at different points in the request lifecycle as well.

While all approaches provide hooks for validation rules, their actual formulation is typically so technical that it requires a developer's rather than a domain expert's skills. In particular, any interdependencies between rules (e.g. visibility vs. validation, or the handling of different issue severities), are not supported by these models and frameworks themselves, but must be implemented explicitly.

6   Conclusion

In this paper, we identified several aspects that have to be considered in the evaluation of user input in RIAs for the purpose of technical and domain-specific input validation, widget visibility and availability. We have shown how these aspects are entwined with each other, and how they are incorporated in the Cepheus framework that generates user input evaluation logic automatically, based on specifications that can be visually modeled by domain experts without the need for programmer assistance. We expect this approach to reduce implementation and maintenance efforts for RIAs considerably, and are striving to obtain more practical evidence to support this hypothesis.

References

1. ICEsoft Technologies, Inc.: ICEFaces, http://www.icefaces.org
2. Ceri, S., Fraternali, P., Bongio, A.: Web Modeling Language (WebML): a modeling language for designing Web sites. Computer Networks 33, 137–157 (2000)
3. Koch, N., Kraus, A.: The expressive power of UML-based web engineering. In: IWWOST 2002: Proc. 2nd Intl. Workshop on Web-oriented Software Technology, pp. 105–119 (2002), http://www.dsic.upv.es/~west/iwwost02/papers/koch.pdf
4. Gómez, J., Cachero, C., Pastor, O.: Conceptual modeling of device-independent web applications. IEEE Multimedia 8(2), 26–39 (2001)
5. Comai, S., Carughi, G.T.: A behavioral model for Rich Internet Applications. In: Baresi, L., Fraternali, P., Houben, G.-J. (eds.) ICWE 2007. LNCS, vol. 4607, pp. 364–369. Springer, Heidelberg (2007)
6. Meliá, S., Gómez, J., Pérez, S., Díaz, O.: A model-driven development for GWT-based Rich Internet Applications with OOH4RIA. In: ICWE 2008: Proc. 8th Intl. Conf. on Web Engineering, pp. 13–23. IEEE Computer Society Press, Los Alamitos (2008)
7. Preciado, J.C., Linaje, M., Morales-Chaparro, R., et al.: Designing Rich Internet Applications combining UWE and RUX-Method. In: ICWE 2008: Proc. 8th Intl. Conf. on Web Engineering, pp. 148–154. IEEE Computer Society Press, Los Alamitos (2008)
8. Linaje, M., Preciado, J.C., Sánchez-Figueroa, F.: A method for model based design of Rich Internet Application interactive user interfaces. In: Baresi, L., Fraternali, P., Houben, G.-J. (eds.) ICWE 2007. LNCS, vol. 4607, pp. 226–241. Springer, Heidelberg (2007)
9. Apache Software Foundation: Struts Validator Guide, http://struts.apache.org/1.2.4/userGuide/dev_validator.html
10. SpringSource: Validation, Data-binding, the BeanWrapper, and PropertyEditors, http://static.springframework.org/spring/docs/2.0.x/reference/validation.html
11. Red Hat Middleware, LLC: JSF form validation in Seam, http://docs.jboss.org/seam/1.1GA/reference/en/html/validation.html
12. ICEsoft Technologies, Inc.: How to Use Validators, http://facestutorials.icefaces.org/tutorial/validators-tutorial.html
13. Red Hat Middleware, LLC: rich:ajaxValidator, http://www.jboss.org/file-access/default/members/jbossrichfaces/freezone/docs/devguide/en/html/ajaxValidator.html

Patterns for the Model-Based Development of RIAs*

Nora Koch[1,2], Matthias Pigerl[3], Gefei Zhang[1], and Tatiana Morozova[1]

[1] Ludwig-Maximilians-Universität München, Germany
[2] Cirquent GmbH, Germany
[3] S.CO LifeScience GmbH, Germany

Abstract. Rich Internet Applications (RIAs) are highly interactive web applications that resemble desktop applications. Modeling RIAs hence requires techniques for web modeling enriched by model elements for powerful user interactions and client-server communications. Many existing approaches provide the required modeling features, but they are still failing short in designer-friendliness and effectiveness. We present a pattern approach for the model-based engineering of RIAs that (1) reduces design efforts maintaining expressiveness of the models, and (2) contributes to model-driven development of RIAs. Our RIA patterns can be easily embedded in existing web modeling methods, which is illustrated with the UML-based Web Engineering.

1 Introduction

Rich Internet Applications (RIAs) are web applications augmented with desktop features and mechanisms of advanced communications. The rich look and feel, better responsiveness, performance, and accessibility enthuse both users and software providers. RIAs improve user interaction facilities like drag&drop, multimedia presentations and avoid unnecessary page reloading. Data handling and operations executed on the client side minimize server requests.

RIAs use the power of client and server and can be implemented using different techniques, such as Asynchronous Javascript with XML (AJAX) for which a set of frameworks have been developed (Flex, Ruby on Rails, etc.). Frameworks are quite helpful for programming, but the development of software requires also support for other phases like design and testing. In particular, model-driven development requires building models during the design and using models as sources of transformations to generate other models or running code. In this paper we focus on modeling RIAs.

Different modeling approaches for RIAs were developed as extensions of existing methods during the last few years (see Sect. 5). The extensions proposed so far consist of creating new model elements for the new RIA features, such as the validation of an input field value as soon as the user moves the mouse out of it. However, they do not alleviate the designer's work, i.e. provide the appropriate model elements of frequent use in the domain with precisely defined semantics.

---

* This research has been partially supported by the projects MAEWA II (WI841/7-2) of the DFG, Germany, and the EC 6th Framework project SENSORIA (IST 016004).

M. Gaedke, M. Grossniklaus, and O. Díaz (Eds.): ICWE 2009, LNCS 5648, pp. 283–291, 2009.
© Springer-Verlag Berlin Heidelberg 2009

Patterns have proved valuable for efficient RIA programming [7]. We propose to apply patterns at a higher abstraction level, i.e. modeling, to achieve the objectives of minimizing the design efforts and maximizing the expressiveness of the models used in the development of RIAs. Our focus is on the use of state machines for the representation of the patterns – a widely used modeling technique. The models of the RIA patterns we specify can be embedded in almost all existing methodologies. In this sense, it is a general approach for all UML conform methods. The use of these RIA patterns only requires the definition of extension points in the methodology, and afterwards the specification of how to integrate the patterns, which makes our patterns easily reusable. In this paper and for demonstration purposes only, we use the UML-based Web Engineering (UWE) [4] as the hosting language.

This paper is organized as follows: Section 2 describes the industrial case study S.CORE used to validate the approach. Section 3 presents RIA patterns. Section 4 describes the integration of RIA patterns in the development using existing web modeling methods; the procedure is illustrated by UWE. In Section 5 we discuss some related work. Section 6 concludes and provides some ideas for future work.

2   Real World Case Study: S.CORE System

Our approach was validated in a real case study: the S.CORE application of the company S.CO LifeScience [11]. S.CORE is a web-based image analysis system. Since the complete service of image analysis is offered totally through the web, no software needs to be downloaded. S.CORE offers standard analysis modules such as cell counting, as well as customized solutions tailored to the customers' need for enumerating, measuring and statistical quantification of images. S.CORE is mainly used in the lifescience area.

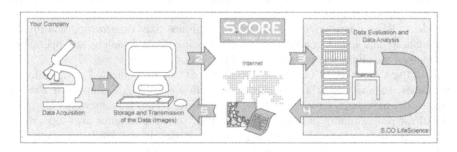

Fig. 1. Image analysis by S.CORE system

The image analysis process supported by S.CORE is shown in Fig. 1. It consists of the following steps: (1) The customer obtains and prepares the digital images of his samples with the appropriate technical tools in his laboratory. (2) With the help of S.CORE, which has a web-based human-machine interface, configured to the specific requirements of the customer, he can upload the images and specifications for performing the desired analysis type in the processing center of S.CO LifeScience. (3) The images are loaded automatically into the Analyzer of S.CORE, where the desired data is extracted from the image and made available on the server. (4+5) The customer can download the results (including the processed image).

Within a collaboration between the Ludwig-Maximilians-Universität München and S.CO LifeScience, the S.CORE system was augmented with Web 2.0 features. This improved the user-friendliness of S.CORE. In particular, input fields supported by auto-completion, the progress of the upload and download functions visualized, images to be analyzed presented as a gallery of images, the result page should show the current status of analysis results. These Web 2.0 features challenged the design of the system with UWE.

3 RIA Patterns

Best practices for the implementation of RIAs include the use of RIA patterns. A RIA pattern is a general reusable solution to a commonly occurring problem in RIA design. It describes the interaction, operation and presentation of a RIA widget [12]. The interaction is the trigger of the RIA pattern, i.e. every pattern starts with a user event or a system event, e.g. *mouseover, onfocus, keyboard stroke* or *time event*. A variety of operations can be triggered by the interaction, such as validate, search and refresh. Finally, the result of the operation implies an update of the user interface.

Bill Scott emphasizes that patterns are great for forming a design vocabulary [12]. However, we stress that these patterns if appropriately generalized and modeled, are more powerful as they could be integrated in the models already built for other concerns of a web application, e.g. presentation and process. This means that the models of the RIA patterns are solutions that could be reused in the development of RIAs. Reuse can be performed manually or in an automated development process, such as model-driven development by model-to-model transformations.

Our pattern-based approach for implementing RIAs then consists in the use of the models of RIA widgets and the embedding of these models of RIAS into the other existing models. Therefore the designer needs (1) models of the patterns describing the RIA features, (2) an event language for the representation of user and system events, (3) model elements to be integrated in the existing web application models, such as the presentation model to indicate which pattern should be applied in which case. Our pattern approach compared to other RIA modeling techniques concern only the abstract presentation. Concrete presentation issues, like multimedia, animation, etc., are handled in the concrete presentation model, for further details see [5]. The separation of abstract and concrete presentation is essential to an MDD process since the abstract presentation model can be easily reused for other platforms [10].

An event language is defined, which includes constructs such as mouseover, onblur, onfocus, onclick, etc. A RIA pattern catalog is created which contains RIA patterns for modern web applications used in S.CORE reference projects [9]. Note this catalog is not exhaustive. It is an open document, which will grow up in the way RIA patterns become more familiar. We illustrate our approach presenting in the following two patterns of the catalog [9].

Auto-Completion. A S.CORE user has to deal with a lot of forms and input fields, There are forms for analysis parameter, search masks or user registration. Similarly to forms of other web applications, some input fields ask for redundant data or data which could be identified after entering the first characters. Unnecessary work would be burdened to the user if he had to fill in every input field. Therefore the application should fill in redundant input fields automatically. Here some examples to concretize the scenario: When a user starts entering the image name, the system should find the analysis name automatically if this image only exists in one analysis (Fig. 3). Obviously all data captured by application logics could only be suggestions in order to allow a better usability. The user is still the last instance for checking the correctness of the suggested data. Therefore he should be able to overwrite every auto-completed input field.

Problem. How could the user of a RIA get an immediate suggestion for values in an input field, after he has entered some initial data or has filled in other related fields?

Motivation. Assistance by filling in input fields and forms. (1) People make mistakes when they type. (2) Typing in data is a tedious work. (3) Typing speed remains a bottleneck; faster user input is aimed by reducing the number of keystrokes.

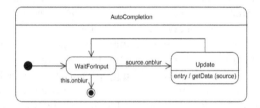

Fig. 2. RIA Pattern auto-completion (UML state diagram)

Solution. Suggest words or phrases that are likely to complete what the user is typing. As soon as the user moves to another input element or even as soon as the user inputs a character, the RIA in the background will try to query databases and find relations to already entered data. If such data could be found and the user has not yet completed it himself, a completed value for the input field is suggested to user. Fig. 2 shows the general pattern for auto-completion: on *source* (e.g. analysis name) losing focus (*onblur*), the RIA goes into the state *Update* to get the relevant data (image name), and then to update the corresponding content of itself. Note that the user can overwrite the suggested value as the widget remains in the *WaitForInput* state.

Examples. (1) Online banking. (2) Sixt car rental system (www.sixt.com).

Periodic/Dynamic Refresh. An S.CORE user can upload several microscope images for image analyses in order to extract statistical data from the uploaded images. Thus inside S.CORE there is a status page where the user can monitor the status and check the approximate finishing time of every analysis process. During the analysis the process runs through different states and also the approximation of the finishing time could change due to unpredictable analysis process events or other analysis with a higher priority being started. The status page should always provide correct and up-to-date information without a permanent reload of the whole page, i.e., change the list of analysis that are currently running, the remaining time for finishing the analysis and the options selected according to the state and type of analysis (Fig. 3).

Scratch Assay   Search image: [   ]   Analysis name: [   ]

Images waiting to be processed

MC-24#3.jpg warning The uploaded file MC-24#3.jpg was analysed on Thursday 12th of February 2009 with the same module. Analyse it a
The filename was MC-24#2.jpg.   **yes / no**

siGLIPR-24HRS.jpg done
U251NT24#2.jpg processing   notify by **sms / email** Estimated time: < 1 min
U251NT24#3.jpg requested   notify by **sms / email** **Cancel**

Start Analysis   Results   F

Fig. 3. S.CORE: Analysis status page

Problem. How could the data embedded in a status page stay permanently updated without reloading the whole page?

Motivation. The status of the page has to be updated dynamically and permanently.

Solution. Periodically a request has to be executed to check if there is new data available. If so, this data has to be processed and the connected data element at the page updated or a new data element created.

Examples. (1) Flight status at Munich airport pages (www.munich-airport.de). (2) Goals during a soccer game at Spiegel online (www.spiegel.de).

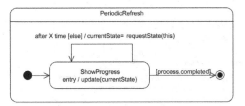

Fig. 4. RIA Pattern periodic refresh (UML state diagram)

4   Embedding RIA Patterns in Existing Web Methods

RIA patterns can be embedded in almost all existing methodologies to achieve considerable reduction of modeling and programming efforts. Our approach requires: (1) definition of extension points in the methodology for including references to RIA functionalities, (2) use of the state machines of the RIA patterns defined in Sect. 3, (3) definition of transformation rules that automatically integrate the behavior defined in the state machines into the models or code of the web application (for model-driven approaches only). Hence, a web developer using our approach only needs to indicate for which user interface (UI) objects of the web application a specific RIA pattern should be applied. He does not need to model the behavior of these UI objects as it is already specified by the state machines. He will afterwards use the state machines, integrating them in the models of the web application. If an automated generation process is followed, e.g. a model-driven approach, the developer will use a set of model transformation rules that automatically add the corresponding behavior defined by the RIA pattern. This procedure and the advantages for the developer are made even clearer by the examples given in the next paragraphs. The use of state machines for the specification of the RIA patterns – a widely used modeling technique – makes the approach easily embeddable. In this paper and for demonstration purposes only, we use UWE as the hosting language, which is extended by RIA patterns.

UML-based Web Engineering. UWE [4] is a method for systematic and model-driven development of web applications. UWE follows the principle of "separation of concerns" by modeling the content, the navigation structure, the business processes, and the abstract and concrete presentation of a web application separately. The model-driven approach implemented by UWE is based on model transformations [1] that generate platform specific models from platform independent models and running programs based on these models [5]. UWE's outstanding feature is its reliance on standards: the modeling language is defined as a UML profile using the extension mechanisms provided by the UML. Model transformations are defined in ATL [5] and generate in the last step of the development process a JSF-based web application.

RIA Patterns in the Design with UWE. The objective of an extension covering a new concern is to augment the expressive power of the modeling language. The inherit risk is that successive extensions may end up with a powerful but not anymore intuitive language. Therefore, one of the main goals of UWE is minimalism and conciseness: web engineers should have to provide as much information as necessary for the generation of code, and as little as possible in order to keep diagrams readable.

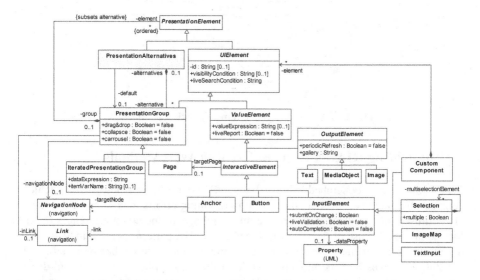

Fig. 5. Extended metamodel of the UWE Presentation Layer

In this sense, our RIA patterns are ideal constructs that provide a specification of the RIA behavior. The specification is given by a UML state diagram as shown in Sect. 3 for auto-completion and periodic refresh. The web engineer does not need to model this behavior each time to define such a RIA feature. It only remains to specify for which UWE elements the auto-completion, the live validation, the period-refresh, etc. apply. This annotation is performed by tags added to existing model elements. A tag at model level implies the definition of a meta-attribute at metamodel level. Fig. 5 shows the metamodel for the presentation package of UWE, providing an overview of all meta-attributes defined so far in the UWE extension for RIAs. It shows how we embed RIA patterns in UWE.

The extension comprises: (1) the *liveSearchCondition* meta-attribute for *uiElement*, i.e. for all model elements that inherit form *uiElement*, (2) the meta-attributes *drag&drop, collapse* and *carrousel* for all *presentationGroups*, (3) *live-Report* for *value-Elements*, (4) meta-attributes *liveValidation* and *autoCompletion* for *inputElements*, (5) meta-attributes *periodicRefresh* and *gallery* for *outputElements*. In addition a new composition association was added to meta-class *Selection* providing the facility of an object to be on the one side multiple selectable and on the other side comprise a set of objects which are single selectable. Fig. 6 shows *auto-completion* of the image search and *periodic refresh* of the analysis status page.

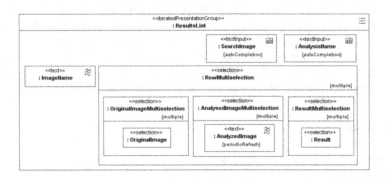

Fig. 6. S.CORE presentation model of analysis status page (excerpt)

5   Related Work

The need of an engineering support for RIA development has been recently addressed by several methods. New model-driven methods for designing RIAs are proposed by e.g. [2]. This method employs interaction spaces, tasks models and state machines. Disadvantage is that in case of reengineering web applications requires modeling from scratch. Several existing method have been extended for modeling RIAs. Toffetti et al. [13] focus on client or server side actions in data-intensive and collaborative RIAs describing events explicitly in WebML. In [14] issues related to behavior, single-page paradigm and content composition are treated extending OOHDM. UWE-R [6] is a light-weighted extension of UWE for RIAs, covering navigation, process and presentation aspects. In contrast to our work, UWE-R uses stereotypes for many of the extensions instead of meta-attributes. OOH4RIA [8] extends the OOH method introducing new model elements and applying to them new transformations. These extensions do not focus on reuse and integration of RIA features in applications automatically.

Another type of approach combines modeling of a web application with an exiting method, such as in [10] where UWE is complemented with the RUX method for the UI design. The approach consists of the transformation of UWE presentation model to a RUX abstract interface model (AIM), which is afterwards enriched with typical RIA user interface actions. In this approach RIA features are introduced into models at a lower level of abstraction than in the current approach. Moreover, RIA requirements and code library based on best practices are also available, like [12].

6 Conclusions and Future Work

We have presented patterns in the form of UML state machines for modeling RIAs. Our approach is general as it can be used on top of virtually every UML conform language. Future work based on our patterns includes an extension of the modeling tool for UWE, MagicUWE (uwe.pst.ifi.lmu.de/toolMagicUWE.html), to support the notation and the integration of the RIA patterns. Furthermore, we plan to extend our work on validating web design models by model checking [3] to cover our patterns, too. The implementation of our real world case study S.CORE was performed by manual translation of the RIA patterns to code. We also plan to implement model-driven code generation out of our patterns using the JSF framework [5].

References

[1] ATLAS Transformation Language & Tool,
     http://www.eclipse.org/m2m/atl/doc/
[2] Dolog, P., Stage, J.: Designing Interaction Spaces for Rich Internet Applications with UML. In: Baresi, L., Fraternali, P., Houben, G.-J. (eds.) ICWE 2007. LNCS, vol. 4607, pp. 358–363. Springer, Heidelberg (2007)
[3] Knapp, A., Zhang, G.: Model Transformations for Integrating and Validating Web Application Models. In: Proc. MOD 2006, LNI P-82, pp. 115–128, GI (2006)
[4] Koch, N., Knapp, A., Zhang, G., Baumeister, H.: UML-based Web Engineering: An Approach based on Standards. In: Web Engineering: Modelling and Implementing Web Applications, HCI (12), ch. 7, vol. 12, pp. 157–191. Springer, Heidelberg (2008)
[5] Kroiss, C.: Model-based Generation of Web Applications with UWE Diploma thesis (in German). LMU (2008)
[6] Machado, L., Filho, O., Ribeiro, J.: UWER: uma extensão de metodologia em Engenharia Web para Rich Internet Applications. II Simpósio de Informática da PUCRS, RS. Hifen Magazine 32(62), 205–212 (2008)
[7] Mahemoff, M.: Ajax Design Patterns. O'Reilly, Sebastopol (2006)
[8] Meliá, S., Gómez, J., Pérez, S., Díaz, O.: A Model-Driven Development for GWT-based RichInternet Applications with OOH4RIA. In: Proc. of ICWE 2008, pp. 13–23. IEEE, New York (2008)
[9] Morozova, T.: Modeling and Generating Web 2.0 Applications. Diploma thesis (in German). LMU (2008)

[10] Preciado, J.C., Linaje, M., Morales, R., Sánchez-Figueroa, F., Zhang, G., Kroiss, C., Koch, N.: Designing Rich Internet Applications Combining UWE and RUX-Method. In: Proc. of ICWE 2008, pp. 148–154. IEEE, New York (2008)

[11] S.CO LifeScience, http://www.sco-lifescience.de/ (Last visited 17.04.2009)

[12] Scott, B.: RIA Patterns. Best Practices for Common Patterns of Rich Interaction, http://www.uxmatters.com/mt/archives/2007/03/ (Last visited 10-02-2009)

[13] Toffetti, G., Comai, S., Bozzon, A., Fraternali, P.: Modeling Distributed Events in Data-Intensive Rich Internet Applications. In: Proc. of ICWE 2007. LNCS, vol. 4607, pp. 593–602. Springer, Heidelberg (2007)

[14] Urbieta, M., Rossi, G., Ginzburg, J., Schwabe, D.: Designing the Interface of Rich Internet Applications. In: Proc. of LA-Web 2007, pp. 144–153. IEEE, Los Alamitos (2007)

Adapting the Presentation Layer in Rich Internet Applications

Irene Garrigós[1], Santiago Meliá[1], and Sven Casteleyn[2]

[1] Universidad de Alicante, Campus de San Vicente del Raspeig,
Apartado 99 03080 Alicante, Spain
{igarrigos,santi}@dlsi.ua.es
[2] Vrije Universiteit Brussel, Department of Computer Science, Pleinlaan 2,
1050 Brussel, Belgium
Sven.Casteleyn@vub.ac.be

Abstract. Rich Internet Applications offer Web surfers a richer user experience, mainly due to better responsiveness and enhanced user interface capabilities. In recent years, existing design methodologies targeting traditional Web 1.0 applications were extended to also support RIAs. These extensions do not yet cover all design concerns typically encountered in state-of-the-art Web applications. One yet unsupported aspect is the personalization of content and presentation to the specific user and his/her context, exploiting the extra capabilities offered by RIAs. This article addresses this hiatus and presents an extension of the OOH4RIA approach to include presentation personalization support, focusing on Rich Internet Applications.

1 Introduction

Rich Internet Applications are an answer to the growing demand for Web applications offering better responsiveness and an extended UI experience. They keep the middle between the traditionally sober (HTML-based) Web applications and the interface, interaction and functionality capabilities of traditional desktop applications.

When designing and implementing Rich Internet Applications, several new requirements and concerns come into play [1, 13], complicating the task of a Web engineer. The Web engineering community is well-aware of these difficult challenges, extending the design methodologies that target traditional Web 1.0 applications to also support RIAs [2, 5, 9, 12]. However, due to their relative recentness, these extensions do not yet cover all design concerns usually encountered in state-of-the-art Web applications. One yet unsupported aspect is the personalization of content and presentation to the specific user and his/her context, specifically for RIAs. UIs of RIAs are typically dependent on the context device rendering them and vulnerable to the limitations they impose: limited screen size, more difficult interaction and poorer multimedia support. In this paper, we aim to overcome some of these problems by personalizing the UI depending on the specificities of the device (i.e. the device context). This device context personalization must consider two important aspects: (1) an interface re-organization to fit the UI layout to the device dimensions, and (2) the

M. Gaedke, M. Grossniklaus, and O. Díaz (Eds.): ICWE 2009, LNCS 5648, pp. 292–299, 2009.
© Springer-Verlag Berlin Heidelberg 2009

transformation of some origin widgets into specific widgets that work more efficiently in the target device.

With this goal in mind, we present an extension to an existing RIA design method called OOH4RIA [5, 8], to support personalization of the RIA user interface for different devices. OOH4RIA defines a model-driven development process based on a set of models and transformations allowing to easily introduce new concerns to the RIA development process. We thus adapt the OOH4RIA process by (1) introducing new personalization models (such a User Model and personalization rules), (2) defining transformations that reduce the effort to redefine new presentation models for each device . These extensions process allows us to obtain different device-aware versions of the same RIA project.

The remainder of this paper is organized as follows. Section 2 discusses how personalization gets differed in RIA from traditional Web applications and outlines related approaches. Section 3 presents the extensions done in OOH4RIA to integrate personalization. Section 4 presents the main contribution of the paper: the personalization of the RIA user interface to different contexts. Finally, Section 5 provides conclusions and future research lines.

2   Personalization: From Traditional Web Applications to RIAs

Personalization has been intensively studied in traditional Web application methods. Typically, content, navigation and presentation are personalized to tailor to the specific user based on his/her preferences, characteristics, context and browsing behavior. Traditional Web applications limit the possibilities to track the user browsing to the requests performed to the server. RIAs provide new client-side capacities, new presentation features and different communication flows between the server and client side. These differences with respect to traditional Web applications must be taken into account in RIAs design, as well as in the specification of personalization strategies.

RIA applications provide richer and more interactive user interfaces, similar to desktop applications. They offer multimedia native support (i.e. no plug-ins are needed to show video and audio) and support animations. As a consequence, from a personalization point of view, the layout and look-and-feel of the application can be personalized but also the system's reaction to user interaction has to be specified accordingly. Recently, existing Web design methodologies were extended to also support RIAs. The most relevant ones are (1) OOHDM [12] which provides the use of ADVcharts to model widget interaction. (2) WebML which extends its conceptual modeling primitives for RIA's [2] and provides support for distributed event-driven RIA's and specific interaction patterns typically occurring in RIAs. (3) RUX [9], a method independent presentation framework for RIAs tackling presentational specificities of RIAs. RUX has been applied to WebML and UWE, lending its presentational capabilities to these approaches and (4) OOH4RIA which we will extend and use as a RIA method in this article.

To the best knowledge of the authors, there is only one approach [11] that provides personalization support specifically targeting Rich Internet Applications. This approach is not in the context of Web engineering and performs on-the-fly adaptation over AJAX pages. The authors combine ontologies to annotate RIAs and adaptation rules which are derived from semantic Web usage mining techniques. This approach however, does not contemplate the personalization of the presentation features, which is exactly the focus of this paper. We thus present a personalization approach founded in a Web application method, and specifically focus on the RIA-specific elements of the presentation layer.

In the next section, we explain how to integrate personalization in the OOH4RIA development process.

3   Integrating Personalization in the OOH4RIA Development Process

OOH4RIA [5] is a model-driven approach whose main target is to cover all the phases of the Rich Internet Application (RIA) lifecycle development for a GWT-based application [4]. This paper presents an extension of the OOH4RIA development process, focusing on the models and artifacts that allow us to introduce the personalization concern into OOH4RIA. The personalization extended OOH4RIA process starts specifying the *OOH Domain Model* in order to represent the domain entities and the relationships between them. This model is the starting point of the main subprocesses: (1) the definition of the RIA server side where a model-to-text transformation generates the business logic and persistence from the domain and navigational entities, (2) the RIA user interface, defining *the OOH Navigation Model* which represents the navigation through the domain concepts and establishes the visualization constraints. Starting from the Navigation Model, the different screenshots, which represent spatial distributions of the widgets rendered in a given moment, of the Presentation Model are defined. A detailed overview of OOH4RIA can be found in [5].

The personalization extension introduced by this work begins defining *the OOH User Model* where the Domain, Navigation and Presentation models are taken as input. The User Model represents the dynamic data structures where the information about the user is stored. This information is used to personalize the website containing information about the user preferences and widget mappings of different contexts. The actual personalization is defined over the Presentation Model for different devices. To do that: we have used the marking technique defined by the MDA guide [6] to introduce information about the spatial arrangement of the layout widgets, which are to be reorganized in the target Presentation Model. This marked Presentation Model, together with the User Model, are the inputs to obtain one or more presentation models according to the devices defined by the User Model. For this aim, a set of transformation rules was defined.

On the other hand, the User Model together with the Navigation, Presentation and Orchestration models are the input that permits to define Personalization Rules, specifying runtime personalization strategies based on user preferences, goals and context. To define these rules we use the PRML language [3], which was defined in the context of OOH to extend it with personalization support. However, due to space constraints, we do not elaborate these rules in this paper; instead, we focus solely on presentation personalization targeting different devices.

The last step consists of defining the model-to-text transformations that will grant us the personalized RIA implementation. The *GWT Server Side* transformation generates the server code from the OOH Domain and the Navigation models, while the *GWT client side* transformation generates the client side code using a specific GWT framework. These model-to-text transformations are written in the MOFScript language which follows the OMG ModelToText RFP for the representation of model-to-text transformations.

4 Device Context Adaptation of the Presentation Model

In this work, we are focused on the device context personalization of the Presentation layer of a RIA, and for this purpose, we must reorganize the layout widgets in the user interface depending on the screen size, and some widgets may need to be transformed into others that better fit the new device screen dimensions.

In OOH4RIA, the layout of the RIA is represented by the Presentation Model, so the adaptation of its elements should be done in order to cope with these issues. As explained, the OOH4RIA Presentation Model is based on the GWT framework, which is composed of widgets and panels (i.e. layout widgets) where the widgets are placed. For personalization purposes, the designer has to specify how these panels and widgets are transformed and/or reorganized for the target application (i.e. specific device). For instance, one screenshot element specified in the original Presentation Model may be split into different screenshots in a mobile screen device. As already explained, we reduce the effort to redefine new presentation models for each device, including these transformations in the OOH4RIA development process.

The OOH4RIA device context adaptation is made up of following steps:

- *Marking the Presentation Model* in order to determine the spatial arrangement of the panels in the target Presentation Model
- *Define the User Model* with the purpose of specifying the target device(s) and to provide specific information on how to transform certain widget types in order to influence the set of transformation rules to be performed.

a) Marking the Presentation Model
The first step the designer has to do is to mark the Presentation Model in order to mark how the elements will be reorganized. Depending on these markings a set of transformation rules will be executed for modifying the spatial arrangement of the elements. Other rules have to be explicitly selected by the designer or are selected depending on the data stored in the User Model (this will be further developed in the ongoing section).

To allow the designer marking the elements, the metamodel of the Presentation Model is extended: each of the panels has a new attribute called *Location* which indicates whether the panel will be placed in a new screenshot or it will be shown in an existing one. The location attribute can have different values:

- **inherits:** this is the default value for all the panels. The panels are nested, all the nested panels will be placed in the same screenshot that their upper panel unless the designer specifies a different value.

- **new:** in this case the designer specifies that the panel will be placed in a separate screenshot.
- **none:** this value would be assigned when the designer wants to exclude the panel, so it will not be visible (and all what is in it) from the target application.
- **all:** the designer would assign this value when he wants to include this panel in all the screens of the target application.
- **containerID:** the designer may also want to show the panel within of another concrete panel of the website.

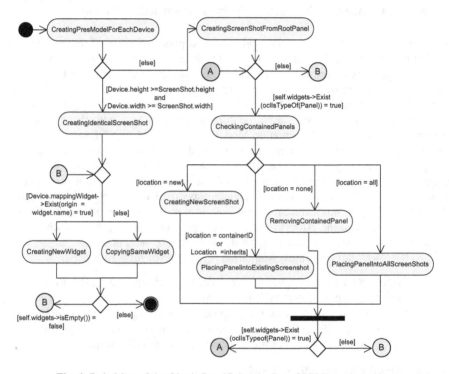

Fig. 1. Rule Map of the ObtainSpecificDevicePres QVT Transformation

Depending on the markings done in the Presentation Model different transformation rules are to be performed. They allow to convert a generic Presentation Model into a specific device Presentation Model. Fig. 1 presents an activity diagram that establishes the execution workflow of the transformation rules defined for this purpose. The execution starts with the root rule called *CreatingPresModelForEachDevice* which creates the Presentation Model element for each Device defined in the User Model. When the dimensions (height and width) of the device are larger than the definition, the transformation invokes the *CreatingIdenticalScreenShot* rule which creates Screenshots identical to the destination model. On the contrary, if the device dimensions are smaller, then the *CreatingScreenShotFromRoolPanel* rule establishes a Screenshot from the container panel with the dimensions adjusted to the device.

Here begins the reorganization of the containers or panels where the transformation checks whether the root panel contains in turn inside panels. If this is the case, the CheckingContainedPanels rule is executed and it decides the destination of the panel according to the value of the location attribute. (1) If location is equals to *new* then the panels requires a new Screenshot, thus executing the CreatingNewScreenshot rule. (2) If the location is equal to the *ID* of a pre-existing panel or is equal to inherits then a new Screenshot will be created within it. (3) However, if we want to eliminate the panel (location equal to *none*), we execute RemovingContainedPanel rule. (4) Finally, if we want the panel to appear in all the Screenshots (location equal to *All*), the PlacingPanelScreenshot rule is executed.

b) Specifying the User Model

In the User Model, information regarding the user characteristics, interest, preferences or context is stored. In this case we store information regarding the device context of the user.

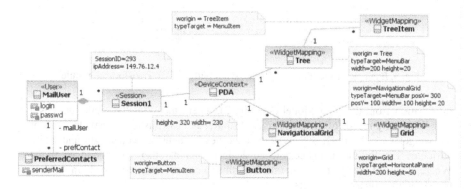

Fig. 2. The User Model of GWT Mail application

In Fig. 2 we can see the User Model needed for defining a sample mobile-aware RIA. In order to deal with the personalization at widget level, the personalization designer must introduce the *WidgetMapping* concept into the User Model which proposes the widget conversion to another widget, giving it similar functionality in the target device. Thus, by defining the User Model, the designer provides information that influences which set of rules is to be executed.

Let's recover the *Pres2DevicePres* transformation at point B where the transformation of simple widgets starts. Here, the transformation checks if there is a WidgetMapping into the User Model for the current Widget, if this is the case, the *CreatingNewWidget* (Fig. 3) rule is executed converting a Widget into another one. However, when there is not a WidgetMapping defined, the original Widget is copied into the target Presentation Model.

Figure 3 presents the *CreatingNewWidget* rule which converts a Widget into another one gathering the information from the WidgetMapping defined by the User Model. Firstly, this rule checks that the source Widget is not a panel in the *When* sentence. From here, the rule creates a new widget that maintains the same name, position and isDisable properties. However, the rule introduces the personalization

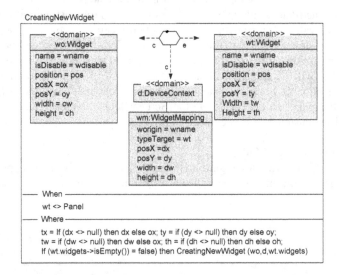

Fig. 3. Example of Pres2Device: CreatingNewWidget QVT Transformation Rule

information from the User Model (see Fig. 2), where the WidgetMapping defines a new Widget by means of the typeTarget attribute, and establishes the new location of the widget with the posX and posy, and the new dimension with height and width attributes. Finally, the rule checks if the Widget contains other nested Widgets in the Where clause of the QVT rule, in this case, this rule is invoked recursively in order to transform the contained widgets.

5 Conclusions and Future Work

In this paper, we presented, in the context of the existing Web design method supporting Rich Internet Applications OOH4RIA, a personalization approach specifically targeting the enhanced presentational capabilities of RIA's. We elaborated on the models and artifacts needed to support personalization in the overall RIA design process. Our approach consists of two steps. During the first step, the personalization designer marks in the Presentation Model which elements will be subject for transformation and what will be their target designation. The second step consists of rule selection. This is done partly automatically, for general rules, based on the information specified in the User Model.and partly manually, for specific rules that will personalize the interface at runtime for each specific user which is out of the scope of the present paper.

Currently, we are developing the OOH4RIA tool which is based on the Eclipse Graphical Modelling framework (GMF). This tool is being completed with the specified personalization transformations presented in this work. Furthermore, we are working on defining the transformation rules that should be performed over the Orchestration Model to complement the work described here.

Acknowledgements

We would like to thank our colleague Sandy Pérez for his pointers on implementation issues and his comments on the work presented.

This work has been co-supported by the ESPIA project (TIN2007-67078) from the Spanish Ministry of Education and Science and the DEMETER (GVPRE/2008/063) project from the Valencia Ministry of Enterprise, University and Science (Spain).

References

1. Bozzon, A., Comai, S., Fraternali, P., Carughi, G.T.: Conceptual Modeling and Code Generation for Rich Internet Applications. In: 6th International Conference on Web Engineering (2006)
2. Comai, S., Carughi, G.T.: A Behavioral Model for Rich Internet Applications. In: Baresi, L., Fraternali, P., Houben, G.-J. (eds.) ICWE 2007. LNCS, vol. 4607, pp. 364–369. Springer, Heidelberg (2007)
3. Garrigós, I. A-OOH.: Extending Web Application Design with Dynamic Personalization, Phd thesis, University of Alicante (2008)
4. Google. Google Web Toolkit (GWT), http://code.google.com/webtoolkit
5. Meliá, S., Gómez, J., Pérez, S., Diaz, O.: A Model-Driven Development for GWT-Based Rich Internet Applications with OOH4RIA. In: Eighth International Conference of Web Engineering, Yorktown Heights, USA (2008)
6. Object Management Group (OMG). MDA Guide (version 1.0.1) (June 2003), http://www.omg.org/docs/omg/03-06-01.pdf
7. Object Management Group (OMG). Software Process Engineering Metamodel (version 1.1) (January 2005), http://www.omg.org/docs/formal/05-01-06.pdf
8. Pérez, S., Díaz, O., Meliá, S., Gómez, J.: Facing Interaction-Rich RIAs. In: The Orchestration Model Eighth International Conference of Web Engineering, Yorktown Heights, USA (2008)
9. Preciado, J.C., Linaje, M., Comai, S., Sánchez- Figueroa, F.: Designing Rich Internet Applications with Web Engineering Methodologies. In: 6th International Conference on Web Engineering (2006)
10. Rossi, G., Urbieta, M., Ginzburg, J., Distante, D., Garrido, A.: Refactoring to Rich Internet Applications. A Model Driven Approach. In: Proceedings of the Eighth International Conference of Web Engineering, ICWE (2008)
11. Schmidt, K., Stojanovic, L., Stojanovic, N., Thomas, S.: On Enriching Ajax with Semantics: The Web Personalization Use Case. In: Franconi, E., Kifer, M., May, W. (eds.) ESWC 2007. LNCS, vol. 4519, pp. 686–700. Springer, Heidelberg (2007)
12. Urbieta, M., Rossi, G., Ginzburg, J., Schwabe, D.: Designing the Interface of Rich Internet Applications. In: 5th Latin American Web Congress (2007)
13. Wright, J.M., Dietrich, J.B.: Requirements for Rich Internet Application Design Methodologies. In: Bailey, J., Maier, D., Schewe, K.-D., Thalheim, B., Wang, X.S. (eds.) WISE 2008. LNCS, vol. 5175, pp. 106–119. Springer, Heidelberg (2008)

Web Site Metadata

Erik Wilde and Anuradha Roy

School of Information
UC Berkeley

Abstract. Understanding the availability of site metadata on the Web is a foundation for any system or application that wants to work with the pages published by Web sites, and also wants to understand a Web site's structure. There is little information available about how much information Web sites make available about themselves, and this paper presents data addressing this question. Based on this analysis of available Web site metadata, it is easier for Web-oriented applications to be based on statistical analysis rather than assumptions when relying on Web site metadata. Our study of `robots.txt` files and sitemaps can be used as a starting point for Web-oriented applications wishing to work with Web site metadata.

1   Introduction

This paper presents first results from a project which ultimately aims at providing accessible Web site navigation for Web sites [1]. One of the important intermediary steps is to understand how much metadata about Web sites is made available on the Web today, and how much navigational information can be extracted from that metadata. Our long-term goal is to establish a standard way for Web sites to expose their navigational structure, but since this is a long-term goal with a long adoption process, our mid-term goal is establish a third-party service that provides navigational metadata about a site as a service to users interested in that information. A typical scenario would be blind users; they typically have difficulties to navigate Web sites, because most usability and accessibility methods focus on *Web pages* rather than *Web sites*. Following the extended principle of Web engineering as *blending into the Web* rather *building Web front-ends* [2], our approach is to first understand the current state of Web site metadata on the Web, before designing our service and data format. This paper describes our analysis of the current state of Web site metadata available on the Web.

Most information resources on the Web are *Web sites*, informally defined as a set of *Web pages* made available by some information provider. While the concept of a Web site is only loosely defined, it is often associated with all Web pages available under one DNS domain name (this could be generalized to all Web pages using the same URI prefix, but for the purpose of this paper, we look at domain-based sites only). For information gathering, Web sites are usually accessed by *Web crawlers* [3] which systematically retrieve Web pages, in

M. Gaedke, M. Grossniklaus, and O. Díaz (Eds.): ICWE 2009, LNCS 5648, pp. 300–314, 2009.
© Springer-Verlag Berlin Heidelberg 2009

most cases to drive later stages of indexing them for eventually driving a search engine. To allow Web sites some level of control over crawlers, the informal robots.txt format [4] — sometimes also referred to as the *Robots Exclusion Protocol (REP)* — is the established way of how a Web site can control crawlers. This format can only be used on a per-domain basis, and specifies rules for all pages under that domain.

The robots.txt format is a simple way of how a site can publish metadata about itself; in that case with the sole purpose of controlling crawler access to the site (most often by limiting access to certain parts of a site). This assumes that crawlers get information about available URIs from other sources; in most cases this happens by following links on already crawled pages. On the other hand, sites often want to be crawled so that their contents are available through search engines, and the *sitemaps* format allows sites to publish lists of URIs which they want to advertise to crawlers. Sitemaps can be made available to crawlers in different ways; they can be directly advertised through user interfaces or an HTTP ping interface to individual crawlers, or they can be specified in the robots.txt file. While the name "sitemap" implies a certain structure to the URIs contained in that information, this information, in fact, is not a map. Despite its name, the sitemaps format only supports the publication of unstructured lists of URIs.

Sitemap information can be useful for exposing the *Deep Web* [5,6], for example, those pages that are accessible only through HTML forms. Because search engine crawlers typically discover pages by following links, large portions of the Web can be hidden from crawlers, and thus might never be indexed, and therefore never show up in search results. Hence, without sitemap information, search engine crawlers might not be able to find these pages. Since sitemap information may be incomplete and/or inaccurate, search engines have to rely on other techniques to completely crawl the deep Web.

The current Web site metadata already allows crawlers to get information about a site's structure, they can do so by using a Web site's URIs as they are listed in the robots.txt and sitemaps files, and if they are associated with a search engine, they can also use click data to learn about a site's popular pages. In that case, site metadata combined with the click data can be used for approximating a site's navigation structure. Figure 1 shows an example for such an algorithmically computed site map.

Site metadata on the one hand greatly improves the interaction of humans with a site, because many tasks on a site require accessing more than one page on the site. On the other hand, even though explicit navigation often is provided through Web page design, IR techniques can be used to algorithmically infer site metadata for tasks other than direct user interaction with a Web site. Google's search results, for example, occasionally include a small "site map" (called "sitelinks") for highly ranked search results (Figure 1 shows an example). This demonstrates the fact that site metadata can have useful applications beyond crawling, and since most Web sites use content management systems to publish their site anyway, exposing site metadata in a richer format than just sitemaps in many cases could be easily implemented by Web sites.

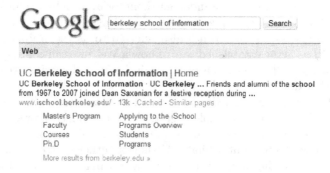

Fig. 1. Algorithmically Computed Site Map

This paper first presents a brief overview of how Web site metadata is managed from a Web engineering perspective (Section 2). We then describe the crawling process for `robots.txt` files and the results from that process (Sections 3 and 4). We continue by describing the crawling process for sitemaps files and the results from that process (Sections 5 and 6). We conclude the paper by describing related and future work (Sections 7 and 8).

2   Web Site Metadata on the Web

The *Robots Exclusion Protocol (REP)* or `robots.txt` format was never published as a formal document, the only "official" reference is an Internet draft [4] and various Web sites. The `robots.txt` has a well-defined discovery method: if a Web site is publishing such a file, it must be available at the URI path `/robots.txt` on that site. The file format itself is very simple; it started out as a way to "protect" certain parts of a Web site (defined by URI prefix) to be excluded from crawler access. And because it is possible that access should only be limited for certain crawlers, these exclusion rules can be made specific for certain user agents (which in case of `robots.txt` are not really user agents, but search engine crawlers).

The informal specification of the `robots.txt` file format only defines the three fields `User-Agent`, `Disallow`, and `Allow`. However, the specification does allow other fields as well, as long as they are based on the same basic syntax. Some other fields that are used are `Noindex`, `Crawl-Delay`, `Request-Rate`, and `Visit-Time` fields, which are defined by specific crawlers, and apparently Web site administrators seem to believe these fields are (at least potentially) interpreted by crawlers. Section 4 contains a more complete list of the fields in our sample of `robots.txt` files, as well as other statistics about that data set.

One additional field that can occur in a `robots.txt` file is `Sitemap`, which points to the URI of a sitemaps file as defined in the sitemaps protocol. While discovery through `robots.txt` is one possible way for a site to publish a sitemap, the protocol also defines the ability to submit a sitemap file to a search engine through a submission interface, or by HTTP ping. In these latter cases, the sitemap file is only known to the search engine it has been submitted to, as there is no well-defined discovery method for it.

Sitemaps can use XML (using a simple schema), plain text, or feed formats (RSS 2.0 and Atom [7]) as their syntax, and it is allowed to compress them on the server side using *gzip* (HTTP transfer encoding works regardless of that, but sitemaps can be served as compressed documents). There are size limitations limiting a sitemap file to no more than 50'000 URIs and no more than 10MB in size. Furthermore, there are size limitations limiting an index file to no more than 1'000 URIs and no more than 10MB in size. For compressed files, these size limits apply to the uncompressed files.

Despite of their name, sitemaps are not really maps, because they do not contain any structure. Sitemaps are simply lists of links a site wants to be crawled, and in addition to the URI, the XML format supports parameters to set last modification data, change frequency, and priority for each URI. It is up to a crawler to decide how to use sitemap information, but it is likely that most search engine crawlers will take their data into consideration when computing their crawling process.

3   Crawling for Robots.txt

Our starting point is Alexa's dataset of the most popular 100'000 domains. This dataset has some bias, based on the way this dataset is collected. Even though the exact method of how the dataset is collected is not published, we chose to accept the bias, because our research does not depend on the exact ranking of popular domains, but instead just depends on a reasonably large set of popular domains. Based on this dataset, our crawling process requests `robots.txt` files from all domains.

Using a simple two-step process (trying `http://domain.com/robots.txt` and `http://www.domain.com/robots.txt` for all domain names), our crawl of 100'000 domains for `robots.txt` files yields 44'832 files (i.e., 44.8% of the domains make `robots.txt` files available); more detailed statistics about these files can be found in Section 4. Various error conditions can be encountered when requesting the files. We do not fully implement error recovery (such as trying to fix corrupted `robots.txt` files and retrying failed connection attempts), because error conditions are only encountered in a small fraction of cases. This means that our crawl yields slightly fewer `robots.txt` files than it could with a more robust crawling mechanism, but that is an acceptable compromise allowing a less complex crawler implementation.

4   Robots.txt Data Analysis

The `robots.txt` files crawled as described in Section 3 are mainly intended as a starting point to find sitemap information, as described in Section 5. However, because the available literature does not present a lot of data about large-scale

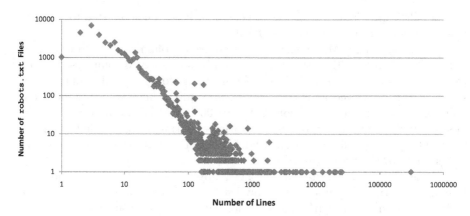

Fig. 2. Distribution of robots.txt Size

collections of robots.txt files, we first present some statistics about the dataset obtained in the first step of our study.

Figure 2 shows the distribution of the size of robots.txt files (in lines) over the number of robots.txt files. It is a heavy-tail distribution with the average size being 29.8 lines ($\sigma = 293.4$) with a median of 7 lines. Since there is a fair number of rather large robots.txt files in our dataset, we want to understand the reasons for these sizes. robots.txt files can become large for two reasons: because they contain individual configurations for a large number of user agents, or because they contain a lot of instructions for one user agent (or a combination of these two reasons). We therefore looked at how many individual configuration sections for specific user agents the robots.txt files contain.

Figure 3 shows the result of this analysis. Again, it is a heavy-tail distribution with an average of 6 sections ($\sigma = 29.5$) and a median of 2. However, in this case there is a noticeable peak in the long tail, with the center at robots.txt files having 120 user agent configuration sections.

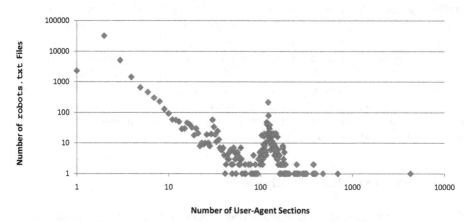

Fig. 3. User-Agent Sections per robots.txt File

Table 1. Popular Fields in `robots.txt` Files

Field Name	#Files	#Fields	Fields/File
1. User-Agent	42'578	225'428	5.29
2. Disallow	39'928	947'892	23.74
3. Sitemap	6'765	10'979	1.62
4. Allow	3'832	23'177	6.05
5. Crawl-Delay	2'987	4'537	1.52
6. Noindex	905	2'151	2.38
7. Host	728	758	1.04
8. Request-Rate	121	127	1.05
9. Visit-Time	89	102	1.15
10. ACAP-Crawler	71	234	3.30

Our assumption is that this peak has its origin in some widely used and reused template that originally had 120 configuration sections, and then was adapted for various sites by adding or removing some of these sections. There is a variety of templates and generators for `robots.txt` files available on the Web, so assuming that one of these gained popularity is a reasonable explanation of the peak around 120 configuration sections.

To better understand how current `robots.txt` files are using fields to steer crawlers, we looked at the overall usage of fields. As stated in Section 2, only the three fields `User-Agent`, `Disallow`, and `Allow` are defined by the `robots.txt` file format, but some other fields also have gained some acceptance. Table 1 contains a list of the ten most popular fields we found (sorted by the number of files containing this field, based on the dataset of 44'832 files), also listing how many occurrences were found in total, and the average number of occurrences per file based on the number of files in which this field was used.

The three standard `robots.txt` fields are among the most frequently used ones, and the popularity of fields drops significantly after the top five. The `Sitemap` field points to a sitemap and is what we use for the second step of our crawling process (described in Section 5). Most of the other fields we found are fields only supported by particular crawlers, so if they do appear in an appropriate `User-Agent` section, they can control that particular crawler. One exception to these crawler-specific fields are `ACAP`-prefixed fields, which are part of the *Automated Content Access Protocol (ACAP)*. ACAP is an initiative of content providers to extend the `robots.txt` format so that it is possible to express more specific policies about the crawled content, mostly about access and usage permissions for copyright-protected content.

The idea of `robots.txt` most often is to restrict crawlers from certain pages and paths on a site. This can make sense because of pages that are frequently updated, because of pages that contain content that should not be indexed (e.g., because of copyright issues), or because of crawlers that interact with the server in unfortunate ways when retrieving pages. This means that while some configurations in `robots.txt` files are global (i.e., apply to all crawlers), there are also some which are for specific crawlers only. We looked at the `User-Agent` fields in our dataset

Table 2. Popular User-Agents in `robots.txt` Files

User Agent	Occurrences	
1. *	46'645	20.70%
2. Mediapartners-Google	3'825	1.70%
3. wget	3'787	1.68%
4. WebZIP	3'014	1.34%
5. Mozilla	2'696	1.20%
6. GoogleBot	2'694	1.20%
7. Microsoft URL Control	2'647	1.17%
8. WebBandit	2'271	1.01%
9. lwp-trivial	2'227	0.99%
10. MIIxpc	2'180	0.97%

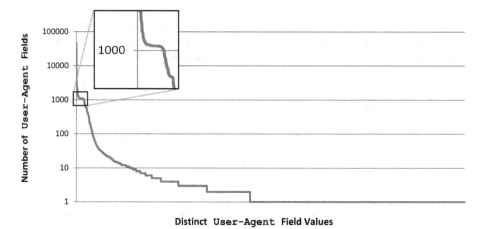

Fig. 4. Distribution of User-Agent Field Values

and counted the various strings listed there, trying to adjust for minor variations such as capitalization, whitespace, or version numbers.

Table 2 lists the top ten User-Agent field values we found in our dataset (the total number of all fields was 225'304, the distribution of those fields across `robots.txt` files is shown in Figure 4). * is the catch-all value which is used to define rules applying to all crawlers; it is by far the most popular value. Mediapartners-Google is the crawler for sites participating in Google's *AdSense* program, and is the most frequently listed named crawler. wget and WebZIP are two similar "crawlers" which usually do not really crawl the Web, but instead are used to download the contents of a site; they are often used to download site contents for offline browsing or post-processing.

Many crawlers do not reveal their identity and use fake User-Agent field values to cloak themselves as browsers. The Mozilla User-Agent value is the most frequently used one and thus is listed in many `robots.txt` files; but if a crawler is misbehaving in the sense that it does not properly reveal its identity, it is unlikely that it will be sufficiently well-behaving to respect `robots.txt` configurations. GoogleBot is Google's search engine crawler (it is using a different identity than the AdSense crawler mentioned earlier). Microsoft URL Control is a default identity used within various Microsoft Web tools, and developers can either change that when they develop software using these tools, or leave it at its default value. WebBandit is a tool similar to wget and WebZIP, in most cases not used as a crawler, but for targeted downloads of Web content. lwp-trivial is the default name used by the Perl module LWP::Simple. MIIxpc is a crawler about which there is no public information available, but apparently it is active enough to be listed in many robots.txt files.

Figure 4 shows the distribution of occurrences of User-Agent fields. The horizontal axis linearly lists all 4'483 distinct User-Agent fields we found (Table 2 lists the top ten) sorted by the number of occurrences. It can be seen that more than half of the User-Agent values only occur once. The tableau in the distribution at about 1'000 occurrences (as magnified in the figure) is something that we believe to be caused by robots.txt files being created using templates or generators, which usually just present a list of predefined User-Agent values, and therefore the values available there will show up in many template-based or generated files.

5 Crawling for Sitemaps

Starting from the robots.txt files obtained as described in Section 3, the next step to get more complete Web site metadata is to crawl for the second Web site metadata format, the sitemaps format. The likelihood of a Web site providing sitemaps is substantially lower than that of it providing a robots.txt file, but on the other hand, the information found in sitemaps typically is more valuable, because it is much more specific in listing a Web site's actual page URIs, whereas robots.txt files typically only specify a small number of URI prefixes.

While we depend on sitemaps being available through robots.txt files, this only provides access to a subset of available sitemap information. Web sites can also directly make sitemaps available to crawlers by uploading them or pinging crawlers to download a sitemap. However, these two methods depend on the Web site explicitly cooperating with the crawler, and therefore is not available to crawlers which have to depend on publicly available information.

Figure 5 shows an overview of the complete crawling process as it starts with the domain dataset and eventually creates a dataset of Web page URIs from those domains. In the starting dataset of 44'832 robots.txt files, 6'268 files (14%) contained Sitemap fields, for a total of 10'029 fields (it is legal for robots.txt files to reference more than one sitemap file; we found one pointing to 530 sitemap files).

Figure 6 shows the distribution of robots.txt files according to how many references to sitemaps they contained (robots.txt files with no references are not shown in this figure). The vast majority of robots.txt files (5'710 or 91%) specify only one sitemap reference, but there also is a considerable number of robots.txt files pointing to more than one sitemap file.

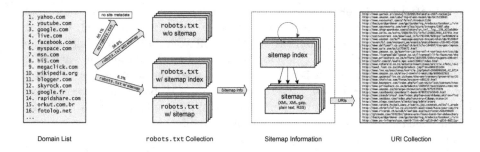

Fig. 5. Overview of the Crawling Process

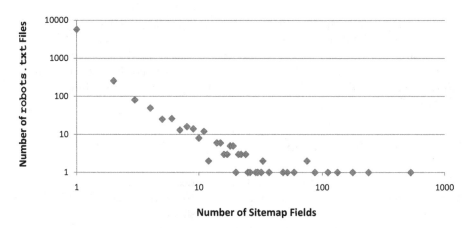

Fig. 6. `Sitemap` Fields per `robots.txt` File

The first task when crawling for sitemaps is to navigate sitemap indices and sitemap files, so that all sitemap information for a given site can be retrieved. The sitemaps specification is silent on whether index files may point to index files, but since it is not specifically disallowed, it is probably allowed, and there are sites that make use of that assumption. As one example of sitemap information crawled from one company, Table 3 shows the number of sitemaps/sitemap indices for various **amazon** domains. It also shows the total number of URIs contained in these sitemaps.

Table 3. Sitemap Information about **amazon** Domains

Domain	#Sitemaps	#URIs
amazon.com	4'945	119'346'271
amazon.ca	2'980	96'476'534
amazon.co.jp	2'933	54'487'651
amazon.co.uk	3'177	44'668'202
amazon.fr	378	15'571'351

Amazon is a good example for the *Deep Web* motivation described in Section 1. Amazon has a large number of products available through its Web site, but most pages are dynamically generated and not statically linked from anywhere. Thus, to make all of these pages available to crawlers, all of these product pages must be listed in sitemaps.

6 Sitemaps Data Analysis

A somewhat surprising discovery is that some big sites do not have any sitemap information. `ebay` and `yahoo` are two examples. Contrast `ebay` to `amazon`, which has by far the largest number of page URIs in its sitemaps. Furthermore, many big sites are only marginally present: Our crawler discovered only 147 URIs for `microsoft`. The reason for this is that Microsoft specifies sitemaps for only a small fraction of its site.

To better understand the usage of sitemap files, it is interesting to look at how many sitemap files an average domain has, and what the distribution is of

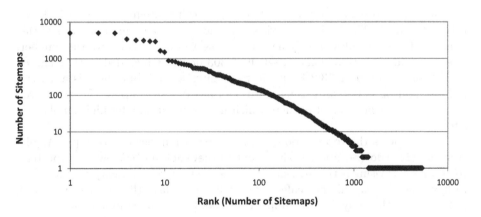

Fig. 7. Distribution of Sitemaps Across Domains

Table 4. Top 10 Domains for #Sitemaps/Domain

Domain	#Sitemaps
1. pricecheck.co.za	5'006
2. ricardo.ch	5'000
3. amazon.com	4'945
4. mailonsunday.co.uk	3'395
5. amazon.co.uk	3'177
6. amazon.de	3'108
7. amazon.ca	2'980
8. amazon.co.jp	2'933
9. alacrastore.com	1'644
10. motofakty.pl	1'505

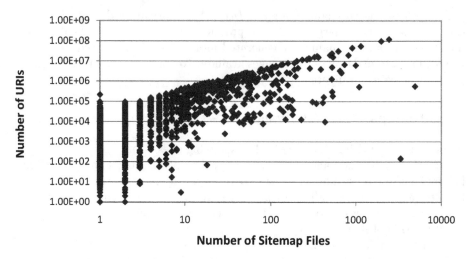

Fig. 8. Number of URIs vs. Sitemap Files

the number of sitemap files for those domains using sitemaps. Figure 7 shows this distribution. The horizontal axis shows the rank of a domain in terms of the number of sitemap files this domain uses. The vertical axis shows the number of sitemap files for that domain. Of the 5'303 domains included in that figure, the majority (3'880 or 73.2%) use just one sitemap file; but there is a heavy-tail distribution of domains using more than just one sitemap file. Furthermore, there is a small number of outliers which use an exceptionally high number of sitemap files.

Table 4 shows the top ten domains in terms of number of sitemaps.[1] While amazon, ricardo (an auction site), and pricecheck are somewhat expected, somewhat surprising is the presence of the news site mailonsunday, which seems to have one sitemap file per calendar day. Each file lists the articles that were published on that day. This example contrasts the variance in sitemap organization: amazon uses a large number of sitemap files because of its sheer size; mailonsunday uses a large number of files in order to better organize its URIs in sitemaps.

To better understand how sitemap files are used on average, it is interesting to analyze the usage of sitemap files for managing large sets of URIs. Figure 8 plots the number of URIs in sitemaps versus the number of sitemap files used for storing these URIs. In theory, there should be no data point above the 50'000 URI mark on the 1 sitemap file line, because of the 50'000 URI per sitemap file limit specified by the sitemaps format.

There is much diversity in how sites beyond 100'000 URIs divide their URIs into sitemap files. For example, pt.anuncioo.com has a sitemap file with more than 200'000 URIs.[2] On the other extreme, ricardo.ch divides its 549'637 URIs

---

[1] The top ten are the easily recognizable outliers visible in Figure 7.

[2] Which is a violation of the sitemaps format that specifies a maximum of 50'000 URIs per file.

into 4'911 files. Really large sites tend to use uniformly large (usually close to the maximum size of 50'000 URIs) sitemap files. Some of the outliers in the bottom right part of the figure are most likely caused by domains where we did have a substantial amount of sitemap files, but downloading the actual files (and then counting the URIs) failed due to timeouts.

7   Related Work

Regarding the analysis of `robots.txt` files, there is early work based on a rather small sample [8] (164 sites), and a specific analysis of corporate Web sites [9], also using a small sample (60 sites), and manual analysis of the results. This early work has been limited by much lower adoption of `robots.txt` files, and by the scale of the studies.

More recently, a study of initially only 8'000 sites [10,11] has been extended in the *BotSeer* project and now covers 13.2 million sites [12]. Their finding (in the initial 8'000 site study) of a 38.5% adoption rate of `robots.txt` files is a little bit smaller than our average of 45.1%, which might be explained by the study's date (October 2006), and also by the fact that the study did not start with the most popular domains, which probably have a higher adoption rate. At the time of writing, the BotSeer Web page reports 2'264'820 `robots.txt` files from 13'257'110 Web sites, which translates to a 17% adoption rate; this considerably lower number may be explained by the fact that the large set of Web sites necessarily contains many rather small sites, which in many cases do not configure `robots.txt` files. In addition to crawling for `robots.txt` files, BotSeer is able to look at the dynamic behavior of crawler by setting up honeypot sites. These sites use `robots.txt` files and act as regular Web sites. BotSeer then logs how ethically crawlers act, i.e. how much of the restrictions defined in `robots.txt` they actually respect. This study of crawler behavior is something that is outside of our scope.

The *Web Modeling Language (WebML)* [13] is an approach to capture the structure of a Web site in a declarative way; it thus would be an ideal starting point for publishing information about site's structure (we do not know how far WebML provides support for this functionality, though). More generally, almost all *Content Management Systems (CMS)* have metadata about a site's content and structure and many support exposing this as `robots.txt` and/or sitemaps. As a popular example, the Drupal CMS supports a module for publishing sitemaps (initially named *Google Sitemap*, the module has been renamed to *XML Sitemap*).

We believe that once the users of richer Web site metadata are there (in the form of crawlers or browsers), it will be easily possible for many Web sites to automatically make that information available. A study by DANIELSON [14] has shown that a more structured overview of a Web site can help significantly in many tasks when interacting with a Web site; however, most approaches for Web site navigation only look at it as a per-site task, rather than looking at it as a fundamental way of how to interact with Web-based information.

To our knowledge, there is no related work in the overlap of the two areas described above, which is our eventual target area: The overlap of crawler-oriented site metadata often investigated in IR-oriented research, and the HCI-oriented question of how to make site metadata available to support navigational tasks on Web sites. Some prior work about looking at the Web graph in general [15] does discuss some questions relevant for our approach, though (specifically, the "URL split" technique presented in that paper). Surprisingly, even the otherwise detailed *Web Content Accessibility Guidelines (WCAG)* [16] say little about how to implement Web site navigation in an accessible may, they are mostly concerned with looking at individual Web pages.

8   Future Work

The work presented in this paper is the first stage of a research project that aims at making metadata about Web site structure available on the Web, as a service that can be provided by a site itself, or by a third party. We believe that this metadata should be available so that it can be used by clients, for example to enhance Web site accessibility. Our approach [1] is twofold:

1. *Data Mining:* Based on the sitemap URIs, it is possible to construct a navigational sitemap of a Web site. We intend to employ approaches based on clustering of URI prefixes. This approach assumes that a site's URI structure reflects the site's navigational structure, and the important question is to find out how appropriate this assumption is, and whether it is possible to reliably detect whether the assumption is true for a given Web site or not.
2. *Data Format:* Based on the sitemaps format, we propose a format that can be used by Web sites to expose their navigational structure, if they want to do so. This site metadata can then be picked up by browsers and other clients, and typically will be more reliable than reverse-engineered data.

The next step beyond this is to set up an experimental service that provides access to data-mined navigational metadata, and to make that data available in a browser. A browser could use the two possible data sources mentioned above, first looking for authoritative navigational metadata provided by the site itself, and then accessing a third-party service inquiring about data-mined navigational metadata. This approach supports a transition strategy to a Web where sites can make their navigational metadata available, but if they don't do it, there still is a fallback provided by a third party.

9   Conclusions

This paper presents detailed analyses of the current availability of Web site metadata. The analyses are based on a starting set of the 100'000 most popular domains, and use data these sites make available through their `robots.txt` files and sitemaps. The analyses show that there is a wealth of Web site metadata available, even though currently its sole purpose is to control and steer Web crawlers. Based on these analyses, we conclude that it is a promising research path to take a closer look at the properties of the available Web site metadata, and our future work proposes to do that with the specific goal of extracting navigational metadata (i.e., metadata intended to improve navigational access to Web sites).

A more detailed presentation of the results can be found in a technical report [17], which is an extended version of the results presented here. We would like to thank Alexa for providing us with their dataset of the most popular 100'000 domains.

References

1. Wilde, E.: Site Metadata on the Web. In: Proceedings of the Second Workshop on Human-Computer Interaction and Information Retrieval, Redmond, Washington (October 2008)
2. Wilde, E., Gaedke, M.: Web Engineering Revisited. In: Proceedings of the 2008 British Computer Society (BCS) Conference on Visions of Computer Science, London, UK (September 2008)
3. Pant, G., Srinivasan, P., Menczer, F.: Crawling the Web. In: Levene, M., Poulovassilis, A. (eds.) Web Dynamics: Adapting to Change in Content, Size, Topology and Use, pp. 153–178. Springer, Berlin (2004)
4. Koster, M.: A Method for Web Robots Control. Internet Draft draft-koster-robots-00 (December 1996)
5. He, B., Patel, M., Zhang, Z., Chang, K.C.C.: Accessing the Deep Web. Communications of the ACM 50(5), 94–101 (2007)
6. Madhavan, J., Ko, D., Kot, L., Ganapathy, V., Rasmussen, A., Halevy, A.: Google's Deep Web Crawl. In: Proceedings of the 34th International Conference on Very Large Data Bases, Auckland, New Zealand, pp. 1241–1252. ACM Press, New York (2008)
7. Nottingham, M., Sayre, R.: The Atom Syndication Format. Internet RFC 4287 (December 2005)
8. Cobsena, G., Abdessalem, T., Hinnach, Y.: WebWatching UK Web Communities: Final Report For The WebWatch Project. Technical Report British Library Research and Innovation Report 146, British Library Research and Innovation Centre (July 1999)
9. Drott, M.C.: Indexing Aids at Corporate Websites: The Use of Robots.txt and META Tags. Information Processing and Management 38(2), 209–219 (2002)
10. Sun, Y., Zhuang, Z., Councill, I.G., Giles, C.L.: Determining Bias to Search Engines from Robots.txt. In: Proceedings of the 2007 IEEE/WIC/ACM International Conference on Web Intelligence, Silicon Valley, California, November 2007, pp. 149–155 (2007)
11. Sun, Y., Zhuang, Z., Giles, C.L.: A Large-Scale Study of Robots.txt. In: Poster Proceedings of the 16th InternationalWorld WideWeb Conference, Bank, Alberta, pp. 1123–1124. ACM Press, New York (2007)
12. Sun, Y., Councill, I.G., Giles, C.L.: BotSeer: An Automated Information System for AnalyzingWeb Robots. In: Schwabe, D., Curbera, F., Dantzig, P. (eds.) Proceedings of the 8th International Conference on Web Engineering, Yorktown Heights, NY (July 2008)

13. Ceri, S., Fraternali, P., Matera, M.: Conceptual Modeling of Data-Intensive Web Applications. IEEE Internet Computing 6(4), 20–30 (2002)
14. Danielson, D.R.: Web Navigation and the Behavioral Effects of Constantly Visible Site Maps. Interacting with Computers 14(5), 601–618 (2002)
15. Raghavan, S., Garcia-Molina, H.: Representing Web Graphs. In: Dayal, U., Ramamritham, K., Vijayaraman, T.M. (eds.) Proceedings of the 19th International Conference on Data Engineering, Bangalore, India, pp. 405–416. IEEE Computer Society Press, Los Alamitos (2003)
16. Caldwell, B., Cooper, M., Reid, L.G., Vanderheiden, G.: Web Content Accessibility Guidelines 2.0. World Wide Web Consortium, Recommendation REC-WCAG20-20081211 (December 2008)
17. Wilde, E., Roy, A.: Web Site Metadata. Technical Report UCB ISchool Report 2009-028, School of Information, UC Berkeley, Berkeley, California (February 2009)

Conceptual Modeling of Multimedia Search Applications Using Rich Process Models

Alessandro Bozzon, Marco Brambilla, and Piero Fraternali

Politecnico di Milano,
Piazza Leonardo Da Vinci, 32 - 20133 Milano, Italy
{alessandro.bozzon,marco.brambilla,piero.fraternali}@polimi.it

Abstract. With the advent of the Web, search has become the prominent paradigm for information seeking, both across the online space and within enterprises. Search frameworks and components can be used to build search-based applications in the most diverse vertical fields. This paper explores Model Driven Development and model transformations as a paradigm for developing search-based applications, considered as process- and content-intensive applications. A rich process model, obtained by extending BPMN, is proposed as the starting point of development, followed by a set of semi-automatic model transformations that lead from the conceptualization of requirements to the running code.

1 Introduction

With the diffusion of the Web, search has become the predominant paradigm for addressing the information needs of users. Nowadays search is not only confined to the online information space, but has assumed a fundamental role also in enterprise application integration, as a practical means to grant unified access to the vast collections of structured, semi-structured, and unstructured contents that constitute the core of modern businesses. This brings about the notion of *Search-Based Application* (SBA), i.e., an application in which searching constitutes the predominant user interface paradigm.

Unlike monolithic search engines, SBAs are mostly tailor-made evolving solutions, because the nature of the searched information and of the user needs vary considerably across different business sectors [13] and in time. The main factors of SBA complexity and variability stem from: *content*, which can span distributed database, document, and audiovisual materials; *content processing*, which involves crawling, transcoding, analysis, annotation, and indexing [1]; and *querying*, which must support multiple paradigms like keyword search, content-based similarity search (query by image, by sketching, by humming, etc), query refinement and enrichment based on the profile of the user and of her community.

The thesis of this paper is that SBA development demands for the same evolution in methods and tools that has characterized in the recent past the progress

---

[1] Annotations are the metadata extracted by analyzing the content: e.g., frequent terms for documents, or features for images, audio, and video.

M. Gaedke, M. Grossniklaus, and O. Díaz (Eds.): ICWE 2009, LNCS 5648, pp. 315–329, 2009.
© Springer-Verlag Berlin Heidelberg 2009

of Web Engineering [8] for "classical" Web applications. We claim that SBAs demand for novel approaches and tools, which combine the benefits of process-driven and data-driven design methodologies, while adding new solutions to specific needs of SBAs. SBAs are undergoing a growth towards complex, tailor-made, personalized, multichannel, and adaptive applications, while retaining a specific flavor, due to the prevailing role of search: they must integrate a complex front-end (for query submission and result presentation) with a complex back-end (content provisioning, annotation, indexing, and distributed query execution). Both aspects involve a lot of search-specific aspects, that cannot be treated by usual approaches: the query and the result list are subject to a specific life-cycle: they must be obtained, reformulated, integrated or enriched, and stored. The same is true for content, which must be provisioned, transcoded, analyzed, annotated, and indexed. These processes vary based on requirements, which may evolve over time or change depending on the business sector.

The approach proposed in this paper is based on the paradigm of Model Driven Development (MDD), where *models* are the core artifacts of the application life-cycle and *model transformations* progressively refine models to achieve an executable version of the system. The core contribution of the paper is twofold: 1) the set of models that can represent the core elements of a SBA; 2) a set of model transformations from the initial model to the executable system.

To cope with the process-intensive nature of the main SBAs' interactions (i.e., content analysis, query management, etc.), we advocate the use of a *Rich Process Model*[20], obtained by extending BPMN with search-specific primitives, as the starting point of both the front-end and the back-end SBA specification. In the terminology of MDA, the Rich Process Model can be seen as a Computation Independent Model (CIM), which specifies SBA requirements. Such Rich Process Model can be semi-automatically transformed into an *Application Model*, encoded using WebML [3], a Platform Independent Model (PIM) that exploits SOA and Web interfaces as a technical space to design data-intensive Web applications. Finally, Java 2 application code can be generated as a Platform Specific Model (PSM), through an extended version of an existing tool [19][2].

To our knowledge, the proposed approach is the first that addresses the Model Driven Development of SBAs through semi-automatic model transformations. General-purpose Web Engineering methodologies have been applied to data-intensive [12,3,16] and process-intensive applications [1,15,18,10]. However, none of these approaches has focused on the specific requirements of SBAs nor implemented the model transformations needed for turning a rich process model into an application.

The paper is organized as follows: Section 2 summarizes the main characteristics of SBAs; Section 3 overviews the SBA models and transformations; Sections 4 and 5 respectively detail the domain model and the process model; Section 6 discusses the CIM to PIM model transformation; Section 7 presents the

---

[2] A detailed discussion about the chosen modeling and deployment technologies is out of the scope of this paper. The reader may refer to [3,20] for further details.

application model; Section 8 reports on implementation experience; Section 9 reviews the related works; and finally Section 10 concludes.

2 Search-Based Applications

Figure 1 shows the multi-tier reference architecture of a SBA. The *Presentation Tier* deals with the rendition of the user interface whereby users can formulate their information need as a query to the system. This level must allow multiple ways of expressing queries: e.g., by means of keywords or by the submission of examples of content similar to the desired ones. The *Frontend Business Logic Tier* is responsible of: 1) receiving the query from the Presentation Tier, pre-processing it, and submitting it for execution to the back-end tier; 2) receiving the result list, postprocessing it and forwarding it to the Presentation Tier for rendition. Examples of query preprocessing are: linguistic or semantic treatment of keywords (e.g., stemming, language identification), query personalization with user's preferences. Examples of result post-processing include: filtering based on access rights, enrichment with external non-indexed information (e.g., content previews), etc. The *Backend Business Logic Tier* manages content acquisition, feature extraction, encoding of features as content annotations, and indexing of such annotations in one or more search engines. It also orchestrates the execution of the query, by brokering it across one or more search engines.

As shown in Figure 1, the SBA architecture supports two major flows of activities, which are the main subject of SBA design: 1) The *Query and Result Presentation* (QUIRP) process, which encompasses query preprocessing, query execution, and results post-processing; 2) The *Content Provision and Annotation* (CPA) process, which gets content from its original location and makes it available to the search engines, together with the appropriate annotations. The rest of the paper will show how to formalize such processes and their supporting data, together with the model transformation to progressively obtain an executable application embodying the desired QUIRP and CPA flows.

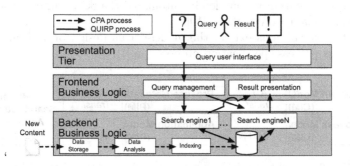

Fig. 1. Architecture and Processes of a SBA

3   Models and Transformations

Figure 2 outlines the models and transformations involved in SBA design. Initially, requirements are conceptualized in 1) a *Domain Model*, which formalizes, using any object-oriented notation (e.g., UML), the essential objects managed by the SBA and their relationships, and 2) a *Process Model* describing the QUIRP and CPA workflows in terms of activities, precedences, and data flows. We describe process models by means of BPMN diagrams [20], coherently with the BPDM metamodel [3], which has been extended with activity and parameter typing. Domain objects support the QUIRP process, the CPA process, and process enactment. The link between the domain and process models is established by the type of objects that flow between activities, and by classifying each activity based on its behaviour.

The Domain Model and Process Model are subject to a first (CIM to PIM) transformation, which produces the *Application Model* and *Process Metadata*. The *Application Model* expresses the design of the SBA application as a set of coordinated services that implement the QUIRP and CPA processes, possibly augmented with hypertext interface to support human-directed activities. We encode the application model in WebML [3], which allows the seamless specification of hypertexts and services. The *Process Metadata*, instead, represents a logical view of the constraints between activities, useful for encapsulating the process control logic in the Application Model. Explicit process metadata simplify the Application Model, because process advancement control logic can be encapsulated in one dedicated operation, which exploits process metadata. The generated Application Model can be refined manually by the designer, to add domain-dependent information on the execution of activities.

The manually refined Application Model is the input of a second (PIM to PSM) transformation, which produces the code of the application for a specific technological platform. The *Implementation Model* (PSM) includes all the needed software artifacts (i.e., running code, database schema and instances, XML configuration files, and so on). The PSM we produce is in the Java2 technical space, based on the MVC framework and relational technology. The PIM to PSM transformation is completely automated thanks to an extension added to the commercial tool WebRatio [19].

These transformations extend the model-driven design of Web applications from business process specification proposed in [1].

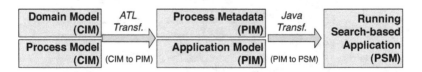

Fig. 2. Model to model transformations from CIM to PIM to PSM

---

[3] http://www.omg.org/spec/BPDM/1.0/

4   Domain Model

The domain model formalizes data and metadata supporting the QUIRP and CPA processes, and comprises the sub-models shown in Figure 3. For the sake of illustration, from now on we assume a SBA case study dealing with multi-modal audiovisual search, supported through three paradigms: matching keyword over content annotation, similarity to an audio sample, and similarity to a person's face.

The main SBA domain sub-models (Figure 3) are: 1) the *Content Model*, which defines the *Content Item*s of interest for the search, associated to *Annotations* and other collateral resources (e.g., transcoded version of audio/video); 2) the *Query Model*, which specifies the admitted types of *Query* (e.g., face similarity, audio similarity); 3) the *Result Model*, which defines the structure of the *ResultSet*; 4) the *Index Model*, which represents the information that is stored in the *Index* of the managed search engines; 5) the *Tracking Model*, which describes the *ActivityInstance*s executed during the enactment of a specific case of the QUIRP and CPA processes (*processCase*); 6) the *User Model*, which reflects the *User* profile and roles (*Groups*).

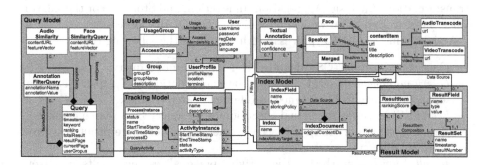

Fig. 3. Example of Domain model for an audiovisual SBA

5   Process Model

The Process Model exploits the BPMN notation [20], extended with SBA-specific information to enable a more precise model transformation towards PIM and PSM models. The classification of activities based on their semantics and the precise typing of data flows permit the generation of PIMs that are very close to a complete solution usable for generating the code of the application.

Figure 4 shows the graphical notation of the extended BPMN activity. An activity is associated with a *Type* (1), which denotes the kind of processing performed (e.g., Data Analysis), and possibly a set of refined *SubType*s (2) (e.g., Music Genre Analysis). The activity performs the processing implied by all the associated subtypes, combined in a domain-dependent way. An activity has a (possibly empty) set of input parameters (3) and output parameters (4). The actual values of input parameters can be assigned from one or more input objects,

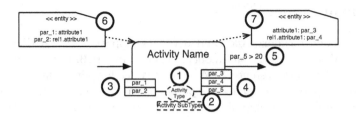

Fig. 4. Extended activity notation

associated to incoming links; the output parameters can take values from some objects produced or modified by the activity. The output flow of an activity can be associated to a guard condition (5), which is an OCL Boolean expression over the values of the output parameters. The target activity of the guarded link can be executed only if the activity source of the link has completed and the condition evaluates to true. Input and output objects (6) (7) correspond to instances of the classes specified in the Domain Model.

Activities in the CPA process can have one of the following types: Retrieval, Transformation, Analysis, Aggregation, Indexation, and Storage. For the sake of conciseness, from now on we will only discuss the QUIRP process[4].

Activities in the QUIRP process can have one of the following types:

- *Query specification* (QS): denotes the submission of a query;
- *Query management* (QM): denotes the manipulation of the query, e.g., for separating parts to be assigned to different search engines;
- *Search* (S): denotes the actual execution of the query by a search engine;
- *Result Aggregation* (RA): the activity merges two or more result sets provided by different search engines;
- *Result Enrichment* (RSE): the activity personalizes the results based on social knowledge and user preferences, inferred from previous searches by the same users or other users connected to her;
- *Result Presentation* (RP): the activity formats results according to the need of the presentation tier.

Such a categorization do not claim for completeness, but it stems from the authors' experience in the field. Nonetheless, new activity types can be added at will, without affecting the validity nor the generality of our approach.

Figure 5 shows an example of QUIRP process where the query can be specified according to three different modalities: by keyword, by audio recognition of the speaker, and by face recognition of the appearing characters. These options are specified as *SubTypes* to be performed within the Query Specification activity. The Query Management activity reshapes the query and assigns each part to the respective Search Activity. Results are then aggregated, enriched and personalized, and finally presented to the user, that can possibly decide to

---

[4] An extended version comprising also discussion and examples of CPA process can be found at http://home.dei.polimi.it/bozzon/ICWE2009/SBAMDD_ICWE2009.pdf

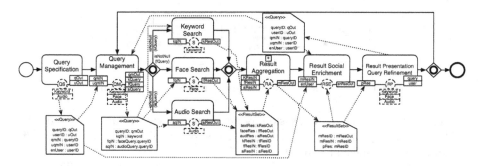

Fig. 5. Process models example: the QUIRP process

refine the query, thus triggering again the Query Management, for addressing the refinement parts of the query.

6   CIM-PIM Model Transformations

The transformation from CIMs to PIMs consists of two sub-transformations:

- BPM to Process Metadata: the business process specifications are transformed to instances of a relational representation of the Process Metamodel shown in Figure 6, for enabling runtime control of activity precedence constraints;
- BPM to Application Model: the business process is transformed to a coarse Application Model, which can be subsequently refined by the designer.

6.1   Process Metadata generation from BPMN

The transformation from BPMN to the relational representation of Process Metadata adheres to the following guidelines:

- each BPMN process is transformed to a *Process* instance;
- each BPMN activity is transformed to a *Activity Type* instance;
- each BPMN flow arrow is transformed to a *nextActivity/previousActivity* relation;
- each guard condition is transformed to a *Condition* instance, whose OCL expression is the expression of the original guard condition;
- each gateway is transformed to a *Condition* instance (in conjunction with the possibly existing guard conditions on the incoming and outgoing arrows).

The conditions generated for the gateway elements are defined according to the BPMN semantics:

- *AND-splits* allow a single thread to split into two or more parallel threads, which proceed autonomously. The condition over the workflow structure is the *TRUE* expression, because as soon as the preceding activity is finished, all the branches can start independently.

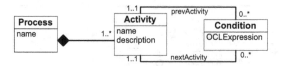

Fig. 6. Metadata describing activity precedence constraints

- *XOR-splits* represent a decision point among several mutually exclusive branches. Its condition will define that one of the alternatives can start iff all the others haven't started yet.
- *OR-splits* represent a decision for executing one or more branches. The condition is the *TRUE* expression, because one or more branches can start independently.
- *AND-joins* specify that an activity can start iff all the incoming branches are completed. The associated condition will allow execution of the next activity iff all the previous ones are completed.
- *XOR-joins* specify that the execution of a following activity can start as soon as one activity among the incoming branches has been terminated. The condition will check this situation to allow the execution of the next activity.
- *OR-joins* specify that the execution of the following activity can start as soon as all the started incoming branches have been terminated. The condition will check this situation.

Process Metadata generation has been formalized as an ATL transformation from the BPDM metamodel to the Process Model of Figure 6[5]

6.2   WebML Model Generation from BPMN

The transformation from Process Models to WebML coarse models of services and hypertext interfaces considers modeling dimensions like actor type (human or automatic), process distribution, managed data objects, and exception handling. The application models produced by the transformation still need manual refinement, to add domain-specific elements that cannot be expressed even in the enriched BPMN notation. However, by exploiting information about the activity type/subtype, a first-cut application model can be generated.

WebML Workflow Primitives. A WebML application model can be either an *hypertext model* or a *service model*. An hypertext model, called *site view*, is a set of navigable pages comprising static or dynamic content elements. Pages, content elements, and executable operations are connected in a graph structure by *links*, which allow navigation and operation execution. A service model, called *service view*, denotes the orchestration of multiple service executions; it is expressed as a graph of operations denoting the receipt of a message, the sending of a message, and the execution of a piece of business logic.

---

[5] A sample ATL fragment that calculates the condition of a XOR split can be found at home.dei.polimi.it/bozzon/ICWE2009/SBAMDD_ICWE2009.pdf

Both site views and service views can be subjected to the constraints of a process model, by exploiting ad hoc operations that denote the starting and closing of an activity (*Start* and *End* units), the storage and retrieval of parameter values (*Assign* and *Retrieve* units), and the computation of the next enabled activities given the current state of the workflow (*Next* unit). These units are discussed in the paper [1], except for the Next unit, which has been defined in this work.

A specific component (*Next* unit) encapsulates the process control logic: it exploits the information stored in the Process Metadata and in the Tracking Domain Model to calculate the current process status and the enabled transitions. Given the *activityID* of the *ActivityInstance* just terminated, the current *caseID* (process instance), and the *conditionParameters* (the values required by the conditions to be evaluated), the *Next* unit queries the Process Metadata to find all the process constraints and enables the execution of the proper activities. If the activities are automatic, they are immediately started. If they involve human interaction, the corresponding hypertext are enabled.

Process Transformation. The *Process transformation* from BPMN to WebML consists of three main rules: the *Process transformation rule*, addressing the whole process; the *Activity transformation rule*, managing starting, closing, and parameters of each activity; and the *Business logics transformation rule*, addressing the internal logic of the activities, based on the activity type/subtype.

The outcome of the *Process transformation rule* is a WebML model that comprises: 1) the process initiation and termination logic, generated from the *Start Process* and *End Process* BPMN events; 2) a site view or service view for each BPMN pool; 3) a set of hypertext pages or a graph of services for each BPMN activity.

The WebML model for *process initiation* (*process termination*) is defined based on the type of BPMN *start* (*end*) event; it creates (consumes) data objects, supplied by the process initiator in order to run the case (returned as a result of process termination). If the *start* (*end*) event is a BPMN *message* events, we assume the process to be exposed as a Web service, with an invocation (response) interface comprising a parameter for every consumed (produced) data object. Otherwise, the transformation produces an hypertext page for inputting the objects needed for initiating the process (for accessing the objects resulting from process termination).

The *Activity transformation* rule is based on the BPMN activity specification, taking into account aspects like the actor enacting the activity (e.g., a user or the system), pre- and post-condition specification, as well as exception management. For each BPMN activity, a set of WebML primitives is generated, as shown in Figure 7. The WebML model is embodied within a siteview named as the BPMN pool containing the activity, and is composed of seven blocks:

- *Inception*, evaluating the set of pre-conditions for the activity through a *Switch* unit. If the condition holds, then the execution can proceed.
- *Initiation*, devoted to starting the activity. It comprises a *Start Activity* unit and, for each consumed data object, a *Retrieve* unit properly configured for

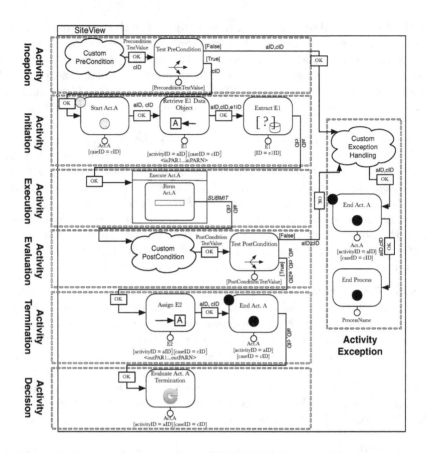

Fig. 7. Skeleton of the result of the BPMN-WebML activity transformation

extracting the needed parameters and a *Selector* unit retrieving the work items;

- *Execution*, depending on the business logic enforced by the specific activity. If no Activity type and subtype are specified at the BPMN level, it is possible to generate only a functionally void set of WebML units, which the designer will later substitute with the needed ones. Otherwise, the *Business logics transformation rule* is in charge of producing a more refined model;
- *Evaluation*, evaluating the set of post-conditions for the activity, similarly to pre-conditions.
- *Termination*, closing the activity. For each created data object, an *Assign* unit is defined, followed by an *End Activity* unit.
- *Decision*, defining the advancement of the process, through the *Next* unit.
- *Exception*, handling exceptional events, by means of compensation activities or by interrupting the process. In our transformation, exceptions are checked during pre- and post-condition evaluation.

The *Business logic transformation rule* is in charge of generating the execution part of the activity. The generated WebML fragment depends on the type of actor, on the distribution of actors, and on the type and operations:

- For user-enacted activities, *activity execution* consists of a user-browsable hypertext, while for automatic activities it consists of a service view.
- Process activities assigned to distributed actors require a communication modeled in BPMN by means of message events. Our transformation assumes Inter-actor communication to be based on Web Services.
- For each *Activty Type*, a specific WebML hypertext pattern is defined as general purpose implementation. Moreover, if one or more *Subtypes* are specified, the pattern is composed by one or more subpatterns, each describing the corresponding operation. For instance, an Activity of type *QuerySpecification* will be transformed to a submission page for the search criteria. If the type is detailed by the *AudioSearch* and *TextSearch* operations, the input interface in the hypertext will be generated accordingly.

The whole approach is specified by an ATL transformation organized into the three above specified rules: a *Process transformation rule* generates the process level actions and then invokes the generic *Activity rule* that manages untyped activities (by generating an activity skeleton as shown in Figure 7). A set of *type-specific Activity rules* inherit from the general transformation and refine it according to the *Activity Type*. These rules also consider the *SubType* and generate the appropriate hypertext elements, according to a composition logics specific for each Activity Type. A skeleton of the generic Activity transformation is available in the extended version of this paper [6].

7   Application Model

The result of the CIM to PIM transformation consists of a coarse Web application model, which needs to be manually refined by the designer. The generated model complies with the already existing WebML metamodel[2], extended with the new SBA primitives. This section exemplifies the refined WebML application models of two representative QUIRP process activities derived from the BPMN example of Figure 5.

Figure 8(a) depicts the WebML model for the *Query Specification* activity, which involves the user interaction and therefore is generated as a WebML hypertext. The *Query Specification* unit (1) sets the activity status to *Active*. The *Search Page* contains a form for each query modality defined as *Activity Sub-Type* in the process model. In our example, the *Keyword* (3) and *Audio Content* file upload (2) forms are created starting from the activity subtypes "Keyword" and "Audio". By navigating the *Submit* link (L1), the user submits his search criteria and triggers the the definition of the new *Query* instance (4) and of the associated *Audio Similarity* term (5,6). The *Assign Query* unit (7) assigns

---

[6] home.dei.polimi.it/bozzon/ICWE2009/SBAMDD_ICWE2009.pdf

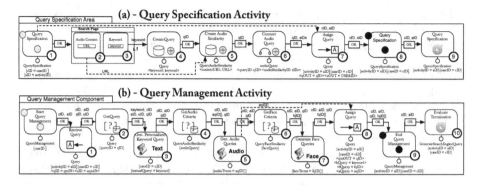

Fig. 8. WebML models of (a) *Query specification* and (b) *Query management* activities

the created query and parameters to the next activities. Finally, the activity ends (8,9).

Figure 8(b) depicts the *Query Management* activity which creates the actual query terms to be submitted to the different search engines. After retrieving *Query* and *User* (1), the *Get Query* (2) and *Gen. Personalized Keyword Query* (3) units address the query keyword terms, by respectively extracting them from the current *Query* instance (2) and generating the textual search engine's query (3), where also user personalization is applied. Then, the *QueryAudioSimilarity* (4,5) and *QueryFaceSimilarity* (6,7) query terms are processed, where the low-level features are calculated and translated in the respective search engines query languages. Finally, the *Assign Query* unit (8) sets the values to be provided as output parameters, the current activity is closed (9), and the *Next* unit (10) triggers the next activities. For the *QUIRP* process of Figure 5, the *Next* unit must evaluate an OR gateway, which means that the activities (i.e., *Keyword Search*, *Face Search* and *Audio Search*) for which a query term is defined are triggered.

8   Implementation and Experience

This section reports our experiences in the extension of WebRatio 5[7], a CASE tool supporting WebML design and code generation of industrial Web applications. The extension regarded all three major component of the WebRatio suite: the modeling editor GUI, the code generator, and the runtime environment.

The *modeling GUI* has been extended by: 1) creating an online workflow editor implementing the SBA-specific extensions of BPMN [8]; 2) adding the SBA-specific units to the WebRatio design environment. The *code generator* has been extended in two directions: 1) the CIM to PIM transformation has been implemented within the toolsuite, to allow seamless transformation of BPMN models to WebML and to the Process Metadata. 2) the PIM to PSM transformation has been enriched by the Process Metadata transformation towards platform

---

[7] http://www.webratio.com.

[8] http://home.dei.polimi.it/mbrambil/SBAwfEditor.htm

specific database tuples and by extending the existing j2EE code generator to cover the new WebML primitives. The *runtime* counterpart of the new primitives has been created too. Since at runtime search applications have to be very efficient, attention must be paid to the implementation issues. SBA applications must exploit ad-hoc optimizations which reduce (or ignore) separation of concerns between architectural modules or execution steps. This issue is partially addressed by our work through the activity subtype concept: if two or more subtypes are declared for one activity, their combination is built by considering as many optimizations as possible. On the opposite, at the moment no generation of optimized combination of separate activities is implemented.

To validate the approach, we have applied it in the context of PHAROS[4] (Platform for searcHing of Audiovisual Resources across Online Spaces), an EU Integrated Project, whose peculiarity consists in being an open framework for developing audiovisual search solutions. Every functionality of the architecture is conceived to be pluggable, according to the SOA paradigm. Our contribution has been twofold: we fostered the adoption of a MDD approach for the specification of the PHAROS platform and we applied our design method for the development of both QUIRP and CPA prototype components that have been plugged into the Pharos platform. Tangible results can be found in the project's Website [9].

9   Related Work

Even if several methodologies and tools exist for Model Driven Development of general-purpose and vertical applications, very few works explored the construction of search-based applications using models and model transformations. Some proposals [21] [5] offer frameworks based on design patterns for meta-search engines or vertical search engines. The idea is to associate the main components of a search engine (e.g., crawlers, text-filters) with reference UML design patterns, to be used in application design. However, the dynamic behavior of SBAs is not captured and no model transformation or code generation capability is provided. Ferreira at al. [6] introduce IRML, Information Retrieval Modeling Language, a formalism based on the UML extension mechanisms, that include a library of modules and code generation based on XML transformations. However, there is no formalization of the composition of IRML modules.

With respect to the above-mentioned works, the approach in this paper goes a step forward: it not only proposes a (data- and process-centric) model of the application requirements, but also formalizes a model-to-model transformation yielding a PIM amenable to be refined by the application designer and to be automatically transformed into running code.

SBA development could be considered as a special case of process- and data-centric application design. Several MDD methods have explored the integration of business process and Web application modeling. The Process Modeling language (PML) [14], for instance, is an early proposal for the automatic generation of simple Web-based applications exploiting process specifications. Koch et al.

---

[9] http://www.pharos-audiovisual-search.eu/

[10] approaches the integration of process and navigation modeling in the context of UWE and OO-H. The convergence between the two models focuses on the requirement analysis phase, where standard UML constructs are used. The design of the application model, instead, is separated. In our work, both approaches are considered: like in UWE, we preserve the *process model* as an additional domain model; as in OO-H, we provide semi-automatic generation of navigational skeletons directly from the process model.

The approach proposed by Torres and Pelechano [17] leverages BPM and OOWS [7] to model process-centric applications; model-to-model transformations are used to generate the Navigational Model from the BPM definition and model-to-text transformations can produce a WS-BPEL process definition. In contrast, our work enriches the representation of the business process with data-centric features and with typed activities, so to encode in the BPMN model more knowledge exploitable in the automatic generation of application models.

Liew at al. [11] presents a set of transformations for automatically generating a set of UML artifacts from BPM. Jonkers et al. [9] presents a more pragmatic implementation of Model-Driven Architecture (MDA) in order to provide semi-automatic generation of enterprise applications starting from business process models, by extending some existing BPM and MDA tools.

With respect to the literature on business process integration within general-purpose Web Engineering methods, our work differs in its specific focus on SBAs, highlighting the core processes behind these solutions and demonstrating applicability of how data-centric and process-centric MDD methods.

10   Conclusions

In this paper we have shown how to exploit MDD methods and tools to support the development of search based Web applications. We proposed a top-down design approach that combines the benefits of (extended) business process design with the advantages of a domain specific language for the Web. We formalized a set of domain-specific BPMN extensions and a set of MDA transformations, thus covering the requirements of SBAs. Future research includes the definition of: a more complete CIM to PIM transformation; the transformation rules of a wider set of Activity Types/Subtypes; and algebraic representation of SBA processes, in order to define a verification framework of search-specific properties.

Acknowledgments. This work is partially supported by the Pharos project funded by the EU within the VII FP. We wish to thank all the partners of the project for the fruitful collaboration.

References

1. Brambilla, M., Ceri, S., Fraternali, P., Manolescu, I.: Process modeling in web applications. ACM TOSEM 15(4), 360–409 (October 2006)
2. Brambilla, M., Fraternali, P., Tisi, M.: A metamodel transformation framework for the migration of WebML models to MDA. In: CEUR-WS.org, (ed.) MDWE 2008, CEUR Proceedings, vol. 389, pp. 91–105 (2008)

3. Ceri, S., Fraternali, P., Bongio, A., Brambilla, M., Comai, S., Matera, M.: Designing Data-Intensive Web Applications. Morgan Kaufmann Publishers Inc, San Francisco (2002)
4. Debald, S., Nejdl, W., Nucci, F., Paiu, R., Plu, M.: Pharos platform for search of audiovisual resources across online spaces. In: CEUR-WS.org. (ed.) SAMT 2006 December 2006, pp. 57–58 (2006)
5. Dorn, J., Naz, T.: Structuring meta-search research by design patterns. In: ICSTC 2008 (March 2008)
6. Ferreira, J., Silva, A., Delgado, J.: A model-based approach to information retrieval systems development. In: Cheng, A. (ed.) Software Engineering and Application (November 2006)
7. Fons, J., Pelechano, V., Albert, M., Pastor, O.: Development of web applications from web enhanced conceptual schemas. In: Song, I.-Y., Liddle, S.W., Ling, T.-W., Scheuermann, P. (eds.) ER 2003. LNCS, vol. 2813, pp. 232–245. Springer, Heidelberg (2003)
8. Ginige, A., Murugesan, S.: Guest editors' introduction: Web engineering - an introduction. IEEE MultiMedia 8(1), 14–18 (2001)
9. Jonkers, H., Steen, M.W.A., Heerink, L., Leeuwen, D.V., Telematica Instituut: Bridging BPM and MDE: On the Integration of BiZZdesigner and OptimalJ. In: Eclipse Summit Europe 2007 (October 2007)
10. Koch, N., Kraus, A., Cachero, C., Meliá, S.: Integration of business processes in web application models. Journal of Web Engineering 3(1), 22–49 (2004)
11. Liew, P., Kontogiannis, K., Tong, T.: A framework for business model driven development. In: STEP 2004, Washington, DC, USA, pp. 47–56. IEEE, Los Alamitos (2004)
12. Merialdo, P., Atzeni, P., Mecca, G.: Design and development of data-intensive web sites: The araneus approach. ACM Trans. Internet Techn. 3(1), 49–92 (2003)
13. Moulton, L.: Enterprise Search Markets and Applications. Capitalizing on Emerging Demand. Gilbane Group, Report & Studies edition (June 2008)
14. Noll, J., Scacchi, W.: Specifying process-oriented hypertext for organizational computing. J. Netw. Comput. Appl. 24(1), 39–61 (2001)
15. Schmid, H.A., Rossi, G.: Modeling and designing processes in e-commerce applications. IEEE Internet Computing 8(1), 19–27 (2004)
16. Schwabe, D., Rossi, G., Barbosa, S.D.J.: Systematic hypermedia application design with OOHDM. In: Hypertext, pp. 116–128. ACM, New York (1996)
17. Torres, V., Pelechano, V.: Building business process driven web applications. In: Dustdar, S., Fiadeiro, J.L., Sheth, A.P. (eds.) BPM 2006. LNCS, vol. 4102, pp. 322–337. Springer, Heidelberg (2006)
18. Troyer, O.D., Casteleyn, S.: Modeling complex processes for web applications using wsdm. In: IWWOST 2003 (July 2003)
19. Web Models S.r.l. WebRatio (2008)
20. White, S.: Introduction to BPMN. OGM - BPM Initiative (2004)
21. Zhang, J., Qu, W., Du, L., Sun, Y.: A framework for domain-specific search engine: Design pattern perspective. In: IEEE Conf. on Systems, Man and Cybernetics, vol. 4(3881) (October 2003)

Zero-Effort Search and Integration Model for Augmented Web Applications

Ryong Lee and Kazutoshi Sumiya

School of Human Science and Environment, University of Hyogo,
Shinzaike-honcho, Himeji, Hyogo 670-0092, Japan
{leeryong,sumiya}@shse.u-hyogo.ac.jp

Abstract. Due to the rapid advancements of mobile web access environments, there are constantly increasing requirements for web searches of real-world spaces. Nevertheless, search methods available for mobile devices are not much different from those currently available in indoor computing environments. Quite often, it is inconvenient to manipulate such small devices in outdoor environments. In this paper, we propose a zero-effort search model composed of zero-query search and zero-synthesis integration. With zero-query search, there is almost no need for users to express their queries explicitly with cumbersome manipulations. In order to reduce the user's efforts to generate search queries with the least amount of interaction, users' intentions are analyzed from sensing information and map databases. Applying zero-synthesis integration, users can browse an interpolated form, requiring less effort to understand. To realize this convenience, media contents will be displayed in an overlaid form over the real world image. With this proposed intuitive platform model, many various web search and browsing applications will be easily realizable in all the stages from design to actual implementation.

Keywords: Zero-Query Search, Augmented Web Space.

1 Introduction

With the advancement of mobile computing environments, today's smartphones or cell-phones are already web-accessible from anywhere. It is universally possible to get information on the spot through mobile web browsers. However, there are still many difficulties in searching for and integrating various kinds of information from mobile devices in outdoor environments. Even though connectivity to the Web is available with mobile devices, there is still work involved in the physical and mental processes of searching, arranging, and matching the information with real-world objects on a small screen with keypads.

For example, in order to find a restaurant in an unfamiliar downtown area, a few words need to be inputted into a cell-phone to begin the process of investigating the town's information from the Web, using an embedded browser. If the phone is equipped with an apparatus to estimate the physical location of the target, the search guides the user directly to a page including a map showing restaurants near the desired location. Once one of the restaurants is chosen, the best route to the restaurant

M. Gaedke, M. Grossniklaus, and O. Díaz (Eds.): ICWE 2009, LNCS 5648, pp. 330–339, 2009.
© Springer-Verlag Berlin Heidelberg 2009

needs to be determined. With the help of a map showing the user's current position, the user is able to navigate toward his goal. This is the type of short mission that is often experienced in everyday life in urban areas.

In order to reduce the physical and mental efforts of mobile web searches, we are developing an Augmented Web Search System based on Augmented-Reality (AR) technology. AR systems [1] have so far been introduced in see-through devices, such as the head-mounted display [3], or other camera-embedded mobile gadgets [7, 8, 9]. These devices can concurrently display real and virtual worlds in a mixed form; virtually created graphics or information are superimposed over outer-world images corresponding to real-world objects or spaces on a see-through screen. Those combined worlds are called mixed reality or augmented reality. Such augmentation from virtual existence to the real world can provide many innovative applications from personal activity assistance by wearable computing systems to front-glass based automobile navigation systems [2, 6]. Recently, certain smartphones, such as iPhone [9] and G-Phone [8], have shown one of their possible usages as an AR system. However, AR systems are still in their infancy. Most of the work done has been in relatively closed platforms under different system requirements to visualize graphic contents in order to achieve various purposes in augmented worlds.

We think that these emerging systems are candidates for the next generation of web browsing systems. Future web browsers do not necessarily need to show web contents pages as they currently do. Rather the contents should be displayed adaptively to suit a given user environment. In mobile systems, it would be better to show the web search results in a mixed form with real-world images that have been drawn in most AR systems. It is a new challenge for browser developers to show page contents and real-world space together. In such cases, if a new kind of media format is not available, it is necessary to fragment the page contents, for an enhanced or more natural display of photos or real-time videos. AR developers need to consider the interoperability issue that web browser developers have been pursuing for the last decade.

In order to extend AR functionality onto current web browsers and to make it possible to share content interoperability between heterogeneous AR systems, we are developing an open and interoperable browsing platform for augmented media that can be easily shared and browsed on any augmented system. Before discussing this common media share platform, the common specifications for AR systems should be considered. For constructing media for AR worlds, in Güven et. al [4], a structured document has been proposed, but there is no concrete or standardized format or system for general web search purposes. However, from most research and the fundamental philosophy of the first work by Azuma et al. [1], the common criteria required would at least be that the platform should combine the real and virtual world and be interactive in real-time. In other words, the media should be strongly related to a real-world space, and occasionally it should be able to react to the user's controls on the spot. Based on this simple policy, a media space where every user has a mobile device to search and browse augmented media can be imagined, assuming that current web spaces are specified as the media and a web browser can display both worlds concurrently, as in an AR system. In this paper, this type of media is denoted as Augmented Web Media, the browser as the Augmented Web Browser, and the share environment as the Augmented Web Space as shown in Fig. 1.

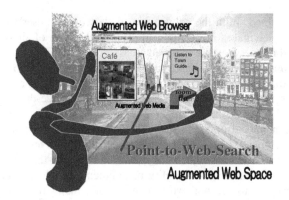

Fig. 1. Concept of Augmented Web Space

With the augmented browser, the search work described above can be greatly improved by reducing unnecessary effort by the user. First, it can be supported by sensing devices and map databases. For example, in order to know a current location, GPS-based latitude and longitude data must be available and used to determine the place name using map databases. Furthermore, if the name of a building in a distant location is required, simply pointing to the geographic object would suffice (the direction data is usable by digital compass and the system searches for the visible object using the map and returns the object name.) In a strict sense, it is not a perfect zero-query. However, this kind of human interaction can reduce efforts to generate queries. It is much easier to just point to target objects than to manipulate the small keypads. The user's effort and time are nearly reduced to zero. For this reason, such a query generation function is called zero-query search model or platform. Although the use of keypads is still required to express users' queries precisely, the targeted goal is to support the query generation by making the most of available context information about the users and their surrounding environments.

The zero-query search model consists of three major components: (1) user motion recognition, (2) environment sensing, and (3) query resolution. In this paper, the main focus is on the 'pointing' action from various human gestures and motions. Especially, the authors investigate which geographic objects are pointed at, and how they can be represented as the next step in high-level queries. We also describe the methodology used to extract visible geographic objects using a digital map rather than simply selecting the nearest geographic objects, which is the most-used method by current location-based systems. Furthermore, with an overlaid display on real-time videos with attached contents, users can understand the captured objects better, with less matching efforts, compared to current browsing methods in normal web browsers. Hence, this function is called zero-synthesis integration support. In order to exactly display searched results or contents from the Web on the screen, the corresponding region on the displayed image should be known. The support of these two zero-effort functions would accelerate application development work for augmented web applications, and would enable performance on a high abstract level for all designs and implements.

In the remainder of this paper, Section 2 introduces emerging augmented web application scenarios and describes a layer-based media integration platform to integrate the web browser and AR systems. Section 3 describes the zero-query search platform using spatial sensing devices and map databases with user-intention reasoning. Section 4 explains the zero-synthesis integration platform for mapping searched results to correspondent regions on displayed images. Lastly, Section 5 concludes the paper with future work.

2 Augmented Web Applications

The advantage to using the Web as a fundamental platform for AR systems is twofold: first, the current open Web platform can be held and its contents managed on the Web servers; second, anyone can participate in the contents service. In other word, there is no restriction to creating and publishing augmented contents. In this section, we describe emerging scenarios by an augmented web browser based on an open media platform for media sharing in real-world space. The assumed media has various types: it can be multimedia, as in photo, audio, or video files; or it can be for applications such as navigation or games with interactive 3D characters. Each media is managed and accessed by a unit of layer. In this study, it is called augmented layer. As in the concept of layers used for map data management, augmented layers can be overlaid to concurrently show a multiple number of layers. For example, a layer showing blogs about a shop can be displayed with another advertisement layer. It is possible to make every augmented layer over a structured file and stored in a uniquely identified location on the Web.

2.1 Layer-Based Augmented Media

Unlike the current web browsers, augmented web browsers need to display web contents over real-time video images. Thus, in order to harmonize both images on a screen, it is necessary to superimpose web contents over a video image, as shown in Fig. 2. This means that the web page cannot be displayed in the author's intended original form. Furthermore, just listing search results in rows is not an effective way to display them. To solve these tangled requirements, we propose a layer-based media that is extracted from searched pages and is able to display the information, together with other results.

The layer-based media we present is quite different from the HTML-based document that is the basic unit for current web browsers. The media included in the layer is somewhat atomic rather than a document. It can be only a photo or audio; but sometimes it also consists of a complex document having these primitive media, which can be drawn on real-world video images. Compared to recent web browsers, it seems that layer-based media shows multiple HTML documents on one screen. This augmentation might reduce the backward or forward operations or the efforts to compare or integrate multiple numbers of contents together. The alignment and accordance of the layers should be considered. For major media formats, the following layer usage scenarios are possible:

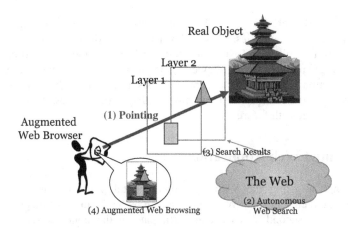

Fig. 2. Layer-based Media for Augmented Web Browsing

- *Photo Layer*: A virtual advertising poster can be attached to a geographical object. While it is accessible only though an augmented media player, these new kinds of media can be beneficial to both advertisers and potential customers. Advertisers can easily and frequently update their content, whereas customers have access to the most recent information.
- *Audio Layer*: A voice can be recorded in a physical space. In [5], they introduce an interesting scenario, using voice guides to warn people of poisonous plant hazards in an unfamiliar forest area.
- *Blog Layer*: With primitive media formats, complex formats, such as blogs, are possible on augmented web space. A blog page, including the primitive media and an opinion article, can be attached to a geographic object. For example, users may find an appraisal on the front door of a shop, attached by another prior visitor.
- *Game Layer*: Interactive applications, such as games, are also realizable in real-world space [10]. For interactivity, operational codes and stable connections are required for synchronization. It would surely require to recognize human behaviors and to give feedback to have people indulge in the best reality in the mixed world.

These are only a few examples of the wide range of possibilities in media applications. As described above, media searched from the Web are able to be concurrently displayed using the layer concept. It surely provides better understanding with less effort, especially for users who have little time to search the Web while engaged in outdoor activities.

3   Zero-Query Search Platform

As described in Section 1, various human gestures and motions are regarded as a query for our augmented web browser, especially, 'pointing.' For each pointing action, it is necessary to find what geographic objects can be pointed at with the help of sensing devices and a map database.

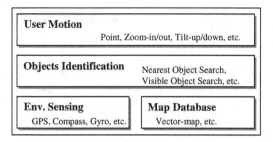

Fig. 3. Zero-Query Generation Platform

The zero-query search platform that we designed and actually implemented is composed of four critical components in three layers, as shown in Fig. 3. In the figure, users' motions previously registered in 'User Motion' are activated by monitoring critical changes of sensing data. For example, if a 'pointing' action is registered, the 'Env. Sensing' component starts to monitor 'direction,' actually azimuth, to determine which direction the augmented browser device is facing (here, a two-dimensional direction is considered, ignoring tilting or rolling of the device.). As the direction is received in real time, the positioning sensor is also activated to determine the current location.

These two sensed data are now converted to an explicit pointed region in real space. Furthermore, the 'Object Identification' layer translates the region query into actual geographic object names with the support of 'Map Database,' for the purpose of searching for the relevant information from the conventional web search sites.

In this section, the process performed by 'Object Identification' is explained; that is, how the user intention is established from the pointing motion with the sensing data and map database. For practical use of the query generation function, it should be performed in real time. In other words, if a user changes his direction, the system needs to detect it as soon as possible to respond in real time.

3.1   Reasoning User Intention from Pointing Action

In order to understand the difference between using location only and using location and direction in AR systems, a representative example is shown. To simplify the discussion, let us assume that we want to automatically tag photographs in the context of location. In order to specify spatial information in a photograph, additional sensors are necessary, since camera devices generally take photographs only in the visual domain.

To accomplish this, integration with GPS has been the approach in many applications; however, this primitive integration is very restricted in its representation of geographic areas of photographs. For example, as shown in the upper-right section of Fig. 4, a photograph is taken from *Kobe Harbor-Land Park* in Japan; fortunately, the camera used here was embedded with GPS and could acquire the exact location coordinates. Hence, it was a simple task to orient the photo to the corresponding location point on the map and the user was able to share the photograph with others over the Web through a photo-sharing site, such as Google Earth or Flickr. The appearance of the *Oriental Hotel* in the background of the photo may provide a good resource for a tourist who wants to visit the hotel later; however, a photograph indexed only by the

Fig. 4. Photo Tagging based on (1) Location-only and (2) Location and Direction

photo-taking position could not be easily found by simple word-based or map-based photo searching. The major problem is that the photograph was not properly tagged to represent the architecture appearing in the background. If such geographic objects in the content of a photograph are 'taggable,' there is a good possibility that object can be searched and the usability of photographs over the Web improved.

In the above example, the greatest limitation in identifying the building is in the difference between the photo-taking location and the location of the hotel. In order to solve the mismatch problem by location-only sensing, we need to apply additional direction information from the photo-taking location to target objects. Direction is usually available using compass and gyro sensors; in 2D real-space, it corresponds to azimuth, and in 3D, it has three attributes—roll, tilt, and yaw. If the photo-taking location and the direction toward the target object are known, it is possible to guess what geographic objects were captured by the camera with a digital map. Furthermore, if other spatial sensing data are available, identification of geographic objects within the camera view range becomes easier, although it would require some additional computational efforts.

4   Augmented Web Browser: Zero-Synthesis Integration

In this section, we describe the later parts of presenting searched results, which augmented browser displays all the searched contents on the real-time video images of the background. To accomplish this, the Zero-Synthesis Integration Model was designed, as shown in Fig. 5. With the zero-query search platform, we could extract the visible object names and their visible angles inside of the camera view angles could be extracted as the set of {<name, (SA,EA)>*} (SA: starting angle, EA: ending angle, managed by the 'Object Mapping Mgt.' component). Based on real-time calculation, we calculated which part of the displayed images was correspondent to each pair of the set by the 'Drawing Object Mgt' component with the results of {<name, drawing_ rectangular region>*}. It is then possible to superimpose the searched results over the correspondent part using the 'Content Display' component. Furthermore, each part on the screen is allocated to a user operation, so that selecting or touching it makes it possible to go for further detailed information (by the 'User Interaction Mgt.' component). In practice, these requirements would be a general interface for construction of augmented web applications. The superiority of current web browsers can be adopted for navigating other pages by following links, with the support of user interaction.

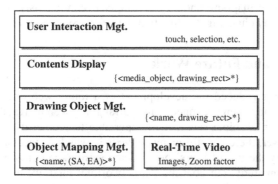

Fig. 5. Zero-synthesis Integration Platform

4.1 Mapping to Display Region

To draw searched results onto the correspondent position of the real-time video image plane, the system uses the angular rate of each object compared to the whole-view angle

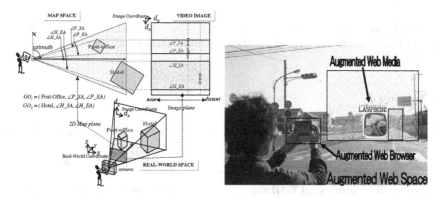

Fig. 6. Mapping geographic object names to the image plane

of the camera to draw position in *x_way*, and the distance from the view_point to the nearest point of each object to draw position in *y_way* as follows and shown in Fig. 6:

$$drawing\_position_{x\_way} = width\_of\_image\_plane \times \frac{visual\_angle(object_i)}{view\_angle}$$

$$drawing\_position_{y\_way} = height\_of\_image\_plane \times \frac{distance\_to\_object}{distance\_of\_query\_range}$$

In order to investigate practical problems and deliver new emerging application scenarios, we are developing a new type of web browser. The only action required by the user is to select a layer and to point to a geographic object. Then, it is able to calculate what spatial area is being targeted with the Zero-Query Search Component. In the browser, this mapping should be computed continuously to respond to the user's movements by changing the direction with Zero-Synthesis Integration.

5   Conclusion and Future Work

In this paper, we introduced the development of a future web browser for outdoor activities, where inputting a query and arranging search results are still an encumbrance. In an absolute sense, it is impossible to predict users' general query intentions. However, there are still many contexts in which unnecessary users' efforts can be reduced by the use of users' profiles and surrounding environmental sensing data. In the present study, our contribution is two-fold: First, we have tried to reason the user-pointing action with position and direction sensing on the map and we have discovered what users want to direct with a visible object search. Such identified geographic object names are used for web search queries. Second, synthesizing web search results with real objects often required when we find paths in urban areas is removed by visualizing searched results directly onto the real video images. In future work, we will study a conversion method from the current web contents to the media drawn in our browser, and also study the accordance between conflicting layers having heterogeneous types of media.

Acknowledgments. This research was supported in part by Grant-in-Aid for Scientific Research from the Ministry of Education, Culture, Sports, Science and Technology of Japan.

References

1. Azuma, R.T.: A Survey of Augmented Reality. Presence: Teleoperators and Virtual Environments 6(4), 355–385 (1997)
2. Barfield, W., Caudell, T. (eds.): Fundamentals of Wearable Computers and Augmented Reality. Lawrence Erlbaum, Mahwah (2001)
3. Feiner, S., MacIntyre, B.T., Holler, A., Webster: A Touring Machine: Prototyping 3D Mobile Augmented Reality Systems for Exploring the Urban Environment. In: Proc. Int. Symp. on Wearable Computers, pp. 74–81 (1997)

4. Güven, S., Feiner, S.: Authoring 3D Hypermedia for Wearable Augmented and Virtual Reality. In: Proceedings of the 7th IEEE international Symposium on Wearable Computers. ISWC, October 21 - 23, p. 118. IEEE Computer Society, Los Alamitos (2003)
5. HP MSCAPE: http://www.hpl.hp.com/mediascapes/
6. Hu, Z., Uchimura, K., Lu, H.: Fusion of Realities for Vehicle Navigation. In: Int. Symposium on Computer Vision, Object Tracking and Recognition, Beijing (2004)
7. Kähäri, M., Murphy, D.J.: MARA - Sensor Based Augmented Reality System for Mobile Imaging. In: ISMAR 2006 (October 2006)
8. Mobilizy: http://www.mobilizy.com/wikitude.php
9. Sekai Camera: http://tonchidot.com/index_info.html
10. Thomas, B., Close, B., Donoghue, J., Squires, J., De Bondi, P., Morris, M., Piekarski, W.: ARQuake: An Outdoor/Indoor Augmented Reality First Person Application. In: 4th International Symposium on Wearable Computers, Atlanta, October 2000, pp. 139–146 (2000)

A Higher Order Generative Framework for Weaving Traceability Links into a Code Generator for Web Application Testing

Piero Fraternali and Massimo Tisi

Politecnico di Milano, Dipartimento di Elettronica e Informazione
P.za L. Da Vinci, 32. I-20133 Milano, Italy
{piero.fraternali,massimo.tisi}@polimi.it

Abstract. Model Driven Engineering is extending its reach beyond the generation of code from Platform Independent Models (PIMs), to all the phases of the software life-cycle. This paper presents an approach to exploit PIMs to ease regression testing, whereby developers can record and replay testing sessions and investigate testing failures on the application model, thanks to traceability links automatically inserted in the generated code. The core of the approach is a modified version of the model transformation for code generation, obtained by applying a Higher Order Transformation (HOT), that is a transformation that takes in input a transformation (the original code generator) and produces another transformation (the augmented code generator). The HOT weaves into the code generator additional rules producing traceability clues that help developers link any error to the model features likely to cause it.

1 Introduction

Model Driven Engineering advocates the use of models as the primary artifact of the software life-cycle. Models incorporate the knowledge about the application at hand, independently of the technological platform of delivery. The knowledge embodied in the model is primarily used for forward engineering, that is, the progressive refinement towards the final implementation code. However, models have a range of application that goes beyond code generation [31]. They can be used as documentation, to estimate the size and effort of application development [4][5], and even as a support to testing [9,7,23,26,28].

In the domain of testing, the use of models mostly concentrates on automating the production and execution of test cases, while other activities, like model-based selective regression testing and behavioral result evaluation are less supported [24]. When testing and debugging an application, developers are used to think in terms of the functionality at the source code level, and want to trace any testing failure directly to the source code elements that are most likely to have caused it. In an MDE environment, the link between the occurrence of a testing failure and the source code is not there; developers specify the application at a high level, and the detailed source code is produced by a model transformation.

M. Gaedke, M. Grossniklaus, and O. Díaz (Eds.): ICWE 2009, LNCS 5648, pp. 340–354, 2009.
© Springer-Verlag Berlin Heidelberg 2009

When a regression test fails, developers should be able to link the failure not to the platform-dependent, low-level code, but to the PIM that they have specified.

This paper presents a framework for addressing the problem of letting Model Driven Engineers manage the testing of their application without exiting the level of abstraction of MDE. The main contributions of the proposed framework consist of:

- An Higher-Order-Transformation (HOT), whereby the model to text transformation that produces the source code of the application from its PIM is modified, so that model traceability clues are automatically weaved into the generated code.
- A Navigation Recorder, whereby the developer can implement a test session as a navigation script. The recorder not only registers the navigation steps of the user, but also encodes correctness assertions automatically, exploiting the model traceability clues weaved into the generated code.
- A Test Session Player, embedded within the same IDE used by the developer for editing the PIM and generating the code, which allows one to modify the model and generate the code, play any previously recorded regression test session, and trace failures back to the PIM elements that have caused them.

The rest of the paper is organized as follows: Section 2 introduces the motivations of this work and presents a case study used throughout the paper; Section 3 illustrates the use of Higher Order Transformations for enabling the production of model traceability clues in a model-to-code transformation; Section 4 presents a browser's extension for recording testing sessions, enabling the automatic production of correctness assertions, and a plug-in extension of a MDE development tool, allowing the seamless integration of change management, code generation and regression testing. Section 5 briefly discusses the implementation work; Section 6 compares our contribution to the related work; Section 7 draws the conclusions.

2   Motivation and Case Study

Regression testing is the activity aimed at detecting software regressions, defined as those situations in which a program functionality that was previously working ceases to do so, as a consequence of a change in the software.

Regression testing is particularly relevant in modern Web development methodologies for several reasons: 1) Web applications are often delivered in short times and are subject to continuous evolution; 2) the enabling technologies are still in motion, which introduces further source of uncontrolled changes; 3) rapid prototyping in the early phase of development is often used, to help the stake-holders compare alternative functionalities.

In Web applications, testing sessions can be encoded as scripts that simulate the user's navigation. Such scripts operate on the platform-dependent realization of the application and reproduce the interaction-evaluation loop typical of Web browsing: the user inputs or selects values using the interface and assesses the response computed by the system; if this is correct, she proceeds in the interaction.

Navigation can be recorded using a state-of-the-practice *Record & Play* tool. Several such tools exist (e.g. Selenium [29] and TestGen4Web [30]), which implement an event-handler that listens to the events occurring inside the browser and then generate a test script (usually in XML format) that contains one or more assertions to be verified after each navigation step. An example of interaction that could be recorded as a test script is:

1. Go to the Google home page
2. Verify that the page title is "Google"
3. Fill the input form with the string "WebTest"
4. Press the "I'm Feeling Lucky" button
5. Assert that the string "WebTest" must appear in the returned page

Specifying an assertion requires an extension of the browser. The test scripts generated by the navigation recorder can then be executed, using one of several Web test environments available, e.g., Canoo WebTest [12], Cactus [32], HTMLUnit [19] and JWebUnit [21], which replay the test session and verify the assertions, highlighting failures.

The problem of this approach is that the evaluation of the testing session breaks the MDE abstraction level, because the testing sessions are defined in terms of the platform-specific realization of the application, and not at the level of the platform-independent models produced by the designers. This semantic mismatch hampers the task of linking failures back to the model elements that are likely to cause them. Furthermore, the testing sessions based on the realization of the system may depend on technological details and not only on the application functions: for example, an assertion on the page content may be sensible to the specific markup used for rendering the application look & feel. After a change of the presentation, such an assertion would fail, even if the functionality and content of the page are still valid.

The present work aims at supporting the definition and evaluation of test sessions in a MDE context, by:

- providing a (possibly automatic) way to preserve the elements of the conceptual model in the definition of the platform-dependent testing session;
- allowing the user to translate the use cases into navigation sessions without worrying about the presence of the models in the background;
- supporting the execution of regression testing from the replay of navigation sequences, with the possibility for the modeler to inspect the failures and trace their possible causes to the model elements.

The proposed approach is illustrated with respect to an exemplary MDE methodology, based on a Domain Specific Language targeted to Web application development, called WebML [13]. We use WebML to model a simplified Web application, derive testing sessions, generate the code with model-to-implementation traceability links, and perform regression testing with the support of the application model. As a case study, we consider a Product Catalog Web application, for publishing and managing content about furniture. The

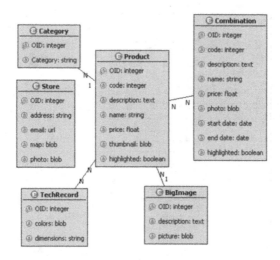

Fig. 1. Data model of the Product Catalog Application

home page contains the product and offer of the day, with a link to access their details, and a form for logging in. From the home page, several other pages are reachable, which allow one to browse the content of the catalog.

Figure 1 shows the data model of the case study, using the simplified E-R notation of WebML; the *Product, Combination,* and *Store* constitute the core entities of the data schema; products are clustered in *Categories* and associated with *Images* and a *Technical Record.*

A Web application is specified on top of a data model by means of one or more *site views,* comprising *pages,* possibly clustered into *areas,* and containing various kinds of data publishing components (*content units* in the WebML jargon) connected by *links.*

Figure 2 shows a fragment of the site view for publishing the content of the Product Catalog application. The *Home* page contains two data publishing components (*data units*), which display selected attributes of a product and of a combination object, and one *entry unit,* which denotes a data entry form. The units have outgoing links, which enable navigation and parameter passing. For example, the *ProductOfTheDay* data unit has an outgoing link that permits the user to reach the *Product Page,* where all the details of the product displayed in the home page are shown. The *Product* page contains further content units, connected to the *Product details* data unit by *transport links* (represented as dashed arrows), which only allow parameter passing and are not rendered as navigable anchors.

The WebML PIMs can be automatically translated into a running application, by means of the WebRatio tool suite [3]. The WebRatio code generator produces all the implementation artifacts for the Java2EE deployment platform, exploiting the popular MVC2 Struts presentation framework and the Hibernate persistence layer. In particular, the View components can utilize any rendition platform

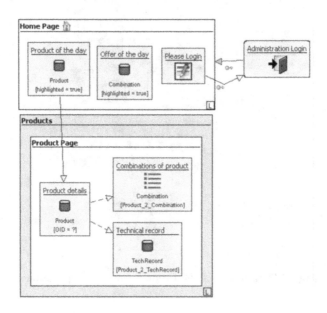

Fig. 2. Site view of the Product Catalog Application

(e.g., HTML, FLASH, Ajax), because the code generator is designed to be extensible: the generative rules producing the components of the View adopt a template-based style and thus can incorporate examples of layout for the various WebML elements (pages and content units) coded in arbitrary rendition languages.

In the case study, a testing session is expressed at high level using the concepts that appear in the application model. In the subsequent Sections, we will use the following example:

1. Go to the Home Page of the Product Catalog
2. Check that the ProductOfTheDay data unit displays the 'Aladdin' item
3. Navigate the outgoing link of the ProductOfTheDay unit

Despite its simplicity, the above test can reveal several bugs. Step 1 checks that the Home page is correctly generated and that the communication between the client and the Web server works properly. Step 2 verifies that the item extracted from the database is correct. Step 3 tests the navigation from the Home Page to another Web page, verifying that the link in the Home Page exists and has proper parameters and that that the destination page is computed properly.

With an implementation-oriented approach, an equivalent case must be encoded manually, by navigating the generated HTML pages and asserting conditions on the HTML content (e.g. images, input forms, strings, etc.). Furthermore, the resulting script depends on the graphical layout. For example, step (3) requires evaluating an XPath expression over the page markup: the evaluation of some XPath expressions may change if the page layout is updated (even if functionality does not change).

3   HOT for Weaving Traceability Links into the Code Generation Transformation

One way of circumventing the semantic gap between the application model and the implementation subjected to regression testing is enhancing the implementation with traceability clues, which have no functional meaning but can help linking the occurrence of a failure to the model elements more likely to bear responsibility.

In the context of MDE, this task can be achieved by a Higher Order Transformation, that is, a transformation that acts on the transformation used for generating the code.

Figure 3 pictorially illustrates the HOT framework: the code generation process can be seen as a model-to-model transformation (T1 in Figure 3) that maps an input model at level M1 (the WebML model of the application) into a an executable model (the Java2EE code). T1 is normally a lossy transformation: since its purpose is to produce the code to be actually executed, no extra information is added to the output model and the links between the input and output artifacts are lost.

Adding traceability to the generative framework of Figure 3 requires preserving the relationship between the elements of the input model and the elements of the output model derived from them. Traceability links can be stored: 1) in the input model; 2) in the output model; 3) in a separate ad-hoc model.

In this paper, we have opted for the second solution, but in our case the transformation T2, which produces an output model comprising the needed traceability links, is dynamically generated from T1. In this way, T1 can still be used to produce the concise and efficient code needed for application execution, but the traceability links needed for regression testing can be obtained by using T2.

With this solution, the major problem is to ensure the consistency between T2 and T1, so that the code produced for testing is exactly equivalent to the production code, modulo the presence of traceability links.

This result can be attained by deriving T2 automatically from T1 by means of a HOT, as depicted in Figure 4.

The input of the HOT is the M2M transformation that produces the implementation code. This transformation can be seen as a model, represented by the

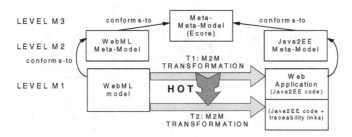

Fig. 3. Using HOT to weave traceability links into the code generator transformation

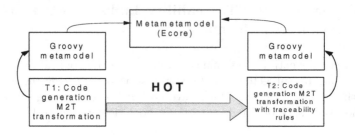

Fig. 4. Input and Output Models of the HOT

chosen transformation language (Groovy, in our case study). The output is another transformation, derived by extending the input model with extra elements (additional code generation rules and templates) for producing the traceability links in the implementation code.

Figure 5 shows the internal structure of the input model of the HOT (i.e., the original Groovy code generation transformation).

The transformation is organized into three sub-transformations.

The *Layout Transformation* generates a set of JSP pages (one for each page of the WebML model) and miscellaneous elements required by the target platform: Struts configuration (i.e. the controller in the Struts MVC architecture), localization bundles, and form validators.

The *Business Logic Transformation* generates a set of XML files (logic descriptors) describing the run-time behavior of the elements of the source model, mainly pages, links, and units. In addition, this transformation produces secondary artifacts, such as the access/authentication logic.

The *Persistence Transformation* produces the standard Hibernate artifacts: Java Beans and configuration mapping (one for each entity of the source model) as well as the overall database configuration.

The sub-transformations are based on Groovy. Being the output a set of structured XML and JSP/HTML files, the Groovy generators use a template-based

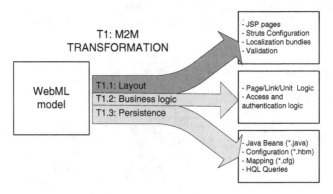

Fig. 5. Structure of T1 transformation

approach: each sub-transformation comprises templates similar to the expected output (e.g., XML or HTML) enriched with scriptlets for looking-up the needed elements of the source model.

The HOT must apply to the relevant original transformation rules and produce extended rules such that: 1) they generate the same output elements as the original rules; 2) they add the needed traceability links to the output.

The design of the HOT requires deciding where to store the traceability links in the output model (the Java2EE code) and what information to use for the trace links. In the present version of the HOT, the following design decisions have been taken:

- The traceability link information amounts to the id, name and published values of the content units appearing within the pages of the WebML model, and to the id, name and parameters of navigable links.
- Such traceability links are stored into the View elements of the output model, so that they can be easily added to the recording of the user's navigation.

The above-mentioned design choices entail that the HOT takes only the layout sub-transformation in input, because this is the only one that produces the View elements. The traceability links are stored within presentation-neutral, transparent elements (e.g., HTML DIV elements) added to the View artifacts of the output model (namely, the JSP pages).

An example can help illustrate the modified behavior of T2 with respect to T1.

The *ProductOfTheDay* data unit of Figure 2 can be represented by the following fragment of the input model[1]:

```
<DataUnit id="dau16" name="Product of the day">
 <Selector id="dau16sel">
   <AttributesCondition attributes="att23"
       name="highlight"/>
 </Selector>
</DataUnit>
```

Transformation T1 (for an XHTML implementation of the View) maps the data unit into JSP code that produces the following mark-up fragment, for a specific product named "Aladdin":

```
<table>
 <tr>   <td>Aladdin</td> </tr>
 <tr>   <td>1500</td> </tr>
 <tr>   <td><img src="images/small_table.jpg"/></td> </tr>
</table>
```

Transformation T2, derived from T1, maps the data unit into JSP code that produces a mark-up fragment enhanced with traceability links:

```
<div id="testUnit id:dau16 name:Product of the day">
 <table>
 <tr>   <td><div id="testAttribute id:att10 name:name
       type:string unitName:Product of the day">
       Aladdin
          </div></td> </tr>
```

---

[1] WebML has both a visual notation and an XML syntax, and is also equipped with a MOF metamodel; for simplicity, in the example, we use the XML syntax.

```
<tr>    <td><div id="testAttribute id:att11 name:price
        type:float unitName:Product of the day">
        1500
            </div></td> </tr>
<tr>    <td><div id="testAttribute id:att12 name:thumbnail
        type:blob  unitName:Product of the day">
        <img src="images/small_table.jpg" />
            </div></td> </tr>
</table>
</div>
```

The trace clues, inserted in rendition-neutral DIV elements, link the output model (e.g., an XHTML table cell containing the string 'Aladdin") to the input model (e.g., the *name* attribute published by the *ProductOfTheDay* data unit).

To show how the HOT is implemented in a generic way, we illustrate the creation of the traceability link for a content unit. The HOT locates the following instruction in T1:

```
<%printRaw(executeTemplate(templateFile.absolutePath,
    ["params" : unitLayout.parameters,
                "templateType" : "unit"])) %>
```

The instruction is an explicit call to the Groovy transformation rules for the unit content. It will be translated by the HOT to a new version in T2 that contains an additional DIV element:

```
<div id="testUnit_id:<%=unitId%>_name:<%=unitName%>_">
        <%printRaw(executeTemplate(templateFile.absolutePath,
            ["params" : unitLayout.parameters,
                        "templateType" : "unit"])) %>
</div>
```

This translation is achieved by the following HOT rule:

```
rule UnitLink {
  from
    matched : GroovyMM!Scriptlet (
    matched.statements->recursiveExists(p |
    p.oclIsKindOf(GroovyMM!MethodInvocation) and s.name='printRaw' and
    s.arguments->exists(e | e.oclIsKindOf('GroovyMM!MethodInvocation')) and
        e.name='executeTemplate' and
        e.arguments->at(2).oclIsKindOf('GroovyMM!Map') and
        e.arguments->at(2).elements->exists(t |
        t.key='templateType' and
        t.value.oclIsKindOf('GroovyMM!String') and t.value.value='unit')
    to
    div : GroovyMM!Tag (
        name <- 'div', attributes <- Sequence{id}, children <- Sequence{c}),
        id : GroovyMM!TagAttribute (
        name <- 'id', value <-'testUnit_id:<%=unitId%>_name:<%=unitName%>_'
    )
    c : GroovyMM!Scriptlet (
        statements <- matched.statements
    )
}
```

The HOT rule matches any Groovy scriptlet that prints the result of an executeTemplate call to a unit template, i.e. a call with a parameter *templateType* = *'unit'*. The output pattern of the rule is a *Tag* named *div* containing a *TagAttribute* named *id* representing an encoding of the traceability link. The matched scriptlet is finally copied as a child of this Tag.

4   Test Session Recording and Execution

The modified T2 transformation produces traceability links in the generated code, so that the resulting application can be exploited to record model-aware testing sessions.

For recording the test sessions, a *Test Session Recorder* has been designed, by extending the TestGen4Web Firefox add-on [30], so to recognize the trace links in the page rendition and save them in the final test script automatically, without any user's intervention.

As an example, consider the testing session of Section 2. Once the recording is stopped, the navigation is saved in an XML file compliant with the syntax of Canoo WebTest, shown below:

```
/*step 1*/
<testInfo type="trace" info="page1"/>
<echo message="Go to the URL: http://www.acme.com"/>
<wrInvoke url="http://www.acme.com"/>

/*step 2*/
<verifyXPath text=".*Aladdin.*"
  xpath="//div[@id='testUnit_id:dau16
          _name:Product of the day_']
     //div[@id='testAttribute_id:att10
     _name:name_type:string
     _unitName:Product of the day_']"/>

/*step 3*/
<testInfo type="input" info="Aladdin"/>
<testInfo type="trace" info="ln30"/>
<wrClicklink fieldIndex="0"
   label="More.." exactmatch="true"
   description="Click the link labeled More.."/>
```

The test script contains, besides the usual Canoo tags, additional information coming from the trace links.

Each step is annotated by the ID of the model element involved (e.g, as in `<testInfo type="trace" info="page1">`). Assertion steps, e.g., step (2), are expressed by means of XPath expressions that do not depend on the graphical layout, but only on the identifiers of the model elements. If the code is regenerated with a different style or layout, the assertion remains valid.

Trace links are also enhanced with dynamic information about the objects appearing in the navigated page. For instance, step (3) shows the case of the navigation of a link, where the `<testInfo type="input" info="Aladdin">` annotation stores the name of the object that is associated with the navigated link as a parameter. In this way, session recording can take advantage of the dynamic information coming from the objects of the data model, and blend it with the information on the user's interactions with the page widgets (e.g, single or multiple selections from indexes, selections from combo boxes, and so on).

The final element of the proposed regression testing environment is the *Regression Testing Plug-in*, a component of the WebRatio tool suite that allow modelers to perform regression testing from within the same tool they use for design and code generation.

The Regression Testing Plug-in executes the recorded scrips using the Canoo WebTest platform and collects the outcome of the execution, linking each step to the model elements it refers to.

The plug-in exploits the information stored inside the test script by the Navigation Recorder to reflect the user's navigation onto the WebML model, thanks to the identifier of the elements; the plug-in can replay a session visually and can overlay the dynamic information on the navigated objects over the model elements, as shown in Figure 6.

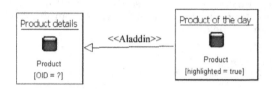

Fig. 6. Visual replay of the testing session with dynamic information overlaid on the WebML model

The replay of a testing session from within the WebRatio IDE is achieved by a client/server connection between the WebRatio Regression Testing Plugin and the Canoo test environment.

The WebRatio plug-in acts as a server and starts the test environment as a client. The client, in turn, opens a new socket to communicate with the server sending to it the testing session trace. Once the test execution ends, the server collects all the identifiers of the WebML elements that have been reached during the test execution together with the information on the outcome of each step. The WebRatio plug-in presents the regression test results in a tabular pane (see Figure 7), where each row displays the identifiers of the WebML elements, their input and a description in natural language of the current step.

Using the provided visualizations, developers can monitor the regression steps and correlate them to the involved elements of the WebML model. In the case of a test failure, the plug-in also catches the exceptions launched from the test

Step #	WebML Element	Input	Description
	page1		Go to the URL: http://localhost:8080/Acme/page1.do
	ln30	Aladdin	Click on the label More... of Aladdin
	page18		Click on the label By price
	ln44	Lucid	Click on the label Details of Lucid
	page1		Go to the URL: http://localhost:8080/Acme/page1.do
	ln30	Aladdin	Click on the label More... of Aladdin

Step #	WebML Element	Input	Description	Error
0	page1		Go to the URL: http://localhost:8080/Acme/page1.do	
	ln30	ERROR	Click on label More... of Aladdin	label More... not found

Fig. 7. Tabular representation of a test: success (top) and failure (bottom)

environment, and reports the cause of the errors in the debugging pane (as shown in the bottom part of Figure 7).

5 Implementation

The HOT has been implemented using the ATL language and the AmmA [10] framework. To integrate the Groovy language in the transformation framework, a Groovy metamodel has been developed extending the JavaAbstractSyntax metamodel provided by the MoDisco project [1].

The Test Session Recorder has been implemented extending the Firefox Test-Gen4Web add-on, using XUL and Javascript. In particular, the Javascript module that generates the output has been modified to produce XML files compliant with Canoo WebTest. Furthermore, its code has been refactored to manage every type of assertions in a separate sub-module.

The WebRatio Regression Testing Plug-in has been implemented by means of: 1) a a Java component that runs the Canoo WebTest environment, taking the test script as input, and elaborates the information received from the test execution; 2) an Eclipse view that visualizes the execution outcome. The communication between the test execution platform and WebRatio is regulated using auxiliary Groovy tags inserted in the test script by the Test Session Recorder.

6 Related Work

The task of optimizing the regression testing phase has been addressed in literature especially from the point of view of selective regression testing [27], i.e. of optimizing the regression test set removing superfluous tests. The importance of model-based specifications, for generating and selecting test cases, is already recognized [15]. The HOT framework presented in this paper, as a general approach to embed high-level information in low level code, can be naturally used to address these concerns. In this paper we presented also an original application of the method that facilitates the manual development of regression test cases.

Our application makes use of traceability links to connect the generated implementation with model-based specifications. The concept of traceability links has been widely investigated in literature. A first classification of traceability has been made between *traceability in the small* and *traceability in the large* [8]. The former is intended to handle the trace information between model elements, i.e. information about how different elements of source and target models are linked together; the latter traces information between models in the whole, in order to have information about relationships between distinct models. In some approaches the traceability mechanism is implicitly embedded in the tool's algorithms [11],[25], while other approaches represent traceability relationships explicitly, e.g., [18]. In this latter case, the location where the links are stored, can be the source and/or target model, or separate (e.g, by means of a GUIDE in each model element and traceability information separate from the source and target models). Our approach realizes traceability in the small representing explicitly the traceability links in the target model.

Transformation frameworks can address traceability during the design of transformations [14], either by providing dedicated support for traceability (e.g., Tefkat [22], QVT [2]), or by encoding traceability as any other link between the input and output models (e.g., VIATRA [33], GreAT [6]). Traceability links may be encoded manually in the transformation rules (e.g., [22]), or inserted automatically (e.g., [2]). The HOT-based approach that we propose can be used to add traceability support to languages like groovy, that do not provide any built-in support to automatic or manual traceability links.

With respect to hard-coding the traceability mechanism when developing the transformation, our use of a HOT favors reusability and extension, because the feature to be weaved into the transformation is managed separately.

A general traceability system using HOTs is already implemented in [20], where the HOT adds to each original transformation rule the production of a traceability link in an external ad-hoc traceability model (conforming to a small traceability metamodel). In other analogous solutions, such as [17], the traceability links are represented by an ad-hoc extension of a standard metamodel for modeling correspondences, the Atlas Weaving Metamodel [16]. Our approach differs from these in merging traceability links within the target metamodel, i.e. the generated implementation code. We showed how this technique is useful in the Web domain to derive model-based test cases from hypertext navigations.

Finally Aspect Oriented Development can be considered as a particular case of HOT. Using a generic transformation language for defining the HOT, our approach has a higher expressing power and flexibility, allowing the definition of complex HOT rules.

7   Conclusions

In this paper we have presented a framework for supporting regression testing in MDE environment. The framework supports the phases of: 1) recording a testing session with a conventional Record & Play tool; 2) replaying the recorded session from within the same IDE that is used for application modeling and code generation; 3) tracing the failures of a test session to the model elements most related to them. The core of the approach is the connection between the conceptual model, which the developer uses to specify and build the application, and the generated code, which is exploited to record and play the testing session. Such a connection is established by traceability links between the input model and the generated code, automatically inserted by a modified version of the code generator. This modified version is itself produced automatically, by exploiting the powerful paradigm of Higher Order Transformation (HOT), which are transformations that operate on other transformation. The resulting framework enables MDE developers to perform regression testing in an effective way, without breaking the level of abstraction entailed by the use of models as the principal artifact of design.

The ongoing and future work will focus on: 1) Extending the HOT to obtain a code generator capable of producing application code instrumented for the step-by-step debugging of the sequences of operations, which are now executed as black boxes; 2) Structuring the HOT in a modular way, so that it is possible to weave different orthogonal aspects in the code generator, e.g., the insertion of performance verification code or of security code (e.g. alternative URL encoding and encryption policies). 3) Supporting selective regression testing [24]: when a change is made, the collaborative work function of WebRatio can be used to identify the list of differences between the original and modified model and to select a minimal set of sessions to execute. From an analysis of differences, it could also be possible to launch the extended code generator and session recorder to automatically synthesize the sessions needed for covering the new parts of the model.

Acknowledgment. We wish to thank Alessandro Baffa for the implementation work and the WebRatio Team for the evaluation of the testing framework.

References

1. MoDisco home page, http://www.eclipse.org/gmt/modisco/
2. QVT 1.0., http://www.omg.org/spec/QVT/1.0/
3. WebRatio, http://www.webratio.com
4. Abrahao, S., Pastor, O.: Measuring the functional size of web applications. Int. J. Web Eng. Technol. 1(1), 5–16 (2003)
5. Abrahão, S.M., Mendes, E., Gómez, J., Insfrán, E.: A model-driven measurement procedure for sizing web applications: Design, automation and validation. In: MoDELS, pp. 467–481 (2007)
6. Agrawal, A., Karsai, G., Shi, F.: Graph transformations on domain-specific models. Technical report, ISIS (November 2003)
7. Baerisch, S.: Model-driven test-case construction. In: ESEC-FSE Companion 2007: 6th Joint Meeting on European SE Conf. and the ACM SIGSOFT Symp. on the Foundations of SE, pp. 587–590. ACM, New York (2007)
8. Barbero, M., Del Fabro, M.D., Bézivin, J.: Traceability and provenance issues in global model management. In: 3rd ECMDA-Traceability Workshop (2007)
9. Baresi, L., Fraternali, P., Tisi, M., Morasca, S.: Towards model-driven testing of a web application generator. In: Lowe, D.G., Gaedke, M. (eds.) ICWE 2005. LNCS, vol. 3579, pp. 75–86. Springer, Heidelberg (2005)
10. Bézivin, J., Jouault, F., Touzet, D.: An introduction to the ATLAS model management architecture. Research Report LINA(05-01) (2005)
11. Briand, L., Labiche, Y., Soccar, G.: Automating impact analysis and regression test selection based on uml designs. In: IEEE International Conference on Software Maintenance, p. 252 (2002)
12. Canoo. Canoo Web Test (2008), http://webtest.canoo.com
13. Ceri, S., Fraternali, P., Bongio, A., Brambilla, M., Comai, S., Matera, M.: Designing Data-Intensive Web Applications. Morgan Kaufmann, USA (2002)
14. Czarnecki, K., Helsen, S.: Classification of model transformation approaches. In: OOPSLA 2003 Workshop on Generative Techniques in the Context of MDA (2003)
15. Dick, J., Faivre, A.: Automating the generation and sequencing of test cases from Model-Based specifications. In: Larsen, P.G., Woodcock, J.C.P. (eds.) FME 1993. LNCS, vol. 670, pp. 268–284. Springer, Heidelberg (1993)

16. Del Fabro, M.D., Bézivin, J., Jouault, F., Breton, E., Gueltas, G.: Amw: a generic model weaver. In: 1ére Journée sur l'Ingénierie Dirigée par les Modèles (IDM 2005) (2005)

17. GMT Project. Amw use case - traceability (February 2008), http://www.eclipse.org/gmt/amw/usecases/traceability

18. Hartman, A., Nagin, K.: The AGEDIS tools for model based testing. SIGSOFT Softw. Eng. Notes 29(4), 129–132 (2004)

19. HTMLUnit Team. HTMLUnit (2008), http://htmlunit.sourceforge.net/

20. Jouault, F.: Loosely coupled traceability for atl. In: European Conference on Model Driven Architecture (ECMDA), workshop on traceability (2005)

21. JWebUnit Team. JWebUnit (2008), http://jwebunit.sourceforge.net/

22. Lawley, M., Steel, J.: Practical declarative model transformation with tefkat. In: Bruel, J.-M. (ed.) MoDELS 2005. LNCS, vol. 3844, pp. 139–150. Springer, Heidelberg (2006)

23. Li, N., Ma, Q.-q., Wu, J., Jin, M.-z., Liu, C.: A framework of model-driven web application testing. In: COMPSAC 2006, Washington, DC, USA, pp. 157–162. IEEE Computer Society, Los Alamitos (2006)

24. Naslavsky, L., Richardson, D.J.: Using traceability to support model-based regression testing. In: ASE 2007, pp. 567–570. ACM, New York (2007)

25. Nebut, C., Fleurey, F., Le Traon, Y., Jezequel, J.: Automatic test generation: A use case driven approach. IEEE Transactions on SE 32(3), 155, 140 (2006)

26. Pretschner, A.: Model-based testing in practice. In: Fitzgerald, J.S., Hayes, I.J., Tarlecki, A. (eds.) FM 2005. LNCS, vol. 3582, pp. 537–541. Springer, Heidelberg (2005)

27. Rothermel, G., Harrold, M.J.: Analyzing regression test selection techniques. IEEE Transactions on Software Engineering 22(8), 529–551 (1996)

28. Saad, M.A., Kamenzky, N., Schiller, J.: Visual scatterUnit: A visual model-driven testing framework of wireless sensor networks applications. In: Czarnecki, K., Ober, I., Bruel, J.-M., Uhl, A., Völter, M. (eds.) MODELS 2008. LNCS, vol. 5301, pp. 751–765. Springer, Heidelberg (2008)

29. Selenium Project. Seleniumhq (2008), http://seleniumhq.org/

30. Vinay Srini. Testgen4web (2008), http://developer.spikesource.com/blogs/vsrini/2008/06/testgen4web_update_10_1.html

31. Stahl, T., Voelter, M., Czarnecki, K.: Model-Driven Software Development: Technology, Engineering, Management. John Wiley & Sons, Chichester (2006)

32. The Apache Jakarta Project. Cactus (2008), http://jakarta.apache.org/cactus

33. Varró, D., Varró, G., Pataricza, A.: Designing the automatic transformation of visual languages. Sci. Comput. Program. 44(2), 205–227 (2002)

Exploring XML Perturbation Techniques for Web Services Testing

Paulo Silveira and Ana C. V. de Melo

University of São Paulo
Department of Computer Science
São Paulo, Brazil
{silveira,acvm}@ime.usp.br

Abstract. This paper presents testing techniques to automatically generate a set of test cases and data for web services. These techniques extend the ones based on Data Perturbation presented by Offutt and Xu, to which are added mutation operators, boundary values considering XML Schema facets, testing cases using relationship defined in the message schema, UDDI integration and an internal database to collect and use values previously captured from messages. Together with these techniques, a tool (*GenAutoWS*) was developed for proof of concepts.

1 Introduction

Most organizations today rely on information systems as part of their business process. The need to exchange data between different applications requires these applications to be more flexible and interoperable. Web Services emerged to support such requirements: services can communicate with each other by passing data from one service to another or by coordinating an activity between two or more services. Web services and SOA (Service-Oriented Architecture), which has been strongly implemented with Web services, have then received substantial attention from academy and industry.

The massive use of SOA and Web services in heterogeneous systems requires a high quality of development standards. Automated test tools, in particular, can help improving such quality. However, systems built on the top of Web services differ from traditional systems and testing techniques and tools applied to the latter cannot be directly applied to former.

Due to the particular features and the widespread use of Web services in industrial software, testing Web services has recently received more attention [11]. In [6], Huang et al. pointed out two major approaches to address the Web services testing problem: automatic testing and model checking. New techniques have been proposed undergoing these approaches since then.

Tsai et al. [11] proposed a hierarchical testing framework to generate test scenarios based on WSDL (Web Service Description Language) specifications, together with some WSDL improvements. Huang et al. [6] presented a model checking process for OWL-S (Web Ontology Language for Web Services) in which

M. Gaedke, M. Grossniklaus, and O. Díaz (Eds.): ICWE 2009, LNCS 5648, pp. 355–369, 2009.
© Springer-Verlag Berlin Heidelberg 2009

the model checker BLAST [2] is extended to cope with concurrency in OWL-S. Some OWL-S extensions were also proposed. Song et al. [10] described a testing framework, named Coyote, that consists of a test master and a test engine. The test master allows the tester specifying test scenarios and cases, performing a set of analysis such as services dependency, completeness and consistency. The test engine interacts with Web services providing traces information.

Regarding the test automation approach, Offutt and Xu [8] presented a Web Services testing technique based on data perturbation. Existing XML (Extensible Markup Language) messages are modified based on message grammars rules and data perturbation on values and interactions. The set of these modified messages are then used as test suites. Concerned with the automation approach, the present work extends the data perturbation testing technique by Offutt and Xu by adding mutation operators, boundary values considering XML Schema facets, testing cases using relationship defined in the WSDL, UDDI (Universal Description, Discovery and Integration) integration, internal database to collect and use values previously captured from messages. As proof of concept, a tool was developed, *GenAutoWS* , embedding the previous and the new techniques presented here.

The forthcoming sections present: some fundamental concepts on Web services and SOA; an existing technique to test Web services; the new testing techniques based on data perturbation; some experimental results regarding the new techniques; and, finally, some concluding remarks on the presented techniques.

2   Web Services and SOA Preliminaries

SOA (Service-Oriented Architecture) is essentially an architectural style to allow a collection of loosely coupled software agents interacting with each other[5]. The most common way of implementing such an architecture is by the use of Web Services.

There are today many definitions for Web Services. According to W3C [15], Web Services are software systems designed to support machine-to-machine interaction over a network via well-defined interfaces. A Web service is specified in a standard way by a *service descriptor* using a service description language, WSDL (Web Service Description Language [14]), for example. Each service descriptor must contain all the information needed to make the service interaction possible, including message format, transportation protocol and binding information.

Web services can interact with other systems in the way described by the service descriptors, using SOAP (Simple Object Access Protocol) to receive and send information. SOAP exchanges XML-based messages over another application layer protocol, normally HTTP (Hypertext Transfer Protocol) or MIME (Multipurpose Internet Mail Extensions). Those messages can differ in style, the two most common messages types are *RPC (Remote Procedure Call)* and *Document*. The RPC messages wrap program methods into the message, allowing them to be remotely invoked. The body contains a single element and all parameters are sub-elements. By contrast, in the Document style, the message content is placed directly into the body element, making Document-based Web services loosely coupled and document driven. A simple example of a Web Service message, using Document style, for a *Movie Rental Store* is shown in Listing 1.1. In this example, the driving license identifies the customer and the message contains a list of movies, each one with an id, price and media type.

Listing 1.1. XML document - Movie Rental Store

```
...
    <id>
    <drivingLicense>S1234-123456-12</drivingLicense>
    </id>
    <moviesList>
        <movie>
            <id>12</id>
            <media>DVD</media>
            <price>3.25</price>
        </movie>
        <movie>
            <id>130</id>
            <media>DVD</media>
            <price>3.25</price>
        </movie>
    </moviesList>
...
```

SOAP depends on XML standards, such as *XML Schema* and *XML Namespaces*. XML Schemas are used to describe messages exchanged by Web services. As such, Schemas define content, structure and semantics of XML documents that can be shared between applications. Restrictions on XML elements are called facets. Listing 1.2 shows an XML schema for the Listing 1.1. In this XML schema, we can see constraints on the elements: *drivingLicense, media* and *price*, it also uses the order indicator *choice* in the element ID and the occurrence indicator *minOccurs* and *maxOccurs* restricting the number of movies in this Web service call.

Listing 1.2. Schema for Movie Rental Store

```
<?xml version="1.0" encoding="UTF-8"?>
<xs:schema xmlns:xs="http://www.w3.org/2001/XMLSchema"
           elementFormDefault="qualified">
  <xs:element name="movieRental">
    <xs:complexType>
      <xs:sequence minOccurs="0" maxOccurs="1">
        <xs:element name="ID">
          <xs:complexType>
            <xs:choice>
              <xs:element name="drivingLicense">
                <xs:simpleType>
                  <xs:restriction base="xs:string">
                    <xs:pattern value="[A-Z][0-9]{4}-[0-9]{6}-[0-9]{2}"/>
                  </xs:restriction>
                </xs:simpleType>
              </xs:element>
              <xs:element name="memberNumber" type="xs:decimal"/>
            </xs:choice>
          </xs:complexType>
        </xs:element>
        <xs:element name="moviesList">
          <xs:complexType>
            <xs:sequence>
```

```
<xs:element name="movie" minOccurs="1" maxOccurs="5">
  <xs:complexType>
    <xs:sequence>
      <xs:element name="id" type="xs:int"/>
      <xs:element name="media">
        <xs:simpleType>
          <xs:restriction base="xs:string">
            <xs:enumeration value="BLURAY"/>
            <xs:enumeration value="DVD"/>
            <xs:enumeration value="VHS"/>
          </xs:restriction>
        </xs:simpleType>
      </xs:element>
      <xs:element name="price">
        <xs:simpleType>
          <xs:restriction base="xs:decimal">
            <xs:fractionDigits value="2"/>
          </xs:restriction>
          ...
```
</xs:schema>

The Universal Description, Discovery and Integration (UDDI) [12] specification is used to catalog the Web Services. The implementation of this specification is called UDDI registry, representing data and metadata about Web Services. UDDI registry includes a set of Web Services to allow service to be published and found.

Web services are rather used in a very distributed and heterogenous contexts and require dynamic integration. Their applications interact in three different ways: **publishing**, the service provider makes a service interface available to other services; **finding**, other services (requesters) must be able to discover the service interface; **binding**, address the ability to connect and invoke services. Many of these features make Web services differ from traditional and web applications and the testing must be performed accordingly. Web services must be tested considering also communication aspects [8,11]: discovering Web services, the data format exchanged, and the request/response mechanisms. Testing SOAP messages addresses request/response mechanism and data format aspects of Web services. WSDL is used to expose interfaces as services available on the Internet. Testing WSDL files can be used to generate test plans to validate services. Testing UDDI registries provides the capabilities of publishing, finding and binding of SOA, giving the way software is integrated.

3   A Web Services Testing Technique Based on Data Perturbation

Data perturbation testing technique consists of changing (perturbing) existing data to create new test sets. For Web Services, Offutt and Xu [8] presented a data perturbation technique based on data value and interaction perturbations. **Data value perturbation** modifies values using data type information, following the boundary value testing approach [1]. For this, a set of rules for XML data types, corresponding to the primitive types in most programming languages, were created. Table 1 shows the data types with the corresponding

Table 1. Data value perturbation

Data Type	Boundary Values
String	Maximum length, minimum length, upper case, lower case
Numeric	Maximum value, minimum value, zero
Boolean	true, false

data value perturbations to be applied. Then, for each test data, new ones are created based on the boundary values.

For **interaction perturbation**, messages are modified according to their types: *RPC* or *data communications*. For RPC messages, testing is focused on data uses and mutation operators. The traditional mutation operators were redefined for Web Services[8], as shown in Table 2.

Table 2. Data type operators

Divide (n)	Change value n to $1 \div n$, where n is double data type
Multiply (n)	Change value n to $n \times n$
Negative (n)	Change value n to $-n$
Absolute (n)	Change value n to $\lceil n \rceil$
Exchange (n_1, n_2)	Substitute value n_1 for n_2 and vice-versa, where n_1 and n_2 have the same type.
Unauthorized (str)	Change string value str to str' OR '1' = '1

For *data communications* (document-based messages), testing focus on relationships and constraints (defined by facets in XML Schemas). To precisely define these, XML Schema are defined using RTG (Regular Tree Grammar), a formal model for XML schemas.

Definition 1. *A regular tree grammar is a 6-tuple $< E, D, N, A, P, n_s >$, where:*

1. *E is a finite set of element types*
2. *D is a finite set of data types*
3. *N is a finite set of non-terminals*
4. *A is a finite set of attribute types*
5. *P is a finite set of production rules with two forms:*
    - *$n \rightarrow a < d >$, where n is non-terminal in N; a is either an attribute type in A or an element type in E, and d is a data type in D;*
    - *$n \rightarrow e < r >$, where n is non-terminal in N; e is an element in E, and r is a regular expression comprised of non-terminals.*
6. *n_s is the starting non-terminal, $n_s \in N$*

Based on the *maxOccurs* attribute of XML schemas (a relationship defined as XML facet - see Listing 1.2, for example), the parent-child associations are acquired and a regular expression for the relationship is created[1]. For these relationships, some testing strategies were defined[8]:

---

[1] In the regular expressions, operators '?', '+', and '*' denote zero-or-one, at least one, and any number of element occurrences, respectively. These operators reflect cardinality constraints in an XML Schema.

- Given a relationship $n \rightarrow e < r >$, if there is an expression α? in r, there will be two test cases: an α and an empty instance.
- Given a relationship $n \rightarrow e < r >$, if there is an expression $\alpha+$ in r, there will be two test cases: an α and a number of α instances.
- Given a relationship $n \rightarrow e < r >$, if there is an expression $\alpha^*\alpha$ in r, there will be two test cases. One contains $\alpha^*\alpha$ and the other contains α^{*-1}, where $\alpha^*\alpha$ duplicates one element instance and α^{*-1} deletes one element instance.

Besides that strategy based on relationships, in [16], a method to generate tests for XML-based communication by modification and further instantiation of XML schemas was presented. Schemas are modified based on predefined perturbation operators. The goal is to perturb XML Schemas to create invalid XML messages. With this aim, seven perturbation operators for XML Schema were defined; some are applied to nodes and others to sub-trees. For nodes, the operators are: insert and delete a new node between two other nodes, insert and delete a new node with a data type under an existing node. The sub-tree operators are: insert and delete a sub-tree below a node and change an edge between two nodes using an edge with different constraints. Almeida and Vergilio [4] extended that work with six new mutation operators for SOAP messages, together with a tool to generate modified messages. Table 3 shows the operators defined by them.

Table 3. Mutation operators - SOAP

Operator name	Brief description
Null(n)	Set to *null* the value assigned to a node n in the SOAP message.
Incomplete(n)	Delete a node n and its child nodes from the SOAP message.
Inversion (n)	Inverts the order of nodes within node n in the given SOAP message.
ValueInversion (n)	Inverts the order of the values assigned to the child nodes of node n in the given XML message.
Mod_Len (n)	Modifies the length of the value assigned to node n in the given XML message.
Space (n)	Set to ' ' the value assigned to node n.

4   A New Technique on Test Cases Generation for Web Services

This section presents a new testing technique based on [8] and [4]. The extensions to the previous works aim to increase the test coverage, creating new messages with information not explored by original works, mainly from XML Schemas:

1. boundary analysis is enlarged with values immediately above and below the data type domain, as defined by Pressman[9] and Myers[7];
2. XML facets are also considered in boundary analysis;
3. new relationship rules are added to data communication perturbation, including choice and all, and the occurrence indicator *minOccurs*; and
4. four new mutation operators are defined for RPC messages.

Either for data value and interaction perturbation, invalid cases are also considered. This means that the Web Service should return an error when test suites corresponding to these test cases are executed. For example, if the valid set of values for a given element is 1, 2 and 3 and the message generated has the value 4, this test case will be classified as invalid. This property intends to help in the oracle test.

4.1 Extending Data Value Perturbation

Web services using literal messages can be defined by XML Schema and the legal values for each simple type can be constrained using XML Schema Facets. There are twelve different Facets. Offutt and Xu [8] has considered only the `maximum` and `minimum` values and the `totaldigits` Facets under valid values. We improved the test of these facets by adding test cases for invalid values (when executed, these messages should receive an error message). Apart from these, all other XML Schema Facets were considered to create new messages. We use these Facets to assist in the data value perturbation. Here, the facets and the corresponding test cases are presented.

Pattern: Defines the valid content for a data type, specified by a regular expression. We use pattern values to generated valid and invalid messages. For the `drivingLicense` type definition showed in Listing 1.2, the new messages in Table 4 corresponds to the test suites generated for the Pattern test cases:

Table 4. Test suites for pattern in Listing 1.2

<drivingLicense>Z9999-999999-99</drivingLicense>	Valid
<drivingLicense>A0000-000000-00</drivingLicense>	Valid
<drivingLicense>9ZZZZ-ZZZZZZ-ZZ</drivingLicense>	Invalid

A *regular expression quantifier* specifies how often that preceding character or group is allowed to occur. A predefined number should be used to create test cases to messages that has the quantifier '*' or '+'.

Enumeration: Constrains the valid values of a data type to a specified set. A message is generated for each value in the given enumeration set. An invalid message is also generated with a value out of this set. For the `media` type definition presented in Listing 1.2, the technique generates the messages showed in Table 5:

Table 5. Test Suites for enumeration

<media>DVD</media>	Valid
<media>VHS</media>	Valid
<media>ZZZZZZZZ</media>	Invalid

FractionDigits: Specifies the maximum number of digits allowed in the fractional part of numbers. The value must be equal or greater than zero. Three messages are generated: one with the maximum number of digits, the second with one digit and an invalid message with oversized fractional digits.

Length: Specifies the number of character or list items are allowed. A valid message and an invalid message are generated. The invalid message has an extra character than the maximum allowed.

TotalDigits: Defines the maximum number of values are allowed by restricting it to numbers expressible as $i \times 10^{-n}$, where i and n are integers such that $|i| < 10^{totalDigits}$ and $0 \leq n \leq totalDigits$. Example: using $totalDigits = 4$, the value of 55.51 is valid, it can be expressed as 5551×10^{-2}, $i = 5551$ and $n = 2$. A valid message is generated using the maximum number of digits allowed and an invalid message is created using a value over this maximum value. An extra message is generated with fractional digits if the facet *FractionDigits* is also specified for this element.

WhiteSpace: Specifies how spaces, line feeds, tabs, and carriage returns will be handled. Depending on `whitespace` value (preserve, replace, collapse) messages are generated including line feeds, tabs and carriage returns.

For all other data type facets (`maxInclusive, minInclusive, maxExclusive, minExclusive, maxLength, minLength`), data value perturbation defined by Offutt and Xu is applied to generate the test cases.

Test cases generated using XML Schema facets will test boundaries values not only based in the data type but also in constrains defined for the element. The more accurate an element is specified, the more effective is the quality of the messages generated. Also, the extensions for data value perturbation based on values immediately above and below the data type domain tests messages for invalid domains.

4.2   Extending Relationship Strategies for Data Communication Perturbation

In Document-based Web services, service consumer and provider interact using complete documents. These documents are typically XML files, defined in a common way, agreed upon schema. Data communications aim at testing Document-based Web service. DCP (Data Communication Perturbation) focus on testing relationship and constraints in this kind of messages. As with [8], here messages are defined using RTG (Regular Tree Grammar) - Definition 1, and the relationships and constraints are the finite set of production rules P in the RTG.

Definition 2. *Given an XML schema $< E, D, N, A, P, n_s >$, a relationship is a production rule in P : $n \rightarrow e < r >$, where n is a non-terminal in N, e is an element in E, and r is a regular expression made up of non-terminals.*

Offutt and Xu used the occurrence indicator *maxOccurs* to specify referential relationships between parent and child elements. Here, this idea is extended with the use of the occurrence indicator *minOccurs*, and the order indicators: *all* and *choice*, and the element *any*. Table 6 describes each of the XML Schema indicator used and the corresponding regular expression.

Table 6. Regular expressions used to represent relationship in the RTG representation

XML Schema indicator	regexp	description
minOccurs, maxOccurs	$\{x,y\}$	at least x and not more than y times
choice	|	one child element or another can occur
all	$\{x_1, .., x_n\}$	the child elements can appear in any order but each must occur only once.
any element	.	element not specified in the XML Schema

Apart from the three testing strategies established by Offutt and Xu (Section 3), the following testing strategies are added:

- Given a relationship $n \rightarrow e < r >$, if there is an expression $\alpha+$ in r, there will be one extra test case that contains no instances of α. This test case expect to receive an error when executed.
- Given a relationship $n \rightarrow e < r >$, if there is an expression $\alpha*$ in r, there will be two extra test cases. One deleting all instances of α, and the other one containing k instances of α, where k is a predefined number representing *unbounded*.
- Given a relationship $n \rightarrow e < r >$, if there is an expression containing '.' in r, there will be one test case. It contains one instance of β, where β represents any element.
- Given a relationship $n \rightarrow e < r >$, if there is an expression $\alpha\{x,y\}$ in r, there will be two test cases. One contains x instances of α and the other contains y instances of α. If y has the value *unbounded*, y will have the value of k, where k is a predefined number.
- Given a relationship $n \rightarrow e < r >$, if there is an expression $\{x_1, .., x_n\}$ in r, there will be two test cases. One contains a random permutation of $\{x_1, .., x_n\}$, and the other one contains $\{x_1, .., x_{n-1}\}$.
- Given a relationship $n \rightarrow e < r >$, if there is an expression $x_1|..|x_n$ in r, there will be $n + 1$ different test cases. The first n tests case contains x_i where i is an integer and $1 \leq i \leq n$. The other test cases will contains all n elements, this last expects to receive an error when executed.

The RTG for the XML Schema showed in the Listing 1.2 contains two relationships:

$$n_{id} \rightarrow ID < n_{drivingLicense}|n_{memberNumber} >$$
$$n_{movieList} \rightarrow movie < (n_{movieId}, n_{media}, n_{price})\{1,5\} >$$

Four test cases for both relationships are shown in Listings 1.3, 1.4, 1.5, 1.6.

Listing 1.3. Test data for choice -2nd element

```
...
<id>
    <memberNumber>1234</memberNumber>
</id>
...
```

Listing 1.4. Test data for all choice elements- An error is expected for this message

```
...
<id>
    <drivingLicense>S1234-123456-12</drivingLicense>
    <memberNumber>1234</memberNumber>
</id>
...
```

Listing 1.5. Test suites for the maximum number allowed for sequence's relationship

```
...
<id>
    <memberNumber>S1234-123456-12</memberNumber>
</id>
<moviesList>
    <movie>
        <id>12</id>
        <media>DVD</media>
        <price>3.25</price>
    </movie>
    <movie>
        <id>130</id>
        <media>DVD</media>
        <price>3.25</price>
    </movie>
    <movie>
        <id>12</id>
        <media>DVD</media>
        <price>3.25</price>
    </movie>
    <movie>
        <id>12</id>
        <media>DVD</media>
        <price>3.25</price>
    </movie>
    <movie>
        <id>12</id>
        <media>DVD</media>
        <price>3.25</price>
    </movie>
</moviesList>
...
```

Listing 1.6. Test suites for the minimum number allowed for sequence's relationship

```
...
<id>
    <memberNumber>S1234-123456-12</memberNumber>
</id>
<moviesList>
    <movie>
        <id>12</id>
        <media>DVD</media>
        <price>3.25</price>
    </movie>
</moviesList>
...
```

4.3   Operator Perturbation

Operator Perturbation relies on the idea of RPC Communication Perturbation[8] and SOAP Perturbation Operators [4]. In [8], mutation operators were only applied to RPC style Web services. In the present work, all mutation operators, presented in Table 2 and 3, are implemented for RPC Web services and, besides that, all of them are redefined and implemented for Document based Web services. Apart from those already defined operators, the following new mutation operators are defined:

Code Injection: Code injection is a technique to introduce some code into a program. The goal normally is to take advantage of some assumption, such as: quotation marks or semi-colons would never appear, only alphanumeric will be entered, use of array index from input, and so on. The following mutation operator were included:

DynamicEvaluation(n) - This mutation operator explores the situation when part of input is used into an *eval* function, Listing 1.7 shows an example of code.

Listing 1.7. Code using function eval

```
$var = "";
eval("\$var=\$inputValue;");
$var = "";
```

Test case: Add the value: *0 ; system(\ "/bin/echo error message\ ");* to the node *n*.

FileInjection(n) - This operator is used to demonstrate errors when an input parameter is used as file name.

Test case: Add a file path as element value.

Numeric Value SQL Injection: To protect against SQL injection, many programmers are escaping or removing quotes, but this does not completely remove the risk in certain programming languages. Consider the following query:

SELECT fields FROM table WHERE id == $id;

The variable *$id* was assumed to be a numeric value and it would expose all users if someone tries: *id = 0 OR 1=1.*

Test case: Add the value *= 0 OR 1=1* to the element value.

Null: XML Schema introduces a mechanism for signaling that an element's content is missing or "null"[13]. This operator only applies for literal messages. Listing 1.8 has an extract of XML Schema that specify nullable and a XML that has a null element.

Test Case: Remove the element value and add the attribute xsi:null="true" to the element.

Listing 1.8. Null example

```
XML Schema:
<element name="middleName" type="string" nullable="true"/>

XML Document:
<middleName xsi:null="true"/>
```

The following mutation operator was included:

Null(n)

Test case: Add the attribute xsi:null="true" to the node n, and delete its contents.

5   Empirical Results

Using the testing techniques presented in this paper, we built a tool, *GenAutoWS*. It can be used by both Web services subscribers and providers. For the former, the test suites are generated based on the service interfaces to certify particular uses of services. Service providers can also be benefited by the use of *GenAutoWS* as a development tool in which messages are automatically generated based on the presented techniques.

Test cases automatically generated by the tool can be included in a test suite. These test suites can actually be executed by the tool which is responsible for sending messages to the Web services and response messages can be checked by the tester. Messages perturbed to create new test cases are automatically saved in an internal database. *GenAutoWS* has a feature, namely "internal data - perturbation", used to create new messages by swapping values with previously saved values.

Regarding connectivity *GenAutoWS* supports UDDI. Bloomberg [3] showed many issues of testing Web services including testing publishing, finding and binding capabilities of SOA. *GenAutoWS* allows UDDI registry inquiries, the WSDL returned is used to create test case messages automatically. The seed message uses values from the internal database or values default based on the element datatype.

GenAutoWS was submitted as a first proof-of-concept to generate test cases for five Web services from two different systems of a financial institution. The first three Web services (WS1, WS2 and W3) belong to an enterprise email application and the other two Web services (WS4 and WS5) are used to verify credit information.

The Web services used in this proof-of-concepts are specified using WSDL and they communicate using SOAP over HTTP. The first four Web services are document/literal and WS5 is RPC/encoded. Both systems were developed in Java. Although they are now used in a production environment, pre-release versions of these systems were used for test. During the tests, the faults found were classified as low, medium and high accordingly to the critical level.

Using the techniques of boundary value [8] and all XML Schema Facets presented in Section 4.1, we generated 162 different tests. Table 7 summarizes the result for this approach. The majority of the observed faults were classified as low level, example: no error message or message incomplete.

The relationship strategies for DCP, shown in Section 4.2, generated 49 tests, the results are presented in Table 8. No tests were generated for WS5 using this technique, since it was not specified by XML Schema.

---

[1] Some faults were found for more than one test cases.

Table 7. Tests - Data Value Perturbation

Number of tests	162
Generated using the new techniques	99
Generated using the previous techniques	63
Total number of faults	32
Medium and high level faults	7
Tests that detect faults [1]	62
From new techniques	48
From previous techniques	14

Table 8. Tests - Data Communic. Perturbation

Number of tests	49
Generated using the new techniques	40
Generated using the previous techniques	9
Total number of faults	12
Medium and high level faults	4
Tests that detect faults [1]	20
From new techniques	16
From previous techniques	4

Table 9. Tests - Mutation Operators

Number of tests	164
Generated using the new techniques	48
Generated using the previous techniques	116
Total number of faults	16
Medium and high level faults	4
Tests that detect faults [1]	44
From new techniques	10
From previous techniques	34

The mutation operators presented in [8,4] and the four new operators proposed in Section 4.3 generated 164 tests. The results are summarized in the Table 9.

Certain faults were detected by multiple tests and were common among the different techniques. The new techniques presented in the present paper generated more test cases/data than the original approach for the DVP and DCP tests. These new tests could reveal faults not detectable by the original techniques. The new testing strategies defined for DCP took advantage of relationships described in XML Schema not considered before. For instance, the order indicators *choice* and *all*. The generation of test cases/data that should cause errors in the application allowed us to validate errors messages returned by the service, either for incorrect or inexistent messages.

The use of other XML Schema constrains (facets) in the DVP technique permitted to create more accurate data within the element domain. For example, for the string element that contain `pattern`: [A-Z]{2,3}-[0-9]{2,3}, a part from the string maximum length from the previous techniques, two new ones were created: ZZZ-999 and ZZZZ-9999. The latter is an invalid message and should receive an error when executed.

6   Conclusion

This paper proposed extensions to testing techniques based on Data Perturbation for Web Services together with a tool to generate the test suites based on the previous and new techniques. For that, new mutation operators, boundary values considering all WSDL facets, testing cases using relationship defined in the WSDL, UDDI integration, internal database to collect and use values previously captured from messages were proposed.

The testing tool *GenAutoWS* was built using these extensions and a first proof-of-concepts using five Web services from a financial institution was carried out. In this proof-of-concepts, DVP tests were shown more efficient compared to the other techniques, founding at least twice the number of faults. Such a result is similar to the one got by Offutt and Xu [8] in their proof-of-concepts.

The test cases added to DVP and DCP previous techniques could generate more messages and reveal more faults than their counterparts in the original approach. The new rules inserted to DCP and the improvements for DCP were able to generate many messages for WS1, WS2 and WS3. These Web Services had many constrains specified using XML Schema facets and XML Schema order indicators testing technique could exploit these features. Although the mutation operators presented in the section 4.3 have a limited scope in the case studies preformed so far, they can produce better results if applied to systems in which security issues are more relevant.

Web Services testing presented here can be applied to existing Web Services without modifying or rewriting any piece of code, or adopting a specific framework. The quality of test cases/data generated, however, depends on how well the Web Services are specified, since the WSDL and schema files are used to generate the messages.

The techniques for data perturbation based on rules for XML Schema can be easily adapted to different kinds of applications that exchange messages in XML format. One possible work is to explore the generation of test cases for REST (Representational State Transfer) with information specified in a WADL (Web Application Description Language) file, a message descriptor for REST Services, using the same techniques presented here.

Acknowledgements. This project has been co-funded by the National Council for Scientific and Technological Development (CNPq - Brazil) - Process:551038/2007-1, the State of São Paulo Research Foundation (FAPESP) and the Ministry of Education Research Agency (CAPES- Brazil) - Process:0671-08-8.

References

1. Beizer, B.: Software Testing Techniques, 2nd edn. International Thomson Computer Press (1990)
2. UC Berkeley. Blast (berkeley lazy abstraction software verification tool) model checker, http://embedded.eecs.berkeley.edu/blast/

3. Bloomberg, J.: Testing web services today and tomorrow. The Rational Edge E-zine for the Rational Community (2002)
4. de Almeida Jr., L.F., Vergilio, S.R.: Exploring perturbation based testing for web services. In: ICWS 2006: Proceedings of the IEEE International Conference on Web Services (ICWS 2006), Washington, DC, USA, pp. 717–726. IEEE Computer Society, Los Alamitos (2006)
5. Harrison, A., Taylor, I.J.: Wspeer - an interface to web service hosting and invocation. In: IPDPS 2005: Proceedings of the 19th IEEE International Parallel and Distributed Processing Symposium (IPDPS 2005) - Workshop 4, Washington, DC, USA, p. 175. IEEE Computer Society, Los Alamitos (2005)
6. Huang, H., Tsai, W., Paul, R., Chen, Y.: Automated model checking and testing for composite web services. In: ISORC 2005: Proceedings of the Eighth IEEE International Symposium on Object-Oriented Real-Time Distributed Computing (ISORC 2005), Washington, DC, USA, pp. 300–307. IEEE Computer Society, Los Alamitos (2005)
7. Myers, G.J.: The Art of Software Testing, 2nd edn. Wiley, New York (2004)
8. Offutt, J., Xu, W.: Generating test cases for web services using data perturbation. SIGSOFT Softw. Eng. Notes 29(5), 1–10 (2004)
9. Pressman, S.R.: Software Engineering: A Practitioner's Approach, 6th edn. McGraw-Hill, New York (2004)
10. Tsai, W.T., Paul, R., Song, W., Cao, Z.: Coyote: An xml-based framework for web services testing (2002)
11. Tsai, W.T., Paul, R., Yu, L., Saimi, A., Cao, Z.: Scenario-based web service testing with distributed agents (2003)
12. OASIS UDDI. UDDI Specification, http://www.uddi.org/specification.html (last access, 2005)
13. W3C. Xml schema part 1: Structures, http://www.w3.org/TR/2000/CR-xmlschema-1-20001024/
14. W3C. Web services description language (WSDL) version 2 part 1: Core language, http://www.w3.org/TR/wsdl20/ (last access, 2006)
15. W3C. Web services glossary (last access, July 2007)
16. Xu, W., Offutt, J., Luo, J.: Testing web services by xml perturbation. In: ISSRE 2005: Proceedings of the 16th IEEE International Symposium on Software Reliability Engineering, Washington, DC, USA, pp. 257–266. IEEE Computer Society, Los Alamitos (2005)

Facilitating Controlled Tests of Website Design Changes: A Systematic Approach

Javier Cámara[1] and Alfred Kobsa[2]

[1] Department of Computer Science, University of Málaga
Campus de Teatinos, 29071. Málaga, Spain
jcamara@lcc.uma.es
[2] Dept. of Informatics, University of California, Irvine
Bren School of Information and Computer Sciences. Irvine, CA 92697, USA
kobsa@uci.edu

Abstract. Controlled online experiments in which envisaged changes to a web site are first tested live with a small subset of site visitors have proven to predict the effects of these changes quite accurately. However, these experiments often require expensive infrastructure and are costly in terms of development effort. This paper advocates a systematic approach to the design and implementation of such experiments in order to overcome the aforementioned drawbacks by making use of Aspect-Oriented Software Development and Software Product Lines.

1 Introduction

During the past few years, e-commerce on the Internet has experienced a remarkable growth. For online vendors like Amazon, Expedia and many others, creating a user interface that maximizes sales is thereby crucially important. Different studies [9,8] revealed that small changes at the user interface can cause surprisingly large differences in the amount of purchases made, and experience has shown that it is very difficult for interface designers and marketing experts to foresee how users react to small changes in websites. The behavioral difference that users exhibit at web pages with minimal differences in structure or content quite often deviates considerably from all plausible predictions that designers had initially made [18,23,21]. For this reason, several techniques have been developed by industry that use actual user behavior to measure the benefits of design modifications [14]. These techniques for *controlled online experiments* on the web can help to anticipate users' reactions without putting a company's revenue at risk. This is achieved by implementing and studying the effects of modifications on a tiny subset of users rather than testing new ideas directly on the complete user base.

Although the theoretical foundations and practical lessons learned from such experiments have been well described [13], there is little systematic support to their design and implementation. In this work, we advocate a systematic approach to the design and implementation of such experiments based on *Software Product Lines* [5] and *Aspect Oriented Software Development* (AOSD) [10]. Section 2 overviews the different techniques involved in online tests and points out their shortcomings. Section 3 describes our approach, briefly introducing software product lines and AOSD. Section 4

M. Gaedke, M. Grossniklaus, and O. Díaz (Eds.): ICWE 2009, LNCS 5648, pp. 370–378, 2009.
© Springer-Verlag Berlin Heidelberg 2009

introduces a prototype tool that we developed to test the feasibility of our approach. Section 5 compares our proposal with related work, and Section 6 presents some conclusions and perspectives.

2   Controlled Online Tests on the Web: An Overview

The underlying idea behind controlled online tests of a web interface is to create one or more different versions of it by incorporating new or modified features, and to test each version by presenting it to a randomly selected subset of users in order to analyze their reactions. User response is measured along an *overall evaluation criterion* (OEC) or *fitness function*, which indicates the performance of the different versions or *variants*. A simple yet common OEC in e-commerce is the *conversion rate*, that is, the percentage of site visits that result in a purchase. OECs may however also be very elaborate, and consider different factors of user behavior.

Controlled online experiments can be classified into two major categories, depending on the number of variables involved: **(i) A/B, A/B/C, ..., A/../N Split Testing.** These tests compare one or more variations of a single site element or *factor*, such as a promotional offer. Site developers can quickly see which variation of the factor yields the highest conversion rates. In the simplest case (A/B test), the original version of the interface is served to 50% of the users (A or *Control Group*), and the modified version is served to the other 50% (B or *Treatment Group*). A/B tests are simple, but not very informative. For instance, consider Figure 1, which depicts the original version and a variant of a checkout example taken from [9][1]. This variant has been obtained by modifying 9 different factors. While an A/B test tells us which of two alternatives is better,

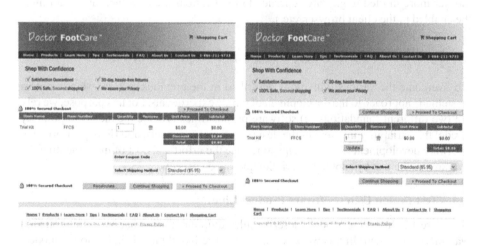

Fig. 1. Checkout screen: variants A (original, left) and B (modified, right)[2]

---

[1] Eisenberg reports that Interface A resulted in 90% fewer purchases, probably because potential buyers who had no promotion code were put off by the fact that others could get lower prices.
[2] © 2007 ACM, Inc. Included by permission.

it does not yield reliable information on how combinations of the different factors influence the performance of the variant. **(ii) Multivariate Testing**. A multivariate test can be viewed as a combination of many A/B tests, whereby all factors are systematically varied. This extends the effectiveness of online tests by allowing the impact of interactions between factors to be measured. A multivariate test can, e.g., reveal that two interface elements yield an unexpectedly high conversion rate only when they occur together, or that an element that has a positive effect on conversion loses this effect in the presence of other elements.

The execution of a test can be logically separated into two steps, namely (a) the assignment of users to the test, and to one of the subgroups for each of the interfaces to be tested, and (b) the subsequent selection and presentation of this interface to the user. Specifically, three implementation methods are currently used: **(i) Traffic Splitting.** Different implementations (variants) are manually created and placed on different servers. Then, user traffic is diverted to the assigned variant using a proxy. This approach is expensive, and both website and the code for the measurement of the OEC have to be replicated across (virtual) servers. Moreover, creating each variant for the test manually is impossible in most multivariate tests. **(ii) Server-side Selection.** The logic that produces the different variants for users is embedded in the code of the site. In particular, branching logic has to be added to produce the different interfaces. Code becomes complex and unmanageable if different tests are run concurrently. However, if these problems are solved, server-side selection is a powerful alternative which has the potential to automate variant generation. **(iii) Client-side Selection.** Assignment and generation of variants is achieved through dynamic modification of each requested page at the client side using JavaScript. The drawbacks of this approach are similar to the ones in server-side selection, but in addition, the features subject to experimentation are far more limited (e.g., only superficial modifications are possible, JavaScript must be enabled in the client browser, etc.).

3   Systematic Online Test Design and Implementation

To overcome the various limitations described in the previous section, we advocate a systematic approach to the development of online experiments. For this purpose, we rely on two different foundations: **(i)** software product lines provide the means to properly model the variability inherent in the design of the experiments, and **(ii)** aspect-oriented software development (AOSD) helps to reduce the effort and cost of implementing the variants of the test by capturing variation factors on aspects.

3.1   Test Design Using Software Product Lines

Software Product Line models describe all requirements or features in the potential variants of a system. In this work, we use a feature-based model similar to the models employed by FODA [11] or FORM [12]. This model takes the form of a lattice of parent-child relationships which is typically quite large. Single systems or variants are then built by selecting a set of features from the model.

Product line models allow the definition of directly reusable (DR) features which are common to all possible variants, and three types of *discriminants* or variation points,

---

F1(MA) The cart component must include a checkout screen.

   – **F1.1(SA)** There must be an additional "Continue Shopping" button present.
       • **F1.1.1(DR)** The button is placed on top of the screen.
       • **F1.1.2(DR)** The button is placed at the bottom of the screen.
   – **F1.2(O)** There must be an "Update" button placed under the quantity box.
   – **F1.3(SA)** There must be a "Total" present.
       • **F1.3.1(DR)** Text and amount of the "Total" appear in different boxes.
       • **F1.3.2(DR)** Text and amount of the "Total" appear in the same box.
   – **F1.4(O)** The screen must provide discount options to the user.
       • **F1.4.1(DR)** There is a "Discount" box present, with amount in a box next to it on top of the "Total" box.
       • **F1.4.2(DR)** There is an "Enter Coupon Code" input box present on top of "Shipping Method".
       • **F1.4.3(DR)** There must be a "Recalculate" button left of "Continue Shopping."

Fig. 2. Feature model fragment corresponding to the checkout screen in Figure 1

namely: **(i) Single adaptors (SA):** a set of mutually exclusive features; **(ii) Multiple adaptors (MA):** a list of alternatives not mutually exclusive (at least one must be selected); and **(iii) Options (O):** a single optional feature.

To define the different interface variants in an online test, we specify common interface features as DR in the feature model. Varying elements are modeled using discriminants. Different combinations of interface features result in different variants. A fragment of such a feature model for our example is given in Figure 2. Variants can be manually created by the test designer through the selection of the desired interface features in the feature model, or automatically by generating all the possible combinations of feature selections. Automatic generation is especially interesting in the case of multivariate testing. However, not all combinations of feature selections are valid. For instance, a single feature selection cannot include both F1.3.1 and F1.3.2 (single adaptor). Likewise, if F1.4 is selected, it is mandatory to include F1.4.1-F1.4.3 in the selection. These restrictions are introduced by the discriminants used in the feature model. If restrictions are not satisfied, the variant is not valid and should not be presented to users. Feature models can be translated into a logical expression by using features as atomic propositions and discriminants as logical connectors. By instantiating all the feature variables in the expression to *true* if selected, and *false* if unselected, we can generate the set of possible variants and then test their validity [17]. A valid variant is one for which the logical expression of the complete feature model evaluates to *true*.

3.2   Implementing Tests with Aspects

Aspect-Oriented Software Development (AOSD) is based on the idea that systems are better programmed by separately specifying their different concerns (areas of interest), using *aspects* and a description of their relations with the rest of the system. Those specifications are then automatically *woven* (or composed) into a working system.

With conventional programming techniques, programmers have to explicitly call methods available in other component interfaces in order to access their functionality, whereas the AOSD approach offers implicit invocation mechanisms achieved by means of *join points*. These are regions in the dynamic control flow of an application (method calls or executions, field setting, etc.) which can be intercepted by an aspect-oriented program by using *pointcuts* (predicates which allow the quantification of join points) to match with them. When a join point is matched, the program runs code implementing new behavior (*advices*) typically *before, after, instead* of, or *around* (before and after) the matched join point. To illustrate our approach, we use PHP [20] and phpAspect [3], which provides AspectJ[3] -like syntax and abstractions. However, our proposal is easily adaptable to other platforms.

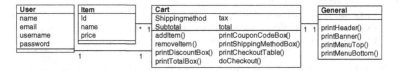

Fig. 3. Classes involved in the shopping cart example

We introduce a simplified implementation of the shopping cart in Section 1 to illustrate our approach: a 'shopping cart' class (`Cart`) allows for the addition and removal of different items. This class contains a number of methods that render the different elements in the cart at the interface, such as `printTotalBox` or `printDiscountBox`. These are private methods called from within the public method `printCheckout-Table`, used to render the main body of our checkout screen. A user's checkout is completed when `doCheckout` is invoked. The `General` class contains auxiliary functions, such as representing common elements of the site (e.g., headers, footers and menus).

Variant implementation. The alternatives used so far for variant implementation have important disadvantages (discussed in Section 2). These include the need to produce different versions of the system code either by replicating and modifying it across several servers, or using branching logic on the server or client sides.

Using aspects instead of the traditional approaches offers the advantage that the original source code does not need to be modified, since aspects can be applied as needed, resulting in different variants. In our approach, each feature described in the product line is associated to one or more aspects which modify the original system in a particular way. Hence, when a set of features is selected, the appropriate variant is obtained by weaving with the *base code* (*i.e.,* the original system's code) the set of aspects associated to the selected features in the variant.

To illustrate how these variations are achieved, consider for instance the features labeled F1.3.1 and F1.3.2 in Figure 2. These two features are mutually exclusive and state that in the total box of the checkout screen, text and amount should appear in different boxes rather than the same box, respectively. In the original implementation (Figure 1.A), text and amount appeared in different boxes, hence there is no need to modify the behavior if F1.3.1 is selected. When F1.3.2 is selected though, we merely have to replace the method that renders the total box. This is achieved by adding the aspect in Figure 4.A, which defines a pointcut intercepting the execution of `Cart.printTotalBox` and applies an `around`-type advice.

---

[3] AspectJ [7] is the de-facto standard in aspect-oriented programming languages.

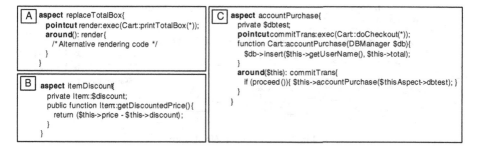

Fig. 4. Aspects: (A) rendering code replacement; (B) item discount inter-type declarations; and (C) data collection

This approach to the generation of variants results in better code reusability (especially in multivariate testing) as well as reduced costs and efforts, since developers do not have to replicate nor generate complete variant implementations. Moreover, this approach is safer and cleaner, because the system logic does not have to be temporally (nor manually) modified, with the risks this represents in terms of security and reliability.

Experimenting with variants may also require the modification of data structures or method additions to some classes. Consider for instance a test in which developers want to monitor how customers react to discounts on products in a catalog. Assume that discounts can be different for each product and that the site has not initially been designed to include any information on discounts, i.e. this information needs to be introduced somewhere in the code. To solve this problem we can use inter-type declarations. Aspects can declare members (fields, methods, etc.) owned by other classes. These are called inter-type members. The aspect on Figure 4.B, introduces an additional `discount` field in our `Item` class, and also a `getDiscountedPrice` method used when the discounted price of an item is to be retrieved.

Data Collection and User Interaction. The code in charge of measuring and collecting data for the experiment can also be written as aspects in a concise manner. Consider a new experiment with our checkout example in which we want to calculate how much customers spend on average when they visit our site. To this end, we need to add up the amount of money spent on each purchase. One way to implement this functionality is again inter-type declarations.

When the aspect in Figure 4.C intercepts the method `Cart.doCheckout` that completes a purchase, the associated advice inserts the sales amount into a database that collects the results from the experiment (but only if the execution of the intercepted method succeeds, which is represented by `proceed` in the advice). It is worth noting that while the database reference belongs to the aspect, the method used to insert the data belongs to the `Cart` class.

4   Tool Support

The approach for online experiments on websites that we presented in this article has been implemented in a prototype tool, called **WebLoom**. It includes a graphical user

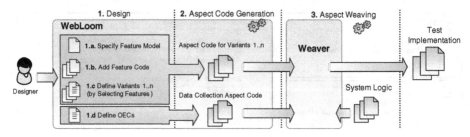

Fig. 5. Operation of WebLoom

interface to build and visualize feature models. Moreover, the user can attach aspect code to features. The tool also supports both automatic and manual variant generation, and is able to deploy code which lays out all the necessary infrastructure to perform the designed test on a particular website.

In Figure 5 we can observe the way in which our prototype tool works. The user enters a description of the potential modifications to be performed on the website in order to produce the different variants under WebLoom's guidance. This results in a basic feature model structure which is then enriched with code associated to the afore-mentioned modifications (aspects). Once the feature model is complete, the user can select features to generate any number of variants, which are automatically checked for validity before being stored. Alternatively, the user can ask the tool to generate all the valid variants for the current feature model. Once all necessary input has been received, the tool gathers the code for each particular variant to be tested in the experiment by collecting all the aspects associated with the features that were selected for the variant. It then invokes the weaver to produce the actual variant code for the designed test by weaving the original system code with the aspect code produced by the tool.

5   Related Work

Feature models and AOSD have already been applied in the construction of Web appli-cations in order to achieve significant productivity gains [22,19]. However, these pro-posals only exploit one of these alternatives and do not pursue a combined approach.

Regarding the combined use of both approaches, Lee et al. [15] and Loughran and Rashid [16] present some guidelines on how feature-oriented analysis and aspects can be combined. Other approaches such as [24] aim at implementing variability, and the management and tracing of requirements to implementation by integrating model-driven and aspect-oriented software development. The AMPLE project [1] takes this approach along the software lifecycle, aiming at traceability during product line evo-lution. Although both combination approaches and our own proposal employ software product lines and aspects, the earlier approaches are concerned with the general process of system construction by identifying and reusing aspect-oriented components, whereas our approach deals with the creation of different versions of a Web application with a limited lifespan to test user behavioral response. Hence, our framework is intended to generate lightweight aspects which are used as a convenient means for the transient modification of parts of the system. In this sense, it is worth noticing that aspects are only involved as a means to generate system variants, but not necessarily present in the original system implementation.

To the extent of our knowledge, no research has so far been reported on treating online test design and implementation in a systematic manner. A number of consulting firms already specialized on analyzing companies' web presence [4,2]. These firms offer ad-hoc studies of web retail sites with the goal of achieving higher conversion rates. Some of them use proprietary technology usually focused on the statistical aspects of the experiments, requiring significant code refactoring for test implementation.

6 Concluding Remarks

We believe that the benefits of our approach are especially valuable for the problem do-main that we address. On one hand, testing is performed on a regular basis for websites to continuously improve their conversion rates. On the other hand, a high percentage of the tested modifications are discarded since they do not improve the site's performance. Therefore, a lot of effort is lost in the process. We believe that WebLoom will save de-velopers time and effort, reducing the amount of work they have to put into the design and implementation of online tests.

A more detailed description of our work can be found in [6]. Regarding future work, we aim at enhancing our basic prototype with additional WYSIWYG extensions for its graphical user interface. Specifically, developers should be enabled to immediately see the effects that code modifications and feature selections will have on the appearance of their web site.

References

1. Ample project, http://www.ample-project.net/
2. Optimost, http://www.optimost.com/
3. phpAspect: Aspect oriented programming for PHP, http://phpaspect.org/
4. Vertster, http://www.vertster.com/
5. Software product lines: practices and patterns. Addison-Wesley Longman Publishing Co., Boston (2001)
6. Cámara, J., Kobsa, A.: Facilitating Controlled Tests of Website Design Changes using Aspect Oriented Programming and Software Product Lines. Transactions on Large Scale Data and Knowledge Centered Systems 1(1) (2009)
7. Colyer, A., Clement, A., Harley, G., Webster, M.: Eclipse AspectJ: Aspect-Oriented Pro-gramming with AspectJ and the Eclipse AspectJ Development Tools. Pearson Education, London (2005)
8. Eisenberg, B.: How to decrease sales by 90 percent,
   http://www.clickz.com/1588161
9. Eisenberg, B.: How to increase conversion rate 1,000 percent,
   http://www.clickz.com/showPage.html?page=1756031
10. Filman, R.E., Elrad, T., Clarke, S., Aksit, M. (eds.): Aspect-Oriented Software Development. Addison Wesley, Reading (2004)
11. Kang, K., Cohen, S., Hess, J., Novak, W., Peterson, S.: Feature-oriented domain analysis (FODA) feasibility study. TR. CMU/SEI-90-TR-21, SEI (1990)
12. Kang, K.C., Kim, S., Lee, J., Kim, K., Shin, E., Huh, M.: FORM: A feature-oriented reuse method with domain-specific reference architectures. Ann. Software Eng. 5 (1998)

13. Kohavi, R., Henne, R.M., Sommerfield, D.: Practical guide to controlled experiments on the web: listen to your customers not to the hippo. In: Proc. of KDD 2007. ACM, New York (2007)
14. Kohavi, R., Round, M.: Front Line Internet Analytics at Amazon.com (2004), http://ai.stanford.edu/~ronnyk/emetricsAmazon.pdf
15. Lee, K., Kang, K.C., Kim, M., Park, S.: Combining feature-oriented analysis and aspect-oriented programming for product line asset development. In: Proc. of SPLC 2006. IEEE, Los Alamitos (2006)
16. Loughran, N., Rashid, A.: Framed aspects: Supporting variability and configurability for AOP. In: Bosch, J., Krueger, C. (eds.) ICOIN 2004 and ICSR 2004. LNCS, vol. 3107, pp. 127–140. Springer, Heidelberg (2004)
17. Mannion, M., Cámara, J.: Theorem proving for product line model verification. In: van der Linden, F.J. (ed.) PFE 2003. LNCS, vol. 3014, pp. 211–224. Springer, Heidelberg (2004)
18. McGlaughlin, F., Alt, B., Usborne, N.: The power of small changes tested -change.html (2006), http://www.marketingexperiments.com/improving-website-conversion/power-small
19. Pettersson, U., Jarzabek, S.: Industrial experience with building a web portal product line using a lightweight, reactive approach. In: Proc. of ESEC/SIGSOFT FSE. ACM, New York (2005)
20. PHP: Hypertext preprocessor, http://www.php.net/
21. Roy, S.: 10 factors to test that could increase the conversion rate of your landing pages (2007), http://www.wilsonweb.com/conversion/sumantra-landing-pages.htm
22. Trujillo, S., Batory, D.S., Díaz, O.: Feature oriented model driven development: A case study for portlets. In: ICSE, pp. 44–53. IEEE, Los Alamitos (2007)
23. Usborne, N.: Design choices can cripple a website (2005), http://alistapart.com/articles/designcancripple
24. Voelter, M., Groher, I.: Product line implementation using aspect-oriented and model-driven software development. In: Proc. of SPLC 2007. IEEE, Los Alamitos (2007)

SOAF – Design and Implementation of a Service-Enriched Social Network*

Martin Treiber, Hong-Linh Truong, and Schahram Dustdar

Distributed Systems Group, Institute of Information Systems
Vienna University of Technology
{treiber,truong,dustdar}@infosys.tuwien.ac.at

Abstract. In this paper, we propose the integration of services into social networks (SOAF - Service of a Friend) to leverage the creation of the Internet of
Services vision. We show how to integrate services and humans into a common
network structure and discuss design and implementation issues. In particular, we
discuss the required extensions to existing social network vocabulary with regard
to services. We illustrate a scenario where this network structures can be applied
in the context of service discovery and highlight the benefit of a service-enriched
social network structure.

1 Introduction

The Internet of services [1] vision focuses on the extension of the existing Internet with
regard to services. In a future Internet of services, information is not static any more,
but dynamically provided by all kind of software services. This development was driven
by the so-called Web 2.0 phenomena, which included the broad adoption of social networks like facebook [1], xing [2] or twitter[3]. Indeed, as Kleinberg observed in his work [2],
social and technical networks converge. In these networks, user generated content, like
folksonomies [3], provides a vast source of information that is able to classify arbitrary
content (e.g., del.icio.us [4]). In this area, the Friend of a Friend project (FOAF) [4] aims
at providing information about relationships between humans in social network structures. FOAF describes relationship structures with RDF [5], thus defining the technical
foundation to access information of social networks in a machine readable form.

Viewed from a business perspective, these developments have a profound impact on
the way businesses are conducted. In his Wired article, Howe shows how the idea of
crowdsourcing [6] can be applied to businesses. With regard to (Web) services, which
already provided by companies, and the integration of humans into common networks,
companies can benefit from these emerging network structures. However, with existing service-oriented infrastructures, this endeavor proves to be difficult to achieve. In

---

* The research leading to these results has received funding from the European Community's
Seventh Framework Programme FP7/2007-2013 under grant agreement 215483 (S-Cube).
[1] http://www.facebook.com
[2] http://www.xing.com
[3] http://www.twitter.com
[4] http://delicious.com

M. Gaedke, M. Grossniklaus, and O. Díaz (Eds.): ICWE 2009, LNCS 5648, pp. 379–393, 2009.
© Springer-Verlag Berlin Heidelberg 2009

fact, SOA (service-oriented architecture) focuses on stable processes that are defined and executed in workflow systems. The gap between SOA and Web 2.0 is widened by the emerging end user driven creation of applications (mashups [7] and situational applications [8,9]) which are playing an important part on the Internet now and become increasingly important for businesses.

One of the main reasons is that there is little support to integrate humans and services into networks to benefit from social connections within such network structures. There exist approaches that support the integration of human activities [10,11] into business processes. These approaches assume that there is already a workflow and that there is repository that can be used to select the required services for a given workflow. The associated service discovery process is well studied in literature [12]. However, with the failure of centralized registries [13] and no Web service standard for the discovery of Web services, the discovery process is fragmented and cumbersome. This leads to a situation in which Web service related information is distributed among several isolated company registries, if this is the case at all. Especially smaller companies hesitate to use registries, because of the overhead involved in maintaining dedicated registries. In such cases, Web services are often published simply by mailing customers the necessary information about the endpoint of a Web service or maintaining simple catalogues with unstructured information of available Web services on company owned web pages.

This practice hinders the creation of Web service marketplaces [14] where one can discover Web services and learn from the experience of others by using a particular Web service. When investigating the process of Web service discovery, one finds that the human factor is dominant in (semi-) automated approaches [15]. Furthermore, structured meta information in form of ontologies [16] suffers from the same limitations concerning availability as centralized registries. Even with available semantic information, the process of discovering Web services requires human activities, since different semantic service descriptions can be provided by different ontologies. These ontologies require mappings which cannot be fully automated due to ambiguities or even contradictions within their content [17].

In the context of Web service discovery, we can learn lessons from humans and how they look for solutions of problems. Humans exploit local information and use links to other persons to ask for pointers or for information when needed. In short, humans ask their friends whether they had a similar problem and how the problem was solved. In our work, we aim to make use of human relations together with service information. We link software services and humans in a common network structure. We refer to this approach as *Service of a Friend* (SOAF) and follow the spirit of FOAF. We believe that the integration of humans and services into networks fosters the creation of Web service ecosystems [18]. Our approach bears several challenges that we are going to address in this paper. First of all, we need a representation of the links between services and humans. Secondly, dynamic changes must be represented in our network, since there are relations that exist only over a certain time (e.g., projects may require collaboration for several months). And finally, we need to consider that past relations provide useful information for potential future use (e.g., a service that was useful for certain tasks in the past may be again useful for new tasks of different users).

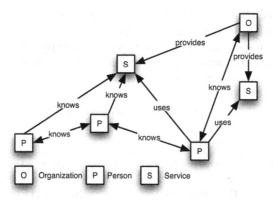

Fig. 1. Overview of SOAF network structure

The rest of the paper is organized as follows. We discuss our approach in Section 2. We provide an analysis and discussion of our findings in Section 3. Afterwards, we introduce our prototype architecture in Section 4. We conclude our paper with related work in Section 5 and an outlook for future research directions in Section 6.

2   Linking Web Services

Due to distributed nature of services and the lack of centralized repositories to search for services, we require meta information that provides information about the connections (links) between services in service networks (see Figure 1). These network structures originate for instance from organizational structures of companies or social networks which model social connections between humans. Thus, links and their associated information are very critical for the traversal of networks efficiently and to facilitate the discovery of distributed services. Therefore, we include meta information into links to make the traversal more efficient. Furthermore, as the linkage between elements of networks is constantly changing, we consider dynamic aspects of the relations between services, organizations and humans as well. These are not static and may change over time. For instance, a person might move from one organization to another or the service provision might depend on the duration of a project (e.g., event notification services). Our approach takes these considerations into account and we discuss our concept in detail in the following sub-sections.

2.1   Extending FOAF

The integration of services and humans in a common information network requires the integration of existing social network structures and service related information. Our idea is to augment FOAF network structures with service related information and to link services and humans in the same network. In particular, we extend the relation mechanisms of FOAF to model relations between services and persons. In SOAF [5] we

---

[5] http://www.infosys.tuwien.ac.at/staff/treiber/soaf/index.rdf

extend the FOAF concepts with a (i) *Service* concept to represent services, a (ii) *uses* relation which denotes the use of a service by a person or other services (iii) and a *provides* relation that specifies the relation between service provider and service. With these extensions, we can establish relations between persons, services and organizations/groups. We summarize the relations in Table 1.

Table 1. Relations between SOAF entities

Relation	Description
Service uses service	Denotes direct service invocation by other services. For instance, in service compositions, a service might call another service directly
Service knows service	Denotes that two services are related within a certain context (e.g., workflows, compositions or mashups) without any direct invocation of each other
Person uses service	Denotes the service use of a person
Person knows service	Denotes mutual knowledge of a service and a person without usage
Person provides service	Denotes the service provision by a person, e.g., a human provided service
Organization provides service	Defines the relation between organizations and their provided services

2.2   Dynamic SOAF

As discussed before, we model three basic relations between entities in a SOAF network (i) knows, (ii) uses and (iii) provides. The latter two imply automatically knows, since it is required to know a service before it can be offered or consumed. *Knows, uses* and *provides* are pairwise related through a simple subset relation: *uses* is a subset of *knows*, since it is required to know a service before a service can be used. Besides, persons/organizations might know more services than they actually use. The *provides* relation is also a subset of the knows relation, since a provider knows obviously the services that are provided and knows/uses additional services.

Viewed from a time based perspective, elements of the *knows/uses/provides* sets are subject to changes. For instance, a service might move from the *knows* set to the *uses* set and vice versa. Consequently, we allow to have multiple links to a single service from a person at any point in time. For instance, as soon as a service is used by a person, a *uses* relation is created. If the service is not used anymore (e.g., the service was used for registration purposes or the access has been revoked due to company changes, etc.) the *uses* relation is not valid any more and its internal state and timestamp are set accordingly. Thus the service moves to the *knows* set.

Notice that the *knows* relation is static: once a person knows another person/service, the relation remains - it is not removed anymore. However, with services we have to pay attention to the fact that a service does simply not exist any more. In these cases, the *knows* relation points to an inactive services that have been used in the past.

An aspect that needs explicitly to be considered is the type of service usage. We identified several types of service usage that we include in our model. We use this kind of information to generate accurate historical information. In particular we consider the usage frequency of a service and classify the usage as summarized in Table 2.

Table 2. Service usage in SOAF

Usage	Description
Once	The service is only used once and then never again during the lifetime of the service (e.g.,a registration/unregistration service is used to subscribe to a mailinglist, a polling service might exist only before a certain event takes place, etc.).
Continuously with pre-defined time to live	The service is used for a certain activity during a pre defined time and is removed afterwards (e.g., a service that provides state information about persons in a project).
Continuously	The service is used continuously without limitations concerning the time of use and frequency.

Complementary to the use of services is their provision. Service provision changes also over the time, but is generally less dynamic than the *uses* relation. In particular we consider three distinct service provision scenarios that are supported by our model (see Table 3).

Table 3. Service provision in SOAF

Usage	Description
Continuously with pre-defined time to live	The service is provided for a certain activity during a pre defined time and is removed afterwards (e.g., a service that provides state information about persons in a project).
Continuously	The service is provided continuously without limitations concerning the time of use and frequency. This includes the case when a service is used only once for registration purposes, but nevertheless is required by different customers to register and thus must be available continuously.
Deprecated	The service is still available but not actively maintained,

Of central importance for the representation of the network dynamics is the connection between entities in the SOAF network. We include additional meta information in the linkage of SOAF entities that is important for management purposes (e.g., creation and deprecation) (see Table 4).

Table 4. SOAF Connection attributes

Attribute	Description
Creation	Date, on which the connection between the entities was established
Removal	Date on which the connection was removed
Active	Flag that indicates if a connection is currently active
Type	Defines the type of connection, either *uses*, *provides* or *knows*

2.3 Managing SOAF Service Networks

The management of dynamic aspects of distributed networks is complex task. The first challenge is to identify a resource in a network in a unique manner. In our approach, we follow the concept of "inverse functional properties" from OWL [19]. We use a functional property that defines the URI of a person, an organization or a service. Services include a functional property that points to the endpoint of the service as well.

Since we do not intend to define a centralized authority that manages available information, we have to rely on all network members to manage their links and to keep the links updated. Still, there is no guarantee that this process works without disruption, since this process relies partially on the intervention of humans. However, since links between entities in the SOAF network imply a certain degree reciprocal agreement (*knows* relation, *uses* relation) we support this by including Atom feed based [20] notification mechanisms. This is an extension to our previous work on service evolution management (SEMF) [21] that is able to manage distributed information of services that change during their life-cycle. Like SEMF, SOAF supports a set of events that can be subscribed to and that can be accessed as Atom feeds (see Table 5).

Table 5. SOAF events

Event	Description
Registration	This event describes the creation of a new SOAF entity in the SOAF network. This event is generated upon the creation of a service, a person or an organization
Change	This event describes changes of SOAF entities
Removal	This event is generated upon the removal of a SOAF entity
Connection	This events is generated if a new connection between two SOAF entities is established

Service Publication, Service Removal. Service publication in SOAF is done locally. A service provider updates its SOAF description with new services that are offered. Since we do not have a central entity that is used for service registration, we do not require service providers to actively contact a registry and provide information. Other SOAF network members that are registered for service publication events receive corresponding notifications, i.e., a registration event that contains service related information. If a network member is interested in this newly registered service, the network member contacts the service after having received the registration event and asks for the service profile. The protocol is shown in Figure 2.

The removal of existing service is closely related to the publication process. To remove a service the provider deletes the service information from its local SOAF description. The propagation of the update follows the same pattern as the publication with regard to the propagation of changes. Upon service removal, the provider obtains a list of all service users. Then, the provider checks its subscribed SOAF network members and informs all service users and the subscribed network members about the service removal with a removal event (see Figure 3).

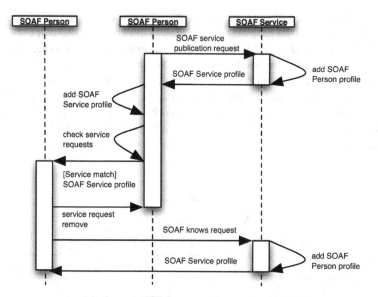

Fig. 2. SOAF publication information protocol

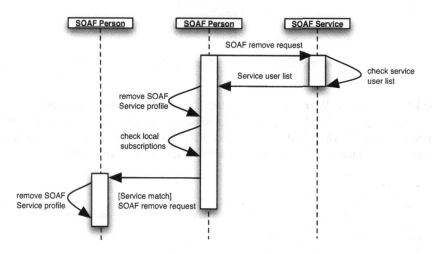

Fig. 3. SOAF removal protocol

It it worth noticing that from a conceptual point of view, SOAF does not limit this approach to humans. Since we envision services as part of the network, and thus providing well formed information, we can extend the notification to services as well.

2.4   Extending the FOAF Datamodel

In this section, we discuss the extensions of the FOAF data model with regard to SOAF concepts. Notice that the mapping is not limited to FOAF in particular, other representations of SOAF concepts are also possible. An alternative could be the use of XML structures that are linked with XLink constructs [22]. However, since FOAF has gained considerable adoption [23] [24] we have decided to integrate our prototype data model into the FOAF data model. SOAF requires new concepts to be added to the main FOAF data model with regard to the needs of services. We include a (i) *Service* class to represent services that inherits from Agent, a (ii) *uses* relation which is similar to the *knows* relation, but provides additional information, (iii) a *provides* relation that defines the connection between service providers (which may be organizations, persons, teams, virtual teams), and (iv) a dedicated *Connection* class (which also inherits from Agent) that encapsulates the connection between services, persons and organizations (see Figure 4).

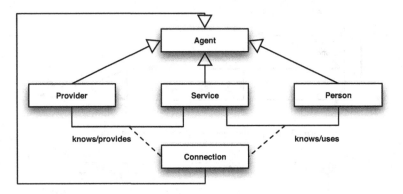

Fig. 4. An implementation moel of the SOAF network structure

SOAF Service Class. We model service related information in the SOAF service class. In our prototype data model, we provide a basic set of information that defines the capabilities service. The SOAF service class offers information about the endpoint of the service, the interface description, version information, etc. (see Listing 1.1).

```
<soaf:Service>
  <foaf:name>SOAFer</foaf:name>
  <soaf:endpoint>...</soaf:endpoint>
  <soaf:description>SOAF Service Profiles Generator</soaf:description>
  <soaf:interface rdf:resource="..."/>
  <soaf:active>true</soaf:active>
  <soaf:version>1.0</soaf:version>
</soaf:Service>
```

Listing 1.1. SOAF service class example snippet

SOAF Connection Class. The introduction of the connection class addresses the major shortcoming of FOAF with regard to connections between persons and services. In our data model, we need to attach additional attributes to a connection like creation date, state of the connection, etc. FOAF uses the *knows* relation to connect persons and this relation does not support additional attributes to further refine the type of connection.

Thus, we modeled connection class as a subclass of the *agent* class. This allows us to seamlessly integrate SOAF connections using the *knows* relation as bridge to FOAF. The connection class acts as a container for the connection between persons and services (see Listing 1.2).

```
<foaf:knows>
  <soaf:Connection>
    <soaf:established>January 23rd 2009</soaf:established>
    <soaf:active>true</soaf:active>
    <soaf:connectiontype>Continuous</soaf:connectiontype>
    <soaf:uses>
      <soaf:Service>
        <foaf:name>SOAFer</foaf:name>
        ...
      </soaf:Service>
    </soaf:uses>
  </soaf:Connection>
  <soaf:Connection>
    <soaf:established>December 1st 2008</soaf:established>
    <soaf:discontinued>December 21st 2008</soaf:discontinued>
    <soaf:active>false</soaf:active>
    <soaf:connectiontype>Continuous</soaf:connectiontype>
    <soaf:uses>
      <soaf:Service>
        <foaf:name>SOAFReporter</foaf:name>
        ...
      </soaf:Service>
    </soaf:uses>
  </soaf:Connection>
</foaf:knows>
```

Listing 1.2. SOAF connection class example snippet

SOAF Uses Relation. The *uses* relation is encapsulated in the SOAF connection class and denotes the service usage of persons, providers and services (see Listing 1.3 for an example of the *uses* relation).

```
<foaf:knows>
  <soaf:Connection>
    <soaf:established>January 23rd 2009</soaf:established>
    <soaf:active>true</soaf:active>
    <soaf:connectiontype>Continuous</soaf:connectiontype>
    <soaf:uses>
      <soaf:Service>...</soaf:Service>
    </soaf:uses>
  </soaf:Connection>
</foaf:knows>
```

Listing 1.3. SOAF uses example snippet

SOAF Provides Relation. Like the *uses* relation, the *provides* relation is encapsulated in the connection class. The *provides* relation describes connections between providers and their services where every connection models the provision of a service (see Listing 1.4).

```
<foaf:knows>
  <soaf:Connection>
    <soaf:established>January 23rd 2009</soaf:established>
    <soaf:active>true</soaf:active>
    <soaf:deprecationdate>July 23rd 2009</soaf:deprecationdate >
    <soaf:connectiontype>Continuous</soaf:connectiontype>
    <soaf:provides>
      <soaf:Service>... </soaf:Service>
    </soaf:provides>
  </soaf:Connection>
</foaf:knows>
```

Listing 1.4. SOAF provides example snippet

3   Discussion

One of the major benefits of the SOAF network is that we are able to create a dynamic ecosystem of services from a bottom up approach. In particular, since we integrate humans and services alike, we can track relations between different stakeholders of Web services [25]. For instance, a service developer might integrate different services into a new service by wiring the respective service invocations in the code of the service. By storing such information into SOAF networks, we provide information about service dependencies and input for creating dependency graphs of services.

Another important aspect is to consider historical information in SOAF which are particular interest for service mashups. These are created for a certain purpose, and this kind of information is reflected by connections of different services and persons that used this particular service mashup. Depending on the amount of meta information provided, we provide the ability to search in SOAF networks for examples of mashups that solved particular problems. These examples can be viewed as best practices and thus serve as blueprint for the creation of other mashups.

Related to historical information is the aspect of network evolution. With the data provided by SOAF, we can observe the development of network connections (*uses, knows, provides* relation) and study the general dynamics of the service network. For instance, we can establish the number of services that oined the network during a certain period of time or how many services where removed, etc. Another example is the creation of metrics that define the attractiveness of services for other members of the SOAF network, based on the data SOAF provides.

As "side-effect" in SOAF, we can observe emerging clusters of well connected services and persons. This allows us to foster communities in a bottom up manner from existing connections between services and persons. In contrast to existing Web service community approaches, we follow the social aspect more closely and do not pre-define the community functionality. We are aware that a social approach brings a certain degree of fuzziness. Furthermore, it is difficult to obtain the overall functionality of communities, since some services might overlap in their functionality. Especially when limited information is available (e.g., WSDL descriptions), a clear description in terms of overall community functionality might not be feasible. However, even with fuzzy information, we are able to define a set of core functions that are used within a community since through the community structure we know which services have the highest connection and usage rates.

SOAF also supports *social based service discovery* which is the translation of human search activities into a service discovery process. To illustrate our approach, consider the following example. Company A needs a service that is able to provide information of public holidays in european countries, for a project meeting planning purposes. Traditionally, an employee of company A would search a public registry or search engine [6] for a service that is able to fulfill this requirements. If no corresponding service can be found, the search is repeated after a while in order to find a service and eventually a service may be found (we assume, that such a service exists in reality and is published during the time the employee searches for it).

When we transform the discovery example from above to a social network oriented approach, person A would ask another person B (colleague from work or friend) if s/he knows a holiday information service. If this is not the case, then person A could ask person B if person B either knows another person that in turn could be asked or if s/he hears from such a service to inform person A about the service. This approach is also known as epidemic protocol [26]. The discovery process we envision in SOAF mimics the process that we described above. First of all, we assume that SOAF provides a link between person A and person B. Furthermore, Person B has connections to services and persons s/he knows and/or uses. By following our example, person A browses all services that person B knows and learns that none of the services known by B is able to provide the required functionality. In this case, person A registers to a feed person B provides in order to get a notification if person B finds a service or if person B is linked with a service of the required functionality. Simultaneously, person A can do the same with other persons in the network and thus distribute the discovery among other network participants by following links.

4 Prototype

We base our prototype on the distributed architecture of previous work [21] and extends it with the required functionality to model SOAF networks. Our prototype uses a XML database [7] to persist SOAF related information, which we organize internally in several different collections (see Table 6). We use XQuery expressions to generate SOAF profiles from the persisted data [8].

Our prototype provides the basic functionality (implemented as REST-based Web services) to manage SOAF data. In order to provide access to events, our prototype generates Atom feeds from SOAF data. We organize the events in three separate feeds as shown in Figure 4. For analytical purposes and to co-relate events, we foresee links between different entries of the feeds.

5 Related Work

From a technical perspective, our approach have similarities with the Web Service Introspection Language [27]. Like WSIL, SOAF also provides a container to store Web

---

[6] seekda.com, strikeiron.com, xmethods.net

[7] eXist XML Database http://www.exist-db.org/index.html

[8] For an example see http://www.infosys.tuwien.ac.at/staff/treiber/ soaf/MartinTreiber.soaf

Table 6. SOAF collections in the XML Database backend

Collection	Description
Service	Stores service related information (e.g., endpoint, link to interface description, etc.)
Person	Stores all person relevant data (e.g., name, surname, etc.)
Connection	Stores connection information (e.g., knows, uses, provides, etc.)
Organization	Contains information about organizations (e.g., name, address, etc.)

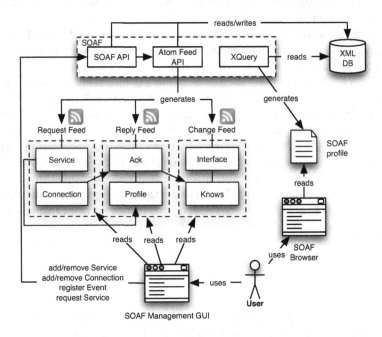

Fig. 5. SOAF prototype framework overview

service related data and supports the linking of services with each other. In contrast to WSIL, SOAF extends the service linkage towards social networks that is not provided by WSIL itself and integrates humans and services into a common network.

Semantic Web service communities as introduced by [28] aim at creating communities of Web services. However, the aforementioned approach focuses on issues like service replaceability and how semantic descriptions of communities can be created. We consider our approach at the other end of the spectrum, since SOAF follows a bottom up approach and doesn't require ontologies to define the available service functionality. Moreover, we explicitly consider humans and services as fundamental part of a network and integrate social structures into of service networks.

The work of Basole and Rouse [29] is related to our work in general. Value Networks [30] are of interest when business aspects are studied, i.e., the value that can be generated by such networks. This is of particular interest when we use our approach to structure available information of humans and services for further analysis with regard to businesses.

Mandelli [31] studies self-organizational aspects that are of importance for our work, since we consider SOAF as environment where we can investigate emergent structures. What distinguishes our approach is the technical focus of our work since we aim to augment existing social networks with service descriptions that we consider this as foundation for the integration of services in a future Internet of Services [32].

Throughout our work, we utilize concepts that originate from connector oriented architectures [33]. In particular, we borrow the concept of connectors to model connections between services and humans in SOAF networks. Furthermore, we also consider dynamic aspects of connections between entities in SOAF networks. With respect to changes, we refer to software evolution which has been studied on software architecture level [34] and evolution languages have been proposed to model software architecture changes. While conceptually similar, our focus lies on the basic support for change mechanisms.

6 Future Work

In this paper, we have presented SOAF (Service of a Friend), which integrates humans and services into a common network structure. We have showed how to model humans and services by extending FOAF and providing a common data model. In future work, we are going to analyze scalability issues in our proposed SOAF network structure. Since we consider humans in the loop we require a simulation model to estimate the human impact in such networks (e.g., during searching). Closely related are human provided services [35] which we are going to investigate in the context of SOAF. In particular we are going to study dynamic aspects like quality of service of human provided services and how to address these issues in SOAF.

Furthermore, we are going to investigate how to generate larger networks from existing data. In order to obtain simulation data, we are going to crawl social networks and to address the important question how to bootstrap SOAF networks from this data. With simulations of larger SOAF networks we are going to study evolutionary aspects of social service networks. Of particular interest is the study of concepts like service fitness in simulations of SOAF networks and the impact analysis of fitness changes in such networks.

References

1. Ruggaber, R.: Internet of services sap research vision. In: WETICE 2007: Proceedings of the 16th IEEE International Workshops on Enabling Technologies: Infrastructure for Collaborative Enterprises, Washington, DC, USA, p. 3. IEEE Computer Society, Los Alamitos (2007)
2. Kleinberg, J.: The convergence of social and technological networks. Commun. ACM 51, 66–72 (2008)
3. Voss, J.: Tagging, folksonomy & co - renaissance of manual indexing? CoRR abs/cs/0701072 (2007)
4. Brickley, D., Miller, L.: Foaf vocabulary specification 0.91 (November 2007)
5. W3C: Resource Description Framework (RDF) (2000)

6. Howe, J.: The rise of crowdsourcing (June 2006), http://www.wired.com/wired/archive/14.06/crowds.html
7. Maximilien, E., Wilkinson, H., Desai, N., Tai, S.: A domain-specific language for web apis and services mashups. In: Krämer, B.J., Lin, K.-J., Narasimhan, P. (eds.) ICSOC 2007. LNCS, vol. 4749, pp. 13–26. Springer, Heidelberg (2007)
8. Saphir, J.: Situational applications - cost-effective software solutions for immediate business challenges (2008), http://knol.google.com/k/jonathan-sapir/situational-applications/
9. Shirky, C.: Situated software (2004)
10. Endpoints, A., Systems, A., Systems, B., Corporation, I., Oracle, SAP: Ws-bpel extension for people (bpel4people), version 1.0 (June 2007)
11. Schall, D., Truong, H.L., Dustdar, S.: Unifying human and software services in web-scale collaborations. IEEE Internet Computing 12, 62–68 (2008)
12. Garofalakis, J.D., Panagis, Y., Sakkopoulos, E., Tsakalidis, A.K.: Contemporary web service discovery mechanisms. J. Web Eng. 5(3), 265–290 (2006)
13. Microsoft: Uddi shutdown (2006)
14. van den Heuvel, W.J., Yang, J., Papazoglou, M.: Service representation, discovery, and composition for e-marketplaces. Cooperative Information Systems, 70–284 (2001)
15. Benatallah, B., Hacid, M.S., Leger, A., Rey, C., Toumani, F.: On automating web services discovery. The VLDB Journal 14(1), 84–96 (2005)
16. Gruber, T.R.: Towards principles for the design of ontologies used for knowledge sharing. In: Guarino, N., Poli, R. (eds.) Formal Ontology in Conceptual Analysis and Knowledge Representation, Deventer, The Netherlands. Kluwer Academic Publishers, Dordrecht (1993)
17. Choi, N., Song, I.Y., Han, H.: A survey on ontology mapping. SIGMOD Rec. 35(3), 34–41 (2006)
18. Barros, A.P., Dumas, M.: The rise of web service ecosystems. IT Professional 8(5), 31–37 (2006)
19. W3C: OWL Web Ontology Language Overview (2004) W3C Recommendation (February 10, 2004)
20. IETF: The Atom Syndication Format (2005), http://tools.ietf.org/html/rfc4287
21. Treiber, M., Truong, H.L., Dustdar, S.: Semf - service evolution management framework. In: Treiber, M., Truong, H.L., Dustdar, S. (eds.) 34th Euromicro Conference on Software Engineering and Advanced Applications. SEAA 2008, pp. 329–336 (2008)
22. W3C: Xml linking language (xlink) version 1.1 (March 2008)
23. Ding, L., Zhou, L., Finin, T., Joshi, A.: How the semantic web is being used: An analysis of foaf documents, p. 113c (January 2005)
24. Golbeck, J., Rothstein, M.: Linking social networks on the web with foaf: A semantic web case study. In: Fox, D., Gomes, C.P. (eds.) AAAI, pp. 1138–1143. AAAI Press, Menlo Park (2008)
25. Canfora, G., Penta, M.D.: Testing services and service-centric systems: Challenges and opportunities. IT Professional 8(2), 10–17 (2006)
26. Demers, A., Greene, D., Hauser, C., Irish, W., Larson, J., Shenker, S., Sturgis, H., Swinehart, D., Terry, D.: Epidemic algorithms for replicated database maintenance. In: PODC 1987: Proceedings of the sixth annual ACM Symposium on Principles of distributed computing, pp. 1–12. ACM, New York (1987)
27. IBM, Microsoft: Web services inspection language (ws-inspection) 1.0 (November 2001)
28. Medjahed, B., Bouguettaya, A.: A Dynamic Foundational Architecture for Semantic Web Services. Distributed and Parallel Databases 17, 179–206 (2005)

29. Basole, R.C., Rouse, W.B.: Complexity of service value networks: conceptualization and empirical investigation. IBM Syst. J. 47(1), 53–70 (2008)
30. Allee, V.: Reconfiguring the value network. Journal of Business Strategy 21(4) (August 2000)
31. Mandelli, A.: Self-organization and new hierarchies in complex evolutionary value networks. IGI Publishing, Hershey (2004)
32. Schroth, C., Janner, T.: Web 2.0 and soa: Converging concepts enabling the internet of services. IT Professional 9(3), 36–41 (2007)
33. Shaw, M., Garlan, D.: Software architecture: perspectives on an emerging discipline. Prentice-Hall, Inc., Upper Saddle River (1996)
34. Oreizy, P., Medvidovic, N., Taylor, R.N.: Architecture-based runtime software evolution. In: ICSE 1998: Proceedings of the 20th international conference on Software engineering, Washington, DC, USA, pp. 177–186. IEEE Computer Society, Los Alamitos (1998)
35. Schall, D., Truong, H.L., Dustdar, S.: The human-provided services framework. In: CEC/EEE, pp. 149–156 (2008)

RESTful Transactions Supported by the Isolation Theorems*

Amir Razavi, Alexandros Marinos, Sotiris Moschoyiannis, and Paul Krause

Department of Computing, FEPS, University of Surrey,
Guildford, Surrey, GU2 7XH, UK
{a.razavi,a.marinos,s.moschoyiannis,p.krause}@surrey.ac.uk

Abstract. With REST becoming the dominant architectural paradigm for web services in distributed systems, more and more use cases are applied to it, including use cases that require transactional guarantees. We propose a RESTful transaction model that satisfies both the constraints of transactions and those of the REST architectural style. We then apply the isolation theorems to prove the robustness of its properties on a formal level.

Keywords: REST, Transactions, Isolation Theorems, Locking.

1 Introduction

Representational State Transfer (REST) is a distributed computing architectural style first defined in 1999 by Roy Fielding [7] as an abstraction of the architectural style that had emerged in the World Wide Web. REST focuses on resources identified by names, a fixed number of methods with known semantics to manipulate those resources, hypermedia as a means of traversing the resources and statelessness in the interactions between client and server. REST has gained traction in addressing many common use cases for distributed systems [4],[13]. As is common with disruptive technologies, REST over HTTP is evolving to compete with WS-* in increasingly advanced scenarios. While REST has made great progress, the WS-* stack is currently the only standardized way to perform arbitrary transactions. A RESTful API has to resort to custom solutions of variable quality in order to address this issue. This paper aims to define a RESTful transaction model that is designed to operate over HTTP. We then apply the Isolation Theorem to prove the correctness of the model.

In terms of RESTful transactions, various approaches have been proposed. The traditional approach is to simply design a new resource that can be used to trigger the desired transaction on the server side. For example, when transferring funds between bank accounts, this approach proposes creating a 'transfer' resource to which new 'transfers' can be POSTed. While this approach can be very simple to implement at design time, it ties users to the ability of the developers to predict usage at design time. Furthermore, in scenarios where a large or even infinite variation of transactions and transaction types may take place, it is not reasonable to expect all the corresponding

---

* This work was supported by the EU-FP6 funded project OPAALS Contract No 034824.

M. Gaedke, M. Grossniklaus, and O. Díaz (Eds.): ICWE 2009, LNCS 5648, pp. 394–409, 2009.
© Springer-Verlag Berlin Heidelberg 2009

resources to have been designed beforehand. Other approaches [14] suggest extending REST to include mutex locks which would require extending HTTP as well. The alternative to these approaches [18] is to introduce locks on resources by modelling them as resources themselves. While this approach looks much more capable, the details of its implementation and its extension into transactions have neither been fleshed out nor proven. The general term 'Transaction' has been introduced by Gray [1] and is defined by the four properties contained in the ACID acronym. These properties guarantee that a system is maintained in a consistent state, even as transactions are executed within it concurrently. This includes situations where one or more transactions fail to commit. When dealing with a sequence of transactions (one transaction executed at a time), each transaction starts with the consistent state that its predecessor ended with. If all the transactions are short, the data are centralised in a main memory, and all data are accessed through a single thread, there is no need for concurrency. The transactions can simply be run in sequence. Real-world interactive systems however, often require execution of several concurrent transactions. Use cases such as distributed environments or dynamic allocation of resources to external developers illustrate this.

While transactions are concerned with the constraints of maintaining the ACID properties, REST adheres to its own set of constraints. These are primarily expressed by the uniform interface constraint, but supported by the following four constraints: Resource Identification; Resource manipulation through representations; Self-descriptive messages; Hypermedia as the engine of application state. Our efforts are directed at creating a truly RESTful transaction model that satisfies both the constraints of REST while possessing the ACID properties. This paper is structured as follows. Section 2 examines classic transactional challenges that appear in distributed systems. Section 3 introduces Isolation theorems, which includes theorems that show the correctness of a transactional system by applying the necessary constraints. Section 4 applies the transaction model in a RESTful framework. In section 5 the proof of correctness of constraints is applied, by using classical isolation theorems.

2 Concurrency Challenges in RESTful HTTP

The classic view of isolation considers the transaction in terms of inputs and outputs [10],[6]. This means that transactions have *read* (input) and *write* (output) operations. Write operations are described as operations that affect the state of resources. On the other hand, REST prescribes a uniform interface for accessing resources. One challenge is therefore to map the traditional input/output perspective with the RESTful approach to the uniform interface. Since our model operates over the HTTP protocol, we must examine its four fundamental operations. GET is the standard retrieve operation. Its execution must be safe; it should have no side-effects. It should also be idempotent; duplicate messages should have no adverse effects. POST is understood as an operation to create a new resource on a server where the target URI is not known. The representation of the resource is sent via POST to the collection that will contain the resource. The server determines its appropriate location and the resulting URI is returned to the client. In this model, we approach POST purely as a creation operation and use it in the mechanics of the model to handle creation of resources such as transactions, locks, and others. However, transactions that include POST operations are outside the scope of our model. PUT can be used for updating resources, by simply instructing the server to apply a new representation as a replacement of the previous one. It can also be used to create a new resource, when a representation is PUT at a URI that was previously unused. In the proposed model, PUT operations on pre-existing resources are the main operations that a transaction can execute, with only the Update aspect within scope. DELETE is used to remove the resource representation at the target URI. While they are used as part of the mechanics of the model, transactions which include DELETE operations are out of scope of the proposed model. From the above discussion it can be extracted that our model is concerned with transactions that are sequences of GET operations or PUT operations, specifically when used for updating resources. While other uses of the above verbs are of interest, this limited scope makes robust theoretical consistency proofs feasible. The limitation to GET and PUT applies only to the target resources, those that will remain after the transaction has committed. For interactions with the transactional resources, those that are created to enable the execution of the transaction, the full range of HTTP operations is utilised. As GET operations do not change the state of resources, when the initial state of a resource is consistent, concurrent GET requests to the same resource, cannot cause inconsistency. On the contrary, PUT operations of different transactions on the same resource, change the state of the resource and may violate consistency or isolation. The basic assumption is that a transaction knows what it is doing in terms of its internal data manipulation, meanwhile if it runs in isolation (without any concurrent transactions), it will manipulate its own resource state correctly. Therefore, sequential PUTs within the same transaction are not problematic [10], [2]. At the same time however, overlap between PUTs of one transaction and GET action of another, can violate isolation and cause inconsistency. Additionally, PUT-related interactions between different concurrent transactions on the same resource can also cause a problem. If we consider GETs operations as inputs of transactions and PUTs operations as output operations of them, this can be expressed as:

$$O_i \cap (I_j \cup O_j) = \emptyset \text{ for all } i \neq j \tag{1}$$

By letting I_i be the set of resources accessed via GET by transaction T_i (its inputs), and O_i be the set of resources altered via PUT by transaction T_i (its outputs). Based on EQ.1, in the set of transactions$\{T_i\}$, when their outputs are disjoint from one another's inputs and outputs, they can run in parallel with no concurrency anomalies. Clearly by applying EQ.1 any transaction scheduler can work. Conventionally for applying EQ.1 each transaction should declare its Input-Output set, then a scheduler is able to compare the new transaction's need to all running transactions and in case of a conflict, initiation of the new transaction would be delayed until the conflicting transactions complete. This approach is called 'Static allocation'. The computing complexity of analysing the inputs and outputs before running transactions causes a bottleneck on scalability. The approach has been abandoned in more modern transactional environments [2], [9]. The 'Dynamic allocation' scheme has been introduced as the substituting approach. Under the prism of dynamic allocations, we can view transactions as sequence of operations on resources. A particular resource is subject to one operation at a time. Each operation of a transaction is either a GET or a PUT. Resources go through a sequence of versions as

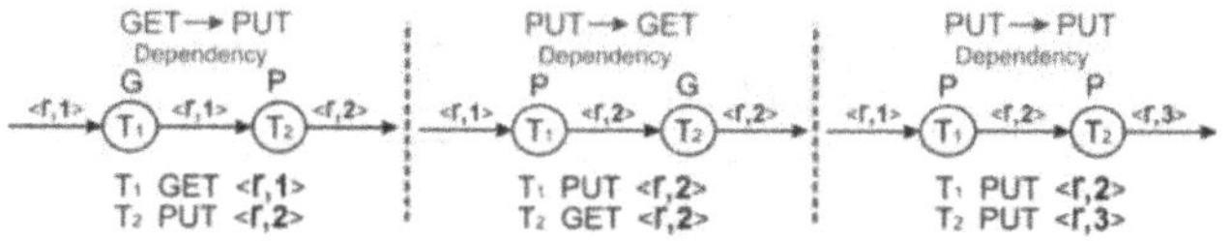

Fig. 1. Different Dependencies

they are updated by PUT operations. GETs do not change the resource version. If a transaction GETs a resource, the transaction depends on that resource version. If the transaction PUTs a resource, the resulting resource version depends on that transaction. When a transaction aborts and goes through the undo logic, all its PUT operations must be undone. These cause the resources to get new versions, as the undo looks like an ordinary new update. In the RESTful model we apply the shadow-based updating, which saves the complexity in terms of aborting the lock. This can be seen in the existence and behaviour of the conditional resource representation in section 4.

Theoretically a dependency graph can be read as a time sequence. The main conclusion of applying the ACID properties is that any dependency graph without cycles implies an isolated execution of transactions. General danger of violating isolation is related to the various dependency cycles. Similar to conventional transactions, REST cycle dependencies are categorised to three generic forms: When two (or more) transactions access the same resource, they may produce two (or more) different versions of that resource (*lost update*), or simply they may work with the out-of-date version of the resource (*dirty* GET and *unrepeatable* GET). More details can be found at the classic references such as [10] or our previous work [21].

3 Isolation Theorems

Isolation theorems include several theorems, which shows the correctness of a transactional system by applying few constraints [10]. The constraints will be explained in sections and after applying them in a RESTful framework, we explain the proof of correctness of constraints, by using classical isolation theorems in section 5. In order to present a theoretical aspect of our model, we define a formal vocabulary that is larger than the standard HTTP operations. We call these formal terms operations. The correspondence with HTTP operations is made explicit in section 4.3 and figure x. More importantly, for avoiding violating consistent access, in term of GET and PUT resources, the SLOCK and XLOCK should be applied on the resources (before GET or PUT) and these locks should be released when the dependency on the resources expires. Therefore, the model should support the major *actions* of GET, PUT, XLOCK, SLOCK, UNLOCK on the resources, as well as generic actions BEGIN, COMMIT, ROLLBACK. GET and PUT have the usual meaning: GET returns the named resource's value to the program, while PUT alters the named resource's state. A *transaction* is any sequence of actions starting with a BEGIN action, ending with a COMMIT or ROLLBACK action, and containing any other BEGIN, COMMIT, or ROLLBACK actions. Figure 2 demonstrates an example in term of a conceptual transactional access to resources R1 and R2.

Fig. 2. Transaction life cycle

Transactions are characterized symbolically by a sequence such as $\langle\langle t, a_i, r_i\rangle | i = 1, ..., n\rangle$. This means that the ith step of transaction t preformed action a_i on resource r_i. To simplify the transaction model, BEGIN, COMMIT, and ROLLBACK are defined in terms of other actions, so that only GET, PUT, LOCK, and UNLOCK actions remain. A *simple transaction* is composed of GET, PUT, XLOCK, SLOCK, and UNLOCK actions. Every transaction, T, can be translated into an *equivalent simple transaction* as follows [10]:

(1) Discard the BEGIN action.
(2) If the transaction ends with a COMMIT action, replace that action with the following sequence of UNLOCKS:

<UNLOCK A | if SLOCK A or XLOCK A appears in T for any resource A>.

(3) If the transaction ends with a ROLLBACK statement, replace that action with the following sequence of PUTs and then UNLOCKs:

<PUT A | if PUT A appears in T for any resource A> ||<UNLOCK A | if SLOCK A or XLOCK A appears in T for any resource A>.

The idea here is that the COMMIT action simply releases Locks, while the ROLLBACK action must first undo all changes to the resources the transaction wrote (PUT) and then issue the resources the transaction wrote (PUT) and then issue the unlock statements. If the transaction has no LOCK statements, then neither COMMIT nor ROLLBACK will issue any UNLOCK statements, as that would risk violating isolation. A transaction is said to be *well-formed* if all its GET, PUT, and UNLOCK actions are covered by locks, and if each lock action is eventually followed by a corresponding UNLOCK action [2], [9]. A transaction is defined as *two-phase* if all its LOCK actions precede all its UNLOCK actions. A two-phase transaction T has a growing phase, $T[1], ...,T[j]$, during which it acquires locks, and a shrinking phase, $T[j+1], ...,T[n]$, during which it releases locks [10]. The simplified Figure 3 (focusing on the formal locks), has been shown in Figure 3 and the concept of well-formed and two phase is indicated.

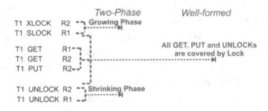

Fig. 3. Two-phase and Well-formed locking

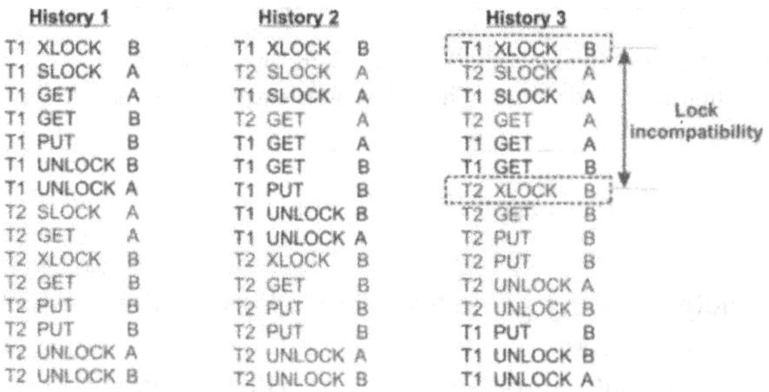

History 1	History 2	History 3

Fig. 4. Different types of histories

First, a *history* is any sequence-preserving merge of the actions of a set of transactions into a single sequence for the set of transactions and is denoted $H = \langle\langle t, a, r\rangle_i | i = 1, ..., n\rangle$. Each step of the history $\langle t, a, r\rangle$ is an action a by transaction t on resource r. A history for the set of transactions $\{T_j\}$ is a sequence, each containing transaction T_j as a subsequence and containing nothing else. A history lists the order in which actions were successfully completed. *Serial histories* are One-transaction-at-a-time histories. In serial histories as no concurrency-induced, there is not any inconsistency and no problem with viewing dirty data by other transactions. As it is expected, a history should not complete a lock action on a resource when that resource is locked by another transaction. But if two or more transactions want to just read (GET) the content of a resource, they do not change the resource version (state). This may not cause any conflict or access to dirty data (data/resource which has been PUT by another transaction) but the transaction has not committed and may change the version of the resource again (2.2). The table 2 shows the lock compatibility. The locking compatibility rules constrain the set of allowed histories.

Legal history: Histories that obey the locking constraints are called *legal*. In Figure 4, three histories are shown, where History 1 and 2 are legal and History 3 is not. History 1 is a serial history. It is obviously legal, as each transaction will be run in sequence and no locks will conflict. History 2 is a non-serial legal history. There are no incompatible locks between T1 and T2 as T2 applies an XLOCK on resource B only when T1 has performed an UNLOCK. Finally, history 3 is a non-serial and not legal history, as resource B has an XLOCK by T1 but T2 applies an XLOCK on the same resource, which is illegal according to Table 1. As a consequence, we can see that T1 then performs a PUT based on its earlier GET and overwrites T2's PUT, which is the case of 'Lost Updates' as discussed in 2.

4 Locks in RESTful HTTP

Having defined the formal language we will use to prove the robustness of our model as well as discussed history well-formedness and legality, we now translate this abstract language into HTTP operations. To handle HTTP concurrency challenges, we introduce the concept of locks. This is done in a way that does not affect the always available and backwards compatible nature of the web. For an API to be characterized as RESTful according to the hypermedia constraint, it must allow a client to interact

```
<lockable>
    <link rel="lock_collection"  href="http://example.org/resource/locks/" />
    <link rel="transaction_collection"  href="http://example.org/transactions/" />
</lockable>
```

Fig. 5. (R) XML Fragment

with the service solely by being given a single URI and understanding of the relevant media types. This enforces loose-coupling and elimination of assumptions.

Ideally, any resource that can be served by an HTTP server should be a **Lockable Resource (R)** regardless of media type. This however would require the HTTP protocol to carry the metadata for the locking mechanism. Since we wish to preserve the HTTP protocol, we can use either prescribe that the resource links to lock collection and the transaction collection, or create custom HTTP headers that contain them. An example of the first approach can be seen in Figure 5. What is important is that the client has access to these resources while not obstructing normal use of the lockable resource.

Lock Resource (R-L): The lock resource is represented by a dedicated media type and should contain the elements in Table 1.

Table 1. Elements of R-L

ResourceURI: a link back to the resource that this lock affects.
TransactionURI: a link to the transaction that controls the lock.
Type: "S" or "X" depending on the type of the lock.
PrevLockURI: a link to the previous lock in the lock sequence.
Timestamp: Server's timestamp when the lock was granted.
Duration: Indicates the interval that the lock has been granted for.
ConditionalRepresentationURI: A link to the representation of the resource that will come into effect once the lock is committed.
InitialRepresentationURI: A link to the initial state of the lock resource.

The type element can take one of two values, X or S, corresponding to the available lock types. X stands for **XLOCK: eXclussive Lock**, and S stands for **SLOCK: Shared Lock**. To place a new lock, the server must authenticate the user as the owner of the transaction that the lock references. The time period of effectiveness that is granted to a lock is dependent on the maximum length of time that the server is prepared to grant a guarantee to the client. Once the duration of the lock expires, the lock is aborted. *To avoid violating 2PL, once a lock of a transaction expires, all other locks of the same transaction expire.* The result of the GET operation does not change until a lock of type X is committed. In this sense, the locks and transactions are transparent to the GET which on commit reacts as if a simple PUT or DELETE was applied. This was a specific design objective. Direct PUT and DELETE operations return a *'405 Method Not Allowed'* HTTP response for the duration of a lock's effect. GET requests should still return successfully. This behaviour maintains backwards compatibility, with the understanding that if a client requires further guarantees on the future state of the resource, the client should seek to place a lock. In all other cases, the semantics of GET are unaffected, as a GET on a resource does not guarantee that the state will remain unchanged for any period of time.

Table 2. Legal lock sequences

		Mode of Preceding Lock	
		Share	Exclusive
Mode Of New Lock	Share	Yes	No
	Exclusive	No	No

Resource Lock Collection (R-Lc): The R-Lc contains locks in sequences that follow the compatibility rules stated in Table 2, rendering the transaction well-formed. The lock collection is represented as an Atom Feed [13]. Since ATOM does not support sequencing entries, we use the 'PrevLockURI' element of the lock resource to create a linked list of locks that can be represented as an ATOM Feed. The client can retrieve the lock collection via GET to determine if the resource is locked. An empty feed indicates an unlocked resource. New locks can be submitted to the resource collection via the POST method.

4.1 Two Phase Locking and Recoverability

Clarifying the scope of each transaction and determining whether it is in a GROWTH or SHRINK phase is necessary. In this part we introduce the required resources. The **Transaction (T)** resource is represented by a dedicated media type and should contain a TransactionCollectionURI, an OwnerURI and a TransactionLockCollectionURI. These 3 elements identify the collections of information vital to the execution of a transaction. The owner of the transaction can GET the transaction resource as a means of locating these collections. The **Transaction Collection (Tc)** is a resource where new transactions are submitted via the POST operation which creates a new transaction and returns the URI for its representation. The resource itself cannot be accessed via GET as the clients that need to know the location of a specific resource are informed at the time of POSTing. The **Transaction Lock Collection (T-Lc)** contains links to the locks that belong to a specific transaction, formatted as an Atom feed. Clients cannot abort single locks directly but must do so through the T-Lc which aborts all the locks of a transaction, leaving the transaction void and is equivalent to aborting the transaction.

Table 3. Available Operations for T-Lc

GET	Returns the collection of locks relevant to a transaction
DELETE	Aborts all the locks of the relevant transaction. This can only be performed by an owner of the transaction.

4.2 Recoverability

Based on the Rollback Theorem, a transaction that unlocks an exclusive lock and then performs a '*Rollback*' is not well-formed and can potentially cause a wormhole unless the transaction is degenerated. As the theorem is well-known, we refer the interested reader to [9] for the actual proof. The important point of the theorem is that we have to degenerate the transaction to effect rollback. For this purpose, our model does not store potential updates on the actual resources but works on the shadow of the locked data, called a *conditional resource representation*. The **Initial Resource Representation (R-L-IR)** is of identical media type as the locked resource and stores the initial state. The initial representation is archived together with the lock to represent the change caused by the commit of the lock and enable rollback. The **Conditional Resource Representation (R-L-CR)** is of identical media type as the locked resource and is essentially the state that will be applied to the resource once the XLOCK is committed.

Table 4. Available Operations for R-L-CR

GET	Returns the representation that will be committed if the relevant XLOCK is committed.
PUT	Creates a new conditional state that will replace the current state of the locked resource once the linking XLOCK is committed.
DELETE	Deletes the conditional state. If the XLOCK is committed, there will be no write action performed.

4.3 Model Overview

Having defined all the resource types, it is easy to see that an interconnected network arises (Figure 6). It can be observed that having a URI for R is enough to locate all other resources in the network. The connection from Tc to T is perforated as there is no GET ability for the Tc resource, for security reasons. The URI of a given T is only returned as a response to the initial POST operation on Tc performed by the transaction's owner. Table 5 summarizes the relevant resource types of our model.

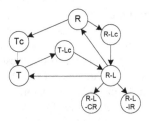

Fig. 6. Resource Hypermedia connections

Table 5. Transaction model resource types

Lockable Resource (R)	A resource that locks can be applied to.
Resource Lock Collection (R-Lc)	The collection of locks that apply to a particular resource.
Lock Resource (R-L)	The representation of a specific lock.
Conditional Resource Representation (R-L-CR)	The potential representation of a locked resource.
Conditional Resource Representation (R-L-IR)	The initial representation of a locked resource.
Transaction Collection (Tc)	The collection of transactions on the server.
Transaction Resource (T)	The representation of a specific transaction.
Transaction Lock Collection (T-Lc)	The collection of locks connected to a specific transaction.

4.4 RESTful Transaction Examples

To illustrate the operation of the transaction model, table 6 shows a scenario where two transactions from clients A and B interact with resources, R1 and R2. Table 7 shows what happens if a third client tries to XLOCK a resource that is already locked.

Table 6. Concurrent transactions

Client	Operation	Resource	Response	Description
A	GET	R2	200 OK	GETting R2 to extract location of TC and R2-LC
A	POST <new transaction>	TC	201 CREATED {Location: T1}	Creating a new transaction
A	POST <LOCK {type:X}>	R2-LC	201 CREATED {Location: R2-L1}	POSTing an XLOCK to R2-LC
B	GET	R1	200 OK	GETting R1 to extract location of TC and R1-LC
B	POST <new transaction>	TC	201 CREATED {Location: T2}	Creating a new transaction
B	POST <LOCK {type:S}>	R1-LC	201 CREATED {Location: R1-L1}	POSTing an XLOCK to R1-LC
A	GET	R1	200 OK	GETting R1 to extract location of R1-LC
A	POST <LOCK {type:S}>	R1-LC	201 CREATED {Location: R1-L1}	POSTing an XLOCK to R1-LC
B	GET	R1	200 OK	GETting the locked representation of R1
A	GET	R1	200 OK	GETting the locked representation of R1
A	GET	R2	200 OK	GETting the locked representation of R2
A	GET	R2-L1	200 OK	GETting R1 to extract location of R2-C
A	PUT <new representation>	R2-C	201 CREATED	iting a conditional Representation of R2
A	DELETE	T1	200 OK	Commiting R2-C to R2 and Unlocking R1 and R2
B	GET	R2	200 OK	GETting R2 to extract location of R2-LC
B	POST <LOCK {type:X}>	R2-LC	201 CREATED {Location: R2-L1}	POSTing an XLOCK to R2-LC
B	GET	R2	200 OK	GETting the locked representation of R2
B	PUT <new representation>	R2-C	201 CREATED	Creating a conditional Representation of R2
B	PUT <new representation>	R2-C	200 OK	Updating the conditional Representation of R2
B	DELETE	T2	200 OK	Commiting R2-C to R2 and Unlocking R1 and R2

Table 7. Attempting to lock an already locked resource

Client	Operation	Resource	Response	Description
C	POST <LOCK {type:X}>	R2-LC	403 Forbidden	POSTing an XLOCK to R2-LC while R2 is locked

5 Applying the Isolation Theorems to REST

As our approach follows two-phase and well-formed locking, in this section, we use
the classical isolation theorems [2], [9], [10] to show its correctness. Since the formal
model introduced in section 3 is fully compatible with Isolation theorems, we apply it
in classical proof of isolation theorems. For doing so, we can start from the main
property of our model; all transactions are well-formed and two-phase. Based on the
Locking Theorem, if all transactions are well-formed and two-phase, then any legal
history will be isolated and based on Wormhole Theorem, A history is isolated if, and
only if, it has no wormhole transactions. By adopting these two theorems, we show
our approach, does not have any wormhole. We start by formulating the wormhole in
the RESTful formal approach, then presenting the wormhole theorem and finally
evoking the Locking theorem in our RESTful formal presentation (see Figure 7).

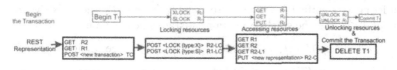

Fig. 7. Mapping Actions to Operations

5.1 Dependency and Wormholes

First we try to have a definition of a clear legal history; transaction t has resource r locked
in SHARED mode at step k of history H, if for some $i < k$ action $H[i] = \langle t, SLOCK, r \rangle$,
and if there is no $\langle t, UNLOCK, r \rangle$ action in the subhistory $H[i + 1], ..., H[k - 1]$,

similarly transaction t has resource r locked in EXCLUSIVE mode at step k is defined analogously. Then we say history h is legal if there is no step $H[k]$ of H at which two distinct transactions have the same resource locked in incompatible mode. In a simple way, we can say any data which has been PUT by the transaction is dirty data until is unlocked. Therefore when we analyse the system behaviour by using the history, easily we can say at each step of history, which resource value have been committed and which are dirty. We can analyse this by using dependency graph. One transaction instance T is said to depend on another transaction T' in a history H if T GET (reads) or PUT (writes) data-resources previously PUT (written) by T' in the history H, or if T PUT (writes) a resource previously GET (read) by T'. We can formalise different dependencies (Fig 1) by Dependency Graph; a directed graph where nodes are 'transactions', Arcs are 'transactions dependencies' and label is 'resource versions'. The *version* of an resource r at step k of a history is an integer and is denoted $V(r,k)$. In the beginning each resource has version zero ($V(r,0)=0$). At step k of history H, resource r has a version equal to the number of writes of that resource before this step. Formally this means:

$$V(r,k) = \left| \{ \langle t_j, a_j, r_j \rangle \in H \mid j < k \text{ and } a_j = PUT \text{ and } r_j = r \} \right|$$

(The outer vertical bars represent the set cardinality function.)

Each history, H, for a set of transactions $\{T_i\}$ defines a ternary *dependency relation* DEP(H), defined as; Let $T1$ and $T2$ be any two distinct transactions, let r be any resource, and let i, j be any two steps of H with $i < j$. Suppose step $H[i]$ involves action $a1$ of $T1$ on resource r, step $H[j]$ involves $a2$ of $T2$ on r, and suppose there is no PUT of r by any transaction between these steps (there is no $\langle T', PUT, r \rangle$ in $H[i+1], ..., H[j-1]$). Then DEP(H) is defined as:

$$\langle T, \langle r, V(r,j) \rangle, T' \rangle \in DEP(H) \text{ if } a1 \text{ is a PUT and } a2 \text{ is a PUT}$$
$$a1 \text{ is a PUT and } a2 \text{ is a GET}$$
$$a1 \text{ is a GET and } a2 \text{ is a PUT.}$$

PUT→PUT, PUT→GET and GET→PUT dependencies.

The dependency relation for a history defines a directed *dependency graph*, where Transactions are the nodes of the graph, and resource versions label the edges. If $\langle T, \langle r, j \rangle, T' \rangle \in DEP(H)$, then the graph has an edge from node T to node T' labelled by $\langle r, j \rangle$. Two histories are equivalent, if they have the same dependency relation.

The dependency of history defines a time order of the transactions. Conventionally this ordering is signified by $<<<_H$, (or simply by $<<<$), and it is the *transitive closure* of $<<<$. It is the smallest relation satisfying the equation:

$$T <<<_H T' \text{ if } \langle T, r, T' \rangle \in DEP[H] \text{ for some resource version } r, \text{ or}$$

($T <<<_H T''$ and $\langle T'', r, T' \rangle \in DEP[H]$ for some transactions T'', and some resource r). Off the record, $T <<< T'$ if there is a path in the dependency graph from transaction T to transaction T'. The $<<<$ ordering defines the set of all transactions that run before or after T;

$$BEFORE(T) = \{T' | T' <<< T\}$$
$$AFTER(T) = \{T' | T <<< T'\}$$

If T runs fully isolated (ex: it is the only transaction, or it GET and PUT resources not accessed by any other transactions), then its BEFORE and AFTER sets are empty (it can be scheduled in any way). When a transaction is both after and before the other distinct transaction, it is called *wormhole transaction* (T' here):

$$T' \in \text{BEFORE}(T) \cap \text{AFTER}(T)$$

Serial histories do not have wormholes as all the actions of one transaction precede the actions of another; the first cannot depend on the outputs of the second.

Wormholes Theorem: Based on wormhole theorem, a history is isolated if, and only if, it has no wormhole transactions. On the other hand, the isolated histories have the *unique* property of having no wormholes. It proves a history that is not isolated has at least one wormhole; $T <<< T' <<< T$. In graphical term, if the dependency graph has a cycle in it, then the history is not equivalent to any serial history because some transaction is both before and after another transaction. (History 3 Fig 4). A wormhole in a particular history is a transaction pair in which T ran before T' ran before T. A history is said to be isolated if it is equivalent to a serial history. As the first part of the proof of the concept, the classical testimony of Wormhole theorem has been recalled [9],[10]; Isolated history has not any wormholes. This proof is by contradiction; Suppose H is an isolated history of the execution of the set of transactions $\{T_i | i = 1, ..., n\}$. By definition, then, H is equivalent to some serial execution history, SH, for that same set of transactions. Without loss of generality, assume that the transactions are numbered so that $SH = T_1 \| T_2 \| ... \| T_n$. Suppose, for the sake of contradiction, H has a wormhole; that is there some sequence of transactions $T, T', T'', ..., T'''$ such that each is BEFORE the other (i.e., $T <<<_H T$), and the last is BEFORE the first (i.e., $T''' <<<_H T$). Let i be the minimum transaction index such that T_i is in this wormhole, and let T_j be its predecessor in the wormhole (i.e., $T_j <<<_H T_i$). By the minimality of i, T_j comes completely AFTER T_i in the execution history SH, so that $T_j <<<_{SH} T_i$ is impossible (recall that SH is a serial history). But since H and SH are equivalent, $<<<_H = <<<_{SH}$; therefore, $T_j <<<_{SH} T_i$ is also impossible. This contradiction proves that if H is isolated, it has no wormholes.

A history without wormhole is isolated: Our adopted proof (like the classic Wormhole theorem [10]) is by induction on the number of transactions, n, that appears in the history, H. The induction hypothesis is that any n transaction history H having no wormholes is isolated (equivalent to some serial history, SH, for that set of transactions). If $n < 2$, then any history is serial history, since only zero or one transaction appears in the history. In addition, any serial history is an isolated history. The basis of the induction, then, is trivially true. Suppose the induction hypothesis is true for $n - 1$ transactions, and consider some history H of n transactions that has no wormholes. Pick any transaction T, then pick any other transaction T', such that $T <<< T'$, and continue this construction as long as possible, building the sequence $S = \langle T, T', ... \rangle$. Either S is infinite, or it is not. If S is infinite, then some transaction T'' must appear in it twice. This, in turn, implies that $T'' <<< T''$; thus, T'' is a wormhole of H. But since H has no wormholes, S cannot be infinite. The last transaction in S-call it T^*- has the property AFTER(T^*) = $\emptyset$, since the sequence cannot be continued past T^*. Consider the history, $H' = \langle\langle t_i, a_i, r_i\rangle \in H | t_i \neq T^*\rangle$. H' is the history H with all the formal actions (RESTful operations) of transaction T^* removed. By the choice of T^*,

$$\text{DEP}(H') = \{\langle T, \langle r, i\rangle, T'\rangle \in \text{DEP}(H) | T' \neq T^*\} \tag{2}$$

H' has no wormholes (since H has no wormholes, and $\text{DEP}(H) \supseteq \text{DEP}(H')$). The induction hypothesis, then, applies to H'. Hence, H' is isolated and has an equivalent serial history $SH' = T_1\|T_2\| ...\|T_{n-1}$ for some numbering of the other transactions.

The serial history $SH = SH'\|T_n = T_1\|T_2\|...\|T_{n-1}\|T^*$ is equivalent to H. To prove this, it must be shown that $\text{DEP}(SH) = \text{DEP}(H)$. By construction,

$$\text{DEP}(SH) = \text{DEP}(SH'\|T_n) = \text{DEP}(SH')\cup\{\langle T', \langle r, i\rangle, T^*\rangle \in \text{DEP}(H)\} \tag{3}$$

By definition, $\text{DEP}(SH') = \text{DEP}(H')$. Using this to substitute equation EQ. 2 into equation EQ. 3 gives:

$$\text{DEP}(SH) = \{\langle T, \langle r, i\rangle, T'\rangle \in \text{DEP}(H) | T' \neq T^*\}\cup\{\langle T', \langle r, i\rangle, T^*\rangle \in \text{DEP}(H)\} = \text{DEP}(H)$$
$$\tag{4}$$

Thus, the identity $\text{DEP}(SH) = \text{DEP}(H)$ is established, and the induction step is proven. The wormhole theorem is the basic result from which all the others follow. It essentially says "cycles are bad". Wormhole is just another name for cycle. The wormhole theorem can be stated in many different ways. One typical statement is called the *Serializability Theorem*: A history H is isolated (also called a *serializable schedule* or a *consistent schedule*) if, and only if, $<<<_H$ implies a partial order of the transactions. (Alternatively: if and only if it defines an acyclic graph, or implies a partially ordered set [6]).

Locking Theorem: If all transactions are well-formed and two-phase, then any legal history will be isolated. As our RESTful framework, use the 'DELETE' operation (section 4), for unlocking resources (Shrinking phase), we can adopt the conventional proof [9] as bellow;

This proof is by contradiction. Suppose H is a legal history of the execution of the set of transactions, each of which is well-formed & 2-phase. For each transaction, T, define SHRINK(T) to be the index of the first unlock step of T in history H ; formally:

$$\text{SHIRINK}(T) = min(i | H[i] = \langle T, \text{UNLOCK}, r\rangle \text{ for some resource}))$$.

Since each transaction T is non-null and well-formed, it must contain an *UNLOCK* step. Thus SHRINK is well defined for each transaction. First we need to prove:

Lemma: if $T <<< T'$, *then* SHRINK(T) $<$ SHRINK(T').

Suppose $T <<< T'$, then suppose there is a resource r and steps $i < j$ of history H, such that $H[i] = \langle T, a, r\rangle$, $H[j] = \langle T', a', r\rangle$; either action a or action a' is a PUT (this assertion comes directly from the definition of $\text{DEP}(H)$). Suppose that the action a of T is a PUT. Since T is well-formed, then, step i is covered by T doing an XLOCK on r.

Similarly, step j must be covered by T' doing an SLOCK or XLOCK on r. H is a legal schedule, and these locks would conflict, so there must be a $k1$ and $k2$, such that:

$i < k1 < k2 < j$ and $H[k1] = \langle T,\text{UNLOCK}, r \rangle$ and

Either $H[k2] = \langle T,\text{SLOCK}, r \rangle$ or $H[k2] = \langle T',\text{XLOCK}, r \rangle$.

Because T and T' are two-phase, all their LOCK actions must precede their first UNLOCK, action; thus, $\text{SHRINK}(T) \leq k1 < k2 < \text{SHRINK}(T')$. This proves the lemma for the $a = \text{PUT}$ case. The argument for the $a' = \text{PUT}$ case is almost identical. The SLOCK of T will be incompatible with the XLOCK of T'; hence, there must be an intervening $\langle T,\text{UNLOCK}, r \rangle$ followed by a $\langle T',\text{XLOCK}, r \rangle$ action in H. Therefore, if $T <<< T'$, then $\text{SHRINK}(T) < \text{SHRINK}(T')$. Proving both these cases establishes the lemma. Having proved the lemma, the proof of the theorem goes as follows; Assume, for the sake of contradiction, that H is not isolated. Then, from the wormhole Theorem, there must be a sequence of transactions $\langle T_1, T_2, T_3, \dots, T_n \rangle$, such that each is before the other (i.e., $T_i <<<_H T_{i+1}$), and the last is before the first (i.e., $T_n <<<_H T_1$). Using the lemma, this in turn means that $\text{SHRINK}(T_1) < \text{SHRINK}(T_2) < \cdots < \text{SHRINK}(T_n) < \text{SHRINK}(T_1)$. But since $\text{SHRINK}(T_1) < \text{SHRINK}(T_1)$ is a contradiction, H cannot have any wormholes.

Locking Theorem (Converse): One may argue about the necessity of well-formed and two-phase history, which our approach warily follows. For proving the necessity of these properties, we use the converse locking theorem [9], [10]; if a transaction is not well-formed or not two-phase, then it is possible to write another transaction such that the resulting pair has a legal but not isolated history (unless the transaction is degenerate). When the classical proof [10], relies on actions on objects (read and write), we modelled the actions in term of RESTful classic operations (GET and PUT) and adopt the proof; first not well-formed history; Suppose that transaction $T = \langle\langle T, a_i, r_i \rangle | i = 1, \dots, n \rangle$ is not well-formed and not degenerated. Then for some k, $T[k]$ is a GET or PUT action that is not covered by a lock. The GET case is proved here; the PUT case is similar. Let $T[k] = \langle T,\text{GET}, r \rangle$. Define the transaction,

$T' = \langle\langle T',\text{XLOCK}, r \rangle, \langle T',\text{WRITE}, r \rangle, \langle T',\text{WRITE}, r \rangle, \langle T',\text{UNLOCK}, r \rangle\rangle$

That is, T' is a double update to resource r. By inspection, T' is two-phase and well-formed. Consider the history;

$H = \langle T[i] | i < k \rangle \| \langle T'[[1], T'[[2], T[k], T'[3], T'[4] \rangle \| \langle T[i] | i > k \rangle$

That is, H is the history that places the first update of T' just before the uncovered GET and the second update just after the uncovered GET. H is a legal history, since no conflicting locks are granted on resource r at any point of the history. In addition, for some j, $\langle T', \langle r, j \rangle, T \rangle$ and $\langle T, \langle r, j \rangle, T' \rangle$ must be in the DEP(H); hence, $T <<_{H T}' <<<_H T$. Thus T is a wormhole in the history H. Invoking the wormhole theorem, H is not an isolated history. Intuitively, T will see resource r while it is being updated by T'. This is a concurrency anomaly. Now it is possible to show, if a history is not two-phase it can be legal but not isolated; Suppose that transaction $T = \langle\langle T, a_i, r_i \rangle | i = 1, \dots, n \rangle$ is not two-phase and not degenerate. Then for some $j < k$, $T[j] = \langle T,\text{UNLOCK}, r1 \rangle$ and $T[k] = \langle T,\text{SLOCK}, r2 \rangle$ or $T[k] = \langle T,\text{XLOCK}, r2 \rangle$.

Define the transaction

$$T' = \langle \begin{array}{c} \langle T',\text{XLOCK}, r1 \rangle, \langle T',\text{XLOCK}, r2 \rangle, \langle T',\text{WRITE}, r1 \rangle, \langle T',\text{WRITE}, r2 \rangle, \\ \langle T',\text{UNLOCK}, r1 \rangle, \langle T',\text{UNLOCK}, r2 \rangle \end{array} \rangle.$$

That is T' updates resource $r1$ and $r2$. By inspection, T' is two-phase and well-formed. Consider the history:

$$H = \langle T[i] | i \leq j \rangle \| T' \| \langle T[i] | i > j \rangle$$

This says that H is the history that places T' just after the UNLOCK of $r1$ by T. H is a legal history, since no conflicting locks are granted on resource $r1$ at any point in the history. In addition, since T is not degenerate, it must GET or PUT resource $r1$ before the unlock at step j and must GET or PUT resource $r2$ after the lock at step k. From this $\langle T, \langle r1, j1 \rangle, T' \rangle$ and $\langle T, \langle r2, j2 \rangle, T' \rangle$ must be in the DEP(H). Hence $T <<< T' <<< T$, and T is a wormhole in the history H. Invoking the Wormhole Theorem, H is not isolated history. Intuitively, T sees resource $r1$ before it is updated by T' and sees resource $r2$ after it is been updated by T'; thus T is before and after T'. This is a concurrency anomaly.

6   Conclusions and Further Work

By adopting conventional isolation theorem, we have provided a RESTful locking framework for business transactions which avoids inconsistency when dealing with a highly concurrent environment. While our detailed discussion shows the most important consistency issues are addressed, recoverability has been out of the scope of this paper. A recoverability extension on the RESTful transaction can be found in our paper at [22]. Meanwhile, long-running transactions and deadlock detection are the other issues which shall be considered as future work of this framework.

References

1. Astrahan, M.M., et al.: A history and evaluation of System R. Communications of the ACM 24, 632–646 (1981)
2. Bernstein, P.A., Hadzilacos, V., Goodman, N.: Concurrency control and recovery in database systems. Addison-Wesley Longman Publishing, Boston (1987)
3. Cabrera, L.F., et al.: Web Services Atomic Transaction (WS-AtomicTransaction). Version 1.0, IBM developerWorks (2005)
4. Castro, P., Nori, A.A.: A Programming Model for Data on the Web. Data Engineering, 2008. In: IEEE 24th International Conference on Data Engineering. ICDE 2008, pp. 1556–1559 (2008)
5. Crockford, D.: JSON: The fat-free alternative to XML. In: Proc. of XML 2006 (2006)
6. Date, C.J.: An Introduction to Database Systems, 5th edn. Addison-Wesley, Reading (1996)
7. Fielding, R.T.: Architectural Styles and the Design of Network-based Software Architectures. University of California, Irvine (2000)

8. Fielding, R., Gettys, J., Mogul, J., Frystyk, H., Berners-Lee, T.: Hypertext Transfer Protocol–HTTP/1.1. RFC 2616, The Internet Engineering Task Force (1999)
9. Gray, J.: Benchmark Handbook: For Database and Transaction Processing Systems. Morgan Kaufmann Publishers Inc., San Francisco (1992)
10. Gray, J., Reuter, A.: Transaction Processing: Concepts and Techniques. Morgan Kaufmann Publishers Inc., San Francisco (1993)
11. Greenberg, S., Marwood, D.: Real time groupware as a distributed system: concurrency control and its effect on the interface. In: Proceedings of the 1994 ACM conference on Computer supported cooperative work, pp. 207–217 (1994)
12. Hadley, M., Sandoz, P.: JSR 311: Java api for RESTful web services. Technical report, Java Community Process, Sun Microsystems (2007)
13. Hoffman, P., Bray, T.: Atom Publishing Format and Protocol (atompub). In: IETF (2006)
14. Khare, R., Taylor, R.N.: Extending the Representational State Transfer (REST) Architectural Style for Decentralized Systems. In: Proc. of the 26th International Conf. on Software Engineering, vol. 23, pp. 428–437 (2004)
15. McGuffin, L.J., Olson, G.M.: ShrEdit: A Shared Electronic Work Space. University of Michigan, Cognitive Science and Machine Intelligence Laboratory (1992)
16. Ramakrishnan, R., Gehrke, J.: Database Management Systems. McGraw-Hill Science/Engineering/Math (2003)
17. Razavi, A., Moschoyiannis, S., Krause, P.: Concurrency Control and Recovery Management in Open e-Business Transactions. In: Proc. WoTUG (CPA 2007), pp. 267–285 (2007)
18. Richardson, L., Ruby, S.: RESTful Web Services. O'Reilly Media, Inc., Sebastopol (2007)
19. Sun, C., Ellis, C.: Operational transformation in real-time group editors: issues, algorithms, and achievements. In: Proc. of the 1998 ACM conference on Computer supported cooperative work, pp. 59–68 (1998)
20. Vinoski, S.: WS-nonexistent standards. IEEE Internet Computing 8, 94–96 (2004)
21. Marinos, A., Razavi, A., Moschoyiannis, S., Krause, P.: RETRO: A Consistent and Recoverable RESTful Transaction Model. In: IEEE 7th International Conference on Web Services (ICWS 2009), Los Angeles, CA, USA (2009) (in the process to be published)

An Optimization Rule for ActiveXML Workflows

Sattanathan Subramanian and Guttorm Sindre

Department of Computer and Information Science,
Norwegian University of Science and Technology (NTNU),
NO-7491 Trondheim, Norway
{sat,guttors}@idi.ntnu.no

Abstract. Web services are used as the de facto standard to develop
the modern business applications that require collaboration and coordination among the business partners. ActiveXML (AXML) is viewed as a
data-oriented workflow language for specifying the Web service calls and
their interactions. The present workflow engines execute the workflow
specifications *strictly* without attempting to optimize the Web service
calls. This paper proposes an optimization approach as a rule called
$\mathcal{SCG}$, to improve the performance of workflows in the context of AXML.
The $\mathcal{SCG}$ groups the Web service calls of AXML documents, and reuses
the existing results of other equivalent Web service calls.

Keywords: ActiveXML, Optimization, Web service, Workflow.

1 Introduction and Related Work

Workflow systems have been in research [11, 13] as well as industry [1] for many
years to support the collaboration among the business processes. The workflows
are often implemented as Web services to cross the boundaries of networks, architectures, platforms, and organizations [7, 8]. A Web service (*service*, hereafter)
based workflow typically contains a number of service calls to perform its tasks.
Due to the control flow nature of workflow systems [14], the service calls are
strictly invoked in an order given in the workflow specification without attempting any optimizations, even when less expensive workflows could be devised that
obtain the same results. Hence, the execution of many such workflows consumes
more time and resources (e.g., bandwidth) than necessary, a clear weakness of the
state-of-the-art. Emphasizing dataflow instead of control flow could help to relax
the execution of workflows. The Active XML (*AXML*) [3] platform facilitates the
data-oriented workflows, where the dataflow is considered as the processing key.
An AXML document is an XML document with the embedded service calls to
the Web services, executed in a peer-to-peer architecture (www.activexml.net).
The present optimization framework of AXML called OptimAX [4, 5, 6] has the
rules to delegate and instantiate the service calls among the peers, to compose
and decompose the simple queries that are available directly, and to eliminate
the redundant computation. This paper extends the OptimAX framework by
proposing a new rule called $\mathcal{SCG}$ to optimize the number of service calls in the

M. Gaedke, M. Grossniklaus, and O. Díaz (Eds.): ICWE 2009, LNCS 5648, pp. 410–418, 2009.
© Springer-Verlag Berlin Heidelberg 2009

AXML documents. Our optimization approach is leveraged from the continuous query optimization [10] of database systems to the AXML by correlating the continuous queries as service calls, which groups the service calls of one with another based on their data source (i.e., Web service) and reuses the existing results received from other equivalent service calls. This improves the execution complexity of the *peer* that executes the service calls of an AXML document, of the *Web service* that provides the actual service, and of the *database* connected behind the Web service. The framework proposed in [13] optimizes a BPEL based workflow into a single SQL activity. Whereas, we specifically intend to optimize the service calls of workflow in the same form. This widens the scope of optimization across the workflows and minimizes the changes required in the execution environment. Lazy query evaluation [2] evaluates the user queries and detects the relevant service calls in an AXML document that can bring data. The $\mathcal{SCG}$ is intended to be applied after detecting such relevant service calls from the AXML document.

We consider a four-tier architecture for the purpose of this paper, i.e., the *clients* to request workflow applications, *AXML peer* to execute the respective AXML document, and *Web services* to process the service requests of AXML peer and deliver back the results after accessing its *databases*. Finally, the AXML peer delivers the results to the respective clients. This paper considers the service calls that carry queries (e.g., SQL) of selection and projection, and one-stage execution of AXML documents, i.e., the new service call sc_i which is returned from the activation of another service call sc_{i-1} is omitted.

The paper is organized as follows: Section 2 shows a motivating example. Section 3 illustrates the idea of $\mathcal{SCG}$ through some examples of relational algebra and shows its algebraic execution. Section 4 concludes the paper.

2   Motivating Example

Consider that there is a *FlightEnquiry* AXML document (shown in the Fig. 1), which is meant for comparing the prices and availability of flights as per the travel requirements of the user. The input of *FlightEnquiry* is `travelDetails` like starting point, destination, date, etc, and output is `flightDetails` like

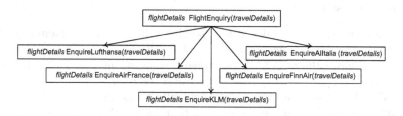

Fig. 1. FlightEnquiry Workflow

price, availability, etc. *FlightEnquiry* has five independent service calls targeting five different flight Web services. Those are, *EnquireLufthansa*, *EnquireAir-France*, *EnquireKLM*, *EnquireFinnAir*, and *EnquireAlItalia*. All these service calls carry the same input and output of *FlightEnquiry*, i.e., `travelDetails` as input and `flightDetails` as output. *FlightEnquiry* is potentially accessible for many users in the Internet through some graphical interfaces. So, many (thousands of) *FlightEnquiry* requests can reach the AXML peer simultaneously. In such situations, the AXML peer and the respective Web services are heavily loaded since all the service calls of the AXML document are processed separately. We understand that the load balancing [9] techniques provide a single domain name from multiple servers by consolidating many HTTP requests of various clients as a single TCP socket to the back-end servers. But, this cannot consolidate the service calls and their associated queries to optimize the execution in the AXML peer, Web services, and databases. Similarly, web caching techniques are useful if the queries associated with the service calls are unique, however, the queries tend to be different in real due to the personalization of users over the web content [12]. For the purpose of discussion, we consider that an AXML peer receives one thousand *FlightEnquiry* requests simultaneously. These one thousand requests internally require five thousand service calls, i.e., one thousand to *EnquireLufthansa*, one thousand to *EnquireAirFrance*, etc. The AXML peer and the servers of Web services like *EnquireLufthansa* are heavily loaded in this case. We also consider that the *EnquireLufthansa* service is implemented on top of a `LufthansaDB` database which has the details of flights, availability, price, etc. So, one thousand *EnquireLufthansa* requests additionally produce one thousand data requests to the `LufthansaDB`. Assuming that the workflow requests arrive at sufficiently close moments in time and their answers can be forcedly synchronized with no perceived disadvantage to the user, the execution complexity of one thousand instances of *FlightEnquiry* can be reduced if the service calls targeting the same service are grouped as "one", i.e., only *one* service call to *EnquireLufthansa* to obtain the required results of one-thousand service calls. Similarly for *EnquireAirFrance*, *EnquireKLM*, *EnquireFinnAir*, and *EnquireAlItalia*. This implicitly optimizes the data requests to the respective databases from the Web services in the same way.

3   Service Calls Grouping

3.1   Idea Illustration

This paper groups many independent service calls of AXML document that target the same Web service into *one* service call. The state-of-the-art way of executing service calls of AXML documents is shown in Fig. 2(a), i.e., independent service calls ($sc_1, sc_2, ..., sc_n$; hereafter we refer this list as $sc_{1..n}$) are activated and its results are received individually although those calls target the same Web service. Also, it can be noticed that each Web service request opens an additional database request as shown in Fig. 2(a). The proposed optimization is shown in Fig. 2(b), where all the independent service calls are grouped as one

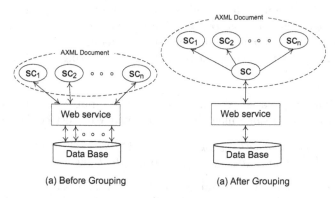

(a) Before Grouping   (a) After Grouping

Fig. 2. Idea of Grouping Service calls

service call (i.e., sc), and similarly to the database access from the Web service. The sc carries all the data constraints of $sc_{1..n}$. The activation of sc receives the results required for $sc_{1..n}$, which are accessed and filtered by $sc_{1..n}$ according to their individual data constraint.

The service calls are grouped by encoding their input parameters as XML trees. The input parameter has a *condition* and a finite set of *output attribute names* for which the values are expected from the Web service. Fig. 3(a) shows the generalized encoded tree format of the service call's input parameter. In that, the *conditional attribute names and its values* are located in the leaf position, the *relational operator* is located as the parent of conditional attribute name and its value, the *logical operator* is located as the parent of relational operator, and the *output attribute names* are located as the parent of logical operator (or relational operator). The output attribute names are always located in the top level of the encoded tree, and the relational operator can be the immediate child of output attribute name when there is no logical operator in the condition. Fig. 3(b) shows the encoded tree form of the following service call's input parameter:

$$\Pi_{ws.weather}(\sigma_{ws.country=\text{``France''} \text{ and } ws.city=\text{``Paris''}}(WeatherService\ ws)).$$

For the sake of simplicity, we use the relational algebra to represent the input parameters of service call including the service name. Also, we use generic

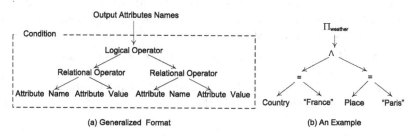

(a) Generalized Format   (b) An Example

Fig. 3. Encoded Input Parameter of a Service Call

examples in this section to illustrate all possible cases of grouping service calls. In the above example, $ws.country = \text{"}France\text{"}$ and $ws.city = \text{"}Paris\text{"}$ is the condition and $ws.weather$ is the output attribute name.

Two (or more) independent service calls are grouped using any of the following two cases,

Gr_1 : **same input parameters and target**. The input parameters of service calls are *exactly same* including the targeted Web service. For example,

$$sc_a = \Pi_{ss.stockRate}(\sigma_{ss.stockName=\text{"}Dell\text{"}}(StockService\ ss)).$$
$$sc_b = \Pi_{ss.stockRate}(\sigma_{ss.stockName=\text{"}Dell\text{"}}(StockService\ ss)).$$

The sc_a and sc_b have the same condition (i.e., $ss.stockName = \text{"}Dell\text{"}$), output attribute name (i.e., $ss.stockRate$), and target (i.e., $StockService$). So, here sc_a or sc_b can be considered as the input parameter of grouped service call.

Gr_2 : **related input parameters but same target**. The input parameters of service calls are different from each other, but the targeted service is same for both. The difference can be in the condition or output attribute name or both. Between the conditions, the difference can be in relational or logical operator or both, or conditional attribute name or its value or both, or both. For example,

$$sc_c = \Pi_{ss.stockRate}(\sigma_{ss.stockName=\text{"}Yahoo\text{"}}(StockService\ ss)).$$

The conditional attribute value differs between sc_a (or sc_b) and sc_c, i.e., sc_a has "$Dell$" as the value for $stockName$, whereas, sc_c has "$Yahoo$" as the value for $stockName$. So, the sc_a and sc_c are grouped as,

$$sc = \Pi_{ss.stockRate}(\sigma_{ss.stockName=\text{"}Dell\text{"}\ or\ \text{"}Yahoo\text{"}}(StockService\ ss)).$$

The sc joins the conditions of sc_a and sc_c as $ss.stockName = \text{"}Dell\text{"}$ or "$Yahoo$", and the output parameter name, i.e., $stockRate$. Now, we consider another input parameter of a new service call,

$$sc_d = \Pi_{ss.stockRate,ss.noOfAvailableStocks}(\sigma_{ss.stockName=\text{"}Yahoo\text{"}}(StockService\ ss)).$$

Here, the output attribute name differs between sc and sc_d, i.e., sc has $ss.stockRate$, whereas, sc_d has $ss.stockRate$ and $ss.noOfAvailableStocks$. It can be observed that the condition of sc is the superset of sc_d's condition. So, sc and sc_d are grouped as,

$$sc = \Pi_{ss.stockRate,ss.noOfAvailableStocks}(\sigma_{ss.stockName=\text{'}Dell\text{'}\ or\ \text{'}Yahoo\text{'}}(StockService\ ss)).$$

Now sc has two output attribute names (i.e., $ss.stockRate$ and $ss.noOfAvailableStocks$) to get the required results of sc_a, sc_b, sc_c and sc_d.

The conditional attribute names of respective input parameters (i.e., sc_a, sc_b, sc_c and sc_d) are added as the output attribute names of sc if it is not available already, i.e., $ss.stockName$ is added as a new output parameter name. The updated sc is,

$$sc = \Pi_{ss.stockRate,ss.noOfAvailableStocks,ss.stockName}$$
$$(\sigma_{ss.stockName=\text{``}Dell\text{''} \text{ or ``}Yahoo\text{''}}(StockService\ ss)).$$

This is done for filtering the service results after the activation of a grouped service call. The intended results of sc_a, sc_b, sc_c and sc_d are filtered from the service results (say, R) of sc after its activation. This filtering is done based on the input parameter of the respective service call. In our example,

$$sc_a,\ sc_b = \Pi_{stockRate}(\sigma_{stockName=`Dell'}(R))$$
$$sc_c = \Pi_{stockRate}(\sigma_{stockName=`Yahoo'}(R))$$
$$sc_d = \Pi_{stockRate,noOfAvailableStocks}(\sigma_{stockName=`Yahoo'}(R))$$

3.2 Rule for AXML

Consider that there are n independent service calls $sc_{1..n}$ in the AXML document d located at the peer p, targeting the Web service ws located at the peer p_1, with the input parameters $t_1, t_2, ..., t_n$ (hereafter, we refer this list as $t_{1..n}$) respectively. For this, the $\mathcal{SCG}$ rule is,

$$eval@p(\sharp x_0@p\langle sc_1@p_1(t_1)\rangle, \sharp x_1@p\langle sc_2@p_1(t_2)\rangle, ..., \sharp x_n@p\langle sc_n@p_1(t_n)\rangle)$$
$$\rightarrow \sharp x_0@p\langle filter@p(\sharp y_0@p, t_1)\rangle, \sharp x_1@p\langle filter@p(\sharp y_0@p, t_2)\rangle,$$
$$..., \sharp x_n@p\langle filter@p(\sharp y_0@p, t_n)\rangle, \sharp y_0@p\langle eval@p(sc@p_1(t))\rangle$$

where, $eval$ is an operation that evaluates the service calls of d, sc is the grouped service call which is grouped from $sc_{1..n}$, t is the input parameter which is grouped from $t_{1..n}$, $filter$ is a newly proposed operation available in the peer p to filter the service results of sc. The optimization is the the first stage of $eval$, which creates sc and replaces $sc_{1..n}$ with $filters$. The inputs of the $filter$ operation are the service results of sc (in our case, it is available at $\sharp y_0@p$) and the input parameter of respective service call which needs the partial results from sc. The pictorial view of this optimization rule is shown in Fig. 4, where the bidirectional arrow line indicates the Web service request and response.

The detailed step-by-step algebraic execution of the $\mathcal{SCG}$ is follows,

$$eval@p(\sharp x_0@p\langle sc_1@p_1(t_1)\rangle, \sharp x_1@p\langle sc_2@p_1(t_2)\rangle, ..., \sharp x_n@p\langle sc_n@p_1(t_n)\rangle)$$

Next, the grouped service call $sc@p_1$ is created at $\sharp y_o@p$ with the input parameter t which is created by grouping the input parameters $t_{1..n}$ of $sc_{1..n}$. The service calls $sc_{1..n}$ are replaced with $filter$ operations. Every filter operation takes the service results that are produced by sc and the respective input parameter of service call sc_1 or sc_2 or ... or sc_n.

$$\rightarrow \sharp x_0@p\langle filter@p(\sharp y_0@p, t_1)\rangle, \sharp x_1@p\langle filter@p(\sharp y_0@p, t_2)\rangle,$$
$$..., \sharp x_n@p\langle filter@p(\sharp y_0@p, t_n)\rangle, \sharp y_0@p\langle eval@p(sc@p_1(t))\rangle$$

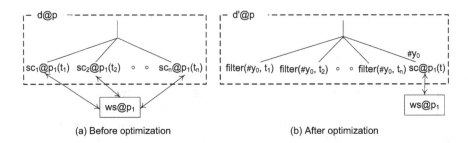

(a) Before optimization   (b) After optimization

Fig. 4. The SCG Rule

Next, the $sc@p_1$ is evaluated at p. This results in *send* and *receive* operations from $(new)@p_1$ to $\sharp y_0@p$. Note that the *send* and *receive* are the predefined services locally available in the peer, used to move the streams of XML data from one peer to another [6]. The *send* service has two parameters: what (represents the data to be sent from one site to another), and where (represents a node id). There are no parameters for *receive*. The symbol $\circ$ indicates the start of an operation, and $\bullet$ indicates the end of an operation.

$$\rightarrow \sharp x_0@p\langle filter@p(\sharp y_0@p, t_1)\rangle, \sharp x_1@p\langle filter@p(\sharp y_0@p, t_2)\rangle,$$
$$..., \sharp x_n@p\langle filter@p(\sharp y_0@p, t_n)\rangle, \sharp y_0@p\langle \circ receive@p()\rangle \ \&$$
$$(new)@p_1 : eval@p_1(send@p_1(\sharp y_0@p, sc@p_1(t)))$$

Next, the *receive* operation ends its operation.

$$\rightarrow \sharp x_0@p\langle filter@p(\sharp y_0@p, t_1)\rangle, \sharp x_1@p\langle filter@p(\sharp y_0@p, t_2)\rangle,$$
$$..., \sharp x_n@p\langle filter@p(\sharp y_0@p, t_n)\rangle, \sharp y_0@p\langle \bullet receive@p()\rangle$$

Next, the *filter* operations start filtering the result available at $\sharp y_0@p$ based on the respective input parameter t_1 or t_2 or ... or t_n.

$$\rightarrow \sharp x_0@p\langle \circ filter@p(\sharp y_0@p, t_1)\rangle, \sharp x_1@p\langle \circ filter@p(\sharp y_0@p, t_2)\rangle,$$
$$..., \sharp x_n@p\langle \circ filter@p(\sharp y_0@p, t_n)\rangle, \sharp y_0@p$$

Finally, the *filter* ends its operation.

$$\rightarrow \sharp x_0@p\langle \bullet filter@p(\sharp y_0@p, t_1)\rangle, \sharp x_1@p\langle \bullet filter@p(\sharp y_0@p, t_2)\rangle,$$
$$..., \sharp x_n@p\langle \bullet filter@p(\sharp y_0@p, t_n)\rangle$$

4   Conclusion and Future Work

This paper has provided an optimization approach for the execution of AXML documents. The proposed SCG rule groups Web service calls that carry selection and/or projection queries. Our optimization approach relates one service call with another based on its target i.e., Web service, and reuses the existing results that are received from other equivalent service calls. This improves the performance of the *workflow server* and the *Web service* including the *database server* that provides the data to Web service. The algebraic executions are shown to illustrate the service calls grouping in the framework of AXML.

Presently, the $\mathcal{SCG}$ is limited to the independent service calls. So, this has to be extended to accommodate the update queries (e.g., insert, delete, modify) that are dependent of one with another. The nested transactions of database systems can be correlated to the service calls in order to maintain the ACID properties while grouping. The open questions related to the performance of $\mathcal{SCG}$ are: (i) what is the execution improvement of an AXML document in a real application?, (ii) what extent the workload of Web service and its associated database server is reduced?, (iii) what is the efficient threshold time of the workflow server to wait and accumulate the workflow requests for applying $\mathcal{SCG}$ in a wider range?, (v) how many service calls can be grouped together in order to match the capacity of a server?, and (vi) how far the $\mathcal{SCG}$ is efficient than the classical web caching techniques especially when the queries are identical?

Acknowledgements

This work was carried out during the tenure of an ERCIM "Alain Bensoussan" Fellowship Programme. First author would like to thank Serge Abiteboul and Ioana Manolescu of INRIA for their initial ideas and suggestions.

References

[1] Aalst, W.M.P.: Trends in business process analysis - from verification to process mining. In: The proceedings of International Conference on Enterprise Information Systems (ICEIS), Madeira, Portugal (2007)
[2] Abiteboul, S., Benjelloun, O., Cautis, B., Manolescu, I., Milo, T., Preda, N.: Lazy query evaluation for Active XML. In: The proceedings of ACM SIGMOD International Conference on Management of Data (SIGMOD), Paris, France (2004)
[3] Abiteboul, S., Benjelloun, O., Milo, T.: The Active XML project: an overview. The VLDB Journal 17(5) (2008)
[4] Abiteboul, S., Manolescu, I., Taropa, E.: A Framework for Distributed XML Data Management. In: The proceedings of International Conference on Extending Database Technology (EDBT), Munich, Germany (2006)
[5] Abiteboul, S., Manolescu, I., Zoupanos, S.: OptimAX: optimizing distributed continuous queries. In: The Proceedings of International Conference on Bases de Donnees Avancees (BDA), Marseille, France (2007) (A French Conference)
[6] Abiteboul, S., Manolescu, I., Zoupanos, S.: OptimAX: Optimizing Distributed ActiveXML Applications. In: the Proceedings of Eighth International Conference on Web Engineering (ICWE), New York, USA (2008)
[7] Andrews, T., Curbera, F., Dholakia, H., Goland, Y., Klein, J., Leymann, F., Liu, K., Roller, D., Smith, D., Thatte, S., Trickovic, I., Weerawarana, S.: Business Process Execution Language for Web Services, Version 1.1. Standard proposed by BEA Systems. IBM Corporation, and Microsoft Corporation (2003)
[8] Benatallah, B., Sheng, Q.Z., Dumas, M.: The Self-Serv Environment for Web Services Composition. IEEE Internet Computing 7(1) (January/February 2003)

[9] Bourke, T.: Server load balancing. O'Reilly & Associates, Inc., Sebastopol (2001)

[10] Chen, J., DeWitt, D.J., Tian, F., Wang, Y.: NiagaraCQ: a scalable continuous query system for Internet databases. In: The Proceedings of ACM International Conference on Management of data (SIGMOD), Dallas, Texas, United States (2000)

[11] Hull, R., Su, J.: The Vortex Approach to Integration and Coordination of Workflows (A position paper). In: The Proceedings of International Joint Conference on Work Activities Coordination and Collaboration (WACC), San Francisco (1999)

[12] Sivasubramanian, S., Pierre, G., Steen, M., Gustavo, G.: Analysis of Caching and Replication Strategies for Web Applications. IEEE Internet Computing 11(1) (January 2007)

[13] Vrhovnik, M., Schwarz, H., Suhre, O., Mitschang, B., Markl, V., Maier, A., Kraft, T.: An Approach to Optimize Data Processing in Business Processes. In: Proceedings of International Conference on Very Large Data Bases (VLDB), Vienna, Austria (2007)

[14] Wang, J., Kumar, A.: A Framework for Document-Driven Workflow Systems. In: van der Aalst, W.M.P., Benatallah, B., Casati, F., Curbera, F. (eds.) BPM 2005. LNCS, vol. 3649, pp. 285–301. Springer, Heidelberg (2005)

Personal News RSS Feeds Generation Using Existing News Feeds

Bin Liu, Hao Han, Tomoya Noro, and Takehiro Tokuda

Department of Computer Science, Tokyo Institute of Technology
Meguro, Tokyo 152-8552, Japan
{ryuu,han,noro,tokuda}@tt.cs.titech.ac.jp

Abstract. Nowadays more and more news sites publish news stories using news RSS feeds for easier access and subscription on the Web. Generally, news stories are grouped by several categories and each category corresponds to one news RSS feed. However there are no uniform standards for categorization. Each news site has its own way of categorization for grouping news stories. These dissimilar categorization can not always satisfy every individual user, and generally the provided categories are not detailed enough for personal using.

In this paper, we proposed a method for users to create customizable personal news RSS feeds using existing ones. We implemented a news directory system(NDS) which can retrieve news stories by RSS feeds and classify them. Using this system, we can recategorize news stories from original RSS feeds, or subdivide one RSS feed to a more detailed level. With the classification information for each news article, we offer customizable personal news RSS feeds to subscribers.

1 Introduction

At present, there are lots of news sites on the Web. Many of them offer news RSS feeds[1] for easier access and subscription. News RSS (Really Simple Syndication) feed is an XML-based format document for sharing and publishing frequently updated Web news. By subscribing to some news RSS feeds using a RSS reader, we can get alerts about publications of new issues. Generally news sites divide news articles to numbers of categories and publish news RSS feeds corresponding with these categories one-to-one.

Unfortunately, there are no uniform standards for categorization, news sites determine how to categorize news articles by themselves. For example, *CNN.com*[2] provides news RSS feeds by fields such as *Science, Sports, Business* and so on, while *allAfrica.com*[3] offers news RSS feeds grouped by countries or regions. As we can see, there are some difference of categorization between various sites. If users happen to find just what they want in the given categories, the categorization is

---

[1] http://cyber.law.harvard.edu/rss/rss.html
[2] http://www.cnn.com/
[3] http://allafrica.com

M. Gaedke, M. Grossniklaus, and O. Díaz (Eds.): ICWE 2009, LNCS 5648, pp. 419–433, 2009.
© Springer-Verlag Berlin Heidelberg 2009

contributing. While if users can not find any appropriate categories close to what
they want, the categorization does not make any sense. For instance, if users want
to subscribe to news about diseases from *allAfrica.com*, they have to subscribe to
all of the news RSS feeds from this site and discriminate the news about diseases
one by one by themselves. So the original categorization of each site can not always
satisfy every individual user. Further, usually categories used in news sites are not
subdivided. They are not detailed enough for personal using. This make users have
to handpick what they really need from the news gotten from RSS feeds.

Some RSS reader tools can let subscribers integrate RSS feeds, however what
these tools could do is only to make a union from selected feeds by users, they
do not make any analysis about the contents in feeds. News alert can also filter
useful news stories for users, while users have to imagine all the presumable
expressions for keywords and connect them together with *OR* during the initial
setting of alerts. It is acceptable when the keywords are technical terms, but we
could know what we omit when the keywords are general words. Further, simple
string matching is used in news alerts, they will give a hit when *ice hockey* occurs
while user wants stories of *hockey*.

In this paper, we propose a method for recategorizing the articles published
from existing news RSS feeds, and using these subdivided news articles, we
provide personal news RSS feeds for users. Personal news RSS feeds can be configured for individual demands like Fig.1. Users can recategorize or subdivide the
news articles gotten from existing news RSS feeds according to their individual

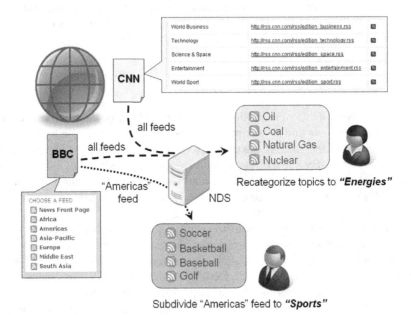

Fig. 1. Overview of personal news RSS feeds

needs. We implemented a news directory system which gives preconditions for re-categorization and subdivision. It retrieves news articles using information from existing news RSS feeds and subdivides news articles into categories automatically. We gave each category used in this system a definition, and constructed automata with these definitions to categorize news articles with high speed. Each definition includes several related expressions (synonyms and abbreviations) of the corresponding category. So users need not make an association of all the expressions of their interested topics. We also avoid miss hits like *hockey* and *ice hockey* using limitation in categories' definitions.

The organization of the rest of this paper is as follows. Section 2 gives an overview of our news directory system. Section 3 presents the mechanism of automatic retrieval and subdivision of news articles, the basis of our work. While section 4 shows directions about how to get personal news RSS feeds using existing ones. Experimental results demonstrating the effectiveness of our approach are in Section 5. Section 6 discusses related work. Finally conclusions and directions for future work can be found in Section 7.

2 Overview of NDS

News directory system can be divided into two subsystems as Fig.2. One is for news retrieval, the other is for classification. System for news retrieval detects news titles and news body from original pages using the information of news titles and URLs. And the system for classification categorizes news stories with automata constructed from definitions of categories. We can get the results of categorization by scanning news stories only one time. We will give introduction about these two subsystems respectively in following section.

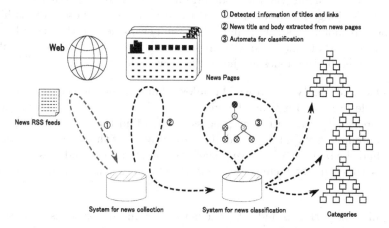

Fig. 2. Structure of News Directory System

3   News Directory System

3.1   Automatic News Collection

In this section, we give a brief introduction about the process of automatic news collection. Detailed explanation can be found in paper [11]. As a general approach, pattern matching is used in extraction from web pages. Considering it need corresponding patterns for various web site, extensibility is low when we get new web sites. We collect news articles by extracting news titles and body from news pages using information in original news RSS feeds.

The initials "RSS" are used to refer to the following formats:

- Really Simple Syndication (RSS 2.0)
- RDF Site Summary (RSS 1.0 and RSS 0.90)
- Rich Site Summary (RSS 0.91)

Although there are a number of different formats of RSS, all of them include the URL and title information in <link> and <title> respectively. These two information fields are the minimum necessary parts of each news item in a RSS feed. We detect these information and extract news articles from original news pages. The phase of the news article extraction consists of the following two parts.

Detection of News Title. The process detects position of the news title in the original news pages. Since the title shown in news feeds is not always same as the real title in original news pages, we have to try to extract news titles from original news pages once again. And because of the difference between titles in RSS feeds and original news pages, exact match is not appropriate for news titles detection. Instead, for each node n in the news pages (an HTML document[4]), we calculate similarity score with the news title in RSS feeds.

If the score is higher than a predetermined threshold, the string covered by the node n is judged as a news title. If there is no node whose score is higher than the threshold, no string is judged as the news title. On the other hand, if there are more than one node with higher score than the threshold, all of the strings covered by the nodes are judged as news titles.

Extraction of Body of News Articles. The process detects a part of the news article body and extract the whole body. Since body of a news article is usually preceded by its title, the process tries to find the news article body in some "contents ranges" at first, and, if it cannot find out the body in the range, it tries to find the body in a "reserve range". "Contents range" and "reserve range" are parts which might include the news article body. They are determined as follows.

- If only one string is judged as a news title in the previous process, the following part and the preceding part are a contents range and a reserve range respectively (Fig.3(a)).

---

[4] http://www.w3.org/TR/html401/

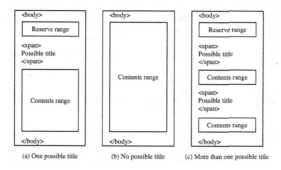

Fig. 3. Contents range and reserve range

- If no string is judged as a news title, the whole part of the news article page is a contents range and no reserve range exists (Fig.3(b)).
- If more than one string are judged as news titles, for each of the strings except the last string, range of between itself and the next string is a contents range. The part preceded by the last string is also a contents range. The part followed by the first string is a reserve range (Fig.3(c)).

At first, we specify a part of news article body. Then we calculate possibility score of each leaf node with non-link text n in each of the contents ranges. If there were some nodes with higher score than a predetermined threshold, we consider the nodes with the highest score cover a part of the news article body. Otherwise, we consider the nodes with the highest score in the reserve range cover a part of the news article body. Since a news article body is usually a continuous text, it can be extracted by taking leaf nodes around the specified nodes. However, in some cases, some information which is not related to the article, such as advertisement, is inserted in the article body. In order to avoid taking such information, we also set limitations to filter them. Finally, we get a list of nodes which cover the whole news article body. The whole body can be extracted by getting the node value (i.e. text) from each node in the list.

3.2 Automatic News Classification

After the news articles extraction, we get the materials for news classification. The next step is to give categories for classification and define them to construct automata.

News Categories. At first we need categories for classification. In news directory systems we use one-level flat directory structures or multi-level tree directory structures. Typical examples of one-level flat directory structures may be as follows.

- Classification of natural disasters such as typhoon and earthquake.
- Classification of human diseases such as diabetes and malaria.

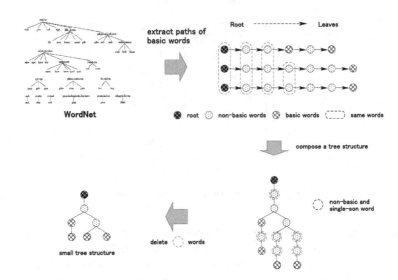

Fig. 4. Composition of a small classification tree

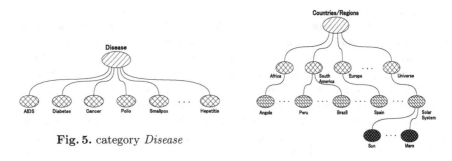

Fig. 5. category *Disease*

Fig. 6. category *Countries/Regions*

Typical examples of multi-level tree directory structures may be as follows.

- Classification of locations such as countries/regions on the earth and outside of the earth.
- A small classification tree constructed from the large classification tree such as *WordNet*[5] [9] or *Wikipedia*[6] structures.

An example of one-level flat directory structure is shown in Fig.5 and an example of multi-level tree directory structure is shown in Fig.6. Users can also build their original directory structures manually. Here we give methods to build directory structures with existing resources.

---

[5] http://wordnet.princeton.edu/
[6] http://en.wikipedia.org/wiki/Main_Page

Method 1. We use open knowledge collection of classifications by humans, such as *Wikipedia* and *WordNet*, to build an initial collection of instance names belonging to one category.

Method 2. Our method of building multi-level tree directory is as follows. We need a small set of basic words. Such a set of basic words may be subject words in *New York Times Topics Index*[7] or a subset of *Longman defining vocabulary*[13] or a subset of *Oxford defining vocabulary*[3]. For a given set of basic words we construct a small classification tree as follows.

1. We retrieve full paths of all basic words in the *WordNet* tree.
2. We construct the initial small tree using the full paths obtained in the step 1.
3. We construct the small tree by deleting all non-basic words having exactly one child node from the initial small tree.

A process of construction of a multi-level tree directory is shown in Fig.4.

Automatic Placement. In order to realize the automatic placement, each category need a definition. Our default definition of a news article A to be contained in a category B is that the article A has an occurrence of the word B. In addition to default definitions of single word occurrences, we use explicit definitions of a news article in a category using the expressions defined by following extended context-free syntax rules with repetition operator {} representing zero or more times of repetitions.

$$expression \rightarrow (term) \ \{OR \ (term)\}$$
$$term \rightarrow factor \ \{AND \ factor\}$$
$$factor \rightarrow (phrase)|(NOT \ phrase)$$
$$phrase \rightarrow word \ \{SPACE \ word\}$$
$$word \rightarrow character \ \{character\}$$

This expression allows us to define news articles having slightly more complicated word occurrences. For example, we may write a definition for category *soccer* using the following expression.

$$((football)\mathbf{AND}(\mathbf{NOT}american\_football))\mathbf{OR}((soccer))$$

This expression means that an article A is to be contained in the category, if A contains the word *football* but not *american football* or A contains the word *soccer*. The same expression may be written briefly as follows.

1. football **AND** (**NOT** american football)
2. soccer

We collect phrases from dictionaries of synonyms and append the **NOT** limitation according to the inclusion relations among the phrases we used. And then

---

[7] http://topics.nytimes.com/top/reference/timestopics/

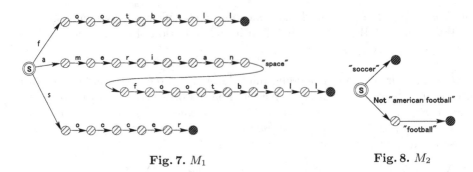

Fig. 7. M_1 **Fig. 8.** M_2

give **AND** limitations where **NOT** appears to create terms. At last connect all the terms for same meaning with **OR** limitation. Using the definitions, we make keywords matching to realize automatic placement. Making simple comparison between target string and source string costs much time. We realize this process more efficiently by using finite-state automata, which allow us to get the results of classification by scanning the news articles only one time.

The task of automatic placement consists of two phases using finite-state automata. In the first phase, we construct an automaton with all the phrases used in category definitions, it can help us to detect which phrases we used in definitions appeared in the news story. And in the second phase, we construct another automaton with all the limitations used in definitions, it can tell us which definitions the new story satisfied. We call these two automata as M_1 and M_2. For the sample expressions of category *soccer*, we can construct M_1 and M_2 shown in Fig.7 and Fig.8. About the details of M_1 and M_2, we introduced in paper [17].

4   Personal News RSS Feeds Generation

After the news extraction and classification, we can use the results of news' classification to help users generate their personal news RSS feeds. We explain the process of personal news RSS feeds generation in this section.

At first, news sites or news feeds should be designated for contents extraction. We offer users about 40 well-known news sites such as *CNN*, *BBC*[8] and so on, and RSS feeds from these sites. While we do not mean to put restrictions on users' sites selection. Users can keep their favorite news sites or news feeds as usual. If only the users favorite news sites publish RSS feeds, and they could designate the URLs of RSS feeds. Then our system will also operate extraction and classification.

Secondly, user can select the categorization or categories which they are interested in. We provide categorization such as *countries/regions*, *human/organizations*, *events/accidents*, and so on. Each categorization has numbers of categories which may have a tree structure. If users could not find a appropriate categorization or categories. They can also input the keywords for filtering

---

[8] http://www.bbc.co.uk

certain topics. In this case, our system will create a personal automaton for classification using the input keywords.

Personal news RSS feeds will be helpful in following two cases.

1. Replace the categorization of original RSS feeds.

   If users wanted to read news articles grouped by countries or regions from a news site which only provides news feeds in categories like *Science, Sports, Business* and so on. Users can designate the URLs of original RSS feeds and subscribe to the categorization of countries or regions. Contents would be sent to users in several RSS feeds and each feed corresponds to a country or region. User can also subscribe to news feeds of certain countries or regions by designating certain categories in the categorization.

2. Subdivide the news of original RSS feeds.

   User can subdivide the news in RSS feeds by operating categories. For example, we can get a news feed which sends news articles about both *whale* and *Japan* by making a intersection set of categories *whale* and *Japan*. The order of intersection will result in different meaning. If we selected *Japan* and then *energy*, we would get news articles grouped by kinds of energy, and all the news articles also belong to category *Japan*. If we selected *coal* and then *Asia*, we would get news articles grouped by countries or regions in Asia, and all the news articles also belong to *coal*.

According to the usages mentioned above, personal news RSS feeds are generated by following steps.

1. Pick up sites and news RSS feeds from the lists we offered. If users' favorite sites or RSS feeds were not in our lists, users can also register the URLs of the new RSS feeds into the system.
2. Select the categories or make intersection sets from the given categories.
3. New personal news RSS feeds are generated according to the results of user's choices. An unique URL is issued for the personal feed.

Once personal news feeds are generated successfully, users can register the feeds' URLs into their RSS reader tools. Our system will send along corresponding news articles to users by the personal news feeds at fixed intervals.

5   Experimental Results

In this section we introduce our implementation in details. We also evaluate our approach using the results of experiments.

5.1   Implementation

We implemented the parts of news articles extraction and classification. The news sites from which we collect news articles are 40 sites from 21 countries or regions and news RSS feeds from these sites are 624 in all. We run the extraction

Table 1. Result of News Extraction

1000 news pages		
successful extraction	extraction failure	
	partially-extracted	non-extracted
902	68	30

at fixed intervals and we can get about 1,500 latest news articles each time averagely. We constructed a directory structure for our news directory system using resources from Wikipedia and other existing resources. We also constructed a small classification tree of 885 nodes with 624 basic words from Longman defining vocabulary and 261 non-basic words from WordNet. Categories are given in methods like *Countries/Regions*, *Sports*, *Diseases* and so on. The max value of the depth in the directory structure is 5. The part of automatic classification is also implemented. We used 2,328 terms in all for the definitions of the 825 categories and automata M_1 and M_2 are generated with 12,801 and 1,666 nodes respectively.

5.2   Evaluation

Using the news directory system, we collect news articles and make them classified. We evaluate our approach and system in following sections.

Automatic News Collection. We selected 1,000 news articles from the results of extraction in random order and compared them with the original news contents in each corresponding news page. Results is shown in Table 1. We found 970 articles were extracted successfully and most of the cases of failure are due to multi-pages, that is, when the contents of a news article is too long to show in one page, most sites will divide the contents into several parts and prepare one Web page for each part. In this case, our approach just extracts the partial contents on the first page. We can also find some advertisement, blog pages or video news in the RSS feeds of some news Web sites, and news articles in some news Web pages can not be viewed until users log into the news sites. Our approach can not extract well from these Web pages.

Automatic News Classification. We manually evaluated the precision rate and recall rate of our automatic classification method using *country/ region* classification of 500 news articles, the results are shown in Table 2. In these

Table 2. Result of Automatic Classification

500 articles		
articles classified appropriately	inappropriate articles	
	not classified	misclassified
453	12	35

Table 3. News count from feeds of *sports*

Name of feed	news count	Name of feed	news count	Name of feed	news count
Sports	219	Golf	28	Archery	55
Athletics	7	Baseball	4	Basketball	1
Boxing	9	Cycling	4	Diving	1
Fencing	1	Gymnastics	1	Hockey	11
Rowing	1	Sailing	1	Swimming	10
Weightlifting	1				

500 news articles, 453 articles are appropriately classified. 12 articles mentioning country/region names are not classified into any category of country/region, because our definitions of corresponding categories did not contain the expressions used in those articles. 35 articles not mentioning country/region names are classified into countries/regions, because company names, event names, and news source names may contain country/region names. Because we did not use semantic analysis, system can not pick out multisense words yet at the present time.

Personal News RSS Feeds Generation. We supposed a user wanted to subscribe news stories about sports from *BBC*. Because there is no RSS feed corresponding to sports from *BBC*, user has to input all the keywords related to sports to set up a news alert. Instead, when we customize a personal RSS feed from all *BBC* feeds with category *Sports*, what we need to do is only to check some checkboxes. We checked this personal feed from Jan, 2009 to Feb, 2009, 219 stories were sent to our RSS reader in 16 kinds of sports as Table 3, and we made a search with keyword *sport* in news articles from *BBC* in this period, there were only 19 hits. We also took same experiments at other sites.

6   Related Work

Our approach contains news extraction and automated classification. So we will mention related work about these two topic respectively and give comparison with other systems.

6.1   News Extraction

There are two opposite approaches to the recognition and extraction problem:

1. Static patterns
   In this approach static patterns (extraction template) need to be defined previously for every source indexed by the system. Each web site has its own source structure of pages and the document location would be different, too. So in the extraction phase the pages of every site are individually processed filtering the documents.

   The advantage of this kind of methods is the computational cost. On the other hand, a lot of human intervention is needed. For every new source to be added to the system, users should analyze the internal HTML structure of the documents and define a custom template. If some site changed something in publication format or the document structure, the corresponding template must be redefined. Thus the system maintenance becomes in a critical task.

2. Automated extraction

Most of the published works belong to this approach. These techniques aim to avoid the human intervention and enable dynamically source adding to the systems. There are mainly two ways to affront the automated solution:

- Adaptation of data extraction

  Traditional techniques based on different clustering techniques as for example tree edit distance [7,18], or use of equivalence classes [2]. The concept over these approaches lie, is that news with common structures will match in the same cluster or class, so after the clustering phase a extraction template could be generated for each cluster.This implies multiple reprocessing of the documents with prohibitive computational cost. Thus this family of techniques is not applicable in real systems, it is only useful in applications where the number of documents managed is reduced and the frequency of content update is low.

- Domain specific approaches

  Other approaches try to combine the previous knowledge in the area of data extraction taking in account the singular characteristics of the news domain. Some works try to exploit the structure of the articles by semantic partitioning [16]. This approach is not still computational efficient and the results of precision and recall claimed by the authors can be improved. Other recent work [9] tries to use the tables present in the documents after assume that the news are present in the larger cell. Actually this assumption is false in most of the cases the news articles are not contained by tables. Also the evaluation methodology used in this work is very poor.

So in this context we present an automated extraction approach based on the provided RSS feeds. With the information of news title and URL, we detect news contents from the original pages. Our method is a tradeoff between computational efficiency and result effectiveness.

6.2   Automated Classification

Automated classification is also a well studied problem. There are two main approaches to realize automatic text classification.

1. Clustering Clustering [14] is a common technique to divide objects into several groups (called clusters). Objects from the same cluster are more similar to each other than objects from different clusters. Usually similarity is assessed according to a distance measure. There were also some experiments [4]taken to apply clustering to classify news articles. Well, this application showed us which news groups (cluster) will occur after analysis. It is unsuitable when users know definitely what kind of news they want.

2. Classification

Classification is distinguished from clustering by whether there are categories given previously before processing. The following two kinds of approaches are mainly applied to realize classification.

- Hand-Crafted Rules

  Google alerts [9] takes this approach to filter information for users. It needs users to give a set of keywords which they think are important to set up. If the occurrences of these keywords were detected, system will notify users.

  The advantage of this approach is that rules can be created simply by listing related words. By the same token, system could only detect the words listed because of the exact matching [1]. In the same way, system will tell us there is a hit when it detects *ice hockey* even we adopted *hockey*. While, when there are numbers of categories, we have to define them one by one, too. So we cannot use this approach directly.

- Machine learning

  Machine learning has demonstrated good performance can be achieved on spam/junk email. For example, *SpamCop*[12] (Pantel & Lin, 1998), using a Naive Bayes approach achieved accuracy of 94%. Sahami [15] applied a Bayesian approach and achieved precision of 97.1% on junk and 87.7% on legitimate mail and recall of 94.3% on junk and 93.4% on legitimate mail. Besides approach of Bayes, TF-IDF [5], K-Nearest Neighbor [19] and SVM [6] are also common applied techniques. Well, using machine learning to classify news article, we need numbers of labeled documents to create a model at first. Labeling must be done by a person, this is a painfully time-consuming process and it is per se unpractical for news categories which are changing momently. No one would like to be ordered to gather numbers of samples when he (or she) plan to create a new category.

In this context, we use the rule-based method and proposed automated method to construct categories and rules (definitions). And we use limitation in definitions to avoid miss matching like *ice hockey* and *hockey*.

6.3   Comparison

Comparing with *Google Alerts*, user do not need list all the expressions of a topic they are interested in with our approach. Because we have considered most of the possibilities of expressions about a category during the process of defining categories already. So the necessary operations become more simple and the recall rate of our approach is higher than that of *Google Alerts*. And another thing, because simple string matching is used in *Google Alerts*, when keyword A is contained by keyword B completely(such as *hockey* and *ice hockey*), there may be some mistakes in the results if users input keyword A. In our approach, we avoid this kind of mistake by using **NOT** relation in categories' definitions.

---

[9] http://www.google.com/alert

NewsKnowledge.com[10] provides a more friendly service. This site allows users create personal news RSS feeds. Categories are subdivided and users can choose their favorite categorization such as *Health, Industries*, and so on. Users can also give keywords for filtering certain topics. However, the source of news feeds are limited, so users can not designate their favorite news feeds or news sites. And the subdivided categories are still in an insufficient degree.

7   Conclusion

In this paper, we have presented an approach for generating personal news RSS feeds from existing news feeds using news extraction and automatic classification. We also proposed methods to realize the news extraction and automatic classification. We implemented the methods and confirmed the availabilities of our approach.

As our future work, we will try the news articles extraction from multi-pages, enrich the news sites and news feeds, the categories in news directory, and improve the precision rate by resolving the problem of multisense words, too. We also plan to develop a RSS reader tool which allow users view news feeds multi-level structure, that is, users can view parts of the directory structure of our news directory. Users can view the other items in the category which contains the item they chose, this could be suggestive for users.

References

1. Aho, A.V., Corasick, M.J.: Efficient string matching: an aid to bibliographic search. CACM 18(6), 333–340 (1975)
2. Arasu, A., Garcia-Molina, H., University, S.: Extracting structured data from web pages. In: Proceedings of the 2003 ACM SIGMOD international conference on Management of data, pp. 337–348. ACM Press, New York (2003)
3. Hornby, A.S., Ashby, M.: Oxford Advanced Learner's Dictionary of Current English. Oxford University Press, Oxford (2005)
4. Das, A., Datar, M., Garg, A.: Google News Personalization: Scalable Online Collaborative Filtering. In: Proceedings of the 16th international conference on World Wide Web. ACM Press, New York (2007)
5. Boone, G.: Concept features in re:agent, an intelligent email agent. In: Second International Conference on Autonomous Agents
6. Brutlag, J., Meek, C.: Challenges of the email domain for text classification. In: Seventeenth International Conference on Machine Learning
7. Reis, D.C., Golgher, P.B., Silva, A.S., Laender, A.F.: Automatic web news extraction using tree edit distance. In: Proceedings of the 13th international conference on World Wide Web, pp. 502–511. ACM Press, New York (2004)
8. Domingos, P., Pazzani, M.: On the optimality of the simple Bayesian classifier under zero-one loss. Machine Learning 29, 103–137 (1997)
9. Zhang, D., Simoff, S.J.: Informing the curious negotiator: Automatic news extraction from the internet. In: Williams, G.J., Simoff, S.J. (eds.) Data Mining. LNCS, vol. 3755, pp. 176–191. Springer, Heidelberg (2006)

---

[10] http://www.newsknowledge.com/home.html/

10. Gonzalo, J., Verdejo, F., Chugur, I., Cigarran, J.: Indexing with WordNet Synsets Can Improve Text Retrieval. In: Proceedings of the COLING/ACL Workshop on Usage of WordNet in Natural Language Processing Systems, Montreal (1998)
11. Han, H., Tokuda, T.: Web News Contents Extraction Using RSS Feeds. In: The Proceeding of Annual Meeting of Japan Society for Software Science and Technology (2007)
12. Pantel, P., Lin, D.: Spamcop: A spam classification & organization program. In: Proceeding of AAAI 1998 Workshop on Learning for Text Categorization, pp. 95–98 (1998)
13. Proctor, P.: Longman Dictionary of Contemporary English. Longman (2005)
14. Berkhin, P.: Survey of Clustering Data Mining Techniques Accrue Software (2002)
15. Sahami, M., Dumais, S., Heckerman, D., Horvits, E.: A bayesian approach to filtering junk e-mail. In: AAAI 1998 Workshop on Learning for Text Categorization (1998)
16. Vadrevu, S., Nagarajan, S., Gelgi, F., Davulcu, H.: Automated metadata and instance extraction from news web sites. In: WI 2005: Proceedings of the The 2005 IEEE/WIC/ACM International Conference on Web Intelligence (WI 2005), Washington, DC, USA, pp. 38–41. IEEE Computer Society, Los Alamitos (2005)
17. Noro, T., Liu, B., Van Hai, P., Tokuda, T.: Towards automatic construction of news directory systems. In: The 17th European-Japanese Conference on Information Modelling and Knowledge Bases, pp. 211–220 (2007)
18. Crescenzi, V., Mecca, G.: Automatic information extraction from large websites. J. ACM 51(5), 731–779 (2004)
19. Yang, S., Jian, H., Ding, Z., Hongyuan, Z., Giles, C.: IKNN: Informative K-Nearest Neighbor Pattern Classification. Practice of Knowledge Discovery in Databases, 248–264 (2007)

A Tag Clustering Method to Deal with Syntactic Variations on Collaborative Social Networks

José Javier Astrain, Francisco Echarte, Alberto Córdoba, and Jesús Villadangos

Dpt. de Ingeniería Matemática e Informática
Universidad Pública de Navarra
Campus de Arrosadía. 31006 Pamplona, Spain
josej.astrain@unavarra.es,
patxi@eslomas.com, {alberto.cordoba,jesusv}@unavarra.es

Abstract. Folksonomies have emerged as a common way of annotating and categorizing content using a set of tags that are created and managed in a collaborative way. Tags carry the semantic information within a folksonomy, and provide thus the link to ontologies. The appeal of folksonomies comes from the fact that they require a low effort for creation and maintenance since they are community-generated. However they present important drawbacks regarding their limited navigation and searching capabilities, in contrast with other methods as taxonomies, thesauruses and ontologies. One of these drawbacks is an effect of its flexibility for tagging, producing frequently multiple syntactic variations of a same tag. Similarity measures allow the correct identification of tag variations when tag lengths are greater than five symbols. In this paper we propose the use of cosine relatedness measures in order to cluster tags with lengths lower or equal than five symbols. We build a discriminator based on the combination of a fuzzy similarity and a cosine measures and we analyze the results obtained.

Keywords: Folksonomies, Fuzzy similarity, Tag Annotation, Tag Clustering.

1 Introduction

Folksonomies offer users an easy way to sort and organize resources by assigning text tags at different resources, such as photos, web pages, documents, etc. User annotations and categorization define collaboratively the semantics of the tags and resources used, causing the emergence of their associated semantics (unstructured knowledge). Folksonomies are based on the assignation of text tags to these resources. Tag annotation allows defining collaboratively the meaning of the annotated resources, and the used tags. Tags provide users new approaches for information search and exploration. Some navigation tools as clouds of tags allow users searching for certain tags and to locate resources tagged by other users. Though folksonomies have a great success in current web, mainly due to their simplicity of use, they also have important drawbacks. The fact of users creating tags and assigning them freely to resources produces the inexistence of any structure among these tags.

M. Gaedke, M. Grossniklaus, and O. Díaz (Eds.): ICWE 2009, LNCS 5648, pp. 434–441, 2009.
© Springer-Verlag Berlin Heidelberg 2009

Users can introduce synonyms, syntactic tag variations or different granularity levels [1] in the tagging process, lowering the quality of folksonomies and making more difficult the exploration and retrieval of information [2,3].

Several works in the literature focus on solving some of the problems associated with folksonomies. Folksonomy browsing is addressed in [4] presenting different ways to display tag clouds; [5] analyze the co-occurrence of labels to improve the quality of tag clouds. Tag clustering is addressed in [6,7]. An in-depth study of semantic tag relatedness is addressed in [8]. The problem of exploring hierarchical semantics from social annotations is studied in [7]; and [6] deals with the conversion of a large corpus of tags into a navigable hierarchical taxonomy using a graph of similarities. Other proposals such as [9] propose to improve the quality of folksonomies supporting users in the task of resource annotation by suggesting tags. Other works as [1,10] relate folksonomies with formal information classification systems as ontologies [11] and personalized recommendation [12].

Most of the above proposals do not take into account that a relevant number of the existing tags corresponds to syntactic variations (erroneous or not) of previously existing tags. The performance of a pre-filtering of the tags before applying an algorithm for tag clustering, as occurs in [13], allows minimizing the effects of syntactic variations increasing the quality of tag clustering. In [13] Specia and Motta create clusters of semantically related tags over a reduced experimental data set, using a previous step in which Levenshtein similarity measure is used to reduce the number of tags identifying syntactic variations. Then the folksonomy is changed replacing each identified variation by a representative tag. Another way to represent these variations is presented in [1, 14]. The use of pattern matching techniques designed to automatically recognize syntactic variations of tags provides mechanisms to improve the quality of folksonomies [15]. Approximate string matching techniques allow dealing with the problem introduced by syntactic variations on folksonomies. The problem consists on the comparison of an observed input string called α, maybe containing errors, and a pattern string ω in order to transform α in ω [16]. Edit operations (insertion, deletion and change of a symbol) allow recovering those errors transforming α in ω. The number of edit operations needed to recover an input string provides a distance measure between the input string and the pattern string. This distance, known as edit distance, can be expressed in terms of similarity and distance (dissimilarity) measures between strings. Imperfect pattern matching techniques perform better when dealing with syntactic variations of tags as indicated in [17]. The use of a fuzzy automaton with ε-moves (FA_ε), as described in [15], allows obtaining correct tag clustering rates greater than 95% when considering large data sets.

The main contribution of this paper is the introduction of a discriminator that combines a syntactic similarity measure based in a fuzzy automaton with ε-moves (FA_ε), and a cosine relatedness measure. This combination improves significantly the performance of the syntactic variations detection, even when considering short length tags (lower or equal than three symbols).

The rest of the paper is organized as follows: section 2 describes the tag clustering process; section 3 describes the experimental scenario and the results obtained; and finally, conclusions and references end the paper.

2 Syntactic Variations Clustering

Folksonomies can be described following different approaches [6,8,17]. A folksonomy F can be defined as a tuple: $F=(U,R,T,f_a:UxRxTx...xT)$, where U, R and T are respectively the finite sets of users, resources and tags defined in the folksonomy; and where the annotation relation f_a relates a user, with a resource and with the set of tags employed by the user to annotate the resource. In order to represent the syntactic variations of tags, this definition must be extended. Then, a folksonomy is defined as a tuple: $F'=(U,R,T,T',f_a:UxRxTx...xT,f_g:T'{\rightarrow}Tx...xT)$. In this model U, R and T keep their meaning and a new set with name T' is used to represent the clustering of T elements, being $T'{\subseteq}T$. This model allows clustering tag variations included in T in a new set of tags T'. Relation f_a keeps the same meaning, relating a user with a resource and a set of tag variations used to annotate the resource by the user. Function f_g represents the relation between T' groups of tags and T tags variations.

A fuzzy finite state automaton with ε-moves FA_ε is a sixtuple $(Q,\Sigma,\mu,\mu_\varepsilon,\sigma,\eta)$ where Q is a non-empty finite set of states; Σ is a non-empty finite set of input symbols (*input alphabet*) where Σ^+ is the set of all non-empty strings over Σ, and $\Sigma^* = \Sigma+U\{\varepsilon\}$; $\mu: QxQx\Sigma \rightarrow [0,1]$ is the state transition function; σ and η are fuzzy sets on Q; and μ_ε is a reflexive binary fuzzy relation on Q representing the state transition function by empty string. For q, $p \in Q$ and $x \in \Sigma$, the value $\mu(q,p,x) \in [0,1]$ represents the degree to which the automaton in state q and with the input symbol x may enter to state p. For $q \in Q$, σ (q) indicates the degree to which q is an initial state, and $\eta(q)$ indicates the degree to which q is a final state.

(1) $\hat{\mu} : \Im(Q)x\Sigma \rightarrow \Im(Q)$

(2) $\hat{\mu}_\varepsilon : \Im(Q) \rightarrow \Im(Q)$ is the fuzzy state transition function by empty string. Given a fuzzy state $V \in \Im(Q), \hat{\mu}_\varepsilon(V) = V \circ \mu_\varepsilon^T$, where μ_ε^T is the T-transitive closure of μ_ε.

(3) $\mu^* : \Im(Q)x\Sigma^* \rightarrow \Im(Q)$ is the extended transition function for the fuzzy finite state automaton with ε-moves. It is defined as follows:

a) $\mu^*(V,\varepsilon) = \hat{\mu}_\varepsilon(V) = V \circ \mu_\varepsilon^T, \forall V \in \Im(Q)$

b) $\mu^*(V,\alpha x) = \hat{\mu}_\varepsilon(\hat{\mu}(\mu^*(V,\alpha),x)) = (\mu^*(V,\alpha) \circ \mu[x]) \circ \mu_\varepsilon^T, \forall V \in \Im(Q), \alpha \in \Sigma^*$, and $x \in \Sigma$

The language accepted by FA_ε, denoted $L(FA_\varepsilon)$, is the fuzzy set on Σ^* such that $L(FA_\varepsilon)(\alpha) = \max_{q \in Q}(\mu^*(\sigma,\alpha)(q) \circ \eta(q)), \forall \alpha \in \Sigma$.

Two tags co-occur if both of them are used by a user to annotate a certain resource. Given a folksonomy $F=(U,R,T,f_a:UxRxTx...xT)$, we can define a co-occurrence graph as a weighted undirected graph whose set of vertices is the set T of tags. Two tags t_1 and t_2 are connected by an edge, if there exists at least one annotation with a f_a relation corresponding to user u, resource r, containing both tags. The weight of an edge $w(t_1,t_2)$ is determined by the number of co-ocurrences of the two tags connected (t_1 and t_2). According to co-occurrences, each tag t can be encoded as a weights vector $v_t \in R^T$ where each position is associated to a tag t' and whose value is determined by the weight of the co-occurrences between both tags (t and t'): $v_{t,t'} = w(t, t') \forall t \neq t' \in T$, where $v_{tt} = 0$. This encoding allows measuring the semantic similarity between to tags using the cosine measure. Given two tags t_1 y t_2 represented by $v_1, v_2 \in R^T$, their cosine similarity is defined as:

$$Similarity \ (t_1, t_2) := \cos(v_1, v_2) = \frac{v_1 \cdot v_2}{|v_1| \cdot |v_2|} \qquad (1)$$

When comparing two tags encoded following their co-occurrences vectors, the measure provided supplies values in the closed interval [0,1] representing the existing angle between both vectors (v_1 and v_2). This measure is independent of the tag length, and its value is 0 whenever both vectors are orthogonal and 1 when both vectors have the same direction.

In [15] we proposed a method that allowed the classification of tags (containing syntactic variations) based on a discriminator which computed similarity measures among a candidate tag and a set of pattern tags contained in a dictionary. The main drawback of similarity measures based on dictionary comparisons is their poor performance when considering short length chains. The proposed fuzzy similarity based on fuzzy automata with ε-moves FA_ε provides low recognition rates whenever the tag lengths are lower or equal than three symbols. In a folksonomy, a syntactic variation in a short length tag (e.g.: *cut* is transformed in *cat*) can imply a great impact in the meaning represented by this tag. In order to deal with syntactic variation of tags grant an adequate clustering, we propose the use of the cosine measure to increase the reliability of the fuzzy similarity when dealing with short length tags. The main problem is how to identify if a tag is a syntactic variation of a pre-existing tag or not. The cosine measure allows identifying if a candidate tag is semantically similar to a pattern tag. Cosine measure allows discriminating a great number of false positives that fuzzy similarity measures can introduce when dealing with short length tags.

In such way, we propose to assist the discriminator with the cosine relatedness similarity measure between tags. Figure 1 describes the process followed by a new candidate tag that is introduced in the system for the first time. The discriminator computes the fuzzy syntactic similarity and the cosine measure among the observed tag and the set of existing tags stored in a dictionary. The occurrence of a new tag not included in the dictionary implies a clustering process. If the discriminator identifies

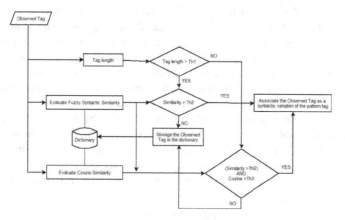

Fig. 1. Syntactic tag variation discrimination, flow diagram

the tag as a syntactic variation of an existing tag, it assigns this new tag to the cluster whose cluster-head is the pattern tag with the higher similarity value (pattern). According to the tag length, the discriminator uses the fuzzy similarity or the fuzzy & cosine similarities. Thresholds Th_1, Th_2 and Th_3 represent the tag length threshold, the fuzzy similarity threshold and the cosine threshold, respectively. Whenever the tag length is greater than Th_1, the discriminator uses the fuzzy similarity measure for the tag clustering process. In other case, the cosine measure is also considered by the discriminator in conjunction with the fuzzy similarity measure. If both, fuzzy and cosine measures provided values greater than Th_1 and Th_2 respectively, then the discriminator identifies the tag as a variation of a certain pattern tag, and performs the tag clustering according to this result. When fuzzy and cosine measures do not agree (values lower than thresholds) the discriminator includes the tag in the dictionary.

3 Experimental Results

In order to evaluate our proposal, we have collected data from the social web *del.icio.us* during the first weak of the year 2009[1], collecting 2,296,300 annotations. Each annotation consists on a tag assigned by a user to a resource, on a given date. We have obtained the 1,000 tags more widely used among the set of annotations. Although these tags only are the 0.64% of the total set of tags (a very small sample size), they represent: (i) the 66.92% of the total set of annotations, (ii) the 78.24% of the set of resources and (iii) the 87.85% of the total sets of users. We have analyzed one by one the 1,000 tags (with fuzzy similarity and cosine measures) adding them to the dictionary (initially empty) when the discriminator identifies them as new tags, and clustering them when the discriminator identifies them as syntactic variations of existing ones. A first experiment focuses on the selection of the adequate threshold values for the hybrid method (fuzzy and cosine). A second experiment focuses on the hybrid method (fuzzy similarity and cosine measures) validation. Figure 2 represents the tag length distribution for the initial set and for the subset of 1,000 annotations more frequently used, respectively. The rate of occurrences of small length tags (lower or equal than five symbols) is near a 15% for the initial set of tags, and increases to 35% when considering more frequently used subset.

The fuzzy similarity measure provides good clustering rates of tag including syntactic variations [15]. Considering the related set of 1,000 annotations, the fuzzy similarity measure provides a correct classified rate (*OK*) of 91.4% for a threshold value of 0.0003. To improve this rate, mainly for short length tags, we analyze the threshold values concerning the cosine measure. Figure 3 (left) shows the correct clustering rate obtained for different threshold values. Better results are obtained for a threshold of 0.7, obtaining a correct clustering rate of 95.5%. As Figure 2 (right) shows, the hybrid method improves the results provided by the fuzzy similarity even if the cosine threshold is not selected properly. The threshold considered by the hybrid method (see Figure 4) determines the weight assigned by the hybrid method to the fuzzy similarity according to the length of the tag considered. The goal of the hybrid method is to improve the correct clustering rate provided by the fuzzy

---

[1] http://www.eslomas.com/index.php/publicaciones/
tagsvariationscombinedmethod

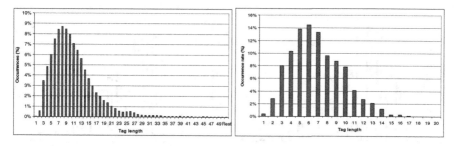

Fig. 2. Tag length distribution for the initial (left) and experimental (right) sets respectively

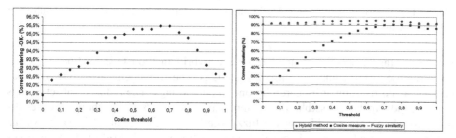

Fig. 3. Threshold selection for the cosine measure (left) and correct clustering rates (right)

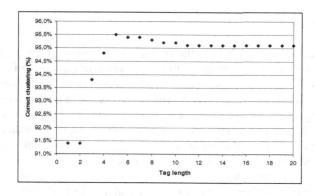

Fig. 4. Hybrid method threshold referred to the tag lengths

similarity when dealing with short tag length. The 91.4% of recognition rate provided by fuzzy similarity increases notably when dealing with tag lengths in the interval [3,10]. Tags with lengths lower than three symbols still provide worse results. A syntactic variation of a symbol often implies a semantic change.

In order to validate the hybrid method, we consider thresholds of 0.0003 and 0.7 for the fuzzy similarity and cosine measures, respectively. These values have been obtained experimentally as described above. In the same way, the threshold value fixed for the hybrid method is five, in order to improve the clustering of tags with lengths of three, four and five symbols. Figure 5 shows the tag clustering results obtained for the experimental subset of 1,000 annotations. Label OK represents the

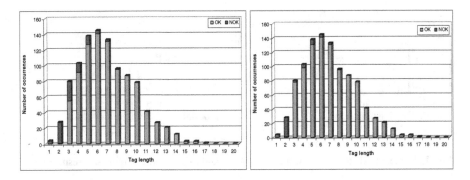

Fig. 5. Tag clustering results provided by the hybrid method for the experimental subset of 1,000 annotations

number of tags correctly grouped using the hybrid method (see Section 2). Label NOK represents the number of misclassified tags. The correct clustering rate (*OK*) has been obtained by comparing carefully one to one all tags. The reduced subset of tags (a thousand) makes possible this comparison. Figure 5 (left) shows the results obtained when only considering the fuzzy similarity measure, and (right) shows the results obtained when considering the hybrid method. The hybrid method improves notably the clustering rates when considering tag lengths between three and five.

4   Conclusions

In this work, we propose a hybrid method to cluster tags using a fuzzy similarity and a cosine measures. The fuzzy similarity discovers syntactic variations of tags allowing the clustering of tags. The cosine measure allows improving the clustering process when dealing with short length tags. A syntactic variation in a short length tag often implies a change in the meaning of the tag, and the cosine measure allows discovering if that occurs. A high cosine similarity value in a short length tag indicates that this tag is a syntactic variation of an existing one, while a low cosine value indicates that this tag must be considered as a new tag. We tune the threshold values and analyze the clustering rates obtaining that the hybrid method improves the tag clustering process when considering tag lengths lower or equal than five symbols.

Acknowledgements

Research partially supported by the Spanish Research Council under research grants TIN2006-14738-C02-02 and TIN2008-03687.

References

1. Echarte, F., Astrain, J.J., Córdoba, A., Villadangos, J.: Ontology of Folksonomy: A New Modeling Method. In: Semantic Authoring, Annotation and Knowledge Markup, Whistler, British Columbia, Canada (2007)

2. Mathes, A.: Folksonomies - Cooperative Classification and Communication Throught Shared Metadata. Computer Mediated Communication (2004)
3. Guy, M., Tonkin, E.: Folksonomies - Tidying up Tags? DLib Magazine 12(1) (2006)
4. Kaser, O., Lemire, D.: TagCloud Drawing: Algorithms for Cloud Visualization. In: Work. Taggings and Metadata for Social Information Organization, Banff, Alberta, Canada (2007)
5. Hassan-Montero, Y., Herrero-Solana, V.: Improving tag-clouds as visual information retrieval interfaces. In: International Conference on Multidisciplinary Information Sciences and Technologies, Mérida, Spain (2006)
6. Heymann, P., García-Molina, H., Collaborative Creation of Communal Hierarchical, Taxonomies in Social Tagging Systems. Stanford Info. Lab. Tech. Report 2006-10 (2006)
7. Zhou, M., Bao, S., Wu, X., Yu, Y.: An Unsupervised Model for Exploring Hierarchical Semantics from Social Annotations. In: Aberer, K., Choi, K.-S., Noy, N., Allemang, D., Lee, K.-I., Nixon, L., Golbeck, J., Mika, P., Maynard, D., Mizoguchi, R., Schreiber, G., Cudré-Mauroux, P. (eds.) ASWC 2007 and ISWC 2007. LNCS, vol. 4825, pp. 680–693. Springer, Heidelberg (2007)
8. Cattuto, C., Benz, D., Hotho, A., Stumme, G.: Semantic Grounding of Tag Relatedness in Social Bookmarking Systems. In: Sheth, A.P., Staab, S., Dean, M., Paolucci, M., Maynard, D., Finin, T., Thirunarayan, K. (eds.) ISWC 2008. LNCS, vol. 5318, pp. 615–631. Springer, Heidelberg (2008)
9. Xu, Z., Fu, Y., Mao, J., Su, D.: Towards the Semantic Web: Collaborative Tag Suggestions. In: Workshop on Collaborative Web tagging, Edinburgh, Scotland (2006)
10. Passant, A.: Using Ontologies to Strengthen Folksonomies and Enrich Information Retrieval in Weblogs: Theoretical background and corporate use-case. In: International Conference on Weblogs and Social Media, Boulder, USA (2007)
11. Gruber, T.: A Translation Approach to Portable Ontology Specifications. Knowledge Acquisition 5(2), 199–220 (1993)
12. Shepitsen, A., Gemmel, J., Mobasher, B., Burke, R.: Personalized Recommendation in Social Tagging Systems Using Hierarchical Clustering. In: 2nd ACM Conference on Recommender Systems, Lausanne, Switzerland, pp. 259–266 (2008)
13. Specia, L., Motta, E.: Integrating Folksonomies with the Semantic Web. In: Franconi, E., Kifer, M., May, W. (eds.) ESWC 2007. LNCS, vol. 4519, pp. 624–639. Springer, Heidelberg (2007)
14. Kim, H.L., Scerri, S., Breslin, J.G., Decker, S., Kim, H.G.: The State of the Art in Tag Ontologies: A Semantic Model for Tagging and Folksonomies. In: 8th Int. Conference on Dublin Core and Metadata Applications, Berlin, Germany, pp. 128–137 (2008)
15. Echarte, F., Astrain, J.J., Córdoba, A., Villadangos, J.: Improving Folksonomies Quality by Syntactic Tag Variations Grouping. In: 24th Annual ACM Symposium on Applied Computing, Honolulu, USA, vol. 2, pp. 2016–2020 (2009)
16. Navarro, G.: A Guided Tour to Approximate String Matching. ACM Computing Surveys 33(1), 31–88 (2001)
17. Echarte, F., Astrain, J.J., Córdoba, A., Villadangos, J.: Pattern Matching Techniques to Identify Syntactic Variations of Tags in Folksonomies. In: Lytras, M.D., Carroll, J.M., Damiani, E., Tennyson, R.D. (eds.) WSKS 2008. LNCS (LNAI), vol. 5288, pp. 557–564. Springer, Heidelberg (2008)

Relating RSS News/Items

Fekade Getahun, Joe Tekli, Richard Chbeir, Marco Viviani, and Kokou Yetongnon

Laboratoire Electronique, Informatique et Image
(LE2I) – UMR-CNRS Université de Bourgogne – Sciences et Techniques
Mirande, Aile de l'Ingénieur, 9 av. Savary – 21078 Dijon Cedex, France
{fekade-getahun.taddesse,joe.tekli,rchbeir,marco.viviani,
kokou}@u-bourgogne.fr

Abstract. Merging related RSS news (coming from one or different sources) is beneficial for end-users with different backgrounds (journalists, economists, etc.), particularly those accessing similar information. In this paper, we provide a practical approach to both: measure the relatedness, and identify relationships between RSS elements. Our approach is based on the concepts of semantic neighborhood and vector space model, and considers the content and structure of RSS news items.

Keywords: RSS Relatedness, Similarity, Relationships, Neighbourhood.

1 Introduction

Really Simple Syndication (RSS) [16] is an XML-based family of web feed formats, proposed to facilitate the aggregation of information from multiple web sources. Merging related RSS news items would allow clients to efficiently access content originating from different providers, rather than roaming a set of news providers and often accessing related or identical news more than once (as existing RSS aggregators[1] do not provide facilities for identifying and handling such items).

In this work, we address *semantic relatedness*[2] [2] between RSS elements/items (labels and contents) and consecutively element semantic relationships with respect to (w.r.t.) the meaning of terms and not only their syntactic properties. To motivate our work, let us consider Figure 1 and Figure 2 showing a list of news extracted from CNN and BBC's RSS feeds. Identifying related news would enable the user to more easily and efficiently acquire and/or merge information. XML news feeds (e.g., RSS items) can be related in different manners:

- A news might be totally included in another news (*inclusion*).
  Example 1. The title content of *CNN1* "U.N. chief launches $613M Gaza aid appeal" includes the title content of *BBC1* "UN launches $613m appeal for Gaza"[3] (cf. Figures 1 and 2).

---

[1] Newsgator, google-reader, etc., allows search, filter or display news in RSS format.
[2] Semantic relatedness is a more general concept than similarity. Dissimilar entities may also be semantically related by lexical relations such as meronymy and antonymy.
[3] After a pre-process of stop word removal, stemming, ignoring non textual values and semantic analysis.

M. Gaedke, M. Grossniklaus, and O. Díaz (Eds.): ICWE 2009, LNCS 5648, pp. 442–452, 2009.
© Springer-Verlag Berlin Heidelberg 2009

- Two news may refer to similar and related concepts (*intersection*).
  Example 2. The description content of *CNN2* "Ford Motor reported that its ongoing losses soared ...." and description content of *BBC2* "US carmaker Ford reports the biggest full-year loss in its history ...." are related and very similar, they share some words/expressions ('Ford', 'report', 'loss', 'US') and semantically related concepts ('fourth quarter', 'year'), ('biggest', 'soar'), ('reiterate', 'say'), ('federal bailout'), and ('government loan').

- News might be opposite but refer to the same issue (*oppositeness*).
  Example 3. "The international youth forum cancel call for stop-war demonstration due to security reason" (description of CNN3) and "International youth forum call demonstration as part of stop the war" (description of BBC3) can be considered as opposite because of the use of antonym expressions 'call' and 'cancel call'.

<item><title>U.N. chief launches $613M Gaza aid appeal</title><description> United Nations Secretary-General Ban Ki-moon on Thursday launched a humanitarian appeal to provide emergency aid to the people of Gaza in the aftermath of Israel's military offensive in the region.</description></item>	*CNN1*
<item><title>Ford reports $5.9 billion loss in the fourth-quarter </title><description>Ford Motor reported that its ongoing losses soared in the fourth quarter, but the company reiterated it still does not need the federal bailout already received by its two U.S. rivals.</description> </item>	*CNN2*
<description>The international youth forum cancels the call for stop-war demonstration due to security reason</description></item>	*CNN3*

Fig. 1. RSS news extracted from CNN

<item><title> UN launches $613m appeal for Gaza </title><description> The UN will launch an appeal for $613m to help people affected by Israel's military offensive in Gaza, the body's top official says </description></item>	*BBC1*
<item><title> Ford reports record yearly loss </title><description> US carmaker Ford reports the biggest full-year loss in its history, but says it still does not need government loans.</description></item>	*BBC2*
<item><title>Youth's form call for demonstration</title><description> International youth forum call demonstration as part of stop the war </description></item>	*BBC3*

Fig. 2. RSS news extracted from BBC

Identifying these relationships is beneficial while defining merging rules and making merging decisions. For instance, (i) merging identical or including news might be reduced to keeping the including news (keeping $title_{cnn1}$ in example 1), (ii) merging intersecting news might refer to keeping the common parts and adding the differences ($title_{cnn2}$ and $title_{bbc2}$) (iii) merging opposite news might be done by keeping both news (i.e. merging *CNN3* and *BBC3*). Hence, the main objective of this study is to put forward a specialized XML relatedness measure, dedicated to the comparison of RSS items, able to identify (*i*) RSS items that are related enough and (*ii*) the relationship that can occur between two RSS news items (i.e., *disjointness, intersection, inclusion, antonomy* and *equality*).

The remainder of this paper is organized as follows. In Section 2, we discuss background and related works. Section 3 defines basic concepts to be used in our measure. In Section 4, we detail how the relatedness and relationships between text values are computed. Section 5 details our RSS relatedness and relationship measures. Section 6 presents experimental result. Finally, Section 7 concludes this study and draws some future research directions.

2 Related Work

Identifying correspondence or matching nodes in hieratically organized data such as XML is a pre-condition in different scenarios such as merging [9]. A lot of research has been done to determine XML document similarity, which we roughly categorize into *structure-based*, *content* and *hybrid* approaches. Most *structure-based* similarity approaches use tree edit distance [1]. Chawathe [3], Nireman and Jagadish [13] , consider the minimum number of edit operations: insert node (insert tree), delete node (delete tree) and update node operations to transform one XML tree into another. Also, the use of Fast Fourier Transform [4] has been proposed to compute similarity between XML documents. With *content based* XML similarity measures [5], similarity is computed based on element contents, disregarding (to a certain extent) the document tags and structural information. Semantic similarity between concepts is estimated either by the distance between nodes [18] or the content of the most specific common ancestor of those nodes involved in the comparison [11] and is evaluated according to some predefined knowledge base(s). In Information Retrieval (IR) [12], the content of a document is commonly modeled with sets/bags words where each word (and subsumed word(s)) is given a weight computed with Term Frequency (TF), Document Frequency (DT), Inverse Document Frequency (IDF), and the combination TF-IDF. In [7], the authors used a Vector Space having TF-IDF as a weight factor in XML retrieval. More recently, there are *hybrid* approaches that attempted to address XML comparison. In a recent work [17], the authors combine an IR semantic similarity technique with a structural-based algorithm based on tree edit distance. However, semantic similarity evaluation is limited only to tag names. In [8], *xSim* computes the matching between XML documents as an average of the elements' matching similarity value. Similarity between two elements is computed as the average of textual content, element name and path (i.e. sequence of node names starting from the root) similarity values without considering semantics.

The relationships between objects such as equality, inclusion, intersection, disjointness, etc. have been used in different applications such as spatial data retrieval, access control and text mining. In [10], Ho-Lam *et al.* stress on the importance of considering relationships (equality, overlap, disjointness and containment or inclusion) between data sources while merging XML documents, without however addressing the issue. Ian Gracia *et al.* [5] used a correlation based approach (applied only to content) to identify relationship among RSS news articles: redundant (equal and inclusion), non-related (disjoint) and related (intersection) relationships. In paper work, we identify equality, inclusion, disjoint, intersection and opposite relationships in addition to measuring relatedness while considering tag name similarity.

3   Preliminaries

An RSS[4] document is a well-formed XML document represented as a rooted ordered labeled tree following the Document Object Model (DOM) [19]. Each node or element of an RSS Tree is a pair having $e = \langle \eta, \varsigma \rangle$ where $e.\eta$ is the element name and $e.\eta$ its content. The content of an element can be another element (complex element) or a text value (simple element). Notice that, different versions of RSS items consistently follow the same overall structure with minor additions and removals (e.g. source is part of RSS 0.9x and guid in RSS 2.0).

3.1   Knowledge Base

A *Knowledge Base* [15] (thesauri, taxonomy and/or ontology) provides a framework for organizing entities (words/expressions, generic concepts, web pages, etc.) into a semantic space. In our study, it is used to assist relatedness and is formally defined as $KB = (C, E, R, f)$ where C is the set of concepts (synonym sets of words/expressions as in WordNet [14]), E is the set of edges connecting the concepts, $E \subseteq C \times C$, R is the set of semantic relations, $R = \{\equiv, \prec, \succ, <<, >>, \Omega\}$[5], f is a function designating the nature of edges in E, $f : E \rightarrow R$.

We introduced two types of knowledge bases to assist simple element relatedness: (*i*) *value-based*: to describe the textual content of RSS elements, and (*ii*) *label-based*: to organize RSS labels. Note that one single knowledge base could have been used. However, since XML document labels in general, and RSS labels in particular, depend on the underlying document schema, an independent *label-based* knowledge base, provided by the user/administrator, seems more appropriate than a more generic one such as WordNet (treating generic textual content).

3.2   Neighborhood

In our approach, the *neighborhood* of a concept C_i underlines the set of concepts $\{C_j\}$, in the knowledge base, that are subsumed by C_i w.r.t. a given semantic relation. The concept of neighborhood, introduced in [6], is exploited in identifying the relationships between text (i.e., RSS element labels and/or textual contents) and consequently RSS elements/items.

Definition 1 [Semantic Neighborhood]: The *semantic neighborhood* of a concept C_i ($N^R_{KB}(C_i)$) is defined as the set of concepts $\{C_j\}$ (and consequently the set of words/expressions subsumed by the concepts) in a given knowledge base *KB*, related with C_i via the hyponymy ($\prec$) or meronymy ($<<$) semantic relations, directly or via transitivity.

---

[4] RSS refers to one of the following standards: Rich Site Summary (RSS 0.91, RSS 0.92), RDF Site Summary (RSS 0.9 and 1.0), and Really Simple Syndication (RSS 2.0).

[5] The symbols in R underline respectively the synonym ($\equiv$), hyponym (Is-A or $\prec$), hypernym (Has-A or $\succ$), meronym (Part-Of or $<<$), holonym (Has-Part or $>>$) and Antonym (Ω) relations, as defined in [6].

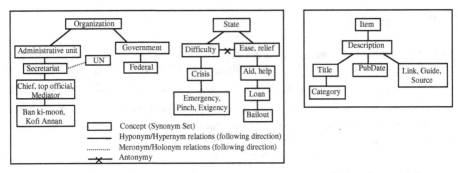

a. Two sample value KBs with multiple root concepts extracted from WordNet

b. Sample RSS labels

Fig. 3. Sample value and label knowledge bases

Definition 2 [Global Semantic Neighborhood]: The *global semantic neighborhood* of a concept C_i ($\overline{N_{KB}}(C_i)$) is the union of each semantic neighborhood w.r.t. all synonymy ($\equiv$), hyponymy ($\prec$) and meronymy ($\ll$) relations altogether.

Definition 3 [Antonym Neighborhood]: The antonym neighborhood of a concept C_i ($N_{KB}^{\Omega}(C_i)$) is defined as the set of concepts $\{C_i\}$, in a given knowledge base KB, related with C_i via the antonymy relation (Ω), directly or transitively via synonymy($\equiv$), hyponymy ($\prec$) or hypernym ($\succ$).

4   Text Relatedness

4.1   Text Representation

A text is represented following the vector space model used in information retrieval [12]. Each text t_i is represented in an n-dimensional vector space such as: $[\langle C_1, w_1 \rangle, \ldots, \langle C_n, w_n \rangle]$ where C_i is a *concept set*, w_i is its weight and n is the number of distinct concepts in both texts. The *concept set* of text t, denoted as *CS*, is a set of concepts $\{C_1, \ldots, C_m\}$, where each C_i (obtained after several textual pre-processing operations such as stop-words[6] removal, stemming[7], and mapping to knowledge base) represents the meaning of a group of terms in $\{k_1, \ldots, k_n\}$, where m is the total number of concepts describing t. The weight of a concept C_i reflects its existence in vector V_i (1 if it exists) or the maximum enclosure similarity it has with a concept C_j in V_j.

$$Enclosure\_sim(C_i, C_j) = \frac{|\overline{N_{KB}}(C_i) \cap \overline{N_{KB}}(C_j)|}{|\overline{N_{KB}}(C_j)|} \quad (1)$$

Enclosure_sim(C_i, C_j) takes into account the global semantic neighborhood of each concept. It is asymmetric, allows the detection of the various kinds of relationships between RSS items, and returns a value equal to 1 if C_i includes C_j.

---

[6] Stop-words identify words/expressions which are filtered out (e.g., *yet, an, but, the, ...*)

[7] Stemming is the process for reducing inflected (or sometimes derived) words to their stem, i.e., base.

Example 4. Consider the *description* element of RSS items *CNN2* and *BBC2* (Figures 1, 2). The partial corresponding vector representations V_1 and V_2 are shown in Figure 4.

	Ford	report	loss	...	Federal	Bailout	Big	say	government	loan
V_1	1	1	1	...	1	1	1	1	1	1
V_2	1	1	1	...	0.67	0.86	1	1	1	1

Fig. 4. Vectors obtained when comparing title texts of RSS items *CNN2* and *BBC2*

For each concept C in V_1 and V_2 its weight is 1 if it exists, otherwise it is updated with the maximum semantic enclosure similarity value. For instance, following the WordNet extract in Figure 3a, the concept 'Government' is included in the global semantic neighborhood of 'Federal', i.e., $government \in \overline{N_{KB}}(federal)$. Hence, *Enclosure_sim*(federal, government) = 1 but in V_2, *Enclosure_sim*(government , federal) = 0.67. Likewise, 'loan' is included in the global semantic neighborhood of 'bailout' i.e. *Enclosure_sim*(loan, bailout) = 1 and *Enclosure_sim*(bailout, loan) = 0.86.

4.2 Text Relatedness and Relations

Given two texts t_1 and t_2, the *Textual Relatedness (TR)* algorithm returns a pair containing the semantic relatedness *SemRel* value and the relationship between the texts being compared. The *SemRel* value is computed using a vector based similarity method (e.g. cosine [12]) after building the corresponding text vector space. *SemRel* is consequently exploited in identifying basic relations (i.e., *disjointness, intersection* and *equality*) between texts. Our method for identifying basic relationships is based on a *fuzzy logic* model using pre-defined/pre-computed similarity thresholds $T_{Disjointness}$ and $T_{Equality}$, as shown in Figure 5.

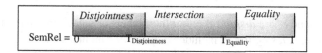

Fig. 5. Basic text relationships and corresponding thresholds

Thus, we identify the relationships between two texts t_1 and t_2 as follows:

- *Relation(t_1, t_2) = Disjointness,* i.e., $t_1 \rhd \lhd t_2$, if there is a minimum relatedness between t_1 and t_2 i.e., *SemRel*(t_1, t_2) $\leq T_{Disjointness}$.
- *Relation(t_1, t_2) = Intersection,* i.e., $t_1 \cap t_2$, if t_1 and t_2 share some semantic relatedness, i.e., $T_{Disjointness} <$ *SemRel*(t_1, t_2) $< T_{Equality}$.
- *Relation(t_1, t_2) = Equality,* i.e., $t_1 = t_2$, if t_1 and t_2 share a maximum amount of relatedness, i.e., *SemRel*(t_1, t_2) $\geq T_{Equality}$.

More intricate relations such as *inclusion* and *oppositeness* are identified as follows.

- *Relation(t_1, t_2) = Inclusion,* i.e., $t_1 \supset t_2$, if the product of the weights of vector V_1 (describing t_1) is equal to 1, i.e., $\Pi_{V_1}(w_p) = 1$. The weight product of V_1 underlines whether or not t_1 encompasses all concepts in t_2.

- **Relation(t_1, t_2) = Oppositeness**, i.e., $t_1 \Omega t_2$, if they intersect ($t_1 \cap t_2$) having at least one concept C_i of CS_1 included in the antonym neighborhood of a concept C_k in CS_2 or vice-versa, and such as neither CS_1 nor CS_2 encompass themselves concepts that are antonym to C_i and C_k respectively (we call this last condition *inner antonymy*), considering the antonym neighborhood.

  Example 5. Considering Example 2, (t_1 of *CNN2* and t_2 of *BBC2*), and thresholds $T_{Disjointness} = 0.1$ and $T_{Equality} = 0.9$, *SemRel(t_1, t_2)* = 0.86 and *Relation(t_1, t_2)* = *Intersection* as no concept of t1 is included in antonymy neighborhood of concept of t2 and vice-versa. Hence, $TR(t_1,t_2) = <0.86, Intersection>$.

  Example 6. Considering Example 3, (t_1 of *CNN3* and t_3 of *BBC3*), and thresholds $T_{Disjointness} = 0.1$ and $T_{Equality} = 0.9$, *SemRel(t_1, t_2)* = 0.612 and $t_1 \cap t_2$ (intersection) and as 'Call' and 'Cancel call' are related with antonymy. *Relation(t_1, t_2)* = *Oppositeness*. Hence $TR(t_1,t_3) = <0.86, Oppositeness>$.

5   RSS Relatedness and Relations

Given two simple elements e_1, and e_2, the Element Relatedness (*ER*) algorithm returns a pair quantifying the semantic relatedness *SemRel* value and *Relation* based on corresponding *TR* label and content values. *SemRel* quantifies the relatedness value between elements, as the *weighted sum* value of label and value relatedness such as:

$$SemRel(e_1,e_2) = w_{Label} \times LB_{SemRel} + w_{Value} \times VR_{SemRel} \qquad (2)$$

where $w_{Label} + w_{Value} = 1$ and $(w_{Label}, w_{Value}) \geq 0$.

Relation exploits a rule-based method for combining label and value relationships as follows:

- Elements e_1 and e_2 are *disjoint* if either their labels or values are disjoint.
- Element e_1 *includes* e_2, if $e_1.\eta$ includes $e_2.\eta$ and $e_1.\varsigma$ includes $e_2.\varsigma$.
- Two elements e_1 and e_2 *intersect* if either their labels or values intersect.
- Two elements e_1 and e_2 are *equal* if both their labels and values are equal.
- Two elements e_1 and e_2 are *opposite* if both their contents are opposite. RSS label oppositeness is not relevant in identifying element oppositeness, especially w.r.t. RSS merging (cf. Example 3 and Figure 3b).

Given two RSS items I_1 and I_2, each made of a bunch of elements, the Item Relatedness (IR) Algorithm returns a pair containing *SemRel* and *Relation*. The *SemRel* is computed as the average of the relatedness values between corresponding element sets I_1 and I_2 as:

$$SemRel(i_1, i_2) = \frac{SemRel(e_i, e_j)}{|i_1| \times |i_2|} \qquad \forall e_i \in I_1, \forall e_j \in I_2 \qquad (3)$$

The *Relation* between I_1 and I_2 is identified by combining sub-element relationships using a rule-based method as follows:

- Items I_1 and I_2 are *disjoint* if all elements $\{e_i\}$ and $\{e_j\}$ are disjoint (elements are disjoint if there is no relatedness whatsoever between them, i.e., $SemRel(I_1, I_2) = 0$).
- Item I_1 *includes* I_2, if all elements in $\{e_i\}$ include all those in $\{e_j\}$.
- Two items I_1 and I_2 *intersect* if at least two of their elements intersect.
- Two items I_1 and I_2 are *equal* if all their elements in $\{e_i\}$ equal to all those in $\{e_j\}$.
- Two items I_1 and I_2 are *opposite* if at least two of their respective elements are opposite.

Example 7. Let us consider RSS items *CNN2* and *BBC2* (Figures 1 and 2). Corresponding item relatedness is computed as follows. Notice that weight value of $w_{label} = 0.5$ and $w_{value} = 0.5$ and Thresholds $T_{Disjointness} = 0.2$ and $T_{Equality} = 0.8$ are used. Below, simple element relatedness values and relationship values are given.

ER	$title_{BBC2}$	$description_{BBC2}$
$title_{CNN2}$	<0.864, Equal>	<0.551, Intersect>
$description_{CNN2}$	<0.555, Intersect>	<0.799, Intersect>

Using (c.f. 3) $SemRel(CNN2, BBC2) = (0.864 + 0.551 + 0.555 + 0.799) / 2 \times 2 = 0.692$, where $|I_1|$ and $|I_2|$ are equal to 2. $Relation(CNN2, BBC2) = Intersection$ since a number of their elements intersect, i.e., $Relation(title_{CNN2}, title_{BBC2}) = Relation(description_{CNN2}, description_{BBC2}) = Intersection$.

6 Experiments

To validate our approach, we have developed a C# prototype entitled R^3 (*RSS Relatedness and Relationship*) encompassing: (a) a KB component that stores value and label knowledge bases (b) RSS input component that allow users to register existing RSS feeds addresses and alos accepts parameters to be used in generating synthetic news. We have conducted a set of experiments in order to conform (*a*) the computational complexity and (*b*) the relevance of our relatedness measure. All the experiments were carried out on Intel Core Centrino Duo Processor machine (with processing speed of 1.73.0 GHz, 1GB of RAM).

6.1 Timing Analysis

Computational complexity of our item relatedness algorithm is polynomial and depends on the number of concept sets in input texts t_1 and t_2 (i.e. n and m), and the value knowledge base size (n_c - number of concepts and d - depth). Figure 6.a shows the timing result without considering knowledge base information while varying the size of the input texts. Timing increases in a liner fashion w.r.t. the number of concepts. Figure 6.b presents timing result considering fixed knowledge information (100 concepts within a depth of 8). The time needed to compute the relatedness between items increases drastically and in a quadratic fashion.

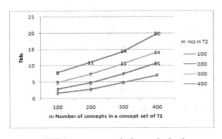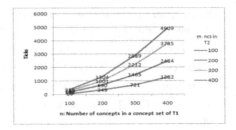

a. Without semantic knowledgebase   b. With fixed semantic (d=8,nc = 100)

Fig. 6. Timing analysis text concept set in t_1, t_2 (n, m)

6.2 Relevance of Measure

In this set of tests, we used our *relationship-aware*[8] *level based single* link clustering algorithm (adapted from classical clustering approaches [7]; not detailed in this paper due to space limitation). The single link clusters at a clustering level l_i (between 1 and 0) produces all items I_i with pair-wise similarity values greater than or equal to l_i. Notice that clustering at level nearer to zero produces very big and less relevant grouping hence should be avoided. We used the popular information retrieval metrics *precision* (PR) and *recall* (R) [12] and an *f-score* value to check the quality of discovered cluster.

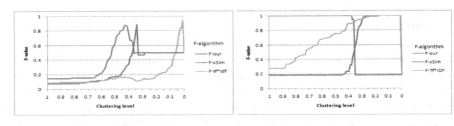

Fig. 7. *f*-score on real data set   **Fig. 8.** *f*-score on synthetic dataset

Two data sets were used to conduct our experiments:

- Real data set: we used 158 RSS news items extracted from CNN, BBC, USAToday, L.A. Times and Reuters, clustered manually into 6 groups: *US Presidential elections 08, Middle-east, Mumbai-attacks, space-technology, oil,* and *football.* Figure 7 shows the *f-score* resulting graph. The average *f-value* computed over the entire clustering level conforms that our semantic relatedness measure provides relevant clustering results (clusters closer to the predefined ones, particularly between levels 1 and 0.37) compared to *xSim* and TF-IDF.

---

[8] Classical clustering algorithms, do not consider the relationship between items, so they may produce clusters having highly related members with lots of intersections which are less relevant during merging. As a result, items related with inclusion and having less relatedness values will belong to different clusters.

- Synthetic data set: we generated 100 synthetic RSS news items using our own random RSS item generator. The generated news belong to 10 disjoint clusters. Each cluster has 10 members and 9 of them are related via the inclusion relationship. Figure 8 shows the f-score graph corresponding to our clustering experiments. Our relationship aware clustering algorithm groups all items related with inclusion in the appropriate cluster (between clustering levels 1 and 0.4, achieving a maximum f-score=1), whereas $xSim$ and TF-IDF generate incomplete clusters, disregarding the inclusion relationship.

7 Conclusions and Perspectives

In this paper, we have addressed the issue of measuring relatedness between RSS items. We have studied and provided a technique for RSS item relatedness computation, taking into account the different kinds of relationships that can occur among texts, elements and items. We have developed a prototype validating the complexity and effectiveness of our relatedness measure. Clustering experiments, conducted on both real and synthetic data show that our measure generates more relevant clusters compared to $xSim$ and TF-IDF. In addition, we have shown the capability of our measure in identifying relationships between items. Currently, we are working on RSS merging, developing relation-aware merging rules. The next step would be extending our work to address XML multimedia merging (SVG, MPEG-7, etc.).

References

[1] Bille, P.: A survey on tree edit distance and related problems. Theoretical CS 337(1-3), 217–239 (2005)
[2] Budanitsky, A., Hirst, G.: Evaluating wordnet-based measures of lexical semantic relatedness. Computational Linguistics 32(1), 13–47 (2006)
[3] Chawathe, S.S.: Comparing hierarchical data in external memory. In: VLDB 1999, pp. 90–101. Morgan Kaufmann Publishers Inc., San Francisco (1999)
[4] Flesca, S., Manco, G., Masciari, E., Pontieri, L.: Fast detection of xml structural similarity. IEEE Transactions on Knowledge and Data Engineering 17(2), 160–175 (2005)
[5] Garcia, I., Ng, Y.: Eliminating Redundant and Less-Informative RSS News Articles Based on Word Similarity and a Fuzzy Equivalence Relation. In: ICTAI 2006, pp. 465–473 (2006)
[6] Getahun, F., Tekli, J., Atnafu, S., Chbeir, R.: Towards efficient horizontal multimedia database fragmentation using semantic-based predicates implication. In: SBBD 2007, pp. 68–82 (2007)
[7] Grabs, T., Schek, H.-J.: Generating Vector Spaces On-the-fly for Flexible XML Retrieval. In: ACM SIGIR Workshop on XML and Information Retrieval 2002, pp. 4–13 (2002)
[8] Kade, A.M., Heuser, C.A.: Matching XML documents in highly dynamic applications. In: ACM symposium on Document engineering 2008, pp. 191–198 (2008)
[9] La Fontaine, R.: Merging XML files: A new approach providing intelligent merge of XML data sets. In: Proceedings of XML, Barcelona, Spain (May 2002)

[10] Lau, H., Ng, W.: A Unifying Framework for Merging and Evaluating XML Information. In: Zhou, L.-z., Ooi, B.-C., Meng, X. (eds.) DASFAA 2005. LNCS, vol. 3453, pp. 81–94. Springer, Heidelberg (2005)

[11] Lin, D.: An Information-Theoretic Definition of Similarity. In: Proceedings of the 15th International Conference on Machine Learning, pp. 296–304. Morgan Kaufmann Publishers, San Francisco (1989)

[12] McGill, M.J.: Introduction to Modern Information Retrieval. McGraw-Hill, New York (1983)

[13] Nierman, A., Jagadish, H.V.: Evaluating structural similarity in XML documents. In: WebDB 2002, pp. 61–66 (2002)

[14] Princeton University Cognitive Science Laboratory. WordNet: a lexical database for the English language, http://wordnet.princeton.edu/

[15] R. Richardson and A. F. Smeaton. Using WorldNet in a knowledge-based approach to information retrieval. Technical Report CA-0395, Dublin, Ireland (1995)

[16] RSS Advisory Board. RSS 2.0 Specification, http://www.rssboard.org/

[17] Tekli, J., Chbeir, R., Yetongnon, K.: A hybrid approach for xml similarity. SOFSEM 07: 783-795

[18] Wu, Z., Palmer, M.: Verbs semantics and lexical selection. In: Proceedings of the 32nd annual meeting on Association for Computational Linguistics, Morristown, NJ, USA, pp. 133–138 (1994)

[19] WWW Consortium. The Document Object Model, http://www.w3.org/DOM

A Layout-Independent Web News Article Contents Extraction Method Based on Relevance Analysis

Hao Han and Takehiro Tokuda

Department of Computer Science, Tokyo Institute of Technology
Meguro, Tokyo 152-8552, Japan
{han,tokuda}@tt.cs.titech.ac.jp

Abstract. The traditional Web news article contents extraction methods are time-costly and need much maintenance because they analyze the layout of news pages to generate the wrappers manually or automatically. In this paper, we propose a relevance-based analysis method to extract the news article contents from the news pages without the analysis of news page layouts before extraction. This method is applicable to the general news pages and we give the implementations of news extraction from different kinds of news sources.

Keywords: News Extraction, Search Engine, RSS Feeds.

1 Introduction

Nowadays, the traditional newspapers have developed significant Web presences. We can extract and analyze the Web news articles to acquire the desired information. Wrappers are generated based on the analysis of layout of news pages by many traditional extraction methods. However, different news sites use the different news page layouts, and each news site uses more than one layout. It is costly and inefficient to analyze the news page layout of each news site for news contents extraction.

In this paper, we propose a novel Web news article contents extraction method, which is independent of news page layout and does not need to analyze the news page layouts before extraction. We calculate the relevance between the news title and each sentence to detect the news paragraphs from the full text of the news page. We give the implementations of news extraction from the general news pages, news site databases, and news aggregation sites. By the experiments, we prove that our method runs conveniently and accurately. The organization of the rest of this paper is as follows. In the next section we give the motivation of our research and an overview of the related work. We explain our Web news article contents extraction method in detail in Section 3. In Section 4, we explain the implementation of our method and give the evaluation. Finally, we conclude our method and give the future work in Section 5.

M. Gaedke, M. Grossniklaus, and O. Díaz (Eds.): ICWE 2009, LNCS 5648, pp. 453–460, 2009.
© Springer-Verlag Berlin Heidelberg 2009

2   Motivation and Related Work

A lot of approaches have been proposed for extracting the Web news article contents. Reis et al. calculates the edit distance between two given trees for the automatic Web news article contents extraction [1]. Fukumoto et al. focuses on subject shift and presents a method for extracting key paragraphs from documents that discuss the same event [2]. However, if a news site uses too many different layouts in the news pages, the learning procedure costs too much time and the precision becomes low. Zheng et al. represents a news page as a visual block tree and derives a composite visual feature set by extracting a series of visual features, then generate the wrapper for a news site by machine learning [3]. However, it uses manually labeled data for training and the extraction result may be inaccurate if the training set is not large enough. Webstemmer [4] is a Web crawler and HTML layout analyzer that automatically extracts main text of a news site without having banners, advertisements and navigation links mixed up. All the analysis can be done in a fully automatic manner with little human intervention. However, this method runs slowly at contents parsing and extraction, and sometimes news titles are missing.

These methods are still not widely used, mostly because of the need for high human intervention and maintenance, or the low quality of the extraction results. They have to analyze the news pages from target news sites before extraction. Moreover, if the target news sites update the layout of news pages frequently and irregularly, or the target news pages come from a large number of different news sites, it is difficult to realize the extraction by these methods. To address these problems, we propose a layout-independent method to realize the Web news article contents extraction. Compared with the developed work, our method is applicable to the general news pages, and can extract the news articles contents from all kinds of news pages conveniently.

3   News Article Contents Extraction

We can collect the news articles from news sites, RSS feeds, search engines, aggregation sites and others. The collected news is shown as a link to news page, which includes the news title and URL of news page usually. As shown in Fig. 1, we use the collected URL to get the news page and use the collected news title to find out the news article contents from news page. Firstly, we split the news title to get the keyword list and use them to detect the position of news title in the news page. Then, we recognize one paragraph of news article by using the news title position and keyword list. Finally, we find all the paragraphs of news article contents and extract them out of the full text of the news page. We explain our algorithm step by step in this section.

3.1   Title Keywords Acquisition

The news title is a piece of important information for the recognition of the news article contents from the full text of news page. If we locate the position

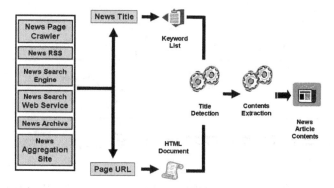

Fig. 1. The outline of Web news article contents extraction

of the news title in the news page correctly, the position of news article contents would be found easily because the contents are a list of paragraphs closely below the title usually. In addition, for a news article, the contents describe the same topic of news title in detail, and the words constituting the title would occur in the news article contents frequently usually. We split the collected title into single words to make a list of keywords as follows. Firstly, we split the news title into a word list using whitespace as the delimiter. Then, we remove the articles, prepositions and conjunctions. Finally, we remove the characters " 's" or " '" from the words ending with " 's" or " '". For example, we replace "Tom's" with "Tom", and replace "parents'" with "parents".

3.2   Full Text Analysis

An HTML document may be represented as a tree structure. A sentence in a Web page is a visible character string, which is the value of a leaf node. It is possible for each sentence to be the title or a paragraph. We use the following steps to analyze the full text of a news page in order to find the most possible title and paragraphs.

1. We split each sentence into a list of words using the keywords acquisition method described in Section 3.1.
2. We set the words list size as an attribute $WordNumber$, and set the occurrence number of the keywords ignoring case considerations within the words list as an attribute $KeyNumber$ of the corresponding leaf node.
3. We count up the $WordNumber$ of the sibling nodes and set the sum as an attribute $WordNumber$ of their parent node.
4. We count up the $KeyNumber$ of the sibling nodes and set the sum as an attribute $KeyNumber$ of their parent node.
5. We repeat the Step 3 and Step 4 until we set the attribute $WordNumber$ and $KeyNumber$ for <body> as shown in Fig. 2.

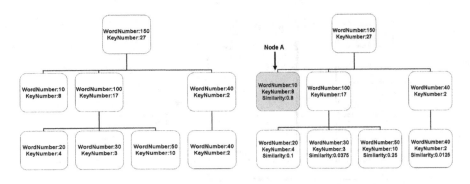

Fig. 2. A full text analysis example   **Fig. 3.** A news title detection example

3.3   News Title Detection

After the full text analysis, we need to find out the real news title in news page.
Usually, the real news title in a news page is same or similar to the collected
news title. We use the following formula to calculate the similarity between each
sentence of the news page and the collected news title.

$$Similarity = \frac{KeyNumber^2}{WordNumber \times TitleKeywordNumber}$$

Where, $KeyNumber$ and $WordNumber$ are the attribute value of the corresponding node of each sentence respectively, and $TitleKeywordNumber$ is the
size of keyword list of the collected news title.

We think a sentence is a possible real news title in the news page if the value
of $Similarity$ is more than a predetermined threshold, and a node whose value
is a possible news title would be a possible title node. Fig. 3 shows a news title
detection example where the size of title keyword list is 8. Assuming that the
predetermined threshold is set to 0.6, the node A is judged as the title node.

However, the collected news title is not always same or similar to the real
news title in the corresponding news page. In some news sites, we even can find
that the collected news title is different from the real news title totally, but same
to the other sentences in the news page. Moreover, some news titles are so short
and simple that we can find two or more same or similar sentences in news pages.
Therefore, there are five different situations about the possible news title and
the real title in a news page: 1. There is no possible news title. 2. There is just
one possible news title, and it is the real news title in the news page. 3. There
is just one possible news title, but it is not the real news title in the news page.
4. There are two or more possible news titles, and one of them is the real news
title in the news page. 5. There are two or more possible news titles, but none
of them is the real news title in the news page.

3.4   News Paragraph Recognition and News Contents Extraction

Usually, the news article contents part is a list of paragraphs immediately below the title. It becomes easier to find the paragraphs after the real news title is found. However, we can not make certain whether the found possible news title is the real news title in the news page as we describe in Section 3.3. The news paragraph recognition can be classified as the following situations.

1. There is no possible news title and the news paragraphs exist between <body> and </body> (Fig. 4(a)).
2. There is one possible news title and the news paragraphs exist between the end tag of possible title node and </body>. If we can not find out the news paragraphs in this range, we would find them in the reserve range which is between <body> and the start tag of possible title node (Fig. 4(b)).
3. There are two or more possible news titles and the news paragraphs exist between the end tag of each possible title node and the start tag of the next possible title node or </body>. If we can not find out the news paragraphs in these ranges, we find them in the reserve range which is between <body> and the start tag of the first possible title node (Fig. 4(c)).

Although each sentence of each selective range, including the link text, has the possibility to be one of the paragraphs, most of the paragraphs are non-link texts. We give a possibility for each non-link sentence and select one with the highest possibility as the final most possible paragraph if the highest possibility is more than a predetermined threshold. If the highest possibility is less than this predetermined threshold, we would find a sentence with the highest possibility in the reserve range and then compare these two possibilities to select one with the higher possibility as the final most possible paragraph. We use the following formula to calculate the possibility of each non-link sentence.

$$Possibility = WordSum \times (KeySum + 1)$$

Where, $WordSum$ is the sum of the attributes $WordNumber$ of each sentence's corresponding node and its related nodes in the same selective range. $KeySum$ is the sum of the attributes $KeyNumber$ of each sentence's corresponding node

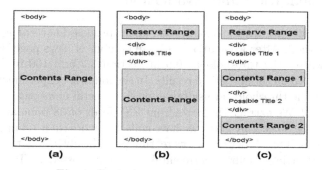

Fig. 4. Contents range and reserve range

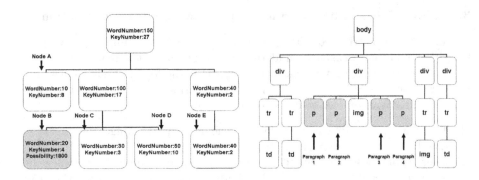

Fig. 5. A paragraph recognition example   **Fig. 6.** A full contents extraction example

and its related nodes in the same selective range. For Node A and Node B, Node B is a related node of Node A if Node B satisfies the following conditions.

1. Node B and Node A are sibling nodes, or their parent nodes are sibling nodes.
2. Node B or its parent node is of one of the following nodes: $\sharp text$, <span>, <a>, <p>, <ul>, <ol>, <dd>, <dt>, <strong>, <h1>, <h2>, <h3>, <h4>, <b>.

Fig. 5 shows a paragraph recognition example. Node B, C, D and E belong to the contents range, and finally the node B is judged as the paragraph node where the predetermined threshold is set to 100. After the paragraph recognition, we get a paragraph of the news article contents. Usually, the full contents of a news article are a list of continuous paragraphs. However, there is advertisement information such as the image advertising among the paragraphs of a news article in some news sites. We get a list of related nodes of paragraph node, and each one represents a paragraph of the news article contents as shown in Fig. 6. We get the node value from each node as a paragraph. The full contents of news article are the extracted continuous node values.

4   Implementation and Evaluation

In this section, we give the implementation of our proposed news article contents extraction method. After we analyzed a large number of news pages from many news sites, we set the threshold as 0.6 in Section 3.3 and 100 in Section 3.4 respectively based on the statistical results. In the following experimental results, we prove that the thresholds are suitable for the general news pages.

Experiment 1 We extract the news from RSS feeds of 38 popular news Web sites periodically. Since May 2007, we have collected more than 1.8 million pieces of news articles. Our experiments were run periodically using the randomly collected news articles. Our experimental results are listed in Table 1. Here, *Success* means that our extraction method extracts the news article contents

Table 1. Experimental results of extraction accuracy rate (long period extraction)

Period	Sum	Success	Failure	Precision
May 2007 - Aug 2007	1000	970	30	97.0%
Sep 2007 - Jan 2008	500	491	9	98.2%
Feb 2008 - May 2008	500	485	15	97.0%
Jun 2008 - Sep 2008	500	488	12	97.6%
Total	2500	2434	66	97.4%

correctly, and *Failure* means that our extraction method extracts nothing or partial paragraphs or other non-news parts such as advertisements and related stories. Although the news sites update the layout of news pages irregularly, our news article contents extraction method works well during each period and the precision of extraction is over 97%. The experimental results prove that our extraction algorithm is highly accurate during a long period.

Experiment 2 We extract and analyze the topic-based Web news articles from news site databases to observe the difference in the various topics. We select the countries and leaders as our test topics. There are 242 countries in the world and most of them have the leaders. We use these country names and leader names as our search keywords. We send these keywords to site-side news search engines one by one, and collect 121,336 news titles and page URLs of matched news published in the past 6 years (from January 1, 2003 to December 31, 2008) from news database of CNN. Finally, we extract the news article contents from these news pages. We select 250 news pages randomly and check them one by one manually. The experimental result is listed in Table 2. We find that 2 news pages can not be obtained (the server responds the message like "page not found"). Among the rest 248 news pages, the news article contents of 240 news pages are extracted correctly. In the 8 extraction failures, some parts of news article contents are not extracted. We also do the similar experiments on the other news sites. Although the news sites updated the layout of news pages many times in the past 6 years irregularly, our extraction method works well from our experimental result. The experimental results prove that our extraction method is suitable for the extraction of topic-based news articles from news site databases.

Experiment 3 We collect the news from a large-scale news sources by collecting the news titles and URLs of news pages from news aggregation sites. We collect one week's news about "Asia" from Google News as our experimental data. The total results include 1,535 news articles extracted from many different news sites. We select 500 news pages randomly and check them one by one manually. The experimental result is listed in Table 3. Among the 500 news pages, the news

Table 2. Experimental result of extraction accuracy rate (news site databases)

Sum	Extracted	Success	Failure	Precision
250	248	240	8	96.8%

Table 3. Experimental result of extraction accuracy rate (news aggregation sites)

Sum	Success	Failure	Precision
500	483	17	96.6%

article contents of 483 news pages are extracted correctly. In the 17 extraction failures, some parts of news article contents are not extracted or other non-news parts are extracted. Although the news pages comes from the different news sites, our news article contents extraction method works well and the experimental result proves that our extraction method can extract the news article contents from news aggregation sites accurately.

We give the implementation of our proposed news article contents extraction method and the experimental results prove that our extraction algorithm is highly accurate. However, in some news pages, a paragraph, usually the outline of news article, shows in different style compared to other paragraphs. This kind of paragraph looks like a non-news part such as an advertisement in text format, and is omitted in the extraction. Moreover, some news article contents are too short to recognize from the news pages. For example, a news flash about baseball game result, which contains just a short paragraph of ten words, maybe can not be extracted correctly. Compared with other developed methods, our extraction method has different implementations including the extraction from crawled news pages, news search engines and news aggregation sites. The extraction system is constructed easily based on our method and does not need any maintenance over the long period extraction. We do not need to analyze the layout of news pages since our extraction algorithm is independent of the layout of Web pages. It does not need to reconfigure extraction even though the news sites update the layout of news pages, and keeps a high extraction precision.

5   Conclusion

In this paper, we have presented a relevance-based analysis method to realize the news article contents extraction without the analyzing the layout of news pages. Our algorithm is applicable to the general news pages, and can extract the news article paragraphs accurately. Our experimental results show that our method works well with a high accuracy rate in different kinds of implementations. As future work, we will modify our algorithm to improve the accuracy rate even further, and extend its implementations to more news related applications.

References

1. de Castro Reis, D., Golgher, P.B., da Silva, A.S., Laender, A.H.F.: Automatic Web news extraction using tree edit distance. In: The Proceedings of the 13th International Conference on World Wide Web (2004)
2. Fukumoto, F., Suzuki, Y.: Detecting shifts in news stories for paragraph extraction. In: The 19th International Conference on Computational Linguistics (2002)
3. Zheng, S., Song, R., Wen, J.R.: Template-independent news extraction based on visual consistency. In: The Proceedings of the 22th AAAI Conference (2007)
4. Shinyama, Y.: Webstemmer (2007),
   http://www.unixuser.org/~euske/python/webstemmer/

HyperAdapt: Enabling Aspects for XML

Matthias Niederhausen[1], Sven Karol[2], Uwe Aßmann[2], and Klaus Meißner[1]

[1] Technische Universität Dresden
Chair of Multimedia Technology
01062 Dresden, Germany
{matthias.niederhausen,kmeiss}@inf.tu-dresden.de
[2] Technische Universität Dresden
Software Technology Group
01062 Dresden, Germany
{sven.karol,uwe.assmann}@tu-dresden.de

Abstract. Aspect orientation offers an intuitive way to specifiy adaptivity for web applications, but despite its advantages, the approach still lacks acceptance. We argue that there are two main reasons for this: First, aspects make implicit assumptions on the underlying system and can thus produce invalid behavior if that system is changed. Second, the lack of concepts for dealing with aspect interactions places a heavy burden on the use of multiple aspects. In this paper we discuss how Hyper-Adapt addresses these problems, paving the road towards a productive use of aspect orientation in the domain of web applications.

1 Introduction

Developing adaptive hypermedia applications is a very challenging and demanding task. In order to achieve a single adaptation goal (e.g., adapting to a special device), many different application parts have to be edited in a consistent way. This process gets even more complicated if there are multiple different adaptation goals. To deal with this complexity, we apply aspect-oriented programming (AOP) to place adaptivity into separate modules – so-called adaptation aspects. The growing number of approaches that leverage aspect orientation to model adaptivity [1,2,3] clearly demonstrates the attractiveness of this solution. In contrast to these existing solutions, we apply aspects not on a model level, but on XML. However, aspect orientation in this context still has several open issues:

1. *Untyped Aspect Weaving.* In hypermedia applications, aspects are usually woven into XML documents. To guarantee validity of the resulting document, weaving operations must support typed weaving.
2. *Interaction of Aspects.* Aspects may conflict if they address the same part of a document. Since it is hard to keep an overview of such conflicts, it is imperative to provide means for detecting and potentially resolving them.
3. *Constrained Aspects.* If a document contains protected parts that should not be adapted, it can be helpful to impose further restrictions on documents or aspects beyond type-safety. Thus, techniques are needed to specify constraints for documents and aspects.

M. Gaedke, M. Grossniklaus, and O. Díaz (Eds.): ICWE 2009, LNCS 5648, pp. 461–464, 2009.
© Springer-Verlag Berlin Heidelberg 2009

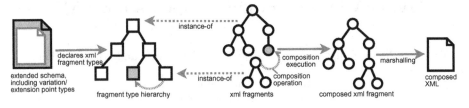

Fig. 1. Invasive composition of XML documents

In the remainder of this paper we explain how HyperAdapt tackles the above issues. Sect. 2 introduces a type-safe aspect weaving approach. Sect. 3 investigates how to detect aspect interactions, while Sect. 4 discusses aspect conflict resolution and constraint-based weaving. Finally, Sect. 5 concludes the paper.

2   Safe Weaving of Web Adaptation Aspects

An appropriate composition technique for safe aspect weaving has to consider the specific properties of XML. At runtime, XML documents are usually represented as trees typed by XML schemas, which are comparatively similar to a context-free grammar describing the abstract syntax of a language.

Invasive Software Composition (ISC) [4] is a powerful technique to create composition systems for tree-shaped components, called fragments in this context. It has proven to be expressive enough to recreate several other component-based concepts and ensures syntactic type-safe composition w.r.t. the component language. ISC has made its way to several orthogonal domains. For instance, the COMPOST[1] system recreates aspect orientation and generics for Java 1.4 . Also, Modular XCerpt provides the XCerpt query language with a module system [5]. To reduce implementation effort, recent research developed grammar-based ISC [6], which allows to declaratively specify composition systems based on markup and extension of context-free grammars. However, the approach has not yet been applied to XML languages. Hence, to be applicable to XML documents, we attune the approach in two ways:

First, we extend grammar-based ISC to support XML, such that every composition step composes fragments according to a given XML schema (see Figure 1). Furthermore, we develop an approach to declare extension and variation points (see filled symbols in Figure 1) in XML documents as well as complex composition operators and evaluate it by means of prototype composition systems. Second, we use a weaving pipeline for composing aspects of general XML-based languages. Each stage in this pipeline provides output parameters and requires input parameters which can be typed according to a given schema. This allows for modular type-safe definitions of composition steps even for different XML dialects. Moreover, it provides a grounding for conflict resolution techniques and constraints imposed on aspects as discussed in Sect. 4.

---

[1] The compost system. http://www.the-compost-system.org

3   Investigation of Aspect Interactions

Typically, aspects resemble adaptation techniques, as identified by the adaptive hypermedia community (e.g., [7,8]), and are applied to components in the web application. Dependant on context parameters and runtime state of the web application, aspects usually crosscut several XML documents. Thus, they are quite similar to aspects in aspect-oriented programming [9], which are applied to a pointcut. However, in contrast to general AOP, a clear separation between static (e.g., some node in the document) and dynamic parts (e.g., the context) of a pointcut exists. We argue that these and other special properties of adaptation aspects can be used to better analyse aspect interactions. To this end, we classify frequently used adaptation techniques by their potential for conflicts. For example, an advice removing a fragment can have an impact on other advices with overlapping pointcuts (subsequent advices cannot match the removed fragment anymore), but this may also be desired by the author. In contrast, an advice replacing all text by a localised version and another one replacing certain images by text have a closer interdependency, as the first should be executed only after the second has taken effect.

In a next step, we plan to extend well-known adaptation techniques by a description that offers semantic information on the technique. Starting from the classification and the semantic description, we can then analyse adaptation techniques and aspects to identify potential conflicts. There are multiple options for doing so: First, conflicts are often found when two advices address the same component, therefore we intend to check on these cases first. Second, we plan to employ a conflict matrix that marks often-found interactions, such as the example given above. Third, we can apply confluence tests to identify whether the order of advices has an influence on the resulting document: if this is not the case, we can be sure that there are no conflicts. And fourth, we can combine static analysis based on type information derived from XML schema and analysis of the semantic description to find conflicts before aspects are deployed.

4   Constraint-Based Adaptation

As discussed in Sect. 3, aspects cannot always be completely orthogonal. Often enough, this is even desired by the author (e.g., internationalising a text and at the same time removing it for unauthorised users). A correct resolution has to bring the involved aspects into the right order. One way to do so is to extend the conflict matrix and supply a proposed weaving order for two given aspects. Another option is to define precedence for aspects, depending on the narrowness of their pointcut. For example, if the author has defined a separate adaptation for one particular document fragment, this should always have precedence over a document-wide adaptation that also includes this joinpoint.

Beyond constraints defined by the aspect author, XML document authors may impose constraints on parts of their document. For example, the author may restrict the replacement of images at certain positions or he may require inserted fragments to adhere to a certain structure (e.g., an altering list of text and images). To provide a framework for definition of such constraints, we borrow concepts from contract-based programming [10]. Preconditions may contain structural information on documents before an aspect is applied, postconditions then describe the resulting structure. Thus, contracts can be used to narrow the application of aspects to certain parts of a document.

5 Summary

In this work, we introduced the problem of aspect interactions in the domain of XML documents. We further proposed strategies for dealing with such interactions (e.g., confluence check) and an extension to AOP such that sophisticated contracts between aspects and the application can be defined. With the help of the suggested approach, aspect orientation unlocks its full potential for documents, allowing to cleanly separate adaptation from the rest of a web application.

As the next steps, we extend grammar based Invasive Software Composition to support XML languages and create a prototype weaving pipeline. Additionally, we will investigate adaptation techniques w.r.t. their conflict potential. These initial steps will then give us important feedback on our design of a contract model for aspects.

References

1. Baumeister, H., Knapp, A., Koch, N., Zhang, G.: Modelling adaptivity with aspects. In: Lowe, D.G., Gaedke, M. (eds.) ICWE 2005. LNCS, vol. 3579, pp. 406–416. Springer, Heidelberg (2005)
2. Schauerhuber, A., Wimmer, M., Schwinger, W., Kapsammer, E., Retschitzegger, W.: Aspect-oriented modeling of ubiquitous web applications: The aspectwebml approach. In: ECBS MBD 2007, Tucson, Arizona (2007)
3. Casteleyn, S., Van Woensel, W., Houben, G.-J.: A semantics-based aspect-oriented approach to adaptation in web engineering. In: HT 2007: Proceedings of the eighteenth conference on Hypertext and hypermedia, pp. 189–198. ACM, New York (2007)
4. Aßmann, U.: Invasive Software Composition, 1st edn. Springer, Heidelberg (2003)
5. Aßmann, U., Berger, S., Bry, F., Furche, T., Henriksson, J., Johannes, J.: Modular web Queries–From rules to stores (2007)
6. Henriksson, J.: A Lightweight Framework for Universal Fragment Composition. Ph.D thesis, Technischen Universität Dresden (2008)
7. Bunt, A., Carenini, G., Conati, C.: Adaptive content presentation for the web. In: Brusilovsky, P., Kobsa, A., Nejdl, W. (eds.) Adaptive Web 2007. LNCS, vol. 4321, pp. 409–432. Springer, Heidelberg (2007)
8. Brusilovsky, P.: Adaptive navigation support. In: Brusilovsky, P., Kobsa, A., Nejdl, W. (eds.) Adaptive Web 2007. LNCS, vol. 4321, pp. 263–290. Springer, Heidelberg (2007)
9. Kiczales, G., Mendhekar, A., Lamping, J., Maeda, C., Lopes, C.V., Loingtier, J.-M., Irwin, J.: Aspect-Oriented programming. In: Aksit, M., Matsuoka, S. (eds.) ECOOP 1997. LNCS, vol. 1241, pp. 220–242. Springer, Heidelberg (1997)
10. Meyer, B.: Applying 'design by contract'. Computer 25(10), 40–51 (1992)

Developing an Enterprise Web Application in XQuery

Martin Kaufmann and Donald Kossmann

ETH Zürich, Systems Group,
Universitätsstrasse 6, 8092 Zürich, Switzerland
{martinka,donaldk}@ethz.ch

Abstract. XQuery is a declarative programming language which can be used to express queries and transformations of XML data. The goal of this paper is to explore the expressive power of XQuery as a general-purpose programming language. To this end, this paper describes how to build an entire enterprise web application in XQuery. It is shown that it is actually possible and quite effective to implement a web application entirely in XQuery and that there are several advantages in doing so. The resulting code has proven to be very concise and elegant. More importantly, the use of XQuery simplifies the overall application architecture and improves flexibility.

Keywords: XQuery, XML, Enterprise Application, Web Application, Programming.

1 Introduction

Today, enterprise web applications play an important role for e-business software and data integration. Companies have demand for software which is well designed and structured to allow short training periods for new developers. The software should be easy to maintain by separation of concerns and extensible for future scaling.

In order to develop large-scale enterprise web applications, the state-of-the-art is to use frameworks such as the Java Enterprise Edition (J2EE) or Microsoft's .Net. These frameworks take advantage of the vast experience of object-oriented software development with programming languages like Java and C#. Using J2EE, for instance, Java objects can be mapped to a relational database using an object/relational persistence and query service like Hibernate. In the .Net framework LINQ [5] can be used in order to embed SQL-style database access into the object-oriented application code.

Yet, both J2EE and .Net suffer from the impedance mismatch between different data models used at different application tiers and from repeated work for the same tasks at different application tiers (e.g., error handling, etc.). The core of this problem stems from the fact that all these frameworks actually make use of a mix of technologies.

A result of this observation was the development of object-oriented database systems. They mitigate the impedance mismatch by providing a unified data model but introduce additional problems like verbose code for implementing complex queries by means of the programming language (e.g. SODA API for DB4o [3]).

M. Gaedke, M. Grossniklaus, and O. Díaz (Eds.): ICWE 2009, LNCS 5648, pp. 465–468, 2009.
© Springer-Verlag Berlin Heidelberg 2009

This paper explores a new approach to develop enterprise web applications. The key idea is to leverage the (unified) technology stack developed by the World Wide Web Consortium (W3C). We argue that a unified technology stack can result in simpler, more flexible, and more efficient application code. A central piece of this new approach to build web applications is the use of the XQuery programming language [9]. XQuery was initially designed to query and transform XML data. The main contribution of this paper is to demonstrate that such a uniform technology stack based entirely on W3C standards can be used in order to build and deploy large-scale enterprise web applications.

The remainder of this paper is organized as follows: Section 2 describes a system architecture of a web application written entirely in XQuery. Section 3 sketches the implementation of our example application called PubZone [7], which is a web based repository for scientific publications. Section 4 describes our experience in the development of PubZone with XQuery. Section 5 discusses related work. Section 6 contains conclusions and avenues for future work.

2 Architecture

For this work, we adopt the traditional three-tier architecture for enterprise web applications. As shown in Figure 1(a), this three-tier architecture is typically implemented using different languages and data models at each tier. According to Figure 1(b), we propose to use, as much as possible, one programming language and one data model throughout the entire application stack.

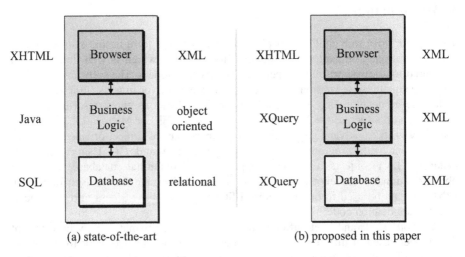

(a) state-of-the-art   (b) proposed in this paper

Fig. 1. Three-tier Application Architecture

The advantage of this approach is that the architecture becomes more flexible, more efficient, and simpler. The architecture of Figure 1(b) is more flexible because it allows for moving code from one tier to another. Simplicity and efficiency is achieved by applying the same programming language to all three application tiers.

3   Implementation

For the implementation and deployment of the PubZone application, we used the Sausalito XQuery application server [8] which integrates an XML database system, the Zorba XQuery engine [10], and the Apache Web Server into a single XQuery application server. In a nutshell, the XQuery application server maps a URL to an XQuery source file (called module) and an XQuery function. The return value of the function is sent back to the client as a result.

According to best practices, we adopt the MVC pattern in order to separate business logic from program control flow and presentation layer. The *Controller* function is the entry point which is called by a defined URL. This function receives an XML input generated from the HTTP request of the web client and carries out checks on the input. If these tests succeed the business logic of the *Model* is called. The result of the business logic is forwarded by the *Controller* to the *View* function which renders the output. [Code 1] shows an example of a *View* function. The result of the *View* is returned to the client by the *Controller*.

Code 1: Module of the *View* to add a new user

```
declare function def:inputForm () {
  let $text := <form method="post" action="/userNew/submit">
    Username: {form:text("uid", 25)}     Group:
    <select name="groupId" size="1">{form:option("", "select...")}
    {for $group in groups:listAllGroups()
      return form:option($group/@id, $group/name)
    } </select><input type="submit" value="Save "/></form>
  return navigation:showPage("Add user", $text)
};
```

For a large enterprise web application it is important to identify reusable components. This code can be implemented as separated XQuery modules that can be used by many functions of the application.

4   Discussion

A considerable amount of time was required to develop standard libraries like modules for pre-filled HTML form elements. When these reusable components had been finished, the development of web applications turned out to be quite effective and fast. Due to clean design and encapsulation of business logic in XQuery modules, this software architecture is expected to scale up for large applications.

Our measurements in terms of runtime performance shows that the XQuery implementation of our example application [7] in average currently is only about 35% slower than the corresponding Java implementation [6]. This result is basically caused by the fact that the XQuery application server [8] is still in a beta state. There is no principal limitation which prevents an application written in XQuery from reaching performance results achieved by state-of-the art technologies like J2EE.

5 Related Work

There has been a great deal of work on XQuery already. XQuery has been implemented by all major database vendors. Furthermore, XQuery is a popular tool for various tasks in the middleware; for instance, BEA's Enterprise Information Bus is based on XQuery and BEA's ALDSP server for enterprise information integration is based on XQuery [1]. XQuery is also used for data stream processing such as RSS streams [2], [4].

6 Conclusion

This paper reported on our experience to develop a complex and customizable enterprise web application entirely using the XQuery programming language and using related W3C recommendations (e.g., XML as a data format, XML Schema to describe data types, and HTTP and REST for remote communication). Overall, the conclusion is that the W3C family of standards is very well suited for this task and has important advantages over the state-of-the-art (e.g., J2EE, .Net, or PHP). Most importantly, using XQuery and W3C standards only ensures a uniform technology stack and avoids the technology jungle of mixing different technologies and data models. As a result, the application architecture becomes more flexible, simpler, and potentially more efficient. Today, the biggest concern in adopting this approach is that there are no mature application servers available, but we believe that the situation will change soon in this regard.

Obviously, this work was only a first step in order to develop complex and large-scale enterprise web applications entirely in XQuery with the help of W3C standards. In the future, more experience with other applications is needed. One important avenue for future work is to introduce a methodology to develop such applications with XQuery.

References

1. BEA AquaLogic Data Services Platform,
   http://edocs.bea.com/aldsp/docs30/
2. Botan, I., Fischer, P., Florescu, D., et al.: Extending XQuery with Window Functions. In: VLDB 2007, Vienna, Austria (2007)
3. Native Java &.NET Open Source Object Database, http://www.db4o.com/
4. Koch, C., Scherzinger, S., Schweikardt, N., Stegmaier, B.: FluXQuery: An Optimizing XQuery Processor for Streaming XML Data. In: VLDB 2004 (2004)
5. LINQ Project,
   http://msdn.microsoft.com/en-us/netframework/aa904594.aspx
6. Kaufmann, M., et al.: PubZone Java implementation, http://java.pubzone.org/
7. Kaufmann, M.: PubZone XQuery implementation, http://xquery.pubzone.org/
8. Sausalito, XQuery Application Server, http://sausalito.28msec.com/
9. Chamberlin, D., et al.: XQuery 1.1, W3C Working Draft,
   http://www.w3.org/TR/xquery-11/
10. The Zorba XQuery Processor, http://www.zorba-xquery.com/

Enhancing WS-BPEL Dynamic Invariant Generation Using XML Schema and XPath Information

Manuel Palomo-Duarte, Antonio García-Domínguez,
and Inmaculada Medina-Bulo

Universidad de Cádiz, Escuela Superior de Ingeniería, c/Chile 1, CP 11003 Cádiz,
Spain
{manuel.palomo,antonio.garciadominguez,inmaculada.medina}@uca.es

Abstract. The dynamic and asynchronous nature of OASIS WS-BPEL 2.0 standard language for web service composition presents a challenge for traditional white-box testing techniques. Takuan is a tool that can help with this problem. It analyzes execution logs of a WS-BPEL process in a real-world WS-BPEL engine to dynamically generate composition invariants. Nevertheless, it suffered some performance issues when handling a large number of variables with complex multidimensional content. We present two techniques implemented to automatically alleviate these issues: dynamic analysis of XPath expressions to avoid inferring nonsensical invariants, and discarding invariants enforced by the XML Schema. We present practical results supporting our work and comment the impact and applicability of these techniques beyond WS-BPEL itself.

Keywords: Web services, service composition, WS-BPEL, white-box testing, dynamic invariant generation.

1 Introduction

The OASIS WS-BPEL (Web Service Business Process Execution Language) 2.0 standard allows programing in the large using web service compositions. However, it presents a challenge [1] for traditional white-box testing techniques, due to the inclusion of WS-specific instructions not found in most programming languages (like those for fault and compensation handling).

Automatic invariant generation [2] has proved to be a successful technique to assist in white-box testing of programs written in imperative languages. Let us note that, throughout this work, *invariant* and *likely invariant* are understood (as in most related works) in their broadest sense: properties which hold always or in the specified test cases at a certain program point, respectively.

We have implemented Takuan [3], an open-source system which dynamically generates likely invariants from actual WS-BPEL composition execution logs. Its automatic workflow takes a WS-BPEL process definition and a test suite specification and outputs a collection of invariants which hold at certain program points in every test case.

M. Gaedke, M. Grossniklaus, and O. Díaz (Eds.): ICWE 2009, LNCS 5648, pp. 469–472, 2009.
© Springer-Verlag Berlin Heidelberg 2009

This paper describes two techniques which aim to reduce Takuan's resource usage (increasing its scalability to larger compositions) as well as the number of uninteresting invariants in its output. We first study their impact and applicability on WS-BPEL and then point out other languages with similar issues.

2   Improving Invariant Generation with XPath

Takuan results were promising [3], but even for slightly complex WS-BPEL compositions there was very high memory and CPU usage depending on the options used. For example, analyzing 7 test cases in a meta-search composition could take over 7 minutes and use over 800 MiB of RAM [4].

The reason was the large number of invariants comprising pairs and triples of variables that had to be checked, many of them nonsensical. For example, the age of an applicant to a loan and its amount can be both integers, but there is no need to waste computational resources trying to relate them in an invariant.

We avoided it by labeling each variable with a so-called *comparability index*: an integer which marks a set of variables as belonging to a specific semantic type, such as a monetary sum or a vector size. This way Daikon (the dynamic invariant generator internally used by Takuan) only infers invariants relating variables that have the same index, avoiding the combinatorial explosion and will even discard uninteresting program points and, optionally, unused variable fields.

We had to extend all steps of the Takuan framework to implement this functionality. Discarding unused variable fields is suitable for any language in which variables from outer scopes are directly used only in a few key program points and control flow is highly structured.

3   Filtering Redundant Invariants

In our experience using Takuan [4], we have observed that a considerable number of the invariants only repeat constraints which are already enforced by the XML Schema declarations of the types used in the composition.

For instance, if XML Schema tells us that a variable has to be in the range $[0, 1]$ an invariant confirming it would only add noise in the resulting invariant list. In fact, if that information relates to a WS-BPEL multidimensional variable that is later mapped into n unidimensional Takuan variables by matrix flattening, we will have avoided generating not one, but n invariants.

We implemented this technique extending Daikon itself, but keeping it as language-independent as possible. Other languages have type systems that include similar information to some parts of XML Schema: statically sized arrays and matrices in C/C++, fixed length strings in FORTRAN, or VARCHAR(N) fields in SQL, for instance.

4   Results

We have studied the impact that each of these two techniques have in the analysis of the meta-search engine composition discussed in [4] with the same test suite.

Table 1. Input, output and performance metrics for each combination of techniques

Mapping [a]	Techniques[b]	P. points[c]	Variables	Memory[d]	Time[e]	Invariants
Slicing	None	64	17,404	656.74	409.98	30,399
	X			646.57	400.15	21,793
	C	48	14,148	561.63	416.72	27,089
	CX			579.81	401.69	18,358
	CF		1,398	25.25	72.96	2,135
	CXF			24.54	75.03	1,559
Flattening	None	64	11,412	291.11	162.00	18,658
	X			280.96	173.40	18,654
	C	48	9,036	261.01	179.39	16,718
	CX			264.54	163.90	16,714
	CF		710	11.18	52.29	942
	CXF			12.29	55.61	940

[a] See [4] for descriptions of these mappings.
[b] C: comparability indices, X: XML Schema invariant suppression, F: unused variable filtering.
[c] Program points with no XPath expressions therein are removed during comparability analysis.
[d] Maximum usage of the JVM heap by Daikon, measured in MiB.
[e] Time required by Takuan's analysis step, including preprocessing, measured in seconds.

We have used each of them separately and in combination. Table 1 shows the computational resources (time and space) required for their analysis, and the length of the invariant list produced by each combination.

The maximum memory used at some point by the preprocessor Perl scripts remains approximately the same at 193MiB for every entry in the table. The test environment consisted of a machine fitted with a dual-core Intel Core Duo T2250 CPU, with 1GiB of DDR2 533MHz RAM and a 80GB 5400rpm HDD. The base system used was a standard GNU/Linux Ubuntu 8.04.1 distribution installation, with its 2.6.24-19-generic default kernel. The active processes during the test suite were mainly those created by the components of Takuan: the Sun 6.0 JRE (with a maximum JVM heap size of 800 MiB), Apache Ant 1.7.0, Perl 5.8.8, Daikon 4.3.4, ActiveBPEL 4.1 and BPELUnit 1.0. During its execution there were no other processes consuming significant CPU time, memory space, or disk throughput.

In our quantitative and qualitative analysis, we see that performing the comparability analysis while only filtering program points does not affect performance as much as expected, but it does improve the quality of the invariants inferred. Likewise, using the information encoded in the XML Schema only presents a minor performance improvement if any, but the number of invariants produced is reduced in some cases over 35%.

In contrast, performance is drastically improved when unused variable fields at each program point are filtered, reducing on average the number of variable fields to be checked over 90% and the running time to a third.

5   Conclusions and Future Work

Takuan is an automated framework for dynamic invariant generation in WS-BPEL compositions. In this paper we have shown two techniques which have been recently implemented into Takuan to reduce computational costs and improve the usefulness and conciseness of the list of invariants inferred. They can be applied to other languages, as little about them is exclusive to WS-BPEL.

Our future work will be validating our findings so far with more complex WS-BPEL process compositions. Once Takuan obtains a satisfying balance between performance and invariant quality, we will focus on the relation between the quality of the invariants generated and the test suite used.

Acknowledgments

This paper has been funded by the Department of Education and Science (Spain) and FEDER funds under the National Program for Research, Development and Innovation. Project SOAQSim (TIN2007-67843-C06-04).

References

1. Bucchiarone, A., Melgratti, H., Severoni, F.: Testing service composition. In: Proceedings of the 8th Argentine Symposium on Software Engineering (ASSE 2007) (2007)
2. Ernst, M.D., Cockrell, J., Griswold, W.G., Notkin, D.: Dynamically discovering likely program invariants to support program evolution. IEEE Transactions on Software Engineering 27(2), 99–123 (2001)
3. Palomo-Duarte, M., García-Domínguez, A., Medina-Bulo, I.: Takuan: A dynamic invariant generation system for WS-BPEL compositions. In: ECOWS 2008: Proceedings of the 2008 Sixth European Conference on Web Services, Washington, DC, USA, pp. 63–72. IEEE Computer Society, Los Alamitos (2008)
4. Palomo-Duarte, M., García-Domínguez, A., Medina-Bulo, I.: Improving Takuan to analyze a meta-search engine WS-BPEL composition. In: SOSE 2008: Proceedings of the 2008 IEEE International Symposium on Service-Oriented System Engineering, Washington, DC, USA, pp. 109–114. IEEE Computer Society, Los Alamitos (2008)

CRUISe: Composition of Rich User Interface Services

Stefan Pietschmann, Martin Voigt, Andreas Rümpel, and Klaus Meißner

Technische Universität Dresden
01062 Dresden, Germany
{Stefan.Pietschmann,Martin.Voigt,Andreas.Ruempel}@inf.tu-dresden.de,
Klaus.Meissner@inf.tu-dresden.de

Abstract. As reuse and technology-independence are key issues of both software and web engineering, web services have gained momentum and are heavily used in modern web-based applications. However, they are only expedient for the business logic layer, while the Web lacks uniform models for the encapsulation and reuse of UI components. Thus, web UIs are usually hand-crafted and static, which complicates both development as well as maintenance and upgrade. We address these issues with a novel approach facilitating dynamic, service-oriented composition of user interfaces for web applications. UI parts therein are provided as reusable services and can therefore be selected, customized and exchanged dynamically with respect to a particular context.

1 Introduction and Motivation

In recent years the Internet has evolved to a stable application platform for a large number or *Software-as-a-Service* (SaaS) solutions, featuring rich UIs and interaction metaphors. This enables location- and time-independent access, but has dramatically complicated application development, especially of the UI.

In the back end, modern web applications use web services – technology-independent building blocks that facilitate reuse and exchange of business logic. There also exist numerous frameworks and libraries that allow for the composition of web-based UIs from components, e. g., Portlets, JSF and WebParts, but they all restrain to specific technologies or platforms with individual interfaces and APIs. Once a choice has been made, it is naturally irrevocable. Future UI changes and updates are costly as there is no uniform model for the technology-independent development and cross-technology integration of web UIs.

Additionally, heterogeneous device, user and usage contexts are decisive factors for a web application UI. "Adaptive Hypermedia" research has addressed this issue for years. Yet, the majority of approaches suffers from the "open corpus" problem [1] – they only work with predefined structures and preindexed or annotated documents – and usually don't support *Rich Internet Applications* (RIA). Despite all these facts, presentation integration, i. e. technology-agnostic UI composition and reuse, has not undergone much research [2]. Thus, the development and maintenance of context-aware RIAs is complicated and hence very time- and money-consuming.

M. Gaedke, M. Grossniklaus, and O. Díaz (Eds.): ICWE 2009, LNCS 5648, pp. 473–476, 2009.
© Springer-Verlag Berlin Heidelberg 2009

To address the above-mentioned problems, we apply the service-oriented paradigm to the presentation level of web applications. In CRUISe[1], a user interface is composed from services providing reusable, configurable components. This greatly simplifies development and maintenance of web UIs. Furthermore, in contrast to present integration concepts (cf. [3,4]), the dynamic, context-aware selection, configuration and exchange of these services enables adaptation of modern web applications at run time.

2 Dynamic, Service-Based Composition of Web UIs

A growing number of applications is built from services which provide data and business logic via generic interfaces or APIs. We argue that future web-based applications can be solely based on services that provide either data, business logic or **user interfaces**. As current solutions do not support such a universal paradigm, the requirements for their deployment and hosting herald the time for a new architectural style, e.g., the "Thin Server Architecture" (TSA) [5].

Figure 1 gives an overview of our concept. Its central idea is the dynamic composition of a web application UI from distributed services to exploit the advantages of service-oriented architectures, like reusability, customizability and technology-independence, at the presentation layer. We do this by encapsulating generic, reusable web UI components as so-called *User Interface Services* that are dynamically selected, configured and integrated into a homogeneous, web-based UI. Conforming to the TSA style, the integration of all services is carried out on the client. Thus, our concept is most suitable for mashup applications aiming at the lightweight service orchestration on the presentation level.

2.1 User-Interface-as-a-Service

User Interface Services. (UIS) form an integral part of our concept. They facilitate the distributed deployment and technology-independent provision of generic, configurable UI building blocks. A trend towards such services for the presentation layer can already be witnessed, prominent examples being Google's Maps or Visualization APIs that allow for the client-side binding and integration of configurable and interactive UI components from a remote server. We generalize such techniques and propose a concept, in which the whole web application UI results from the integration and composition of UIS, or, more precisely, the UI components provided by them.

Specific APIs and technologies are hidden behind a generic UIS interface, which is used for their configuration and initialization and covers the typical functionality exposed by certain class of UI component, e.g. a *Map UIS*. Furthermore, it facilitates interoperability and run time exchangeability of UI parts. Of course, this requires the definition of universal UIS interfaces beforehand. In

---

[1] The CRUISe project is funded with means of the BMBF under promotional reference number 01IS08034-C.

contrast to classic integration systems, we can rely on browser technologies (especially JavaScript) as "glue code" . Due to the openness and simplicity of this approach, the majority of components and services available on the Web (based on JavaScript, JavaFX, Flash, etc.) can be provided as UIS.

UIS metadata is stored in a *UIS Registry* and used to match application requirements and context data with available UIS at run time to enable context-aware web user interfaces.

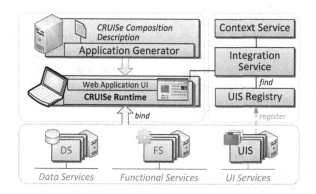

Fig. 1. Architectural overview of the CRUISe infrastructure

2.2   Dynamic, Context-Aware UI Composition

To build a UI based on UIS, a developer declaratively specifies configuration, composition and control flow between them. This *Composition Description* is processed and transformed into an executable web application by the *Application Generator*. It contains "placeholders" for UI parts provided by UIS with their associated configuration parameters, and runs within the *CRUISe Runtime*.

When the application is initialized, the Runtime passes requirements and parameters specified for each placeholder to an external *Integration Service* (CIS). This task can be carried out on the server, as well as on the client. The CIS is responsible for finding those UIS in the UIS Registry that match the given application requirements and context, ranking them by their accuracy of fit and returning the integration code for the best match. In our application domain this is typically a script which is embedded in the application and interpreted dynamically on the client. Conflicts and redundancies between UIS and underlying libraries are resolved by the Runtime, as well.

Once the integration process has finished, the Runtime controls the event and data flow between UI parts as specified in the composition description. It also serves as a homogeneous access layer that facilitates binding of backend services to the UI services. Furthermore, it monitors context data on the client (e. g., device capabilities and user interactions) and sends them to the Integration Service for later use in the discovery and ranking phase. In the end, it also carries out dynamic adaptations, like UIS reconfigurations and exchange.

3   Implementation

To verify our concepts we built an exemplary web application used to manage contacts and track their current locations. To this end, a number of UIS were developed, encapsulating UI components of different technologies, including JavaScript (Google Maps, Dojo Tables) and Flash (Flex Datagrid). In our prototype, they are dynamically integrated on the server side by an Integration Service based on Axis2. The client-side Runtime was realized as a JavaScript component using the widget framework jMaki.

This prototype exemplifies the run time composition of a web UI including data binding with the back end (contact data is provided by application services), communication between UI parts as well as the technology-independence of UIS used. It forms the basis for our current work towards the dynamic, context-aware UI adaptation. Lessons learned include, that a client-side binding of the Integration Service might be advantageous for pure TSA applications.

4   Conclusion

Our concept implies the dynamic, context-aware composition of web user interfaces based on so-called *User Interface Services*. Those provide arbitrary UI parts and are integrated and composed via a uniform configuration and communication interface. This facilitates reusability and technology-independence and offers a great simplification of the development and maintenance of web application UIs. Furthermore, it allows for context-aware rich web UIs by dynamically selecting and configuring UIS depending on the user and usage context.

At the moment, we are evaluating our prototype against other integration and mashup approaches to derive requirements for the composition description and client-side service binding. We are further working on a classification and a semantic description language for UIS to allow for semantic run time matching between web and UI Services. Future work includes the development of an authoring tool and more sophisticated, dynamic adaptation mechanisms.

References

1. Brusilovsky, P., Henze, N.: Open Corpus Adaptive Educational Hypermedia. In: Brusilovsky, P., Kobsa, A., Nejdl, W. (eds.) Adaptive Web 2007. LNCS, vol. 4321, pp. 671–696. Springer, Heidelberg (2007)
2. Daniel, F., Yu, J., Benatallah, B., Casati, F., Matera, M., Saint-Paul, R.: Understanding UI Integration: A Survey of Problems, Technologies, and Opportunities. IEEE Internet Computing 11(3), 59–66 (2007)
3. Liu, X., Hui, Y., Sun, W., Liang, H.: Towards Service Composition Based on Mashup. In: IEEE Congress on Services, pp. 332–339 (2007)
4. Yu, J., Benatallah, B., Saint-Paul, R., Casati, F., Daniel, F., Matera, M.: A Framework for Rapid Integration of Presentation Components. In: WWW 2007: Proc. of the 16th Intl. Conf. on World Wide Web, pp. 923–932 (2007)
5. Prasad, G., Taneja, R., Todankar, V.: Life above the Service Tier (October 2007)

An Online Platform for
Semantic Validation of UML Models

Marco Brambilla[1] and Christina Tziviskou[2]

[1] Politecnico di Milano, Dipartimento di Elettronica ed Informazione,
V. Ponzio 34/5, 20133 Milano, Italy
marco.brambilla@polimi.it
[2] Università di Bergamo, Ingegneria dell'Informazione e Metodi Matematici,
V.le Marconi 5, 24044 Dalmine, Italy
christina.tziviskou@unibg.it

Abstract. The Web is becoming the development platform for applications, thus making desktop IDE and CASE tools obsolete. We propose a first example of online support to application designers, consisting in a tool for online validation of UML models based on semantic formalization and reasoning. We base our work on a formalization of the UML models and we exploit Web engineering methods and techniques, applied to Semantic Web technologies, for providing a set of components and patterns that allow management and verification of UML diagrams.

Keywords: WebML, UML, conceptual modeling, Semantic Web, reasoner, ontology, validation, class diagram, pattern, component.

1 Introduction

The Web is becoming the platform of choice for almost any kind of distributed, as shown by the continuous spreading of *online office suites* offered as *software as a service* (SAAS), leading to international web-based collaboration and virtual teamwork. In the medium period the Web will become a platform for the *development* of applications too: the Eclipse project has transformed the world-famous IDE to the Web platform, and an IBM AlphaWorks project is ongoing to develop a Web browser-based interaction with the Eclipse IDE, under the name EcliFox[1].

We propose a first example of online support to application designers: a tool for online validation of UML models based on semantic formalization and reasoning. It allows for verification of properties and correctness of UML models. It is used at development time by designers for verifying that the devised conceptual models do not contain inconsistencies, and is also used at runtime once instances of the model are changed, to verify that property correctness still hold for the overall application.

Our choice combines UML class and object diagrams. We formalize them with the DL sROIQ [4], supporting nominals, role inclusion axioms, and transitivity.

---

[1] http://www.alphaworks.ibm.com/tech/eclifox

M. Gaedke, M. Grossniklaus, and O. Díaz (Eds.): ICWE 2009, LNCS 5648, pp. 477–480, 2009.
© Springer-Verlag Berlin Heidelberg 2009

Reasoning tasks are carried out by Pellet [7], an open-source Java reasoning engine, offering: incremental update of instances, knowledge base debugging, and optimization reasoning techniques. We exploit Web engineering methods, applied to Semantic Web technologies, for providing a set of components and patterns for managing UML diagrams. We adopt WebML [2], a Domain Specific Model for Web application design and development based on data and Semantic Web Services [1]. The WebML specification of a Web application consists of a *data schema,* and a set of *site views,* expressing the Web interfaces in terms of *pages,* which in turn contain *units,* the atomic publishing primitives that extract contents from the data source. *Links* between units define the navigation paths and carry data. Updating the underlying data and performing other actions is specified through *operation units.*

The critical situations of UML models that we resolve with our platform are: *unsatisfiable classes,* their instantiation would violate some constraints, *inconsistent models,* contain contradictions among instances and their definitions, and *inferred elements,* deducted from the modeled elements. These are not automatically identified by traditional type checking tools, leading to possibly system inconsistencies.

Other works have addressed the implementation of automatic tools for UML consistency checking ([3], [6], [8]). They either deal with different type of inconsistencies or they do not provide the means for automatic corrections. In all cases, their reasoning capabilities cannot be integrated automatically in applications.

2 Web Validation Platform

The proposed platform mediates between Pellet and the UML developer: it translates UML models to logical axioms in the knowledge base and vice versa, and provides semantic inferences while the developer is unaware of the DL-based mechanisms. Fig. 1 depicts the platform architecture: the *Platform Hypertexts* (PHs) represent the front-end application accessed by the user for exploring and managing UML models, and the *Platform Components* (PCs), representing the back-end services for interfacing the front-end with the Knowledge Base (KB).

The components are configurable software artifacts that allow the access and manipulation of UML primitives within the developed application. These primitives refer to a meta-conceptualization as defined by the UML metamodel in [5]: Class,

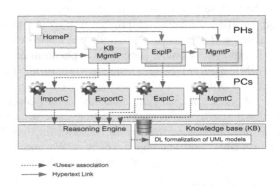

Fig. 1. General architecture of the Web Validation Platform

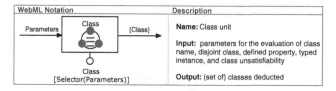

Fig. 2. WebML notation for the semantic Class component

Datatype, Property, Generalization, and Instance. A component is configured upon a UML model. Its execution extracts or modifies UML elements. The *Class Component* (Fig. 2) defines a set of extraction rules for retrieving UML classes. It explores the DL axioms and deducts classes filtered by selection conditions based upon these axioms.

The components are reusable pieces of code that can be easily combined together and integrated in the WebML specification of applications as predefined patterns to provide a reusable definition of hypertextual solutions for knowledge management. In Fig. 3, we exemplify the usage of "*Class and its classification*" WebML pattern: (i) the *Class Component* configured with a *Name* selection condition retrieves the input class, and (ii) the *Class Hierarchy Component* configured with a *Super.Class* condition deducts its ancestor tree. By selecting a more generic class, the *Inclusion Explanations* page is computed. If the inclusion is asserted in the KB, it is displayed and the user may drop the assertion by navigating to the *Remove Component*. Otherwise, the assertions causing the inclusion are presented.

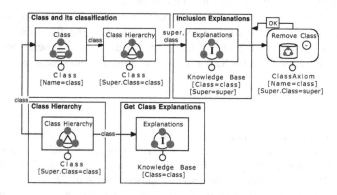

Fig. 3. WebML Class Hierarchy hypertext

2.1 Wines UML Model Case Study

To exemplify the usage of the platform, we describe the user navigation upon a Wines UML model, in order to recognize and resolve a class unsatisfiability: the *Ice Wine* class cannot be instantiated since its instances should have two disjoint parents. The situation becomes known to the developer by exploring the *Class Hierarchy* page. There, the Ice Wine is presented as unsatisfiable (Fig. 4). By selecting it, the popup window of the *Get Class Explanations* page appears with the asserted axioms causing the unsatisfiability: Ice Wine has parents the Red Wine and the Dessert Wine, and the

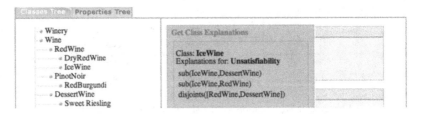

Fig. 4. Explanations pages for the unsatisfiable class Ice Wine

disjoint constraint between them, implies they cannot share instances. A classification can be dropped by the designer invoking the *"Class and its classification"* pattern.

3   Conclusions and Future Work

In this paper we presented a Web platform that allows semantic validation of static UML designs. It is an online tool to be used at development time and at runtime for continuous verification and correctness checking on the application data status.

The resulting Web Platform has three levels of reuse: its Web interfaces can be used for semantic validation of UML models; the patterns can be reused as abstract specifications of exploration and management interfaces for UML models; and the components can be integrated in existing WebML models for providing general purpose reasoning upon the application data semantics.

Future works aim at implementing patterns that resolve the remaining situations in UML models, enable keyword-based search augmenting the flexibility of the user interface, and investigate the use of the components within general-purpose Web applications, to enable them for Semantic Web or Linked Data scenarios.

References

[1] Brambilla, M., Ceri, S., Facca, F., Celino, I., Cerizza, D., Della Valle, E.: Model-Driven Design and Development of Semantic Web Service Applications. ACM TOIT 8(1) (2007)
[2] Ceri, S., Fraternali, P., Bongio, A., Brambilla, M., Comai, S., Matera, M.: Designing Data-Intensive Web Applications. Morgan Kaufmann, San Francisco (2002)
[3] Fillottrani, P., Franconi, E., Tessaris, S.: The new ICOM ontology editor. In: Int.l W.shop on Description Logics (2006)
[4] Horrocks, I., Kutz, O., Sattler, U.: The Even More Irresistible SROIQ. In: KR 2006, pp. 57–67 (2006)
[5] OMG UML, Unified Modeling Language: Superstructure version 2.1.1. ptc/2007-02-03. OMG document (2007), http://www.omg.org/cgi-bin/doc?formal/07-02-03
[6] Simmonds, J., Bastarrica, C.M.: A tool for automatic UML model consistency checking. In: International Conference on Automated Software Engineering, pp. 431–432 (2005)
[7] Sirin, E., Parsia, B., Grau, B.C., Kalyanpur, A., Katz, Y.: Pellet: A practical OWL-DL reasoner. Journal of Web Semantics 5(2), 51–53 (2007)
[8] Zapata, C.M., Gonzalez, G., Gelbukh, A.: A Rule-Based System for Accessing Consistency Between UML models. In: MICAI Artificial Intelligence, pp. 215–224 (2007)

Efficient Building of Interactive Applications Guided by Requirements Models

Begoña Losada, Maite Urretavizcaya, and Isabel Fernández de Castro

Dpt. of Computer Languages and Systems, University of the Basque Country
649 p.k.- 20018 Donostia-San Sebastián, Spain
{b.losada,maite.urretavizcaya,isabel.fernandez}@ehu.es

Abstract. The analysis of functional and non-functional requirements of an interactive application not only encompasses the descriptive aspects of its functionality and the user and system restrictions, it must also satisfy user needs, such as usability, along with system needs, such as reliability. InterMod is an interactive application-design methodology with agile characteristics which proposes the use of incremental models to define requirements, configure presentation and develop functionality. This poster is focused on the requirements of the InterMod methodology for the efficient construction of interactive applications. These models include user, system, task and dialog models. An example created with a tool that follows these principles and illustrates our approach to the dialog model is presented.

Keywords: Requirements analysis, methodology, user model, system model, task model, dialog model.

1 Introduction

Techniques for programming functionality have traditionally taken precedence over human-computer interaction techniques. Therefore, it is common for users to feel that their needed functions are difficult to understand or unnatural.

The requirements capture stage identifies the capabilities that the software system must have in order to meet user needs. In this phase, user participation is particularly active. Thus, a language mutually understood by all people involved should be used in order to allow accurate evaluation.

According to [1], user requirements and user interface design should drive the overall development process. In addition, we believe that requirement gathering and prototype stages help to organize and check information presented in the interface as well as to plan, guide and verify the development process. In order to do this, user characteristics and behaviour should be taken into account along with the physical limitations of the device and the system's reactions.

Below, we present a brief introduction to the InterMod methodology and the models of detailed requirements. After that we provide an example of a dialog model. Finally, we present our conclusions.

M. Gaedke, M. Grossniklaus, and O. Díaz (Eds.): ICWE 2009, LNCS 5648, pp. 481–484, 2009.
© Springer-Verlag Berlin Heidelberg 2009

2 The Requirements Models in the Intermod Methodology

The objective of the InterMod methodology [2] is to facilitate the design of quality interactive applications. InterMod follows the Object Management Group's Model Driven Architecture proposal [3]. We propose interactive software development based on user-centred models generated and evaluated during different phases. Two noteworthy characteristics of InterMod are (a) its use of an Intermediate Language Description, which allows information generated in different models to be stored, and (b) its iterative nature, much like that of an agile process [4].

InterMod models make it possible to quickly produce incremental prototypes by adapting the design according to the modifications prompted by both user and software developer evaluations.

Figure 1 shows a diagram of InterMod's model connections. The user interface models have been separated from the functionality models. Despite this, the InterMod process promotes the early integration of interface models with system functionality.

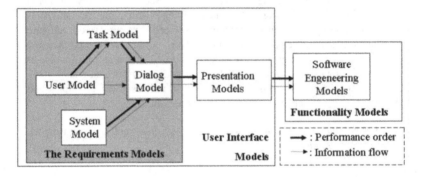

Fig. 1. InterMod models

When it comes to the requirements models, the user model, system model, task model and dialog model are all marked. First of all, the user model, which recognizes properties and limitations of the user, is created. The task model, which describes user performance in completing each task, follows the user model. The system model deals with the properties and limitations of the system. Finally, a dialog model is proposed using information from the other three requirements models.

The dialog model, known as the action-reaction model, represents user actions and system responses. The information in the dialog model affects the user interaction process, particularly the established order of navigation.

The software prototypes that are obtained from the models and tested at different times become the primary measure of progress. In addition, we suggest organizing and dividing the entire project by means of the dialog model, which should include the general overview of the navigation and the connections between user tasks and system actions.

Although UML use cases [5] are the usual means of capturing software system requirements, our proposed dialog model uses a task hierarchy that is not centred on establishing the programme's complete semantics. Our interest resides in identifying the critical aspects of navigation during user-system interactions. In this way, the interface and software analyses are facilitated through the use of early prototypes with user actions and the critical system responses that alter the normal flow of navigation.

An example of a dialog model

A dialog model created with a tool which implements InterMod specifications by means of XML descriptions can be seen in Figure 2. User actions are shown in square boxes while system reactions are represented by ovals.

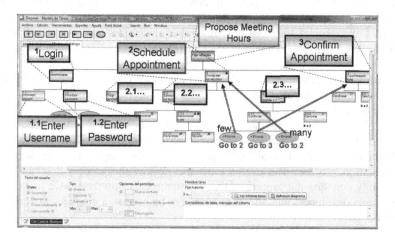

Fig. 2. An example of a dialog model

In this example, the task hierarchy of task "Propose Meeting Hours" is illustrated. The established subtask order is: (a) "1.Login", (b) "2.Schedule Appointment" and "3.Confirm Appointment". However, before progressing to (b), subtasks "1.1.Enter Username" and "1.2.Enter Password" must be completed. In order to progress to the next subtask, tasks 2.1, 2.2 and 2.3 must be carried out, and so on. The dialog model includes different task orders depending on the characteristics of user actions. The action-reaction model of the login task is explained step-by-step, as follows:

1. First, the user identifies herself (task 1).
2. Next, the user completes the next iterative task: "2.Schedule appointment".
3. This task ends when the user confirms the action in subtask 2.3. At this point, the system responds with a predetermined answer or message:

a. In this example, when the user has either too few or too many appointment hours scheduled, the system does not execute the task that usually follows and instead produces a change in interface navigation and in the logic application. A message informs the user of the reason for the change.

b If the correct amount of hours is scheduled, the system executes task "3.Confirm appointments".

This model represents the semantics of the application through interface navigation. When this model is created, verifications of usability and the automatic creation of prototypes are possible. This prototype facilitates user and programmer communication. Like Constantine [6], we believe that close coordination between user interface designers and programmers is essential. Therefore, we have incorporated such communication in the requirements analysis.

3 Conclusions

InterMod is a methodology based on user-centred models with iterative development cycles and the inclusion of phases for early integration of the user interface in the development process. Additionally, the analysis process permits and facilitates the division of the project into tasks. Using a requirements capture process such as InterMod allows the development process of interactive applications to be agile and reliable.

The requirements models in InterMod include a user model, a system model, a task model and a dialog model. This allows end users and developers to guide, organize and check development.

It is worth noting that this methodology involves developers in navigation design and invites them to participate in dialog model descriptions. This allows for the establishment of critical evaluation points at early stages for the subsequent implementation process. The use of tools that follow the process described in the methodology converts the capture of these requirements into the bridge that connects end users and developers and allows this stage to be used as a guide and a verification of the process.

Acknowledgments. This project has been partially supported by the Spanish Ministry of Education and Science grant TIN2006-14968-C01; and by the University of the Basque Country UPV-EHU, grant EHU06/111.

References

1. Mayhew, B.: The Usability Engineering Lifecycle. Morgan Kaufmann Publishers, San Francisco (1999)
2. Losada, B., Urretavizcaya, M., Fernández de Castro, I.: The InterMod Methodology: Integrating Software Engineering Processes in Interface Engineering. In: Macías, J.A., Granollers, T., Latorre, P. (eds.). New Trends on Human-Computer Interaction. Springer, Heidelberg (2009)
3. Object Management Group. Model Driven architecture. Technical report (2003)
4. Larman, C.: Agile & Iterative Development. A manager's Guide. Addison-Wesley/Pearson Education, Boston (2004)
5. Booch, G., Rumbaugh, J., Jacobson, I.: The Unified Modeling Language User Guide. Addison Wesley Longman Inc., Amsterdam (1999)
6. Constantine, L.L., Lockwood, L.A.D.: Usage-Centered Engineering for Web Applications. IEEE Software Magazine 19(1), 42–50 (2002)

WAB*: A Quantitative Metric Based on WAB

Ana Belén Martínez, Aquilino A. Juan, Darío Álvarez, and Mª del Carmen Suárez

University of Oviedo, Department of Computing,
Calvo Sotelo s/n 33007 Oviedo, Spain
{belenmp,aajuan,darioa,macamen}@uniovi.es

Abstract. Web accessibility metrics are crucial for the quantitative evaluation of web sites. We present a new automatic metric called WAB, based on the WAB metric with extensions inspired from the UWEM metric. The first results are encouraging as we have obtained better precision when calculation the accessibility level measured for a site.

Keywords: Accessibility, Metrics, Evaluation.

1 Introduction

We need quantitative evaluations of accessibility [1] to compare accessibility levels of two sites (or for different versions of the same site). Quantitative evaluations are also needed to analyze the evolution over time of accessibility with the changes done during the life of the site (monitorization). For these measurements we can use automatic metrics (no human judgment is involved to calculate an accessibility score) such as WAB [2] or WAQM [1], or semi-automatic, such as Failure_Rate [3] or UWEM [4].

We focused on two of these metrics: WAB and UWEM. The first one is popular in accessibility studies [5] because it is fully automatic. We focused on the second because it is being sponsored by the European Union as part of the Unified Web Evaluation Methodology to evaluate accessibility (EIAO Project [6][7]). We performed some studies using these metrics [8][9] using our own flexible tool called Iris that performs the quantitative evaluation of web sites using different metrics. These studies were able to discover deficiencies in each metric that we tried to solve. Such is the goal of this work: to propose a new metric called WAB*, fully automated, which is based on the WAB metric with some UWEN-like extensions, that retains the automatic feature of WAB and improves the precision of the accessibility score using more detailed checkpoints.

2 Related Work

The following is a brief summary of the features of the two metrics considered: WAB and UWEM.

M. Gaedke, M. Grossniklaus, and O. Díaz (Eds.): ICWE 2009, LNCS 5648, pp. 485–488, 2009.
© Springer-Verlag Berlin Heidelberg 2009

2.1 Web Accessibility Barrier (WAB)

WAB metric [10] yields a quantitative score that looks at 25 checkpoints based on WCAG 1.0 (5 of Priority 1, 13 of Priority 2 and 7 of Priority 3). The number of violations of the checkpoints is the basis for the score:

$$WAB\ score = \frac{\sum_p \sum_v \left(\dfrac{n_v}{N_v} \times W_v \right)}{N_p}$$

With p = Total pages of a Website, v = Total violations of a Web page, nv = Number of violations, Nv = Number of potential violations, Wv = Weight of violations in inverse proportion to WCAG priority level, and Np = Total number of pages checked.

WAB scores greater than 5.5 denote a web site with serious accessibility problems [2]. A score of zero denotes that the Web site does not violate any Web accessibility guideline and should not present any accessibility barrier to persons with disabilities.

2.2 Unified Web Evaluation Methodology (UWEM)

The UWEM [11] describes a methodology for evaluating conformance of Web sites with the WCAG 1.0 guidelines. Currently it is designed to be conformant with WCAG 1.0 priority 1 and 2 checkpoints, and provides manual and automatic evaluation. For automatic evaluation, it applies a set of checkpoints marked as "fully automatable" by the methodology.

One of the outputs is a score computed using the following metric:

$$F(s) = \frac{Bp_1 + Bp_2 + \ldots + Bp_n + \displaystyle\sum_{t\_on\_site\_level} B_{st}}{Np_1 + Np_2 + \ldots + Np_n + \displaystyle\sum_{t\_on\_site\_level} N_{st}}$$

With $F(s)$ = UWEM score for the site s, Bpi = Total number of "fail" results from all tests within page pi and Npi = Total number applications of all tests within page pi. Bearing in mind that some UWEM tests apply to the web site as a whole and not to individual pages, Bst = Total number of "fail" results from all tests on site level, Nst= Total number applications of all tests on site level.

The UWEM metric (Fs) value is a number between 0 and 1. A score of zero denotes that the Web site should not present serious problems of accessibility.

3 WAB*

As mentioned before, the WAB metric evaluates 25 checkpoints from the 3 priority levels. However, the tests performed to evaluate the checkpoints are sometimes vague when specifying the way to determine the number of potential violations of each checkpoint. This is owed mostly to the evolution of the technology used in the construction of web sites. Table 1 shows some examples.

Table 1. Some of the most vague checkpoints in the WAB metric

CheckPoint	Number of potential violations
Each frame should reference a HTML file	Every \<frame\> → **does not include iframe**
Each frame should have a title	Every \<frame\> → **does not include \<iframe\>**
Do not use the same link sentence when pointing to different URLs	Number of \<a\> → **does not include \<area\>**
Use relative position and size instead of absolute	Every **\<table\>, \<th\>, \<td\>, \<frame\> → does not include \<div\> or \<iframe\>**

On the other hand, the UWEM metric specifies priority 1 and 2 checkpoints of greater precision than the ones used in WAB (as seen in Table 2) when identifying the number of potential violations. However, the downside of this metric is that no priority 3 checkpoint is used.

Table 2. Some important checkpoints of the WAB metric

CheckPoint	Number of potential violations
Each frame should reference an HTML file	Every \<frame\>, \<iframe\>
Each frame should have a title	Every \<frame\>, \<iframe\>
Do not use the same link sentence when pointing to different URLs	Every \<a\>,\<area\>
Use relative position and size instead of absolute	Every\<table\>, \<th\>, \<td\>, \<frame\>, \<iframe\>, \<div\>, \<object\>, \<applet\>, \<frameset\>
Valid formal CCS 1.0 or CSS 2.x schema	Every CSS
Do not use CSS rules that produce blinking	Every CSS

Taking into account these deficiencies, we have developed WAB* extension of the WAB metric. A summary of the most important features follows:

1. WAB* considers all 3 priority levels (as WAB), and not only 2.
2. WAB* uses the same WAB metric (with the same weights).
3. WAB* has all WAB checkpoints but updated to eliminate deficiencies. For example:
   a. Not only frames, but iframes are tested.
   b. Not only table, th, td, and frame are tested for relative size and position, but also div, iframe, object, and applet.
4. Besides, WAB* includes eleven automatic checkpoints from the UWEM metric.

The final result is a metric with 36 fully automatic, evaluable checkpoints. 6 are priority 1, 23 are priority 2, and 7 are priority 3. The complete table is not included for space reasons.

4 A Practical Case: Evaluating the Accessibility of the European Banking Sector

We performed an accessibility study of the European Banking Section (some results are published in [9]) using the Iris tool previously mentioned. Among other goals, we evaluated the behaviour of the new WAB* metric with relation to WAB and UWEM. We took the Dow Jones EUROSTOXX TMI Banks list and selected 51 banks belonging to 11 countries. The tool allowed us to evaluate 30,600 pages (51 sites x 200 pages in each site in 3 different depth levels x 3 metrics). The conclusions drawn from the study state that the new WAB* metric results are alongside WAB and UWEM, but the scores are more detailed, and always higher than WAB, mostly because of more exhaustive tests included.

5 Conclusions

We have introduced WAB*, a new fully-automatic metric. It is based on WAB but has a much more severe accessibility evaluation, using also UWEM-inspired checkpoints. It evaluates 36 checkpoints against WAB's 25, and with more precision. The first results from studies performed using the new metric show it provides more precise markers for accessibility levels than the other two metrics.

References

1. Vigo, M., Arrue, M., Brajnik, G., Lomuscio, R., Abascal, J.: Quantitative Metrics for Measuring Web Accessibility (W4A), pp. 99–107. ACM Press, New York (2007)
2. Hackett, S., Parmanto, B., Zeng, X.: Accessibility of Internet Websites through Time. In: ACM SIGACCESS Accessibility and Computing, pp. 32–39 (2003)
3. Sullivan, T., Matson, R.: Barriers to Use: Usability and Content Accessibility on the Web's Most Popular Sites. In: Conference on Universal Usability, pp. 139–144. ACM Press, New York (2000)
4. Wab Cluster. Unified Web Evaluation Methodology (UWEM),
   http://www.wabcluster.org/deliverables.html
5. Freire, A.P., Bittar, T.J., Fortes, R.P.: An Approach Based on Metrics for Monitoring Web Accessibility in Brazilian Municipalities Web Sites. In: ACM Symposium on Applied Computing, pp. 2421–2425 (2008)
6. European Internet Accessibility Observatory (EIAO), http://www.eiao.net/
7. Holmesland, M.S., Ulltveit-Moe, N., Balachandran, A., Goodwin, M.: A Proposed Architecture for Large Scale Web Accessibility Assessment. In: Miesenberger, K., Klaus, J., Zagler, W.L., Karshmer, A.I. (eds.) ICCHP 2006. LNCS, vol. 4061, pp. 234–241. Springer, Heidelberg (2006)
8. De Andres, J., Lorca, P., Martínez, A.B.: Social Responsability versus Efficiency Gains: Which are the Factors that Underlie in the Implementation of Web Accessibility by Listed Firms? In: IASK E-Activity and Leading Technologies 2008 & InterTIC, pp. 49–58 (2008)
9. De Andrés, J., Lorca, P., Martínez, A.B.: Economic and Financial Factors for the Adoption and Visibility Effects of Web Accessibility. The Case of European Banks. Journal of the American Society for Information Science and Technology (accepted, 2009) (publication pending)
10. Parmanto, B., Zeng, X.: Metric for Web Accessibility Evaluation. Journal of the American Society for Information Science and Technology 56(13), 1394–1404 (2005)
11. Nietzio, A., Strobbe, C., Velleman, E.: TheUnified Web Evaluation Methodology (UWEM) 1.2 for WCAG 1.0. In: Miesenberger, K., Klaus, J., Zagler, W.L., Karshmer, A.I. (eds.) ICCHP 2008. LNCS, vol. 5105, pp. 394–401. Springer, Heidelberg (2008)

A Web-Based Mashup Tool for Information Integration and Delivery to Mobile Devices

Prach Chaisatien and Takehiro Tokuda

Department of Computer Science, Tokyo Institute of Technology
Meguro, Tokyo 152-8552, Japan
{prach,tokuda}@tt.cs.titech.ac.jp

Abstract. The immense popularity in mobile internet has driven part of classic web information and services to transform and shrink themselves to match the diversity of web-capable mobile devices. This paper will present a Web-based mashup tool to work with range of Japanese domestic mobile handsets and their variety of limited functionalities. Our purpose is to provide users an alternative option to customize information to be displayed and to integrate available services for their mobile phone. Three major working components, functionality tester, service aggregator and output simulator will aid users in understanding the capability of their mobile device and selecting corresponding functionalities. Successfully simulated and simplified information services will be accessible via user's mobile phones with correct configurations.

Keywords: Mobile Devices, Web-based, Customization, Integration, Mashup.

1 Introduction

The popularity of mobile phones has begun to build up due to their capability of web access. One of the great challenges for mobile developers is dealing with devices' specification. A web page of application which works and displays correctly on one mobile phone may not work or display correctly on another. Classic web information and service may not be easily accessible on a mobile phone. In this paper, we are proposing a web-based tool which can help users build a mashup mobile application from specific information sources, select integratible web services and compile them into his/her personal mobile web service. The primary objective is to aid the user in creating a mobile phone mashup application which matches the user's preferences.

2 Research Backgrounds and Related Works

While Japanese mobile technologies gain major success in the domestic market, rigid rules for designing mobile web services need to be adhered. Even though in many other countries, internet and mobile technology are converging, the current Japanese mobile technology still has obvious drawbacks and compatibility problems. Various case studies have been observed the i-Mode services outside Japan [1], [2]. The latest

M. Gaedke, M. Grossniklaus, and O. Díaz (Eds.): ICWE 2009, LNCS 5648, pp. 489–492, 2009.
© Springer-Verlag Berlin Heidelberg 2009

report shows that European mobile operators have begun to discontinue their i-Mode services. The main reason behind the discontinuation is that i-Mode comes with a fixed business model [3].

Consequently, Japanese mobile users are having no choice but to follow the regulation from carrier-dependent services and profile-specific phones. This research proposes an alternative option to deliver independency to combine internet technology and the ability to create mashup applications from applicable services for mobile phones. A system overview is shown in Fig. 1.

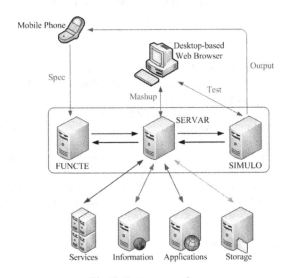

Fig. 1. System overview

1. Our assumption is that users know how to operate their mobile phone browser to a certain level. In some cases, we still require minimal effort from users to run a specification test or make some adjustments which will help the system run correctly on their mobile phone.

2. Specification detection via the user agent string and HTTP headers will be conducted after the mobile phone was registered and accessed the initial page in FUNCTE. The system will automatically detect working functions from this process. Some specifications may need to be tested if they are not available.

3. Users are facilitated by a narrowed choice of mashup modules from the specification detection. All configurations will be passed to the main web mashup engine called SERVAR and match the working services in association with mobile phone's carrier. Using a desktop browser, users can choose applicable services, information and select compatible web application to create their mashup application.

4. After users finish adjusting their mobile service components, simulation of the output page will be display on SIMULO. As soon as the user has completed his/her tuning, the mobile web service page is ready to be published and accessed online.

Although several methods in detecting mobile phone specification have been presented and used worldwide, there is still no central standard for Japanese domestic mobile phones. The user agent profile (UAProf) [4] is a set of XML documents that contains information about the agent type and device capabilities. On the other hand, there is an open-source project intended for developers working with the WAP and wireless protocol called WURFL [5]. In fact, it is a manually imported UAProf with additional sources and fixes submitted by other developers. A mobile device web service database called DetectRight [6] provides free and paid subscribers with APIs and analyzer tools which can be integrated with a mobile communication server.

Technology for mobile customization is being developed alongside technology for desktops. The combination of Yahoo pipes and iPhone [7] is suitably leveraging a creation of mobile mashup application via a visual editor. Christian S. Jensen et al [8] demonstrate an idea of user-generated content for mobile services by introducing the STREAMSPIN which enable users to generate their own mobile services from text/photo posting and geospatial information.

3 Mashup Example and Discussion

Retrieve Location Information. Similar to the technique applied by Google Map but using the carrier's geo-location web service as a substitute. Some backup service such as DoCoMo Open i-Area, which makes use of radio tower triangulation, may not provide as precise a location as the GPS-based one does. A virtual coordinate rectangle will be used to search for nearby places of interest. Location information are fetched from Wikipedia. The user can also display details of these locations by clicking on the marked dots or switching to text display and links as in Fig. 2.

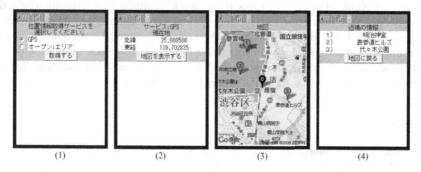

Fig. 2. Screenshots from mashup example. (1) Select a service from available location-based services (2) Current coordinates (3) Display the map with marked dots (4) Links for details.

Discussion. In our mashup example, there are many untested components which are still in development. We now review some of the limitations of the components used in this evaluation.

1. In our example, we only use HTML. However, some mobile phones can display extended HTML which would allow development of a better user interface.

2. Network latency of each web resource need to be tested and revised. The current method reduces the amount of data received and transmitted. The connection time between the mobile phone and the server was very variable. This is because the server has to wait for a response from the requested web service.

3. In providing a map image to the user, the zoom level is not adjustable. This adjustment has to be made manually by the user to fit his/her display area.

4. Search result is limited to a short description. Our intention is not to provide the user with an extra mobile search engine but to have it integrated for other uses.

4 Conclusion and Future Work

In order to converge mobility and mashup information, there are several approaches which need to be considered. Most mobile applications are bound with devices' specifications and with the web services they use. Mobile service carriers in Japan tend to keep their services strictly exclusive. Therefore, we developed a web system that addresses device configuration problem at first hand and provides users an option to mash and use their application independently.

Technically, the current system is able to test mobile phone specifications or make specification detection using the user agent string and HTTP headers. Integratible services will be listed during the mashup application creation process. Specifications which have been tested by users are stored on the server and are used as a resource for further development. There are still some components currently under development which include an output simulator, a look and feel configurator and feature adjustability. We are planning to revise the APIs to improve their speed, size and stability in practical use. Using the same ideas, we plan to extend our system to be compatible with more handsets available worldwide.

A mobile phone does not just support text input. It would be interesting to use the microphone and camera on the mobile phone, for example, to support speech recognition or for scanning 2D barcodes. Better mashup applications could be created for JavaScript-capable phones with accessible low level APIs such as those appeared for the Android or iPhone platforms. Indeed, this study ultimately needs more flexible access to lower level device APIs and higher level web APIs.

References

1. O'Brien K.J.: Forerunner of mobile Internet, i-mode is fading in Europe, International Herald Tribune (2007),
   http://www.iht.com/articles/2007/07/17/business/imode.php
2. Suri, V.R., Sawhney, H.: The internet and its wireless extensions in Japan: the portentous interface between chaos and order. Info. 10(3), 10–21 (2008)
3. Ishii, K.: Internet Use via Mobile Phone in Japan. Telecommunications Policy 28(1), 43–58 (2004)
4. UAProf profile repository,
   http://w3development.de/rdf/uaprof_repository/
5. WURFL, http://wurfl.sourceforge.net/
6. DetectRight, http://www.detectright.com/
7. Trevor, J.: Doing the Mobile Mash. Computer 41(2), 104–106 (2008)
8. Jensen, C.S., Vincente, C.R., Wind, R.: User-Generated Content: The Case for Mobile Services. Computer 41(12), 116–118 (2008)

UWE4JSF: A Model-Driven Generation Approach for Web Applications

Christian Kroiss[1], Nora Koch[1,2], and Alexander Knapp[1]

[1] Ludwig-Maximilians-Universität München, Germany
[2] Cirquent GmbH, Germany
{kroiss,kochn,knapp}@pst.ifi.lmu.de

Abstract. Model-driven engineering is a promising approach, but there are still many hurdles to overcome. The tool UWE4JSF solves the hurdles for the model-driven development of web applications designed with UWE. It builds upon a set of models and domain specific annotations – in particular an abstract and a concrete presentation model. It is completely integrated in Eclipse, implemented as a set of plugins supporting model transformations and fully automatic code generation.

1 Introduction

The aim of model-driven development (MDD) is to raise the level of abstraction at which software is developed in order to save time and to reduce the amount of redundant programming work. MDD approaches are based on models that become first-class citizens in the development process, and on metamodels and model transformations requiring appropriate tool support. UWE4JSF [2] is such a CASE tool that was developed for the generation of web applications within the scope of the UML-based Web Engineering approach (UWE)[1].

UWE4JSF focuses on the automated generation of web applications, similarly to UWEATL [1] – first MDD approach for UWE – but differs in several conceptual and implementation aspects. In particular, (1) UWE4JSF is integrated in the Eclipse IDE using Eclipse-based transformation technologies. (2) It automatically generates web applications for the JSF[2] platform, a component-based technology which provides a flexible and powerful mechanism for the implementation of user interfaces (UI) of arbitrary complexity by means of component libraries. (3) UWE4JSF makes use of OGNL[3] that is an open-source expression language for Java. (4) The generation of the UI is based on a revisited version of the UWE presentation metamodel and an additional *concrete presentation model*.

To summarize UWE4JSF provides a human-readable, debuggable and high-performance approach that supports fully automated generation of web applications.

---

[1] UWE — http://www.pst.ifi.lmu.de/projekte/uwe
[2] Java Server Faces — http://java.sun.com/javaee/javaserverfaces/
[3] Object-Graph Navigation Language — http://www.opensymphony.com/ognl/

M. Gaedke, M. Grossniklaus, and O. Díaz (Eds.): ICWE 2009, LNCS 5648, pp. 493–496, 2009.
© Springer-Verlag Berlin Heidelberg 2009

2   Extending UWE for Model Driven Development

UWE follows the principle of "separation of concerns" by modeling the content, the navigation structure, the business processes, and the presentation of a web application separately as shown in Fig. 1. UWE is mainly based on standards, like UML and MDA[4]. The models are built using the UWE profile, which is a UML extension defined using the extension mechanisms provided by UML. For example, classes with a stereotype «navigationClass» represent navigable nodes for information retrieval; associations stereotyped with «navigationLink» model direct links. For more details the reader is referred to [2].

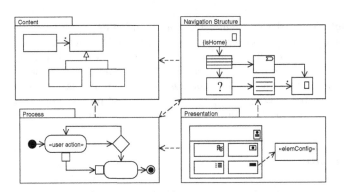

Fig. 1. UWE model types: overview

To use an UWE model for automatic transformation and code generation, it has to be augmented with explicit information that is not necessary if the model is only used for communication or documentation purposes. For example, the input data for navigation nodes has to be specified, together with the selection rules that are executed when links are followed. Information like this is specified by means of OGNL, combined with some UWE-specific functions. OGNL is also used in the activities of the process model to specify guard expressions and data handling actions. Unlike many other approaches, UWE also provides a UML extension for the explicit modeling of the user interface. First of all, the *(abstract) presentation model* is represented in UML using composite structure diagrams containing stereotyped classes and properties as representations for UI elements like text input fields or buttons. The resulting diagrams are very well suited to illustrate the basic layout and functional structure of the UI.

The elements of the presentation model must be mapped to UI components of the target platform. Many MDD approaches like WebML/Webratio[5] use template-based mechanisms for this purpose. However, in modern web applications, the selection of concrete UI components often strongly affects the usability, e.g. a date could be entered in a text field or with a dynamic calendar component.

---

[4] OMG — MDA Guide, http://www.omg.org/docs/omg/03-06-01.pdf

[5] http://www.webml.com

Therefore, in UWE this mapping is regarded as an important part of the application's design and recorded in a dedicated UML-based model, called the *concrete presentation model*. The basic idea is that platform specific UI components are modeled as stereotyped UML classes and corresponding instance specifications represent *concrete component configurations*. An example for a component that requires configuration like this might be a rich table whose column headers can be clicked to switch between different sorting criteria – the latter would be defined using attributes of the component configuration. It is also possible to build composite tree structures of component configurations, which might be used, for example, to add labels or headers to input or output elements. The mapping of abstract presentation model elements to element configurations can be established in two ways: (1) by associating mapping rules to meta-classes in *default element configurations* or (2) by linking individual elements of the abstract presentation model to element configurations with UML dependencies. In the sense of the MDA, these individual mappings could be seen as *markings* that guide the transformation process.

3   Tool Chain for Automatic Generation

The concepts described above were realized in the transformation and code generation tool UWE4JSF[6]. Its applicability has been demonstrated with several example applications, e.g. a simplified MP3 web store. UWE4JSF is implemented as a set of Eclipse plugins and supports automatic generation of JSF-based web applications from UWE models as well as model validation using constraints specified in the Object Constraint Language (OCL). UWE4JSF uses EMF[7] for the storage of (meta-)models and for the exchange with third party UML CASE tools, using a widely supported data format called EMF-UML. The model transformations were realized using ATL[8] for model-to-model (M2M) and JET[9] for model-to-text (M2T) transformations. Both Eclipse-based technologies were combined in a transformation chain that is illustrated in Fig. 2.

The process starts with a UML source model (with applied UWE profile) that contains both the platform-independent model (PIM) and individual element mappings of the concrete presentation model. A first model-to-model transformation converts it to an instance of the UWE metamodel which is then validated using a set of OCL constraints. If the validation succeeds, a next transformation generates a platform-specific model (PSM) by processing the UWE source model together with an additional input model containing the default UI element configurations of the concrete presentation model. This PSM is finally used as input for a model-to-text transformation that generates the application's source code which consists of Java classes, page specifications and configuration files. These generated artefacts build upon an intermediate platform, called the UWE4JSF

---

[6] http://www.pst.ifi.lmu.de/projekte/uwe/uwe4jsf
[7] Eclipse Modeling Framework — http://www.eclipse.org/modeling/emf
[8] Atlas Transformation Language — http://www.eclipse.org/m2m/atl/
[9] http://www.eclipse.org/modeling/m2t

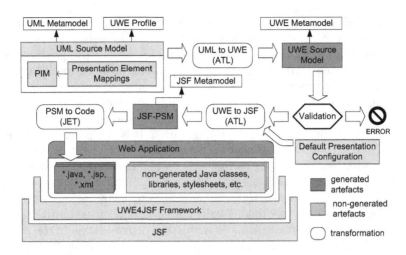

Fig. 2. UWE4JSF Generation Process

framework, that resides on top of JSF and is designed to reduce the complexity of the generated code and the transformation rules. Finally, the application can be augmented with non-generated Java classes to implement complex process actions or persistence layer operations.

4   Conclusions and Future Work

We presented the MDD tool UWE4JSF that allows fully automatic generation of JSF-based web applications from UWE models. The chosen platform provides high extensibility and UWE's concrete presentation model can be used to exploit the vast amount of available JSF component libraries that provide means to create rich user interfaces. JSF also offers a flexible architecture for supporting simultaneously multiple platforms like browsers technologies and mobile devices. Future work includes efforts to incorporate mechanisms like pattern substitution and to extending the validation engine. Last but not least, the MagicUWE[10] project aims to create an elaborate integration of UWE/UWE4JSF into a professional UML CASE tool.

References

1. Kraus, A., Knapp, A., Koch, N.: Model-Driven Generation of Web Applications in UWE. In: MDWE2007 - 3rd International Workshop on Model-Driven Web Engineering, July 2007. CEUR-WS, vol. 261, pp. 23–38 (2007)
2. Kroiss, C.: Model-based Generation of Web Applications with UWE (in German). Diploma Thesis. Ludwig-Maximilians-Universität München, Germany (June 2008), http://www.pst.ifi.lmu.de/projekte/uwe/publications/CKroissDA08.pdf

---

[10] http://www.pst.ifi.lmu.de/projekte/uwe/toolMagicUWE.html

On Using Distributed Extended XQuery for Web Data Sources as Services*

Muhammad Intizar Ali[1], Reinhard Pichler[1], Hong-Linh Truong[2],
and Schahram Dustdar[2]

[1] Database and Artificial Intelligence Group, Vienna University of Technology
{intizar,pichler}@dbai.tuwien.ac.at
[2] Distributed Systems Group, Vienna University of Technology
{truong,dustdar}@infosys.tuwien.ac.at

Abstract. DeXIN (**D**istributed **ex**tended **X**Query for data **IN**tegration) integrates multiple, heterogeneous, highly distributed and rapidly changing web data sources in different formats, e.g. XML, RDF and relational data. DeXIN is a RESTful data integration web service which integrates heterogeneous distributed data sources, including data services (DaaS – data as a service). At the heart of DeXIN is an XQuery extension that allows users/applications to execute a single query against distributed, heterogeneous web data sources or data services. In this system demo, we show how DeXIN can provide an optimized, distributed and parallel query processing and data integration at the same time.

1 Introduction

In recent years, there has been an enormous boost in Semantic Web technologies and Web services. Web applications thus have to deal with huge amounts of data which are normally scattered over various data sources using various languages. Hence, these applications are facing two major challenges, namely (i) how to integrate *heterogeneous* data and (ii) how to deal with *rapidly growing* and continuously changing *distributed data sources*.

The concept of providing data as a service (DaaS) [1] enables applications to expose data sources as Web services that can be consumed by Web clients within a corporate network and across the internet. In this paper, we demonstrate DeXIN, a RESTful Web Service for data integration of heterogeneous and distributed data sources. DeXIN receives a user query in extended XQuery syntax as presented in [2], this extension enables DeXIN to execute a single query in XQuery language, which can contain multiple sub-queries of SPARQL or SQL. Data sources supported by DeXIN can be Web services or databases which provide a query interface based on Web services and XML wrapping facility for results. Supporting Web services based on databases is important as current database management systems increasingly provide REST/SOAP APIs for querying hosted data. The integrated results of all the data sources are presented in XML. Currently available heterogeneous data integration approaches normally work

* This work was supported by the Vienna Science and Technology Fund (WWTF), project ICT08-032.

M. Gaedke, M. Grossniklaus, and O. Díaz (Eds.): ICWE 2009, LNCS 5648, pp. 497–500, 2009.
© Springer-Verlag Berlin Heidelberg 2009

either (i) by transforming the data sources into common format [3,4] or (ii) by query rewriting [5]. In contrast, DeXIN executes distributed parallel queries towards native data sources, without fetching all the data sources into one centralized place or transforming data sources. These features make DeXIN a powerful tool for data integration in a highly distributed, peer to peer, heterogeneous and rapidly changing Web environment, providing the user with a uniform access to this data.

2   Overview of DeXIN

An architectural overview of DeXIN is depicted in Figure 1. The main task of DeXIN is to provide an integrated access to different distributed, heterogeneous, autonomous data sources. DeXIN provides a single entry point to access different data sources by using our extension of XQuery [2]. The DeXIN service can be utilized by many web applications which require an integrated access to heterogeneous web data sources. Distributed, parallel query execution and avoiding data transformation make it a strong tool for data integration and optimized query execution in distributed and peer to peer networks. Normally, the user would have to query each of these data sources separately. With the support of DeXIN, he/she has a single entry point to access all these data sources. In total, the user thus issues *a single query* (in our extended XQuery language) and receives *a single result*. All the tedious work of decomposition, connection establishment, document retrieval, query execution, etc. is done behind the scene by DeXIN.

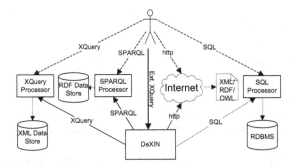

Fig. 1. Architectural overview of DeXIN framework

3   Distributed Extended Query for Data Integration

3.1   DeXIN: Data Integration Web Service

DeXIN is a RESTful data service which takes a single query in extended XQuery syntax as input, decomposes the query into sub-queries, executes each sub-query independently on its appropriate distributed data source at remote locations and outputs the integrated results from all data sources in XML format. Consider an example of a web application which needs to provide the integrated access to the distributed and heterogeneous Web data sources dynamically. Typical data integration approaches e.g. warehousing, mediation or ontology based, do not provide the desired results because they

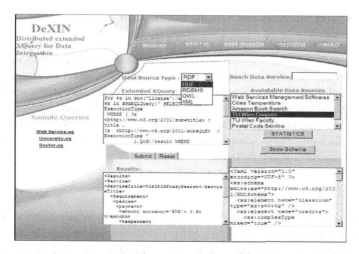

Fig. 2. User Interface of DeXIN

require some prior knowledge about the data sources. DeXIN can ideally serve such applications because it provides integrated access to heterogeneous distributed web data sources dynamically. Figure 2 shows the user interface of the DeXIN service. The user can write a query in extended XQuery format and gets the accumulated results of all the data sources. Currently, DeXIN supports two types of sub-queries inside XQuery namely, (i) SPARQL for RDF, OWL and (ii) SQL for relational data.

3.2 Searching Available Data Services

Many service providers have started to expose their data as a service by implementing the Resource Oriented Architecture (ROA). Some Database Management Systems also provide access to their data using Query Language + REST/SOAP. DeXIN can communicate with Data Service directories to find out the appropriate data service. The user can initiate a keyword search for the required data service, and all the available data services are listed by DeXIN to help the user to select an appropriate data service.

3.3 Registration of Data Sources

The registration of data sources at DeXIN is not mandatory because DeXIN can interact with any data service at runtime, but providing some metadata about data sources by following the registration procedure makes querying simpler from the user's perspective. Different Data Sources (e.g. RDF,XML,OWL or RDBMS) can register at DeXIN to benefit from the integration facilities provided by DeXIN. Each data source must provide a unique name, should have one of the DeXIN supported data types, querying interface with connectivity facility and XML converter for query results. Data providers can provide additional information about schema, user privileges, license and legal issues to facilitate the users to interact with their data sources effectively. It is worth mentioning here that utilizing the concept of Data as a Service greatly eases the process of registration, because it uses the standard HTTP protocol to interact with the data sources and XML for data transfer.

3.4 Data Source Statistics and Schema Information

DeXIN stores some metadata and statistics about registered data sources, which are helpful for the selection of the best available service from the user's perspective. The user can select any data service from the list of available data sources shown by DeXIN (see top right of Figure2) and can see its statistics which are either stored in DeXIN or retrieved by DeXIN after communicating with the Service Management System.

If the data service provider provides some schema information about data sources, the user can click on "Show Schema", to see the schema information, which is helpful for designing queries for that particular data source.

3.5 Query Execution

Once the user submits a query to DeXIN in extended XQuery format, DeXIN (i) decomposes the query into multiple sub-queries for distributed, heterogeneous data sources (ii) connects with the data sources mentioned in the query (iii) dispatches queries to their particular data source at remote locations (iv) displays integrated results of all the sub-queries into XML format.

4 Conclusion

In this demo, we present DeXIN, a web based system to integrate data by executing distributed XQuery over Heterogeneous Data Sources. We demonstrate typical use cases of heterogeneous data integration which show that DeXIN is a simple but powerful tool to integrate rapidly changing heterogeneous data sources dynamically. DeXIN can be utilized by many applications where the data sources are unknown at design time, and it eases the integration process from the user's perspective by not requiring prior knowledge of data sources.

References

1. Zhu, F., Turner, M., Kotsiopoulos, I.A., Bennett, K.H., Russell, M., Budgen, D., Brereton, P., Keane, J., Layzell, P.J., Rigby, M., Xu, J.: Dynamic data integration using web services. In: ICWS, pp. 262–269 (2004)
2. Ali, M.I., Pichler, R., Truong, H.-L., Dustdar, S.: DeXIN: An extensible framework for distributed XQuery over heterogeneous data sources. In: Proc. ICEIS 2009, pp. 172–183 (2009)
3. Gandon, F.: GRDDL Use Cases: Scenarios of extracting RDF data from XML documents. W3C Proposed Recommendation (April 2007)
4. Groppe, S., Groppe, J., Linnemann, V., Kukulenz, D., Hoeller, N., Reinke, C.: Embedding SPARQL into XQuery/XSLT. In: Proc. SAC 2008, pp. 2271–2278 (2008)
5. Akhtar, W., Kopecký, J., Krennwallner, T., Polleres, A.: XSPARQL: Traveling between the XML and RDF Worlds - and Avoiding the XSLT Pilgrimage. In: Bechhofer, S., Hauswirth, M., Hoffmann, J., Koubarakis, M. (eds.) ESWC 2008. LNCS, vol. 5021, pp. 432–447. Springer, Heidelberg (2008)

Automatic Generation of RIAs Using RUX-Tool and Webratio*

Marino Linaje[1], Juan Carlos Preciado[1], Rober Morales-Chaparro[2],
Roberto Rodríguez-Echeverría, and Fernando Sánchez-Figueroa[1]

[1] Quercus SEG, Escuela Politécnica, Universidad de Extremadura
Avda. de la Universidad S/N, Cáceres, Spain
mlinaje@unex.es
[2] R&D Department, Homeria Open Solutions, S.L.
Vivero de Empresas
Avda. de la Universidad S/N, Cáceres, Spain
robermorales@homeria.com

Abstract. This work describes RUX-Tool, an MDD-based tool that gives support to the modeling and automatic code generation of User Interfaces for Rich Internet Applications (RIAs) with multidevice and multiplatform capabilities. This tool is mainly thought to be used with other tools based on Web methodologies such as it is the case of WebRatio that automatically generates the content structure and the business logic.

Keywords: Rich Internet Applications, User Interfaces, CASE Tool.

1 Introduction

The future of the Web is being built using technologies such as Rich Internet Applications (RIAs) [1] which, on the one hand, offer all the advantages of traditional Web applications and, on the other hand, add the flexibility and user-friendliness of desktop solutions. RIAs offer online and offline capabilities, sophisticated user interfaces, augmented storage and processing capabilities at the client side, high levels of user interaction, usability and personalization and they minimize bandwidth usage through the separation of presentation from content at the client side.

Some of the most well-known technologies used for developing RIAs are AJAX [5], Flash [5], Flex [5] and OpenLaszlo [5]. However, while RIA technologies are reaching maturity and a growing number of Web 2.0 applications are being developed based on them, there is a lack of comprehensive models and methodologies for the systematic development of RIAs [5].

Many of the RIA features are related with User Interfaces. With no doubt, they are the most appreciated features by users. The main contribution of this paper is introducing a visual and intuitive tool for the design of RIA User Interfaces on top of existing applications developed with a Web methodology. This tool, called RUX-Tool,

* Developed under Spanish Research Projects: TSI-020501-2008-47 and TIN2008-02985.

M. Gaedke, M. Grossniklaus, and O. Díaz (Eds.): ICWE 2009, LNCS 5648, pp. 501–504, 2009.
© Springer-Verlag Berlin Heidelberg 2009

gives support to the automatic code generation for different devices (PC, Mobile, PDA, etc) and different platforms (AJAX, Flex, OpenLaszlo).

RUX-Tool works together with WebRatio, the WebML CASE Tool. Once the application has been developed using WebRatio, one can use RUX-Tool to obtain from the WebRatio model the data structure and business logic information. Then, the process of modeling the User Interface begins, as described below.

2 RUX-Tool

RUX-Tool is based on RUX-Method [4] (Figure 1). According to [3] the design of the UI is divided into 4 levels: *Concepts and Tasks, Abstract Interface, Concrete Interface and Final Interface*. In RUX-Method Concepts and Tasks are provided by the underlying Web model and each level is composed by Interface Components which are specified in the RUX Components Library.

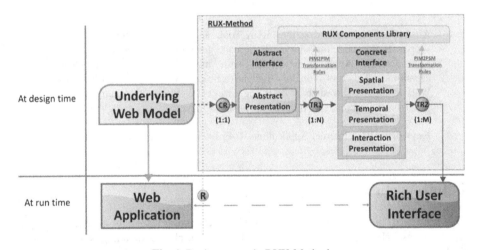

Fig. 1. Design stages in RUX-Method

The development process in RUX-Method has four main stages: connection with the previously defined underlying Web model, definition of the Abstract Interface, definition of the Concrete Interface and specification of the Final Interface which ends in code generation.

So, the first stage in RUX-Tool deals with the connection with the WebRatio model. At this stage, the presentation elements and the relationships among them are extracted, as well as the defined operations on the WebRatio model. On the basis of the results offered by the Connection Rules (CR in Figure 1), RUX-Tool builds the Abstract Interface, which is independent from the platform and the final display device. Applying to the Abstract Interface the first set of Transformation Rules (TR1 in Figure 1), the Concrete Interface, which allows the appearance, spatial arrangement, temporal and interactive behavior, is obtained. Finally, from the Concrete Interface and through the second set of Transformation Rules (TR2 in Figure 1), the Final Interface

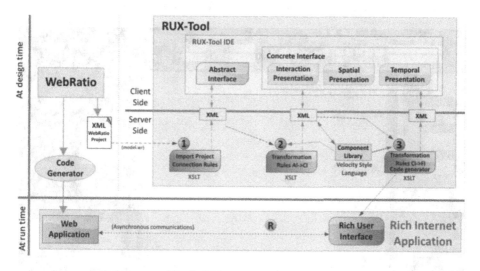

Fig. 2. RUX-Tool architecture

is obtained. The Abstract and the Concrete Interface levels can be modified by the modeler before performing the next stage.

RUX-Tool is not a desktop application. It is itself a RIA, so it is accessed from a browser, and allows working on-line in a cooperative way.

The general architecture of the tool can be seen in Figure 2. RUX-Tool, as a typical RIA, has two sides: client side and server side. The client side includes a graphic UI for redesigning the different levels of User Interfaces once they have been automatically obtained from their corresponding previous stage. The client side also includes different wizards and dialogs to configure the tool, to import the WebRatio project and to specify the chosen devices and platforms for the final code generation.

On the other hand, the server side is in charge of performing the required transformations between interface levels and the connection with the underlying WebRatio application. This implies the communication between client and server sides to interchange the representation of the different interface levels. This is done by means of XML.

The Component Library is also at the server side. It has a plug-in based architecture favoring an easy management of components (deletion, insertion, etc). Each component is implemented using a template based on Velocity Style Language.

3   RUX-Tool in the Market

Currently, RUX-Tool is being used with Webratio 5.1. It is being developed between the University of Extremadura and Homeria Open Solutions, (spinoff of the same university) as a consequence of a Spanish Research project from the Industry Department.

RUX-Tool has being used in several projects such as a Virtual Campus, a Content Management System or Virtual Shop Management System. Figure 3 shows a

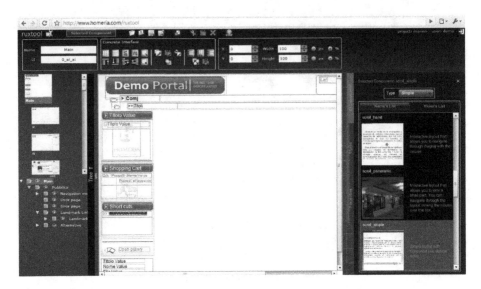

Fig. 3. RUX-Tool

snapshot of the tool at the client side when designing a simple Web portal with a shopping cart.

We refer to the reader to the RUX-project site (www.ruxproject.org) for more details on RUX-Tool (video-demos, examples, etc).

References

1. Bozzon, A., Comai, S., Fraternali, P., Toffetti Carughi, G.: Conceptual Modeling and Code Generation for Rich Internet Applications. In: International Conference on Web Engineering ICWE, pp. 353–360. ACM, New York (2006)
2. Ceri, S., Fraternali, P., Bongio, A., Brambilla, M., Comai, S., Matera, M.: Designing Data-Intensive Web Applications. Morgan Kauffmann, San Francisco (2002)
3. Limbourg, Q., Vanderdonckt, J., Michotte, B., Bouillon, L., Lopez, V.: UsiXML: a Language Supporting Multi-Path Development of User Interfaces. In: Bastide, R., Palanque, P., Roth, J. (eds.) DSV-IS 2004 and EHCI 2004. LNCS, vol. 3425, pp. 207–228. Springer, Heidelberg (2005)
4. Linaje, M., Preciado, J.C., Sanchez-Figueroa, F.: Engineering Rich Internet Application User Interfaces over Legacy Web Models. IEEE Internet Computing 11(6), 53–59 (2007)
5. Preciado, J.C., Linaje, M., Sanchez, F., Comai, S.: Necessity of methodologies to model Rich Internet Applications. In: IEEE Int. Symposium on Web Site Evolution, pp. 7–13 (2005)

MagicUWE – A CASE Tool Plugin for Modeling Web Applications*

Marianne Busch[1] and Nora Koch[1,2]

[1] Ludwig-Maximilians-Universität München, Germany
[2] Cirquent GmbH, Germany
busch@cip.ifi.lmu.de, kochn@pst.ifi.lmu.de

Abstract. Adequate tool support is a crucial factor of success for a software development method or technique. In this paper, we present the MagicUWE tool, that supports systematic design of web applications with the UML-based Web Engineering (UWE) approach. It provides assistance to the designer for the modeling activities using the UWE profile and the semi-automatic generation of models. MagicUWE is implemented as a plugin for the CASE tool MagicDraw. Focus of the development of the plugin was the usability, adaptability and extensibility of the tool.

1 Introduction

The Unified Modeling Language (UML)[1] provides a rich set of modeling elements and diagram types to cover the specification needs of all kinds of software. In particular, it offers an extension mechanism for the definition of domain specific modeling languages (so-called profiles). The UML-based Web Engineering (UWE) profile is such an extension and therefore, all UML CASE tools can be used to build UWE models. In order to provide an augmented assistance to the UWE modeler, we implemented a plugin for the MagicDraw[2] tool - called MagicUWE [1] [2]. In contrast to our previous tool ArgoUWE [3], it is based on the UML2 metamodel.

MagicUWE supports the UWE notation and the UWE development process, i.e. it comprises (1) extensions of the toolbar for comfortable use of UWE elements including shortcuts for some of them, (2) a specific menu to create UWE default packages and new diagrams for the different views of web applications (content, navigation, presentation and processes), and to execute model transformations, (3) additional context menus not only for the containment tree but also within navigation diagrams. MagicUWE is easy to install and easy to extend, and the usability is mainly given by intuitive icons, different types of menus and helpful hints.

---

* This work has been supported by the DFG Project MAEWA II, WI 841/7-2, and the EU FET-GC2 IP project SENSORIA, IST-2005-016004.
[1] OMG - Unified Modeling Language. http://www.omg.org/docs/formal/09-02-02.pdf
[2] MagicDraw. http://www.magicdraw.com/

M. Gaedke, M. Grossniklaus, and O. Díaz (Eds.): ICWE 2009, LNCS 5648, pp. 505–508, 2009.
© Springer-Verlag Berlin Heidelberg 2009

2   Modeling with MagicUWE

In order to get a general idea of MagicUWEs main functionalities, the extensions
of the toolbar, the menu and the context menus are introduced in this section.
The plugin[3] can be downloaded from the UWE website[4], where a tutorial to
UWE and a tabular reference of MagicUWE can be found.

Toolbar. MagicUWE allows selecting model elements for modeling web applications defined by stereotypes directly from the toolbar (see Fig. 1(a)) like navigation classes, and navigation links, index, and all kinds of presentation elements
as page, presentation group and presentation properties, input and output user
interface elements, etc. In particular, before drawing a presentation property, an
element has to be chosen, which should afterwards contain the new property.
The name of the new class and property can easily be typed into an input field
provided by the plugin, as shown in Fig. 1(b). Properties can be nested and are
graphically represented by nested class diagrams.

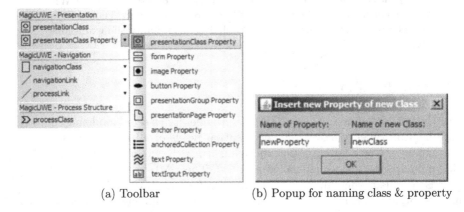

(a) Toolbar   (b) Popup for naming class & property

Fig. 1. MagicUWE: Insertion of property from toolbar

An example of the simplification of such a common operation, is the comparison to an insertion of an UWE property without MagicUWE. The user has to
include the UWE profile[5] manually and one stereotype from the UWE profile
has to be added to a new class. The properties derived from this class, can be
drawn only in elements, that have the `Suppress Structure` value set to `false`
in the `Symbol(s) Properties`.

MagicUWE Menu. MagicDraw's main menu provides the functionalities to
create the default UWE packages (which are also predefined in the MagicUWE

---

[3] UWE - MagicUWE. http://www.pst.ifi.lmu.de/projekte/uwe/toolMagicUWE.html
[4] UWE - UML-based Web Engineering. http://www.pst.ifi.lmu.de/projekte/uwe/
[5] UWE - Metamodel and Profile.
    http://www.pst.ifi.lmu.de/projekte/uwe/publicationsMetamodelAndProfile.html

template) and to store new UWE diagrams in this hierarchy. On the one hand, it is possible to create new empty diagrams like in all UML tools. On the other hand, transformations are available in order to generate step by step drafts of diagrams based on another view of the web application:

- *Content-to-Navigation transformation:* Creates a new «navigationClass» class (in the navigation package) for each class in the content diagram, gives the new class the same name, adds «navigationLink» associations, and finally visualize them in a new navigation diagram.
- *Navigation-to-Presentation transformation:* Generates a new class for each class of a navigation diagram using a presentation specific stereotype. In this case, the «presentationClass» stereotype is added.
- *Navigation-to-ProcessStructure transformation:* Creates a new process structure diagram including a symbol of each class stereotyped «processClass» that is part of a navigation diagram. This is not a complex task, but a convenient method to avoid repetitive tasks to be performed by the modeler.
- *Navigation-to-ProcessFlow transformation:* Prepares a new process flow (an activity diagram) for each «processClass» of a navigation diagram. The new diagrams are labeled like the classes (with the appendix "Workflow").

Context Menu. If more than one diagram should be transformed, the context menu of the containment tree is the most flexible solution, because several diagrams can be selected as source for one kind of transformation. Two more MagicUWE context menus are located over the classes and associations of navigation diagrams, as can be seen in Fig. 2. The checked menu makes it possible to switch the tagged values {isHome} and {isLandmark} to true or false.

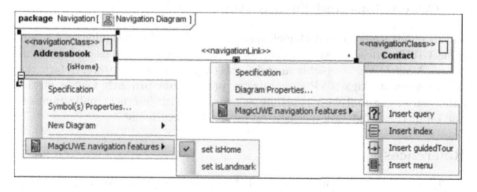

Fig. 2. MagicUWE: Context menus of navigation diagrams

The insertion of access primitives like index and query, is a challenge for the plugin, because it depends on the selected stereotype as well as on the number of associations the user selected before. A concrete example is the insertion of an index and a menu. An index is inserted, if an instance of a class should be selected, i.e. one end of a single association between navigation classes has the multiplicity '*', whereas a menu connects one main class with several classes. A menu will be added with a composition between the menu and the main class.

3   Usability, Adaptability and Extensibility

The aim of MagicUWE is to make the design of web applications with UWE and MagicDraw really easy, therefore an intuitive user interface is essential. In order to support valid models, it is especially important to show advices, e.g. if presentation elements are drawn into a navigation diagram. This check is based on the type recognition of the current UWE diagram and compares predefined substrings with the name of the diagrams parent package.

MagicUWE's hint messages can be configured (or even disabled) separately for all UWE diagram types (e.g. the standard for the package of navigation diagrams is packNavigation=nav). Thus, adaptability is another main goal of MagicUWE. It is possible to change the name of the included UWE profile, to determine the shortcuts for the toolbar entries and to decide which presentation stereotypes should be displayed in the toolbar as property or as class. Further characteristics of usability are a convenient installer for MagicUWE and the integration of the plugin in the GUI of MagicDraw. In particular, the modeler can also create all UWE diagram types out of MagicDraw's "New Diagram" context menu and not only use the familiar toolbar with its *last used* functionality, but also quickly select the required item, recognisable by its stereotype symbol.

In order to cope with new features of UWE and the next versions of MagicDraw, MagicUWE is designed in a very modular way, the code is well documented and a complex build script is used to create and launch new versions of the plugin automatically. Therefore, the tool is easily extensible and adaptable, which is welcome in the continuous improvement process of the CASE tool.

4   Conclusions and Future Work

In this paper we presented MagicUWE – a CASE tool for designing and generating UWE models characterized by its usability. Implemented as a MagicDraw plugin, MagicUWE is a highly modular and easy to extend software. In fact, the development of MagicUWE is an ongoing project that currently focuses on the extension of the tool with modeling elements for rich internet applications [4] and on further validation mechanisms for model consistency.

References

1. Blagoev, P.: MagicDraw-Plugin for Modelling and Generating Web Applications. Master's thesis, Ludwig-Maximilians-Universität München (2007)
2. Busch, M.: Migration and Extension of the MagicDraw Plugin MagicUWE (German). Project report, Ludwig-Maximilians-Universität München (2009)
3. Knapp, A., Koch, N., Zhang, G., Hassler, H.-M.: Modeling Business Processes in Web Applications with ArgoUWE. In: Baar, T., Strohmeier, A., Moreira, A., Mellor, S.J. (eds.) UML 2004. LNCS, vol. 3273, pp. 69–83. Springer, Heidelberg (2004)
4. Koch, N., Pigerl, M., Zhang, G., Morosova, T.: Patterns for the Model-based Development of Rich Internet Applications. In: Gaedke, M., Grossniklaus, M., Díaz, O. (eds.) ICWE 2009. LNCS, vol. 5648, pp. 283–291. Springer, Heidelberg (2009)

A Model-Based Approach Providing Context-Sensitive Television Interaction

Pieter Bellekens[1], Lora Aroyo[2], Geert-Jan Houben[3], and Annelies Kaptein[4]

[1] Eindhoven University of Technology, Den Dolech 2, Eindhoven, The Netherlands
p.a.e.bellekens@tue.nl
[2] VU University Amsterdam, De Boelelaan 1081, Amsterdam, The Netherlands
l.m.aroyo@cs.vu.nl
[3] Delft University of Technology, Mekelweg 4, Delft, The Netherlands
g.j.p.m.houben@tudelft.nl
[4] Stoneroos Digital Television, Sumatralaan 45, Hilversum, The Netherlands
annelies.kaptein@stoneroos.nl

Abstract. With this demonstrator of iFanzy, a Personalized Electronic Program Guide, we want to show how we approached the integration problem between various devices and various heterogeneous data sources in the television domain. Engineering applications in the world of television introduces on one hand some new problems like interfacing with a television set-top box combination via a remote control, and on the other hand asks for new approaches to known challenges like dealing with cold start issues. In this paper we discuss these problems and conclude with some user tests both in progress as well as planned in the near future.

1 Introduction

For years, the television platform did not really witness structural or conceptual changes. People watched their favorite programs and went to their computer if they wanted more information, interaction or services. However, after the steep technological rise of the Internet with concepts and approaches like the existing Web 2.0 and the envisioned Web 3.0[1], the television domain has gained momentum as the new platform where these new engineering techniques can also be applied. In this paper we present iFanzy, a Personalized Electronic Program Guide (PEPG), where user modeling and smart metadata aggregation via Semantic Web techniques [1] are introduced to provide an integrated ubiquitous approach reinventing the television experience.

2 iFanzy

iFanzy is the first practical approach trying to facilitate a ubiquitous environment providing access to television content. To do so, the iFanzy framework consists out of a set-top box application controlled by the remote control, an

---

[1] http://dsiegel.blogs.com/thoughts/2007/05/defining_web_30.html

M. Gaedke, M. Grossniklaus, and O. Díaz (Eds.): ICWE 2009, LNCS 5648, pp. 509–512, 2009.
© Springer-Verlag Berlin Heidelberg 2009

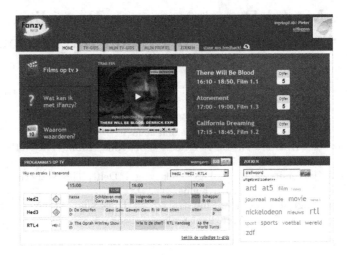

Fig. 1. The iFanzy Web interface

online Web application[2] and a application running on a mobile (currently a prototype running on the iPhone). Together these three platforms aim at helping the user selecting his or her ideal television experience. Each of these applications is specifically tailored to provide the functionality mostly expected from that particular platform. The Web application for example, is mainly built to provide a wide overview of all channels via a PEPG (Personalized Electronic Program Guide), enabling program ratings, setting favorites, reminders and alerts, etc. In figure 1 we see a part of in the UI including some movie tips at the top (including trailer) ranked by the user's estimated interest in these movies, a small overview of three channels in the lower left and a search cloud on the lower right. Some programs in the channel list are colored in different shades of orange. The intensity of the tone indicates how good this program fits with the profile of the currently logged-in user, where a darker tone indicates a better match.

While the Web application benefits from the versatility of the computer, the set-top box application solely depends on interaction via a remote control. This leads to the fact that the set-top box interface is much more limited in the available features and possibilities. Therefore, enabling exactly those features mostly expected by the user on this platform is key. Moreover, since a person watching television is usually much less proactive then when using a computer, we need to enable the features he values most and make them function with as few button presses as possible. In figure 2 we see the iFanzy interface of the set-top box UI. Above the three most favorite channels (the order is personalized), we see the 6 top recommendations for the current user with the option to see more if necessary. Just like in the Web interface, programs get a tone of orange indicating how well they fit the current user. At the bottom of the screen we see the well known colored remote control buttons (red, green, yellow and blue)

---

[2] http://www.ifanzy.nl/

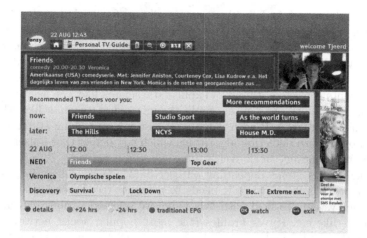

Fig. 2. The iFanzy set-top box interface

providing application shortcuts e.g. to see all program details, etc. Next to these, a dedicated button allows the user to immediately start watching the program.

3 Engineering Techniques

Working with various clients providing one integrated service to the user asks for a centralized approach to the engineering of the applications. This is among others reflected in the model-based approach of the application development. Behind the scenes, all three clients connect to the same server assuring their mutual synchronization of data. Thereby guaranteeing that every action performed on any of the platforms, has an immediate effect on all. However, the combination of a domain which is very time-sensitive (e.g. timed broadcasts), the usage of different clients and the user displaying different behavior at different times and situations, leads to the fact that a good interpretation of contextual information in iFanzy is vital. Knowing in which context or situation (with respect to various factors like time, location, etc.) a statement was uttered is invaluable for e.g. generating more appreciated recommendations. This approach is a much more dynamic one than some other more static TV recommender systems [2]. Therefore, in iFanzy, all the information amassed from the user, is accompanied by the user's current context to be able to draw more fine-grained conclusions.

All user feedback like e.g. ratings, setting of favorites or watching content is associated with a set of concepts like programs, genres, channels and various involved people (e.g. actors, directors, etc.) which are all defined in our central conceptual model. The conceptual model in iFanzy is based on the TV-Anytime specification[3] and is enriched with domain-specific ontologies as shown in [1]. Semantic Web techniques are applied to make the interconnections between these vocabularies and the content, resulting in an RDF/OWL knowledge structure.

---

[3] http://www.tv-anytime.org/

A user model, which is defined to contain all user feedback, is a dynamic representation of the user aggregated by our application by observing and learning from the user behavior as well as explicit user knowledge. The user model acts as a view over the conceptual model superimposing an extra layer containing all aggregated user statements together with the correct associated context. These user statements consists both out of explicit statements like 'the user rated program P with value x', as well as implicitly inferred statements like 'the user has a liking for program P with value x'. These inferred liking statements are generated by pattern detection algorithms which e.g. detect that a user watches the same program every week over again.

Just like most systems depending on user data, iFanzy suffers from the so-called *cold start* problem when it needs to generate recommendations for new users in the system. To deal with this issue, we selected various external user data sources like e.g. Hyves profiles (the most popular social network in the Netherlands), MovieLens[4] movie ratings and IMDb[5] ratings. Afterwards, we matched all retrieved concepts from these sources to our internal data graph. By doing so, we could exploit the semantics of the concepts to initialize the profiles of new users with the ratings gathered from these external sources.

4 Conclusions

In this paper we briefly introduced iFanzy, which is developed in close collaboration with Stoneroos Interactive Television. To further legitimate our approaches we are currently extensively testing the platform. A previous test already has shown that the recommender produces results with an average MAE (Mean Absolute Error) of 0.94 on a 5 star ratings scale. While there is definitely room for improvement there, these first results were encouraging. As part of the future work, next month we will start a user test of iFanzy on the set-top box running at 5000 households in the Netherlands. Here we will focus on the integration between the set-top box application and the Web interface.

References

1. Bellekens, P., Van der Sluijs, K., Van Woensel, W., Casteleyn, S., Houben, G.J.: Achieving efficient access to large integrated sets of semantic data in web applications. In: ICWE 2008: Proceedings of the 2008 Eighth International Conference on Web Engineering, Washington, DC, USA, pp. 52–64. IEEE Computer Society, Los Alamitos (2008)
2. Das, D., ter Horst, H.: Recommender systems for tv. In: Recommender Systems Workshop, Madisson, WI, pp. 35–36. AAAI Press, Menlo Park (1998)

---

[4] http://www.grouplens.org/
[5] http://www.imdb.com/

Model-Driven Development of Audio-Visual Web Search Applications: The PHAROS Demonstration

Alessandro Bozzon, Marco Brambilla, and Piero Fraternali

Politecnico di Milano, Piazza Leonardo Da Vinci, 32 - 20133 Milano, Italy
{alessandro.bozzon,marco.brambilla,piero.fraternali}@polimi.it

Abstract. PHAROS[1] is an EU-founded project aimed at building a platform for advanced audiovisual search applications. In this demo we show the application of a Model-Driven Development (MDD) approach to the PHAROS demonstrator, which consists of an audio-visual Web search portal. The demo highlights the peculiar needs of search based applications and describes how existing MDD approaches can help fulfilling such needs, through visual modeling and automatic generation of RIA code for the front-end and business processes for the back-end.

1 Introduction

Due to the tremendous growth in the amount of digital data on the Web, search has become the default paradigm for interacting with contents. Multimedia search portals, which are now the access channels of choice, typically comprise two major flows of activities: 1) the *Query and Result Presentation* (QRP) process, which encompasses query preprocessing, query execution, and results post-processing, and 2) the *Content Provisioning* (CP) process, which gets content from its original location, analyzes (or annotates) it, and makes it available to the search engines for later search.

Depending on the targeted application domain, the QRP and CP processes have to be tailored to a wide spectrum of functional and non functional requirements, that put at stake the advantages of current Web Engineering approaches [5] [7].

Some typical challenges are related to the complexity deriving from: (i) the adopted query modality (e.g., keyword-based, similarity search, etc.), (ii) the required user interaction patterns (e.g., searching, monitoring, and browsing [2]), (iii) the presence of social interaction features (e.g., tagging), (iv) the need for flexible and distributable composition of annotation technologies (imposed by business or performance requirements), (v) highly competitive and quickly changing marketing strategies typical of the Web environment, etc. The design, development and integration of search engines systems therefore result in an articulated, complex task, involving different knowledge and skills. This demonstration will show that such needs might be fulfilled by adopting and extending

---

[1] http://www.pharos-audiovisual-search.eu

M. Gaedke, M. Grossniklaus, and O. Díaz (Eds.): ICWE 2009, LNCS 5648, pp. 513–517, 2009.
© Springer-Verlag Berlin Heidelberg 2009

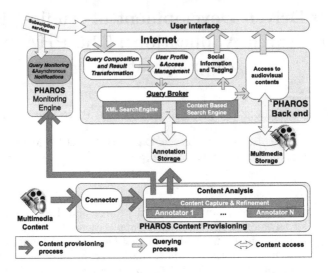

Fig. 1. A high-level view of the PHAROS platform architecture

the methods and tools that Web engineering provides for conceptual modeling of traditional Web applications.

2 Demonstration Scenario

Our work stems from the requirements gathered within PHAROS (Platform for searcHing of Audiovisual Resources across Online Spaces) [4], an Integrated Project funded by the European Union in the Sixth Framework Programme; its goal is to. Figure 1 depicts a high level view of the PHAROS platform architecture, comprising a set of components that interact according to the SOA paradigm for performing the CP and QRP and execution flows.

In PHAROS, contents are represented both by manual metadata (e.g, title and description) and annotations automatically generated by the PHAROS platform during the CP process (e.g speech-to-text transcriptions, speaker's gender or name, music mood and rhythm, etc.). Annotations refer to temporal segments of occurrence, which is exploited in the QRP process to enable navigation of videos according to the temporal segment of occurrence for a given query match. The PHAROS QRP process supports several combinations of user interaction patterns and query modalities, like content-based queries based on music, images and faces, browsing based on automatically generated annotations, search by user-generated tags, etc.

This demonstration includes: (i) the description of the MDD approach adopted for the design of the QRP process, based on the WebML notation, that allow to produce rich web interfaces; (ii) the description of the MDD approach for the

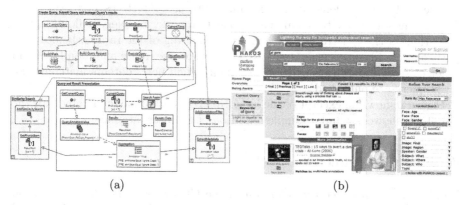

Fig. 2. (a) Hypertext model excerpt for the PHAROS QRP process; (b) Rendition example of the generated QRP Web interface

design of the CP process, based on *ad hoc* workflow models for multimedia content provisioning; (iii) an in-depth tour of the generated Pharos demonstrator, comprising several usage scenarios such as keyword- and content-based search, similarity search, faceted search, social and personalized content management, multi-modal and multi-channel user interfaces, provision of new contents, and update on the CP process.

For conceptual modeling of the user interface level of the QRP we exploit the Web Modeling Language (WebML) [6], a visual Domain Specific Language for the specification of contents, business processes, hypertexts, web service interaction [3], and visual presentation (including rich interface modeling[1]) of a Web application, and WebRatio[2], a MDE tool that provides WebML design and code generation facilities.

The specification of the CP process is based on the BPMN notation[3] for business process design. We support a subset of the complete BPMN semantics (coarsely, the part that maps to BPEL), and we extend it with search-specific aspects.

3   The QRP Process

Starting from a high level specification of a query, the QRP process automatically generates MPQF[4] expressions for (i) keyword-based queries, (ii) annotation-based queries and results' filtering, (iii) user-specified tags, and (iv) similarity-based search on audio, images and faces. Queries can be iteratively built as an arbitrary combination of such options. Example of expressible queries are: a) find all the videos related to tourism in Bavaria, b) find the videos talking about Al Gore and where the speaker is Al Gore himself, c) find all the video containing faces similar to the uploaded one.

---

[2] WebRatio, http://www.webratio.com
[3] Business Process Management Notation, http://www.bpmn.org
[4] MPEG Query Format, http://www.mpqf.org

The QRP process demo application offers two user interfaces: one for desktop PC and one for mobile terminal. The application performs query building, query execution on the PHAROS back-end, and rendering of the results. It also supports aspects like user-generated tags, queries storage, reuse and monitoring, in order to receive notifications (SMS or email) when new contents matching the given query are published.

Figure 2 shows an excerpt of the hypertext conceptual model designed for the PHAROS showcase, and a sample rendition of the user interface.

4   The CP Process

To allow easy and effective definition of the CP process, the BPMN notation is extended with search specific information to enable a more precise model transformation towards the running code. Every BPMN activity is associated with a *type*, describing the semantics of its behaviour, and a set of properties that describe the execution details (e.g., the service to be invoked and the parameters to be passed on). Examples of activity types : Retrieval (R), Transformation (T), Analysis (ANA), and Indexing (IDX) of content. An activity has a (possibly empty) set of input parameters and output parameters. The output flow of an activity can be associated to a guard condition, which is an OCL Boolean expression over the values of the output parameters. Figure 3 shows a simplified example of CP Process specified according to our extended notation. The design of the models is supported by a visual design tool and the CP process models configure a simple workflow engine that processes new contents.

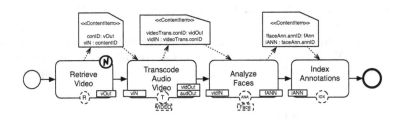

Fig. 3. Process model example for the Content Provisioning

References

1. Bozzon, A., et al.: Conceptual modeling and code generation for Rich Internet Applications. In: ICWE 2006, pp. 353–360 (2006)
2. Bates, M.: Toward an integrated model of information seeking and searching. The New Review of Information Behaviour Research 3, 1–15 (2002)
3. Brambilla, M., Ceri, S., Fraternali, P., Manolescu, I.: Process modeling in web applications. ACM TOSEM 15(4), 360–409 (2006)

4. Debald, S., Nejdl, W., Nucci, F., Paiu, R., Plu, M.: Pharos, platform for search of audiovisual resources across online spaces. In: SAMT 2006 (2006)
5. Koch, N., Kraus, A., Cachero, C., Meliá, S.: Integration of business processes in web application models. J. Web Eng. 3(1), 22–49 (2004)
6. Ceri, S., Fraternali, P., Bongio, A., Brambilla, M., Comai, S., Matera, M.: Designing Data-Intensive Web Applications. Morgan Kaufmann, San Francisco (2002)
7. Torres, V., Pelechano, V.: Building business process driven web applications. In: Dustdar, S., Fiadeiro, J.L., Sheth, A.P. (eds.) BPM 2006. LNCS, vol. 4102, pp. 322–337. Springer, Heidelberg (2006)

beContent: A Model-Driven Platform for Designing and Maintaining Web Applications*

Antonio Cicchetti[1], Davide Di Ruscio[2], Romina Eramo[2], Francesco Maccarrone[2], and Alfonso Pierantonio[2]

[1] School of Innovation, Design and Engineering
Mälardalen University,
SE-721 23, Västerås, Sweden
antonio.cicchetti@mdh.se

[2] Dipartimento di Informatica
Università degli Studi dell'Aquila
Via Vetoio, Coppito I-67010, L'Aquila, Italy
{diruscio,romina.eramo,francesco.maccarrone,alfonso}@di.univaq.it

Abstract. Model Driven Engineering (MDE) is increasingly gaining acceptance in the development of Web Applications as a mean to leverage abstraction and render business logic resilient to technological changes. This paper describes the beContent project with its modeling languages and tools, which aims at the automated generation of rich Web applications.

1 Introduction

The beContent project [1] aims at defining an infrastructure (see Figure 1) consisting of a coordinated collection of languages and tools which permit to shorten systems' life-cycle and ease maintainence tasks. The gluing element of the project is the beContent metamodel (BMM) which is based on a previous work of the authors [2]. The metamodel defines the abstract syntax of the modeling languages: a diagrammatic and a textual concrete syntax, called beContent modeling language (BML) and beContent textual language (BTL), respectively, endowed with a round-tripping mechanism. In other words, they can interchangeably be used for specifying a system and, for instance, whenever a diagrammatic specification undergoes a modification the textual counterpart is consistently updated and the other way round. This has been possible by using the AMMA framework [3] and an additional component such as GMF [4]. The models can be edited by means of a visual and textual editor realized as Eclipse plugins as described in Sect. 3.

2 beContent Models

A beContent model consists mainly of the declarative and coordinated specification of three different concerns:

---

* Partially supported by the European Communitys 7th Framework Programme (FP7/2007-2013), grant agreement n° 214898.

M. Gaedke, M. Grossniklaus, and O. Díaz (Eds.): ICWE 2009, LNCS 5648, pp. 518–522, 2009.
© Springer-Verlag Berlin Heidelberg 2009

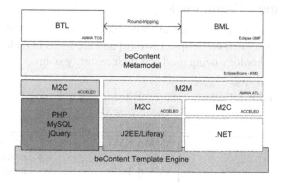

Fig. 1. The beContent infrastructure

- the *data* view is the description of the relational model of the data, in essence it describes the metadata of the application;
- the *content* view describes the data sources and how the content is retrieved and aggregated in pages; and finally
- the *interaction* view specifies how to manipulate the information entered in the forms (e.g., a textual content can be edited by means of text fields, textareas, or rich-text editors), the validation constraints, and additional information which may affect the interaction between the user and the application.

An example of specification is given in Figure 2, where a simple description of *news* is illustrated as a composition of three main model elements: the entity, the form, and the content. In particular, the form is contained in a *manager page* which indicates that the code for managing all the interactions (creation, update, and deletion) are encapsulated in an individual page. Starting from models conforming to BMM *model-to-code* transformations written in Acceleo [5] are capable of generating the whole corresponding applications. The generated artifacts and the model transformations are illustrated in the next section.

Fig. 2. Sample *news* model

3   The beContent Framework

The framework consists of a number of tools which have been implemented (or are planned to be implemented) on Eclipse EMF [6] and are listed in table 1 together with the specific EMF technology being used and their maturity status.

Table 1. Platform components and related technologies

Description	Technology	Status
BMM	AMMA KM3	*advanced*
BML	GMF	*advanced*
BTL	AMMA TCS	*incubation*
J2EE/Liferay code generation	Acceleo	*incubation*
LAMP code generation	Acceleo	*advanced*
Model Repository	EMF Teneo	*preliminary*
Versioning + Co-evolution	EMF Compare, AMMA ATL	*incubation*
Workflow Metamodel	AMMA KM3	*preliminary*

In particular, BMM has been defined by means of KM3, a metamodeling language part of the AMMA framework. As aforementioned, models are edited by means of a visual and textual editors: the former is an Eclipse plugin (realized with GMF) which assists the designer in editing the diagrammatic descriptions; whereas the latter is defined using TCS which uses text-to-model trace-links that are created during parsing to allow hyperlinks and hovers for references within the text. Once created, the models can be mapped onto several platforms (see Figure 1) by means of automated transformations

Fig. 3. Generated *news* interaction and content

which generate the corresponding assets. The model-to-code transformations have been written by means of the Acceleo templating language, which provides enough flexibility and model navigation functionalities. The platforms currently supported are the typical LAMP and J2EE/Liferay portal platform, although the latter is still in a preliminary stage of the development. As an example, consider the model in Figure 2, which can be transformed by the LAMP model-to-code to obtain the functionalities depicted in Figure 3. All the tools have been released under an open source license scheme and can be freely downloaded at [1].

4   Additional Features

Additional aspects of the platform include an advanced *user management* which is reflected in the metamodel and mapped on the choosen target platform. Moreover, users are allowed to interact one with another by means of processes which are described conforming to the *workflow* metamodel extension which is currently under development. The topology of processes are given by means of a restriction of UML activity diagrams (in essence, it is limited to non parallel processes) which are mapped to specific workflow engines integrated with the corresponding platforms.

Analogously to any other software artifacts, Web applications are subject to a heavy evolutionary pressure. Therefore, we are currently designing and implementing a specific support to *model repository*, *versioning*, and *co-evolution*. In particular, as models are considered *first-class* artefacts, they can also be compared to detect the changes a model underwent during its life-cycle. This provides beContent with an evolution support able to *a)* calculate by means of EMF Compare the differences between two versions of the same model, *b)* represent the evolution as a model, and *c)* automatically generate from this model a refactoring procedure which migrates the application and its data (schema and contents) [7].

5   Conclusions and Future Work

This paper described a number of aspects of the beContent project. The approach has been validated on the LAMP platform by producing the following sites

- http://www.abruzzo24ore.tv, a news portal whose features include multimedia and rich-text content, registered users, RSS feeds, and forums;
- http://www.di.univaq.it, the official site of the Computer Science Department at the University of L'Aquila where the project has been initiated;
- http://www.univaq.it, the official site of the University of L'Aquila.

We also briefly illustrated a transformational approach to the co-evolution of applications, i.e., when certain aspects of a model changes then other components are requested to be adapted to remain valid. Future works includes the implementation refinement/enhancement and how to map the beContent metamodel to well-known frameworks, such as *rails*, *django*, and *spring*.

References

1. Pierantonio, A.: beContent (2006), http://www.becontent.org
2. Di Ruscio, D., Muccini, H., Pierantonio, A.: A Data Modeling Approach to Web Application Synthesis. Int. Jour. of Web Engineering and Technology 1(3), 320–337 (2004)
3. Bézivin, J., Jouault, F., Rosenthal, P., Valduriez, P.: Modeling in the Large and Modeling in the Small. In: Aßmann, U., Aksit, M., Rensink, A. (eds.) MDAFA 2003. LNCS, vol. 3599, pp. 33–46. Springer, Heidelberg (2005)
4. Eclipse project: GMF - Graphical Modeling Framework,
   http://www.eclipse.org/gmf/
5. Obeo: Acceleo, http://www.acceleo.org
6. Budinsky, F., Steinberg, D., Merks, E., Ellersick, R., Grose, T.: Eclipse Modeling Framework. Addison-Wesley, Reading (2003)
7. Cicchetti, A., Di Ruscio, D., Eramo, R., Pierantonio, A.: Automating co-evolution in model-driven engineering. In: 12th IEEE Intl. EDOC Conference, pp. 222–231 (2008)

InSCo-Gen: A MDD Tool for Web Rule-Based Applications

Joaquín Cañadas[1], José Palma[2], and Samuel Túnez[1]

[1] Dept. of Languages and Computation, University of Almeria, Spain
{jjcanada,stunez}@ual.es
[2] Dept. of Information and Communications Engineering, University of Murcia, Spain
jtpalma@um.es

Abstract. Rules and ontologies are widely used in software development since they provide semantic web applications with meaning and reasoning features. This demonstration paper presents InSCo-Gen, a Model-Driven Development (MDD) tool for Web rule-based applications, which constructs a functional Web architecture integrating a rule engine for reasoning tasks. Development process is based on conceptual models composed of ontologies and production rules. These models are the source for the MDD process, which automatically generates implementation of the Web application.

Keywords: MDD, Web Engineering, Rule-based systems.

1 Introduction

In Semantic Web context, development of rule languages and inference engines to provide Web information systems with reasoning capabilities is an important research topic. Production rules (if-conditions-then-actions) play a leading role in this aim, since they enable declarative representation of domain expert knowledge and business logic. Rule engines deal with rule bases and execute several inference methods for firing appropriate rules in order to deduct new information and achieve results [1].

This demo presents InSCo-Gen, an MDD tool for building Web rule-based applications. It supports the development process starting from the specification of conceptual models in Conceptual Modeling Language (CML), the formalism for knowledge representation defined by the CommonKADS methodology [2] for knowledge-based system development. A model-driven approach is then applied to produce the implementation of a functional Web architecture which integrates a rule engine for reasoning tasks. The tool was developed for supporting InSCo [3], a software development methodology that interweaves knowledge engineering and software engineering approaches.

This paper is organized as follows: Section 2 introduces the model-driven approach applied in InSCo-Gen. Next, the architecture of the Web rule-based application generated is described in Section 3. Finally, the main conclusions and future work are summarized.

M. Gaedke, M. Grossniklaus, and O. Díaz (Eds.): ICWE 2009, LNCS 5648, pp. 523–526, 2009.
© Springer-Verlag Berlin Heidelberg 2009

2   The *InSCo-Gen* Model-Driven Approach

The *InSCo-Gen* model-driven approach is based on conceptual models created in CML, a knowledge modeling language which entails simplified specification of ontology and production rules. A CML conceptual model is basically composed of two parts, domain schemas and knowledge bases. Domain concepts, binary relationships, rule types and value types (enumerated literals) are modeled in a domain schema. A knowledge base is composed of instances of concepts, instances of relationships called tuples, and instances of rules.

The main difference with other conceptual modeling languages is the possibility of modeling production rules through rule types and rule instances. A rule type describes the structure of a set of rules defining the concepts bound to the rule antecedent and to the rule consequent. Rule types are particularized into rule instances that represent specific, logical dependencies between concept attribute values of rule antecedent and consequent.

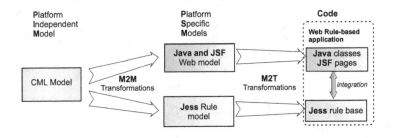

Fig. 1. MDD schema for Web rule-based system generation

Figure 1 shows a simplified schema of the two MDD processes implemented in *InSCo-Gen*. Two different results are found using a single CML model. On one hand, a Jess [4] rule base is generated, a text file that contains the rules converted to Jess syntax. On the other hand, a set of JavaBeans and JSP web pages, making up a JavaServer Faces (JSF) [5] architecture that integrates the Jess rule engine in a rich Web application.

Both MDD processes can be executed separately. Since the decision logic of rule-based applications may change frequently, the tool enables independent generation of a new rule base, which can be deployed in the Web application server without having to modify anything else in the architecture.

InSCo-Gen was developed using MDD tools provided by the Eclipse Modeling Project[1]. Models and metamodels are defined using EMF[2] (Eclipse Modeling Framework). Three metamodels are needed, the CML metamodel for conceptual modeling, the Jess-Rule metamodel used for representing Jess platform-specific models and the Java/JSF metamodel used by Web-based specific models.

---

[1] http://www.eclipse.org/modeling/
[2] http://www.eclipse.org/modeling/emf/

Conceptual models based on the CML metamodel are created using the built-in EMF reflective editor. To improve model editing, the reflective editor was customized using Exeed (EXtended Emf EDitor) [6], a plugin which enables default icons and labels to be modified by using the Exeed annotations in the metamodel.

Two model-to-model (M2M) transformations are designed with ATL[3] (Atlas Transformation Language). The first one (bottom flow in Fig. 1) maps a CML model to a Jess platform-specific model. The second one (top flow in Fig. 1) transforms a CML model into a Java/JSF Web specific model.

The outputs of both ATL transformations are the respective inputs of two model-to-text (M2T) transformations implemented in JET[4] (Java Emitter Templates). As a result, *InSCo-Gen* automatically produces the application code. On one hand, source text files with Jess rules and facts, and on the other hand, the Web application components, the faces-config.xml and web.xml configuration files, the Java Beans for model classes, and a Jess-Engine Bean which uses the Jess Java API (Application Programming Interface) to integrate the rule engine into the architecture. Moreover, a set of JSP/JSF web pages are generated for the user interface. These pages are based on the RichFaces library [7], an open source framework that adds AJAX (Asynchronous JavaScript And XML) capability to JSF applications.

3   Architecture of Web Rule-Based Applications

Figure 2 shows the target architecture for Web rule-based applications generated by *InSCo-Gen*.

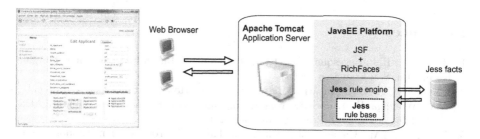

Fig. 2. Architecture of a Web rule-based application

The integrated rule engine manages the Jess rule base and the text file containing persistent instances of concepts, called *facts*. The Web application enables the user to perform four basic predetermined functions, create new instances, read the current list of instances, update and delete instances. That functionality makes the application generated a CRUD system (Create, Read, Update,

---

[3] http://www.eclipse.org/m2m/atl/
[4] http://www.eclipse.org/modeling/m2t/?project=jet

Delete). In general, current tools for automatic generation of CRUD systems perform those operations on relational databases. The contribution of our approach is that CRUD operations are executed on the Jess rule engine working memory, enabling the inference mechanism to fire appropriate rules when necessary. The rule engine executes a forward-chaining inference mechanism to drive the reasoning process, firing the rules with conditions evaluated as true, and executing their actions to deduct new values or modify existing ones.

The use of both rules and AJAX technology improves the creation and edition of instances in the Web application. Since Web forms are implemented with AJAX RichFaces components, each single form value can be validated and submitted individually as it is entered. This facility entails the rule engine firing suitable rules and deducting new information that drives the instance creation or edition, for example, updating choice-field values.

4   Conclusion and Future Work

This demo presented $InSCo\text{-}Gen^5$, a real example of MDD applied to rich Web system development, incorporating a rule engine for reasoning tasks.

The tool is being evaluated within the development of a Web decision-support system for pest control in agriculture, which makes recommendations to growers and technicians about treatment for a specific pest or disease in grapes.

Our current work extends the tool with relational database facilities to provide a complete persistence layer. Also, a deliverable version of the tool as an Eclipse plugin will be available soon. Future incorporation of other semantic Web languages, such as OWL (Web Ontology Language) and SWRL (Semantic Web Rule Language) is planned.

References

1. Brachman, R.J., Levesque, H.J.: Knowledge representation and reasoning. Morgan Kaufmann, San Francisco (2004)
2. Schreiber, G., Akkermans, H., Anjewierden, A., de Hoog, R., Shadbolt, N., de Velde, W.V., Wielinga, B.: Knowledge Engineering and Management: The CommonKADS Methodology. The MIT Press, Cambridge (2000)
3. del Águila, I.M., Cañadas, J., Palma, J., Túnez, S.: Towards a methodology for hybrid systems software development. In: Proceedings of the Int. Conference on Software Engineering and Knowledge Engineering (SEKE), pp. 188–193 (2006)
4. Sandia Lab.: Jess, http://herzberg.ca.sandia.gov/jess/
5. Geary, D., Horstmann, C.S.: Core JavaServer Faces, 2nd edn. Prentice Hall, Englewood Cliffs (2007)
6. Kolovos, D.S.: Exeed: EXtended Emf EDitor - User Manual (2007), http://www.eclipse.org/gmt/epsilon/doc/Exeed.pdf
7. JBoss: RichFaces (2007), http://www.jboss.org/jbossrichfaces/

---

[5] This work is supported by two research projects, TIN2004-05694 funded by the Spanish MEC, and P06-TIC-02411 funded by the Junta de Andalucia.

A Tool to Support End-User Development of Web Applications Based on a Use Case Model

Buddhima De Silva, Athula Ginige, Simi Bajaj, Ashini Ekanayake,
Richa Shirodkar, and Markus Santa

University of Western Sydney, Locked Bag 1797, Penrith South DC, 1719, NSW, Australia
bdesilva@scm.uws.edu.au, a.ginige@uws.edu.au

Abstract. Many Small to Medium Enterprises (SMEs) tend to gradually adopt Web based business applications to enhance their business processes. To support this gradual adoption we need a framework that supports iterative development. Further processes that have been supported by web based business applications can change and evolve requiring applications to be changed accordingly. One way to facilitate these requirements is to empower SMEs to make changes to the web application to accommodate the required changes while using that web application. This paper presents a requirement specification tool and a Use Case model of a Web based application which can be used to specify and create the Web applications. This approach will bring the formalism to ad-hoc end-user development by including requirement specification phase. In this approach an application is viewed as a collection of packages. A package consists of related set of use cases. A scope list is developed at the package level. This will assure the required functionality of the application is completely specified. This will also provide a framework to validate the requirements. We have developed this tool in Component Based Development/ Deployment System (CBEADS). Now we are in a process of testing it.

Keywords: Web application, Requirement specification, Use Case model.

1 Introduction

AeIMS research group at University of Western Sydney has been working with SMEs in Western Sydney region to investigate how Information and Communication Technologies (ICT) can be used to enhance their business processes to become competitive in a global economy [1, 2]. In this research the challenge we had was to find a way to develop web based business applications that can evolve with changing business needs [3]. Also we had to develop these applications rapidly as well as in a cost effective manner [4]. The development approach should also needs to reduce the gap between what the users actually wanted and what is being implemented in terms of functionality [5].

To address above mentioned issues it is very important to empower end users to get involved in the original design of the application during design time and be able to

M. Gaedke, M. Grossniklaus, and O. Díaz (Eds.): ICWE 2009, LNCS 5648, pp. 527–530, 2009.
© Springer-Verlag Berlin Heidelberg 2009

modify the application as a result of evolving requirements during the use time [6]. If we are to empower end users to actively participate during design time and to be able to modify the application during use time rather than developing a specific application we need to provide a set of tools and a framework that they can use to develop and change the application in response to changing needs. However, such tools need to focus on analysis and design process as well as the construction process of an application for the success of end-user development [7]. Therefore, the fundamental challenges to end-user development have gradually shifted from basic syntactic adjustment required to help during construction towards semantic challenges including the need to convey an understanding of design and engineering principles relevant to end-users [8]. We are developing a use case driven approach to face the semantic challenge with the specification and the design of the requirements. All the functional requirements are specified as use cases or functions. We have developed a use case model and a form based tool to capture the different aspects of the use cases/ functions. These are discussed in section 2 and section 3. Using this captured information most of the application can be auto generated.

2   Use Case Model of an Application

Fig.1. shows the high level model of an application used in the use case driven approach. Application consists of one or many packages. A package groups a set of related functions of an application. A package has a list of scopes. Scope list is a list of processes that must be carried out to accomplish the goal. This defines what the project will deliver and what it will not deliver and its boundary (organisational, functional, technical, system or individual user) by specifying them for individual processes. This helps to identify the use cases, actors, workflow, some of the data objects and the relationships between the objects required in the functions. Use cases are specified using user interfaces and user actions associated with the user interfaces. We also define the business rules associated with a package which is used in the implementation of use cases.

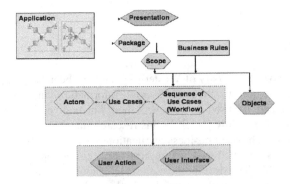

Fig. 1. High level model of an application

3 Requirement Specification Tool

Based on the above use case model we have developed a form based tool to specify the Requirements. This tool also includes some guidelines and examples for the users to specify the requirements of a Web based application. This tool is shown in fig. 2. This tool provides form based interfaces to specify the packages with in an application, scope list of a package, use cases/ functions, actors and objects. A form based interface is also provided to specify the interfaces related to the use cases. Using above information the application is semi-automatically generated. Table 1 shows how the captured information is mapped into the physical implementation.

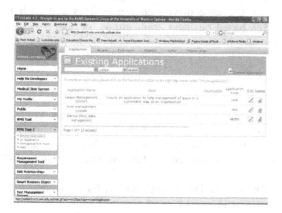

Fig. 2. Requirement Specification tool

Table 1. Purpose and corresponding realization of the inputs

Form Input		Purpose	Corresponding Realisation
Form Name	Input		
Application	Name, description, acronym	Acronym is used for namespace and folder name to store files for the application.	Folder structure for the application
Scope	Name and description	Scope defines the list of processes to be carried out in the system.	
Function/ use case	name, description	Function name used as the primary navigation to the function.	Menu link
Actor	Actor name, description	Used to conceptualise the use cases.	
Objects and Object Relationships	Application, Object Name, Attributes, relationships	Objects with the attributes are created within the application namespace. Data about Relationship is used to create the relationships.	Database, Table and Table columns and Foreign keys, Associa--tive tables.
User Interface	Name,UI attri--butes, actions	UI for function is created with UI elements and actions.	file

This tool is implemented in Component based E Application Development and Deployment System (CBEADS) [3, 9]. Components and engines of CBEADS framework are used to map the specification of the application into the implementation. For example, this tool depends on CBEADS User Management component for binding the users with the created application. Also SBO [10] (Smart Business Objects) is used to map the objects and relationships to the data base tables.

4 Conclusion

We have developed a tool to specify the requirements of a Web based Business Applications based on use case driven approach. This approach is well suited to specify and create web based business applications for SMEs as it supports iterative development. We are now in the process of evaluating the tool.

References

1. Ginige, A.: Collaborating to Win - Creating an Effective Virtual Organisation. In: International Workshop on Business and Information, Taipei, Taiwan (2004)
2. Ginige, A.: From eTransformation to eCollaboration: Issues and Solutions. In: 2nd International Conference on Information Management and Business (IMB 2006), Sydney, Australia (2006)
3. Ginige, A.: New Paradigm for Developing Software for E-Business. In: Proceedings of the IEEE 2001 Symposia on Human Centric Computing Languages and Environments (HCC 2001). IEEE Computer Society, Stresa (2001)
4. Ginige, A.: Re Engineering Software Development Process for eBusiness Application Development. In: Software Engineering and Knowledge Engineering Conference -SEKE 2002, San Francisco Bay, USA (2002)
5. Epner, M.: Poor Project Management Number-One Problem of Outsourced E-Projects, in Research Briefs, Cutter Consortium (2000)
6. Fischer, G., et al.: Meta Design: A Manifesto for End -User Development. Communications of the ACM 47(9), 33–37 (2004)
7. Rosson, M.B., et al.: Design planning in end-user web development. In: IEEE Symposium on Visual Languages and Human-Centric Computing, Couer d'Alene, Idaho (2007)
8. Repenning, A.: End-User Design. In: Workshop on End-User Software Engineering (WEUSEIII), Dagstuhl Seminar Proceedings 07081 (2007)
9. Ginige, A., et al.: Smart Tools to support Meta-Design Paradigm for Developing Web based Business Applications. In: Baresi, L., Fraternali, P., Houben, G.-J. (eds.) ICWE 2007. LNCS, vol. 4607, pp. 521–525. Springer, Heidelberg (2007)
10. Liang, X., Ginige, A.: Smart Business Objects: A new Approach to Model Business Objects for Web Applications. In: 1st International Conference on Software and Data Technologies, Setubal, Portugal (2006)

MODiCo: A Multi-Ontology Web Service Discovery and Composition System

Duy Ngan Le[1], Bao Duy Tran[1], Puay Siew Tan[2],
Angela Eck Song Goh[1], and Eng Wah Lee[2]

[1] Nanyang Technological University (NTU), Singapore
{leduyngan,TRAN0001,ASESGOH}@ntu.edu.sg
http://www.ntu.edu.sg
[2] Singapore Institute of Manufacturing Technology (SIMTech), Singapore
{pstan,ewlee}@SIMTech.a-star.edu.sg
http://www.simtech.a-star.edu.sg

Abstract. Web services have been employed in a wide range of applications and have become a key technology in developing business operations on the Web. In order to leverage on the use of Web services, Web service discovery and composition need to be fully supported. Several systems have been proposed to meet this need. However, these systems usually support either discovery or composition of Web services but not both. Moreover, these systems assume the Web services are based on the same ontology. Existing Web service discovery systems are not able to discover heterogeneous ontology Web services. This paper introduces a Web service discovery and composition system which supports Web services based on different OWL-S ontologies. The discovery process is executed first in order to search for a single Web service that satisfies a requester. If a single Web service cannot be found, multiple Web services are composed to satisfy the request.

Keywords: OWL-S, Web service discovery, Web service composition.

1 Introduction

Semantic Web service [1], an enhancement of current Web services by employing semantics to describe the service, has become an important technology in e-business due to its strength in discovery and composition. Discovery is a process that locates an individual advertised Web service that satisfies a requested Web service's requirement. With the same function, composition is a process that *composes* multiple advertised Web services to satisfy the request. Hence, discovery and composition are two very important tasks, as advertised Web services are useless if they cannot be found.

Researchers have developed several discovery and composition techniques. However, current discovery and composition systems have two major drawbacks: (i) they usually support either discovery or composition but not both and (ii) they only support Web services based on the same ontology. In the real world, a Web service

M. Gaedke, M. Grossniklaus, and O. Díaz (Eds.): ICWE 2009, LNCS 5648, pp. 531–534, 2009.
© Springer-Verlag Berlin Heidelberg 2009

provider should be able to service the requester even though the ontologies of the requester and provider are dissimilar. Moreover, the discovery and composition operations should be conducted simultaneously.

A system that supports both discovery and composition of Web services based on different ontologies is the motivation behind this work. This paper proposes a Multiple Ontologies Web service Discovery and Composition system termed MODiCo. The proposed system supports OWL-S[1] recommended by W3C[2] as it is currently the most popular description language for semantic Web service. The rest of the paper is as follows. Section 2 describes the system algorithm. Our proposed demonstration of the MODiCo system is presented in section 3, followed by the conclusion.

2 MODiCo Algorithm

2.1 MODiCo Overall Architecture

MODiCo overall architecture is presented in figure 1. Providers advertise their Web services by publishing them to MODiCo repository. A requester describes its requirements via a request Web service in order to locate a suitable advertised Web service. Whenever a request is sent to MODiCo, the *discovery* component is executed first to match the requested Web service against individual advertised Web services in its repository. If an advertised service is found, no composition is needed. Otherwise, the *composition* component is executed to compose the advertised services to satisfy the requirement.

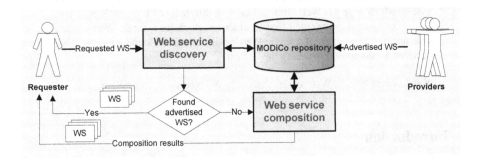

Fig. 1. MODiCo overall architecture

2.2 Web Service Discovery

The core of the discovery algorithm [2] is a matching process which measures the similarity between a requested and an advertised Web service. In turn, the Web service similarity is calculated based on the similarities between input, output, and operation of the two Web services, respectively.

---

[1] Semantic Markup for Web Services: http://www.w3.org/Submission/OWL-S/
[2] World Wide Web Consortium:www.w3.org

In the input matching, we determine how inputs of the advertised services are satisfied by the inputs of the requested services. The input matching operates as follows: for each input of the advertised service, the algorithm tries to find an input of the requested service that has the highest similarity. Both output and operation processing are carried out in the same manner as input. The final matching result is a combination of the input, output, and operation matching. The best 'matched advertised service', which has the highest similarity, is then compared with a threshold. It must be greater than the threshold; otherwise, the discovery is unsuccessful.

Since input, output, and operation of a Web service are nothing more than ontological concepts, matching these elements is eventually measuring similarity between two concepts. By employing the method to measure concept similarity described in [3], the system has an advantage, it considers the relationship as well as context of the two ontologies. The concept similarity is measured based on four sub-similarity components, namely *syntactic, property, neighborhood,* and *context* similarity.

2.3 Web Service Composition

The composition algorithm [4] is a progressive AI-planning-like algorithm which proceeds in a recursive depth-first manner. The algorithm composes the advertised Web services by connecting their inputs and outputs based on their similarity. The resultants are expressed in the form of directed multi-graphs of advertised Web services and inter-connecting edges. Similar to the discovery algorithm, the similarity between input and output of Web services is calculated based on the method introduced in [3]. The 'best solution' is the one with the highest similarity between matching connections. This similarity must exceed the threshold; otherwise, the composition is unsuccessful.

Composition solutions are constructed recursively in a solution tree which is constructed to facilitate tracking of alternative solutions of a progressive state space search algorithm. The requested (desired) output is used as a starting point of the solution tree. The matching algorithm described in [3] is employed to search for an advertised service that best matches the requested output. A short listed advertised service becomes a branch in the solution tree. Its input becomes the new "requested output" and a recursive search for another advertised service begins. Branches are added recursively to the solution tree until a pre- determined number of branches (i.e. the maximum tree depth) is attained.

At every recursive call, the algorithm checks if the advertised services can be connected to the required outputs based on the concept matching algorithm [3]. The similarity of a solution is measured based on the similarity of each connection and its length depth. The algorithm also keeps track the depth of recursion and alternative solutions in the form of a search tree. The tree nodes track the evolution of various solution branches.

3   MODiCo Demonstration

As there is no standard test data or benchmark available, we developed 100 Web service profiles. Using these 100 profiles, we ran the test data for five times and each time chose a profile as a requester, the remaining Web service profiles were treated as providers. In this way, we obtained 500 matching Web service pairs. The "ground truth" of Web service similarity is the expected value which has been derived manually based on the knowledge related to the Web services given by the colleagues in NTU. *Error rate* which is the differences between the MODiCo results compared against the ground truth is measured. The average *error rate* of the 500 pairs is *0.030435*.

Experiments of matching 500 Web service pairs were carried out and a series of tests were conducted to validate the designed and developed MODiCo. However, in order to preserve conciseness and succinctness in the demo, only a comprehensive test scenario together with a detailed example will be presented, illustrated, and discussed for each component.

With each component, we will first show the developed ontologies and Web service derived from the ontologies. Prototype of MODiCo as well as prototypes of discovery and composition components will be introduced. Thereafter, after running the discovery and composition, the outcomes will be analyzed and discussed. For example with the composition component, results were obtained in the form of a composition graph and then compared with an 'expected' composition graph. These scenarios and examples will illustrate how the algorithms work.

4 Conclusion

MODiCo is a prototype system for Web service discovery and composition which supports services based on identical or different ontologies. The system searches for a single advertised Web services matching the requester's requirement. If this fails, advertised Web services in its repository are composed instead based on an AI based approach algorithm. Concept similarity computation which is the core of the proposed system has four major components, namely, syntactic, properties, neighborhood, and context similarity. Experiments confirm the validity of the system. In the demo, test data, prototype of MODiCo, and the outcome will be presented.

References

1. Honglei, Z., Son, T.C.: Semantic Web Services. Intelligent Systems (IEEE) 16, 46–53 (2001)
2. Le, D.N., Goh, A.: Matching Semantic Web Services Using Different Ontologies. In: Lowe, D.G., Gaedke, M. (eds.) ICWE 2005. LNCS, vol. 3579, pp. 302–307. Springer, Heidelberg (2005)
3. Ngan, L.D., Hang, T.M., Goh, A.: Semantic Similarity between Concepts from Different OWL Ontologies. In: 2006 IEEE International Conference on Industrial Informatics, Singapore (2006)
4. Tran, B.D., Tan, P.S., Goh, A.E.S.: Composing OWL-S Web Services. In: IEEE International Conference on Web Services (ICWS), Salt Lake City, Utah, USA (2007)

Author Index